10,001

FOOD FACTS, CHEFS' SECRETS

& HOUSEHOLD HINTS

10,001

FOOD FACTS, CHEFS' SECRETS

& HOUSEHOLD HINTS

Dr. Myles H. Bader

Reader's Digest

Reader's Digest Association, Inc.
Pleasantville, New York / Montreal

Reader's Digest Project Staff

Editorial Director Fred DuBose
Senior Editor Martha Schueneman
Production Technology Manager Douglas A. Croll
Editorial Manager Christine Guido

Contributors

Senior Project Designer Martha Grossman
Illustrator Brian Jensen
Copy Editors Karen Tsakos, Webster Williams
Indexer Felice Levy

Reader's Digest Illustrated Reference Books

Editor-in-Chief Christopher Cavanaugh
Art Director Joan Mazzeo
Operations Manager William J. Cassidy

Published by The Reader's Digest Association, Inc. 2000, by arrangement with
Michael Friedman Publishing Group, Inc.

Copyright © 2000 Dr. Myles H. Bader
Based on 10,001 Food Facts, Chefs' Secrets, & Household Hints, copyright © 1998, Dr. Myles H. Bader

Library of Congress Cataloging in Publication Data
Bader, Myles.
  10,001 food facts, chefs' secrets, and household hints/Myles H. Bader.
  p.cm.
  ISBN 0-7621-0301-9
  1. Food—Miscellanea. 2. Cookery—Miscellanea. 3. Home economics—Miscellanea. I.
  Title: Reader's digest 10,001 food facts, chefs' secrets, and household hints. II. Reader's
  Digest Association. III. Title.
TX355 .B32 2000
641.3—dc21   00-055347

Address any comments about 10,001 Food Facts, Chefs' Secrets, & Household Hints to:
  Dr. Myles H. Bader, c/o Editor-in-Chief, Illustrated Reference Books
  Reader's Digest Road
  Pleasantville, NY 10570

To order additional copies of 10,001 Food Facts, Chefs' Secrets, & Household Hints, call 1-800-846-2100.

You can also visit us on the World Wide Web at: www.readersdigest.com

Printed in the United States of America

A Word About the Author

Dr. Myles H. Bader, a preventive care specialist whose expertise in nutrition has earned him the moniker "the Wizard of Food," is the author of several best-selling books, including *To Supplement* or *Not to Supplement*, *The Wellness Desk Reference*, *2,001 Food Secrets Revealed*, *8,001 Food Facts and Chefs' Secrets*, and an earlier edition of *10,001 Food Facts, Chefs' Secrets, & Household Hints*. Dr. Bader is also a frequent guest on television and radio programs throughout the United States and Canada.

Dr. Bader received his Doctoral Degree from Loma Linda University and is board certified in Preventive Care. He is internationally recognized as a leader in the fields of nutrition, weight control, exercise physiology, and stress managment, and he lectures extensively on nutrition and anti-aging. In recent years, Dr. Bader has established preventive and executive health programs for numerous safety departments, city governments, and Fortune 500 companies. Presently, Dr. Bader practices Preventive Care in association with Health Quest Medical Services in Las Vegas, Nevada.

Contents

COOK IT RIGHT
9

STORE IT RIGHT
37

IT'S PARTY TIME
45

BAKING BASICS
51

HOW SWEET IT IS
95

THE SKINNY ON FATS
113

NUTS AND GRAINS
127

SEASON TO TASTE
145

SPUD FACTS
173

FRUITS AND VEGETABLES
181

MEATY MATTERS
289

FOWL PLAY
317

SOMETHING'S FISHY
329

ALL ABOUT CHEESE
355

EGG-CELLENT FACTS
365

DAIRY DELIGHTS
377

BEVERAGES
391 ■

CLEAN UP YOUR ACT
■ 499

SOUPS, STEWS, & GRAVIES
419 ■

GRAB BAG
■ 519

LOOKING GOOD
429 ■

PETS AND PESTS
■ 533

FEELING GOOD
435 ■

COMMON HOUSEHOLD PRODUCTS
■ 539

EAT WELL EATING OUT
453 ■

VITAMINS, MINERALS, & SUPPLEMENTS
■ 549

SUPERMARKET SMARTS
461 ■

WHAT'S IN YOUR FOOD?
■ 569

SAFETY FIRST
471 ■

INDEX
■ 582

HOUSE AND GARDEN HINTS
487 ■

INTRODUCTION

WHILE SPENDING 22 YEARS AS A PREVENTIVE CARE SPECIALIST counseling in the fields of nutrition, health, and weight control, I was handed an unexpected bonus: thousands of food and nutrition facts given to me by my patients. At first, the facts were grandmothers' and great-grandmothers' secrets about different foods and their preparation. It wasn't long before collecting these interesting tidbits became of hobby of mine, and I started asking my patients to bring me any facts about food that were worth knowing.

I didn't want "old wives' tales" but only food facts that were usable. So the ones I received started ranging from choosing vegetables and fruits to cooking and preparation techniques for every kind of food imaginable.

After 18 years of compiling these hints and tips, I was urged by one of my patients to combine all the information in a book so that all of my patients and the community could use them. But I knew that if I were to undertake the task, I would have to gather more hints, facts, and advice to make the book well rounded. To accomplish this, my family and I contacted chefs from all over the world and asked them to share their secrets. The result was a book called *4,001 Food Facts and Chefs' Secrets*. It was sold at bookstores throughout northern California, which led to interviews on a number of radio stations. Within a few months, the book took off like a rocket and went national.

After the book caught the attention of television personalities like Oprah Winfrey and Crook and Chase, plus the Discovery Channel, America's Talking, and other stations, people across the country began flooding my mailbox with hints and tips. The book grew larger and larger, progressing with every new edition from the figurative 4,001 hints and tips to 6,001, 8,001, and finally 10,001.

Reader's Digest likes *10,001 Food Facts, Chefs' Secrets, & Household Hints* enough to dress it up in this new edition. To them, I say "Thank you"— and to you, the reader, "Enjoy!"

Myles H. Bader, DPH

COOK
IT
RIGHT

VEGETABLE COOKING

Baking or Roasting

Root vegetables—carrots, potatoes, winter squash, jicama, and beets—are well suited to baking and roasting. Make sure that the vegetable has a high enough water content, or it will dry out quickly when cooked. Leave the skins on to preserve most of the vegetables' nutrients. Roast softer vegetables, like broccoli florets and asparagus, for 10 to 15 minutes.

Pressure Cooking

It can be difficult to pressure-cook vegetables; overcooking is common. Follow the directions that come with your appliance.

Stir-Frying

This is a fast method, provided the wok or skillet is well heated first. Because foods cook so rapidly, you're more likely to retain heat-sensitive vitamins, such as A and E.

Waterless Cooking

Best for green leafy vegetables, using only the water that clings to their leaves after washing. Usually takes only three to five minutes.

Boiling

When you boil vegetables, follow these guidelines:

◆ Vegetables should always be added to water that is already boiling. The shorter the time in the water, the more nutrients will be retained. Vitamin C is lost very quickly.

◆ The water should boil for two minutes before the vegetables are added to release some of the oxygen. Oxygen causes nutrient loss.

◆ If possible, cook the vegetables whole and unpeeled. The more surface that is exposed, the more nutrients will be lost.

Slow-Cooking

Avoid slow-cookers for vegetables. During prolonged cooking, most of the nutrients will be lost because of the heat.

Microwaving

Vegetables cook rapidly, so nutrients are retained. The water content of the vegetables will determine just how well they will cook. Microwave ovens should have a turntable so that the food will cook evenly. Foods cooked in a microwave may need to be rotated or stirred to ensure that they are cooked thoroughly and properly.

Measurement Facts

60 drops = 5ml. = 1 teaspoon

3 teaspoons = 1 tablespoon

2 tablespoons = 30 ml. = 1 fl. oz.

8 tablespoons = ½ cup

5 large eggs = 1 cup

1 oz. = 28 g.

Steaming

This method cooks vegetables in a short period and retains most of the nutrients. Start with denser vegetables such as carrots or Brussels sprouts, then add the softer ones, like broccoli florets, later.

Are You Steaming?			
VEGETABLE	TIME	VEGETABLE	TIME
Artichokes	20–25 minutes	Carrots	6-8 minutes
Green beans	10–20 minutes	Cauliflower	5 minutes
Beets	30 minutes	Corn on the cob	7 minutes
Broccoli florets	3–5 minutes	Green peas	5 minutes
Brussels sprouts	6–8 minutes	Pearl onions	20-30 minutes
Cabbage	10 minutes	Potatoes (all)	20-25 minutes

THERMOMETERS

To check the accuracy of a food thermometer, place it in boiling water for three to four minutes. The temperature should read 212°F.

Deep-Fat/Candy

The bulb should be fully immersed in the candy or fat and should never touch the bottom of the cooking container.

Instant-Read

These thin, pointed thermometers have many applications and advantages. Use them to measure water temperature for baking or internal temperatures of many cuts of meat or baked-egg dishes. They register temperatures almost immediately; their small shafts and sharp points mean that little of a meat's juices will escape. Just be sure you don't put these thermometers in the oven!

Meat

Insert the thermometer into the center or thickest part of the meat, making sure that it is not touching bone or a pocket of fat or connective tissue. These thermometers can go into the oven. If you have an instant-read thermometer, you don't need a meat thermometer.

Freezer/Refrigerator

These thermometers read from -20°F to 80°F. Frozen foods should always be stored at 0°F or below to slow nutrient loss and to maintain the quality of the food for a long time.

Oven

These thermometers check the accuracy of your oven. If the temperature is not accurate, it can affect the results of the food being prepared, especially baked goods. The thermometer should be placed in the middle of the center rack. If it the thermostat and the thermometer give different readings, you can either adjust the thermostat when you bake or roast, or have your oven's thermostat recalibrated.

Cooking Temperatures			
FOOD	**TEMPERATURE**	**FOOD**	**TEMPERATURE**
BEEF, LAMB, VEAL		GROUND BEEF, PORK, LAMB	160°F.
Rare	140°F. (not recommended)	**FOOD**	**TEMPERATURE**
Medium-rare	145°F.	POULTRY	
Medium	160°F.	Ground	165°F.
Medium-well 165°F.		Whole	180°F.
Well-done	170°F.	Parts	170°F.
FOOD	**TEMPERATURE**	Stuffing (alone or in bird)	165°F.
PORK AND HAM		**FOOD**	**TEMPERATURE**
Medium	160° F.	Egg dishes	160°F.
Well-done	170° F.	Leftovers	165°F.
Precooked (ham)	140° F.		

OIL CHANGE

To coat food with a very thin layer of oil, use a spray bottle with oil in it (there are special misters that can accommodate the viscosity of oil). This beats using a brush and reduces the amount of oil used.

SWEET HOME AROMA

To help control unpleasant cooking aromas, dampen a cloth with a 50-50 mixture of vinegar and water. Drape it over the cooking pot, taking care that the edges are far from the flame or intense heat.

PUNCTUATION

When baking potatoes, pierce the skin with a fork to allow the steam to escape. Your reward will be a wonderfully fluffy texture.

CRISP IT

If you would like a crisp topping on your casserole, leave it uncovered for the last 15 minutes of baking.

SAFETY FIRST

If a child accidentally turns on the microwave when it's empty, damage may occur to its mechanism. To avoid any problems, just keep a cup of water in the microwave when it is not in use.

KEEP THE ENERGY FOCUSED

To brown meats in the microwave, you'll have to use a special dish. The dish should always be preheated for the best results. If you don't have a browning dish, brush the meat with soy or teriyaki sauce.

If the meat has a bone, more energy will go to the bone than to the meat, and the meat may not cook evenly. If possible, remove the bone.

WHEN USED PROPERLY . . .

A microwave oven is just as safe as a conventional oven. However, make sure you never place a sealed container in a microwave. The pressure can build up, and the container can explode (this is also why you should prick egg yolks and potatoes before microwaving them).

AN ALL-AROUND BREADING

The following breading blend can make any food taste better and enhance its flavor. Mix the ingredients together and refrigerate the mixture until needed. Use about ½ cup at a time, and let the breaded food stand at room temperature for 20 minutes before cooking.

2 cups whole-wheat pastry flour	1 teaspoon ground black pepper
½ tablespoon paprika	1 teaspoon dried basil
1 tablespoon dry mustard	1 teaspoon dried marjoram
¾ teaspoon finely ground celery seed	¾ teaspoon dried thyme

DOUBLE DUTY

Keep a shaker filled with a ratio of 75 percent salt and 25 percent pepper next to the range or food-preparation area.

DON'T BE AN EGG POPPER

Never try to hard cook eggs in the microwave—whole eggs may explode. When cooking an egg with a whole yolk, prick a small hole in the yolk with a pin. The yolk won't break, but you'll allow for its expansion.

CANOLA TO THE RESCUE

To sauté or fry with butter, margarine, or lard, add a small amount of canola oil to raise the smoke point. This will keep the solid fat from breaking down at lower temperatures.

NOT AN OLD WIVES' TALE

To keep a pot from boiling over, stick a toothpick between the lid and the pot. Other tricks include placing a wooden spoon across the top of the uncovered pot or rubbing butter around the inside lip of the pot.

FAT REDUCTION

Frying meat in oil does not lower the fat content—any fat that renders out will be replaced by oil that is absorbed. However, all other methods of cooking will lower the fat content.

WIPE IT

Cast iron and other pans with a high iron content may rust. To prevent this, wash and dry the pan thoroughly, then wipe the inner surface with a thin layer of vegetable oil after each use.

PAPER TOWELS, BEFORE AND AFTER

Use paper towels to blot dry any foods that will be fried or sautéed before cooking; this prevents spatters. Also, set fried foods on paper towels for a few minutes before serving to allow the excess oil to drain off.

GIVE ME AIR

Always use a shallow pot for cooking roasts. This will allow air to circulate more efficiently. Elevating the meat by cooking it atop celery ribs, carrot sticks, or ¼ to ½-inch-thick onion slices also helps.

AN UPLIFTING EXPERIENCE

Sometimes food sticks together when you're deep-frying. To prevent this, lift the basket out of the fat several times before allowing it to stay in the fat. And don't try to fry too much at once—the fat may bubble over from the temperature difference of the cold food and the hot fat. And speaking of hot fat, be sure it's 300°F to 375°F before you add the food.

THE SKINNY ON PUDDING

Laying a sheet of wax paper directly onto a custard or pudding while it is still hot will keep a layer of skin from developing.

CHOP, CHOP

Your market has only canned whole tomatoes and you need chopped? Not a problem. Simply insert a pair of scissors into the can and snip.

THE WHOLE TRUTH

Cooking vegetables whole slows down nutrient loss. For example, carrots that are boiled whole will retain up to 90 percent of their vitamin C and most of their minerals. Sliced carrots will lose almost all of their vitamin C and niacin content when boiled.

DAMAGE CONTROL

Don't add baking soda to foods while they are cooking. It may destroy certain B vitamins, and it turns some vegetables a grayish color.

LOW HEAT IS BEST

Dairy products can curdle if cooked over a high heat. Take care to keep the heat low—no higher than 180°F—so that the food doesn't boil.

DID YOU KNOW?

Acid, heat, and salt are the three main causes of curdling. Older dairy products have higher levels of lactic acid, so use fresh milk and cream in sauces.

POSITION IS EVERYTHING

When you happen to be microwaving foods that are not uniform in shape or thickness, be sure to arrange the larger, thicker, or tougher areas toward the outside of the pan.

FRUIT AND VEGETABLE PREPARATION

Washing and Soaking

Water-soluble vitamins are very delicate and can be lost if vegetables or fruits are left to soak for too long. Dieters often store carrots or celery in a bowl of water in the refrigerator for easy access, but the natural sugars, most of the B vitamins, vitamin C, and vitamin D—not to mention all minerals except calcium—may be lost. It's best to wash vegetables just before you use them.

Slicing and Shredding

When you shred vegetables for salads you will lose 20 percent of the vitamin C content. Then, if you allow a salad to stand for one hour before serving it, you will lose another 20 percent.

COOKWARE ALTERNATIVES

Aluminum

The majority of cookware sold in the United States is aluminum, which is an excellent heat conductor. Recent studies report that there is no risk from using this type of cookware unless your pans are deeply scratched, which allows aluminum to be released into the food.

Iron

Iron cookware will impart a fair amount of dietary iron. It can react with acidic foods such as tomato sauce or citrus fruit to produce off flavors. Iron pots and pans absorb and retain heat very well.

Stainless Steel

This metal is a poor heat conductor unless made with a copper or aluminum bottom. Stainless steel does not react with acidic foods.

Nonstick Cookware

These are made of a type of fluorocarbon resin that may react with acidic foods. If you do chip off a small piece and it gets into the food, don't be concerned; it will pass harmlessly through the body if you swallow it.

Never allow any brand of pan with a nonstick-cooking surface to boil dry. The pan may release fumes that are fatally toxic to pet birds like parakeets if heated above 530°F for long periods.

Glass, Copper, Enameled Cookware

Copper is one of the best heat conductors and is preferred by many chefs. Copper pans, however, should be purchased only if they have a liner of tin or stainless steel for safety; otherwise they may leach metals into the food. Glass and enameled cast iron are nonreactive. Glass heats up very slowly, but retains heat very well. When you bake or roast food in glassware, remember to reduce the oven temperature by 25°F.

Clay Pots

Always soak both the top and bottom of clay pots in lukewarm water for at least 15 minutes before using them. Don't preheat the oven when using a clay pot—put it into a cold oven, then turn on the heat; if sudden temperature changes occur, the cookware may be cracked. Never place a clay cooker on top of the range.

A Note on Convection Ovens

This appliance utilizes a fan that continuously circulates hot air. As a result, food cooks more evenly, and up to 25 percent faster than in a conventional oven. Convection ovens are great for baked goods and roasts, but be sure to follow the manufacturer's recommendations to the letter, especially concerning temperature. Baked goods are easily browned and need to be watched closely.

BYE-BYE, EYEBROWS

Coat your grill with a spray vegetable oil *before* starting the fire, and then clean it shortly after you are through. Never spray the oil on the grill after the fire has started—it may cause a flare-up.

Spray window cleaner on a grill that's still warm to make cleanup easier.

COAL HARD FACTS

◆ To add flavor to barbecued foods, place herbs on the hot coals. The best are savory, rosemary, or dried basil seedpods.

◆ If the coals become too hot or flare up, spray them with water from a mister, or squirt them with water from a bulb baster.

◆ Store charcoal briquettes in airtight plastic bags, because they absorb moisture very easily.

DID YOU KNOW?

Parcooking means to cook a food partially. You can parcook by boiling, blanching, steaming, or microwaving.

SAUTÉING

◆ When sautéing, make sure you only use a small amount of oil, and heat it to a high temperature before adding the food. To test the temperature of the oil, drop a small piece of food into the pan; if it sizzles, it is hot enough for sautéing.

◆ Food will brown faster and cook more evenly if it is not just out of the refrigerator. Cold foods tend to stick to the pan. But for food safety, never keep raw eggs, meat, fish, or poultry at room temperature for more than 20 minutes. During the sautéing process, the food should be stirred constantly to ensure that the browning will be even.

◆ Before sautéing carrots, potatoes, or any dense food, parcook it first. This ensures that the inside will be cooked before the exterior burns.

◆ Foods that are to be sautéed should be dry. Too much moisture on the surface can cause oil to spatter, and it can prevent the surface of the food from browning.

◆ Before sautéing meats, sprinkle a tiny amount of sugar on the surface of the meat. The sugar will react with the juices and then caramelize, causing a deeper browning as well as improving the flavor.

◆ Never crowd a pan with food. Overcrowding causes poor heat distribution, which will result in food that is not evenly browned.

◆ If the foods render too much fat, remove the excess with a bulb baster.

◆ Never cover a pan when sautéing. Steam tends to build up and the food may become mushy.

THE CHEMISTRY OF COOKING

When you heat food, you are increasing the speed of the molecules in that food. The faster the molecules move, the more they collide—and the more heat is generated, the hotter the food gets. This changes the texture, flavor, and even the color of the food. As a matter of fact, for every 20°F you raise the temperature over the normal cooking temperature, you increase the molecular activity by 100 percent.

MOIST HEAT OR DRY?

Less tender cuts of meat that contain a large percentage of connective tissue, or have a tough fibrous structure such as those found in certain vegetables, should be cooked using moist heat. This method helps to break down the fibers of the food, which will tenderize it. There are, of course, exceptions to the rule, two of which are if the meat is heavily marbled or frequently basted. In these cases, dry heat is acceptable.

QUICK, SHUT THE DOOR

If you worry about the amount of heat escaping when you open the oven door when something's cooking, relax. When the door is opened or left ajar for a few minutes it usually takes 40 to 50 seconds for the oven to return to the preset temperature.

WHO GRILLS, MOM OR DAD?

When it comes to slaving over a hot grill, it's Dad who gets the chore 60 percent of the time. However, Mom chooses what goes on the grill almost 100 percent of the time. Her most frequent choices: burgers, chicken, hot dogs, and corn on the cob.

PUT A LID ON IT

When you boil water, cover the pot and the water will come to a boil faster—once it reaches 150°F. At this point, the water is generating steam, which when trapped heats the water faster. Raising 1 gallon of water from 60°F to 212°F (the boiling point) on a gas range top takes 23 minutes with the lid on; without the lid it takes about 35 minutes.

BETTER SAFE THAN SORRY!

In 1996, 525 Americans were killed and thousands became ill from carbon monoxide poisoning. The odorless gas is produced from faulty heating and cooking units. Every home should be equipped with a carbon monoxide detector. It's similar in appearance and function to a smoke detector and costs from $40 to $80.

ARE THERE DIFFERENT TEMPERATURES OF BOILING?

When water boils, the temperature is 212°F (give or take one degree), whether it's boiling gently or rapidly. Food cooks more evenly and retains more nutrients if the water is at a slower boil. Hard water, due to its high mineral content, will reach boiling 1°F to 2°F above soft water.

NEVER SALT FOODS TO BE FRIED

Salt draws moisture from foods. If a food is salted before it goes into the fryer, the salt will draw moisture to the surface and cause the food to spatter when it is placed into the heated oil.

NEVER REUSE FRYING OIL

When oil is used for frying, the temperature is raised to such a high level that a percentage of the oil breaks down (which happens as the oil begins smoking) and decomposes into free fatty acids. Even the oil from a brand-new bottle can break down in a matter of minutes. As a result, it's always best to use fresh oil each time you fry.

NEVER CROWD WHEN DEEP-FRYING

When you add food to hot oil, the temperature of the oil will be lowered. The more food you add, the more the temperature will drop, and the longer it will take to return to normal frying temperature. When this happens, the food will absorb oil and become greasy. There are two steps to preventing this. First, never add too much food to the oil at one time: Not only does it lower the temperature of the oil, but the overcrowding will also prevent the food from frying evenly. Second, be sure the food is close to room temperature before placing it in the fryer: If the food is too cold the oil may drop down to the greasy range of about 300°F to 325°F and may never get back to the proper temperature.

HOT SPOT, COLD SPOT

Cooking pans should be made of a material that will distribute the heat evenly throughout the bottom of the pan so that the food will cook evenly. Not all pans conduct heat evenly. To see whether a pan has hot spots, mix about 4 to 5 tablespoons of sugar with 2 tablespoons of water and pour it into the pan, swirling or spreading to cover the bottom in an even layer. Set the pan over medium heat. The syrup over the hot spots will caramelize and turn brown, creating a visible pattern. Ideally, you won't see a pattern of hot spots, and the sugar will caramelize at the same time. If you do see a pattern, use a heat diffuser under the pan or try the same test using a lower heat setting.

SMOKE, FLASH, AND FIRE POINTS OF OILS

The so-called smoke point of an oil is the point at which the oil starts deteriorating—that is, the oil starts to convert into free fatty acids. All oils have different smoke points; those with the highest are best for frying. Most neutral-flavored cooking oils have the highest smoke points; oils from nuts or fruits, such as walnut oil, hazelnut oil, or olive oil, tend to have lower smoke points.

The flash point is the temperature at which a small amount of flame starts to emanate from the surface of the oil. This usually occurs at about 600°F and is a clear signal that the oil temperature has reached a dangerous level. The fire point is about 700°F. If oil gets this hot, it will ignite. Remember, never use water to put out a grease fire. Cover the pan with a lid, dump in a box of baking soda, or use a fire extinguisher.

Smoke Points of Fats	
FAT	SMOKE POINT
Safflower oil	450°F.
Peanut oil	450°F.
Soybean oil	450°F.
Canola oil	435°F.
Corn oil	410°F.
Sesame oil	410°F.
Sunflower oil	390°F.
Olive oil	375°F.
Lard	361–401°F.
Vegetable shortening	356–370°F.
Unclarified butter	350°F.

GO FOR GAS

Gas ranges for home kitchens burn hotter than electric ranges, and professional gas ranges burn the hottest of all. Gas heat is also easily controlled, and this is why most chefs prefer it. With electric ranges, it's more difficult to make small changes in temperature.

COOKING STUFFED TURKEY

The best temperature for cooking stuffed turkey is 325°F. At lower temperatures, the stuffing doesn't get out of the danger zone of 40°F to 140°F, giving bacteria more time to multiply. Higher temperatures bring the turkey and stuffing to safer temperatures sooner, but may shorten the cooking time so that not all bacteria are killed. Slow overnight cooking with the dressing in the bird causes numerous cases of food poisoning.

CANDY-MAKING SECRET

Candy makers know that keeping the sugar from crystallizing during cooking is a big problem. There's a simple solution to this: Heat the sugar over low heat, without stirring, until the sugar is completely dissolved. To dissolve any sugar crystals that cling to the sides of the pan, cover the pan with a tight-fitting lid and continue cooking the syrup for three to four minutes. The steam that is generated will melt the sugar crystals.

TESTING YOUR METAL

There are a number of materials that are used to manufacture pots and pans, many of which are better for some tasks than for others. Remember, the thicker the gauge of the metal the more uniformly it distributes heat. The finish on the metal will also affect the efficiency of the cookware.

Copper

Copper cookware provides excellent, even heat. It is difficult to keep clean, since black carbon deposits will affect the heat distribution significantly. Copper pots are usually lined with tin, and must be relined if the tin becomes worn; otherwise excess copper may leach into the food.

Copper is reactive, which means that acidic foods may develop off flavors or colors; if the food is high in vitamin C, copper may interfere with it. If you're thinking about purchasing a stainless-steel pan with a copper bottom, be careful—you get what you pay for. Inexpensive pans often have as little as $\frac{1}{50}$-inch-thick copper coating, which is much too thin to distribute heat efficiently and uniformly.

Aluminum

Aluminum cookware stains very easily, especially if you are cooking with hard water. Certain foods, such as potatoes, will also cause the pans to stain easily. Cooking high-acid foods such as tomatoes, onions, wine, or lemon juice, will probably remove some of the stain. However, if the pan is stained when the acidic food is cooked, the stain may transfer to the food and turn it a brownish color. Aluminum pans also tend to warp if they are subjected to rapid temperature changes, especially if they are made of thin-gauge aluminum. Heavy-gauge pans are excellent heat conductors and will not rust.

Cast Iron and Carbon Steel

These are both nonstainless-steel, iron-based metals that have a somewhat porous, jagged surface. These pots need to be seasoned. To accomplish this, you need to rub the cooking surface with canola oil and heat it in the oven to 300°F for 40 to 50 minutes, and then allow it to cool to room

DID YOU KNOW?

Copper cookware tends to be pricey, and it requires care to look its best. A paste of lemon juice and coarse salt makes an inexpensive copper cleaner.

temperature before using it. The oil seals the pores and provides a somewhat nonstick surface. Once the pan is seasoned, the oil forms a barrier that keeps water out and rust at bay. These pots should be washed right after each use using mild soap (heavy scrubbing can remove the seasoning), and then dried immediately. Never use salt to clean the pot, since this may cause rusting. If a cleaner is needed, be sure it is a mild one.

Teflon and Silverstone

These nonstick surfaces are the result of a chemically inert fluorocarbon plastic material baked onto the inside of the cookware or other type of cooking utensil. The surface is commercially seasoned, which produces the final slick coating. The food is actually cooked on jagged peaks that protrude from the pan, which keep the food from sticking. The major benefits of nonstick cookware are that you can use less fat, and cleanup is frequently much easier. Less expensive nonstick cookware usually has a very thin coating and will not last very long with everyday use. With frequent use and cleaning, the coating will eventually wear thin.

Multi-Ply

The bottoms of these pans usually have three layers. They are constructed with a layer of aluminum between two layers of stainless steel. Stainless steel does not have a hot-spot problem, and the heat will be more evenly diffused by the aluminum.

Enamel-Coated

These pans are metal coated with a thin layer of enamel. The coating is produced by fusing powdered glass into the metal surface, which is in most instances cast iron. The cookware resists corrosion, but the enamel can chip easily if hit against another object or dropped, and can even shatter if removed from a very hot range and placed into cold water.

Glass Cookware

Rapid temperature changes may cause glass to crack or break. Glass has a very low "heat-flow" efficiency rating, so the heat that is transferred from the bottom of the cookware will travel slowly to the top of the pot. Because of this, the bottom of the pot will swell and the top of the pot does not expand, creating a structural type of stress where a crack is very likely. Although some glass pots are obviously intended for use on top of the stove, most glass will shatter when exposed to direct heat and should not be used on the stove or under the broiler. Check the product literature and heed the manufacturer's directions.

CRUCIFEROUS COOKING

When you cook cruciferous vegetables such as broccoli, cabbage, or cauliflower, never use an aluminum or iron pot. The sulfur compounds in the vegetable will react with the metal. For instance, cauliflower will turn yellow if cooked in aluminum, and brown if cooked in iron.

THE PRESSURE OF PRESSURE COOKING

Pressure-cooking is especially beneficial for people who live in higher altitudes. At 5,000 feet above sea level, water boils at 204°F, so foods take longer to cook at higher elevations. A pressure cooker allows the water to reach 250°F by increasing the atmospheric pressure in the pot and using the steam to cook the food faster. Steam conducts heat better than air and forces the heat into the food.

BAG THE BROWN BAG

You may remember your mom or grandmother cooking turkey in a brown bag, but don't do it today! Most supermarket brown bags are produced from recycled paper containing a number of harmful chemicals. When heated, these chemicals can be released into the foods and may produce toxic free radicals.

COOKING WITH ALCOHOL

The boiling point of alcohol is 173°F, much lower than the boiling point for water (212°F). When alcohol is added to a recipe it will lower the boiling point until it evaporates.

SALTING YOUR COOKING WATER

Adding 1 teaspoon salt to about 2 quarts of cooking water it will raise the temperature by one or two degrees. Sugar and many other ingredients will also raise the temperature of the water. Just don't add salt to water when you're cooking dried beans—it may toughen them.

HOW A CONVECTION OVEN WORKS

Standard and convection ovens are quite similar; the notable difference is that convection ovens have a fan that increases the distribution of the heat molecules, providing heat to all areas more evenly and rapidly. Because of the efficiency of the heat circulation, convection ovens usually require a lower temperature, thereby conserving energy. Roasts especially do well in a convection oven—because of the lower heat, the meat tends to be juicier.

BOILING POINT VERSUS ALTITUDE

As the altitude increases, the atmospheric pressure decreases. This places less pressure on water that is trying to boil. When this occurs it makes it easier for the water to boil and the water molecules are released more easily.

Altitude (feet)	Fahrenheit	Celsius
0	212°	100°
1,000	210°	99°
2,000	208°	98°
3,000	206°	97°
4,000	205°	96°
5,000	204°	95°
10,000	194°	90°

GETTING BREADING TO STAY PUT

Keeping breading on foods can be a challenge, but there are a few tricks to try. First, make sure that the food that is to be breaded is very dry. Use eggs at room temperature, and beat them lightly. If you have time, refrigerate the breaded food for an hour, then let the food sit at room temperature for 20 minutes before cooking. Homemade breadcrumbs are better than store-bought because of their uneven texture.

WHY PANS WARP

Metal pans have two advantages over other materials: they have a higher heat-flow efficiency rating and they have a tougher internal structure. However, metal pans will warp if exposed to sudden changes in temperature. Thinner pans are less able to withstand the structural stress than thicker ones, so are more likely to warp.

THE SECRET OF WORLD-CLASS GRAVY

Home cooks often use flour to thicken gravy. Because flour thickens somewhat slowly, the temptation is to use too much. Since gravy thickens as it cools, it can become unappealing by the time you're ready for seconds. It can also taste "floury" rather than having the flavor of the meat juices it's made with. Chefs rarely use flour, but deglaze the roasting pan with water, and then add a small amount of butter before reducing the mixture over high heat, stirring frequently, until it is the right consistency.

HOW DOES HEAT COOK FOOD?

There are three main methods of transferring heat to food: radiation, convection, and conduction. Radiant heat is in the form of electromagnetic waves that travel 186,000 miles per second. This form of energy does not require any assistance from air or water. Toasting is an example: Heat radiates from the coils of your toaster to the bread, cooking it. Convection cooking employs circulating molecules, which are propelled by currents of heated air, water, or other liquids. The heat moves from the bottom of the food or liquid and rises, allowing the colder food or liquid to fall toward the heat. Rangetops are a form of convection cooking. Conduction cooking utilizes a medium where the hotter molecules pass along the heat from the surface to the interior of the food. When an aluminum spike is inserted in a potato, the heat passes along the spike to the inside of the food, so it cooks from both the inside and the outside at the same time.

NEVER USE PLASTIC WRAP IN A MICROWAVE

When heated, plastic wrap can release chemicals that migrate into the food. ("Microwave-safe" food wrap won't melt when it comes into contact with hot foods, but it may release fumes.) The wrap may also stick to the foods, especially fatty or sugary ones. Waxed paper, paper towels, or paper plates are good substitutes.

STICKING-LID SOLUTION

When you cook a food in a covered pot, the air inside the pot increases in pressure, raising the lid ever so slightly so heated air can escape. When you turn off the heat, the air pressure decreases along with the temperature and may become lower than the air pressure outside the pot. This decrease in pressure, along with the water from the steam, creates a vacuum around the lid and seals it tight. The longer the lid is left on, the tighter the seal. If this occurs, just try setting the pot over moderate heat for a minute or two. Why? Because the heat will increase the air pressure in the pot, loosening the lid's seal.

GAS OR ELECTRIC?

As with most debates, there's no clear winner. Gas is superior for stovetop dishes; you can make incremental changes in temperature, and the adjustments are immediate. Electric ovens, however, heat up more rapidly than do gas ones, and because the heat is constant (gas heat fluctuates), electric ovens are more accurate.

MICROWAVE MAGIC?

A microwave oven works by emitting high-frequency electromagnetic waves from a tube called a magnetron. This radiation is scattered throughout the inside of the oven by a stirrer, a fan-like reflector that causes the waves to penetrate the food. This, in turn, reverses the polarity of the water molecules billions of times per second, making them bombard one another—which creates the friction that heats the food.

TO MICROWAVE OR NOT TO MICROWAVE, THAT IS THE QUESTION

Microwave cooking is less expensive than most other methods. However, it is desirable only for certain types of foods. Meats, for instance, seem to end up a little mushy and don't attain the brown color we find appealing. Frozen foods will take longer to cook, because it is difficult to agitate the water molecules until they have thawed considerably.

THE SECRET OF SELF-CLEANING OVENS

Electric ovens are capable of much higher temperatures than gas ovens, and self-cleaning ones can get as hot as 1000°F during the self-cleaning phase. In self-cleaning ovens, any food or grease particles disintegrate into dust that only needs to be wiped away.

WOK THIS WAY

Stir-frying foods in woks dates back 2,000 years to the Han dynasty in China. It was developed due to a lack of cooking oil. The stir-fry technique cooks food rapidly in a minimum of oil. Following are some pointers to ensure success when cooking with a wok:

DID YOU KNOW?

Some appliance manufacturers are making ranges with gas cooktops and electric ovens, so home cooks can have the best of both worlds.

◆ Freeze beef, pork, or chicken for about 20 to 30 minutes so it will be easy to cut thin, even-size pieces.

◆ For great flavor, marinate the sliced meat briefly while you are preparing the vegetables. Adding a small amount of cornstarch to the marinade will protect the meat from the high heat and make the meat more tender and juicy.

◆ Vegetables should be cut into uniform bite-size pieces so they will cook evenly. Denser vegetables like carrots and peppers will need to cook longer than vegetables like broccoli florets and snow peas.

◆ Use oil very sparingly. One tablespoon (enough for four servings) is just enough to coat the bottom of the wok.

◆ For the best results, never stir-fry more than ½ pound of food at a time.

QUICHE ME, QUICK!

Quiches, especially those made with onions and mushrooms, should not be allowed to cool. Both of these vegetables have a high water content, which will be released into the quiche as it cools. The result: a soggy crust and runny filling. Let onion or mushroom quiches stand about 10 minutes before cutting them, though, or like any quiche, they'll ooze.

WHEN WAS THE MICROWAVE OVEN INVENTED?

In 1942, Dr. Percy Spencer, an engineer at Raytheon Laboratories, was working with a magnetron tube, which produces microwaves. He had a candy bar in his pocket; when he went to eat, he found that it had melted—although there was no heat source that could have melted it. The only thing he could think of that might possibly have melted the candy was the magnetron tube he was working with.

Dr. Spencer then tried placing a small amount of popcorn near the tube. It popped in a matter of seconds. He then tried focusing the beam through a box at an egg, which exploded on one of his associates, much to both his and the associate's surprise. Twenty-five years later, in 1967, the first microwave oven for home use was introduced to the marketplace.

SLOW AND STEADY

Rival invented the slow-cooker, which it markets as the Crock Pot, in 1971. Many people question whether the pot is safe or a breeding ground for bacteria because it uses low temperatures to cook foods. Most slow-cookers have settings that range from 170°F to 280°F; most bacteria die at

140°F. However, if the lid is left off, the food may not cook fully, so it could potentially harbor bacteria. To minimize the risk of food poisoning:

◆ Do not attempt to cook frozen or partially thawed foods. Foods at refrigerator temperature are safe.

◆ Cook only cut up pieces of meat, not whole roasts or fowl, to allow the heat to penetrate fully.

◆ Make sure that the cooker is at least half to two-thirds full or the food may not absorb enough heat to kill any bacteria.

◆ Cover the food with enough liquid to generate sufficient steam.

◆ Always use the original lid, and be sure it fits tightly.

◆ When possible, cook on the high setting for the first hour, then reduce it to low if necessary.

◆ Never use the cooker to reheat leftovers.

◆ Always follow the manufacturer's directions for temperature settings.

I'D LIKE TO PROPOSE A TOAST . . .

Although Egyptians began toasting bread with long-handled forks in 2500 B.C., Charles Strite received a patent for the toaster in 1918. However, the toaster didn't really work as well as he would have liked. After a few more years of research and refinement, Strite finally produced the first pop-up toaster in 1926 with the brand name of Toastmaster. This toaster also featured a timer, and sales went through the roof. The U.S. Congress was so impressed that in 1927, they declared March as National Toaster Month.

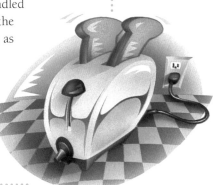

THE CUTTING EDGE

One of the most important utensils in a kitchen is the knife. There are a number of different materials used to make knife blades, which vary widely in price, durability, and weight, among other factors. Make sure the handle is secured with at least three rivets. Always test a knife before you purchase it by making sure it feels comfortable in your hand.

Carbon Steel

This is by far the best metal for having the sharpest edge. However, if the blade is not constantly kept dry, it will rust. Acids in foods may also take their toll and turn the blade black, and the flavor may be passed to foods.

Stainless Steel

This metal has the ability to resist rust and acid from foods. It is much stronger than carbon steel, but it is very difficult to get an extremely sharp edge on a stainless steel blade.

High-Carbon Stainless Steel

This is the most expensive and the one most chefs and serious cooks prefer. It will not rust or stain. It does not have to be washed and dried continually when in use. High-carbon stainless steel can be sharpened to a sharper edge than either of the other steel knives.

LOOK SHARP!

The preferred equipment for sharpening knives is a whetstone, which takes some practice to master. A grinding wheel or electric sharpener can restore the edge, and a sharpening steel keeps the edges in alignment.

If you have a problem keeping an edge on your knife it may mean that you are not using the steel as frequently as you should; you may have to use a grinding tool, such as a wheel or an electric sharpener, to restore the edge. Once your knife is sharp, run both sides of your knife along the sharpening steel at a 20-degree angle before each and every use; wipe off the blade on a clean towel to remove any metal fragments.

WHAT IS THE PROPER WAY TO STORE A KNIFE?

Two of the best places to store knives are on a magnetic rack or in a wooden countertop knife block. Never store knives in a drawer with other utensils. Not only do you risk injury, but the knife blades may become nicked and dented beyond repair.

WHAT SHOULD I LOOK FOR WHEN BUYING A KNIFE?

A top-quality knife is a worthwhile investment for any cook. Purchase either stainless steel or high-carbon stainless steel knives that have good name-brand recognition (ask a knowledgeable salesperson or an accomplished cook for recommendations). Be sure the blade and the handle are forged from one piece of steel. Always hold a knife in your hand before you buy it to be sure it's comfortable. A salesperson might insist you need an 8-inch chef's knife, but you might prefer one with a 6-inch blade.

DID YOU KNOW?

A sharp knife is actually safer than a dull one. Dull knives are more likely to slip off foods, resulting in cut fingers.

YOUR KNIFE COLLECTION

The four basic knives to own are a chef's knife (also called a French knife) for chopping and julienning, a paring knife, a slicer, and a boning knife. Additional knives you might want include a serrated knife for slicing bread, a cleaver, a fish filleting knife, and a pair of kitchen scissors.

BUYING POTS AND PANS

When shopping for pots and pans, always look for a thick, heavy bottom so that the heat will be evenly distributed. To test for heaviness, simply pick up the pot to see how heavy it feels. Another piece of advice: Buy the biggest size pot or pan you need, since you can cook small quantities in a large pan, but not the other way around.

KITCHEN GADGETS

One of the best new gadgets of the last few years is the hand-held blender. It quickly liquifies food directly in the pot or pan you're using. The blender also makes milkshakes in an instant, directly in the glass. Other products include food processors, which come in all sizes and do more than just blend and chop; non-mechanical pastry blenders, for easily cutting butter or shortening into flour; and egg slicers, which evenly slice a hard-boiled egg in a quick, single motion (it's all in the wrist).

HOW TO CHECK YOUR OVEN TEMPERATURE WITHOUT A THERMOMETER

Put about 1 tablespoon flour on a baking sheet and set it into a preheated 350°F oven for five minutes. If the flour turns light tan, the temperature is 250°F to 325°F. If the flour turns golden brown, the oven is 325°F to 400°F. If it turns dark brown, the temperature is 400°F to 450°F. An almost a black color means the oven is 450°F to 525°F.

PASTA, NOT BASTA

When the weather is bad and stormy, the atmospheric pressure goes down. The lower the pressure, the lower the boiling temperature of water. It only decreases by one or two degrees, but you may notice that it takes a little longer to cook pasta.

ACROSS THE POND

If you're an American using an English cookbook, you may well find certain ingredients unfamiliar. Most are actually common on this side of the Atlantic, but go by different names. This chart should help in translating from one country to the other.

British Food	American Food
Plain flour	All-purpose flour
Strong flour	Bread flour
Single cream	Light cream or half-and-half
Double cream	Whipping cream
Caster sugar	Superfine sugar
Demerara sugar	Brown sugar
Treacle sugar	Molasses
Dark chocolate	Semisweet chocolate
Sultanas	Golden raisins
Courgette	Zucchini
Swedes	Turnips
Gammon	Ham
Capsicum	Bell pepper
Aubergine	Eggplant
Minced beef	Ground beef
Cornflour	Cornstarch
Wholemeal flour	Whole-wheat flour
Rocket	Arugula
Mangetout	Sugar snap pea

COMMON SUBSTITUTIONS

Unless otherwise noted, use the substitution in equal measure to the ingredient called for in the recipe.

IF THE RECIPE CALLS FOR	SUBSTITUTE
ACTIVE DRY YEAST (one ¼-ounce envelope)	1 cake compressed yeast
AGAR-AGAR	Plain unflavored gelatin (use more)
ALLSPICE	1 part ground cinnamon + 2 parts ground cloves or ground nutmeg (for baking only)
ANISE SEED	Fennel seed (use equivalent amount)
APPLES (1 cup chopped)	1 cup firm chopped pears + 1 tablespoon lemon juice.
APPLES (1 pound)	4 small, 3 medium, or 2 large or 2⅔ cups sliced or chopped
ARROWROOT	Use 2 tablespoons flour for every 4 teaspoons arrowroot
BAKING POWDER (one teaspoon, double-acting)	⅝ teaspoon cream of tartar + ¼ teaspoon baking soda or ¼ teaspoon baking soda + ½ cup sour milk or buttermilk. (Must take the place of other liquid.)
BASIL (dried)	Tarragon, summer savory, thyme, or oregano
BAY LEAF	Thyme
BLACK PEPPER	Cayenne pepper (use much less; start with a pinch)
BRANDY	Cognac or rum
BULGUR	Cracked wheat, kasha, brown rice, couscous, millet, or quinoa
BUTTER (in baking) Do not use oil in baked goods.	Hard margarine or shortening
BUTTERMILK (1 cup)	1 cup milk + 1¾ tablespoons cream of tartar or 1 tablespoon lemon juice + milk to make 1 cup (let stand 5 minutes) or sour cream
CAKE FLOUR (1 cup)	1 cup minus 2 tablespoons unsifted all-purpose flour
CAPERS	Chopped green olives
CARAWAY SEED	Fennel seed or cumin seed
CARDAMOM	Cinnamon or mace
CAYENNE PEPPER	Ground hot red pepper or chili powder

IF THE RECIPE CALLS FOR	SUBSTITUTE
CHERVIL	Parsley, tarragon, or ground anise seed (use less)
CHIVES	Onion powder (small amount) or finely chopped leeks or shallots (small amount) or scallion greens
CHOCOLATE, BAKING, UNSWEETENED	3 tablespoons unsweetened cocoa powder + 1 tablespoon (one ounce or square) butter or 3 tablespoons carob powder + 2 tablespoons water
CHOCOLATE, SEMISWEET (6 ounces chips or squares)	9 tablespoons unsweetened cocoa powder + 7 tablespoons sugar + 3 tablespoons butter
CILANTRO	Parsley and lemon juice
CINNAMON	Allspice (use less) or cardamom
CLOVES (ground)	Allspice, nutmeg or mace
CLUB SODA	Sparkling mineral water or seltzer
CORNMEAL	Polenta
CORNSTARCH	Flour, as thickener
CORN SYRUP (1 cup, light)	1 ¼ cup granulated sugar + ¼ cup more of the liquid called for in recipe
CRÈME FRAÎCHE	Sour cream in a most recipes or ½ sour cream + ½ heavy cream in sauces. Note that crème fraîche can be boiled but sour cream cannot.
CUMIN	1 part anise + 2 parts caraway or fennel
DILL SEED	Caraway or celery seed
EDIBLE FLOWERS (garnish)	Bachelor buttons, blue borage, calendula petals, chive blossoms, mini carnations, nasturtiums, pansies, rose petals, snapdragons, or violets
EGGS, WHOLE	2 yolks + 1 tablespoon water
EVAPORATED MILK	Light cream or half-and-half or heavy cream
FLOUR (thickeners, use up to 2–3 tablespoons only)	Baking mix, quick-cooking tapioca, cornstarch, arrowroot (use small amount), potato starch, instant potato flakes, or pancake mix
GARLIC (1 medium clove)	¼ teaspoon minced dried garlic or ⅛ teaspoon garlic powder or ¼ teaspoon garlic juice or ½ teaspoon garlic salt (omit ½ teaspoon salt from recipe)
GHEE	Clarified butter

IF THE RECIPE CALLS FOR	SUBSTITUTE
HONEY (1 cup, in baked goods)	1 ¼ cups granulated sugar + ¼ cup more of the liquid called for in recipe
JUNIPER BERRIES	Gin (use small amount)
LEMONGRASS	Lemon juice or lemon zest or finely chopped lemon verbena or lime zest
LOVAGE	Celery leaves
MARJORAM	Oregano (use small amount), thyme, or savory
MASA HARINA	Cornmeal
MASCARPONE	8 ounces cream cheese whipped with 3 tablespoons sour cream and 2 tablespoons milk
MILK (in baked goods)	Fruit juice + ½ teaspoon baking soda mixed in with the flour
MILK (1 cup)	½ cup evaporated milk + ½ cup water or ¼ cup powdered milk + ⅞ cup of water. (If whole milk is called for, add 2 ½ teaspoons melted and cooled butter.)
MILK, EVAPORATED	Light cream or half-and-half or heavy cream
MOLASSES	Honey
NUTMEG	Allspice or cloves or mace
OREGANO	Marjoram or thyme
PANCETTA	Lean bacon (cooked) or very thin sliced ham
POLENTA	Cornmeal or grits (corn)
POULTRY SEASONING	Sage + a blend of any of these: thyme, marjoram, savory, black pepper, and rosemary
ROSEMARY	Thyme
SAFFRON (⅛ teaspoon)	1 teaspoon dried yellow marigold petals or 1 teaspoon safflower petals or ½–1 teaspoon turmeric (adds color)
SAGE	Poultry seasoning or savory or marjoram
SELF-RISING FLOUR (1 cup)	1 cup all-purpose flour + 1 ½ teaspoons baking powder + ⅛ teaspoon salt
SHALLOTS	Small scallions or leeks or yellow onions

IF THE RECIPE CALLS FOR	SUBSTITUTE
SHORTENING (1 cup, in baked goods only)	1 cup butter or 1 cup stick margarine
SOUR CREAM (1 cup)	1 tablespoon white vinegar + milk to make 1 cup (let stand 5 minutes before using); or 1 tablespoon lemon juice + evaporated milk to make 1 cup; or 1 cup plain yogurt if it is being used in a dip or cold soup; or 6 ounces cream cheese + 3 tablespoons milk; or ⅓ cup melted butter + ¾ cup buttermilk; or ⅓ cup melted butter + ¾ cup plain yogurt
TAHINI	Peanut butter
TARRAGON	Anise (use small amount) or chervil (use larger amount) or parsley (use larger amount) or a pinch of fennel seed
TOMATO PASTE (1 tablespoon)	1 tablespoon ketchup or ½ cup tomato sauce providing you reduce some of the liquid in recipe
TURMERIC	Mustard powder
VANILLA EXTRACT (in baked goods only)	Almond extract or other extracts that will enhance the flavor of the dish
VINEGAR	Lemon juice in cooking and salads only or grapefruit juice, in salads or wine, in marinades
YOGURT	Sour cream or crème fraîche or buttermilk or mayonnaise (use in small amounts)

2

STORE
IT
RIGHT

FOOD PRESERVATION

Food can be preserved only if the microorganisms that cause spoilage are destroyed or their growth is controlled. There are a number of methods for doing this: drying, dehydrating, salting, smoking, irradiating, heating, freezing, and using chemical preservatives.

The microorganisms that cause food spoilage are in the water, in the air, and on preparation and storage surfaces. They may be brought home on other foods and may even be in the product itself. In many cases, the contamination is a natural occurrence, such as when salmonella is present in the chicken ovaries. Microorganisms can exist in two forms: First, in colonies that are visible to the naked eye, such as molds on bread, cheese, or fruits and vegetables; second, in small spores that are carried in the air and are for the most part invisible.

There are three kinds of microorganisms: molds, yeast, and bacteria.

◆ Molds are usually airborne spores or seeds that may alight on food products and start to multiply. They tend to send out feelers or filaments and grow in colonies that may appear in many colors, depending on their food source. Mold spores will move from one food to another, especially among fruits, so it is wise to check all your produce when you bring it home to be sure it is mold-free.

◆ Yeast is a one-celled fungus that produces enzymes that convert sugars to alcohol and carbon dioxide in a process called fermentation.

◆ Bacteria are microscopic organisms that need only a small amount of organic material and moisture to grow and multiply. They grow by dividing their cells. When there is no moisture, or if the available moisture is used up, all of these microorganisms will stop growing, and they will dry up and become dormant until moisture is again introduced.

SHOULD I FREEZE IT?

Most people are uncertain about whether to freeze or refreeze a particular food, and, if it is frozen, about how long it will retain not only its nutrient value, but also its flavor and consistency. Many foods do not do freeze well: some become tough when defrosted, others quickly develop ice crystals, which can cause them to become mushy when defrosted.This chapter provides some information on food storage, and if you follow these tips you should be successful. If you have any doubts, freeze a food in small batches.

TIPSY FOODS: SLOW FREEZERS

If you are going to freeze any food that has alcohol in it, such as an ice cream or sorbet, remember that alcohol will not freeze like water, and the food may need to be frozen at a lower temperature.

CLOSE IT UP, SEAL IT UP

The longer a food is frozen, the more nutrients it will lose. Seal all foods to be frozen as tightly as possible to avoid freezer burn and the formation of ice crystals. Ice crystals cause thawed food to become mushy.

VACATION TRICK

When you go away on vacation, fill a zip-close plastic bag with a few ice cubes and put it in the freezer. If a power failure occurs while you are away, the ice will melt and refreeze in a solid block, alerting you that your frozen food has been defrosted.

COLD DAMAGE

A number of foods, including garlic, onions, shallots, potatoes, and tomatoes, should never be refrigerated because the cold will cause sprouting, loss of flavor, or conversion of their starch to sugar. Garlic, onions, shallots, and potatoes should all be stored in a cool, dark place; tomatoes should be stored at room temperature.

READY TO EAT

If you freeze a sandwich the night before and remove it from the freezer in the morning, it will thaw by lunchtime. (For safety, pack your sandwich in an insulated bag.) If the bread is buttered before freezing, it will not become soggy or absorb any filling. Do not freeze sandwiches that contain jelly, salad dressing, or mayonnaise.

WAS NAPOLEON RESPONSIBLE FOR FOOD PRESERVATION?

The men in Napoleon's army became sick and many of them died from scurvy and other diseases related to a lack of essential nutrients in their diet. Because they were far from any source of fresh food on their long marches, all they could carry with them were salted meats. Napoleon offered a reward equal to $250,000 in today's money to anyone who

DID YOU KNOW?

Freezer temperature is critical for maintaining quality of foods. Keep your freezer set at 0°F.

could develop a method for preserving foods. After 14 years of trial and error, Nicolas-François Appert, a Paris confectioner, finally discovered a method that worked. He placed the food to be preserved in a glass jar, allowing enough room for expansion, and placed a hand-hewn cork in the jar, attaching it firmly with a piece of wire. Each jar was then wrapped in a burlap sack and lowered into a pot of boiling water. The boiling time varied with the type of food to be preserved. Appert was successful in preserving eggs, milk products, fruits, vegetables, and meats. He was awarded the prize money in 1810 and became known as "the man who discovered the art of making the seasons stand still."

WHO MADE THE FIRST TIN CAN?

Peter Durand, an Englishman, invented the tin can in 1810—the "tin canister." The can made it possible to transport foods to outlying areas without the breakage that occurred with glass jars. The cans were handmade, with workers cutting them from sheets of tin, then soldering them together, leaving a hole in the top. After the food was put in the can, the hole was covered with a small tin disk and soldered closed.

The United States started its first commercial canning operation in the 1820s, and within 20 years foods were being canned all over the country. In 1860 Isaac Solomon, in Baltimore, discovered that if he added calcium chloride to boiling water he could raise the temperature from 212°F to 240°F, thus reducing the time required for processing canned foods from about six hours to 30 minutes. The oldest canned food that has been safely eaten was a 114-year-old can of meat—but try to use canned food within a year for best nutrition and flavor.

WHO CAME UP WITH THE NAME BIRDSEYE?

Clarence Birdseye, an American businessman who invented a way to freeze foods in small packages, founded the Birdseye food company. He discovered the process by accident while hunting in Labrador in 1914. The dry Arctic air froze some portions of caribou and fish, and when thawed they were tender and still tasty. He developed a freezing method that duplicated the Arctic conditions and founded Birdseye Seafoods in 1923. In 1929 Birdseye sold the company to Postum Co. and Goldman Sachs Trading Co. for $22 million; the following year, the first Birdseye Frosted Foods—frozen peas and spinach—were sold in supermarkets.

NEGATIVE EFFECTS OF FREEZING FOODS

When food is frozen, ice crystals form and grow, puncturing the cells of the food and absorbing the water; when the food thaws, water that had been in the food is released from the ice crystals. This is the result of osmosis, the process by which a liquid passes through a semipermeable membrane (cell wall) in order to equalize the pressure inside and outside the cell. This occurs in all foods regardless of the method of freezing or the type of wrap. Because the flavor of the food is distributed among all the cells, this causes some of the flavor to be lost. Meats, fruits, and most seafood are more negatively affected by osmosis than are vegetables.

BE SMART WHEN FREEZING FOODS

There are a number of important facts you should know if you wish to freeze foods successfully:

◆ When preparing most vegetables for freezing, be sure they are blanched, or briefly steamed or boiled. This will lessen the enzymatic activity in the vegetable, and reheating will complete the cooking.

◆ After blanching, vegetables should be plunged into ice water and drained before freezing.

◆ Vegetables such as pumpkins, winter squash, and sweet potatoes should be fully cooked before freezing.

◆ Freezing tends to intensify the flavors of certain foods, such as garlic, peppers, and cloves. Use less in a dish that you will freeze, and when reheating, taste and add more as needed.On the other hand, use more onion than you would otherwise, because freezing tends to cause onion to lose its flavor. Herbs and salt also tend to diminish in flavor, so it's best to add them after freezing, when you're reheating the dish.

◆ Never use quick-cooking rice in a dish that will be frozen, as it becomes mushy when reheated. Use regular or converted rice.

◆ Artificial flavorings and sweeteners do not freeze well.

◆ Don't add toppings to dishes to be frozen; add when serving.

◆ Freezing causes russet or Idaho potatoes to fall apart; always use red-skinned or potatoes with waxy flesh in dishes that are to be frozen.

◆ Avoid freezing sauces. Egg-based sauces and those high in fat tend to separate when reheated, and cheese- or milk-based sauces are prone to curdling. Most gravies will thicken considerably when frozen, but they can be thinned when reheated.

◆ Cool already-cooked foods in the refrigerator before freezing.

A FULL FREEZER, PLEASE, SIR!

A full freezer works more efficiently than a half-full freezer because the cold in the foods themselves will help to maintain the temperature, saving you considerable money in electricity.

BLANCHING BEFORE FREEZING: A MUST!

The enzymes in vegetables, even those previously stored under refrigeration, may remain active and cause changes in the color, texture, and taste when they are frozen. To prevent this from happening, blanch or steam them briefly. The vegetables will not be cooked, but the enzymes will be inactivated. Of course, the enzymes are also important nutrients, and it is always desirable to eat fresh rather than frozen vegetables.

CHEST VERSUS UPRIGHT FREEZERS

The answer to this ongoing debate is actually quite simple. The chest freezer, even though its door may be larger, will retain its cold setting longer when the door is opened because cold air is heavier than hot air and tends to stay put when the door opens up. The upright freezer tends to release most of its cold air the minute the door is opened.

SMOKE-CURED FOODS

The use of smoke to cure foods is one of the oldest methods of preservation, but one that provides a number of risks because of the toxins that may be introduced into the food from the smoke. Smoke may contain as many as 200 different chemical components, including alcohols, acids, phenolic compounds, pyrobenzine, and other carcinogenic chemicals. Many of these toxins are, in fact, the very substances that retard microbial growth, which is why smoking works as a method of preservation. Salt-curing and smoking are frequently used in combination to minimize the oxidation of fats that causes foods to turn rancid. Eaten in moderation, smoked foods should not present problems, but they should never be the mainstay of your diet.

NEW STORAGE BAGS: A MUST FOR EVERY KITCHEN

A new type of plastic bag, marketed under the name Evert-Fresh (yes, the spelling's correct!), is great for storing fruits and vegetables. The bag con-

DID YOU KNOW?

If you don't want to freeze a sandwich, freeze a juice box and pack it in your lunch bag. It will act as an ice pack to keep foods cold but should thaw by lunchtime.

tains hundreds of microscopic holes that allow air to circulate around the produce. The bag is also impregnated with a natural substance that absorbs the ethylene gas that produce releases as it ripens and that eventually causes it to spoil; reducing the amount of gas keeps the food fresher longer. The bags are also tinted green to prevent the permeation of light, which would reduce the potency of the vitamins in the food.

These bags will keep produce fresh three to 10 times longer than standard plastic storage bags, and tests done over a 12-day period show that produce stored in these bags retain 50 percent more vitamin C.

STORING MARGARINE

Inside the fridge, margarine quickly absorbs odors from other foods. It should be tightly sealed and will keep 4 to 5 months in the refrigerator or for one year frozen at 0°F.

Freezer Storage Times for Meats at 0°F			
MEAT	MONTHS	MEAT	MONTHS
Bacon, sliced	1	Hot dogs	2
Bacon, unsliced	1	Organ meats	1-2
Beef, roasts	9	Pork, chops	6-9
Beef, steaks	9	Pork, ribs	6-9
Cold cuts	1	Pork, roasts	9
Duck	4-6	Poultry, parts	6-9
Fish, fatty	3	Poultry, whole	6-12
Fish, lean	6	Rabbit	6-9
Goose	4-6	Sausage	2
Ground beef	2-3	Shrimp or shellfish	4-6
Ground pork	2-3	Turkey, whole	6-12
Ham	3	Turkey, parts	3-6

PROBLEMS WITH ALUMINUM FOIL

Because aluminum foil is a great insulator, it tends to slow down the transfer of heat (or cold), so that foods wrapped in foil will take longer to freeze. As a result, bacteria will have more time to grow and may not be killed when the food is reheated. In addition, when you crinkle the aluminum foil to place it around the food, the foil may develop tiny cracks, which will allow air and moisture to penetrate the food; heavy-duty foil tears and cracks less easily and is better for freezing. If you plan to store food covered in foil for more than two to three days in the refrigerator, wrap it first in plastic. Aluminum foil will also react with acidic or salty foods, causing them to taste unpleasant.

WHICH IS BETTER, A THERMAL BOTTLE OR A VACUUM BOTTLE?

A hot beverage placed in a container for storage loses its heat to the air outside through conduction, and a cold beverage will become warmer as a result of the same process. Both thermal and vacuum bottles slow the transfer of heat and cold between the beverage and its surroundings by placing a barrier between the beverage and the environment. Thermal bottles are not as efficient as vacuum bottles, but they will not break as easily because they do not have a glass interior.

COLD FACTS

◆ If ice cream thaws it should not be refrozen; bacterial growth is possible if it is.
◆ Jelly, salad dressing, and mayonnaise do not freeze well.
◆ The freezer in your refrigerator is not the same as a supermarket freezer. The home freezer is best for storing foods for short periods only.
◆ Foods should be cooled as quickly as possible, and then frozen. This prevents bacterial growth.
◆ Potatoes in stews or casseroles become mushy when frozen because their cells have a high water content and tend to break down easily. Mashed potatoes, however, freeze well.
◆ Do not freeze any bakery item with a cream filling because it will become soggy.
◆ Custard and meringue pies do not freeze well. The custard tends to separate and the meringue becomes tough.
◆ Waffles and pancakes may be frozen, thawed, and reheated in the toaster.

3

IT'S PARTY TIME

DIP HOLDERS

For a pretty dip holder, use a large green, red, or yellow bell pepper. Remove the top and scrape the pepper clean of ribs and seeds. A scooped-out cucumber or small squash will work as well. Another idea: Hollow out a round loaf of pumpernickel bread and fill the crust with your favorite spinach dip. Cut the bread into cubes and dunk them in the dip.

EASY FINGER SANDWICHES

Slice a loaf of French bread lengthwise, fill with filling of choice, and use an electric knife for easiest slicing.

CHEESE IT

Homemade pizzas often lack the crispness of pizzeria pies. Here's one tip that should help: Add the cheese *before* the tomato sauce. Cheese has a lower water content than tomatoes do, and the crust won't get as soggy.

GOBBLE, GOBBLE

If you have ever wondered how many appetizers each guest will consume, wonder no more. At a cocktail party (no meal served), figure 10 to 12 mouthfuls per person. If you're serving dinner, figure four to five mouthfuls. If you are having a wine and cheese gathering, figure 4 ounces of cheese per person. If you're serving a dip and crackers or chips, 1 cup of dip will serve eight people if you are serving other nibbles (each person will eat about 2 tablespoons). Four cups of dip will provide about 160 cracker-size servings (each serving being a little over a teaspoon). If you're having a picnic, figure on three beers or soft drinks per person.

FRESH IDEA

For the buffet table, hollow out a melon, orange, or grapefruit and fill it with cut-up fruits and miniature marshmallows. For a more attractive holder, you can scallop the edges, or cut it in the shape of a basket.

A CHILLING SOLUTION

To keep ice cubes from melting at a party, put them in a bowl, and then set that bowl in a larger one filled with dry ice.

BEFORE IT TURNS TO VINEGAR

Freeze leftover wine in ice cube trays (store the cubes in freezer bags). Use the cubes in wine coolers and any dish that calls for wine.

WHO-O-OSH

Serving a dessert that's flambéed? Soak sugar cubes briefly in lemon or orange extract that contains alcohol, and then set them on the dessert. Carefully ignite the cubes with a match.

THE SANDWICH OF MANY COLORS

Color cream cheese with powdered or liquid food coloring to use it as a filling for dainty rolled sandwiches. Try a different color for each layer, then slice as you would a jelly-roll cake.

CHILLY CHERRIES

For children's drinks, freeze red or green maraschino cherries in ice cubes; for adult drinks, freeze cocktail onions or olives in the cubes. Or, freeze lime or lemon rinds in cubes for a nice twist. Inserting toothpicks before freezing makes for easy retrieval.

KEEPING REAL CO-O-OL

One of the easiest ways to keep a large punch bowl cold is to make large ice cubes in coated paper milk cartons (remove the paper label before using). The larger the ice cube, the slower it melts.

YOU'RE IN TROUBLE IF YOU RUN OUT

When you buy ice cubes in the bag, you will get about 10 cubes per pound. The average person at a party will go through 10 to 15 cubes depending on the type of drink.

JOLLY-GOOD FOOD

Instead of using a pastry shell around the filet when preparing Beef Wellington, try using refrigerated crescent-roll dough. Do not separate the dough into triangles, but keep it one whole piece.

THIS WILL SURPRISE YOU

Here's a great-tasting, super-fast, high-fiber dip: Puree 1 cup of drained cooked white beans with a package of herb-flavored soft cheese.

NATURAL EGG DYES

It's easy to make natural Easter-egg dyes. Use grass for green, onion skins for yellow and deep orange, or beets for pink. Add to the water when you boil the eggs. If you plan to eat the eggs, be sure to use plants that haven't been fertilized or treated with pesticides or other chemicals.

CHILDREN'S TREAT

Surprise the kids with sandwiches in the shape of animals or objects. It's as simple as using animal-shaped cookie cutters.

AVOIDING A CRUSTY SOLUTION

To keep your meat or cheese hors d'oeuvres moist, cover them with a damp paper towel, then cover loosely with plastic wrap. Many fillings (as well as bread) dry out very quickly.

IT'S LIKE MAGIC

Have you ever had a problem with soda fizzing over the top of an ice-filled glass? The cubes will fizz less if you put them in the glass and rinse them for a few seconds, and then pour out the water. You will have changed the surface tension of the ice, and then the soda won't fizz over.

A REALLY BIG BARBECUE

Fifty folks coming for a backyard barbecue? Start with 17½ pounds of ground beef for hamburgers and 70 buns; then buy 20 pounds of hot dogs and 100 hot-dog buns. For the traditional side dishes, buy 2 gallons of baked beans, 6 quarts of potato salad, and 10 pounds of cole slaw.

DISINTEGRATION

If you have a cork stuck inside of a wine bottle and want to keep the bottle, pour a small amount of ammonia into bottle and place it outside for two to three days. The ammonia should dissolve the cork.

DID YOU KNOW?

If you're hosting an Easter egg hunt, be sure that no one eats any hard-cooked eggs that have been out of the refrigerator for more than two hours.

BEULAH, FROST ME A GRAPE

Choose some really nice sized grapes, wash them, and dry them thoroughly. Dip them in a solution of ½ cup granulated sugar and ½ cup ice water, then freeze. Don't freeze for more than one day for the best results.

SWEET IDEA

To save money, purchase solid chocolate bunnies after Easter or Santas after Christmas when they are half price. Store them in the freezer. To use, shave off chocolate with a potato peeler whenever you need chocolate.

A GOOD OLD SQUEEZE

To make fancy butter pats for a party, soften the butter (don't melt it completely), and then put it in a pastry bag with a decorative tip, such as a rosette. Squeeze the butter onto a baking sheet and refrigerate until hard.

MAKING BUTTER BALLS

If you would like butter balls, set a melon baller in very hot water for five minutes, then scoop out butter from a 1-pound brick, dropping each ball in a bowl of cold water with ice cubes. Store in the refrigerator.

WHOA, DISH

The dishes set on a buffet table tend to move around when people scoop food from them. Just set a damp cloth napkin or dish towel under the dishes to solve this problem.

THE RIGHT TEMPERATURE

At buffets, keep cooked foods either hot or cold, not lukewarm. Hot foods should be kept at 140°F in a warming tray or in a chafing dish. Cold foods should be kept at 40°F or cooler.

WANT ENTERTAINMENT?

If you decide you want to have live entertainment at a party, it may be easier than you think. Often, musicians and singers can be found through a local college, a music school, or a church that is known for its music.

SHOPPING FOR A PARTY?

The following chart is for 20 guests; adjust the quantities accordingly.

What You Need		
TYPE OF FOOD	**SERVING SIZE**	**AMOUNT NEEDED**
Butter/margarine	1 tablespoon	3 sticks
Cake	1/12 cake	(2) 13-x 9-inch cakes
Canned vegetables	1/2 cup	6 pounds
Coffee	1 cup	1 pound
Ice cream	1 cup	5 quarts
Mashed potatoes	1/2 cup	6–8 pounds
Olives	4	1 quart
Pasta	1 cup, cooked	2 pounds, uncooked
Pickles	1/2 pickle	10 medium pickles
Pie	1/6 pie	(4) 9-inch pies
Pizza	1/3 of 12-inch pie	(7) 12-inch pizzas
Potato salad/slaw	1/2 cup	3 quarts
Potato/corn chips	1 ounce	1 1/4 pounds
Soft drinks	12 ounces	(4) 2 liter bottles
Soup	1 1/2 cups	(6) 50 oz. cans
Spaghetti	1 1/2 cups	3 1/2 pounds, uncooked
Tea, iced	1 cup	1 1/2 gallons (or 30 tea bags)

4

BAKING
BASICS

FLOUR FACTS

Flour is most often ground from grains, but fruits, vegetables, beans, nuts, herbs, and seeds can also be used. Primarily, flour is used in breads, muffins, pies, cakes, cookies, and other baked goods. It is also used to thicken soups, stews, gravies, and sauces. Many foods are floured before they are breaded to help the breading adhere better.

Most commercial flour is milled by the roller process. High-speed rollers and sifters crack grain, separate it from the bran and germ, and then grind it to a fine consistency.

Wheat flours are more popular than other types because they contain gluten. This protein gives wheat its strength and elasticity, which is important in the production of breads.

TYPES OF FLOUR

All-Purpose Flour

A blend of hard- and soft-wheat flour. It has a balanced protein and starch content, which makes it an excellent choice for breads, rolls, and pastries. It may be used for cakes when cake flour is unavailable (use $7/8$ cup all-purpose for every cup of cake flour). Presifted all-purpose flour has been milled to a fine texture, is aerated, and is best for biscuits, waffles, and pancakes. However, it can settle during shipping so it should be sifted before use if called for in the recipe.

Bleached Flour

A type of all-purpose flour.

Bran Flour

A whole-wheat flour that can have a drying effect on baked products.

Bread Flour

Made from hard wheat. It has a very high protein, or gluten, content and is used to make breads.

Brown Rice Flour

Contains rice bran as well as the germ and has a nutty flavor.

Cake Flour

A very fine white flour, made entirely of soft wheat. It is best for baking cakes and soft cookies. Produces soft-textured, moist baked goods.

Corn Flour

A very starchy flour used to thicken sauces; it has a slightly sweet flavor. It is not the same thing as cornstarch.

Gluten Flour

A very strong white flour that has twice the strength of standard bread flour. Used as an additive with other flours.

Instant Flour

A very finely milled white flour that pours and blends easily with liquids. It is used mainly as a thickener for sauces, gravies, and stews. It is rarely used for baking due to its fine, powdery texture.

Pastry Flour

Has a gluten content between cake flour and all-purpose white flour; it is best for light pastries and biscuits.

Potato Flour

Used mainly to thicken stews, soups, and sauces. Because it produces a moist crumb, it is used in some baked goods.

Rice Flour

Excellent for making delicately textured cakes.

Self-Rising Flour

A soft-wheat, white flour that should not be used in yeast-leavened baked goods. Contains a leavening agent that tends to cause deterioration. The flour should be used within one to two months of purchase.

Semolina

A somewhat coarsely ground flour made from durum wheat. Used mainly in commercial pasta and bread. Has a high protein content.

Soy Flour

A gluten-free flour produced from lightly toasted soy beans, which have a somewhat sweet flavor. Baked goods made from soy flour tend to stay fresh longer than those made with other flours.

Whole-Wheat Flour

Ground from the entire wheat berry, including the bran and germ. It is sometimes sold as graham flour and has small specks of brown. Because it is slightly higher in fat than other flours, it should be stored in the freezer or refrigerator to retard spoilage.

BAKING PANS MUST RISE TO THE OCCASION

Choose your baking pans carefully—they're an important part of the baking process. The pans should be thick or insulated (heavy-duty pans don't warp) and light in color. Dark or nonstick pans absorb heat, and can result in cookies, cakes, breads, and pastries that are burnt, tough, or dry. Lighter pans reflect heat. The bottoms of cookies will be more likely to remain golden if you bake them on a shiny metal pan.

THE TASTE TEST

Not sure whether the flour in the canister is self-rising or all-purpose? Taste it. Self-rising flour will taste salty because it contains baking powder.

ARE BREAD AND TOAST NUTRITIONALLY DIFFERENT?

The answer is yes, but not different enough to matter. When bread is toasted, a chemical reaction that caramelizes the sugars and proteins on the surface takes place, turning it brown. (This is called the Maillard reaction, after the French scientist who first noted it.) A piece of bread that weighs 23 grams (just less than one ounce) provides 2.1 grams of protein and 11.5 grams of carbohydrate; the same size slice of toast provides 2.4 grams of protein, 13.6 grams of carbohydrate. Those who make their own bread can boost the protein by replacing 2 tablespoons of regular flour with an equal amount of soy flour.

CAN POPPY SEEDS GIVE YOU A POSITIVE DRUG TEST?

Poppy seeds are commonly derived from the same poppies used to make morphine and codeine, so they may indeed cause a positive urine test for opiates. In one incident, a Michigan woman ate a lemon poppy-seed muffin which resulted in a positive urine test. She was in trouble until the authorities and the University of Michigan solved the mystery.

DEBUGGING YOUR FLOUR

It is almost impossible to purchase any flour without some sort of bug infestation. In fact, it is so unavoidable that the FDA allows an average of 75 insect fragments per 50 grams (about 2 cups) of grain. At this level, your health is not in danger. Insects and their eggs may set up residence when the grain is warehoused, during transit, or even in your home. To reduce the risk of infestation, store your grains and flour in the freezer to prevent eggs from hatching.

DRYING OUT

Baking is a dry-heat method of cooking that surrounds the food with heated air. Baking dries the food, and it is important to control the amount of moisture lost.

WORK FAST

Remember, on humid or very hot days, yeast dough can rise faster than you expect and can become very hard to knead. When this occurs, there is a loss of elasticity.

VICE VERSA

The ingredients for baking cakes and cookies should always be warm, never cold, to start. For pastry it is just the opposite: The ingredients should be cold.

LOOKS FUNNY, TASTES GREAT

For a different type of toast, lightly butter a slice of bread on both sides and cook it in a waffle iron.

WHO STOLE THE COOKIE . . .

Rinse out coffee cans and store cookies in them. Use the original lids, or stretch plastic wrap across the top and seal with a rubber band.

BUT IT'S HEALTHIER

Whole-wheat bread dough will not rise as high as bread dough made from all-purpose or bread flour. Whole-wheat flour is denser because it's not as refined. This is why most whole-wheat bread recipes blend whole-wheat flour with either bread or all-purpose flour.

DOWN, DOUGH, DOWN!

Electric stand mixers are a boon for bakers, because the dough hook attachment reduces or eliminates the need to knead. To keep the dough from climbing up the hook, spray the dough hook with nonstick cooking spray or vegetable oil before turning the mixer on.

DID YOU KNOW?

You can freeze bread dough. Let it rise once, and then punch it down, wrap well, and freeze. Don't forget to label it!

USE THE BEST BOARD FOR THE JOB

A wooden board is your best bet for kneading bread, but other surfaces will work. Just be sure to flour the board and your hands adequately.

OVERSIZE BAGELS

In 1999, Americans spent more than $617 million on bagels. Most bagel-shop and deli bagels weigh between 4 and 8 ounces, turning a formerly low-calorie breakfast into a high-calorie one.

FRISBEE, ANYONE?

Take advantage of leisurely weekend mornings. If you're making French toast, waffles, or pancakes, cook some extras and freeze them. On harried weekday mornings, just pop them in the toaster for an easy breakfast.

BREAD BASICS

Don't be fooled by bread labels—be sure to read ingredient lists to be sure you're buying what you really want.

◆ If the package reads wheat flour or wheat bread it is probably made from white flour. Most flour is made from wheat, so "100 percent wheat" does not mean the same as "100 percent whole-wheat."

◆ Rye bread typically contains mostly white flour and very little rye flour. A bread made only from rye flour would be heavy and dense—almost inedibly so. But read labels and avoid those with artificial coloring.

◆ To purchase the highest quality white bread, make sure the list of ingredients reads "unbleached flour" or "enriched flour."

BAKING SMART

For best results, preheat the oven for at least 20 minutes before baking. Another tip: In most instances, it is best to bake the food on the center of the rack so heat can circulate evenly.

PANS NEED THEIR SPACE, TOO

Never set pans next to each other on the same oven rack. Air space between pans is important, so the hot air can circulate.

PUCKER UP!

To speed whole-wheat bread dough's rising time, add one tablespoon of lemon juice to the dough as you are mixing it.

TIMING IS IMPORTANT

Make sure you turn pancakes as soon as air bubbles appear on the top. Why? Because if you wait until the bubbles break, gas escapes, and your pancakes won't be as light or fluffy.

STARCH IT

When you boil potatoes, save the cooking water. It contains just the right amount of starch to substitute for water you might use in a bread recipe. It will also help keep the bread fresher for a longer period.

VITAMIN C TO THE RESCUE

Adding a bit of ascorbic acid (vitamin C) to the flour when you bake bread can help to strengthen weak flour. For every 6 cups flour, add a pinch of powdered ascorbic acid to the yeast.

TRICK OF THE TRADE

When you make pancakes, waffles, or latkes, always stir the batter between batches. This keeps the ingredients from settling and keeps the batter aerated.

AN OLDIE BUT GOODIE

If you find icing too sweet or too rich, try this cake topping: Set a paper lace doily on the cake, and then dust lightly with confectioners' sugar. Carefully lift the doily off the cake. Try colored confectioners' sugar or a mixture of confectioners' sugar and cocoa powder.

EASY DOES IT

If you make bread with 100 percent whole-wheat flour, it will be moister if you add the flour to the water slowly and mix gently. Whole-wheat flour absorbs water at a slower rate than do other types of flour. Reserve ¼ cup of flour and knead in a tablespoon or so at a time as needed.

RISING TO ANY OCCASION

Yeast is a living single-celled organism. In a single pound, there may be up to three trillion cells. They prefer to live on sugar in any form (including starch and complex carbohydrates) and produce alcohol and carbon dioxide, which is what causes dough to rise. When you use flour or wheat starch, the enzymes actually produce the sugar for the rising to take place.

COLD STORAGE IS BEST

Always store yeast in the refrigerator. The cold slows down deterioration. Bringing the yeast to room temperature will help it dissolve faster.

SOURDOUGH SECRETS

Sourdough bread is made from a live bacterial culture that is called a starter. Once upon a time, starters were fermented mixtures of water, flour, and airborne yeasts, but today they are often made with a special sour-dough yeast. As the starter ferments, it becomes sour. Starters may be kept for years. Only a small portion is removed when needed for making each loaf, and the starter can be "fed" or added to.

CURSES, FOILED AGAIN

Serving fresh-from-the-oven rolls or bread for dinner? Here's a trick to keep them warm: Tuck a small piece of aluminum foil under the cloth in the breadbasket. It helps the food retain the heat.

COOL IT!

After you've removed bread from the oven, always cool it on a wire rack. This will allow air to circulate around the bread and should eliminate any soggy areas in the loaf.

GOING UP

A little heat does wonders when it comes to cutting down on rising time. Set the dough (either in a bowl or a loaf pan) on a heating pad set on medium, or over the pilot light on a gas stove.

DID YOU KNOW?

Muffins will come out of the baking pan more easily if you place the hot pan on a cool, wet towel for about 30 seconds.

FATTY LITTLE STICKS

It's always a good idea to read the list of ingredients and nutrition labels to check the fat content before you purchase bread sticks. They may contain up to 40 percent fat.

TOO CHEWY?

One secret to light biscuits: Handle the dough gently. Overworking the dough and rerolling the scraps makes for tough biscuits.

A LITTLE DIP WILL DO YA

If you dip a biscuit cutter in flour, the dough won't stick to it. And when you cut biscuits out, don't twist the cutter. The motion seals the edges of the biscuits, keeping them from rising high.

UP, UP, AND AWAY

Substitute buttermilk for milk in a muffin or quick-bread recipe. You'll be amazed at how light they are.

LESS EXPOSURE FOR SOFTNESS

For soft biscuits, brush them with milk or melted unsalted butter, and then arrange them in a cake pan so the sides touch one another.

ZAPPING A SANDWICH

When you heat a sandwich in the microwave, you'll get the best results if you use a firm textured bread such as French or sourdough. The filling should be heated separately. If the filling is heated in the sandwich, be sure to spread it evenly over the bread and very close to the edges. Wait a few minutes before eating the sandwich, as the filling may remain very hot even if the bread is cool to the touch.

A NO-NO

Most bread machines are timed for the use of dry yeast. Compressed fresh yeast should never be used in bread-baking machines. If you have a bread machine, look for special bread-machine yeast.

GOOD OLD BREAD BOX

Keeping bread in the fridge can prevent mold developing, but the refrigerator's dry air draws moisture from the bread, so it will go stale faster. Freezing maintains the freshness, but when the bread thaws, ice crystals rupture and the texture of the bread suffers. The best place to store bread? That depends on how long it will take you to use it. For up to five or six days, wrap it in waxed paper or a paper bag; if you have a bread box, perfect—otherwise leave it on the counter. Avoid plastic bags, which can make the crust soggy. If it will take you more than six days to use the bread, it should go into the freezer.

CRUNCHY-CRUST SECRET

If you prefer bread with a crispy crust, here's a secret: Put some ice cubes in a shallow pan and put this in the oven when you put in the bread. This will produce a dense steam, and as the water evaporates, the crust becomes hard and crispy. The steam also will allow the bread to rise more evenly, giving you a nice firm, chewy inside.

THE ROLE OF SALT IN BREAD MAKING

Salt makes bread crust a little crisper and is essential for flavor, but it also slows down the growth of yeast, which prevents the dough from rising too fast. If this happens, the air pockets will be larger and your bread will have a coarser texture.

LOWER FAT, HIGHER PRICE

A reduced-fat Oreo contains 47 calories and 1.67 grams of fat. The original Oreo has 53 calories and 2.33 grams of fat. Not a big savings calorie-wise, and because reduced-fat foods often cost more than their original counterparts, your pocketbook may be the only thing that's lighter.

DOING THE TWIST

About 1,400 years ago in a monastery in northern Italy, a monk made the first pretzel. It was during Lent, when he was forbidden to use any type of fat, eggs, or milk. He made a dough of flour, salt, and water and formed it into the shape of what he thought were two arms crossed in prayer. He named the bread *pretiola,* which is Latin for "little gift," and gave the treat to the town children as a special reward for saying their prayers.

WHAT DO SWEETENERS DO?

Sweeteners such as honey, molasses, and sugar are imperative in bread-making. Yeast can produce carbon dioxide only if sugar is present. Omitting or reducing the amount of sugar in your recipe can be tricky business—your bread may be heavier or take longer to rise.

LITTLE BOYS, LIKE LITTLE GIRLS, LIKE LITTLE OREOS

Hands down, America's favorite cookie is the Oreo, which was first marketed by the National Biscuit Company of Hoboken, New Jersey in 1912. The Oreo Biscuit, as it was originally known, was described in the company literature as "a biscuit with two beautifully embossed, chocolate-flavored wafers with a rich cream filling." The company has manufactured 362 billion Oreos since they were introduced, which is an average of more than 4.1 billion every year for 85 years. If you are counting calories, that amounts to more than eight trillion calories.

WHY THE FRENCH BUY BREAD TWICE A DAY

Authentic French bread is made without fat. Fat coats the strands of gluten in the flour, retarding their development, and tends to slow down moisture loss in bread. As a result, French bread can get stale in as little as six hours.

THE RISE AND FALL OF A SOUFFLÉ

When you beat egg whites, you incorporate air into them. The air bubbles are trapped, and when a soufflé is placed in the oven, the air expands, causing the soufflé to rise. If the soufflé is punctured or shaken, the air will be released too early and the soufflé will collapse.

TWO TWINKIES A DAY?

Twinkies were invented by James Dewar in 1930. Mr. Dewar lived to be 88 years old, and supposedly attributed his long life to the fact that he ate two Twinkies every day since he invented them. How long do you think he would have lived without them?

DID YOU KNOW?

You can keep the top of your bread from cracking if you slash it first. Use a single-edge razor blade to make two or three shallow diagonal cuts across the top.

CHESS, ANYONE?

Chess pie is a specialty of the southern United States. It has a rich, smooth, translucent filling made of eggs, sugar, butter, and buttermilk. In the 1800s, the pie was made with molasses because sugar was hard to come by. It remains fairly flat when baked and traditionally is flavored with vanilla or lemon.

HOW MUCH BREAD DOES A BREAD PLANT BAKE?

Most large bread-baking companies can bake 20,000 loaves every hour. A typical plant uses raw materials literally by the trainload: It is not unusual for a large plant to have two million pounds of flour delivered every week in steam-sterilized boxcars or specially equipped tankers. The flour is then stored in sealed silos until used, with each silo carefully dated. Bakeries that use this much flour have very strict rules regarding sparks or the lighting of a match, because flour dust may be ignited under the right conditions.

WHEN IS A CAKE A COOKIE?

Mexican wedding cakes are really very rich, buttery, cookies filled with pecans or almonds. The cookies are coated with confectioners' sugar when they are warm and then again after they are cooled. In some bakeries they're called Russian tea cakes.

HOW DOES BREAD BECOME STALE?

When bread is baked, water accumulates in its starch. As bread ages, water is released from the starch and evaporates, so the texture of the bread becomes more crumbly and firm. The longer bread lasts, the more water is released from the cells—resulting in an increasingly dry, hard loaf. Reheating bread allows the moisture that remains to be redistributed into the starch. The trick to reheating bread is to warm it just enough to move the water back into the cells—if it is heated too much, the water will evaporate. Keep the moisture in by heating the bread in a sealed container or in foil, and don't let the temperature go above 140°F.

WHY SOURDOUGH BREAD IS SOUR

Standard baker's yeast does not work well in an acidic environment; sourdough yeast thrives in an acidic environment. Baker's yeast works by breaking down maltose. The bacteria in sourdough breads also require maltose, but do not break it down. The acids that are found in sourdough bread are 75 percent lactic and 25 percent acetic acid. The bacteria prefer a temperature of 86°F and a pH of 3.8 to 4.5 as ideal. Standard bread yeast prefers a pH of 5.5. Starters for sourdough have lasted for hundreds of years and are thought to be protected by a bacteria that is related to the penicillin mold in cheese.

HOW DOES BAKING POWDER WORK?

Baking powder is a mixture of leavening agents. The primary ingredients are calcium acid phosphate or cream of tartar, which act quickly at low temperatures; sodium aluminum sulfate, which reacts at high temperatures; and sodium bicarbonate. When this mixture of acids and alkalis come into contact with water, it produces carbon dioxide. This gas either enters air pockets that already exist in the batter or dough, or it creates minute air pockets.

When the dough or batter is heated, the baking powder releases even more carbon dioxide, and the trapped carbon dioxide expands, creating steam. This pressure swells the dough or batter, and it expands or rises.

DRY BEFORE WET, THE SAFER BET

Never put a wet measuring spoon into a baking powder tin. Use 1 teaspoon of baking powder for each cup of flour.

FRESHER IS BETTER

Baking powder loses potency over time. If you can't remember when you bought it, you should test it before using it. Put ½ teaspoon of baking powder in a small bowl, then pour in ¼ cup of hot tap water. The more vigorously it bubbles, the fresher the baking powder. Try this test on a fresh box of baking powder so you will be familiar with the activity level of the fresh powder. Be sure to check the expiration date on the box when you first purchase it to be sure it's fresh. Once opened, baking powder will remain fresh for up to a year.

THE BEST THICKENERS FOR THE BEST PIES

The best thickener for fruit pies is 3 to 4 tablespoons of minute tapioca. Just mix it with the sugar before adding to the fruit.

BAKING WITH BUTTERMILK IN LIEU OF MILK

Don't substitute buttermilk for milk measure for measure in baking recipes. Chemically, the two are quite different, which you need to accomodate. Buttermilk is much more acidic than regular milk and will interfere with the leavening agent, reducing the amount of carbon dioxide.

  To offset the additional acid, reduce the amount of baking powder by 2 teaspoons and replace it with ½ teaspoon of baking soda for every cup of buttermilk you use in place of milk.

HOW MANY EGGS DOES A BAKER CRACK OPEN EVERY DAY?

At large baking companies, bakers rarely take the time to break open every egg. Instead, frozen whole eggs are used. Frozen eggs are delivered at −15°F and must be thawed before use. Defrosting takes six to eight hours in a special tank of cool, running water.

LOW-FAT CAKES

Although there are a few substitutions you can use to replace fat in baked goods—and there are many excellent cookbooks outlining the fine points of this—it is important to realize that fat performs several important functions. It extends shelf life, adds tenderness and flavor, and contributes to the texture of baked goods. When fat is replaced, baked goods may be altered to an unacceptable degree. Replacements include: skim milk, egg whites, pureed cooked fruits such as applesauce or prune puree, and syrups; professional bakeries may use certain starches and gums. These can rarely replace all the fat, but they do help to retain moisture and may reduce the total calories.

HOME FORMULA FOR BAKING POWDER

No baking powder? No problem. Here's the formula to mix the equivalent of 1 teaspoon: use ⅝ teaspoon of cream of tartar and ¼ teaspoon of baking soda. If you plan to store a quantity of this mixture for a few days, add ¼ teaspoon of cornstarch to absorb moisture from the air. This formula tends to work more rapidly than do commercial baking powders. When you use homemade baking powder, plan to get the food in the oven as quickly as you can.

SOLVING THE MYSTERY OF CAKE PROBLEMS

Shortened Cakes

These are made by creaming shortening (usually butter) and sugar together. Eggs are then beaten into the mixture, and then dry and liquid ingredients are added alternately in increments.

If your cake is coarse-textured, heavy, and dense, you most likely didn't cream the sugar and fat long enough. These ingredients need to be mixed together very thoroughly for best results. Be sure the butter is at room temperature.

Overbaking can cause cakes to become dry; be sure to check the doneness after the minimum baking time.

Elongated holes mean you may have overmixed the batter when you added the flour.

Angel Food, Chiffon, and Sponge Cakes

These are foam cakes—that is, they are made by beating egg whites just until the peaks bend over. If your cake isn't high, you may not have beaten the egg whites long enough, or you may have overmixed the batter when you add the flour. The ingredients should be gently folded in and combined until the batter is just smooth.

If an angel food cake falls, it's probably because you opened the oven door to test the cake for doneness before the proteins coagulated enough for it to hold its shape when the temperature changed. Other causes may be overbeaten egg whites, or you may have forgotten to cool the cake upside down (this lets the steam dissipate throughout the cake, so it's lighter and fluffier).

Tough cakes result from overmixing when you add the dry ingredients. Ingredients should be blended only until they are mixed.

If your sponge cake has an uneven texture, you didn't beat the egg yolks long enough. They should be beaten until thick and lemon colored.

If your chiffon cake has yellow streaks, you probably added the yolks directly into the dry ingredients instead of making a well in the center of the dry ingredients and then adding the oil and egg yolks.

If your chiffon cake is uneven, you may have either overbeaten or underbeaten the egg whites. Beat the egg whites only until peaks bend over.

HARD WATER WOES

The high mineral content of hard water may retard yeast fermentation by causing the gluten in the flour to become tough. The minerals prevent the protein in the flour from absorbing water the way it normally would. There are a number of solutions: using bottled or unchlorinated water, adding a small amount of vinegar to reduce the pH, or adding more yeast. Water that is too soft can cause the dough to be sticky.

PANCAKE SECRETS—REVEALED!

Short-order cooks and chefs have a host of tricks to make the lightest pancakes; here are a few:
- Replace the liquid in the recipe with an equal amount of club soda. This increases the amount of air in the pancakes and make them fluffier. But take note: batter with club soda won't keep, so you'll need to use it all after you mix it.
- Don't overmix the batter—leave a few lumps—so the gluten doesn't overdevelop and so the carbon dioxide doesn't escape.
- Refrigerate the batter for up to 30 minutes. This further slows the development of the gluten and the leavening action.
- Always, always, stir the batter before you pour it onto the griddle. The ingredients can settle; stirring recombines them and aerates the batter.
- If you like brown-on-the-outside pancakes, add a little extra sugar. The sugar caramelizes, giving a browner color to the pancakes.

GET IT HOT

Pancakes should be cooked on a 325°F griddle. But how do you know when it's that hot? Flick a few drops of water on the heated griddle. The droplets should skitter and dance—steam causes the drops to rise, but gravity brings them back down. If the griddle is too hot the water drops will be propelled off the griddle; this usually occurs at about 425°F.

BLEACHED VERSUS UNBLEACHED

When flour is processed, it can retain an unappealing yellowish tint. Bleaching removes the yellow, but it also destroys the vitamin E. Flour is bleached with chlorine dioxide gas. Higher-quality flours are naturally aged, so the oxygen in the air bleaches them.

DID YOU KNOW?

You can make a pancake syrup by mixing 1/3 butter, 1/3 cup sugar, and 1/2 cup frozen orange juice concentrate. Heat, stirring constantly, until the sugar has dissolved and the mixture is syrupy.

SHOOFLY, PLEASE BOTHER ME

Shoofly pie is an old Pennsylvania Dutch specialty. It's a single-crust pie with a sweet, spicy custard filling made from molasses, brown sugar, butter, and boiling water. It is usually covered with a crumb topping made with brown sugar and a variety of spices; its flavor is reminiscent of gingerbread. Sometimes the custard is on top and the crumbs are inside. There are several stories about how the name originated—some say the pie was so sweet you had to shoo the flies away, others say the pie was originally made to lure flies from other foods.

FOOLS RUSH IN . . .

This is actually a classic British dessert made from fruit and whipped cream. The fool is usually made with a cooked-fruit puree that is chilled, sweetened, and then folded into whipped cream and served in a tall glass. The traditional fruit of choice is the gooseberry. Fools probably originated in the fifteenth century.

YEAST AND ITS USES

A cake of yeast is composed of millions of one-celled organisms. Put yeast in a warm (ideally 110°F to 115°F), moist environment and feed them sugar or starch, and they'll multiply like crazy. Yeast causes carbohydrates to convert into a simple sugar, glucose, which then ferments into alcohol and carbon dioxide. It is the carbon dioxide that leavens, or raises, the baked goods by expanding the air and creating steam. There is no risk from the production of alcohol, because the heat from the baking evaporates the alcohol as well as kills the live yeast cells.

A SLUMP TO GET INTO

A slump is a deep-dish fruit dessert with a biscuit-like crust that dates back to Colonial times in New England. The name slump came about because the dessert does not hold its shape well and usually slumps over when served.

ANOTHER ONE FOR THE MICROWAVE

Bread bakers take note: You can cut the rising time by one-third if you use your microwave oven. Here's how to do it for one standard loaf: Set ½ cup of hot water in the back corner of the microwave. Place the dough in a well-greased microwavable bowl and cover it with plastic wrap, and then cover the plastic wrap with a damp towel. With the power level set at 10 percent, cook the dough for 6 minutes, and then let it rest for 4 to 5 minutes. Repeat the procedure if the dough has not doubled its size. Do *not* heat the dough at higher than 10 percent power setting—the dough will turn into a half-baked glob. The only downside to this quick-rising trick is that the flavor of the bread may not be as full. When bread rises slowly, the flavor has more time to develop and permeate the dough.

Another quick-rising method is to heat the dough at 100 percent power for 1 minute, and then leave the oven door closed and let the dough stand 15 minutes. If you don't have a turntable, rotate the dough a quarter turn, and then repeat the process.

NO LITTLE WHITE HOCKEY PUCKS

If your biscuits are heavy and dense, check your baking powder for freshness and make sure that you sift all the dry ingredients together. If you don't have a sifter, put the dry ingredients into a large sieve and shake them into the mixing bowl, or whisk them. It's the even blending of the ingredients that's key. Shortening is also the preferred fat for biscuits. Butter makes for a more solid biscuit, and oil makes them greasy.

YOU NEED TO KNEAD

Don't skimp when kneading bread—it's what distributes the yeast and other ingredients evenly throughout the dough. If dough isn't kneaded properly, it won't rise evenly. Electric bread machines, stand mixers and food processors, however, can make short work of this important task; many recipes are written specifically for these appliances.

WHAT IS FONDANT ICING?

Fondant icing is made from corn syrup, granulated sugar, and water that is cooked to 238°F, then quickly cooled to 140°F and rapidly worked until it is white, creamy, and very smooth. It is then cured for as little as a day to as long as a week; it is reheated over a double boiler before using.

DON'T SNICKER, DOODLE

The snickerdoodle is a cookie that originated in the 1800s in the north-eastern United States. It is buttery and filled with dried fruit nuts, and spices, usually nutmeg or cinnamon. The top of the snickerdoodle is sprinkled with cinnamon sugar before it is baked, which gives it a crinkly top. Snickerdoodles can be crispy or chewy.

ANOTHER CAKE CURE

If your cakes "dome" when baked, it may be caused by one of three things: The oven temperature was too high (use an oven thermometer and adjust the temperature accordingly), your pan was too small (be sure to use the exact size specified in the recipe), or the balance of liquid, egg, flour, and fat was off (always measure accurately).

REMOVING BREADS AND CAKES FROM PANS

When breads and cakes are baked, steam builds up inside, which needs to be released after they are removed from the oven. If the steam cannot escape, it will revert to water as it cools and will be absorbed back into the baked good, which will become soggy. To avoid this problem, remove the pan from the oven and cool the food in the pan for a few minutes. Then transfer the baked good to a cooling rack so air can circulate on all sides, evaporating the steam.

DRY AND COMPRESSED YEAST

Compressed yeast has a higher level of moisture, about 72 percent compared with the standard dry yeast at 8 percent. Compressed yeast should be stored in the refrigerator and lasts for only about two weeks before losing its effectiveness. Dry yeast should always be stored in an airtight container because it absorbs water rather easily. The yeasts are inter-changeable, with 1 packet of the active dry yeast equaling the leavening power of 1 cake of the compressed yeast.

BAKING POWDER AND CHOCOLATE MAKE A BAD CAKE

Chocolate is acidic enough to upset the balance between the acid (cream of tartar) and the alkali of baking powder. Baking soda (sodium bicarbonate) may make a chocolate cake too alkaline, so most recipes also call for a sour-milk product such as yogurt, sour cream, or buttermilk to ensure that the batter will not be too alkaline. If the batter becomes too alkaline, the cake will be red instead of brown, and it will taste bitter.

THE SECRET TO MAKING FLUFFY BISCUITS

When you cut out biscuits from the dough, be sure to press the cutter straight down—don't twist it even slightly. Doing so seals the edges of the biscuits and they won't rise as high.

THERE'S NO CREAM IN IT

Cream of tartar is derived from grapes during and after fermentation. A pinkish crystalline sediment remains in wine casks after the wine has fermented; it is argol, which collects on the sides of the cask. (Lees are another by-product of fermentation; they are the thick layer of dead yeast and grape residue that sinks to the bottom.) Argol and lees are crude tartar; argol is preferred for making cream of tartar. Crude tartar is then decrystallized by cooking in boiling water and then allowing the remains to crystallize again. This substance is then bleached pure white and further crystallized. As this process concludes, a thin layer of very thin white crystals forms on the surface. The name cream of tartar is derived from this thin top layer that looks like cream. Cream or tartar is used to produce baking powder when mixed with baking soda.

WHAT IS BAKING SODA?

Baking soda is actually bicarbonate of soda, which is composed of carbon and oxygen molecules that combine to form carbon dioxide gas when mixed with a liquid. If a batter is sufficiently acidic, then only baking soda is needed to produce carbon dioxide. If the batter does not have sufficient acid, then baking powder, which carries both acid and alkali, is needed.

About 90 percent of the baking soda in North America is mined from the mineral trona, which is found in Green River, Wyoming. The large deposit was discovered in the 1930s. Trona is actually composed of sodium bicarbonate and sodium carbonate, a very close relative. The ore is mined, crushed, rinsed, and heated to produce sodium carbonate. The sodium carbonate is then dissolved in water and carbon dioxide is forced through the solution, releasing the sodium bicarbonate crystals, which are then washed, dried, and packaged as baking soda.

When baking soda is added to a recipe, it has an immediate rising action, which means that your oven must be preheated and your pans greased before you even combine the ingredients. Baking soda should be added to dry ingredients, and they should be combined with the wet ingredients just before the food goes into the oven.

If you are not sure how old your baking soda is, test its activity level. Stir ¼ teaspoon into about 2 teaspoons of white vinegar; it should bubble vigorously. If it doesn't, throw it out.

Sodium bicarbonate is also produced in the human body to assist in maintaining the acidity (pH) level of the blood. It is also found in saliva and will neutralize plaque acids that might otherwise dissolve our teeth. It also neutralizes stomach acid, and assists in the breathing process by transporting carbon dioxide from the tissues to the lungs for disposal.

MAKING TURKISH DELIGHT

This chewy, rubbery dessert is made from fruit juice, honey, sugar, cornstarch, and gelatin. It is colored pink or green and usually contains a variety of nuts for texture. An old-fashioned treat, Turkish Delight is usually found in squares and covered with powdered sugar.

THE CASE OF THE UNRISEN DOUGH

One of the most frequent problems bread bakers encounter is yeast dough that doesn't rise adequately. There are a number of reasons for this.

◆ The dough may be too cool, which reduces the level of yeast activity. Dough can rise at lower temperatures—even in the refrigerator—but it takes several hours or overnight to attain the same volume that it can at 80°F to 90°F in an hour or two.

◆ The yeast may have been prepared with water that was too hot, which can kill it. The water must be around 115°F for optimum results.

◆ The yeast may have been too old. Proof the yeast before using it to be sure it's not ready for retirement.

JUMBLE, JUMBAL—IT'S NOT A DANCE CRAZE

Whether you spell it *jumble* or *jumbal,* you'll love this tasty cookie that dates all the way back to colonial America. It is a sugar cookie baked in a ring shape, flavored with sour cream, and then scented with rose water. Sometimes nuts are added to the top.

DID YOU KNOW?

Baking soda will last for about six months so long as you keep it in an airtight container in the fridge or in a cool, dry place.

YEAST, DEAD OR ALIVE?

Yeast should always be tested, or proofed, before using it. To proof yeast, dissolve a little sugar in warm water; sprinkle in the yeast. The mixture should begin bubbling within about 5 to 7 minutes. If it doesn't, the yeast are either dead or too inactive to provide the leavening function.

THE NAPKIN TEST

There is an easy method of determining whether baked goods are high in fat: the napkin test. Set the baked good on a paper napkin or paper towel. If the item leaves a grease stain, it contains more than three grams of fat. To reduce the fat on a slice of pizza, blot the top with a paper napkin.

HERMITS ARE CHEWY

The hermits in question are chewy, spicy cookies that are usually flavored with brown sugar, cinnamon, nutmeg, and cloves. Chopped fruit or raisins and nuts are typically added.

TO BLEACH OR NOT TO BLEACH

Unbleached flour is the best choice for most baking projects. It has a more natural taste because it lacks the chemical additives and bleaching agents used in bleached flour. Bleached flour is less expensive to produce because it doesn't require aging. Aging, however, strengthens the bonds among the gluten of unbleached flour. Don't skimp when buying unbleached flour; not all companies allow the flour to age adequately.

WHY DOESN'T BREAD COLLAPSE ONCE THE STEAM IS RELEASED?

Some food science: The structure of the bread is supported by the coagulation of the proteins and the gelatinization of the complex carbohydrates. If this did not occur, all baked goods would collapse once they started to cool and the steam and carbon dioxide dissipate.

WHAT IS A BATH BUN?

It is a yeast-risen roll that is filled with candied citrus peels and raisins or currants. Bath buns are usually topped with powdered sugar and occasionally caraway seeds. They are commonly found in England and originated in the town of Bath.

MAKING IT WITH A TWIST

Pretzels are made from a stiff, thin, yeast-risen dough that is baked so that the pretzel will have a hard surface. Once the pretzel dough is shaped, it is sprayed with a 1 percent solution of lye (sodium hydroxide) or sodium carbonate that is heated to 190°F. It is this process of spraying and heat that causes the surface starch to gelatinize. The surface is then lightly salted or left plain and baked at a high heat for 4 to 5 minutes. The gelatinized starch hardens and leaves a shiny surface. The lye creates an alkaline condition on the surface, which causes the intense brown color. The lye reacts with carbon dioxide while it is cooking to form a baking soda. The final cooking stage occurs at a lower temperature and takes about 25 minutes, at which point the pretzel is hard and crisp; a shorter cooking time will produce a soft pretzel.

DOUGH THE RIGHT THING

Cookie dough is fairly high in sugar and fat, and has little liquid. Bread dough has less fat and sugar than does cookie dough, and more liquid. Batter has more liquid than dough.

COOKIE FACTS

Because cookie dough has less water than bread dough, the starch has less opportunity to gelatinize and the gluten has less opportunity to develop. With most cookies, you mix the shortening, eggs, sugar, and liquid together, and then gently fold in the flour and leavening agent. For puffier cookies, use vegetable shortening instead of butter and cake flour instead of all-purpose, and chill the dough before baking.

MARGARINE MADNESS

When you use margarine to make cookies, the firmness of the dough will depend on the type of margarine you use. Be sure to use a stick margarine, not one in a tub. Margarine made from 100 percent corn oil will make the dough softer. When using margarine you may need to adjust the chilling time and may have to place the dough in the freezer instead of the refrigerator. If you're making cutout cookies, the chilling time should be at least one hour in the refrigerator. Dough for drop cookies and bars does not have to be chilled.

YOU'VE GOT TO LOVE A GRUNT

This grunt was first developed in the late 1700s in America; it is a type of cobbler. It was most often made with berries and topped with a biscuit dough, and then steamed in a covered kettle that hung over an open fire. Water was added to the fruit, and as it steamed sugar formed a syrup on top of the fruit. The name grunt comes from the sound that the fruit makes as it releases steam. Grunts are still popular in New England, where they are served with ice cream on the side.

HEAT MATTERS

Baked goods should always be baked at the temperature specified in the recipe, with one notable exception: If you are using a glass baking dish, reduce the specified oven temperature by 25°F. Glass heats slowly but it retains heat well; failing to lower the temperature can result in burned bottoms. Oven thermometers are inexpensive and are available at most supermarkets and hardware stores—if you are at all unsure how accurate your oven is, they're an easy way to tell.

THE FASTEST GROWING BAKED GOOD

Tortillas and tortilla chips are the fastest-growing segment of the baked-goods industry. People in the United States now consume more tortillas than they do bagels, English muffins, and pitas combined. In 1998, we consumed more than 75 billion tortillas (not including tortilla chips), totaling over $3.5 billion in sales. According to the Tortilla Industry Association, this equates to 290 tortillas per person annually.

HOW OLD IS THE BAGEL?

The name for New Yorkers' favorite bread comes from the German word *beugel,* which means "a round loaf of bread." The first mention of the bagel was in 1610 in Kracόw, Poland, when a piece of literature referred to it as something to give to women in labor.

Sources For Baking Equipment

Albert Uster Imports, Inc. 9211 Gaither Rd. Gaithersburg, MD 20877 (800) 231-8154	Dean & DeLuca 560 Broadway New York, NY 10010 (800) 221-7714 www.deandeluca.com
The Kitchen Witch Gourmet Shop 127 N. El Camino Real, Ste. D Encinitas, CA 92024 (619) 942-3228	Williams-Sonoma P.O. Box 7456 San Francisco, CA 94120 (800) 541-2233 www.williams-sonoma.com
C.A. Paradis, Inc. 1314 Bank St. Ottawa, Ontario K1S 3Y4 Canada (613) 731-2866	The King Arthur Flour Co. 135 Route 5 South P.O. Box 1010 Norwich, VT 05055 (802) 649-3881 www.kingarthurflour.com

WHAT IS A ONE-BOWL CAKE?

It is a cake made by mixing the batter in one bowl. When this is done you omit the step of creaming the shortening or butter and the sugar. Using the one-bowl method, you add the shortening, liquid, and the flavorings to the dry ingredients and beat. The eggs are then added and the batter beaten again. What you gain in simplification and easier cleanup, you lose in texture—one-bowl cakes tend to be coarser.

DOES YOUR PASTRY HAVE PUFFY ENDS?

Puff pastry dough is made from flour, butter, and water. A small amount of butter is layered between dough that is folded several times to form as many as 700 layers. When you cut puff pastry dough, be sure to use a very sharp knife and cut straight down; never pull the knife through the dough or cut the dough at an angle. Doing so will cause the ends to puff up unevenly as the pastry bakes.

WHAT IS A MOON PIE?

A Moon Pie is simply marshmallow between two graham cookies. In the early 1900s, a man named Earl Mitchell had a store that catered to miners who wanted a solid, filling snack for their lunch pails. When Mitchell asked the miners how big this snack should be, one looked at the rising moon and said, "About that big."

It was known as the largest five-cent snack cake on the market. It was a regional bakery novelty that had its origins in Chattanooga, Tennessee, at the Chattanooga Bakery. The snack cake caught on nationally and has sold over two billion since its creation in 1917. Moon Pies are still manufactured by the Chattanooga Bakery on King Street, which produces 300,000 Moon Pies every week.

CHOOSE YOUR LIQUID WISELY

Liquids tend to impart different characteristics to bread. Water, for instance, will cause the top of the bread to be crisp, and it significantly intensifies the flavor of the wheat. Potato water (saved after you've boiled potatoes) adds a unique flavor, makes the crust smooth, and causes the bread to rise faster due to the high starch content. A liquid dairy product imparts a rich, creamy color and leaves the bread with a fine texture and a soft, brown crust. Eggs provide a moist crust.

A liquid sweetener such as molasses, maple syrup, or honey will cause the crust to be dark brown and will keep it moist. Vegetable or meat broth will give the bread a special flavor and provide you with a light, crisp crust. Alcohol of any type will give the bread a smooth crust with a flavor that may be similar to the alcohol used, especially beer; just don't use too much or you'll kill the yeast. Coffee and tea are commonly used to provide a dark, rich color and a crisp crust.

THE BAKER'S SECRET

Recipes for baked goods may call for greased and floured pans. The standard method is to grease the pan with oil and then sprinkle flour in and tap or shake the pan to distribute the flour as evenly as possible (don't forget the sides). Some recipes call for baking pans to be lined with a piece of waxed paper or parchment paper.

If you bake a lot, take a tip from professional bakers and mix up a batch of "baker's magic": Mix ½ cup of room temperature vegetable shortening, ½ cup of vegetable oil, and ½ cup of all-purpose flour. Blend the mixture well and use it to grease pans. The mixture can be stored in an airtight container in the refrigerator for up to six months.

THE FOUR TYPES OF BREAD

Batter Breads
These breads are leavened with yeast. They are always beaten instead of kneaded.

Quick Breads
These are leavened with baking powder or baking soda instead of yeast. They require no rising time, and in fact should be put into the oven almost immediately after mixing dry and wet ingredients.

Unleavened Breads
These have no leavening whatsoever and are easily identifiable because they are flat.

Yeast Breads
These are leavened with yeast and are always kneaded to stretch the gluten in the flour.

CHEWY! PHOOEY!

Read commercial baked goods labels to see if the ingredients include hydrogenated oil or partially hydrogenated oil. Such items will have a chewier texture, but will also be higher in saturated fat and trans fat.

TAKE A PEEK

Always check cake or bread at least 10 to 15 minutes before the baking time is completed. If your oven temperature is off, it may be done before (or after) the baking time stated in the recipe.

WRAP 'EM UP

To reheat biscuits or rolls, sprinkle them lightly with water and wrap them in foil. It should take about 5 minutes in a preheated 350°F oven.

TIMBER!

If your bread rises too high, or rises and then collapses, you may have added too much yeast or water. Remember, a small amount of sugar will feed the yeast and make the dough rise faster. If you use too much sugar, though, it can actually inhibit the rising.

BREAD MAKING 101

For the best results, never use a shiny bread pan. It is best to bake bread in a dull aluminum pan. A dark pan may cook the bread too quickly, resulting in burned bottoms. A shiny pan reflects heat to such a degree that the bread may not bake evenly.

A GAS LEAK

Occasionally dough rises too much before the bread starts to bake, thus causing the gluten strands to become weak and thin, leading to the escape of carbon dioxide gas. When this happens, the bread may rise and then collapse, leaving a sunken top.

EVEN THINGS OUT

Never omit the salt from your bread recipe—salt strengthens and tightens the gluten, keeping bread from becoming crumbly.

TUCKING IN THE BREAD

If you are going to freeze a loaf of bread, make sure you include a paper towel in the package to absorb moisture. This will keep the bread from becoming mushy when thawed.

ARTIFICIAL COLOR?

Some pumpernickel bread is made from white flour, a little rye flour, and caramel or other coloring agents. The better pumpernickel breads are made from a high proportion of rye flour and a small amount of white flour. Sometimes molasses is used to add color and flavor.

WHAT A CUTUP

One of easiest ways to cut a pizza is to use scissors with long blades—you can cut from top and bottom, and you can cut through the pizza quickly.

Make sure they are sharp and only used for food. Pizza cutters do work fairly well, provided they are always kept very sharp. However, most tend to dull quickly because they are made of poor-quality metal.

THE OCTOPUS MOLD

If you see the slightest sign of mold on baked goods, throw the item out. Mold often sends out "feelers" that cannot be seen in most instances.

JUST A TEASPOON OF SUGAR . . .

If you like biscuits and rolls to be a rich golden color, add a teaspoon of sugar to the dry ingredients. It helps the crust caramelize, and it only adds 16 calories to the whole batch.

SLOWING DOWN THE RISING

If you would like to slow down the rising time, put your bread dough in a cool place—even in the refrigerator. The yeast will still be active (assuming it's alive in the first place), but it will be much more sluggish.

OR USE A BELLOWS

If you want the lightest popovers every time, puncture them with a fork when you remove them from the oven to release the air inside.

IT'S A WRAP

When bread dries out, it hardens. To replace the moisture, wrap the loaf tightly in a damp paper towel for two to three minutes, and then remove the towel and heat the bread in a 350°. oven for 15 to 20 minutes. When French or Italian bread hardens, sprinkle the crust with cold water and heat at 350°F for 8 to 10 minutes.

A FAST BREAK

To remove muffins or rolls from a pan, set the pan on a damp towel for about 30 seconds. Use an old towel, because the pan might stick.

DID YOU KNOW?

You can make lightly scented garlic bread by adding 1 teaspoon of garlic powder to the flour when you're making white bread.

YOU KNEAD TO KNOW

If your dough is thick and difficult to knead, rub a small amount of vegetable oil on your hands.

SEALING IT UP

One of the best methods of keeping the insides of a cake from drying out is to place a piece of fresh white bread next to the exposed surface. The bread can be affixed with a toothpick or a short piece of spaghetti.

KEEPING IT ALL TOGETHER

If you have problems keeping a layer cake together when you are icing it, stick a few bamboo skewers into the cake through both layers; remove them as you're frosting the top.

THINNING IT OUT

Frosting tends to become thick and difficult to work with after a short period. If this happens, just stir in a drop or two of liquid.

UNSALTED IF YOU PLEASE

Next time you make chocolate icing, add one teaspoon of unsalted butter to the chocolate while it is melting to improve the consistency.

NO HANGERS-ON HERE

To keep the frosting from sticking to your knife as you cut the cake, dip your knife into a glass of cold water between each cut.

WHIP IT UP

When you whip cream, add a small amount of lemon juice or salt to the cream to make the job easier. For a unique flavor, add just a small amount of honey at the very end of whipping.

GETTING ARTISTIC

Before you put rolls in the oven, glaze their tops: Lightly beat an egg white with a tablespoon of milk and brush on. To glaze a baked cake, dissolve a little brown sugar in 1 tablespoon of milk and brush on.

HELP, I NEED AIR

When your recipe calls for cream cheese, be sure it is at room temperature before you start, and make sure you beat it so it's light and fluffy before adding any other ingredients, especially eggs.

TOSS IT!

If a cake gets hard and stale, throw it out—don't try to repair it. Or, whirl pieces (without icing) in the blender to use as an ice cream topping.

THROW IN THE COLD TOWEL

When baked foods stick to the bottom of the pan, wrap the pan in a towel while it is still hot. You can also set the pan on a cold, wet towel for a few minutes.

POOR BUBBLES

If you have bubbles in your cake batter, hold the pan an inch or two above the counter and tap it two or three times. Be careful—the batter might spatter.

CHEESECAKE TO DIE FOR

When preparing a cheesecake, go exactly by the recipe and don't make any substitutions. You'll have a better chance at success if you follow the recipe to the letter. Here are some other pointers.

◆ Be sure that the cheese is at room temperature before using it.

◆ When you bake a cheesecake at a lower temperature, there's less chance of it shrinking from the sides of the pan.

◆ Don't open the oven for the first 25 to 30 minutes when baking cheesecake; the cheesecake may develop cracks or partially collapse.

◆ Cheesecakes crack because they overcook. They're done when the center of the cake is still wobbly and shaky—it will look underdone.

◆ Flourless cheesecakes need to be baked in a pan of water (called a water bath or bain marie). The water keeps the eggs from coagulating.

◆ Cheesecake cracks can be repaired with creamed cream cheese or sweetened sour cream, but you'll be able to see the repair. It's better to top the cheesecake with berries.

◆ Never substitute a different size pan for a cheesecake recipe, use the exact size recommended.

STAYING SOFT

To keep boiled icing from hardening, just add a very small amount of white vinegar to the icing after it is whipped.

YOUR CAKE RUNNETH OVER

If you sprinkle a thin layer of cornstarch on top of a cake before you ice it, the icing won't run down the sides.

THE BEST FLOUR FOR CAKES

Cake flour is made from soft wheat; because of its low gluten content, it will make a lighter cake. If you don't have any cake flour, use all-purpose flour, but use ⅞ cup all-purpose flour (1 cup minus 2 tablespoons) for each cup of cake flour.

BEAT ME, BEAT ME

When your recipe calls for creaming butter or shortening with sugar, be sure you beat it for the entire time specified in the recipe. Shortening the time may yield a coarse-textured or heavy cake.

WORKS, BUT NOT A HEALTHY TIP

If you don't have to worry about your cholesterol count, substitute two egg yolks for one whole egg. The cake will be very rich—but it will also be a little denser, because the yolks won't hold as much air as the whites.

GIVE ME ROOM, LOTS OF ROOM

Remember, never fill a baking pan more than half to two-thirds full. Cakes, muffins, and other baked goods need room to expand.

CAKEQUAKE

Hold off checking your cake until about 15 minutes before the time specified in the recipe—the cake may fall from the sudden change in temperature. But always check a few minutes early, just in case your oven temperature is too high and the cake is baking faster than you expect.

HEAVENLY FOOD

An angel food cake may be left in the pan and covered tightly with foil for up to 24 hours or until you are ready to frost it.

BE THE FLAKIEST!

There a number of ways to make a flaky pie crust; here are just a few:
- Add a teaspoon of vinegar to the pie dough with the ice water.
- Substitute sour cream or whipping cream for any water.
- Replacing the shortening or butter with lard. Lard has larger fat crystals and three times the polyunsaturates as butter.

FAT MATTERS

Reduced-fat margarine, margarine spreads, and whipped butter should not be used for baking. They have too much water and air, which can cause cakes or cookies to collapse or flatten out. Always use the type of fat called for in the recipe.

MAKE THE RIGHT GRADE

If your cookbook doesn't specify what size egg to use, go with large eggs. The volume difference in a small egg compared with a large egg can be enough to change the consistency and the quality of the item.

JUST WHAT THE RECIPE NEEDED

Here's pastry chefs' trick to add flavor to a lemon tart or pie: Rub a few sugar cubes over an orange or lemon, then include the cubes in the recipe as part of the total sugar. The sugar tends to extract just enough of the natural oils from the peels of the fruits to add some flavor.

ROOM TEMPERATURE WORKS BEST

To keep cookies or butter cakes from becoming too heavy, be sure the butter is at room temperature before you cream it with the sugar. Shortening of any type does not cream when it is cold.

DID YOU KNOW?

You can add flavor to pie crust by adding a little ground spice or minced herbs to the flour. Use cinnamon or ginger with an apple pie, and try finely chopped parsley with a meat pie.

TENDER CAKES

The texture of a cake depends on the type of sweetener and fat used. These ingredients affect how tender the cake will be, so be sure you use the right ones. Never substitute granulated sugar for confectioners' sugar; granulated sugar is recommended for baking most cakes. Cakes made with oil are very tender and moist—oil doesn't hold air as well as butter or shortening, so eggs and other thick ingredients must trap the air.

FOLLOW INSTRUCTIONS TO THE LETTER

When baking cakes, be sure to read the instructions about greasing pans carefully—a number of cakes need to climb the sides of the pan, and only the bottom of the pan should be greased.

BATTER UP

When mixing batter, spray the beaters with a vegetable oil spray before using them and the batter won't climb up the beaters.

BUTTER BEWARE

Don't melt butter unless your recipe directs you to do so. Most recipes, especially cake recipes, will have a better texture if the butter is just softened.

GUARANTEEING A DRY BOTTOM

If you have a problem with fruit or fruit juices soaking the bottom of your pie crust and making it soggy, brush the bottom crust with egg white before adding the filling. This will seal the pie crust and solve the problem. Other solutions include prebaking the pie crust, partially cooking the filling, or brushing the crust with jelly before you fill it.

When using a cream filling in a pie, sprinkle the crust with granulated sugar before adding the filling. This usually eliminates a soggy crust.

MAKE A COOL CRUST

When making pie crust, be sure the kitchen and all your ingredients and equipment are cool. A hot kitchen will affect the results. All pie ingredients should be cold when preparing a crust.

JUST RIGHT

Low-gluten flour such as pasty flour is the best choice when you're making pie crusts. Cake flour is too soft and won't give the crust the body it needs, and bread flour contains too much gluten content to make a tender crust. As a substitute for pastry flour, combine 2 parts all-purpose flour and 1 part cake flour or instant flour.

NO SMOOTHIES WANTED HERE

Add some sugar to your pastry recipe to help tenderize the dough. Pastry dough should look like coarse crumbs after you cut in the fat.

CHILLING OUT

Be sure the liquid going into your pie crust is ice cold. Ice-cold sour cream instead of ice water will result in a flakier crust.

KEEPING IN SHAPE

Never stretch pie dough when you are placing it in the pan. Stretched dough usually shrinks from the sides.

OUCH! THAT HURT!

If you have a problem with burning the bottoms of cookies when baking a number of batches, let the baking sheets cool between batches; when you start with too hot a surface the cookies may burn. Two to three minutes cooling time is usually long enough. Another alternative is to line the baking sheets with parchment paper—simply lift the cookies, still on the parchment paper, onto the cooling rack.

TYPES OF COOKIES

Bar Cookies
Made by pressing dough into a shallow pan and then cutting into small bars after baking.

Drop Cookies
Made by dropping small mounds of dough onto a baking sheet.

Hand-Formed Cookies
Made by shaping cookie dough into balls or other shapes by hand.

Pressed Cookies

Made by pressing the cookie dough through a cookie press or pastry bag with a decorative tip to make fancy designs or shapes.

Refrigerator Cookies

Made by shaping cookie dough into logs, then refrigerating until firm. The logs are sliced before baking.

Rolled Cookies

The cookie dough is rolled to a thickness of about ¼ inch. Cookie cutters are then used to make different shapes.

HELP, LET ME OUT!

Cookies can go from just right to burned in no time. To lessen the chance of this happening, take the cookies out of the oven when they are not quite done, but don't transfer them to the cooling rack right away. Let them sit on the hot pan for a minute or two to finish baking. (This also lets the pan cool, lessening the chance that the next batch will burn.)

DOUBLE DECKER

If you don't have an insulated or a thick baking sheet, there's a simple solution: Try baking the cookies on two sheets, stacked one on top of the other. It will eliminate burned bottoms.

RACK 'EM UP

Cookies should be transfered to a wire rack to cool completely, not left in the pan. Just be sure the cookies are fully cooled before you store them; otherwise, they risk becoming soggy.

SAME ADVICE FOR BISCUITS

When you mix cookie dough, don't overstir. The reason? Because overstirring can cause the cookies to become tough.

IT NEVER TASTES THE SAME

Unbaked cookie dough may be frozen for up to one month. Wrap as airtight as possible in a freezer bag.

STAYING SOFT

If you prefer chewy cookies, they'll stay soft if you add a half an apple or a slice of white bread to the jar. This will provide just enough moisture to keep the cookies from becoming hard.

PERK UP YOUR PEAKS

Here are hints for making world-class meringue and high peaks.

◆ Make sure that your egg whites are at room temperature. As you beat, add 2 to 3 tablespoons of superfine or granulated sugar for each egg used. Keep beating until the peaks stand up without drooping.

◆ To keep the peaks firmer for a longer period, add ⅛ teaspoon of white vinegar per egg white while beating.

◆ Remember, if the weather is bad, rainy, or even damp out, the meringue peaks will not remain upright.

VALENTINE'S DAY SPECIAL

A heart-shaped cake is easier to make than you might think. Simply divide your cake batter between one round pan and one square one. When the cakes are cool, cut the round cake in half. Turn the square cake so it looks like a diamond and set the half-rounds on the two top sides.

HEAVENLY CAKES

Never bake an angel food cake on the top or middle rack of the oven. It will retain moisture better if baked in the lower third and always at the temperature specified in the recipe. The best tool to cut the cake? An electric knife or unwaxed dental floss.

CRUNCHY, CRUNCHY

When you make oatmeal cookies, boost the oatmeal's flavor by toasting it lightly on a baking sheet before adding it to the batter. Sprinkle the oatmeal on a baking sheet and heat it in a 300°F oven for about 10 minutes. The oats should turn a golden-brown.

SWEET TRICK

If you want sugar cookies to remain a little soft, try rolling the dough out in granulated sugar instead of flour.

WATER RETENTION?

If you are having a problem with icing drying out or stiffening before you're done frosting the cake, just add a pinch of baking soda to the confectioners' sugar. This will help the icing retain some moisture and it will not dry out as fast.

ELIMINATING MERINGUE TEARS

Occasionally meringue will develop small droplets of water on its surface shortly after it is removed from the oven. Beading is caused by overcooking. To prevent this, bake meringue at a high temperature (between 400°F and 425°F) for a short time—4 to 5 minutes.

FRUIT PIE TIP

The acid in fruits may react with metal pan and discolor a pie or tart. Always use a glass dish when baking a fruit pie or tart; remember to lower the temperature of the oven by 25°F.

THE INCREDIBLE SHRINKING PIE

Most recipes tell you to be sure pie dough is chilled before putting it in the pie plate. Why? Cold will help to firm up the fat and relax the gluten in the flour. This will help it to retain its shape and reduce shrinkage.

A MUST TO REMEMBER

When you need to grease a baking pan, be sure you always use vegetable shortening. Butter has a low smoke point and burns easily, and salted butter can cause food to stick to the pan.

ACCURACY COUNTS

A cup of flour can vary by several grams by weight depending on how much it has settled. For this reason, professional pastry chefs never use measuring cups—they weigh ingredients, especially flour, because accuracy is so important.

GOOD RULE TO FOLLOW

You've heard it before, and it's true: A soufflé must be served as soon as it is removed from the oven. Soufflés begin to collapse as soon as they start to cool down. So it's best to serve them in the baking dish.

A CLEAN GRIDDLE IS A HEALTHY GRIDDLE

Pancakes will never stick to the griddle if you clean it after every batch with coarse salt wrapped in a piece of cheesecloth. The salt will provide a light abrasive cleaning and won't harm the surface if you're gentle.

TO CRUNCH OR NOT TO CRUNCH

If you are using 100 percent whole-wheat flour and want the crunchiest cookies ever, try using butter instead of another shortening. Never use oil, as it will make the cookies spread too fast when baked.

RUNNY IS NOT FUNNY

If you have a problem with juices bubbling or oozing out when baking a pie, try adding a tablespoon of tapioca to the filling. This will thicken the filling just enough. Another method is to insert a tube of wide macaroni, such as ziti or rigatoni, in the center of the top crust to let air escape (though you still need to thicken the filling).

OLD NEW ENGLAND TRICK

Vermonters can tell you that a tablespoon of pure—and only pure— maple syrup added to your pancake batter will really improve the taste.

POP GOES THE MARSHMALLOW

For a unique pumpkin pie, put small marshmallows on the bottom of the pie. As the pie bakes, the air in the marshmallows expands and the marshmallows rise to the top.

TRY BLENDING IN

When baking, it is important that all the ingredients be blended well, without being blended too much. If you need to sift flour, add the other dry ingredients (such as leavening and salt) to the flour before you sift.

GOING UP?

When cookies do not brown properly, bake them on a higher rack in the oven. Other techniques to boosting the browning of cookies: substitute a tablespoon or two of corn syrup for the sugar, use egg for the liquid, or use unbleached or bread flour in the recipe.

ONE FOR THE COUNTY FAIR

If you want to try something different, enhance cake flour by adding 2 tablespoons of cornstarch to every cup of cake flour, sifting them together. This will produce a light, moist cake.

GRAPE WORKS BEST

Keep soft cookies moist and the maintain the moisture in cakes and pan-cakes by adding a teaspoon of jelly to the batter.

SLICK MOVE

Spray a small amount of vegetable oil on your knife before cutting a pie with a cream filling. This will stop the filling from sticking to the knife.

WORLD'S GREATEST DOUGHNUT

Doughnut dough should be allowed to rest for about 20 minutes before frying. The air in the batter will have time to escape, so the doughnuts will have a better texture. This will also allow the doughnut to absorb less fat. To reduce the fat in a doughnut, drop it into boiling water for 3 to 5 seconds immediately after you remove it from the oil. Any fat clinging to the doughnut drops off in the hot water. Drain the doughnuts on a wire rack. Fry doughnuts at 375°F for about 2 to 3 minutes on each side. Never turn them more than once, and allow room for them to expand in the frying vat.

CRISPY CRITTERS

If you want crisp cookies, be sure your cookie jar has a loose-fitting lid. This allows air to circulate and evaporates any moisture.

DIP IT, DIP IT

To get a sharp edge on your cookies when using cutters, dip the cutter in flour or warm oil occasionally during the cutting.

A CENTER CUT

Next time you cut a cake, cut it from the center out so that you can move the pieces together, keeping the edges moist.

CHILLY DOUGH

Cold cookie dough will not stick to the rolling pin. Refrigerate the dough for no more than 20 minutes for the best results.

WELL SLIVER MY CANDY

If you like the look of chocolate curls, all you have to do is run your vegetable peeler on a chocolate bar.

WORKS LIKE A CHARM

Pies with graham cracker crusts can be difficult to remove from the pan. However, if you dip the pan in warm water for 5 to 10 seconds, the pie will come right out without any damage.

BE GENTLE

The best way to cool an angel food cake is to turn it upside down on an ice-cube tray or set it upside down in the freezer for just a few minutes.

FOWL FACT

Never allow anyone in your family to sample batter that contains raw eggs. More than 3,200 people in the United States became ill in 1997 from tasting batter, homemade eggnog, and Caesar salad dressing made with raw eggs. Chicken ovaries may be contaminated with salmonella, and eggshells are porous—the bacteria can pass through.

SUGARTIME

Sprinkle a thin layer of sugar on a plate before you put a cake on it. This keeps the cake from sticking, and makes the bottom crunchy.

YOU'LL NEVER TASTE THE WINE

Here's a trick to keep waffles from sticking to the waffle iron: Beat a tea-spoon of white wine into the batter.

INCREASING THE HUMIDITY

If you are having a problem with bread browning too fast, set a dish of water on the oven rack just above the bread. The added humidity in the oven will slow down the browning. This will work with cakes as well.

STAY FRUIT, STAY

Dried fruits sink to the bottom of cakes, muffins, and the like because they lose some moisture and become more solid during baking. If you coat them with a little flour, though, they will stay put.

A BIG ONE WORKS BEST

Fill a salt shaker with confectioners' or colored sugar for dusting candy or cookies. Choose one with large holes for best results.

FAT REDUCTION

Substituting light cream or reduced-fat sour cream for the liquid in a packaged mix will yield the same results in most instances.

A SIMPLE SOLUTION

A gelatin salad will be easy to unmold if you spray the mold with non-stick cooking spray before making the gelatin.

A COOL TRICK

If you are going to cut an unfrosted cake to arrange it into different con-figurations, try freezing the cake first. This will make it much easier to slice. Fresh cakes, especially those made from a mix, often crumble easily.

AN APPLE A CAKE

If you need to store a cake more than a day or two, put half an apple in the cake saver. The apple will provide just enough moisture to keep the cake from drying out too soon.

GETTING HIGH

When baking at an altitude over 3,500 feet, you need to increase the oven temperature 25°F and add 1 tablespoon of flour to the recipe. Increase the flour by 2.5 percent at 3,500 feet, increasing to 10 percent at 8,000 feet. Decrease the baking powder by ⅛ teaspoon at 3,000 feet; by ⅛ to ¼ teaspoon at 5,000 feet, and by ¼ teaspoon at 7,000 feet.

NOT VERY PROFESSIONAL

Warped baking pans should be discarded. The uneven surface will spoil the quality of the baked goods.

LET THE ARTIST OUT

A baker's trick to make it easier to decorate the top of a cake: With a toothpick, trace the pattern, picture, or lettering before you pipe the icing.

ATTACK OF THE SPORES

If you don't plan to use a loaf of bread within a week, wrap it in waxed paper and store it in the refrigerator. The bread will not get moldy as fast as it would on the counter.

SOUFFLÉS

When preparing a soufflé, be sure to use a soufflé dish with straight sides. This will force the soufflé to expand upward. Also, always use the exact size dish called for in the recipe.

CALL THE PARAMEDICS

Always beat the egg whites in such a way as to ensure the highest amount of air is trapped. Follow these guidelines:
◆ Use fresh eggs, without a speck of yolk or any other fat.
◆ Be sure your beaters and mixing bowl are spotlessly clean.
◆ Use a mixer attachment with wire tines.
◆ Replace up to one-fifth of the total volume of egg whites with water to increase the volume.
Never overbeat egg whites, or they'll become dry and collapse. You'll know it's time to stop when the foam slips a little when you tilt the bowl.

CURIOSITY KILLED THE SOUFFLÉ

Never open the oven door during the first three-fourths of the soufflé's baking time, or else it may fall.

WHAT IS FOCCACIA?

This Italian yeast bread, from Genoa, is similar to pizza and is newly popular in the United States. Foccacia is thicker and chewier than pizza crust, and usually has fewer toppings. An Italian cookbook will give you the recipe for foccacia dough, and you can have a field day with the toppings: pesto, tapenade (a thick paste made from anchovies, capers, ripe olives, olive oil, and lemon juice), or your favorite pizza toppings (as long as you use less of them). Depending on their size, foccacias are usually baked in a 350°F oven for about 45 minutes, or until the crust is golden.

5

HOW SWEET IT IS

SUGAR SHOCK OF A DIFFERENT SORT

Around the 1880s, Americans consumed just less than nine pounds of sugar per person per year. Today, we consume, on average, more than 20 teaspoons of sugar every day—which comes to 153 pounds per year.

"Wait!" You say. "I never reach for the sugar bowl. How could this be?" Sugar is hidden in thousands of foods, as well as in medicines, even lipstick or lip balm. In fact, nearly all packaged or processed foods contain some form of sugar (though it often goes by a name other than "sugar"), and it occurs naturally in fruits, vegetables, and other foods.

The only health problem sugar causes in and of itself is dental cavities. However, it supplies no nutrients other than calories (in the form of simple carbohydrates). Consuming too much sugar can mean that you don't eat enough nutrient-rich foods, and it can lead to obesity—which can lead to a significant number of very serious health problems.

Keep An Eye Out		
Sugar has many names; here are a few of the more common ones:		
Beet sugar	Hexatol	Mannitol
Cane sugar	High-fructose corn syrup	Molasses
Corn syrup	Honey	Sorghum
Dextrose	Lactose	Sucrose
Fructose	Levulose	Turbinado
Glucose	Maltose	Xylitol

Who Would've Guessed?		
You'll find sugar in the strangest places:		
Baby foods	Lipstick	Soup mixes
Bacon	Lip gloss	Soy sauce
Canned fish	Peanut butter	Stamp adhesives
Cough drops	Pickle relish	Vitamins
Laxatives	Pickles	Waffle mixes

CORN SYRUP

Because corn syrup is very inexpensive to produce, it's one of the most common sweeteners. It is made from a mixture of starch granules derived from corn, which are then processed with acids or enzymes that convert it into a heavy, sweet syrup. The syrup is then artificially flavored and used in literally thousands of foods, from pancake syrup to applesauce. The fact that corn syrup tends to retard crystallization makes it a good choice for candies, preserves, and frostings.

HONEY FACTS

◆ Honey is sold in three varieties. Liquid honey is extracted directly from the honeycomb; chunk-style honey contains pieces of the honeycomb; and comb honey contains a larger section of the honeycomb.

◆ Honey is about as sweet as granulated sugar. One pound of honey measures 1⅓ cups.

KEEP IT FLOWING

Honey should be stored in as airtight a container as possible since the sugars attract moisture and absorb water from the air easily, especially if the relative humidity is more than 60 percent. Honey tends to crystallize easily, which releases the glucose from the sugars. Heating the honey slightly will force the glucose back into the sugar molecules and return the honey to a liquid. Microwaving it for about 30 seconds can liquefy crystallized honey. Never allow honey to boil or get too hot, because it will break down and then must be discarded.

CERTAIN HONEY CAN BE DANGEROUS

Honey that is produced from nectar from flowers of families of plants such as the rhododendron, azalea, and laurel may cause symptoms of excessive perspiration, low blood pressure, irregular heart rhythms, vomiting, and muscle weakness. Farmers call this type "mad honey." These symptoms are rarely fatal and typically last no more than 24 hours.

Honey is unique in that it will not grow bacteria. However, it may harbor botulism spores, so it should not be fed to children younger than one year old; their digestive systems are too immature to process it properly. Older children and adults are able to digest it without harm.

THE REMARKABLE HONEY STORY

Bees gather honey by drawing the flower nectar into their proboscis (a tube extending from their heads). The nectar then passes through their esophagus into a honey sac (storage pod) located just before the intestine. The nectar is stored until the bee returns to the hive. While the nectar is in the sac, the bee secretes enzymes that begin to break down the starch into simple sugars and fructose. The hive contains one mature queen, about 100 male drones, and 20,000 female workers. The bees utilize eight pounds of honey for daily activities for every pound that reaches the market. For every gallon of honey the bees consume, they travel 7 million miles, or 7 million miles to the gallon if you prefer. When a worker returns to the hive, it pumps and mixes the nectar in and out of its proboscis until the carbohydrate concentration is about 50 to 60 percent, and then it is deposited into the honeycomb.

THE REAL SAP, MAPLE SYRUP

The sap run is one of the mysteries of nature. Pure maple syrup is the product of the rock maple tree, which is the only tree that produces high-quality syrup. The amount of sap available depends on whether the leaves are able to convert the right proportions of sunlight, water, and carbon dioxide into sugar. Sap is collected only between the first major spring thaw and the time the leaf buds begin to burst. If the sap collection is not discontinued at this point, the syrup will have a bitter flavor.

Conditions must be nearly perfect to have a good sap run. The winter must be severe enough to freeze the trees' roots, the snow cover must extend into the spring to keep the roots very cold, the temperature swings must be extreme from day to night, and the tree must have excellent exposure to sunlight.

Maple sap is about 3 percent sucrose, and each tree produces 10 to 12 gallons of sap on average per spring season. Early in the season, it takes 20 gallons of sap to produce one gallon of pure maple syrup; as the season progresses, it can take as many as 50 gallons. Pure maple syrup is composed of 62 percent sucrose, 35 percent water, 1 percent glucose, 1 percent fructose, and 1 percent malic acid. The longer the syrup is boiled during processing, the darker the syrup becomes; this is due to a reaction between the sugars and proteins.

DID YOU KNOW?

Maple syrup has a very pronounced flavor. Use it only when called for in recipes—never substitute it for honey, brown sugar, or any other sweetener.

THE REAL THING

Maple syrup is best stored in the refrigerator after it is opened to retain its flavor and retard the growth of mold. If it granulates, just warm it up slightly. It should last about one year from the time it is opened, and is best used at room temperature or slightly heated.

Read the label well! Make sure it doesn't read "maple-flavored," "maple-blended," or "imitation." The real thing is expensive and contains nutrients such as iron and calcium. Typical pancake syrup is almost always pure corn syrup and artificial maple flavoring.

Maple sugar must contain a minimum of 35 percent pure maple syrup. Look for pale maple sugar. The lighter the color, the higher the quality.

MOLASSES

When sugar cane is processed to make white sugar, it undergoes a complex process that removes virtually all nutrients except calories. The residue that remains after processing is molasses. Whether a molasses is sulfured or unsulfured depends on whether sulfur was used during processing. Unsulfured molasses is lighter in color and has a cleaner flavor than either sulfured or blackstrap molasses. Blackstrap molasses is the result of the third boiling and is the dregs of sugar production. It is only slightly richer in iron, calcium, and potassium than its more refined cousins.

If a recipe calls for dark molasses, you can use light molasses without a problem. If you use molasses in place of another sweetener in baked goods, be sure and reduce the heat about 25°F, or the food may over-brown. Molasses has a degree of acidity that can be neutralized by adding 1 teaspoon of baking soda to the dry ingredients for every cup of molasses the recipe calls for. Molasses is best used in gingerbread, gingersnaps, and baked beans, where its robust flavor can really shine.

If you need to measure molasses, coat the measuring utensil with non-stick spray so it will flow better and have a more accurate measurement.

RAW SUGAR (TURBINADO)

Despite its name, this is almost exactly like refined white sugar—it's partially processed, so a little molasses is left on the surface for color, and its grains are often larger than granulated. It has no advantage over granulated sugar, and its price is higher. As with all sugar, it can be labeled "natural" to make you think that it is more healthful than it really is.

ARTIFICIAL SWEETENERS

Acesulfame K

This noncaloric sweetener is sold under two brand names, Sunett and SweetOne. It provides sweetening and cannot be metabolized by the body, but passes through and is excreted. It has an advantage over aspartame in that it can be used at high temperatures for baking and cooking. It is about 200 times sweeter than sugar and is commonly used in chewing gums, beverage mixes, candies, puddings, and custards. Acesulfame K received FDA approval in 1988 and is used worldwide.

Aspartame

Best known by its trade names Nutrasweet and Equal. This sweetener is produced from two amino acids—phenylalanine and aspartic—and methanol. When aspartame was approved in 1981, the FDA set a maximum recommended amount of 50 milligrams per kilogram of body weight per day. This equates to a 140-pound person drinking 20 diet drinks per day or the equivalent in food. The World Health Organization recommended a maximum of 40 milligrams per kilogram of body weight for adults. A child who consumes artificially sweetened gum, candy, puddings, and beverages could easily exceed the *adult* maximum amounts.

It has been implicated in animal laboratory testing in contributing to nerve disease. However, testing is not conclusive and the studies were conducted using high dosages, which may have skewed the outcome. Recent negative study results by leading universities and the Arizona Department of Health Sciences were regarded by the FDA as "unfounded fears." Future testing may prove more conclusive.

Caution must be taken when aspartame is heated, because a percentage may turn into methyl alcohol. It is not recommended for use in baked goods or any drink that requires a liquid being brought to a boil.

Cyclamates

Are banned by the FDA.

L-Sugars

These contain no calories or aftertaste. Can be substituted cup for cup for granulated sugar in recipes.

Saccharine

Has been around since 1879 and is 300 times sweeter than sugar. It is used in many common products such as mouthwashes and lipsticks. Saccharine has long been suspected of causing cancers. Recently, however, it was determined that the cancers developed by laboratory animals are not the type developed by humans. In fact, no tumors or cancers in humans were linked to saccharine in more than 20 years of study.

Stevia

New to the United States, Stevia has been used in South America and Japan for years as a calorie-free sweetener. Stevia is an extract from a member of the chrysanthemum family that is sold in health-food stores as a dietary supplement. Because it is a natural herbal product, the Dietary Supplement Act of 1994 applies, and Stevia was allowed into the country. It is unapproved as a food additive—Stevia cannot be promoted for use as a sweetener, but can be sold as a dietary supplement. However, the FDA is still not sure of any potential problems that might arise since testing is not yet conclusive. Research from Japan says it is safe and may even prevent yeast infections, boost energy levels, and doesn't pro- mote tooth decay. The extract is concentrated and is 200 to 300 times sweeter than table sugar. It is being used for cooking and may leave a licorice- flavored aftertaste.

Sucralose

A concentrated form of granulated sugar that has been approved by the FDA; it is 600 times sweeter than regular sugar and has no calories. It is very stable in foods and carbonated beverages. In Canada, it is sold under the brand name Splenda.

A GOOD SWEETENER?

Fruit is high in the sugar fructose. However, all studies show that there is no risk factor involved with this sugar and consumption of fruit does not have to be—in fact, should not be—limited. Fructose breaks down at a slower rate than most sugars, giving the body more time to utilize it before it is completely broken down to glucose.

CHOCOLATE FACTS

- ◆ Adults purchase more than 50 percent of all chocolate sold in the United States. Americans consumed about $3.9 billion worth of candy products in 1997 and more than 1.6 billion pounds of chocolate bars.
- ◆ Fry & Sons invented the chocolate bar in 1847 in England.
- ◆ Almost 75 percent of American chocolate eaters prefer milk chocolate.
- ◆ Dark chocolate must contain at least 15 percent chocolate liquor and no more than 12 percent milk solids.
- ◆ Dark chocolate can be sweet (sometimes called German chocolate), semisweet, or bittersweet.

◆ Milk chocolate must contain at least 10 percent chocolate liquor and a minimum of 12 percent milk solids.

◆ Unsweetened chocolate, sometimes called baking chocolate, must contain at least 50 percent cocoa butter.

DID YOU KNOW?

Starchy foods like soda crackers and graham crackers can be bad news for oral hygiene. They stick to your teeth, and then the starch changes to sugar, which bacteria thrive on.

OFF TO THE GYM

Americans consume about 237,000 calories of sweeteners annually. This is enough calories to put 67 pounds on the average person.

CHOCOHOLICS BEWARE

The chemical theobromine, found in chocolate, may reduce the amount of available protein that is absorbed through the intestinal wall. Sugar also reduces the body's ability to destroy bacteria.

DENTISTS' RETIREMENT FOOD

Sucking on hard candy or lollipops causes a greater risk of tooth decay than consuming large quantities of cake, ice cream, or doughnuts. Hard candy dissolves slowly and surrounds each tooth with a layer of sugar for a longer period. Sticky foods like raisins have a similar effect.

OVERWORKING YOUR LIVER

Many candies, especially those that are multicolored, contain a number of additives. These include red dyes #3 and #40, green dye #3, blue dye #2, yellow dye #5, and glycerides. Check your favorite candy for any of these additives. Remember, your liver is the organ that must cleanse these potentially toxic chemicals from the body.

PRECISION COUNTS

If you're making candy, be sure to follow recipe directions to the letter. Candy recipes are very exacting and variances can compromise quality. Candy must be cooked at the recommended temperature—never try to speed up the process by increasing the heat. The lower the final temperature of the candy after it is cooked will determine the softness of the final product. In fact, most candy-making cookbooks stress the importance of waiting for a cool, dry day.

A BAD-MOOD RELIEVER

Fudge should be stirred vigorously or beaten with a wooden spoon from its glossy, thin consistency to a slightly thick consistency; depending on the recipe, this can take a good 20 minutes. If the fudge doesn't set when cooked, add a few tablespoons of water and cook it again.

CRYSTAL CLEAR

If you add water to a candy recipe, always add very hot water for a clearer candy. Most homemade candy will remain fresh for two to three weeks.

PUFF, PUFF, DRINK, DRINK

Smokers frequently consume more sugar than nonsmokers do, possibly because smokers are more likely to drink sweetened coffee.

SUGAR DISASTER

Freezing has a negative effect on many candies. Their flavors can change and the candies may even lose their consistency: Hard candies may crumble, jellies become granular, and the rest lose their original consistencies due to the expansion of the liquid in their cells.

TONS AND TONS OF SUGAR

In 1997, 60 million chocolate bunnies and 600 million marshmallow bunnies and chicks were sold in the United States at Eastertime.

MAKING CANDY? COOL IT!

If the weather is hot and humid, don't try to make candy, especially chocolates, unless your kitchen is air-conditioned. The best temperature for making most candies, including chocolate truffles, divinity, hard candy, and fudge, is between 62°F and 68°F, with low humidity. These candies absorb moisture from the air very easily.

FRESH AND FRUITY

Jams and jellies can be produced from a number of artificial ingredients, so it's best to read labels and purchase those made from real fruit. If they are and are labeled "light," so much the better—that's an indication that the sugar content has been reduced.

SNIP, SNIP

Store marshmallows in the freezer. Just cut them with a scissors that have been dipped in very hot water to get them apart.

MOISTURIZE ME

Add a slice of very fresh white bread or half an apple to a bag of marshmallows to soften them. Just leave them alone for one to two days until the marshmallows absorb the moisture.

DE-LUMPING YOUR SUGAR

Brown sugar loses moisture rather quickly and develops lumps easily. To soften it, put the sugar in the microwave with a slice of fresh white bread or half an apple, cover the dish tightly and heat for 15 to 20 seconds; let it stand five minutes before using. The moisture from the bread or apple will produce enough steam to soften the sugar without melting it. Store brown sugar in the freezer to keep it from getting lumpy in the first place.

THE LOW-TECH METHOD

Your brown sugar's hard but you don't have a microwave? Wrap the entire box tightly in a towel and hit it on the counter a few good whacks.

THAT'S A FEW EXTRA CALORIES

In 1997, Americans spent approximately $2.6 billion on ice cream; each person consumed an average of 23.2 quarts.

YOU WON'T BELIEVE IT UNTIL YOU TRY IT

Frustrated with syrup running down the sides of the bottle? If you don't buy the type in squeeze bottles, try this trick: Rub the threads at the neck of the bottle with a small amount of vegetable oil.

HEAT KILLS

Strawberries and oranges are sky-high in vitamin C, but if you think that the strawberry jelly or orange marmalade you spread on your toast will provide you with this nutrient, you're wrong! Vitamin C is very sensitive to heat, and the processing kills almost all of it.

Kind Of Scary, Isn't It?	
The percent of sugar in some common foods, by weight:	
Candy corn	89.6 percent
3 Musketeers	76.8 percent
Milky Way	71.6 percent
Breakfast cereals	up to 46 percent
Oreo cookie	39.4 percent
Ketchup	22.3 percent
Flavored gelatin	18 percent

IT'S NOT THE REAL THING

Despite its name, white chocolate does not include any chocolate liquor and thus is not really chocolate. It is produced from sugar, milk solids, cocoa butter, lecithin, and vanilla.

THE NOSE KNOWS

Candies stored in the refrigerator can pick up odors from other foods. Keep them in an airtight container.

FREE FLOWING

Granulated sugar clumps less than brown sugar, but it can still become lumpy. Keep this from happening by sticking a few salt-free crackers in the canister to absorb the moisture; replace the crackers every week.

BUBBLE, BUBBLE, TOIL AND TROUBLE

Few burns are as nasty as those that result from boiling sugar syrup. To keep syrup from boiling over when you make candy, be sure to use a pot large enough to hold the volume of syrup once it starts boiling.

JUST A SPOONFUL OF SUGAR . . .

The chemicals used to produce cough medicine—syrup or lozenge—are incredibly bitter. To make them palatable, the sugar content can be as high as 50 percent. In fact, about one-third of all cough syrups and drops contain at least 25 percent sugar.

A REAL SURPRISE

The three most popular desserts in the United States are pie, cheesecake, and ice cream, in that order.

POP A CUBE, BUT NOT TOO OFTEN

If you must satisfy a sugar craving, don't opt for a high-fat candy bar or cookie. Instead, eat a sugar cube. One provides a mere 10 calories and contains no fat or preservatives.

KEEP 'EM WORKING

Consuming too much sugar reduces the effectiveness of the body's healing mechanism. Normally, white blood cells go to the site of the injury and assist the body by removing debris and starting the healing process. When there is an overabundance of sugar in the bloodstream, white blood cells get lazy, so to speak, and don't want to go to work.

A WEIGHTY MATTER

By weight, almost 98 percent of food additives are corn syrup, ground black pepper, mustard, baking soda, sugar, citric acid, salt, or a natural or artificial coloring agent.

HOW SWEET IT IS

In a recent study at the University of California at Davis, Dr. Andrew Waterhouse found that chocolate contained phenols, the same antioxidant compound in red wine that is thought to lower the risk of heart disease. The study found that cocoa powder prevented the oxidation or breakdown of LDLs (bad cholesterol). When LDLs break down, they can turn into arterial plaque, which causes artery walls to harden. A 1½-ounce chocolate bar has the same amount of phenols as a 5-ounce glass of red wine; dark chocolate has more than milk chocolate.

YOU WERE BORN WITH A SWEET TOOTH

Babies that are only one day old can detect the taste of sweet; they do not respond to the taste of salt until they are six weeks old. In adults, taste buds are able to detect sweetness in foods that have only one part sweetness in 200. Saltiness can be detected in foods with only one part in 400.

ELIMINATE A SWEET CRAVING

There are two ways to eliminate the craving for sweets. One way is to place a small amount of salt on your tongue. The second: Dissolve about a teaspoon of baking soda in a glass of warm tap water, then rinse your mouth out and don't swallow. The salt or baking soda tends to stimulate the production of saliva, which eliminates the craving for sweets.

WHAT IS PLASTIC CHOCOLATE?

It sounds disgusting, but this is actually a pliable decorating paste made from a mixture of chocolate and corn syrup that has a texture similar to marzipan. It is used to wrap around the outside of cakes, to make ribbons, ruffles, decorative flowers, or any other complex design. It can be rolled into a thin layer with a rolling pin.

WAS THE BABY RUTH CANDY BAR NAMED AFTER BABE RUTH?

Many people think that the Baby Ruth candy bar was named after the famous baseball player, especially since he did wish to produce a candy bar with his name on it. The candy bar was actually named in honor of the daughter of President Grover Cleveland.

DOES YOUR CHOCOLATE STIFFEN?

When you melt chocolate, water droplets, condensation, and high temperatures may cause the chocolate to seize or stiffen. To alleviate this problem, add 1 teaspoon vegetable shortening per ounce of chocolate and stir. More oil can be added if needed to ensure proper consistency.

THE CANDY MAN CAN

The Hershey Candy Company produces 2,200,000 Kisses every day. The Dutch, however, outdo Americans when it comes to candy consumption. They consume 64 pounds of candy per person annually, while Americans consume a mere 25.2 pounds.

ORIGIN OF CHEWING GUM

A variety of gums, resins, and plant latexes have been chewed for thousands of years. The oldest known gum was found in 1993 in what is now western Sweden. It was a 9,000 year-old blob of resin sweetened with honey, and it bore the toothmarks of a teenager. Commercially, chewing gum as we know it today was first produced in Bangor, Maine, in 1848 by John Bacon Curtis, with only mediocre results. However, in 1869, a New Yorker by the name of Thomas Adams used chicle, the dried latex material of the Central American sapodilla tree. In 1871, Adams received a patent for chicle gum.

In 1885, William J. White of Cleveland further refined and improved gum by adding corn syrup and peppermint. Chicagoan William Wrigley invented Juicy Fruit and Spearmint gums in 1893. In 1900, Frank Fleer of Philadelphia placed a hard shell on the gum and called it Chiclets; 28 years later, Fleer invented bubble gum.

WHY DOESN'T CAROB POWDER MELT?

Most forms of chocolate and cocoa contain fat, which allows it to melt (cocoa powder is an exception). Carob does not contain any fat; therefore it will not melt, only burn. When carob powder is heated with water, the starch granules absorb moisture and rupture. This releases a gum that is used as a stabilizer and thickener in processed foods.

THE JELLY-BEAN RULE

Jelly beans have zero fat, no cholesterol—and with the exception of calories, virtually no nutritive value whatsoever. Toward the end of the twentieth century, jelly-bean manufacturers, hoping to tap into the fat-free food frenzy, began to tout the candy as a healthful food, which is, to put it kindly, stretching the facts. The FDA put a stop to this with a rule that's actually called the "jelly-bean rule." For a food to be labeled healthful, it must contain a minimum of 10 percent of the Daily Values for vitamins A and C, iron, calcium, protein, or fiber (a main dish must have 10 percent of two of these nutrients; a meal must have 10 percent of three of them). In addition, a healthful food must be low-fat, low in saturated fat, and be low in sodium and cholesterol.

THE DIFFERENCE IN CANE, BEET, WHITE, AND BROWN SUGAR

Chemically, all table sugar is sucrose, a simple carbohydrate that the body breaks down into glucose in a short period. Cane and beet sugars are not noticeably different in appearance or taste. Brown sugar contains traces of molasses, which is a by-product of the sugar refining process. The nutritional difference between white and brown sugar is insignificant, but the additional moisture in brown sugar can be very important in recipes; be sure to use what the recipe calls for.

WHAT IS SORGHUM?

Many people think sorghum is just another type of molasses, but there is a difference. While molasses is produced from the juice of the sugarcane stalk, sorghum is made from the juice of the sorghum plant, which is normally grown for animal feed. Molasses is usually darker and may be a slight bit bitter because much of the sugar is refined out.

A TRICK TO STOP SYRUP FROM CRYSTALLIZING

When boiling syrup, one of the more frequent and annoying problems is that it crystallizes. The easiest way to avoid this is to put a pinch of cream of tartar in the syrup while it's cooking. This adds a small amount of acidity—just enough to prevent crystals from forming.

WHAT IS BLOWN SUGAR?

If you've ever seen animals or other shapes made of sugar and painted with food coloring, you may have wondered how they were made. Sugar is cooked to a point just below the hard-crack stage, and then poured onto a marble slab and worked with a metal spatula until it has cooled enough to be worked by hand. The sugar is "satinized" by pulling it back and forth until it has a glossy, smooth sheen. It is then formed into a ball. A blowpipe is inserted, and as air is gently blown in, the ball expands, similar to glass blowing. After cooling and painting, the items are used for display or consumed. They can be kept indefinitely.

DID YOU KNOW?

Another way to prevent sugar syrup from crystallizing: Once the sugar melts, cover the pan. The condensation that forms on the pot lid will melt the crystals.

CAROB, THE CHOCOLATE ALTERNATIVE?

Do you feel guilty for eating chocolate? Do you think you "should be" enjoying a carob bar instead? Carob, also known as St. John's bread and locust bean, comes from the pulp inside of pods from a tropical tree. The pulp is dried, roasted, and then ground into a powder. The carob powder used to make confections is less than 1 percent fat but may contain as much as 48 percent sugar. Cocoa powder used to make chocolate bars is 23 percent fat, but only 5 percent sugar. When they're processed into candy bars, the differences between carob powder and cocoa powder are pretty much erased. In fact, some carob bars contain a higher level of saturated fat than a chocolate bar and more sugar than a scoop of regular ice cream. Unlike chocolate, however, carob does not contain caffeine.

SUGARLESS GUM, FRIEND OR FOE?

Sugarless gums sweetened with sorbitol or mannitol are suspected to play a role in tooth decay. Neither artificial sweetener actually causes tooth decay, however, they simply provide nourishment for *Streptococcus mutans,* a bacteria that sticks to your teeth and is relatively harmless until it comes into contact with sugar or one of these sweeteners. Dr. Paul Keyes, founder of the International Dental Health Foundation, reported this.

However, the American Dental Association reports that chewing sugarless gums sweetened with sorbitol after eating can significantly reduce the incidence of dental caries. The ADA recommends chewing sugarless gum as a way to contribute to improved oral hygiene without any harmful nutritional consequences.

HOW MUCH DO YOU DRINK?

The Coca-Cola Company is the world's largest purchaser of sugar and vanilla. Every day in more than 35 countries, Coca-Cola is consumed more than 190 million times.

In 1997, the average American consumed about 575 12-ounce servings of soda, which came to 54 gallons of soft drinks per person.

A SERIOUS INVESTIGATION?

The M&M Mars company actually does on-going research to determine the colors and the number of each color that will be found in their packages of M&Ms. The following is the current breakdown in percentages, which changes as their research is updated at regular intervals:

COLOR	PLAIN	PEANUT
Brown	30	20
Yellow	20	20
Red	20	20
Green	10	10
Orange	10	10
Blue	10	20

HOW MANY POUNDS OF CANDY ARE YOU EATING?

In 1980, Americans consumed 16.1 pounds of candy per person; by 1993, this number had leaped to 21.9 pounds. The candy industry had set its sights on a goal of "25 by '95," which it didn't meet. However, by 1998 we were eating 25.2 pounds per person. In other words, we're eating the equivalent of 195 candy bars per year.

CUT IT OUT!

You can often reduce the amount of sugar in a recipe for cookies, cakes, pies, and other baked goods by up to one-third without having a negative affect on the results of the recipe.

ON THE DECLINE

Consumption of table sugar has actually declined in the last 20 years in the United States—but that's not cause for celebration. Food manufacturers are using more high-fructose corn syrup (it costs less than sugar), and artificial sweeteners and sugar substitutes have become more popular.

CANDY BY ANY OTHER NAME

Our word *candy* is from the Arabic pronunciation of *khandakah,* the Sanskrit word for sugar. Commercial production of candy can be traced to marzipan, which was brought to Europe by Arabs and Moors during the Middle Ages.

WHAT A HEADACHE

A naturally-occurring compound in chocolate called phenylethylamine can cause migraines in susceptible individuals. This substance has effects similar to those of amphetamines.

BETTER EAT MORE B'S

Although honey contains small amounts of some vitamins, eating it can actually cause a negative vitamin balance. How? B vitamins are used up when our bodies convert carbohydrates and fats into energy. Because honey contains such minute amounts of the vitamins used up, each serving of honey uses more of these vitamins than it provides.

6

THE
SKINNY
ON
FATS

A CRASH COURSE IN FAT CHEMISTRY

Fats are substances such as oils, waxes, lard, butter, and other compounds which are insoluble, or unable to mix with water. Some fats are easily visible—butter, gravy, vinaigrette dressing, and marbling in steak. Others, like the fats in egg yolks, nuts, avocados, and milk, are less obvious.

Fats are composed of fatty acids. The type of fat depends on the specific mixture of these fatty acids. Many of these fatty acids are vital to good health, hence the term "essential fatty acids." The body uses fat as its energy storage reserves, insulation, padding to protect organs, and as a precursor to hormone-like compounds called prostaglandins.

Fats fall into three categories:

Simple fats are basic fats, one group of which is called triglycerides and are composed of a glycerol base with three fatty acids.

Compound fats are a combination of fats and other components, one of the more important being lipoproteins, which are fats that combine with proteins. Because fat is insoluble, it needs a vehicle to carry it around the body, and lipoproteins are the main transport system for fats. Compound fats may contain cholesterol, triglycerides, neutral fats, and fatty acids.

The third type is *derived fat,* which is produced from fatty substances through digestive breakdown.

The fats you eat are composed of three elements: carbon, hydrogen, and oxygen. The carbon atoms are like a skeleton and can be compared with the framework on a house. In a saturated fat, all the carbon atoms are completely surrounded by hydrogen and oxygen atoms. Because the carbon atoms are totally saturated, this type of fat is solid at room temperature.

In polyunsaturated fat molecules, some of the carbon atoms have a free space where a hydrogen atom could be attached. This is the reason that polyunsaturated fat is always liquid. Monounsaturated fat, which the body uses more efficiently than other types, is liquid only at room temperature.

THE THREE MAJOR TYPES OF FATS

Polyunsaturated Fatty Acids (PUFA)

This type of fat always remains in a liquid state, whether at room temperature or in the refrigerator. Examples are safflower, corn, and peanut oil.

Monounsaturated Fatty Acids (MUFA)

These tend to thicken when refrigerated but are still liquid at room temperature. Examples are olive and canola oil. Recent studies show that MUFA oils may be more effective in lowering harmful blood cholesterol levels than PUFA oils.

Saturated Fatty Acids (SFA)

Normally, these are either solid or semisolid at room temperature. Examples are butter, lard, shortening, and stick margarine. The exceptions to the rule are tropical oils like coconut and palm, which are sludge-like at room temperature. SFAs tend to raise cholesterol levels, even though they may not actually contain cholesterol.

HYDROGENATION

Vegetable oils are liquid at room temperature. To make margarine or shortening, hydrogen gas is introduced in the presence of a nickel catalyst to saturate the carbon atoms. This hardens the fat, which alters the texture of the food to make it more palatable and possibly last longer. The problem is, this process negates the benefits of liquid oils—and can introduce a host of other health problems. Hydrogenated fats are high in trans-fatty acids, which can be more harmful than saturated fat.

THE BAD PARTS OF A GOOD FAT

Sometimes good fats may have a bad side. For example, say you go to a fast food restaurant and order a potato patty for breakfast. Because it is early morning, and the frying vat has just been filled with fresh vegetable oil (we hope), the majority of the fat will probably be polyunsaturated. However, when you go back to that same restaurant for lunch, the oil has been used for hours, and it may have deteriorated into free fatty acids.

CIS-FORM FATTY ACIDS

These are horseshoe-shaped molecules of polyunsaturated fat that occur naturally in nature and are normally incorporated into a healthy cell wall. In fact, the health of the cell wall depends on an adequate supply of cis-form fatty acids. When these acids are not available, the cell wall is constructed with abnormal openings that may allow foreign substances to enter and allow a disease process to get started.

TRANS-FORM FATTY ACIDS

Instead of the normal horseshoe shape that fatty acids take, the trans-fatty acids are found in a straight line. This form of fat is hard for the blood cell to utilize in the construction of a healthy wall. Trans-fatty acids have been shown to increase LDL (low-density lipoproteins, or "bad" cholesterol levels) and lower HDL (high-density lipoproteins, or "good" cholesterol), and may be even more harmful than saturated fats. Margarine may contain up to 54 percent trans-fatty acids.

INCREASING THE FAT

Fast food corporations often partially cook French fries when they are manufactured, before they are shipped to restaurants. Although this saves time, it may translate to higher levels of trans-fatty acids in the fries.

GOOD TO THE LAST DROP

If you really want to get all the shortening out of a can, pour 2 cups boiling water into the container and swirl it gently until the fat melts. Refrigerate the container until the shortening solidifies on the water's surface, then just lift or skim it off with a knife blade or a sharp-edged spoon.

LOGJAM AHEAD

Never pour used oil down the drain; it may solidify and cause clogging. Pour the oil in a metal can. When it cools, cover it and throw away.

FOR BETTER BUTTER

If you would like to have your butter ready and spreadable at all times, go to a kitchen-supply store and purchase a British-style butter dish—a butter dish made from terra-cotta. The top of the dish needs to be soaked in cold water every day for butter to be kept spreadable.

BUTTER FACT

The highest quality butter in the United States is U.S. Grade AA, which is produced from fresh sweet cream. U.S. Grade A is almost as good but has a lower-quality rating (the ratings are based on flavor, body, texture, color, and salt content). U.S. Grade B is usually produced from sour cream. The milk-fat content of butter must be at least 80 percent.

SUCKING UP TO FAT

If you know you'll be broiling steaks or chops, save a few slices of stale, dried bread and set them in the bottom of the broiler pan to absorb fat drippings. This will eliminate smoking fat, and it should also reduce any danger of a grease fire.

AN OLIVE OIL PRIMER

Expect to pay top dollar for extra-virgin cold-pressed olive oil. It is made from plump, Grade A olives, has the best flavor, and is processed by pressing the oil from the olives with as little heat and friction as possible. The next best is virgin olive oil, which is also from the first pressing and has an acidity of 3 to 4 percent. Pure olive oil is a rougher oil, or a blend of refined and virgin oils. Beware of labels touting "cold-processed"—unlike cold-pressing, cold-processing may mean the oil is extracted from the olives with a chemical solvent.

DON'T LET OLIVE OIL HAVE A BREAKDOWN

Olive oil is inherently healthful as oils go, but it has a low smoke point, which means that it will break down rapidly when exposed to heat. You can increase the smoke point of olive oil by adding a small amount of canola oil, which has a very high smoke point. For example, if your recipe calls for you to sauté in a tablespoon of olive oil, use 2½ teaspoons olive and ½ teaspoon canola oil.

AVOID THE SMOKE POINT

Never allow oil to heat to the smoke point, as it may ignite. It can make the food taste bitter and may even irritate your eyes. The oils with the highest smoke points are canola, safflower, peanut, and soybean oil.

STEER CLEAR OF RECYCLED FATS

Oil should never be reused. Tricks like "cleaning" the oil with a few slices of raw potato before storing are the kitchen equivalent of old wives' tales—they don't work.

DID YOU KNOW?

Olive oil is one of the more healthful fats, but that doesn't give you license to overindulge. It still packs in 119 calories per tablespoon.

LIGHTEN UP

When making a batter for foods for deep-frying, try adding ½ teaspoon of baking powder for every ½ cup of flour. The coating will be lighter.

FAT'S IN THE FIRE

If the frying fat is not hot enough to cook food as soon as whatever it is you're cooking is added to a pot, the food will absorb more fat. On the other hand, if the fat gets too hot, it will smoke and burn. Use a deep-frying thermometer to be sure it's at the recommended temperature (usually between 350°F and 375°F.) before you add the food.

LOVE LARD OR LEAVE IT

Lard comes from pig fat. Leaf lard is derived from the kidney area and is higher quality than other types; it's best for pie crust, pastries, and biscuits. Most other types of lard are used in chewing-gum bases, shaving creams, soaps, and cosmetics.

PUTTING ON THE RITZ

Some of the highest-fat content crackers are butter-flavored (either round or oval shaped) and small ones shaped like fish. Both types contain about 6 grams of fat per ounce.

LARD HAS LARGER FAT CRYSTALS

Lard can be refrigerated for six to eight months. It can become rancid quickly and should never be stored at room temperature. If you substitute lard for butter or shortening, reduce the amount you use by 25 percent.

MAYONNAISE FACTS

Mayonnaise must contain at least 65 percent oil by weight; any less and it must be called salad dressing. Most fat-free mayonnaise contains more sodium than full-fat mayonnaise. A tablespoon of mayonnaise contains only 5 to 10 milligrams of cholesterol, because very little egg yolk is used.

KEEPING PIGS WARM

Pigs in blankets (sausages wrapped in biscuits or pancakes) are 60 percent fat, almost all of which is saturated fat. If this is a breakfast favorite at your house, switch to lower-fat vegetarian or poultry-based sausages.

EASY GREASING

When you grease a baking pan, make sure you use a light touch, or else you may cause the food to overbrown.

FAT VS. CARB CALORIES

Every ounce of fat contains two and a quarter times more calories than an ounce of carbohydrate or protein.

TRY BUTTERMILK IN PASTRY

Buttermilk can be substituted for 2 percent or whole milk in most pastry or bread recipes. Buttermilk is less than 1 percent fat, almost equal to skim milk, but it has a thicker consistency.

BEAT ME, BEAT ME

Butter will go further and have fewer calories per serving if you beat it well, increasing the volume with air. Unless you happen to churn your own butter, look for whipped butter—but use it only as a spread, not in recipes for cooking or baking.

YOLKS AWAY

To cut fat and cholesterol in a recipe, replace the egg yolks with an equal amount of egg substitute, or just reduce the number of yolks.

THINK TWICE BEFORE EATING JUST ONE

A 6- to 7-ounce bag of potato chips contains a little less than the equivalent of ⅓ cup of oil—more than half a stick of butter!

NEEDS SHADES

Always purchase oils in opaque containers, never clear bottles. Oil is very sensitive to light and will deteriorate more rapidly when exposed to it. If you can't find it in an opaque container, transfer it to one at home.

DID YOU KNOW?

Whipped unsalted butter or soft-tub margarine (look for "trans-fat free" on the label) are the best spreads for your health.

WHY CAROB?

When carob is made into candy, fat is usually added to improve the texture. This usually brings the fat content close to—if not above—that in real chocolate. In fact, cocoa butter is 60 percent saturated fat, while the fat used in a carob candy is 85 percent saturated fat.

MARGARINE FACT

Most stick margarines contain 80 percent fat. Diet margarines usually contain 40 percent fat, 38 to 57 percent water, 2 percent salt, and 2 percent non-fat milk solids, and a minute amount of coloring.

A FATTY SEPARATION

If you are going to make mayonnaise, be sure to check the weather report. High temperatures or humidity can cause the mayonnaise to come out heavier and greasier than normal.

THE GREAT DEBATE

Which is better for you, butter or margarine? If you answered margarine because butter contains saturated fat and cholesterol, you should know that margarine has come under the gun lately. Margarine can be high in trans-fatty acids, which some food and nutrition experts believe are even worse than saturated fat.

DIETARY FIASCO

A 13-ounce burrito that contains 5 ounces of ground beef (like those in your grocery-store freezer) topped with sour cream and guacamole, may contain up to 1,000 calories and 63 percent calories from fat—70 grams. Add cheese sauce and you'll have 300 calories and 23 grams of fat.

THE BIG C

Diets high in total fat and trans-fatty acids have been linked to cancers of the colon, prostate, and breast. Studies are also showing that a high-fat diet can impede the efficiency of the immune system. Most doctors and nutrition experts recommend that you get 30 percent of your total daily calories from fat, even though you can survive on as little as 5 percent dietary fat *if* all the fat you consume is the essential fatty acid type.

OFF TO A SLUGGISH START

The stomach can digest approximately 10 grams of fat per hour. Two scrambled eggs, toast (with 1 tablespoon of butter), coffee, and milk contain about 42 grams of fat—which means that you'll probably start in on lunch before you've digested just the fat from your breakfast! And please don't eat a bacon-cheddar burger for lunch, because each of those burger toppers is 75 percent calories from fat.

No Wonder Obesity Is On The Rise			
SALAD AND COOKING OIL USE		**MARGARINE USE**	
1909	1.5 pounds per person	1950	6 pounds per person
1972	18 pounds per person	1972	11 pounds per person
1990	29 pounds per person	1990	16 pounds per person
1995	33 pounds per person	1995	18 pounds per person
1997	34 pounds per person	1997	19 pounds per person

MAKE THAT "FAT" TOOTH

Studies show that dieters miss fats more than sweets. How unlucky we are to crave the things that aren't good for our health!

EDUCATION A MUST

In 1972, North Americans consumed 53 pounds of hard fats (meats, etc.), shortenings (baked goods, etc.) and cooking fats (oils, etc.) per person. In 1997, consumption rose to 68 pounds. Poor nutrition education and increased eating out at fast-food restaurants are the primary culprits.

HOPE FOR THE FUTURE

Recent studies have shown that stearic acid, a saturated fat found in beef and lamb fat and cocoa butter, has little effect on raising cholesterol levels. As laboratory tests become more sophisticated, expect to hear more information about which fats will actually raise your cholesterol. Then we can avoid only those foods that may be harmful.

TOP FRYING OIL

Rape is a member of the mustard family that is grown in the United States and Canada as animal fodder. Rapeseed oil, also called canola (the name derives from Canada, oil, with an *a* on the end), is high in monounsaturated fat and has a fairly high smoke point.

THE COLOR OF FAT

People have "brown fat" and "white fat" inside the body. Current studies show that if your body is higher in brown fat, you may find it easier to control your weight than do people with higher amounts of white fat. The only way to determine brown fat deposits is with a thermographic skin measurement. But because the relationship between brown fat and obesity is still under study, you would probably need to be a participant in a research study to undergo this test.

INSOMNIA?

Most fat should be consumed either at breakfast or lunch. High-fat meals late in the day may cause the digestive system to overwork while you are sleeping, disturbing your sleep patterns.

SUGAR IN, FAT OUT—CALORIES THE SAME

Don't be duped by reduced-fat peanut butter. It has the same number of calories per serving as does regular peanut butter (about 190 per serving). The fat was replaced with sweeteners.

CREAM IT

To make a creamy salad dressing without the cream, put all the dressing ingredients except the oil into a blender and turn it on. Then, very slowly, pour in cold-pressed olive oil.

WORK LIKE A PRO

Purchase plastic-squeeze condiment bottles to use for storing your cooking oils. They are opaque, which will prevent deterioration of the oil, and the narrow opening makes it easy to pour when you're preparing a dish. Label the bottles with a permanent felt-tip marker.

FAT SCIENCE

When some oils are refrigerated, they become cloudy due to the buildup of harmless crystals. Manufacturers will sometimes prechill the oils and remove the crystals in a process known as winterization. These oils will remain clear when refrigerated.

TYPICAL AMERICAN DIET

The average North American diet is about 44 percent fat. Dietary guidelines suggest no more than 30 percent of total calories. But try for no more than 20 percent, with an emphasis on monounsaturated fats. The 30 percent figure is workable if the fat calories are all from olive or canola oil, which may be difficult for most people.

GOOD FAT?

Medium-chain triglycerides are sold in health-food stores for people who have digestive disorders and problems absorbing fats. These are produced primarily from coconut oil, have a very low smoke point, and do not produce free fatty acids when heated.

FAT SUBSTITUTES

Within the past decade, a good number fat substitutes have been used in food manufacturing. The following two synthetic products should be viewed with caution and used in moderation only.

Olestra

A synthetic fat molecule that is so large it passes through the intestinal tract undigested. As of this writing, Olestra has been approved for use only in snack foods. Chips and snacks made with Olestra have about one-third the calories of the traditional varieties. As with many lower-fat foods, people often eat more, consuming same number of total calories.

As it goes through the system, Olestra tends to bind with the fat-soluble vitamins A, D, E, and K. Products containing Olestra are fortified with these vitamins, but that may not solve the potential vitamin deficiency.

A more significant problem may be that the class of nutrients called carotenoids are also fat soluble, and Olestra may sweep some of the more than 500 carotenoids out of the body. These include beta-carotene, alpha-carotene, lutein, and lycopene. The carotenoids are believed to prevent many different types of cancer, yet foods containing Olestra are not forti-fied with carotenoids.

The most immediate problem with Olestra, however, is that the increase of undigested material may cause diarrhea. The FDA requires that foods containing Olestra be labeled with the following warning: "This product contains Olestra. Olestra may cause abdominal cramping and loose stools. Olestra inhibits the absorption of some vitamins and other nutrients. Vitamins A, D, E, and K have been added."

Hydrolyzed Oat Flour

A fat substitute, developed by the United States Department of Agriculture, which may have some health benefits. It is oat flour that has been treated with water to break down the starches into individual sugars. This causes the texture of the flour to change, and the result is similar to the "mouth feel" that fat imparts to foods. Oat flour is high in beta-glucan, which may have the ability to absorb cholesterol. It contains a mere 1 calorie per gram instead 9 calories per gram in actual fat.

One study has shown a definite cholesterol lower-ing correlation in the 24 volunteers. More than 40 new products using this substance are being developed, and it will be necessary to read the label to find it. It may also be called hydrated oat flour or have the brand name Oatrim. It is currently used in cookies, cheeses, and low-fat hot dogs and lunch meats. It has not been shown to cause digestive problems or interfere with vitamin absorption, but you cannot fry with hydrolyzed oat flour.

SHORTENING VS. OIL

Shortening is a fat that is always a solid at room temperature. The term "pure shortening" means that the product contains vegetable or animal fat, or a combination of the two. If it is labeled "pure vegetable shortening" it must be made from only vegetables sources. If the shortening does not have the word "pure" on the label, then it contains a number of additives to increase its shelf life; however, these additives frequently lower the smoke points, and such products should be avoided. Shortenings that are made from vegetable sources are hydrogenated, which means that hydrogen is added to a liquid fat until it becomes a semisolid.

CLEARING THINGS UP

If you wear eyeglasses when frying, you may have noticed that the oil droplets collect on the inner surface of the lens as well as the outer surface. The reason? Minute droplets of oil become airborne when heated. If you are bending over while you work, the oil droplets can land on the inside of the lenses as gravity pulls them back to earth.

WHY OIL CAN'T BE USED FOR BAKING

Because of its liquid nature, oil tends to collect instead of distributing evenly through the dough. This may cause baked goods to become grainy. When a solid fat is used, baked items tend to be flakier and retain their moisture better. Bottom line: Use the fat your recipe calls for (some will specify vegetable oil).

FRYING TEMPERATURES ARE CRITICAL

Oil needs to be at the proper temperature whether you're sautéing or deep-frying. If the temperature is too low, the food will absorb too much oil and become greasy, not crispy. If the oil is too hot, the food may burn on the outside and not cook through. Most breaded foods are normally fried at 375°F, but check the recipe. Chicken should be fried at 365°F for 15 to 20 minutes for white meat, 20 to 25 minutes for dark.

WHATEVER HAPPENED TO CASTOR OIL?

Up until the 1930s, castor oil was regularly used for the most common ailments: constipation, tummy aches, colds, and skin problems. Commercially, the oil was extracted from castor seeds by means of cold compression and steam treatment. The seeds are from the castor plant (*Ricinus communis*), and contain ricin, a dangerous poison—but they are denatured during the extraction process, making the oil safe to use. Castor oil fell out of favor not only because of its harsh taste but because the pharmaceutical industry came up with more specialized products.

FATS IN FOLK MEDICINE

A lot of animal fats were used in North American folk medicine. In winter, many children were sent to school with foul-smelling bags of camphor and goose grease around their necks so they wouldn't get the flu (was it the grease or the smell that kept the germs away, I wonder?). Warmed chicken fat was sometimes fed to babies and children who had croup. On the mammal side, suet was put on burns. Mutton tallow, which is melted sheep fat, was mixed with white pine resin for skin sores or was mixed with lemon juice for use as a hand lotion. Raw bacon and salt pork were placed on the skin to help draw out infection or poison.

Fat Calories in Common Foods

The following is information regarding fat in relation to total calories in a person's diet.

FOODS	% OF CALORIES FROM FAT	FOOD	% OF CALORIES FROM FAT
Bacon, butter, margarine, lard, mayonnaise, solid shortenings, cooking oils, olives, baking chocolate, cream cheese	90-100	Most baked goods, lean hamburger, ground turkey, Canadian bacon, ham, steak, whole milk, round steak	35-50
Macadamia nuts, salad dressings, pecans, walnuts, avocados, sausages, corned beef, coconut	80-90	Low-fat yogurt, 2 percent milk, veal chops, loin and rump cuts of beef, sweet breads	20-35
Hot dogs, peanuts, most chips, blue cheese, cashews, lunch meats, peanut butter, prime rib, oil-packed canned tuna, Swiss cheese, sunflower seeds	65-80	Crab, baked chicken without skin, most shellfish, water-packed canned tuna, low-fat cottage cheese, low-fat broiled fish	10-20
Hamburger, rib steak, chicken with skin, canned ham, salmon, trout, bass, veal cutlet, eggs, ice cream	50-65	Buttermilk, skim milk, beans, rice, cereals, potatoes, pasta, fruits, vegetables, egg whites	Very small amount

SOURCE: Nutritive Values of Foods, USDA 1994.

7

NUTS
AND
GRAINS

THE GOODNESS OF GRAINS

Familiar with the Food Pyramid? Then you know you should be getting six to 11 servings of grain-based foods every day. While eating your quota from this group isn't as challenging as others—one slice of bread or half an English muffin counts as one serving—eating an adequate amount of nutrient-rich whole grains can be difficult. To obtain optimum health a person should consume five to six servings of whole-grain—not refined—foods every day.

The typical American diet includes only 25 percent complex carbohydrates; in comparison, a typical Japanese person's diet is 65 percent. In recent years, Americans have begun to realize the importance diet plays in overall health; unfortunately it took an increase in cancer and heart diseases to bring this realization about.

Grains are composed of three parts: the bran, the endosperm, and the germ. The outer covering, or bran, contains most of the grain's nutrients and almost all the dietary fiber. The endosperm is the heaviest part of the grain; it contains most of the protein and carbohydrates. It is this portion that is used to make white flour. The germ contains polyunsaturated fat and is rich in vitamin E and the B complex vitamins. Because it is so high in fat, it is usually removed to avoid rancidity.

GRAIN VARIETIES

Amaranth

Was first grown by the Aztecs. The seeds are incredibly small—there are about 700,000 in one pound. Amaranth is the only grain that contains adequate amounts of the amino acid lysine. When this grain is consumed with rice, wheat, or barley, it provides a biologically complete protein containing all the essential amino acids.

Barley

An excellent source of B vitamins and soluble fiber. Half the barley grown in this country is used as animal fodder; 30 percent is used in brewing beer or distilling liquor. Of the remaining 20 percent, most is sold pearled or whole, but some is available as barley grits. Malted barley can be purchased in health-food stores.

Buckwheat

Actually the seed of a leafy plant related to rhubarb. It has a strong nutlike flavor and is especially high in the amino acid arginine. Considered a minor crop in the United States, it is primarily prepared as kasha. Kasha, or buckwheat groats, is buckwheat kernels that are hulled and crushed. It can be prepared the same as rice, and it has a high nutritional value.

Corn

A grain native to the Americas. It is high in fiber and yellow varieties are a fairly good source of vitamin A. Corn is popular in many forms, from fresh on the cob and kernels to ground preparations like grits and cornbread—even distilled into bourbon.

Millet

The only grain higher in B vitamins than whole wheat or brown rice. It is also an excellent source of copper and iron. People with wheat allergies can usually eat millet without a problem. Millet is popular in North Africa, China, India, and Ethiopia, where it is used to make flatbread.

Oats

Were first grown in the United States in the 1600s. By the 1880s, they were packaged and sold, with oatmeal being the most popular breakfast food of that time. In 1997, the annual consumption of oats per person was approximately 15 pounds. Oat bran is known to contribute to lowering cholesterol levels. It is high in a number of vitamins and minerals, and is an excellent source of soluble fiber, which can reduce the risk of heart disease. Besides oatmeal, oats are used in granola and muesli cereals.

Quinoa

This grain is s related to chard and spinach; its leaves can be cooked similarly for a nutritious green. The grain has a delicate flavor and can be substituted for most other grains. It quadruples in volume when cooked and is usually found in natural foods stores. Quinoa is high in potassium, iron, and riboflavin and has good levels of zinc, copper, and manganese.

Rice

Comes in more varieties than nearly any other food. There are hundreds of types of long-, medium-, or short-grain rice grown around the world. Rice is popular in the United States; Americans consume about 25 pounds per person, annually. In Japan, annual consumption is about 30 pounds per person. Rice was first cultivated in Thailand around 3,500 B.C., however, China produces almost 90 percent of all the rice grown worldwide.

Rice is an excellent source of the B complex vitamins and a number of minerals. Long-grain rice is just slightly more nutritious than short- and medium-grain rice. Brown rice is more nutritious and higher in B vitamins and fiber than white rice. Of all rices, only brown provides vitamin E.

Quick-cooking brown rice is available, and though its texture isn't quite as chewy, it cooks in 15 minutes. If you soak brown rice 8 to 10 hours or overnight before cooking, it will cook in about 22 minutes. White rice has had the outer husk and bran removed. Because the bran portion is higher in fat, brown rice may go rancid if not used quickly.

Rye
This grain is higher in protein (75 percent higher than brown rice), iron, and the B vitamins than whole wheat. Most rye breads are usually made from a combination of rye and wheat flour because rye has no gluten—a loaf made just of rye flour will be too dense and strongly flavored. Only 25 percent of the rye crop goes into human food production; the balance is used for whisky and animal fodder.

Triticale
A hybrid of wheat and rye that is high in protein and B vitamins. It may be used in breads due to its excellent gluten content. Triticale can be found in most natural-food stores.

Wheat
The number-one grain crop in the world and used mainly in breads and pastas. The majority of wheat is processed into white flour; whole wheat is very high in the B vitamins and numerous minerals, including iron. Researchers are currently studying the effects wheat fiber might have in decreasing the risk of colon cancers.

WHITE IS OUT, BROWN IS IN

When the bran is removed to make white rice, nutrients are not added back to fortify the grain. Even though rice may be sold as "enriched," the number of nutrients replaced is minimal. When the rice is cooked, most of those additional nutrients are lost. In terms of nutrition, instant rice is your worst bet.

AVOID THE BURN

If your rice burns, spoon the unburned rice into a clean pot and set a slice of white bread on top for 5 minutes, then remove and discard. The white bread will absorb the burnt odor.

TYPES OF OAT PRODUCTS

Instant Oats
Are sliced into very small pieces, and then cooked and dried. Some varieties "cook" when mixed with hot water, others require brief cooking. Instant oats cannot be used in recipes that call for rolled or quick-cooking oats. They lack the texture we find so appealing in cookies, for example.

Oat Bran

The ground outer casing of the grain. It is very high in soluble fiber and can help to lower cholesterol levels.

Oat Flour

Very finely ground oats. It must be mixed with wheat flour in breads an the like, as it does not contain gluten and will not rise if used alone.

Quick-Cooking Oats

Sliced into smallish pieces, and then steamed and flattened. These oats take only five minutes to cook.

Rolled Oats

Are steamed, flattened, and flaked. These oats take about 15 minutes to cook. Both quick-cooking and rolled oats can be used interchangeably with no problem in recipes.

Steel-Cut Oats

Are cut instead of rolled. They are not steamed and take about 30 minutes to cook. They have a very chewy texture.

CLEAN 'EM OUT

Unless the instructions explicitly direct you to rinse rice before cooking, don't—most rice sold in the United States is coated with a fine powder that contains the B vitamins thiamine and niacin. If you rinse the rice, you wash these nutrients down the drain.

COOKING RICE

If you're cooking long grain-white rice, here's an easy formula to determine how much water you need—twice as much water as you have rice. Once the water comes to a boil, add the rice, and then reduce the heat to a simmer and cook for 15 minutes. If you like dry, fluffy rice, once the rice is cooked, wrap the lid with a cotton dish towel and set it on the pot for about 15 minutes. The cloth will absorb the steam.

HOW DO THEY PUFF CEREALS?

Alexander P. Anderson invented puffed cereals in the early 1900s. He was interested in the nature of starch granules and while experimenting, some of the grains exploded into puffy masses of starch. The starch or dough is compressed and cooked to gelatinize the starch, and then placed under high pressure steam until the water vapor expands, puffing out each small morsel. Quaker Oats was the first company to market puffed cereal,

DID YOU KNOW?

Toast oatmeal before using it in cookies and breads: Spread it in a thin layer in a baking pan and bake at 350°F for about 10 minutes, shaking the pan once or twice.

which they introduced to the public in 1904 at the World's Fair in St. Louis and sold as a popcornlike snack. In 1913, Puffed Rice and Puffed Wheat were sold as breakfast cereals.

FAUX CORN

Jasmine rice smells and tastes something like popcorn. Try it as a side dish for a different treat. It pairs nicely with simple grilled chicken or fish.

FLUFFIER BEATS MUSHIER

Converted rice is actually parboiled rice—that is, it has been soaked, steamed, and dried in such a way as to ensure it cooks up fluffy every time. Despite the fact that it is partially cooked, it does take slightly longer to cook than does regular rice.

THE RICE THAT ISN'T

Wild rice is not a grain, but actually a seed of a shallow water grass. It was a staple food of the Chippewa and Dakota. Wild rice has one-third more protein than does long-grain white rice and is high in B vitamins when cooked. Wild rice has a fairly high moisture content and can become moldy in high humidity; it should be stored in the refrigerator.

TOP OF THE LINE

The best pasta is made from durum wheat, and the finest pasta wheat grown in the United States comes from North Dakota, which grows more than 90 percent of this wheat in United States (Russia leads the world in production of durum). Durum has a very high protein content. Like all hard wheats, it has fewer starch grains, and those it has are smaller than those in softer wheats. Because the protein molecules run more continuously through the grain, they are stronger.

DON'T RINSE

When you make pasta, don't rinse it after it's cooked. Sauce will cling better, and you'll retain more nutrients.

THE ANCESTOR OF WHEAT

There are more than 30,000 varieties of wheat; all are descended from a plant called wild einkorn. All commonly consumed wheat grown today is from the species *Triticum aestivum*. There are fourteen species of wheat; two others can be found in natural-food stores: kamut and spelt. Scientists disagree on which species kamut came from, but spelt is the species *Triticum aestivum spelta*.

THE GOOD GERM

Wheat germ is high in nutrients and fiber. Because wheat germ can go rancid quickly, once you've opened the vacuum-sealed jar, store it in the refrigerator. It will stay fresh for six months. It's easy to tell if the jar of wheat germ in your fridge has gone rancid: If it tastes bitter, toss it. Fresh wheat germ should taste sweet.

HEALTHY CHOICE

Cracked wheat can be a nutritious substitute for rice in many dishes. It is prepared by toasting whole-wheat berries (the bran and germ are kept intact), which are then broken into coarse, medium, and fine fragments.

NO GERMS HERE

When you purchase hot cereals, be aware that most of these products are degerminated—that is, the germ is removed—to make them more palatable. The bad news is this also makes them less nutritious.

ISN'T BULGUR CRACKED WHEAT?

Bulgur is not the same thing as cracked wheat. Cracked wheat is uncooked wheat that is dried and coarsely milled, which cracks it apart. Bulgur wheat is steamed, dried, and then crushed into three different sizes. The coarsest wheat is used for bulgur pilaf and stuffings, the finest in breads or desserts, and the medium granulation for tabbouleh and other side dishes, and for cereals.

DID YOU KNOW?

If you want the nutrients of whole-wheat flour but want a lighter texture for your baked goods, use whole-wheat pastry flour.

TASTY DISH

Tabbouleh is a traditional dish in the Middle East. It is prepared from bulgur wheat and includes lemon juice, olive oil, parsley, mint, tomatoes, and onions. Sometimes other vegetables are added.

FOR HEALTH'S SAKE, READ THE LABEL

When you buy bread, be sure to read the list of ingredients on the label. White flour is made from wheat, so any bread made from white flour is a wheat bread—but it won't be as nutritious as whole-wheat bread. If you want whole-wheat bread, look for labels that read "whole wheat" or "whole grain" flour. Whole-wheat flour will keep only for about two months at room temperature before it goes rancid. Under refrigeration, it will keep for about five months. If you freeze it, whole-wheat flour should last one year; just be sure to bring it to room temperature before you use it.

WHERE THE GOOD STUFF IS

The healthiest portion of the wheat is the bran. It contains 86 percent of the niacin, 73 percent of the pyridoxine, 50 percent of the pantothenic acid, 42 percent of the riboflavin, 33 percent of the thiamine, and 19 percent of the protein. When wheat is made into white flour, all is discarded.

SHAKE IT UP

Whole-grain flours should be sifted through a coarse sifter or wire-mesh sieve when the recipe instructs you to do so.

FOODS CONTAINING WHEAT

Many people are allergic to wheat or have celiac disease, a condition where ingesting gluten and similar proteins in rye, oats, barley, and triticale, damages the lining of the small intestine. Wheat can lurk in a surprising number of foods that you might not suspect:

Beer	Sanka	Graham flour	Bouillon cubes
Malt liquor	Whisky	Rye flour	Gravy
Malted milk	Candy bars	Gluten flour	Soy sauce
Gin	Pudding	Patent flour	
Postum	Corn flour	Lima-bean flour	

NUTS AND SEEDS

Nuts are full of vital nutrients like protein, potassium, vitamin E, B vita-mins, and iron. The only drawback to nuts is their fat content: Most nuts range between 50 and 70 percent fat. At 72 percent fat, macadamia nuts are the highest, with coconut and Brazil nuts not too far behind. Coconut gets nearly all its fat in the form of saturated fats. Peanuts, which are really a member of the legume family, and pinenuts are good sources of protein. Shelled nuts go rancid more quickly than do nuts that are in the shells, because the shells protect the oils from oxidizing.

Seeds of many plants are edible and contain an excellent level of nutrients, especially trace minerals that can be difficult to obtain from other foods. The most popular seeds for eating are pumpkin, sesame, and sunflower. Poppyseeds come from a plant related to opium poppies, so eating two poppyseed bread rolls (or about 1.5 grams of seeds) can cause urinalysis to be positive for opiates.

BUT THEY DON'T HARM YOUR LUNGS

Sunflower seeds produce a similar reaction on the body as smoking a cigarette: Both cause the body to produce adrenaline, which goes to the brain, resulting in a pleasant feeling. The seeds, however, must be raw, not roasted, for this to take effect.

ALMOND PASTE AND MARZIPAN

Both of these are made from blanched ground almonds and are used in pastries and confections. They are not the same, however. Marzipan is almond paste with sugar and unbeaten egg whites; it is stiffer and lighter in color. Almond paste contains more blanched almonds, and it costs more.

THE ALMIGHTY ALMOND

In California, almond orchards are second only to grapes in agricultural space—480,000 acres are devoted to growing almonds. Almonds are California's major food export.

WILD ABOUT WALNUTS

Walnuts have been grown in Persia for millennia. Franciscan missionaries brought walnuts to the United States and planted the first walnut trees in California in 1867. California's Central Valley produces 98 percent of the total U.S. crop and 66 percent of the world's crop.

135

WHAT IS MASA HARINA?

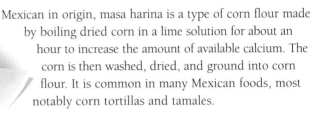

Mexican in origin, masa harina is a type of corn flour made by boiling dried corn in a lime solution for about an hour to increase the amount of available calcium. The corn is then washed, dried, and ground into corn flour. It is common in many Mexican foods, most notably corn tortillas and tamales.

USE YOUR BEAN

Have you heard of beanut butter? It is made from soybeans and, like regular peanut butter, provides high-quality protein. It contains sufficient quantities of estrogen-like substances called isoflavones, which may be effective in reducing the symptoms of menopause such as hot flashes; lowering cholesterol levels; boosting bone density, thus reducing the risk of osteoporosis; and may provide antioxidant properties, possibly protecting against cancers of the bladder, prostate, colon, and breast. The fat content of beanut butter is 11 grams per 2 tablespoons compared with 16 grams in regular peanut butter and has two-thirds the saturated fat. The fat tends to separate as in natural peanut butter and can be poured off to reduce the fat content even more.

TYPES OF NUTS

Roasted Nuts

Often thought to be higher in fat than dry-roasted nuts, but are only slightly so. They are dipped into and out of the oil so rapidly that they actually absorb very little, and the excess oil is drained off after roasting.

Dry-Roasted

These are never cooked in oil. All nuts, however, are naturally high in fat. Most dry-roasted nuts are high in salt.

Raw Nuts

Commonly packaged in cans (which keep them fresh longer), because they tend to go rancid very easily. Raw nuts should be stored in the refrigerator or freezer to slow down deterioration.

Defatted ("Lite") Peanuts

These are processed to reduce their fat content, but don't be fooled—they are still not a low-fat nibble.

A HEALTHIER WAY TO GO

In the early twentieth century our grandparents and great-grandparents were getting twice as much protein from grains and cereals than we get now. We would be healthier if this were still the case.

THE HIGH-CALCIUM NUT

Almonds are an good source of calcium—but they're no substitute for milk. One ounce of dry-roasted almonds provides 80 milligrams of calcium but has 166 calories. A half-cup of fat-free milk provides 228 milligrams of calcium and has about 45 calories.

CRUMMY SOLUTION

Can't quite see your way to buying bread crumbs? Set aside a special jar and pour in the crumbs from the bottom of cracker boxes or low-sugar cereal boxes. Make low-in-sodium seasoned bread crumbs by adding dried herbs to suit the flavors of your dish.

THEY'LL NEVER GO NUTS

Botanically, peanuts are more like beans than nuts; they are members of the legume family. The two most popular varieties of peanuts are Spanish and Virginia. Unshelled peanuts will last for six months if you wrap them in a plastic bag and keep them in the refrigerator.

DOES PEANUT BUTTER CONTAIN A CARCINOGEN?

Yes. Aflatoxin is a carcinogen that can be present in almost all peanut butters on the market. A study that was performed by Consumers Union showed that the major brands had less aflatoxin than most store brands. The biggest offender turned out to be freshly ground peanut butter, which had ten times the levels of the major brands. The FDA allows no more than 20 parts per billion (ppb) of aflatoxin. If you stick with the major brands, there's little reason to worry. Virtually all shipments of peanuts into the United States are tested by the USDA to ensure that peanuts and peanut butter are not contaminated with aflatoxin.

CHEF'S SECRET

Next time you chop nuts in a blender, try adding a small amount of sugar. The nutmeats won't stick together.

THE OLD SWITCHEROO

When a recipe for a dessert topping or a coating (say for chicken) calls for a coarse bran or bread crumbs and you don't have any (or if you just want to try something new), substitute your favorite unsalted nut. Chop it as finely as possible.

SLOWS THE RANCIDITY

Once natural peanut butter is opened, it spoils much more rapidly than highly processed commercial brands. It will stay fresh for one year if unopened. Once opened, natural peanut butter will stay fresh for up to four months, stored in the refrigerator upside down. The oil in natural peanut butter separates because there are no chemical stabilizers.

THE HEALTHIER WAY TO GO

A 12-ounce broiled sirloin steak provides 104 grams of protein—almost double the daily requirement—and tips the scales at 684 calories, 28 grams of fat (12 of them saturated), and not a shred of fiber. A meal of white rice and black beans—one cup of each—provides 21 grams of protein (about one third of the daily requirement), a mere 494 calories, 2 grams fat—zero of which are saturated—and 11 grams dietary fiber.

A SINKING FEELING

Always test grains for freshness before cooking them. Just pour a small amount of water into a pan and add a small amount of grains. Fresh grains sink to the bottom, and older grains float to the top.

THE NOSE KNOWS

Nuts, beans, whole grains, corn, and peanut butter should be discarded if there is even the slightest sign of mold or unusual odor. They may contain the dangerous carcinogen aflatoxin.

CHOCK-FULL OF PROTEIN

Lentils are small dried members of the legume family called pulses that are a good source of protein. They do not need to be soaked before cooking and can be on the table in about a half hour, though they will take longer if cooked with highly acidic foods such as tomatoes.

HEAV-V-VY

One ounce of sunflower seeds contains 160 calories and 14 grams of fat. They're a good source of magnesium, folate, and zinc. Although they may be considered a health food, they're not a diet food!

SUPERMAN TO THE RESCUE

Cooks (and squirrels) love the taste of black walnuts, but they can be almost impossible for people to crack open (squirrels have no problem). If you have a trash compactor, place a piece of wood on the bottom high enough so that when the compactor lowers it will crush the nuts. Be sure to have a clean bag in it. The low-tech solution: Set the nuts on a rock, then hit them with a hammer.

WHY IS BARLEY A COMMON THICKENER FOR SOUPS AND STEWS?

Barley contains starch molecules called amylase and amylopectin. When cooked to 140°F, the amylase and amylopectin relax, and some of their internal bonds come apart and form new bonds. This new network is capable of trapping and holding water molecules, which causes the starch granules to swell. The barley softens and provides bulk. If the barley is cooked to higher temperatures, the granules rupture, releasing some of the amylase and amylopectin, which are able to absorb more water, making the soup or stew thicker.

B IS FOR BARLEY

Barley is high in B vitamins, which are leached out of the grain and into the water when the grain is cooked. To retain most of these vitamins, be sure to consume the liquid as well as the barley.

DID YOU KNOW?

If you're having problems shelling nuts, put them in the freezer for about an hour. You'll find the nuts much easier to crack.

COMPETING WITH THE SQUIRRELS?

Acorns were a popular food during the golden age of Greece, and were consumed by various Native American tribes. They do contain a high level of tannin, which can be removed by soaking the nuts in several changes of hot water. The acorn pulp can then be mashed and made into flat cakes, similar to tortillas.

BRAZIL NUT BASICS

The Brazil nut comes from trees that can only be grown in the Amazon; attempts to grow the trees in other parts of the world have failed. Most of the trees are in the wild, because commercial plantations have great difficulty raising the trees. The trees grow to heights of 150 feet with a diameter of about six feet. The Brazil nut is actually the seed of a pod that resembles a coconut. Each pod is about six inches across with between 12 and 20 seeds. Each pod weighs about five pounds and harvesters must wear hard hats or risk being killed. Brazil nuts have a high fat content and three nuts have about the same number of calories as one egg.

PEANUT BUTTER, BY PRESCRIPTION?

In 1890, Dr. Ambrose Straub of St. Louis, Missouri patented a peanut-grinding machine. At the World's Fair in St. Louis in 1904, peanut butter was first introduced to the North American public. Peruvian Indians and African tribes, however, had been enjoying peanut paste for centuries.

THE POPULAR PEANUT

Peanuts are commonly grown in the southern United States; almost 50 percent of the country's crop is used to make peanut butter.

THE POISONOUS CASHEW

Cashews are among the most popular nuts worldwide. The cashew is related to poison ivy, which is one reason you never see cashews in the shell. The shell contains an oil that is a skin irritant. The oil is driven off by heat processing before the cashew nut can be extracted without becoming contaminated. The extraction process is a delicate operation, because no oil residue can come into contact with the nut. The oil is then used in paints and as a rocket lubricant base.

IF YOU CAN'T EAT 'EM . . .

The cashew is the seed of a fruit that resembles an apple; the cashew seed sits on top of the fruit. In some countries the cashew nut is discarded because it is so hard to extract it from the shell; these cultures simply consume the fruit or ferment its juice and use it to make an alcoholic beverage.

FLAXSEED, A REAL DISEASE-FIGHTER?

The National Cancer Institute is studying flaxseed in relation to breast, colon, and prostate cancer; it is an important source of lignans, which are plant compounds that provide a specific fiber that may contain anticancer properties. Flaxseed is also rich in omega-3 fatty acids and is the richest plant source of alpha-linolenic acid, an essential fatty acid. In a recent study, men who daily ate six slices of bread containing 30 percent flaxseed reduced their cholesterol levels by 7 percent and LDLs (bad cholesterol) by 19 percent, without lowering their HDLs (good cholesterol).

NO SIMPLE MATH

Unlike rice, which triples when cooked, there's no simple formula for converting a measure of uncooked pasta to cooked—a cup of tiny pastina or alphabet shapes will cook up quite differently than a cup of the large, irregularly-shaped bow ties, for example, and how would you measure a cup of uncooked spaghetti? What is constant is this: A cup of cooked pasta provides you with about 7 grams of protein.

A LITTLE OF THIS AND A LITTLE OF THAT

When eating pasta, try to balance the meal with some protein. This will allow the blood-sugar levels to be normalized.

PASTA POUNDAGE

In 1997, the average American consumed 24 pounds of pasta. In the same year, the typical Italian ate 62 pounds.

EAT THE VEGGIE

Spinach and other vegetable pastas contain very little of the vegetable: A cup of spinach pasta contains less than one tablespoon of spinach. Vegetable pastas are barely higher in nutrients than unflavored pasta.

PASTA TRICKS

Cook pasta only until it is slightly chewy (what the Italians call *al dente*, or "to the tooth"). The longer you cook pasta, the less nutrients it will retain and the mushier it will become. Always use plenty of water, and keep the water at a rapid boil—the pasta needs to move around as it cooks to keep it from sticking together.

WAIT FOR GOOD WEATHER

Making pasta from scratch? Don't make it if it's rainy or very humid. Like bread dough, the pasta dough will be very difficult to knead.

YOU'RE GETTING SLEEPY

A large pasta meal may help you relax by increasing a chemical in your brain called serotonin.

GOOD FOR YOUNG AND OLD

Most pasta is easily digested and has a fairly low fiber content, making it a good food for children, the elderly, and those with digestive problems. Most pastas are salt- and fat-free. Just be careful with your sauce and you'll have a healthful dinner.

NO PEEKABOO

Pasta is fortified with vitamins that are light sensitive. If you transfer pasta from the cardboard cartons to decorative glass jars, use it within one or two months. To store it longer, keep it in airtight containers in the dark. Pasta will keep for about 18 months.

PASTA PRESTO!

Capellini and capelli d'angelo, or angel hair pasta, cook up in as little as two minutes. Keep either on hand for times when you need a speedy dinner. Just top these delicate strands with a light sauce.

DID YOU KNOW?

Always follow the cooking directions on the pasta box, especially regarding cooking times. They can vary considerably from brand to brand.

Pasta Shapes

THIN STRANDS	WHAT THE NAME MEANS
Bavette	"Little dribbles." Another name for linguine.
Capelli d'angelo	"Angel's hair." Very thin pasta strands.
Capellini	"Very fine hair." Slightly thicker than capelli d'angelo.
Capelveneri	Flat, medium-width noodles
Fedelini	Another name for capellini.
Linguine	"Little tongues." Flat, narrow ribbons.
Spaghetti	"Little strings." Long, thin strands.
Spaghettini	Very thin spaghetti.
Vermicelli	"Little worms." Between spaghettini and capellini in thickness.
THICK STRANDS	**WHAT THE NAME MEANS**
Bucatini	"Pierced." Hollow thin strands.
Fettuccine	Flat ribbons, sometimes made with eggs.
Fusilli	Corkscrew-shaped pasta.
Gemelli	"Twins." Pasta strand folded in half and twisted together.
Lasagna	Very long, broad noodles.
Mafalda	Ripple-edged flat, broad noodles.
Pappardelle	"Gulp down." Wide noodles with rippled sides.
Perciatelli	Thin, hollow tubes, about twice as thick as spaghetti.
Tagliarini	Pasta shaped like ribbons, usually paper thin.
Tagliatelle	Very long, flat egg noodles.

Gemelli

Lasagna

Tagliarini

Mostaccioli

Cavatelli

Ditalini

Pasta Shapes	
TUBES	**WHAT THE NAME MEANS**
Cannelloni	"Large tubes." Up to 4 inches long.
Magliette	Short, curved pasta tubes.
Manicotti	Tubes between 4 and 5 inches long.
Mostaccioli	"Little mustaches." Tubes about 2 inches long with a slight curve.
Penne	"Quills." Tubes that are diagonally cut, about 2 inches long.
Rigatoni	"Ribbed." Larger than penne, with grooved sides.
Tubetti	Very tiny hollow tubes.
Ziti	"Bridegrooms." A very short tubular-shaped pasta.
OTHER SHAPES	**WHAT THE NAME MEANS**
Anellini	"Small rings."
Cavatappi	"Corkscrews." Short spiral-shaped macaroni.
Cavatelli	"Little plugs." Short, shells with a rippled edge
Conchiglie	"Shells" Available in a variety of sizes.
Ditalini	"Little toes." Used in soup.
Farfalle	"Butterflies." Shaped like a bowtie. Sold in two sizes, large and small.
Orecchiette	"Little ears." Small dimpled circles.
Orzo	Small pasta slightly larger than rice.
Pastina	Very, very small pasta, usually used in soups.
Radiatore	"Radiators." Short and thick, with several ridges.
Ruote	"Wheels." Round pasta with spokes, sometimes called rotelle.

8

SEASON
TO
TASTE

FLAVOR BOOST

Crushing dried herbs before using them will boost their flavor. You can also intensify their flavor by soaking them for a few seconds in hot water. This also works well if they have lost their flavor.

HERBS AND AROMATICS THAT IMPROVE THE TASTE OF MEATS

Beef

Garlic, onion, basil, thyme, summer savory, and rosemary

Buffalo

Rosemary, basil, garlic, and sage

Veal

Rosemary, garlic, thyme, tarragon, and basil

Lamb

Mint, ginger, rosemary, garlic, and basil

Pork

Sweet marjoram, sage, garlic, thyme, rosemary, and basil

Poultry

Sage, basil, sweet marjoram, chervil, onion, and summer savory

Fish

Sage, fennel, parsley, dill, basil, and chives

TO SEASON OR NOT TO SEASON, THAT IS THE QUESTION

When doubling or otherwise changing the yield of a recipe, do not increase the seasonings proportionately. If, for example, you are doubling the recipe, increase the seasonings only by one-and-a-half; if you are tripling the recipe, double the amount of seasoning.

TWO DON'TS

◆ Never increase the sugar in tomato-sauce dishes.
◆ Never increase salt in a recipe by more than a pinch or two at a time.

PROTECTING YOUR HERBS AND SPICES

Herbs and spices contain volatile oils that oxidize easily. It is best to store dried seasonings in a cool, dry spot away from heat and out of direct sunlight; they'll maintain optimal flavor for up to six months. Two of the worst locations are near a microwave exhaust fan and over the stove. If you store herbs and spices in the refrigerator, remove them at least 30 minutes before you plan to use them to release their flavor and aroma.

EASY RETRIEVAL

When you cook with whole garlic cloves that you plan to remove before the dish is served, stick a toothpick firmly in the garlic so it will be easy to take out. Put herbs that fall apart during cooking in a tea infuser to make them easy to remove.

ALLSPICE

The flavor of this spice has hints of cinnamon, cloves, and nutmeg. Jamaica is the largest producer of allspice, but it also comes from Central and South America, and it is sold both whole and in ground form. It is used in pickling and to flavor meats, fish, baked goods, relishes, puddings, and fruit preserves. Allspice is commonly used in a number of ready-to-serve foods such as hot dogs, soups, and baked beans.

ANISE

This herb, imported mainly from Mexico and Spain, has a licorice-like flavor. It is found in licorice candy (as a substitute for real licorice), and in cookies, pickling spices, and soft drinks. It is also used to make anisette (the anise-flavored liqueur) and can be used as a substitute for ginger in some recipes. It is commonly available as the spice aniseed.

BASIL

There are more than 60 varieties of this herb found worldwide; these include lemon basil, cinnamon basil, and opal basil, which has purple leaves. The basil we're most familiar with is sweet basil, which is grown primarily in California for commercial purposes. It is a common seasoning for fish, meat, tomato dishes, soups, stews, pizza sauce, and salad dressings.

A member of the mint family, basil should be stored in the refrigerator wrapped in a damp paper towel and sealed in a plastic bag. It should retain its flavor and aroma for about five days.

Basil tends to lose most of its flavor after about 15 minutes of cooking, so it should be added no more than 10 minutes before the food is done.

DID YOU KNOW?

Drying intensifies the flavor of herbs, so fresh herbs are milder than dried.

BAY LEAF

Bay leaves, sometimes called bay laurel, are usually sold whole rather than ground and are commonly used in stews, sauces, soups, dill pickles, meat dishes, veal, and poultry. They are also used in numerous ready-to-serve foods.

Remember to remove bay leaves from foods before you serve them. If someone eats a piece, it will be like eating a mouthful of straw. Never crumble a bay leaf when using it in a recipe and stir the dish gently so as not to break the leaf up.

The Turkish variety of bay leaf has a milder flavor and is wider and shorter than the California variety.

CAPERS

These are the buds of a shrub native to the Mediterranean. Capers are almost always sold pickled in brine; some gourmet markets sell them packed in salt. The tiny capers called nonpareils are from France; larger capers are from Italy. If you are on a sodium-restricted diet, be sure to rinse capers before you use them. Capers are commonly used in smoked fish, chicken, eggs, or veal dishes.

CARAWAY

With a flavor somewhat similar to anise, caraway seeds are harvested at night before the dew evaporates. The majority sold in the United States are imported from the Netherlands. Caraway seeds are commonly used in rye bread, cookies, organ meat dishes, dips, cabbage, sauerkraut, soft cheese spreads, sweet pickles, and sauerbraten.

CARDAMOM

A member of the ginger family with a pungent aroma and slight lemon flavor, cardamom is used in pickling, pastries, pumpkin dishes, and sweet potatoes. Available as pods or ground, cardamom is often imported from India and is popular in Scandinavian cooking as well as Indian. If you are making a stew or curry, the shells of cardamom pods will disintegrate during cooking. Cardamom is an effective cover for bad breath.

CAYENNE PEPPER

A common spice, also called ground red pepper, cayenne is sold crushed, ground, or whole. It is used in curries, relishes, salsas, chili powders, many Mexican dishes, Italian and Indian foods, sausages, and dressings.

CELERY FLAKES

Celery flakes are made from the dehydrated leaves and ribs of the celery plant and are used in the same dishes as celery seed.

CELERY SEED

This is used for pickling, and in soups, stews, salad dressings, fish dishes, salads such as cole slaw, and many vegetable dishes. Celery salt is a blend of ground celery seed and salt.

CHERVIL

This herb is a member of the parsley family; it is more common in France than in the United States. It can be used in salad dressings or any dish that would also be flavored with parsley.

CHILI PEPPERS

To prepare chili peppers for cooking, spear them with a long-handled fork and singe them over a gas-stove burner (if you don't have a gas stove, broil the chilies) until the skin blisters. Wrap the singed peppers in a cloth towel or foil and let them steam. The skin will relax and pull away, making it easy to peel the chilies and to remove the seeds and veins. (Always wear gloves when you do this, as a compound in hot chilies can irritate skin.) The pulp will be very spicy, but the seeds and veins are even hotter. Don't use too many of the seeds unless you want a really fiery dish.

CHILI POWDER

Chili powder is often blended from cumin seed, dried hot chili peppers, oregano, coriander, cloves, and garlic. It is available in a variety of heat levels, from mild to hot. Some gourmet shops sell pure chili powder, which is made from ground chili peppers with no other spices included.

CHIVES

Chives have a light oniony flavor and are used to flavor dips, sauces, soups, and baked potatoes, or to replace the flavor of onion in a recipe.

CILANTRO

The leaf of the coriander plant, cilantro looks very much like flat-leaf, or Italian, parsley. It is used in certain Mexican and Thai dishes, to flavor salad dressings, and in salsa.

CINNAMON

Real cinnamon is not common in the United States. Imported from China and Indonesia, it is harvested from the bark of the laurel tree. The color is the giveaway. True cinnamon is actually a light tan color. Most cinnamon sold in the United States is actually cassia, which is usually imported from Vietnam; it is a dark reddish-brown.

It is used in its whole form for preserving; to flavor spiced beverages, such as cider or hot wine drinks; in meat or chicken dishes; in puddings; and for pickling. The ground form is used in baked goods, ketchup, vegetables, apple butter, mustards, and spiced peaches.

CLOVES

Tanzania is the largest producer of cloves, which are usually sold whole or ground. This is a strong spice and should be used only in small amounts. Cloves are often used in baked beans, pickling, ham, sweet potatoes, baked goods, puddings, mustards, soups, hot dogs, sausages, and barbecue sauces.

CORIANDER

A relative of the carrot family, coriander has a sweet, musky flavor. The seed or ground form is used in gingerbread, cookies, cakes, biscuits, poultry stuffing, pork dishes, pea soup, and cheese dishes.

CUMIN

This is used mainly in its ground form in curry, chili powder, soups, deviled eggs, fruit pies, stews, soft cheeses, and chili con carne.

DID YOU KNOW?

To tell flat-leaf parsley from cilantro, rub a leaf between your fingers. This will release the herb's fragrance—and if it's cilantro, you'll know at once.

CURRY POWDER

Curry powder is a blend of up to 20 spices and herbs. The ingredients may include chili peppers, cloves, coriander, fennel seed, nutmeg, mace, cayenne, black pepper, sesame seed, saffron, and turmeric; this last spice gives curry its distinctive yellow color. Curry powder is common in Indian cooking, poultry, stews, soups, sauces, and meat dishes.

DILL

Sold either as dill seed, dried dill, or as a fresh herb, dill comes into its own as a flavoring for cottage cheese, chowders, soups, sauerkraut, salads, fish, meat sauces, potato salad, and spiced vinegar, and for pickling. It's also great for livening up egg salad.

FENNEL

The flavor of fennel is similar to that of anise, but it is somewhat sweeter. It is usually used in pork dishes, squash, Italian sausage, sweet pickles, fish dishes, candies, cabbage, pastries, oxtail soup, and pizza sauce.

When you buy fresh fennel, make sure you choose clean, crisp bulbs that are not browning. The stalks and green fronds should be removed, but you can use the fronds as you would dill. The bulb, also known as finocchio, can be used raw in salads, or it can be braised.

FENUGREEK

Sometimes used in curry powder, fenugreek is used as a component of imitation maple syrup and in tea form as a digestive aid.

GARLIC

This member of the Allium (lily) family is sold fresh, chopped and packed in jars, or processed into garlic salt or garlic powder. Garlic is used in thousands of dishes in all cuisines and has been used throughout history as a medication. There are hundreds of varieties of garlic grown world-wide. Most of the garlic used in the United States is grown in Gilroy, California, the "Garlic Capital of the World."

◆ Elephant garlic is another member of the Allium family. As you might surmise from the name, elephant garlic is much larger than common garlic. Also, its flavor is milder.

◆ To make garlic easy to peel, soak it in very hot water for two to three minutes, or rinse the garlic under hot water to loosen its skin.

◆ For special flavor, rub a clove of crushed garlic on the sides of your salad bowl before mixing your salad.

◆ A head of garlic should keep for eight to 10 weeks in a cool (as close to 50°F as possible), dark, dry location. It will lose its flavor more quickly if stored in the refrigerator. When garlic sprouts, some of the flavor will go into the sprouts; however, the sprouts can then be used for salads. If a garlic clove is damaged or nicked with a knife it must be used or it will develop mold very quickly. Garlic should not be frozen.

◆ Garlic has little aroma until the tissues are disturbed and the sulfur-containing amino acid cysteine is released. Make garlic vinegar by mincing two to three cloves and combining with a pint of white-wine vinegar in a sterilized jar. Let this stand for for at least two weeks before using. If you make garlic oil, be sure to use it at once. If stored for more than a day or so, garlic oil can develop botulin spores.

HEAVY-HANDED WITH THE GARLIC

If you have added too much garlic to your soup or stew, add a small quantity of parsley and simmer for about 10 minutes. To remove the odor of garlic from your hands, sprinkle salt on a slice of lemon, and then rub this on your hands.

READ THE LABEL

Once it is processed, garlic is more perishable than most other aromatics. Garlic products should contain an antibacterial or acidifying agent such as phosphoric acid or citric acid. If one of these is not listed on the label, the product should be sold and stored under refrigeration.

MORE THAN A REPELLENT FOR VAMPIRES

Studies published in *The American Journal of Clinical Nutrition* have shown that garlic inhibits blood coagulation, reduces the level of LDL (bad cholesterol), and raises the level of HDL (good cholesterol) in the blood. This study was done using garlic oil in which the active compounds were retained. When subjects consumed the equivalent of 10 cloves of garlic daily, their total cholesterol levels dropped 7 percent and their LDL levels decreased by 4.6 percent. Don't rely on garlic tablets from the health-food store, though. The active compounds in fresh garlic have often been removed or are present in very small amounts in these products.

GINGER

Grown in Jamaica, India, West Africa, and China, ginger has a pungent, spicy flavor. It is available fresh or ground and is used in pickling spices, conserves, fruit compotes, gingerbread, and pumpkin pie.

MACE

Mace is the dried husk of the nutmeg shell. In its ground form, it is used in cakes, beverages, chocolate dishes, jellies, pickling spices, ketchup, baked beans, soups, deviled chicken, and ham spreads.

MARJORAM

Marjoram is part of the oregano family and has a sweet flavor. It can be purchased in leaves and is imported primarily from the Nile Valley. It is usually combined with other herbs and used in soups and sauces, salad, potato dishes, stews, fish dishes, and as poultry seasoning.

MINT

Mint grows in Europe and the United States and is used to flavor lamb, fish, stews, soups, peas, sauces, desserts, and jellies. For an instant breath freshener, try chewing a few fresh mint leaves. Mint flakes, the dried leaves of peppermint and spearmint plants, have a strong, sweet flavor.

MUSTARD

◆ Yellow or white seeds will produce a mild mustard, while brown seeds produce the more spicy variety. Mustard oil, which is pressed from brown mustard seeds, is extremely hot and sometimes used in Chinese or other Asian dishes. Mustard powder has almost no aroma until it is mixed with a liquid.

◆ Mustard has hundreds of uses and is one of the most popular spices around the world. Mustard seeds will keep for up to one year. Store mustard powder for up to six months in a dry, dark place.

◆ If a recipe calls for a particular mustard, it is best not to substitute another variety. When you use a different mustard, you risk altering the taste of the finished dish.

TYPES OF PREPARED MUSTARD

American Mustard

The typical hot-dog mustard, this variety is produced from mild yellow mustard seeds combined with a sweetener and vinegar; it gets its vivid yellow color from turmeric. It has a very smooth texture.

Chinese Mustard

This is made from brown mustard seeds, mustard powder, water, and strong vinegar. Because there is no sweetener, it packs quite a wallop. In fact, Chinese mustard is the most pungent of all prepared mustards.

Dijon Mustard

Originally from Dijon, France, this is produced from brown mustard seeds, white wine, unfermented grape juice, and a variety of seasonings. It typically has a smooth texture and is usually a dull yellow color; when made with whole mustard seeds, Dijon mustard is called coarse-ground or country-style.

English Mustard

This mustard is produced from both white and black mustard seeds, a small amount of flour, and turmeric for coloring. It is one of the hottest mustards on the market.

German Mustard

Produced from a variety of mustard seeds, German mustard can range from sweet and mild to quite hot. It is usually made with a small amount of sugar, which tempers its bite. German mustards vary in color but are most often a brownish-yellow.

NUTMEG

A relatively sweet spice imported from the West Indies, nutmeg is available whole and ground. It is commonly used in sauces, puddings, custards, in creamed foods, eggnogs, whipped cream, sausages, frankfurters, and ravioli. Freshly grated nutmeg is more aromatic and flavorful than that which is sold ground. Special nutmeg graters are sold in specialty kitchenware shops.

OREGANO

Oregano is a member of the mint family. It is commonly sold in both leaf and ground forms. Oregano is found in many Italian dishes, including pizza and spaghetti sauces. Try it on a grilled cheese sandwich and you will never eat another one without it.

PAPRIKA

Paprika is made by grinding sweet red pepper pods; the best paprika is imported from Hungary, but Spain, South America, and California also produce paprika. This spice is used in a wide variety of dishes, including cream sauces, vegetables, mustards, salad dressings, ketchup, sausages, and fish preparations. It also makes an excellent garnish. Hot paprika is indeed hot—if it's all you have, use it sparingly.

PARSLEY

There are more than thirty varieties of parsley, but the two most common are curly and flat-leaf, which is also called Italian parsley. Of these two, flat-leaf has better flavor. This variety is grown in the United States and Southern Europe and is used in countless dishes, including cheese sauces, marinades, salads, soups, vegetable dishes, chicken potpies, and herb dressings. It is high in nutrients, especially vitamins A and C, though you would have to eat it as more than a garnish to get the effects. Curly parsley, which has much less flavor, is used mainly as a garnish to decorate serving platters. Parsley will alleviate bad breath.

PEPPER

- Pepper, one of the most popular spices in the world, comes from India and Indonesia. It is harvested at various stages of ripeness and is sold whole, cracked, or ground.
- After pepper is ground, it loses its flavor rather quickly. Use a pepper mill so your pepper will always be fresh and flavorful.
- White pepper has had the black shell removed. Use it in light-colored dishes, such as cream sauces, if you don't want little black flecks. Its flavor is milder than that of black pepper.
- Szechuan pepper berries, harvested from the prickly ash tree, have very tiny seeds and a mildly hot taste.
- Pink peppercorns, harvested from the Baies rose, have a very pungent odor and a somewhat sweet flavor.

GREEN, BLACK, AND WHITE PEPPERCORNS

These are the same item, harvested at different times of maturity and processed differently. Green peppercorns are picked before they are fully ripe. They are preserved in brine and used mainly for pickling and in dishes that do not require a strong pepper flavor. Black peppercorns are

DID YOU KNOW?

Hot paprika is always labeled such; sweet paprika is often just labeled "paprika."

155

picked when they are almost fully ripe. White peppercorns are picked when fully ripe, and the pungent black shell is removed. Their flavor is somewhat milder, and they have a smooth surface. Use them when black pepper would detract from the color of the dish.

PEPPERMINT: AN HERB AND MORE

Peppermint contains the oil menthol. Menthol is used in cigarettes, candies, liquors, toothpaste, mouthwash, and many other products. In low concentrations, menthol will increase the temperature of skin, paradoxically making a warm area feel cool. It has also been used as an anesthetic.

If you have a problem with mice, try this: Saturate cotton balls with a small amount of oil of peppermint, and then set these as near as you can to their hole. It will rid the area of pests. This also works for underground rodents.

POPPY SEED

With their rich, nutlike flavor, poppy seeds are used in Indian dishes, salads, cookies, pastry fillings, muffins, and other baked goods.

POULTRY SEASONING

Composed primarily of sage, thyme, marjoram, and savory, this seasoning is commonly used to flavor poultry stuffings and soups.

ROSEMARY

A sweet, fragrant, spicy herb with a pungent aroma, rosemary is used in stews, meat dishes, salad dressings, and meat and poultry stuffings. It is common in many southern European and Mediterranean cuisines, including Italian, Greek, Spanish, Portuguese, and Provençal.

SAFFRON

This is one of the more difficult herbs to harvest and, not surprisingly, also one of the most expensive. It is extracted from the stigma of the flowering crocus. The best saffron is imported from Spain. It is used in moderation in poultry, baked goods, and rice dishes.

SAGE

A very pungent herb that is a member of the mint family, sage is available in whole leaves or ground form. It is commonly used in veal dishes, pork dishes, stuffings, salads, fish dishes, and pizza sauces.

SALT

While salt is a seasoning containing important minerals that are beneficial to the body, in excess it may be detrimental to your health. Here's an easy test to see whether you might be eating too much salt: Eat a piece of bacon. If it doesn't taste salty, take a look at your diet—you may need to lower your sodium intake.

The distribution of fluids in the body depends on the location and concentrations of sodium and potassium ions. Our kidneys regulate blood sodium levels and provide the bloodstream with the exact amount required. When blood levels rise due to excess sodium ingestion, the body's thirst receptors are stimulated and our fluid intake increases to balance the sodium-to-water ratio. The excess sodium and water are then excreted by the kidneys. When this balance cannot be maintained, the result might be high blood pressure and increased deposits of atherosclerotic plaque material. (When excess sodium builds up in the bloodstream, the kidneys are unable to clear the excess water. An increase in blood volume occurs, and the heart has to work harder, causing higher blood pressure.)

The American Heart Association estimates that more than 50 million Americans have some degree of high blood pressure. Because sodium is found in thousands of food items, it is recommended that added salt be avoided to help control one's total sodium intake. Regular table salt contains 40 percent sodium while "lite" salt contains 20 percent.

Kelp can be ground up and used in a shaker to replace salt. It only contains 4 percent sodium and the taste is very similar.

When salt is processed commercially, certain natural minerals are stripped away. The salt may then be enriched with iodine; dextrose is added to stabilize it, sodium bicarbonate to keep it white, and anticaking agents to keep it free-flowing. Kosher salt and pickling salt contain no additives. Fine-grained pickling salt dissolves quickly, but kosher salt rarely dissolves completely.

SALT, THE MICROBE INHIBITOR

For thousands of years, salt has been used to preserve foods because of its ability to inhibit microbial growth. It does this by drawing water out of bacterial and mold cells.

◆ Hundreds of years ago, the English preserved meats by covering them with large grains of salt known as "corn," hence the name corned beef.

◆ Fast food restaurants may use high levels of salt to hide the unpleasant flavor of low-quality foods.

SALT OF THE EARTH

The average person consumes about six to 15 grams of salt daily, which amounts to about 2 teaspoons. The body requires only 500 milligrams, or half a gram, daily unless you are perspiring heavily. The American Heart Association recommends no more than 2.4 grams, or 2,400 milligrams.

It is necessary to read labels and be aware of the many ingredients in packaged foods that contain sodium. MSG is one of the leading ones, and many commercial spice blends also contain sodium. Following is a list of some spices and flavorings that are sodium-free:

Sodium-Free Seasonings	
Allspice	Nutmeg
Almond extract	Paprika
Bay leaves	Parsley
Caraway seeds	Pepper
Cinnamon	Pimiento
Curry powder	Rosemary
Garlic	Peppermint extract
Ginger	Sage
Lemon extract	Sesame seeds
Mace	Thyme
Maple extract	Turmeric
Marjoram	Vanilla extract
Mustard powder	Vinegar

DID YOU KNOW?

Canned peas have 100 times the sodium of raw peas.

Foods to Avoid on a Low-Sodium Diet

MEATS AND LUNCHEON MEATS	SNACK FOODS
All pickled products	Candy bars and nuts
All smoked products	Corn chips
Canned meat and fish	Olives
Cold cuts	Pickles
Dried beef (jerky)	Potato chips
Frankfurters	Pretzels
Ham and pork	Salted crackers
Luncheon meats	Salted nuts
Pastrami	Salted popcorn
Salami	Tortilla chips
Sausages	**SOUPS**
SEASONINGS AND CONDIMENTS	Bouillon cubes
All salts, including "lite"	Broth
Chili sauce	Canned soups
Commercial salad dressing	Dehydrated soups
Dried packaged seasoning	**MISCELLANEOUS**
Ketchup	Canned tomato products
MSG	Commercial gravies
Meat tenderizer	Commercial sauces
Packaged pasta mixes	Fast-food sandwiches
Prepared mustard	French fries
Seasoned salts	Instant hot cereals
Soy sauce	Processed foods
Steak sauce	Ready-to-eat meals
Tomato juice	Softened water
Worcestershire sauce	Mineral water

Sodium Content of Common Foods (in milligrams)

	SERVING SIZE	SODIUM
Macaroni & cheese (frozen)	1 cup	1,290
Turkey dinner (frozen)	1 large	990
Dill pickle	1 large	833
Tomato soup	1 cup	730
Bologna	2 slices	620
Pancakes (mix)	Three 4" cakes	560
Pretzels	1 ounce	486
Beef frankfurters	1 regular	458
Cottage cheese (creamed)	½ cup	457
Cheese pizza (frozen)	1 medium slice	412
American cheese (processed)	1 ounces	406
Mashed potatoes (instant)	½ cup	380
Corn flakes	1 cup	305
Tuna (oil-packed)	3 ounces	301
Angel food cake (mix)	1/12 cake	255
Peanuts (roasted in oil)	2 ounces	246
Doughnut (packaged)	1 medium	205
Carrots (canned)	½ cup	177
Whole milk	1 cup	120
Margarine (salted)	1 tablespoon	102
Mayonnaise	1 tablespoon	80
Turkey (roasted)	3 ounces	70
Egg	1 medium	62
Fruit cocktail	½ cup	8
Orange juice	½ cup	2
Fruit (canned)	½ cup	1
Oatmeal (cooked)	3 ounces	1
Macaroni (cooked)	1 cup	1

TYPES OF SALT

The majority of salt used in the United States is mined from deposits that were laid down thousands of years ago and are readily accessible.

Iodized Salt

Standard table salt with iodine (sodium iodide) added. Iodine is the nutrient that prevents hypothyroidism. However, some people find it adds an unpleasant taste to salt.

Kosher Salt

Is additive-free and has excellent flavor and texture. Kosher salt has larger crystals with a more jagged shape than table salt, which means they will cling to food better. Because of these characteristics, kosher salt has the ability to draw more blood from meats; kosher meats must be as free of blood as possible to meet strict Jewish dietary laws.

Pickling Salt

A fine-grained salt that is additive-free and used in the preparation of pickles and sauerkraut.

Rock Salt

A poorly refined salt that is grayish in color, with very large crystals. It is rarely used in cooking—one of its few culinary uses is to make the ice melt faster in old-fashioned ice-cream makers.

Sea Salt

Has a fresh flavor and is available fine- or coarse-grained. It is usually imported and is preferred by many chefs and serious cooks for its pure flavor. Sea salt, as its name implies, is acquired by allowing salt water to accumulate in pools where the sun evaporates the water, leaving a stronger-flavored salt with a few more trace minerals than regular table salt. It can be quite a bit more expensive than table salt.

Table Salt

A highly refined, fine-grained salt that contains additives to make it flow freely but has not been fortified with iodine.

SAVORY

A member of the mint family with a slightly peppery flavor, savory is commonly sold in both leaf and ground forms. There are two varieties: Summer savory is milder than winter savory, but both can be quite strong and are best used judiciously. Dried savory is typically made from summer savory. This herb marries well with eggs, meats, poultry, and fish.

SESAME SEEDS

These seeds have a rich, nutlike flavor and a high oil content. They are also high in many nutrients—by weight, sesame seeds have more iron than liver does; they are also high in calcium. However, we seldom eat enough sesame seeds to provide nutritional benefits.

Sesame seeds are commonly used to flavor many Chinese dishes, and in Middle Eastern dishes like halvah (a dessert made with ground sesame seeds and honey), hummus (a spread made from ground chickpeas), and tahini, which is ground sesame seeds. It is also used as a topping for many baked goods.

TARRAGON

Although this herb is native to Siberia, Arabs were the first to use it in cooking. Most tarragon sold in the United States is grown in California. Tarragon has a strong flavor similar to licorice and is used in bearnaise sauce, meat dishes, salads, herb dressings, and tomato casseroles.

THYME

There are nearly as many varieties of fresh thyme as there are of basil. Available in both leaf and ground forms, thyme has a strong, nicely spicy flavor and is used to flavor tomato-based soups, stews, sauces, chipped beef (an old army favorite), mushrooms, sausages, clam chowder, herb dressings, and mock turtle soup. If you live near a specialty greengrocer or farmer's market, keep an eye out for lemon thyme. This herb has a pleasantly astringent flavor and can perfume a simple broth or sautéed vegetables with an appetizing lemon fragrance.

TURMERIC

Imported from India and the Caribbean, turmeric is ground from the root of a tropical plant similar to ginger. Turmeric is used in chicken and meat dishes, pickles, salads dressings, curry powder, Spanish rice, relishes, and mustards. It imparts a vivid yellow color to the foods it is used in and is, therefore, sometimes substituted for the more expensive saffron (although their flavors are nothing alike).

VANILLA

Vanilla beans grow on trees that are a member of the orchid family. The reason real vanilla is so expensive is that the plants are hand-pollinated when grown commercially; in the wild they are pollinated by only one species of hummingbird. More than 75 percent of all vanilla beans are grown in Madagascar, where the pods are actually marked with the grower's brand to prevent vanilla bean rustlers from stealing the crops.

Pure vanilla extract is made by soaking chopped beans in a solution of alcohol and water. Imitation vanilla is produced from the chemical vanillin, which is a by-product of the wood-pulp industry.

TYPES OF VANILLA

Vanilla Beans

These are long, thin, dark brown beans. They are expensive and not as easy to use as vanilla extract. To use the bean, you must split it and scrape out the seeds. Vanilla beans will keep up to six months when stored in plastic wrap, sealed in an airtight jar, and refrigerated. Put a vanilla bean in your sugar bowl to impart a subtle flavor to the sugar.

Pure Extract

If the label says "pure vanilla extract" it must be made with vanilla beans; however, the taste will be less intense than that of the bean itself. Still, pure vanilla extract has an excellent flavor.

Imitation Extract

Imitation vanilla extract is produced from artificial flavorings and has a stronger, harsher taste than pure vanilla. Imitation extract should be used only in dishes where the vanilla flavor will not predominate.

Mexican Extract

Some Mexican extract has been found to contain the blood thinner coumarin, which is banned in the United States. There is no way to tell which Mexican vanilla contains coumarin and which does not, so it's best to avoid this entirely.

VINEGAR

Despite the literal translation of its French root *vinaigre* and contrary to popular belief, vinegar is not sour wine. Vinegar is produced from wine, beer, or cider fermented with the bacteria acetobacter, which feeds on the alcohol, converting it into acetic acid (vinegar). Vinegar is a stimulant to the palate, making the taste buds more receptive to other flavors.

TYPES OF VINEGAR

Apple Cider Vinegar

This is produced from apple juice and is a good, all-purpose vinegar. It has a mild, somewhat sweet, fruity flavor.

Balsamic Vinegar

This is made from white Trebbiano grape juice. Balsamic vinegar is aged in wooden barrels for three to 12 years before being sold. (The real thing, from Modena in Italy, can be aged for decades.) The aging produces a dark brown vinegar with a mellow, very sweet flavor. Most balsamic vinegar sold in supermarkets is red wine vinegar that has flavorings and colorings added to it. It is best used in salad dressings and will bring out the flavor of many vegetables. Sprinkle it on fresh fruit to perk up their flavors.

Distilled White Vinegar

This is produced from grain alcohol and is too harsh for most cooking, but is excellent for pickling.

Flavored Wine Vinegar

Made by steeping herbs or other flavorings in white-wine vinegar. Chefs commonly use tarragon wine vinegar for flavoring shellfish and poultry dishes. Rosemary wine vinegar is excellent with lamb dishes. Garlic vinegar adds a pleasant bite to salad dressings.

Malt Vinegar

Produced from malted barley. Used in chutneys, fish dishes, sauces, pickling, and as a condiment with French fries.

Raspberry Vinegar

This vinegar, made by soaking raspberries in white-wine vinegar, has a pleasant fruity flavor. Use it in sauces, salad dressings, and on fruits.

Rice Vinegar

Produced from fermented rice, this has a slightly sweet flavor and is used in fish marinades, Asian sauces, sushi, and pickles.

Sherry Vinegar

A product of sherry fermentation. Its flavor is somewhat nutty, and sherry vinegar is used mainly in vegetable dishes.

Wine Vinegar

Produced from red or white wine. The red is used for meat dishes and the white for poultry and fish dishes. It is also frequently used in marinades and salad dressings.

HOW SHOULD HERBS BE ADDED TO A DISH?

Herbs provide both aroma and flavor. Chefs know how to appeal to your sense of smell when preparing a dish and will add either some or all of the herbs just before the dish is served, because the flavor and aroma can dissipate during the cooking process.

CAN THE OIL OF A SPICE BE SUBSTITUTED FOR THE SPICE ITSELF?

Although you might think this is a good idea, it's difficult to execute successfully. Oils are so concentrated that it is almost impossible to calculate the amount needed to replace the spice and obtain the same degree of flavor. A good example is cinnamon, whose oil is 50 times stronger than the ground spice. If you did want to use cinnamon oil to replace ground cinnamon, you would need only 1 to 2 drops of oil to replace ½ teaspoon of ground cinnamon in candy or frostings.

LICORICE, SWEETER THAN SUGAR

The word *licorice* actually means "sweet root." The plant is a member of the legume family and was used by the Egyptians for medicinal purposes more than 4,000 years ago. Throughout the ages, licorice has been used as a mild laxative and to treat coughs, colds, sore throats, bronchitis. Today, it is most commonly used in candy and tobacco.

Licorice extract is produced by boiling the yellow roots of the plant in water, and then extracting the solids by evaporating the liquid. The black solid mass has two components, the oil anethole, which contributes the flavor, and glycerrhetic acid, which is the sweet component. Glycerrhetic acid is derived from glycerrhizin, found in the raw root, which is 50 times sweeter than table sugar (sucrose). Ancient Egyptians chewed the raw root for its sugary flavor.

SPICE ROAST

Allspice berries and peppercorns should be roasted before use to intensify their flavor. Roast them in a 325°F oven on a small cookie sheet for 10 to 15 minutes and you will be surprised at the difference in their flavor and aroma. They can also be pan-roasted over medium-high heat for about five minutes. Other whole spices can be pan-roasted as well.

165

Substituting Herbs and Spices	
HERB OR SPICE	SUBSTITUTE
Allspice	Cinnamon, plus a dash of cloves
Aniseed	Fennel seed
Basil	Oregano
Caraway seed	Aniseed
Chives	Scallion tops
Cinnamon	Nutmeg
Cloves	Allspice
Cumin	Chili powder
Dillweed	Fennel tops
Ginger	Cardamom
Mace	Allspice
Parsley	Tarragon
Thyme	Rosemary

IT'S TURKEY TIME

Poultry seasoning is the one ingredient that really makes stuffing taste great. All poultry seasonings are not alike; there are big differences in the freshness of the herbs, the methods of blending, and the way the seasoning is stored before shipping. The finest poultry seasoning was created in the 1860s by William Bell and is produced by Brady Enterprises of East Weymouth, Massachusetts. It is still marketed today. Bell's Seasoning is more potent than what you may be used to, so if you use it, remember that a little goes a long way.

THE COLOR OF PESTO

Pesto sauce tends to turn brown in a very short time. This browning is caused by enzymes in the stems and leaves of the basil plant. When nuts, such as walnuts, sunflower seeds, or pine nuts are added to the sauce, it will turn almost black. There is little to be done to keep pesto green, so it's best to serve the pesto immediately after it is prepared.

A WORD OF WARNING ABOUT FLAVORED OIL

You might think of storing herbs or garlic in olive oil to prolong their shelf life or to flavor your oil, but don't do it. Serious health hazards may result from this practice. Flavored oils may contain the deadly *Clostridium botulinum* bacteria, which is present in the environment and may be present on some herbs. The bacteria does not thrive well in oxygen but loves an anaerobic environment such as that provided by the oil.

When you put an herb or garlic in oil, the bacteria has a perfect oxygen-free place to multiply. The FDA has warned that a number of people have become ill from putting chopped garlic in oil. Ideally, any flavored oil should be used immediately. Any leftovers should be refrigerated and used within three days to be considered safe.

When an herb and olive oil mixture is sold in the market, the label must state that the product has to be refrigerated, and the mixture will also contain a preservative, probably phosphoric acid or citric acid.

CHINESE FIVE-SPICE POWDER

This fragrant spice mixture is common in Chinese cooking. It is a blend of cinnamon, star anise, fennel seed, Szechuan peppercorns, and cloves. To make your own, grind the spices and combine in equal measure. You can also purchase it in supermarkets.

THE ROYAL BREATH CLEANSER

In 300 B.C., the Chinese emperor had a breath problem and was given cloves to sweeten his breath. Cloves contain eugenol, which is the chemical used in a number of commercial mouthwashes. Eugenol (oil of cloves) is also used to alleviate toothache pain.

The Ten Top Selling Medicinal Herbs			
1.	Chamomile	6.	Ginger
2.	Echinacea	7.	Ginkgo
3.	Ephedra	8.	Ginseng
4.	Feverfew	9.	Peppermint
5.	Garlic	10.	Valerian

DID YOU KNOW?

If flavored oil looks cloudy— anything but perfectly clear—do not consume it. It may be tainted and should be discarded at once.

UNSAFE HERBS

The following herbs, many of which have been used medicinally, are classified as unsafe for human consumption and should not be used in any food or beverage. This is only a partial listing of the hundreds of unsafe herbs.

NAME	SCIENTIFIC NAME	DANGER
Bittersweet, woody nightshade, climbing nightshade	*Solanum dulcamara*	Contains the toxin glycoalkaloid solanine as well as solanidine and dulcamarine.
Bloodroot, red puccoon	*Sanguinaria canadensis*	Contains the poisonous alkaloid sanguinarine as well as other alkaloids.
Buckeye, horse chestnut	*Aesculus hippocastanum*	Contains the family of toxins saponin glycoside, of which aesculin is one.
Burning bush, wahoo	*Euonymus atropurparens*	Contains evomonoside, a digitalis-like cardioactive glycoside. Also contains peptide and sesquiterpene alkaloids.
Belladonna, deadly nightshade	*Atropa belladona*	Contains the toxic tropane alkaloids hyoscyamine, atropine, and hyoscine.
European mandrake	*Mandragora officinarium*	Contains a substance similar to belladonna as well as the alkaloids hyoscyamine, scopolamine, and mandragorine. Considered very dangerous for internal use.
Heliotrope	*Heliotropium spp.*	Contains alkaloids that may cause liver damage.
Hemlock, spotted hemlock, California or Nebraska fern	*Conium maculatum*	Contains the poisonous alkaloid coniine. Slows the heartbeat leading eventually to coma and death.

NAME	SCIENTIFIC NAME	DANGER
Henbane, hog's bean, devil's eye	*Hyoscyamus niger*	Contains the alkaloid hyoscyamine as well as atropine.
Indian tobacco, asthma weed, emetic weed	*Lobelia inflata*	Contains the alkaloid lobeline.
Jalap root, High John root, St. John the Conqueror root	*Ipomoea purga*	Usually found in Mexico, this plant's resin contains a powerful poison.
Jimson weed, thornapple, tolguacha	*Datura stramonium*	Contains the alkaloid scopolamine.
Lily of the valley, May lily	*Convallaria majalis*	Contains the toxic cardiac glycoside convallotoxin.
American mandrake, mayapple, wild lemon	*Podophyllum peltatum*	A poisonous plant containing more than 15 biologically active compounds, including a violently purgative substance.
Mistletoe	*Viscum album*	Contains toxic polypeptides, toxic amines, and toxalbumins that inhibit protein synthesis in the intestinal wall.
Morning glory	*Ipomoea tricolor*	Plant contains a purgative resin. Seeds contain lysergeic acid.
Periwinkle	*Vinca major, Vinca minor*	Contains toxic alkaloids that can injure the liver and kidneys. The entire plant is considered very dangerous for herbal use.
Pokeweed, pigeonberry, skoke	*Phytolacca americana*	Contains phytolaccigenin, phytolaccin, and phytolaccatoxin, which cause abdominal cramps, vomiting, and in severe cases, convulsions and death.

NAME	SCIENTIFIC NAME	DANGER
Broom, scotch broom	*Cytisus scoparius*	Contains the toxin sparteine and other alkaloids.
Spindle tree	*Euonymus europaeus*	Produces violent purges.
Sweet flag, sweet cane, sweet root	*Acorus calamus*	Asarone, a volatile oil from the root, is potentially harmful and has been implicated as a tumor-causing agent.
Tonka bean	*Dipteryx odorata*	Seeds contain coumarin. Can cause serious liver damage.
Water hemlock, poison parsnip, spotted cowbane wild carrot	*Cicuta douglasii* *Cicuta maculata* *Cicuta virosa*	Holds the distinction of being the most violently poisonous plant in the North Temperate zone. Contains an unsaturated alcohol called cicutoxin.
White snakeroot, snakeroot, richweed	*Eupatorium rugosum*	Contains a toxic alcohol called tremetol.
Leopard's bane, Mountain tobacco, wolfsbane	*Arnica montana*	Contains helenalin, which causes dermatitis in some people. Also a potent cardiotoxic agent. Arnica can also cause violent gastroenteritis, neuropathies, collapse, and death. The entire plant is considered unsafe for internal use.
Wormwood, madderwort	*Artemisia absinthium*	Contains oil of wormwood, a psychotropic drug or hallucinogen. The liquor absinthe contains worm-wood and is banned in the United States and many parts of the world.
Yohimbine	*Cornynanthe yohimbe*	Contains toxic alkaloids.

SALT SAVERS

If you're on a reduced-sodium diet, you probably already rely on herbs and spices to perk up flavors—but beware of commercially prepared seasoning blends. Many are loaded with sodium. You're better off reading the ingredient lists and concocting your own, with less—or no—added salt. Here are some of our favorites; store them out of direct sunlight and use within six months for best flavor.

Poultry Seasoning

Mix 2 teaspoons dried crumbled rosemary leaves, 2 teaspoons dried crumbled sage leaves, ½ teaspoon ground ginger, ½ teaspoon dried thyme leaves, and ¼ teaspoon freshly ground black pepper.

Cajun Seasoning

Mix 2 crumbled bay leaves, 1 teaspoon filé powder, ½ teaspoon salt ½ teaspoon freshly ground black pepper, ½ teaspoon ground white pepper, ½ teaspoon dried thyme leaves, ¼ teaspoon cayenne pepper, ¼ teaspoon dried crumbled sage leaves, and ¼ teaspoon dry mustard.

Italian Seasoning

Mix 1 tablespoon dried oregano, 4 teaspoons parsley flakes, 4 teaspoons dried basil, and 1½ teaspoons dried crumbled sage leaves.

Mexican Seasoning

Mix 1 teaspoon chili powder, ½ teaspoon salt, ¼ teaspoon ground cumin, ¼ teaspoon dried oregano, and, depending on how hot your chili powder is, ¼ teaspoon freshly ground black pepper and a pinch or two of cayenne pepper.

THE DATING GAME

Dried herbs and spices lose their potency over time; most retain peak flavor for about six months. When you open a new jar, write the date on it so you'll know when it's time to replace it.

THEY WON'T SUFFOCATE

To keep fresh herbs at their best, put them in a glass of water (as though you were putting flowers in a vase) and cover the glass with a plastic bag. Stash in the refrigerator and use within a week. Or wrap fresh herbs in damp paper towels and put this bundle in a plastic bag.

WHAT IS BOUQUET GARNI?

In classical French cooking, a bouquet garni is a bunch of herbs (traditionally parsley, thyme, and bay leaf) tied in a bundle or wrapped in cheesecloth and used to flavor broths, soups, and stews. The bouquet is removed before the dish is served. If you don't have cheesecloth, put the herbs in a tea ball.

DRYING HERBS

If you have more fresh herbs than you can use, hang them upside down to dry. (Tie them together and hang them from a peg.) In about a week, you'll be able to crumble off the leaves. The flavor won't be quite as wonderful as that of fresh herbs, but it will still be much better than commercial dried herbs.

HERBES DE PROVENCE

This blend of dried herbs is original to the south of France, hence its name. Most typically made of basil, fennel, lavender, marjoram, rosemary, sage, summer savory, and thyme, herbes de Provence is available in gourmet markets and better supermarkets. Sprinkle the mixture on cooked vegetables, rub it into pork chops before cooking, or stuff it under the skin of poultry before roasting.

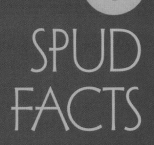

9
SPUD
FACTS

THE POTATO

White potatoes originated in South America and were introduced to Europe in the 16th century. They are one of the most nutritious vegetables: They contain more of the essential amino acids than whole wheat does; they contain iron, magnesium, and calcium, and are high in fiber (provided you eat the skin), vitamin C, and the B vitamins. They're also low in sodium and fat-free. Potatoes are a member of the nightshade family. North Americans consume approximately 125 pounds of potatoes per person annually, with the United States producing 35 billion pounds per year. In the past 30 years, North Americans have reduced their consumption of fresh potatoes by 40 percent.

SWEET POTATOES

Yams evolved separately in tropical Asia, Africa, and America. Sweet potatoes are a member of the morning glory family and despite their similarity to yams, the two are entirely unrelated.

Sweet potatoes are usually available around Thanksgiving; yams are available year-round. Sweet potato skins are normally a light copper color, while yam skins range from reddish brown to a dirty white.

Don't buy either sweet potatoes or yams if you see any soft spots, mold, or white areas on the skins. Sweet potatoes and yams tend to decay faster than white potatoes due to their high sugar content.

THE SWEET NATURE OF SWEET POTATOES

Sweet potatoes tend to become sweeter the more you cook them because some of the starch converts to sugar when the potato is heated. The cells in a sweet potato are not as strong as those in a white potato; when boiled, the sweet potato readily absorbs water and swells.

Sweet potatoes contain the same number of calories as white potatoes; however, they contain more vitamin C and three times the beta-carotene.

The best sweet potato is called a Boniato; it has a very light yellow flesh.

DROP THEM SKINS

To peel sweet potatoes easily, boil them 15 to 35 minutes, depending on their size, then immediately immerse them in a bowl of ice cold water for 20 to 30 seconds. The skins should fall off almost by themselves.

SPUD STORAGE

Sweet potatoes are a root, whereas yams and white potatoes are enlarged stems called tubers that extend underground. The tuber is where the plant stores excess carbohydrates. If white potatoes are stored below 40°F., they tend to release more sugar and turn sweet. Potatoes will last longer and remain solid longer if they are stored in a cool, dry spot, preferably at 45° to 50°F. Air must circulate around potatoes; otherwise, moisture will cause them to decay.

FREEZER FACTS

White potatoes do not freeze well because a large majority of the cells will burst, causing the potato to become mushy and watery when thawed. Commercial frozen potatoes are specially processed to avoid this.

Cooked, peeled sweet potatoes can be frozen without becoming mushy. Store them in a tightly sealed plastic container with as little air as possible (use the smallest container they'll fit in), and then put the container into a tight-sealing plastic freezer bag. They will keep for 10 to 12 months.

BAKED POTATO—MAYBE A BAD CHOICE

If you have a stuffed baked potato at a fast-food restaurant, don't do it for your health—you're better off ordering a specialty burger. One chain's bacon-and-cheese baked potato packs 730 calories and 43 grams of fat, 15 of which are saturated. By comparison, a Burger King Whopper has 630 calories and 38 grams of fat, 11 of which are saturated.

WHO INVENTED POTATO CHIPS?

In the summer of 1853, a man named George Crum was the chef at the Moon's Lake Lodge in Saratoga Springs, New York. A guest who had ordered French fries complained that they were too thick. Chef Crum sliced up another, thinner batch of potatoes, and served them, only to have the customer reject them again. In a fit of pique, Chef Crum decided to slice the potatoes paper-thin, which crisped when cooked. The guest was delighted with the thin potatoes. They became a hit (and the signature dish of the restaurant) and were called Saratoga Chips. In 1997, the Frito-Lay Company used 7 million pounds of potatoes a day in 35 plants to keep us supplied with potato chips.

HOT POTATO, BAKED POTATO

Many people wrap a potato in foil thinking that it will speed up the baking time. After trying to bake potatoes a number of ways to determine the speediest method, I was surprised to find that a faster method was to rub the skin lightly with vegetable oil—the potato baked in less time than when wrapped in foil. The only method that significantly sped up the cooking time was inserting an aluminum nail into the potato, thereby transferring heat inside.

MAKE IT PRETTY

If you would like a richer color to your potato salad, try adding a small amount of mustard when you are mixing it.

HIDE AND SEEK

Potatoes should be stored at cool room temperature away from light. Never refrigerate potatoes, because that tends to turn potato starch to sugar. However, if the potato is removed from the refrigerator and left at room temperature for a few days, the sugar will convert back to starch.

VARIETY IS THE SPUD OF LIFE

There are many varieties of potatoes, such as the Russet, White Rose, Red Pontiac, Katahdin, and Yellow Finn. The most popular is the Russet, which is mainly grown in Idaho and may weigh up to a pound or more.

STAYING FRESH LONGER

It is best to purchase potatoes in bulk bins—not in bags, which make it hard to determine which are bruised. If you store fresh ginger with potatoes it will help keep them fresh longer. Half an apple stored with potatoes will stop the sprouting by absorbing moisture before the potato does.

POTATO TRICKS

◆ To keep peeled potatoes from discoloring, place them in a bowl of cold water, add a few drops of white vinegar, then refrigerate. Drain before cooking. Add a small amount of sugar to the cooking water to revive some of the lost flavor.

◆ Potatoes prefer to be stored in panty hose (so do onions). Just cut a leg off and drop the potatoes in, tying a knot between them. Hang in a cool, dry spot, cutting just below the knot to get to the potatoes.

OLD POTATO, NEW POTATO, BEST POTATO?

A new potato has more moisture than an older one does, and each has its strengths. Use new potatoes in dishes such as potato salad; they absorb less water when boiled and less mayonnaise when prepared (your salad will have better flavor and less fat) and they're less likely to break when you mix the salad. Older potatoes are better for baking and making french fries. They are drier, meatier, and starchier, so they have a lighter texture when baked. Their lower water content means the oil will spatter less when you fry them. When baking a potato, make sure you pierce it so steam can escape; otherwise, it may become soggy.

ARE GREEN POTATOES SAFE TO EAT?

Avoid potatoes with a greenish cast to them, unless you peel or cut away the green part. Overexposure to light causes a chemical reaction that increases a chlorophyll buildup (which is not harmful) and encourages the production of an alkaloid called solanine. Solanine imparts a bitter taste to the potato, and ingesting high levels can actually cause symptoms such as abdominal discomfort, nausea, and diarrhea. Store potatoes in a dark location to avoid solanine buildup.

WHY SOAK FRIES IN WATER?

The surface of a cut potato deteriorates very quickly when exposed to air. When this occurs a layer of sticky starch forms on the potatoes as soon as they're placed into the frying vat. The potatoes may stick to one another as well as the pan and will be almost impossible to serve. Soaking the potatoes in ice water for five to seven minutes before frying will wash off a lot of the surface starch and the sticking problem will be avoided. Just be sure to pat them dry thoroughly with paper towels before you put them in the hot oil to prevent spatters.

MASHED-POTATO EDUCATION

There are number of hints to follow when preparing mashed potatoes.
◆ Never pour cold milk into cooked potatoes. It will change the taste of the starch, giving it an unpleasant flavor, not unlike cardboard. The

DID YOU KNOW?

Many cooks swear the best fries are twice fried, once at a lower temperature to cook them through, then at a higher temperature to make them crispy.

milk should be warmed in a pan with a small amount of chives for flavor before being added.

◆ Buttermilk will give the potatoes a great flavor. If you're watching your weight, save some of the cooking water from the potatoes and use that instead of butter or cream.

◆ A pinch or two of baking powder will give mashed potatoes extra fluff. Never put baking soda in potatoes; it will turn them black.

◆ Never overmix or overcook potatoes. The cell walls will rupture, releasing an excess of starch and resulting in soggy, sticky potatoes. Potatoes should be mashed with a vertical motion, not stirred in a circular motion, to minimize the damage that occurs by crushing the cells on the wall of the bowl.

◆ Try adding powdered milk or instant potato flakes for extra fluffy mashed potatoes.

WHAT IS A NEWLEAF POTATO?

The Monsanto Company has genetically engineered this potato to have a natural resistance to the Colorado potato beetle, reducing the need for additional pesticides. The JR Simplot company is working on a new potato that will absorb less fat when made into French fries.

THE CASE OF THE EXPLODING POTATO

It is not unusual for a potato to pop open during baking if the skin is not pierced. It doesn't really explode; however, it may crack open and make a mess because potatoes build up a good head of steam as they bake. It is best to prick the skin with a fork before baking.

AFTER COOKING, NEVER BEFORE

Onions should never be stored with potatoes because moisture from the onions can cause potatoes to sprout. Onions also release gases that will alter the flavor of a potato.

THEY TASTE BETTER, TOO

Cooked potatoes are easier to digest, and because cooking breaks down the cell walls of the potatoes, the body is better able to use the nutrients. Potatoes should never be cooked in aluminum or iron pots—they will turn yellowish—nor should they be sliced with a carbon-steel knife. Cook potatoes in a stainless-steel, glass, or enamel pot for a nice pale color.

SHORTER IS BETTER

If you store a boiled or baked potato in the refrigerator for three to four days it will lose approximately 90 percent of its nutrient value. Potatoes should only be stored for one to two days.

BOILING BASICS

When boiling potatoes, put them into a mesh frying basket to make them faster to remove and drain; they soften quickly after cooking.

THE HARD TRUTH

Uh-oh—you've reached the bottom of the potato barrel and what's left is a little soft. Don't despair (or run out to the store). To firm soft, uncooked potatoes back up, soak them in ice water for about a half hour or until they become hard.

THE SKINNY ON SKIN

Cooking a potato in its skin will retain of most of its nutrients. This is true whether you bake or boil the spud.

A FRENCH FRY FIT FOR A KING

For the greatest French fries, soak cut potatoes in ice cold water in the refrigerator for an hour; this will harden them so that they absorb less fat. Dry them thoroughly, then fry them twice. First cook them for six to seven minutes, drain them well, then sprinkle them lightly with flour (this step makes them extra crispy and crunchy). Then fry them one to two minutes, until they are golden brown.

TAKING A BIG LOSS

Attention hosts and hostesses: Mashed potatoes that sit out on a buffet will lose significant amounts of their vitamins after one hour. The loss is due to the constant heat, lights, mashing, exposing more of the surface to oxidation, and cooking in boiling water.

DID YOU KNOW?

Potatoes can turn green if exposed to light. It's best to avoid the green parts, which can be toxic in large amounts.

TWO GOOD TIPS

If you have problems peeling a boiled potato, drop it into a bowl of ice water for a few seconds to loosen the skin. To keep peeled potatoes white during cooking, add a small amount of white vinegar to the water.

HOT POTATO, COLD POTATO

The cold potato soup called vichyssoise was actually invented in New York City. Chef Louis Diat of the Ritz-Carlton Hotel adapted his mother's recipe of *soupe bonne femme* to make a chilled soup of the white part of leeks and potatoes in a base of cream and milk. The name of the soup comes from Vichy, the spa near Diat's home in Bourbon.

WATCH OUT FOR THE RADICALS

Potato chips are cooked in 75-foot-long vats of oil; the oil is filtered but rarely changed. Present day production is about 200 pounds an hour. The high temperature (375°F) causes the oil to deteriorate, so it contains a high proportion of free fatty acids, which are potentially unhealthy. Potato chips, corn chips, and tortilla chips contain 10 times more fat than pretzels or air-popped popcorn; in fact, most potato chips get 61 percent of their calories from fat.

THE REAL THING

To make a wonderful potato chip, cut potatoes in half crosswise, exposing two flat surfaces. Use a vegetable peeler to cut paper-thin slices. Spray them lightly with vegetable oil and arrange in a single layer on a baking sheet. Bake at 450°F for about 10 to 12 minutes or until they are a light golden brown. Finally, place the chips in a brown paper bag with a small amount of sea salt (1/4 teaspoon per potato) and shake. This seasons them lightly and also removes some of the fat.

10

FRUITS AND VEGETABLES

PICK OF THE CROP

When selecting fruits, choose the healthiest looking. If possible, check the box the fruit originally was shipped in to see whether it was graded U.S. Grade No.1, or at least had a USDA stamp. To preserve the nutritional quality of frozen fruits, leave them in their original packaging material. This will reduce the risk of exposure to air, which might result in a loss of flavor and cause discoloration.

Bruised areas on fruits mean that the sensitive inner flesh has been exposed to air, oxidation has taken place, and the vitamin C content has been lost. Brown discoloration of the flesh can be reduced if you slice bananas, apples, plums, and peaches with a stainless-steel knife and then either combine them with any citrus fruit or sprinkle them with lemon or pineapple juice. The citric acid from the lemon or pineapple neutralizes the effects of the oxidation.

GETTING RESULTS

Baking soda added to the cooking water will help vegetables retain their color, but it will also cause them to lose texture and vitamins. To keep their color, cook vegetables for no more than 5 to 7 minutes.

SOFT TOUCH FOR SOFT SKINS

Because they have soft skins, most fruits and vegetables easily lose their nutrients. It takes very little to bruise them or to damage their flesh—even air, light, and heat have their effects. When cooking or preparing produce, it is best to leave it in the largest possible pieces until you are ready to serve it. Exposing the surface of any fruit or vegetable will cause nutrients to be lost immediately, and the longer the surfaces are exposed, the greater the nutritional loss. Surprisingly, the vitamin C in some fruits can be completely lost in less than one hour of exposure to air.

PECTIN, A.K.A. SOLUBLE FIBER

The nutrition buzzword these days is pectin. Studies report that pectin, also called soluble fiber, has the ability to lower LDL (bad cholesterol) levels and is being used to treat bowel diseases. These studies may well be valid, and pectin supplement sales are on the rise. There are, however, many natural sources for pectin. At right are a few of the better ones.

Pectin Levels in Certain Foods (in grams)

FOOD	QUANTITY	PECTIN
Soybeans	1 cup, cooked	2.6
Figs	5 fruits, dried	2.3
Orange	1 medium	2.2
Chestnuts	1 ounce, dried	2.1
Pear	1 medium	1.8
Potato	1 medium	1.8
Sweet potato	½ cup, mashed	1.3
Brussels sprouts	½ cup, cooked	1.1
Apple	1 medium	1.1
Papaya	½ fruit	1.1
Broccoli	½ cup	1.0
Banana	1 medium	1.0
Strawberries	1 cup	0.9
Tomato	1 medium	0.9
Lima beans	½ cup, cooked	0.9
Hazelnuts	1 ounce, raw	0.9
Carrot	1 medium	0.8
Pistachios	1 ounce	0.8
Peach	1 medium	0.7
Peas	½ cup, cooked	0.6
Almonds	1 ounce	0.6
Walnuts	1 ounce	0.6
Green beans	½ cup, boiled	0.5
Summer squash	½ cup, boiled	0.5
Grapefruit	½ medium	0.3
Spinach	½ cup, raw	0.2

TO REFRIGERATE OR NOT?

The majority of fruits and vegetables handle cold fairly well. Naturally enough, the exceptions are tropical fruits, whose cells are just not used to the cold. Bananas will suffer cell damage and release a skin-browning chemical, avocados don't ripen when stored below 45°F, and oranges will develop brown-spotted skin. These fruits (bananas, avocados, and all citrus), as well as squash, tomatoes, cucumbers, melons, bell peppers, and pineapples, are best stored at 50°F. Most other vegetables, including lettuce, carrots, and cabbage, prefer 32°F. Humidity is also an important factor, and most fruits and vegetables should be stored in the refrigerator crisper bins, which will prevent them from drying out.

DOUBLING UP

Any salad that has a dairy product in a dressing should be kept cold. The easiest method is to place a larger bowl with ice or dry ice under the food dish. This will keep the salad cold enough so bacteria growth will be slowed while it is out of the refrigerator.

STORING TOMATOES

Don't put tomatoes in the fridge, which stops ripening cold. Keep them stem-side down in a cool place, spaced so that they're not touching.

WAX COATS

A thin coating of wax on fruits and vegetables helps seal in moisture, which not only extends storage life but also reduces weight loss, thus assuring a higher profit to greengrocers. A secondary benefit to markets is that wax gives produce an appealing sheen. The wax coating is safe to eat but may give the produce an off-flavor. Another drawback is that wax makes it more difficult to clean the produce, which is especially troublesome if pesticide residues lurk under the wax.

THE BROWN-BAG TRICK

Fruit normally gives off ethylene gas, which hastens ripening. Some fruits give off more gas than others and so ripen faster. Other fruits are picked before they are ripe and need a bit of help. If an unripe fruit is placed in a brown-paper bag, the ethylene gas it gives off does not dissipate into the air but is trapped and concentrated, causing the fruit to ripen faster.

DID YOU KNOW?

Some varieties of vegetable seeds sold in garden catalogs were developed for commercial growers, not home gardeners. Avoid varieties that stress "firm" or "long shelf life."

PREVENTING BROWNING

Fruits contain a phenolic compound that turns the exposed flesh brown when the fruit's skin is broken by cutting or biting into it. This happens fairly rapidly, especially to apples, bananas, pears, potatoes, and avocados. The browning is caused by the enzyme polyphenoloxidase, which causes the phenolic compound in the cells to oxidize. This is similar to the action that occurs when your skin is exposed to the sun's rays. (Citrus fruits and melons lack the enzyme, but if these fruits are allowed to sit out with their flesh exposed to oxygen for any length of time, they will turn brown through normal oxidation.)

The browning can be slowed down by refrigerating the fruit at 40°F; however, boiling destroys the enzyme. Salt will also slow down the enzyme but will negatively affect the flavor. Placing the fruit in cold water will slow the process by keeping the surface from the air. Brushing lemon juice on the cut surface or dipping the fruit in acidulated water (water mixed with lemon juice or vinegar) also works well.

CAN VITAMIN C SURVIVE IN COMMERCIALLY PREPARED JUICES?

The methods of preparation and packaging will determine the level of vitamin C that remains in a commercial juice. Frozen orange juice loses only about 2 percent of its vitamin C over three months of home-freezer storage. If the juice is sold in glass bottles, it will retain almost 100 percent of its vitamin C; however, if it is stored in plastic or waxed cardboard containers, oxygen will pass through the container and reduce the potency of the vitamin C over time. Your best bet is to buy fresh-squeezed orange juice, if possible. Those in northern climes, though, cannot know how long it's been since the oranges were harvested or how long they've been in transit from the groves to the store. All commercial bottled juices are pasteurized, and natural enzymes are killed by the heat.

CAN PRUNES REALLY RELIEVE CONSTIPATION?

Prunes contain the organic chemical dihydroxyphenyl istatin, which is a relative of another compound, bisacodyl, that is the active ingredient in some over-the-counter laxatives. Bisacodyl tends to increase the secretion of fluids in the bowel and will stimulate contractions of the intestines, thereby pushing waste material on its way. Prunes are also a good source of minerals, and a natural laxative is almost always better for you than a laboratory-produced chemical concoction.

WHAT IS THE CHINESE LANTERN FRUIT?

The fruit is *Physalis peruviana,* which is a round berry encased in a pod that resembles a Chinese lantern. It is also known as the Cape gooseberry and is used as an ornamental garden plant. The berry is cultivated in South Africa and Peru and is an extremely rich source of vitamin A as well as an excellent source of vitamin C.

HAIRY FRUIT?

The rambutan is one of the most unusual-looking pieces of fruit you will ever see. It is oval, about three to four inches long, is crimson red—and is covered with what looks like hair. The name of the fruit comes from the Malayan word for hairy. The skin, however, is harmless and peels off easily, and the fruit is usually sold in cans; look for it in Asian markets. Its taste is slightly acidic, like a grape.

PUCKER UP!

If you have ever bitten into an unripe piece of fruit or tried eating a lemon, or even taken a sip of strong tea, you have experienced a quality known as astringency. Astringency causes dryness of the mouth and puckering and constricting of the lips, and this is just how your mouth feels as it comes in contact with a class of phenolic compounds called tannins. The tannins affect the protein in the saliva and mucous membranes of the mouth, causing puckering.

WHAT IS THE OLDEST KNOWN CITRUS FRUIT?

The oldest known citrus fruit, the citron, originated in Hadhramaut, which is located in a mountainous region of the Arabian peninsula. And for reasons lost to history, the citron was cultivated as a sacred fruit at Nippur, the religious capital of the Sumerians.

Too sour for eating raw, citron is grown for its thick peel, which is candied and used in baking. The fruit itself looks like a yellow-green, knobby lemon and may be sold in a variety of sizes, depending on the country where it is grown. There are a number of varieties, one of which is the Etrog, which is used in the Jewish festival called the Feast of the Tabernacles. If you happen to live in a part of the country where citrus is grown, you may find citron at a farmers market.

WHAT IS A FEIJOA?

The feijoa is a small, green-skinned fruit with a taste similar to that of a guava. It has black seeds and a cream to tan pulp. This fruit is popular in the southwestern United States as well as in South America and New Zealand. The New Zealand crop is available from spring to early summer; California's crop is in stores in the fall.

ACEROLA

The acerola, also called Barbados cherry or pitanga, is a fruit that resembles a cherry. Too sour to be eaten raw, acerolas grown on thick bushes that are used as hedges in some hot climates. The fruit is native to Brazil and has become very popular in Florida. Nutritionists believe it may be the richest fruit source of vitamin C. There are approximately 4,000 milligrams of vitamin C in 3.5 ounces of the fruit.

WHAT IS A MOG INSPECTOR?

Grapes that are shipped from vineyards to wineries are routinely checked for MOG (material other than grapes). The people who perform this inspection are called MOG inspectors; they look mainly for leaves, rocks, and snakes, and when these items are found, the vineyard is fined.

WHAT IS A JACKFRUIT?

This is the largest fruit known to exist. It can measure up to three feet long and 20 inches across and can weigh up to 100 pounds (40 kg). It has a hard, green-colored skin with pointed warts and large seeds that can be roasted and are similar to chestnuts. The seeds are high in calcium and contain protein. Jackfruit is indigenous to India and East Africa.

BABÁCO AS A MEAT TENDERIZER

A recent arrival in supermarkets is the tropical fruit babáco, which is indigenous to Ecuador. A relative of papaya, it has a golden-yellow skin when ripe and pale yellow flesh. Unlike papaya, the babáco has no pips, and the skin is edible. Babáco is high in vitamin C, has a low sugar content, and contains the enzyme papain that is used as a meat tenderizer.

FRESH PRODUCE AND BACTERIA

As more and more produce is being imported from foreign countries, more outbreaks of food-borne illnesses are reported, especially those relating to the strain of bacteria called E. coli 0157:H7. This often deadly strain of bacteria usually results from the fecal contamination of meat during slaughtering and processing, but is now showing up on vegetables and fruits. In 1996, four outbreaks related to lettuce were reported by the Centers for Disease Control and Prevention. Salmonella has also been found on melons and tomatoes, and other dangerous bacteria have been found on cabbage and mushrooms. In one instance, more than 245 people in 30 states became ill from eating cantaloupe. Seventy percent of all produce is now imported from developing nations.

When buying fresh produce, make sure you purchase only as much as you need for a short period. If bacteria are present in or on the fruit, the longer you store the produce, the more the bacteria will multiply. Always wash your hands before handling produce, and then wash the produce thoroughly using a clean vegetable brush before cutting it with a knife. Alternatively, use an organic produce cleaner, which can be found in health-food stores and many supermarkets.

SWEET AND SOUR FRUIT

Sugar is the primary source of energy stored in fruit, which uses the sugar to synthesize other organic material. The sugar content of most fruits averages 10 to 15 percent by weight. The lime, however, has only 1 percent sugar, while the date has more than 60 percent.

The sugar is produced by starch, which is stored in the plant's leaves and, as the fruit ripens, is converted into sugar. In addition, fruits contain a number of organic acids, including citric, malic, tartaric, and oxalic acids. As the fruit ripens, its acid content declines, making it less sour.

DANGEROUS CITRUS PEELS

Unless citrus has been organically grown, it would be wise not to eat any product that has citrus peel, including the zests that are often grated for use in recipes. Citrus crops in the United States are routinely sprayed with a number of carcinogenic pesticides and fungicides, which tend to remain in the skin, even if the citrus has been thoroughly cleaned and scrubbed.

JUJUBE: CHEWY CANDY OR DATE?

A jujube isn't only a candy. It is also a fruit, known as a Chinese date, that is unrelated to the date we are used to seeing in the market. It is not even a member of the same botanical family, although it is similar in texture. The Chinese date is high in vitamin C and is usually sold as a dried fruit.

PAUL BUNYAN'S FRUITS AND VEGETABLES

The largest watermelon that has ever been grown weighed in at 262 pounds. The world's longest zucchini grew to almost 70 inches. The world's largest squash was 654 pounds. The largest cabbage was 123 pounds. The world's largest lemon was 5 pounds, 13 ounces, and the world's largest tomato tipped the scales at 4 pounds, 4 ounces.

COOKING FRUITS

The last thing a cook wants is mushy fruit. This problem can be resolved by adding some sugar to the cooking syrup. The sugar will draw some of the fluid back into the cells to maintain equilibrium in the sugar concentration. The fruit will retain a more desirable and appealing texture.

PRESERVES AND PECTIN

Many a cook still believes that preserves acquire their smooth, semi-solid consistency from the amount of sugar added to the fruit. Actually, the consistency is also controlled by the level of pectin extracted from the cell walls of the fruit. Pectin is similar to cement in that it holds the cell walls together and forms a stringlike network that traps liquids and converts them into solids. A number of fruits, such as grapes and a few varieties of berries, contain enough pectin to gel on their own. Other fruits, including apricots, peaches, and cherries, need additional pectin to gel.

Commercial pectin used for home preserving is derived from apples or the white layer just under the skin of citrus fruits. In making preserves, the balance between sugar and pectin is very delicate. The optimum pH is between 2.8 and 3.4. Pectin concentration should be no more than 0.5 to 1.0 percent, with a sugar concentration of no more than 60 to 65 percent. Because of these exacting percentages, it is best to follow your recipe to the letter. Reduced-calorie preserves are made with a special pectin that contains calcium ions and gels, and they use very little sugar.

DON'T BE FOILED

Never wrap acidic fruits such as lemons, oranges, tomatoes, and grapefruits in aluminum foil. A chemical reaction may take place that will corrode the foil. A common method of preparing meat loaf is to place tomato sauce on top while the meat is cooking and then cover it with foil, but tomato sauce or paste can eat right through the foil.

HOW DO FRUITS AND VEGETABLES MAKE VITAMINS C AND A?

All plants manufacture vitamin C from sugars that are derived from their leaves and produced by photosynthesis. The more light a plant gets, the more pigments (chlorophylls and carotenoids) are needed to process the additional light energy, so the plant's leaves and stems become darker. The darker the leaves, the more carotene (vitamin A precursor) the plant has to devote to the production of vitamin A.

WHAT IS A KIWANO?

The kiwano is a member of the cucumber family and is actually an African horned melon. Although it is grown in California, it was originally exported from New Zealand, hence its Maori name.

The shape of the kiwano is similar to that of a large gherkin; however, it is bright orange with a number of small horns protruding from the skin. The pulp has a jellylike texture, and the flavor is somewhat like a combination of cucumber, banana, and lime. Available in some specialty markets, the kiwano fruit is very tasty and should become more popular and less expensive as the demand increases.

CAN A SWEET LEMON BE GROWN?

There is a fruit that is called a limetta, which is a sweet lemon grown in Italy and California. It resembles a cross between a lemon and a lime and is so sweet it will never make your mouth pucker. Limettas taste a lot like lemonade and are actually excellent for making lemonade, pie filling, and lemon sauces. The California variety is called the Millsweet, but it has not so far become popular at the markets.

WHAT IS THE MOST POPULAR CHINESE FRUIT?

There is really no contest. Even though China grows many wonderful fruits, the litchi is definitely the most popular. It is said that an ancient Chinese poet bragged about his litchi habit, claiming to eat at least 300 every day, and as many as one thousand in one day.

The first book about the cultivation of fruit was written in 1056 A.D. and was devoted entirely to growing litchis. They have a tough, bright-red, scaly skin that peels easily. They may be found either fresh or dried in Chinese markets, or in cans in most supermarkets.

ZESTY FRUIT

The rind of a citrus fruit is made of bitter white pith and a thin zest, which is the outermost layer. The zest contains flavorful aromatic oils and is often called for in recipes. The tool used to remove that outer rind without any of the bitter white pith is called a zester. It has tiny holes that peel off the zest in thin strips.

WHAT PIE IS SERVED NEAR THE KILAUEA VOLCANO?

A fruit called the ohelo is grown on the Big Island of Hawaii. The ohelo is a berry related to the American huckleberry or blueberry, but it's much sweeter. It is used to prepare the jams and pies that are served at the Volcano House on the rim of the Kilauea crater. Be sure to try this unique pie if you ever visit the Big Island.

EXPOSURE

Peeling thin-skinned fruits like peaches, tomatoes, plums, or nectarines will be easier if you first place them in a bowl, cover them with boiling water, and allow them to stand for 1 to 2 minutes. You'll be able to remove the skin with a sharp paring knife. You can also spear the food with a fork and hold it about 6 inches above a gas flame until the skin cracks.

Peeling thick-skinned fruits or vegetables is much easier. Simply cut a small portion of the peel from the top and bottom, set the food on an acrylic cutting board, and then remove the balance of the peel in strips, working from top to bottom.

DID YOU KNOW?

You can remove citrus zest with a vegetable peeler, but you'll probably end up with some pith. Scrape it off with a paring knife before mincing or slicing the zest.

UNIQUE FLAVOR

Grate the zest from an orange and mix it with orange juice and light sour cream to create a tasty dressing for fruits.

CLERK ALERT

Whether you or a clerk bag your purchases at the supermarket, be sure that produce and meats (including poultry and fish) are in separate bags. Meat packaging can leak and might contaminate the produce.

IT'S THE PITS

The pits of a number of fruits, including apricots, apples, pears, cherries, and peaches, contain the chemical amygdalin. If a pit containing amygdalin is crushed and heated, it may release cyanide in very small amounts.

DRIED FRUITS

◆ Vitamin C is lost when fruits are dried or dehydrated. However, most other vitamins and minerals are retained.

◆ The sulfites commonly used to preserve dried fruits may cause an allergic reaction in susceptible individuals.

◆ Dried fruits are graded Extra Fancy, Fancy, Extra Choice, Choice, and Standard, based on size, color, and water content.

◆ If frozen in a liquid, dried fruits should be thawed in the same liquid to retain their flavor.

◆ If you store dried fruits in airtight containers they will keep for up to one month at room temperature. If placed in a cool, dry location or refrigerated, they will last for about one year.

◆ Refrigeration places the cells of dried fruits in a state of suspended animation, which helps preserve their flavor. For best taste, allow cold fruit to stand at room temperature for about 30 minutes before eating it.

Order of Nutritional Levels of Fruits
1. Fresh, if brought quickly to market
2. Dehydrated, if Grade A or No.1
3. Freeze-dried, if packaged at the site where grown
4. Frozen, if packaged within 12 hours of harvest
5. Canned

JELLY PRESERVATION

If you add a small pat of butter when cooking fruits for preserves and jellies, there will be no foam to skim off the top. The fat acts as a sealant and prevents the air from rising and accumulating on top as foam. For safety's sake, always make jellies and preserves in a large pot. Boiling-hot, sugary fruit can be a dangerous mess if it boils over a too-small pan.

SET UP, JELLY!

If you have problems getting fruit jelly to set, pour the jelly back into the pot and cook it again until it reaches 220°F. Be sure to resterilize the jars and use new lids.

HEALTHY FRUITS

- In Australia you can purchase a green plum that contains 3,000 milligrams of vitamin C per 4-ounce serving. (The average orange has only 70 milligrams.)
- In Tanzania, enjoy the kongoroko fruit. It contains 526 milligrams of calcium. (An 8-ounce glass of milk has only 290 milligrams of calcium.)

ACKEE

The ackee is grown in Jamaica and is very popular throughout the Caribbean. When mature, the fruit splits open, exposing the edible white aril—the outer covering of the seed.

APPLES

- Certain varieties of apple may have a different taste at different times of year. If you buy apples in large quantities, it would be best to taste a few first. They should be firm, with no holes and no bruises, and they should have a good, even color.
- If an apple is not ripe, leave it at room temperature for a day or two, but not in direct sunlight.
- Apples will ripen very quickly at room temperature. If you are not sure of their level of ripeness, leave them out for two to three days before refrigerating them.
- Apples should be stored in the refrigerator to stop the ripening process. Wash them, dry, and place in a plastic bag. When refrigerated, apples will stay fresh for two to four weeks but risk becoming mealy.

DID YOU KNOW?

Three of the most nutritious fruits are papayas, strawberries, and cantaloupes.

◆ The ideal way to store apples is in a barrel with sawdust, in a cool, dry location. Stored this way, they will last four to six months. The apples should never touch one another.

◆ Apples to be frozen must first be cored, peeled, washed, and sliced. Spray them with a solution of ½ teaspoon ascorbic acid (vitamin C) mixed with 3 tablespoons of cold water and place the apple slices in a container with ½ inch of space at the top.

APPLE VARIETIES

Akane

These should be used shortly after purchasing. They have a sweet-tart flavor, and their skin is thin and usually tender enough so it doesn't need peeling. Akanes retain their tartness when they are cooked. Good for eating and making applesauce.

Braeburn

These store exceptionally well. The skin is tender, and the flavor is moderately tart. Good for eating raw, applesauce, and pie.

Cortland

Cortlands are very fragile and must be separated when transported and stored to avoid bruising. They resist browning better than most other apples. Normally very thin-skinned, with a tart-sweet taste, Cortlands keep their shape well when baked.

Criterion

These should be a nice yellow color. They are very fragile, and are difficult to handle without bruising. They resist browning. The skin is tender, and their flavor is so sweet they are sometimes called "candy apples." Criterions are good for baking.

Fuji

These store well when firm. They have a tangy-sweet flavor and retain their shape when baked. The shape is similar to that of an Asian pear.

Gala

These apples have a tender yellow skin with light reddish stripes. They are sweet, with a hint of tartness. They hold their shape well when baked; however, they tend to lose flavor when heated. Best eaten as a snack.

Golden Delicious

These will store fairly well for three to four months in a very cool location, but they spoil fast at room temperature. They should be light yellow, not greenish. Their skin is tender and the flavor is sweet. They resist browning, and they retain their shape well when baked. There are more than 150 varieties of Red and Golden Delicious apples grown worldwide, more than any other apple.

Granny Smith
Grannies should be a light green color, perhaps with a slight yellow tint, but they shouldn't be intensely green. The flesh resists browning. A good all-purpose apple, they hold their shape when cooked.

Idared
This apple stores exceptionally well and becomes sweeter during storage. Idareds resemble Jonathans and have tender skin. They bake well and will retain their full flavor. A good all-purpose apple.

Jonagold
A hybrid of Jonathan and Golden Delicious, Jonagold tends to have a good sweet-tart balance and is very juicy with tender skin.

Jonathan
Grown mostly in California and harvested around mid-August, they tend to become soft and mealy very quickly. Thin skinned, Jonathans cook tender and make a good applesauce. They do not bake well.

McIntosh
Most McIntosh are grown in British Columbia. Early harvests are mostly green with a red blush. Later harvests are good for cooking, especially applesauce, and for eating out of hand. Should be peeled before cooking as their skin is quite tough. Good for baking.

Melrose
Grown mainly in the Pacific Northwest, these apples tend to store very well, and their flavor actually improves after one to two months of storage. They have a well-balanced, sweet but somewhat tart flavor and retain their shape well when cooked.

Mutsu
These may be sold as Crispin. They resemble a Golden Delicious but are greener and more irregular in shape. Mutsus store well and have a sweet but spicy taste with a firm, fine texture. Good for applesauce.

Newton Pippin
The color should be yellowish-green; wait until you find them a light green for the sweetest flavor. They keep their shape well when baked or used in pies and make a nice, thick applesauce.

Northern Spy
These are tart, green apples that are especially good for pies. They are excellent in all kinds of cooking and baking.

Red Delicious
May range in color from pure red to red-striped. They will store in the fridge for up to 12 months but will not last long at room temperature; the longer they are stored, the mealier they become. They are normally sweet and mellow, with just a hint of tartness. Unlike their Golden counterparts, Red Delicious apples do not cook or bake well. Good eaten out of hand.

Rhode Island Greening
These are among the best pie apples, but they are rarely available. They can be found only in October and November on the East Coast.

Rome Beauty
These do not store for long periods and become bland and mealy quickly. They are very mild and have a low acid level, which means that they brown easily. The skin is fairly thick but tender, and they are excellent for baking because they hold their shape well.

Spartan
Cannot be stored for long periods without getting mushy and mealy. They are sweet and very aromatic, but their flavor dissipates with cooking, so they are not recommended for baking.

Stayman Winesap
These tend to store well. They are crisp, with a spicy-tart flavor and a thick skin that separates easily from the flesh. Good cooking apples that retain their flavor well, they are excellent for baking and pies.

WHAT IS THE DIFFERENCE BETWEEN APPLE JUICE AND CIDER?

In both products the apples are pressed and the juice extracted. Apple juice is strained, clarified, and usually pasteurized. Cider is pasteurized less frequently, although the outbreaks of contaminated juices in recent years mean that cider available in supermarkets will be pasteurized more often now. Apple cider sold at roadside stands is often without the protection of pasteurization. Pasteurized cider will be slightly less flavorful, but because of potential health risks, it should be your cider of choice. Cider must be labeled as such; if it isn't, it's just apple juice in a jug.

ETHYLENE GAS—A NATURAL

Never store an apple near a banana unless you wish to ripen the banana very fast. Apples tend to give off more ethylene gas than most other fruits (except green tomatoes) and will hasten the ripening of many other fruits and vegetables. Ethylene is a natural gas that all fruits and vegetables release as they ripen. In fact, it has been used for centuries to hasten the ripening of fruits and vegetables.

Ethylene increases cell membrane permeability, allowing the cell to breathe more and use the oxygen it takes in to produce carbon dioxide up to five times faster than it would ordinarily. This increased cellular activity causes the fruit or vegetable to ripen faster.

WHY DOES AN APPLE COLLAPSE WHEN COOKED?

If you place a whole apple in the oven and bake it, the peel will withstand the heat and retain its shape for some length of time. The peel contains an insoluble cellulose, which reinforces it and keeps it intact. The flesh of the apple, however, will partially disintegrate as the pectin in its cell walls is dissolved by the water being released from the cells. The cells then rupture, and the apple turns to applesauce. The reason apples stay relatively firm in commercial apple pies is because of the acid sulfite bath they are given before they are frozen.

DO APPLES HAVE ANY MEDICINAL USE?

Apples have been used for hundreds of years as a folk remedy for diarrhea. Raw apples contain a high level of pectin, which is one of the main ingredients in over-the-counter antidiarrheal medications.

IT'S DUNKING TIME

If you've ever wondered why we bob for apples and not for other fruits, here's why: Apples float because 25 percent of their volume is made up of air pockets between the cells.

OLD AGE?

To prevent baked apples from wrinkling, peel the top third or cut a few slits in the skin to allow for expansion.

PUCKER UP

The tartness of an apple is derived from the balance of malic acid and the fruit's natural sugars.

DID YOU KNOW?

Avoid all bruised fruit, and never place a bruised one next to an unbruised one.

REVIVAL TIME AGAIN

If apples are dry or bland, slice them and put them in a dish, and then pour cold apple juice over them and refrigerate for 30 minutes.

NATURAL IS BEST

Commercially prepared sweetened applesauce can contain up to 97 calories per half-cup serving; the same amount of unsweetened applesauce contains a mere 52 calories.

WE'RE EVEN

Nutritionally, there is no difference between natural (unfiltered) and regular apple juice; even the fiber content is the same. However, apple juice is not high on the nutritional scale. Most varieties of apple juice contain only a small amount of natural vitamin C.

AN APPLE A DAY . . .

Americans consume approximately 19 pounds of fresh apples per person annually, and another 28.2 pounds of processed apples. But take note: As many as 43 different pesticides were discovered to be present in 33 percent of all apples tested by the USDA.

APPLES AS A STRESS RELIEVER?

Researchers at Yale University recently discovered that sniffing apple spice fragrance has a calming effect on human beings. Smelling mulled cider or baked apple actually reduced anxiety attacks. Try it; you'll like it!

REPORTED HEALTH BENEFITS

Studies have shown that apples stimulate body secretions. Apples contain malic and tartaric acids, which may help to relieve disturbances of the liver and aid general digestion. Kidney stones are very rare among populations that drink unsweetened apple juice on a regular basis. The low acidity level in apples tends to stimulate gum tissue and salivary flow. Studies also indicate that consuming apples daily will reduce the severity of arthritis and asthma. The skin of the apple contains a high level of pectin, which is active in raising HDL (good cholesterol) levels.

CAN APPLE SEEDS POISON YOU?

Apple seeds contain cyanogen, which is converted to cyanide when the seeds are damaged and an enzyme in the seeds that liberates the cyanide comes into contact with the cyanogen. Fortunately, apple seeds will pass through the digestive tract undigested. Even if a seed were to split open, the amount of cyanide released would not place you at any risk. Other fruit seeds, such as those of apricots and peaches, also contain cyanogen. Although these seeds split more easily than apple seeds do, they still do not pose any risk to a healthy person.

AN APPLE FOR THE TEACHER

A survey performed by *USA Today* asked teachers what apple they would prefer a student to bring them. The results were as follows:

TYPE OF APPLE	PREFERRED BY
Red Delicious	39 percent
Golden Delicious	24 percent
Granny Smith	20 percent
McIntosh	10 percent

APRICOTS

◆ The apricot, a relative of the peach, is usually the first fruit of the summer season.

◆ Three fresh apricots contain enough beta-carotene to supply 25 percent of your daily requirement of vitamin A.

◆ Apricots were originally grown in China more than 4,000 years ago and were brought to California by the Spanish in the late 18th century. California is still the largest producer of apricots, with more than half the crop being canned because of their short growing season.

◆ Unripe apricots will ripen quickly at room temperature. Once ripe, they should be refrigerated.

WORD TO THE WISE

Dried apricots are more than 40 percent sugar. When buying dried apricots, look for the unsulfured variety if you are allergic to sulfur.

DID YOU KNOW?

Fruit consumption in the United States rose from 101 pounds per person in 1970 to 130 pounds in 1995.

WHY IS IT SO HARD TO FIND A FRESH APRICOT?

In the United States, apricots are grown mainly on 17,000 acres in California's Santa Clara Valley. Because they are so fragile and bruise so easily, they do not travel well or last very long once they ripen. For these reasons, and because they are so difficult to transport from the West Coast to Midwest and Eastern markets, many people in this country have never tasted a fresh, ripe apricot.

REPORTED HEALTH BENEFITS
Apricots have been used topically as a folk remedy to smooth out wrinkles and lighten age spots.

WHAT'S AN ATEMOYA?

This unusual fruit is grown in Florida and is available in markets from August through October. The atemoya is pale green and should not be purchased if it is cracked. This fruit looks like an artichoke and has a cream-colored flesh that is sweet and almost fat- and sodium-free. The atemoya is an excellent source of potassium.

AVOCADOS

◆ Originally from Central America, avocados were first grown in the United States in the 1800s in Florida and California. California produces 90 percent of all avocados now sold. The most popular varieties are the Fuerte and Hass.

◆ Approximately 71 to 88 percent of the calories in avocados come from fat. However, most of the fat is monounsaturated, the same type found in olive oil and canola oil.

◆ Avocados are available year-round. They range in color from bright-green to purple-black. They should feel heavy for their size and be slightly firm. Avoid those with soft spots and discolorations.

◆ Avocados will ripen quicky if placed in a brown-paper bag and set in a warm location. They will ripen even faster if you place them in a wool sock. Refrigerate them once they are ripe, and they will keep 10 to 14 days. Pureed, they can be frozen for three to six months.

HOW GREEN I AM

Have you ever heard someone say that leaving the avocado pit in the guacamole will prevent it from turning black? You have probably tried it—without success, unless you covered the entire dish tightly with plastic wrap. It's the plastic wrap, not the pit, that does the trick by preventing the fruit from oxidizing. Guacamole (with lemon juice) will oxidize on the surface in about 60 to 90 minutes if it is left uncovered.

CAN YOU COOK AN AVOCADO?

It would be a rare event to see a recipe calling for cooked avocado. The heat will cause a reaction that releases a bitter chemical compound. When restaurants do serve avocado in a hot dish, they add it just before serving or cook it just briefly. Simply slicing an avocado releases the enzyme polyphenoloxidase, which causes it to turn brown. Ascorbic acid will neutralize or slow this reaction.

EN GARDE

To remove an avocado pit, thrust the blade of a sharp knife into the pit, twist slightly, and the pit will come right out.

FAUX RIPE

If an avocado is too hard and you want to use it right away, try placing it in the microwave on High for 40 to 70 seconds. Prick the skin before cooking it, and flip it over half way through. This won't ripen the avocado, but it will soften it.

> **REPORTED HEALTH BENEFITS**
> Avocados contain significant amounts of protein and beneficial fats,
> which stimulate tissue growth and regeneration.

BANANAS

◆ Bananas are available year-round because they grow in a climate with no winter. They should be plump, and their skins should be free of bruises as well as brown or black spots.

◆ As soon as a banana ripens at room temperature, it should be stored in the refrigerator to slow down the ripening process. The skin will turn black, but this will not affect the flesh for a number of days.

◆ Bananas can be frozen up to six or seven months if left in their skins, but they will be a bit mushy when thawed (wait to peel them until they've thawed). Then again, a frozen banana makes a delicious treat.

◆ The new miniature bananas have more taste than many of the larger ones and can be used for cooking in the same manner as the full-size ones. Cinnamon and nutmeg are delicious with bananas.

◆ Bananas chips are not a healthful snack food because they are usually fried in oil derived from saturated fat. One ounce of fried banana chips can contain 150 calories and up to 10 grams of fat, most of which is saturated. It would be best to eat air-dried chips, if you can find them.

◆ Americans consume 11 billion bananas annually. The majority of the bananas being exported to the United States today are from Latin America. Uganda is the leading producer of bananas in the world.

◆ Although bananas are a tropical fruit, they are also grown in Iceland, in soil heated by volcanic steam vents.

BERRY INTERESTING

Bananas contain less water than most other fruits. They are actually a type of berry, and grow on a tree classified as an herb. The tree can grow up to 30 feet high and is the largest herb in the world with a woody stem.

RIPENING TIDBITS

If you wish to ripen bananas quickly, wrap them in a wet paper towel and place them in a brown-paper bag. Or place a ripe banana next to the green ones. If you keep apples and bananas in a fruit bowl on the counter, the bananas will ripen very quickly, because apples give off more ethylene gas than other fruits.

BROWN SPOTS ON BANANAS TELL THE SUGAR CONTENT

Bananas are always picked when they are green. If they are allowed to ripen on the tree they tend to lose their taste and become mealy. The sugar content starts to go up as soon as the banana is picked and increases from 2 percent to 20 percent as it ripens. The yellower the skin becomes, the sweeter the banana. Brown spots indicate the sugar level has increased to more than 25 percent. The more brown spots, the higher the sugar.

CAN YOU GET HIGH FROM SMOKING BANANA PEELS?

Smoking dried banana peels became very popular in the 1960s, when scientists announced that they contained minute amounts of certain psychoactive compounds such as serotonin, norepinephrine, and dopamine. The peels were dried, ground into a fine powder, rolled in cigarette wrappers, and smoked. But the fad didn't last very long, because the effects are so minimal that few people actually feel any effect.

OUCH!

If you are not sure whether a banana is ripe, insert a toothpick in the stem end. If it comes out clean and with ease, the banana is ripe. Alternatively, look to see whether it has brown spots.

BANANA VARIETIES

Cavendish
The standard curved banana that we normally purchase. These are imported mainly from South America.

Manzano
Known as the finger banana, this variety tends to turn black when ripe.

Plantain
Very large, green bananas with a high starch content. These are more palatable when prepared as a vegetable. In South America, plantains are used as a starchy vegetable, much as potatoes are used in North America.

Red Banana
Usually straight instead of curved like the standard banana, these tend to turn a purplish color when ripe, and they have a sweet flavor.

REPORTED HEALTH BENEFITS

Historically, potassium-rich bananas have been reported to improve conditions such as stomach ulcers, colitis, diarrhea, hemorrhoids, and even to increase energy levels. The inner surface of the banana's skin has antibacterial properties and has been used to heal burns and boils.

BERRIES

◆ All berries should be firm and brightly colored. They do not ripen after picking, should be refrigerated, and should never be allowed to dry out. For best flavor and nutritional value, berries should be used within two to three days of purchase.

◆ Choose only bright red strawberries and plump, firm blueberries that are light to dark blue.

◆ Always check the bottom of the container to be sure it is not stained from rotting or moldy berries. Mold tends to spread quickly, and you should never leave a moldy berry next to a good one.

◆ Never hull strawberries until after they are washed, or they will absorb too much water and become mushy and waterlogged.

◆ Frozen berries can be defrosted by placing them in a plastic bag and immersing them in cold water for 10 to 12 minutes.

> **REPORTED HEALTH BENEFITS**
> Blackberry leaves have been used to relieve the symptoms of arthritis, weak kidneys, anemia, gout, and minor skin irritations, as a blood cleanser, an antidiarrhetic, to reduce inflammations, and to alleviate menstrual disorders. Strawberries have been used effectively to cleanse the skin and blood, as well as to relieve the symptoms of asthma, gout, and arthritis, and to benefit the cardiovascular system.

BOTTOMS UP

If you're making a cake with a recipe that calls for berries, be sure the batter is thick enough to hold the berries in suspension. Berries added to thin batters just sink to the bottom.

HEALTHY BERRIES

Blueberries and strawberries are higher in vitamin A than most berries. Strawberries are one of the more nutritious berries, with just one cup containing only 45 calories and considerably more calcium, phosphorus, vitamin C, and potassium than blueberries and raspberries.

A LOTTA BERRIES

In 1997, California grew enough strawberries to circle the Earth 15 times. The largest strawberry ever grown weighed 8.17 ounces.

WHAT HAPPENS WHEN YOU SPRINKLE SUGAR ON A STRAWBERRY?

Strawberries are naturally sweet, but you can sweeten them further by sprinkling them with powdered sugar and allowing them to stand for a short time. When the sugar is placed on the surface of the berry, it mixes with the moisture that is naturally being released, producing a solution that is somewhat denser than the liquid inside the berry. Through osmosis, the liquid with the lesser density flows toward the liquid that is denser, so the sugar sweetens the berry juice as it is released.

BERRY, BERRY, INTERESTING

Wild blueberries grow in profusion in Maine. The biggest producers of cultivated blueberries are Arkansas, Michigan, New Jersey, North Carolina, Oregon, and Washington. Blueberries are second only to strawberries in berry consumption in the United States.

CRANBERRIES

- Cranberries are usually too tart to eat raw, and are, therefore, used in making sauces, relishes, and preserves.
- Only 10 percent of the commercial crop in the United States is sold in supermarkets; the balance is made into cranberry sauce or juice.
- Canned cranberry sauce has only 14 percent of the vitamin C found in fresh berries and three times the calories.
- Cranberries contain ellagic acid, a tannin that contributes the tart, astringent taste to raw cranberries.
- When purchasing fresh cranberries, try to see whether one will bounce (another name for cranberries is bounceberries). Cranberries should be hard, bright light- to dark-red, and sealed in plastic bags. If frozen, they will keep for up to one year.

POP GOES THE CRANBERRY

Cranberries will not absorb much heat before the water inside produces enough steam to burst the berry. When a cranberry bursts, it is best to stop the cooking process; otherwise, the berries will become bitter and very tart. A teaspoon of unsalted butter added to the water for each pound of cranberries prevents boiling over by reducing the amount of foam that develops. Adding lemon juice and sugar to the cooking water will help to preserve the color.

IS CRANBERRY JUICE HELPFUL FOR BLADDER PROBLEMS?

Recently, Israeli researchers have found that a substance in cranberries may interfere with the ability of bacteria to adhere to the surface of the bladder and the urinary tract. In addition, a study conducted in Boston found that people who drank 12 ounces of cranberry juice cocktail every day for six weeks had fewer bacteria and white blood cells in their urine.

REPORTED HEALTH BENEFITS

In folk medicine, cranberries have been used to alleviate numerous skin disorders and liver and kidney disorders, as well as to reduce high blood pressure. They have been used extensively for more than 150 years to reduce the symptoms of urinary tract infections.

IS THERE A BLACK RASPBERRY?

Raspberries are actually grown in three colors: the traditional red that we see in the markets during the summer; the black; and the golden or yellow berries that are relatively common in some areas of the country.

BREADFRUIT

This fruit looks like a large melon and may weigh from two to 10 pounds. It is high in starch and vitamins and is a staple food for the Pacific Islanders. It has a greenish, scaly skin and pale-yellow flesh. When ripe, it is very sweet. Make sure you choose a relatively hard breadfruit and allow it to ripen at room temperature until it has some give when pressed. It is usually cooked and eaten as a vegetable.

CANTALOUPE

- ◆ Cantaloupes are at their prime between June and September. They should be round, smooth, and have a depressed scar at the stem end. Be aware that if the scar appears rough or the stem is still attached, the melon was picked too early and will not ripen well.
- ◆ The stem spot should be somewhat soft, but make sure that the melon is not soft all over.
- ◆ Cantaloupes are best if the netting of the skin is an even, yellow color with little or no green.

◆ Melons can be left at room temperature to ripen, but they do not ripen under refrigeration. The aroma will usually indicate if a cantaloupe is ripe and sweet. Once it reaches this point, it should be refrigerated as soon as possible.

◆ Whole melons will last for a week if kept refrigerated. Cut melons, wrapped in plastic and refrigerated with the seeds left in place, are best eaten within two to three days.

◆ One average cantaloupe will produce about 45 to 50 melon balls, or about 4 cups of diced fruit.

REPORTED HEALTH BENEFITS
Cantaloupes have been used to lower fevers, reduce blood pressure, relieve the symptoms of arthritis, alleviate bladder problems, and maintain bowel regularity. They also can alleviate jaundice, inflammation, sunburn, and other burns.

CARAMBOLA

The color of the skin of a ripe carambola should be golden-yellow. When sliced, the fruit yields perfect star-shaped sections. It has a sweet but somewhat tart flavor and may be purchased green and allowed to ripen at room temperature. It is an excellent source of vitamin C.

CHERRIES

◆ Cherries are grown in 20 countries worldwide. The United States grows more than 600 million pounds of cherries annually, 375 million pounds of which are sweet cherries and 251 million pounds of which are sour cherries.

◆ Most of the cherries grown are canned or frozen.

◆ Cherries were a favorite fruit of the Romans, Greeks, and Chinese thousands of years ago. They originated in Asia Minor and were named for the Turkish town Cerasus, which is presently called Giresun and is located on the Black Sea.

◆ It is believed that birds brought cherry pits to Europe from Asia Minor. Europeans enjoy a chilled cherry soup as a summertime treat.

◆ French colonists from Normandy brought cherry pits to the New World, which they planted along the Saint Lawrence River and throughout the Great Lakes area.

- Sweet cherries are primarily grown on the West Coast, while sour cherries are grown in the Great Lakes region, in New England, and on the Great Plains.
- Cherries should be stored in the refrigerator with as much humidity as possible. Under these conditions, they will keep for about four days.
- For best flavor, place cherries unwashed in a plastic bag and allow them to stand at room temperature for 30 minutes before eating. If you freeze cherries, they must be pitted first and sealed airtight in a plastic bag; otherwise they will taste like almonds.

CHERRY VARIETIES

Montmorency

A sour cherry, usually round but slightly compressed. Very juicy, with a clear, medium-red color. Excellent for pies, tarts, and jams. This is the most widely grown sour cherry in the United States.

Early Richmond

A sour cherry. Round, medium-red in color, with tender flesh and a tough, thin skin. Grown in the Midwest and eastern United States.

Morello

A sour cherry. Round in shape and very deep red in color, becoming almost black. The flesh is red, tender, and somewhat tart. This variety is not grown commercially in large quantities in the United States.

Republican (Lewellan)

A sweet cherry. Small to medium-sized, heart-shaped, with crisp flesh ranging from very red to purplish-black. The juice is very dark and sweet.

Royal Ann (Napoleon or Emperor Francis)

A sweet cherry. These are heart-shaped and light golden in color. The flesh may be pink to light red. Usually firm and juicy, with excellent flavor. The light-fleshed variety is used commercially in canning.

Bing

A sweet cherry. These are usually very large, heart-shaped, with flesh that ranges in color from deep red to almost black. The skin is usually smooth and glossy.

Schmidt

Similar to a Bing cherry.

Tartarian

A sweet cherry. Very large, heart-shaped, with purplish to black flesh. Very tender and sweet, thin-skinned, and one of the most popular cherries of the mid season.

Chapman

A sweet cherry. Large, round, with purplish-black flesh. Produced from a seedling of the Tartarian variety. The fruit matures early in the season.

Lambert

A very large, usually round cherry with dark to very dark red flesh. Very firm and meaty.

REPORTED HEALTH BENEFITS

Cherries are very high in magnesium, iron, and silicon, making them valuable for treating arthritis and gout, as a blood cleanser, as well as preventing cancer and reducing the risk of heart disease and stroke. They tend to stimulate the secretion of digestive enzymes. Numerous people have reported that consuming eight to 10 Bing cherries per day relieved their symptoms of arthritis, but this claim has not been scientifically substantiated.

COCONUTS

Coconuts are available in many markets year-round. When choosing one, be sure that it's heavy for its size and that you can hear the sound of liquid when you shake it. If the eyes are damp, do not buy it. Coconuts can be refrigerated for up to one month, depending on how fresh they are when purchased. If you are going to grate coconut for a recipe, make sure you first place the meat in the freezer for at least 30 minutes. This will harden the meat and make it easier to grate.

A COCONUT SEPARATION

Coconut juice, or water (the clear liquid inside the fruit), should be removed before you crack open the fruit. First, pierce two of the three eyes with an ice pick. One hole will allow air to enter as the coconut juice comes out the other one.

To separate the outer shell from the inner meat, bake the coconut for about 15 minutes at 400°F, then tap the shell lightly with a hammer. The moisture from the meat will try to escape in the form of steam and will establish a narrow space between the meat and the shell, separating them.

DATES

◆ Dates contain more sugar than any other fruit; some varieties get 70 percent of their dry weight from sugar. Dates are a concentrated source of calories and should not be considered a diet food.

◆ California and Arizona are the major suppliers for the United States; however, Africa and the Middle East have been cultivating dates for 5,000 years. Spaniards brought the date to California in the 17th century.

◆ Date palms need a lot of tender care if they are to produce maximally— about 100 pounds of dates every year.

◆ Dates are classified as either soft, semisoft, or dry. Semisoft dates are the most common ones sold in the United States, and Deglet Noor is the most common semisoft variety. Two of the other popular date varieties are Zahidi and Medjool.

◆ A date cluster can hold between 600 and 1,700 dates and can weigh up to 25 pounds.

◆ Ounce for ounce, dates supply 1,144 percent more potassium than an orange and 165 percent more than a banana.

◆ Medjool dates will last for up to one year if refrigerated.

REPORTED HEALTH BENEFITS
Dates have been used in cases of anemia, to raise low blood pressure, to cure colitis, to relieve constipation and aid digestion, and to improve sexual potency. Crushed dates have been made into syrup for coughs and sore throats.

FIGS

Figs, one of the oldest commonly eaten fruits, are native to Asia Minor. The majority of the figs grown now are sold dried, with less than 10 percent reaching markets in their fresh form. They were brought to California by the Spaniards, and most are still grown in California. The most common variety found in supermarkets is the Calimyrna. Other varieties include Black Mission, Kadota, Brown Turkey, and Smyrna. Dried figs are very high in calories relative to their size. Figs are pollinated by a small fig wasp.

Fig concentrate is sold in health-food stores and some specialty stores. It is a syrupy, seedless puree of figs that is used as a topping for ice cream and to flavor cakes and other desserts.

IS IT TRUE THAT FIGS CAN TENDERIZE A STEAK?

Yes. Fresh figs contain the chemical ficin, which is a proteolytic enzyme, one that is capable of breaking down proteins with an action similar to that of papain (found in papayas) or bromelain (found in pineapples).

Ficin is effective in heat ranges of 140°F to 160°F, which is the temperature range for simmering stews. If fresh figs are added to the stew, they will help tenderize the meat and will impart excellent flavor. Canned figs will not work because they are heated to very high temperatures during the sterilization process.

REPORTED HEALTH BENEFITS
Figs are beneficial for curing constipation, anemia, asthma, gout, and a number of skin irritations. They also help to lower blood pressure, control cholesterol, and prevent colon cancer. Fig juice makes an excellent natural laxative and can be made into a poultice for boils.

GRAPEFRUIT

The heavier the grapefruit, the juicier it will be. Florida grapefruits are usually juicier than those from the southwestern states; however, those grown in the western United States have thicker skins, which makes them easier to peel. When refrigerated, grapefruits should last for up to two weeks. When you buy them, they should be firm and their skin should be unblemished, with no discoloration. Fruits that are somewhat pointed at the end tend to be thick-skinned and have less meat and juice.

White grapefruit has a stronger flavor than the pink variety. Grapefruits from Arizona and California are at their peak from January through August; the Florida and Texas crops are best from October to June.

REPORTED HEALTH BENEFITS
Grapefruit has been used to dissolve the inorganic calcium found in the cartilage of the joints of people with arthritis. Fresh grapefruit contains organic salicylic acid, which is the active agent in aspirin. Grapefruit also relieves cold symptoms, helps prevent cancer, reduces bruising, and helps prevent heart disease and stroke. Recent studies have shown grapefruit pectin to be effective in lowering the LDL cholesterol levels.

GRAPEFRUIT AND DRUGS: DO THEY MIX?

Recent studies have shown that grapefruit will increase the absorption rate of a number of drugs. A researcher at the University of Western Ontario found that grapefruit juice caused a five-fold increase in the

A small amount of salt will make a grapefruit taste sweeter.

absorption rate for a blood pressure medication. Some of the drugs that are affected this way are the calcium-channel blockers Procardia and Adalat, the immunosuppressant Cyclosporine, the short-acting sedative Halcion, and the estrogen Estinyl. Naringen, a substance found in grapefruit, deactivates an enzyme in the small intestine that helps the body metabolize certain drugs.

GRAPES

- The grape industry—growing table, raisin, wine, and juice grapes—is reported to be the largest single food industry in the world.
- All varieties of grapes are really berries and are native to Asia Minor, where they have been cultivated for 6,000 years. Grapes are now grown on six continents. The growing of grapes is known as viticulture. Of all the European varieties grown in the United States, California produces 97 percent and Arizona 3 percent.
- Grapes should be plump and firm and attached to a green stem. They should have good color and should never appear faded.
- Grapes do not ripen off the vine—so if possible, try and taste a grape from the bunch you have selected before you buy. But be aware that this can get you arrested in some stores.
- Grapes will stay fresh only for three to five days, even if refrigerated. They should be stored, unwashed, in a plastic bag in the coldest part of the refrigerator, but they must be washed very well before eating.
- Grapes do not freeze well because they have a high water content and would become mushy when thawed. They can, however, be eaten frozen (they're especially tasty treats), and frozen grapes can be used in cooking. They will keep in the freezer for about one year.

GRAPE VARIETIES

Black Beauty
A seedless black grape.
Calmeria
A green grape with a thick skin and a rich, tangy flavor.
Champagne
These are wonderfully sweet, tiny grapes. You're more likely to find them in gourmet food markets.

Concord
A common variety of American grape. Concords are usually blue-black with a sweet but somewhat tart flavor.

Delaware
A small pink grape with a tender skin.

Emperor
A very popular small grape. They are reddish-purple with small seeds.

Exotic
A blue-black grape with seeds.

Flame Seedless
These are deep red, seedless, and about the same size as the Emperor variety, but somewhat more tart.

Italia
Green-gold, with a sweet, full-bodied flavor. Has seeds.

Niagara
These large, amber-colored grapes may be somewhat egg-shaped and are not as sweet as most other varieties.

Perlette Seedless
A green grape grown in desert areas of California.

Queen
A large red grape that has a mild, sweet flavor.

Red Globe
A very large grape with seeds and a delicate flavor.

Red Malaga
A thick-skinned, reddish grape that is usually fairly sweet.

Ribier
One of the larger grapes. It is blue-black, with tender skin.

Ruby Seedless
A very sweet, deep-red grape.

Steuben
A blue-black grape that resembles the Concord variety.

Thompson Seedless
The most common grape sold in the U.S. and the one most commonly used to make raisins. This is a small, green grape with a sweet flavor.

Tokay
A much sweeter version of the Flame Seedless grape.

THE POPULAR DRIED GRAPE

Raisins are just dried grapes and may be dried either artificially or naturally. They are sold in a number of varieties, such as:

Golden Seedless

These are produced from Thompson Seedless grapes but are somewhat tart. Sulfur dioxide is used to bleach them.

Muscat

These raisins are made from Muscat grapes and are always sun-dried. They are larger than Thompson Seedless, darker in color, and naturally very sweet.

Natural Seedless

Sun-dried, always dark brown in color, and very sweet, these are produced from Thompson Seedless grapes and are the most common variety of raisin.

Sultana

The British word for golden raisin.

Zante Currants

Produced from the black Corinth grape, these are always sun-dried and are smaller than most other grapes. They are dark and somewhat tart. Because of their size, zante currants are used mainly for baking.

CHUBBY RAISIN

To plump raisins, place in a small baking dish with a little water, cover, and bake in a preheated 325°F oven for 6 to 8 minutes. Or, pour boiling water over the raisins and let them stand for 10 to 15 minutes.

HOME OF THE RAISIN

A good half of the raisins eaten in the world are grown in California. The grapes grown there are either sun-dried or mechanically dehydrated. Golden raisins are dried with artificial heat, which makes them plumper.

STORING RAISINS

Raisins will last for several months if they are wrapped tightly in plastic wrap or a plastic bag and kept at room temperature. They will last for up to a year in the refrigerator if kept in a tightly sealed plastic bag.

UNSTICK THOSE RAISINS

Raisins will not stick to knives and such if they are first soaked in cold water for 10 minutes.

HONEYDEW MELON

The most desirable honeydews have creamy white or pale yellow skin with a slightly silky finish. They are at their prime between July and September. A faint smell usually indicates ripeness. The blossom end (opposite from the stem) should be slightly soft. Like most melons, honeydews taste better if left unrefrigerated for a few days; whole ones will keep in the refrigerator for up to five days. Store cut half-melons with their seeds intact in plastic bags and eat them within two days. Do not purchase half-melons whose seeds have been removed unless you intend to eat them the same day.

REPORTED HEALTH BENEFITS
Honeydews have been used to lower the risk of birth defects and heart disease (because of their high levels of folate) and to help keep blood pressure low (because of their potassium).

KIWI

- Although it is now closely connected with New Zealand, the kiwi actually originated in China and was formerly called the Chinese gooseberry. It was brought to New Zealand in 1906 and renamed for the New Zealand bird. It is also grown commercially in California, and because California and New Zealand have opposite seasons, kiwis are available year-round.
- Kiwis are two to three inches long, with a furry brown skin and lime-green flesh. They are easily peeled with a vegetable peeler.
- Firm kiwis, left at room temperature, soften and sweeten in three to five days. To ripen them more quickly, place them in a brown paper bag with an apple or a banana.
- Ripe kiwis feel like ripe peaches. Refrigerated, they stay fresh for weeks.
- Two kiwis contain as much fiber as a half cup of bran flakes, and they are an excellent source of vitamin C.

KIWI, A GREAT MEAT TENDERIZER?

While we are familiar with the tenderizing properties of the enzymes in papaya and pineapple, we rarely hear about the kiwi, which contains the enzyme actinidin, also an excellent meat tenderizer. Pureed fresh kiwis can be used as a marinade for any type of meat or poultry. Rub it on the meat and refrigerate it for about 30 minutes before cooking. The meat will not pick up the kiwi flavor.

Actinidin will also prevent gelatin from setting, so kiwis should not be added to gelatin dishes until just before serving; they should preferably sit on the top. Cooking the fruit, however, will inactivate the enzyme.

LEMONS AND LIMES

DID YOU KNOW?

Ponce de Leon planted lemon trees in Florida in 1513.

◆ Lemons and limes were probably brought to this country by one of the early explorers and were first grown in Florida in about the 16th century. The commercial lemon-growing industry was started in about 1880, and limes were first grown commercially in about 1912. California is now the largest producer of lemons in the United States.

◆ There are two types of lemons, the very tart and the sweet. We are more used to the tart because sweet lemons are cultivated mostly by home gardeners.

◆ Limes and other citrus were first cultivated in India. Key limes are a smaller variety with a higher acid content. The California variety of limes are seedless and known as Bears.

◆ If refrigerated in plastic bags, lemons and limes will last for 10 days. Frozen, both their juice and grated peel will last about four months.

◆ Look for lemons and limes with the smoothest skin and the smallest points on each end. These will have more juice and a better flavor. Also, submerging a lemon or lime in hot water for 15 minutes before squeezing it will produce almost twice as much juice. Warming a lemon in the oven for a few minutes will also work.

◆ If you only need a few drops of juice, puncture one end of a lemon or lime with a skewer, squeeze out the desired amount of juice, and return the fruit to the refrigerator. The hole will seal itself and the rest of the fruit will still be usable.

◆ Lemons and limes will keep longer in the refrigerator if you place them in a clean jar and seal the jar well. After using half of a fruit, store the other half in the freezer in a plastic bag. This reduces the loss of moisture. The texture will suffer, but you'll be able to use the juice.

◆ Using lemon as a flavoring tends to eliminate the craving for additional salt. Lemon and lime skins contain the oil limonene, which may cause skin irritations in susceptible people.

> **REPORTED HEALTH BENEFITS**
> The flesh—but not the skin—of lemons and limes is an astringent. It can be used as a diuretic, an antioxidant that blocks cancer, and to heal cuts and bruises. It is used as a natural antiseptic to destroy harmful bacteria and as a topical agent for relief of acne and other skin irritations.

THE MYTH REGARDING LIME JUICE

In Latin America, marinating raw fish in lime juice is common. The dish called ceviche is made from raw fish or shellfish marinated in lime juice. Don't believe that the acid in lime juice is strong enough to kill bacteria. Lime juice will not kill E.coli, nor will it kill any parasites that are in the fish's flesh. If the raw fish is commercially frozen well below 0°F for three days, it may be safe to eat.

MAMEY

Sometimes called the national fruit of Cuba, the mamey resembles a small coconut. It has a brown, suede-like skin and bright yellow flesh. The pulp is scooped out and eaten or added to milk and made into a shake.

MANGOES

◆ Mangoes originated in India, which is still the largest producer. Mangoes come in hundreds of varieties and a number of shapes and sizes. The majority of the mangoes sold in the United States are imported from Mexico, Central America, and Hawaii. Only about 10 percent of the commercially sold fruit is grown in Florida.

◆ The most popular mango variety is the Tommy Atkins.

◆ The flavor of mangoes is somewhat of a combination of peach and pineapple, with a flowery aroma.

◆ Mangoes are at their peak from May to September and are an excellent source of vitamins A and C. They are also one of the best sources of beta-carotene, containing 36 percent more per serving than cantaloupes and 66 percent more per serving than apricots.

◆ Mangoes will last for a couple of days if refrigerated in a plastic bag. Underripe fruit can be placed in a paper bag and ripened at room temperature for a few days.

REPORTED HEALTH BENEFITS
Mangoes may help to alleviate the symptoms of kidney diseases as well as to reduce acidity and aid digestion. They are also used for reducing fevers and asthmatic symptoms, and they prevent heart disease and cancer. When crushed and made into a paste, they help to cleanse the pores of the skin.

NECTARINES

◆ Nectarines have been around for hundreds of years. The Greeks gave them the name nectar, from which nectarine is derived.

◆ There are more than 150 varieties worldwide, and California grows 98 percent of all nectarines sold in the United States. Their peak season is July and August.

◆ Nectarines are related to peaches. Their color should be brilliant yellow, blushed with red.

◆ Avoid very hard, dull-looking nectarines. If they are too hard, allow them to ripen at room temperature for a few days; the fruits will not ripen in the refrigerator.

REPORTED HEALTH BENEFITS
Nectarines are used as a digestive aid and to relieve flatulence. They have been used to lower blood pressure and to alleviate the symptoms of arthritis.

ORANGES

◆ Commercial orange growing began to thrive when the United States acquired Florida in 1821. Oranges were first grown commercially in St. Augustine, Florida, in 1820. Florida now grows more citrus than any other state and still produces 70 percent of the Unites States' orange crop.

◆ The color of an orange does not necessarily indicate its quality, because oranges are sometimes dyed to improve their appearance. Brown spots on the skin, in fact, indicate a good-quality orange.

- Pick a sweet orange by examining the navel; those with the largest navel will usually be the best. If you place an orange in a hot oven for two to three minutes before peeling it, the pectin will melt into the flesh and no white fibers will be visible.
- Mandarins are a very close relative to the orange. They peel more easily, have more pronounced sections, and come in a number of varieties.
- The zests of citrus fruits should be stored in a tightly sealed jar and refrigerated. They may be grated and used for flavoring cakes, frostings, and cookies. However, you should remove the zest before you cut the fruit; it is very difficult to zest a citrus fruit after it has been sliced or halved.

GREEN ORANGES?

Oranges that look green have undergone a natural process called regreening, which occurs when a ripe orange absorbs chlorophyll pigment from the leaves. Such oranges are usually very sweet and make excellent eating. Florida oranges are normally greener than oranges from California or Arizona because the warm Florida days and nights allow the orange to retain more of the chlorophyll. A number of companies that sell Florida oranges dye them because we tend to think they are not ripe. When oranges are dyed they must be labeled "Color Added" on the shipping container. The cooler nights in California and Arizona remove the green; however, both states have laws prohibiting adding any color to citrus fruits.

THE NO-WASTE ORANGE

The orange-juice industry uses every bit of every orange it processes. Everything, including the pulp, seeds, and peel, is used in food products such as candy, cake mixes, and soft drinks.

ORANGE JUICE AND ANTACIDS DON'T MIX

If you take antacid that contains aluminum, avoid any kind of citrus juice for at least three hours. A half cup of orange juice can cause a ten-fold increase in the absorption of the aluminum from antacids. Aluminum can collect in tissues, and at high levels, it may affect your health.

Did You Know?

The word "orange" comes from the Sanskrit word "naranga," which means "fragrance."

HOW DO YOU MAKE ORANGE JUICE FIZZ?

Add ¼ teaspoon of baking soda to eight to 10 ounces of orange juice, lemonade, or any other acidic fruit drink. Stir the drink well, and it will do a great deal of fizzing, much to children's delight. It will also reduce the acidity level of the drink.

ORANGE VARIETIES

Blood
Has blood-red flesh derived from anthocyanin pigments and is sweet and juicy. Blood oranges are grown in California.

Hamlin
Grown primarily in Florida and best used for juicing. The Hamlin averages 46 milligrams of vitamin C per 3.5-ounce serving.

Jaffa
Imported from Israel and similar to the Valencia, but sweeter.

Navel
A large, thick-skinned orange that is easily identified by its "belly button," located at the blossom end. It is seedless and sweet, easily peeled, and a favorite in the United States.

Parson Brown
A good juice orange from Florida. This variety averages 50 milligrams of vitamin C per 3.5-ounce serving.

Pineapple
These oranges were named for their aroma, which is similar to that of a pineapple. They are very flavorful and juicy, and average 55 milligrams of vitamin C per 3.5-ounce serving.

Temple
A sweet-tasting juice orange that averages 50 milligrams of vitamin C per 3.5-ounce serving.

Valencia
The most widely grown of any orange, Valencias are used mostly for juice. They average 50 milligrams of vitamin C per 3.5-ounce serving.

REPORTED HEALTH BENEFITS
Oranges are recommended for relief of asthma, bronchitis, arthritis, and to reduce high blood pressure. They can lower the risk of heart disease and stroke, stop inflammation, and fight cancer. Drinking orange juice reduces the desire for alcohol.

PAPAYAS

◆ The papaya is sometimes called the pawpaw, but they are two different fruits. Papayas are native to North America and are now grown extensively in Hawaii, the continental United States, and Mexico.

◆ The fruit can weigh from one-half pound to as much as 20 pounds and comes in a variety of shapes, from pear to oblong.

◆ Papaya seeds are edible and can be used as a garnish for fruit salads or to make salad dressings. They may also be dried, ground, and used as you would pepper.

◆ Hawaiian papayas are the sweetest and those most commonly found in markets. Mexican papayas are much larger and not as sweet.

◆ Papayas contain the enzyme papain, which is an excellent meat tenderizer. Only papayas that are not fully ripe contain sufficient papain to be useful for tenderizing; the riper the papaya, the less papain it contains. The leaves also contain this enzyme, and in Hawaii meat is commonly wrapped in papaya leaves for cooking.

◆ When ripe, papayas are completely yellow. They will take three to five days to ripen at room temperature.

REPORTED HEALTH BENEFITS
Papayas are used to reduce the risk of heart disease and cancer, and to aid digestion because the enzyme papain is also an intestinal cleanser. The juice has been used to relieve infections of the colon and has a tendency to break down mucus.

PEACHES

◆ Peaches are native to China. They were brought to the United States in the 1600s and planted along the eastern seaboard. They have been grown commercially in the States since the 1800s. Although the first commercial peach plantings were in Virginia, it is Georgia that has become known as the Peach State.

◆ To ripen peaches, place them in a box covered with newspaper or in a paper bag. The gasses they give off will be sealed in and the peaches will ripen in two to three days.

◆ Peaches rarely get sweeter after they are picked; they will just become softer and more edible.

◆ Peach skins are easily removed with a vegetable peeler. Also, you can put them in boiling water for a few seconds and the skins will peel off.

◆ There are two main varieties of peaches: clingstone and freestone. The clingstones are best for canning, making preserves, and general cooking. The freestones are the best for eating because the meat separates easily from the pit.

◆ Peaches are an excellent source of vitamin C and are available in many varieties, the favorite being the Alberta.

◆ Never cook peaches with the pit in, because it may impart a bitter taste to the finished dish. The reddish area around the pit may also be bitter and should be removed as well.

WHERE DID THE FUZZY PEACHES GO?

The facial hair of young boys nearing the age when they start shaving has been dubbed peach fuzz, after the fuzzy skin of the fruit that is a nuisance to many people who otherwise love peaches. The peach industry, unable to develop a fuzzless peach, has come up with a machine that gently brushes the surface of the peach, removing most of the fuzz.

> **REPORTED HEALTH BENEFITS**
> Peaches are valuable for curing anemia because of their high vitamin and mineral content. They have also been used to reduce high blood pressure as well as to cure bronchitis, skin ailments like boils and carbuncles, constipation, congestion, fever, asthma, bladder and kidney stones, and for de-worming.

PEARS

◆ Pear trees, which were brought to the Americas by early European settlers, will live and produce for approximately 90 years.

◆ Pears are actually a member of the rose family.

◆ Pears are an excellent source of fiber.

◆ One medium-sized pear provides about 10 percent of the daily requirement for vitamin C—but because most of this nutrient is concentrated in the skin, pears should not be peeled before eating.

◆ Ripen pears by placing them in a brown-paper bag with a ripe apple for two to three days. Punch a few holes in the bag and leave it in a cool, dry spot. Apples give off ethylene gas, which will help speed the ripening of most fruits. As pears ripen, their starch content turns to sugar and they may become somewhat mealy.

PEAR VARIETIES

Anjou

A winter pear with a smooth, yellow-green skin, the Anjou is not as sweet as most other pears.

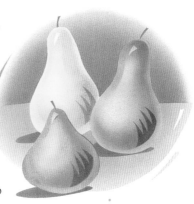

Bartlett

A summer pear and one of the most popular in the United States, accounting for 65 percent of all commercial production. The Bartlett pear is large and juicy and is best when purchased golden-yellow or allowed to ripen to that stage.

Bosc

Has a brown skin and long, tapering neck. Excellent for baking.

Comice

This is the sweetest pear and a favorite for dessert recipes. This is the pear that is usually found in gift baskets.

Other pear varieties include Red Bartlett, Seckel, Asian Pear, and Clapp.

> **REPORTED HEALTH BENEFITS**
> Pears are excellent for constipation and as a digestive aid.
> They lower cholesterol, improve memory and alertness, and keep bones strong, and have also been used to cure skin irritations.

PERSIMMONS

The persimmon is a native of Japan, and is widely grown there. Persimmons are high in vitamins and minerals but have never really caught on as a popular fruit in the United States. The Japanese persimmons sold in the United States are Hachiya and Fuyu. The Fuyu is the smaller of the two and is shaped like a tomato.

Persimmons are available in markets from October through February. They have a smooth, shiny, bright-orange skin, which is very sour and should be removed before eating.

REMOVING THE PUCKER FROM PERSIMMONS

Persimmons are high in tannins and, therefore, very astringent. That astringency is somewhat dissipated when the fruit ripens, and the Fuyu in particular is not at all astringent when ripe. Persimmons should be very soft, almost liquid, when fully ripe. They smell luscious and sweet.

PINEAPPLE

◆ Pineapples originated in South America and were brought to the Hawaiian Islands for cultivation in the 1700s. The pineapple became the main crop of Hawaii and was canned there for the first time.

◆ Pineapples are similar to melons in that the starch, which converts to sugar as a fruit ripens, is found only in the stem until just before the fruit reaches maturity. The starch then converts to sugar and enters the fruit.

◆ The fruit will not become any sweeter after it is picked.

◆ To check for ripeness, gently pull out a leaf anywhere on the stem. If the leaf comes out easily, the pineapple is ripe. It should also smell sweet.

◆ Pineapples are available year-round, but are best from March through July. Buy ones that are as large and heavy as possible, and be sure the leaves are deep green. Do not purchase pineapples with soft spots, and refrigerate them as soon as possible.

◆ Fresh pineapple contains the enzyme bromelain, which will prevent gelatin from setting. This enzyme may also be used as a meat tenderizer. Future studies may also show that bromelain is effective in reducing arterial plaque.

◆ Keeping a pineapple at room temperature for a few days will reduce the acidity, though the fruit will not become any sweeter.

DRIED PINEAPPLE FROM TAIWAN

Most of the dried pineapple sold in the United States is imported from Taiwan and is saturated with refined sugar. The sugar-sweetened dried pineapple will be very plump and will have a coating of sugar crystals, while the naturally sweetened dried pineapple will look somewhat mottled and fibrous, and will lack the surface crystals.

DID YOU KNOW?

Always rinse fruit before cutting it to get rid of any traces of pesticides that might remain on the skin.

PLUMS

- There are hundreds of varieties of plums grown worldwide. The majority of the United States' crop is the Santa Rosa variety, which was developed by Luther Burbank in 1907.
- Dried plums are prunes.
- Plums are available from May through October. Buy only firm to slightly soft plums; hard plums will not ripen well.
- The flavor of plums ranges from sweet to tart.
- To ripen plums, allow them to stand at room temperature until fairly soft. Do not place them in a window where they will be in direct sunlight, as this will dissipate what little vitamin C they have.
- Plums should be refrigerated after ripening and last for only two to three days.

REPORTED HEALTH BENEFITS
Plums are used for liver disorders and constipation, as well as to relieve flatulence and bronchitis and to heal cold sores.

WE'VE BEEN HOODWINKED

The traditional English plum pudding no longer contains plums. Today this tasty steamed cake is filled with currants and raisins.

POMEGRANATE

This has always been a difficult fruit to eat and has never gained popularity. The seeds and pulp are edible (though the pulp is quite bitter), but it is best to juice the fruit to obtain its vitamins and minerals. Pomegranate juice is used to flavor grenadine syrup. Pomegranates are an excellent source of potassium and are available from October through November.

REPORTED HEALTH BENEFITS
Pomegranates are used as a blood purifier and for worm infestations, especially tapeworm. They may also have some benefit for alleviating the symptoms of arthritis.

PRICKLY PEAR

The prickly pear is a type of cactus fruit. It has a green to purple-red skin and light-yellow to deep-golden flesh, and is covered with spines. It has a sweet, somewhat bland taste, similar to that of watermelon, and a melon-like aroma. Other names it may go by are Indian fig and barberry fig.

SAPOTE

Also called chayote or custard apple (and, in Louisiana, mirliton), these fruits have a greenish-yellow, scaly skin and creamy, white pulp. They are a good source of vitamin A and potassium.

STAR APPLE

Also called caimito, this fruit has a skin that is usually dull purple or light green. A cross section reveals a star shape. The star apple is used in jellies and is eaten like an apple.

TANGELO

These were produced by crossing a grapefruit with a tangerine. They have pinkish-orange flesh, are nearly seedless, and are sweeter than grapefruits. Sometimes called Ugli fruit, the tangelo originated in Jamaica and is now grown in Florida. Choose a fruit that is heavy in the hand. It has a yellow, pebbly skin with green blotches that turns orange when the fruit ripens. They make excellent eating and are high in vitamin C, but they look ugli!

WATERMELON

- ◆ The exterior of a ripe watermelon should be a smooth, waxy green, with or without stripes.
- ◆ If the watermelon has been cut, choose one with a bright, crisp, even-colored flesh. Whole melons will keep in the refrigerator for no longer than one week. Once cut, they should be kept refrigerated and covered with plastic wrap.
- ◆ A good test for ripeness is to snap your thumb and third finger against the melon; if you hear a sound like "pink" in a high tone, the melon is not ripe. If you hear "punk" in a deep, low tone, the melon is more likely to be ready to eat and should be sweet.

WATERMELON POPCORN?

In China, watermelon seeds are a treat and are roasted, salted, and eaten like popcorn. But there's a catch with this tasty snack. Watermelon seeds happen to be a high-fat treat, with 65 percent of the 535 calories in a 100 gram serving coming from fat.

INSULATOR

It's likely that a watermelon is going to be the biggest food item you try to squeeze into the fridge. If you're pressed for refrigerator space, a chilled watermelon will stay cold in a double brown-paper bag for up to one hour.

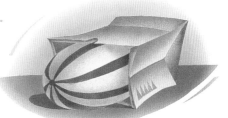

WHAT ARE THE TOP 20 NUTRITIOUS VEGETABLES?

The list of vegetables in the chart below starts with the most nutritious and is based on how much of the 10 most important nutrients—protein, iron, calcium, niacin, vitamins A and C, potassium, phosphorus, thiamine, and riboflavin—they contain. Each of the vegetables listed contains all 10 of these valuable nutrients.

The Top Twenty		
1. Collard greens	11.	Mustard greens
2. Lima beans	12.	Swiss chard
3. Peas	13.	Parsley
4. Spinach	14.	Tomatoes
5. Sweet potatoes	15.	Corn
6. Turnip greens	16.	Beet greens
7. Winter squash	17.	Pumpkin
8. Broccoli	18.	Okra
9. Kale	19.	Potatoes
10. Brussels sprouts	20.	Carrots

THE EGGPLANT OF THE MUSHROOM WORLD

Puffball mushrooms can be found dried or can be picked from the forest floor during the hot, humid, summer months. They are called the eggplant of the mushroom world because they are very large, and their flesh is similar to the eggplant's.

VEGGIE STATS

The following are the latest (1997) statistics on the consumption of vegetables in the United States:

Per Capita Consumption of Vegetables	
VEGETABLE	POUNDS
Potatoes	87
Lettuce	29
Onions	17
Tomatoes	18
Carrots	8
Sweet potatoes	7
Broccoli	4

WHAT IS CHOW-CHOW?

Popular in the southern United States, chow-chow is a relish made from chopped vegetables—usually cabbage, peppers, cucumbers, and onions. It is packed in a sugar-and-vinegar solution and seasoned with pickling spices. It is typically served with meats and sausages.

WHAT IS A JOHNNYCAKE?

Johnnycake is a homemade bread or pancake made from cornmeal, salt, and cold milk or boiling water. It originated with Native Americans, and the name is derived from the Indian word "joniken." Purists believe that johnnycake can be made only with a special type of low-yield Indian corn from Rhode Island, called flint corn.

REDUCE THE RISK OF STROKE

A study of 800 middle-aged men who participated in the Framingham Heart Study found that those who ate three servings of vegetables a day reduced their risk of stroke by 22 percent.

AROMATIC VEGETABLES?

The carrot family includes more than 3,000 species, many of which—including coriander, anise, cumin, dill, caraway, fennel, and parsley—have strongly scented, oil-rich seeds.

WHAT ARE THE BEST GREENS?

The following vegetables are listed in descending order of the nutritional value provided by a half cup cooked portion, except where noted.

How Greens Rate			
VITAMIN A (IU)		**CALCIUM (milligrams)**	
Spinach	7,371	Turnip greens	99
Dandelion Greens	6,084	Dandelion greens	73
Kale	4,810	Swiss chard	51
Turnip greens	3,959	Kale	47
Beet greens	3,672	Arugula (raw)	16
Mustard greens	2,122	**IRON (milligrams)**	
Arugula (raw)	237	Spinach	3.21
VITAMIN C (milligrams)		Beet greens	1.37
Kale	27	Dandelion greens	0.94
Turnip greens	20	**FIBER (grams)**	
Mustard greens	18	Turnip greens	2.5
Dandelion greens	10	Spinach	2.2
Spinach	9	Mustard greens	1.4
Arugula (raw)	2	Kale	1.3

CHOOSING THE MOST NUTRITIOUS GREENS

Dandelion

Young leaves are the best. Buy them from a reputable source to be sure they have not been exposed to weed killers.

Arugula

Has a slightly peppery flavor. Often used in salad blends.

Kale

Young leaves are the best. Look for thin stems and small, frilly leaves. Best in winter.

Romaine

One of the best lettuces.

Spinach

High in nutrients, but contains oxalates.

Beet

Small, young leaves are best.

Endive

A type of chicory that grows in a smaller, cone-shaped head. Very pale leaves, somewhat bitter flavor.

A CANCER-CAUSING FERN THAT LOOKS LIKE ASPARAGUS

There is an asparagus look-alike fern that is sometimes difficult to distinguish from real asparagus. This is a dangerous coincidence, because the look-alike fern contains a potentially cancer-causing agent called quercetin, or ptaquiloside. Occasionally, cows will eat the fern and develop bone-marrow damage as well as inflammation of the bladder membranes.

SOME VEGGIES MAY FORM CARCINOGENS FROM NITRITES

Certain vegetables—including cabbage, cauliflower, lettuce, beets, celery, eggplant, radishes, spinach, and collard and turnip greens—contain nitrites that, when they enter the stomach, may convert to nitrosamines, which are known carcinogens. An adult with a healthy immune system will not have a problem with these foods, although they may not be recommended for infants whose intestinal tracts do not yet contain the acid-producing bacteria necessary to inhibit nitrite formation.

ARE FIDDLEHEAD FERNS SAFE TO EAT?

The young fronds of the fiddlehead fern (also known as ostrich fern) are shaped like the scroll at the end of a violin. Fiddleheads are about two inches long and about $1\frac{1}{2}$ inches in diameter. Their texture is similar to that of green beans, with a flavor somewhere between asparagus and green beans. Fiddleheads are safe to eat if cooked; they can be stir-fried or steamed, but they should never be eaten raw. Cook fiddleheads for no more than 5 minutes for best flavor and texture.

NO FROST ON THE PUMPKINS

Frost on pumpkins is a nice image in a poem, but frost on packages of frozen vegetables is not. It's a sign that the food has thawed and refrozen, and a percentage of moisture has already been lost. The fact that one package of a particular product is damaged indicates there's a good chance the rest of the shipment has also deteriorated.

DOES COOKING CHANGE GARLIC?

When garlic is heated, the sulfur compound diallyl disulfide, which provides its unique flavor, is partially destroyed. If garlic is allowed to sprout, most of this chemical will enter the new sprouts and the garlic will become milder. Always discard sprouts before cooking the garlic, though, as they are very bitter.

STORING COOKED VEGETABLES

The best way to store cooked vegetables is in tightly sealed plastic containers in the refrigerator, where they will last three to five days. To freeze cooked vegetables, seal them in an airtight freezer bag or in a container from which most of the air has been removed.

Because cells will burst when vegetables thaw, releasing some of their liquid, they will be a bit soggy when thawed, but they can be used in soups and stews. Vegetables frozen this way will last from 10 to 12 months.

DON'T BE FOOLED

Lots of snack chips made from vegetables other than potatoes have come onto the market in the last few years, but many are no more healthful than everyday potato chips—most are fried in oil. Any fried chip will be high in calories and fat and almost devoid of nutritional value. If the chip is baked, it will have fewer calories; however, because of the high heat used in baking, the nutritional value will be significantly reduced.

TENDERIZING VEGETABLES

The major component in the cell walls of fruits and vegetables is a complex carbohydrate called cellulose. The higher the cellulose content, the firmer the fruit or vegetable. Heat and moisture weaken the cell wall's ability to retain and release moisture, which causes a structural breakdown resulting in tenderness. (Heat and moisture also dissolve some of the pectin that holds the cell walls together.) Some veggies, however, have different levels of cellulose in various parts. Stems have more than tips, which is why it is necessary to peel the stems before cooking broccoli; otherwise the tips become mushy by the time the stalks are tender.

LOSING COLOR IN VEGETABLES

The acid that is released in vegetables during the cooking process causes a chemical reaction that results in a loss of pigment. After a while, the cooking liquid may deplete the acid and turn alkaline, changing the color of the vegetable again. In green vegetables, the acid that is released reacts with the chlorophyll, lightening the color. In red cabbage the pigment anthocyanin may change from red to purple, depending on the acid or alkaline nature of the liquid. Adding baking soda to the water will help reduce and neutralize the effects of the acid and keep some vegetables close to their natural color, but it will also destroy a number of vitamins, especially C and thiamine. The best way to make make sure vegetables keep their original color is to steam them.

NEW NAMES TO LEARN

Cross breeding has produced new vegetables, such as broccoflower, the cross between a broccoli and a cauliflower. Sea vegetables have been eaten in other countries for a long time, but they are new to American markets. Two that you might find are wakame and kombu, which are derived from seaweed and have a very high mineral content.

DID YOU KNOW?

Another name for cellulose is insoluble fiber.

MAKING THE GRADE

All canned, frozen, and dried fruits and vegetables are sold in three grades: U.S. Grade A Fancy; U.S. Grade B, or Extra Standard; and U.S. Grade C Standard. Grades B and C are just as nutritious as Grade A but have more blemishes.

FRESH PRODUCE GRADING

Fresh fruits and vegetables can also be found in three grades: U.S. Fancy, U.S. Fancy #1, and U.S. Fancy #2. These grades are determined by the product's size, color, shape, maturity, and the number of visible defects.

NO MORE SOGGY SALADS

You will never have another soggy salad if you just place an inverted saucer in the bottom of the salad bowl. The excess water that is left after washing the vegetables and greens will drain under the saucer and leave the greens high and dry.

THE JURY'S OUT

To salt the cooking water or not? Some feel that salting the water when cooking a vegetable will draw out some of the liquid; this may change the consistency, and the food may not cook evenly. Others, however, believe that salting improves the flavor of the vegetables, and that the vegetables absorb a minimal amount of salt—the sodium content will not be appreciably affected. If you do decide to cook vegetables in salted water, the proper ratio is 1½ tablespoons salt to 4 quarts water.

PAIN IN THE JOINT

A study conducted by Rutgers University has found an association between arthritis pain and the ingestion of solanine. Solanine is a toxin that forms just under the skin of potatoes that have been exposed to light during storage; the potatoes' skin turns green in places. If you cut away the green parts, though, the potatoes are safe to eat.

HARMFUL LITTLE CRITTERS

Home-canned vegetables should always be cooked before eating because bacterial contamination is very common.

NO NEED TO WORRY

The thyroid gland is very sensitive to certain chemicals. Cabbage, turnips, kale, watercress, and rapeseed (the source of canola oil) contain a harmful chemical called a thioglucoside, which may adversely affect the gland. But this chemical is destroyed by cooking, and the role of these substances in goiter appears to be minimal.

KEEP YOUR BONES STRONG

Certain plants, such as spinach, beet greens, chard, and rhubarb, are high in oxalic acid, which may inhibit the body from absorbing the calcium these vegetables contain. If you eat a dish with both spinach and cheese, such as lasagna, your body will still be able to absorb the calcium from the cheese. In a balanced diet that includes adequate amounts of calcium, the binding that occurs is not believed to be a problem.

EATING VEGETABLES? STAY INSIDE

Parsnips, fava beans, and sweet potatoes contain a chemical called phytoalexin, which may cause your skin to become sensitive to sunlight.

CLEAN 'EM UP REAL GOOD

During a routine sampling of domestic and imported produce in 1996, the FDA found pesticide residues in 33 percent of the 3,750 vegetables tested. The FDA, however, can test only about 1 percent of all vegetables sold in the United States. Laws regarding the use of pesticides are not very well regulated in most foreign countries.

GIMME AIR

Wrap all produce loosely; air circulating around fruits and vegetables reduces spoilage. A sealed perforated plastic bag is ideal.

MAD SCIENTIST

Avoid using baking soda around fruits and vegetables. Baking soda is alkaline, and many fruits and vegetables are somewhat acidic. Cooking vegetables in baking soda results in mushy texture and reduces the vitamin C and thiamine content of the veggies.

RENDER UNTO CAESAR

The Caesar salad was not invented in France by a renowned chef. It was named after a restaurateur named Caesar Cardini, who lived in Tijuana, Mexico. One day he ran out of food, so he put everything he had left over in the restaurant in the bowl and served it as Caesar salad. Egg substitutes may be used to replace the raw eggs in a Caesar salad in order to eliminate the risk of salmonella poisoning.

PEA-YEW!

Unless you really like the smell, try placing a few unshelled pecans in your saucepan when cooking kale, cabbage, or collard greens to reduce the odor. When cooking onions or cabbage, boil a small amount of vinegar in another pan to eliminate the odor. Take care you don't overcook the vegetables so they won't get odoriferous.

GETTING THE LITTLE CRITTERS OUT

When washing vegetables, place a small amount of salt in a sink full of cold water to draw out any sand and insects.

SWEETENS THEM UP TOO

Caramelizing vegetables will make the flavors and colors more intense. If you toss them in extra virgin olive oil and roast them in a 400°F oven for 10 to 30 minutes, they should turn a nice golden brown. The plus of caramelizing: great flavor. The minus: A big loss of nutrients.

JUST A WEE BIT

Adding a small amount of salt to vegetables while they are cooking will bring out their flavor. This is especially true for corn.

STAMP OUT SOG

If your uncooked celery, carrots, or potatoes get soft and limp, put them in a bowl of water with ice cubes and set them in the refrigerator for 45 minutes. Sometimes adding a small amount of lemon juice also helps.

MOLD-AWAY

It is always a good idea to line the crisper bins of your refrigerator with a few paper towels to absorb excess moisture. Mold spores love moisture.

POPULARITY CONTEST

The most popular salad items are tomatoes, cucumbers, and carrots, in that order. The least popular are lima beans and peas.

SHAPE UP!

Baking stuffed apples, tomatoes, or bell peppers in well-greased muffin tins will help them to hold their shape.

ARTICHOKES

DID YOU KNOW?

To crisp cut-up greens, soak them in cold water for 15 to 20 minutes.

- ◆ The artichoke originated in Italy and was brought to the United States in the 1800s. Almost all of the artichokes sold in the United States are grown in California.
- ◆ The artichoke is actually the unopened flower bud of a thistle-like plant. The most tender and edible part is the heart or center of the plant. Artichokes tend to vary in size, but size does not indicate quality.
- ◆ There are 50 varieties, and it is best to purchase them from March through May. Choose those with compact, tightly closed heads and green, clean-looking leaves. Avoid ones that have brown leaves or show signs of mold. Leaves that are separated indicate that the artichoke is old and will be tough and bitter.
- ◆ Wear rubber gloves when working with artichokes to avoid being pricked by the sharp ends of their leaves. Artichokes should never be cooked in an aluminum pot as the metal can turn them gray.
- ◆ Artichokes should be steamed or cooked in boiling salted water; however, they are also easy to overcook. Use stainless steel knives to cut them; carbon blades tend to react with the chemicals in the artichoke and darken the flesh.
- ◆ For best flavor, add a small amount of salt to the cooking water. The artichokes will be sweeter and will retain their color better.
- ◆ Artichokes can be refrigerated in a plastic bag for up to one week.

THE PROPER WAY TO EAT AN ARTICHOKE

This large, globelike vegetable tends to scare people away, and many people never get to taste one. When you eat an artichoke, remember that the part to eat is the flesh at the *base* of the leaf. The rest of the leaf is bitter and tough. Place the leaf in your mouth upside-down and draw it through your front teeth, removing the tender meat. After eating all the leaves, you will be left with the choke and the heart of the artichoke. Scrape way the hairy choke and eat the succulent heart with a fork.

ARTICHOKES: A REAL SWEET TREAT

Artichokes contain the chemical cyanarin, which stimulates the taste buds that are linked to sweetness and keeps them stimulated for three to four minutes—but only in people who have a genetic predisposition to be sensitive to cyanarin. Any food that these people consume immediately after eating an artichoke will, therefore, taste sweet. To avoid this aftertaste, rinse your mouth with water after eating an artichoke.

THE COLOR OF ARTICHOKES

When an artichoke is cooked, the chlorophyll in the leaves reacts with the acids in the artichoke and forms the compound pheophytin, which turns the leaves olive-brown. This is why many cooked artichokes have a bronze tint. Much research has been conducted to preserve the green color, but nothing has been found that really does the trick.

A few methods to try include rubbing the leaves with the cut side of a lemon after they have been trimmed, or soaking the artichokes for 20 to 30 minutes in a quart of water with 1½ tablespoons of white vinegar. The vinegar will stabilize the chemical that produces the color—and not only that, it will also improve their taste.

REPORTED HEALTH BENEFITS
The juice of artichoke leaves has been used as a powerful diuretic as well as to treat liver disorders and to relieve bad breath. Other uses include relieving arthritis, atherosclerosis, liver problems, memory loss, neuritis, and glandular disorders.

ASPARAGUS

- Asparagus can be traced back to ancient Greece and has been referred to as the aristocrat of vegetables. A member of the lily family, it is excellent source of vitamins and minerals.
- There are two types of asparagus: white and green. White asparagus is planted under a mound of soil that prevents the sun from reaching the vegetable, so photosynthesis cannot take place.
- Canned asparagus contains less vitamin C than fresh because the nutrient is dissipated by the heat used in the canning process and by the water in the can. If you use the water in the can in other dishes, you can retrieve some of the heat-sensitive and water-soluble nutrients.
- The stalks of large asparagus spears may be fibrous and should be peeled. Asparagus loses approximately 50 percent of its vitamin C content along with some of its sugars within two days of picking. Fresh asparagus should be eaten within a day of purchase.
- Put asparagus in a pitcher of water, then refrigerate. Refrigeration will help to retain the nutrients. As the natural sugars are lost, the asparagus becomes tougher.
- When choosing asparagus, look for stalks that are green, with compact, closed tips. Avoid flat stalks or those that contain white streaks.
- The best time of year to purchase asparagus is March through June.
- To freeze asparagus, remove the bottom 2 inches of the stalk and blanch the vegetable in boiling water for 2 to 4 minutes or steam it for 3 to 5 minutes, depending on the thickness of the stalks. Freeze it first on a tray or baking sheet before transferring it to a plastic bag to keep the tips in good condition.
- The greener—or whiter—the asparagus, the more tender it will be.
- Asparagus contains a sulfur compound that develops an unpleasant odor during the digestive process. Everyone who eats asparagus excretes this compound in their urine, but the ability to smell this odor varies from one person to the next.

MALE AND FEMALE ASPARAGUS

The male asparagus flower has a stamen that produces a spore. The female asparagus flower has a pistil, or ovary. Male asparagus plants are higher yielding than female plants.

TOPSY-TURVY

Asparagus is usually canned upside down; it would be wise to read the top of the can before opening it.

CHOP, CHOP

If you've overcooked your asparagus, try cutting it into small pieces and adding it to a can of creamed soup.

THIS WILL STRAIGHTEN THEM OUT

Raw asparagus spears that are too limp can be revived by soaking them in cold water with ice cubes for 30 to 45 minutes.

THE TASTIER, THE BETTER

The flavor of fresh asparagus is one of the pleasures of spring. But if you ever want to doctor the taste, try adding a bouillon cube or a small amount of soy sauce to the cooking water.

> **REPORTED HEALTH BENEFITS**
> Asparagus juice has been used to break up oxalic acid crystals in the kidneys. It has also been used to alleviate symptoms of arthritis and hypertension, and as a cure for lip sores, blackheads, and constipation.

EDIBLE-POD BEANS

◆ Edible-pod beans are picked before they are fully ripe, as the inner seed (bean) is just starting to form. These immature seeds contain high levels of beta-carotene and vitamin C. The dried seeds are high in protein and carbohydrates.

◆ Bean pods may be green, purple, or yellow; the best for eating will have no scars or discolorations.

◆ When broken open, beans should have a crisp snap. Beans are available year-round, but are best from May through August.

◆ Refrigerate beans whole to retain their nutrient content. Never leave beans soaking in water.

DID YOU KNOW?

Since the 1950s, Americans have reduced their purchase of fresh vegetables by 12 percent and increased their purchase of frozen and canned by 50 percent.

239

LEGUMES: A PAIN IN THE ABDOMEN?

Almost all legumes, including beans, peas, and lentils, contain a substance called lectin, which can cause abdominal pain, nausea, diarrhea, and severe indigestion. To destroy the lectin, legumes must be cooked at a rolling boil for 10 minutes before lowering the heat to a simmer. Peas and lentils need to boil for only 2 to 3 minutes.

CHILI-MAKING: IT'S BEAN A SECRET

The first secret to making chili is to soften any beans you add without having them fall apart. The cell walls have to be weakened and the starch granules have to be gelatinized. Initially, the beans are soaked in water for three to four hours. The beans are then cooked in boiling water with ⅛ teaspoon of baking soda (per cup of dried beans) until they are tender but not too mushy. The texture of the beans will remain more stable if the cooking is performed in a somewhat alkaline solution. That is why you add the baking soda to the cooking water. Chili sauce is acidic, and the beans will not continue to soften after they are added to the sauce. Many cooks who try to save time rely on the acidic chili sauce to complete the cooking of the beans and end up with hard beans.

ROASTED BEANS

Only two legumes—soybeans and peanuts—are commonly roasted. This is because their high oil content compensates for the dryness that occurs during roasting. When roasted, both legumes change flavor and texture. The low water content and high temperature used for roasting are responsible for the browning of the outer coating.

Soak the beans for 12 hours, and then drain the water and roast at 250°F for 1 hour 10 minutes, stirring occasionally to avoid burning the surface before the inside is done.

GOODBYE TO FLATULENCE

After eating beans, there's often the problem of flatulence. Gas is produced by the fermentation of complex sugars called raffinose sugars, which are found in beans and some other vegetables. The small intestine does not have the proper enzyme to break down this sugar, so it passes into the large intestine, where bacteria break it down and ferment it, producing hydrogen, methane, and carbon dioxide gases.

Flatulence was first studied when it became a problem for pilots (the higher the altitude, the more gas expands). At 35,000 feet, it will expand to 5.4 times more than at sea level, causing pain and discomfort. Almost 50 percent of the gas is nitrogen, about 40 percent is carbon dioxide produced by aerobic bacteria in the intestinal tract, and the rest is a combination of methane, hydrogen sulfide, hydrogen, ammonia, and the real odor makers—indoles and skatoles. Believe it or not, in the late 1960s one of the criteria for selecting astronauts was whether they produced large amounts of gas after eating beans.

There are now gas-free lima beans, which contain less of the hard-to-digest complex sugar that causes the problem.

FLATULENCE CAUSED BY COMMON BEANS

The chart below provides information that was released by the USDA's Western Laboratory in Berkeley, California. The beans are listed in descending order on a scale of 10 to 1, beginning with those that produce the most intestinal gas. Those at the top of the list are also higher in sugar, which is what causes the problem in the first place.

The Miracle Fruit			
Soybeans	10	Great Northern beans	5
Pink beans	9	Lima beans (baby)	4
Black beans	8	Garbanzos (chickpeas)	3
Pinto beans	7	Lima beans (large)	2
Small white beans	6	Black-eyed peas	1

POD BEAN VARIETIES

Chinese Long
These mild-tasting beans can grow as long as three feet and are sometimes called yard-long beans. They are best when young and tender.

Haricots Verts
A slender variety of snap bean originally developed in France, haricots verts is French for green beans.

Italian Green
Also known as Romano beans, these have a broad, flat, bright green pod and are among the most popular for freezing.

Purple Wax
Has a dark purple pod that changes to green when cooked. Looks similar to a small, yellow wax bean.

Scarlet Runner
Has broad, flat, green pods and black-and-red speckled seeds. The blossom is also edible.

Snap
These beans have tender, crisp pods that snap in half easily. The ends are usually snapped rather than cut off. These are the familiar green beans or yellow wax beans formerly known as string beans. The string has been bred out and their name has been changed.

> **REPORTED HEALTH BENEFITS**
> Pod beans have been used to alleviate hemorrhoids and to offset anemia.

STORING BEANS

Cooked pod beans have a refrigerator life of approximately three to four days. If you boil the beans whole without even removing the ends, you will retain 50 percent more of their nutrients. A very small amount of salt added to the cooking will bring out the flavor. Baking soda added to the water will reduce the nutrient content of the beans. Acidic foods, such as tomatoes, will turn the beans a drab olive color.

SHELL BEANS

These are actually mature, fresh seeds that are in the development stage between fresh seeds and dried seeds. Dried beans are higher in protein, potassium, and iron. Shell beans should have a bulging, tightly closed pod. If the pods are sealed, they should last for two to three days.

SHELL BEAN VARIETIES

Cranberry
These beans are have red markings on the white pods and the bean.

Fava
Similar to lima beans in taste and texture, but with longer pods. These have also been called broad beans and are popular in salads. Individual beans must be peeled.

Lima

The most common shell bean in the United States, limas originated in Peru. Almost all of the U.S. crop is used for canning or freezing. Limas are very perishable and should be used as soon as purchased. A tiny bit of salt added to the cooking water will help to bring out their flavor.

POISONOUS LIMA BEANS?

Lima beans produce an enzyme called cyanogen, which is a form of cyanide. Some countries have laws that restrict the growing of certain varieties. European and American farmers have developed new varieties of lima beans that do not produce as much of the toxin and are safer to eat. These potentially harmful toxins may be removed by boiling the beans in a pot without a lid, allowing the hydrogen cyanide gas to escape with the steam. Neither lima beans nor their sprouts should be eaten raw.

ONE LO-O-ONG BEAN

The yard-long bean, also called the asparagus bean, has pods that grow up to three feet long. But they'll taste better if harvested at 18 inches.

SOYBEANS

◆ Usually sold dried in the United States, fresh soybeans are more popular in Asia. They are high in protein and mild in flavor. Soybeans contain the highest quality protein of all the legumes and approach meat in their amino acid balance.

◆ Soybeans are now the third largest crop in the United States, after wheat and corn, and are the largest source of protein meal for livestock. They are also used to make vegetable oil.

◆ Soybeans originated in China, and the ancient Chinese considered them one of the five sacred grains necessary for life. They became popular in the United States after Commodore Matthew Perry's expeditions brought back two varieties from the Far East in 1854.

◆ The bean has a protein content of 40 percent protein and fat content of 20 percent. The oil derived from soybeans was originally used in paints, soaps, and varnishes but was not used in foods until the process of hydrogenation was invented, making its taste more acceptable. The food industry first used soybean oil to make margarine as a replacement for butter during World War II.

SOY FOODS

Soy is all the rage, but is it the miracle food it's claimed to be? The jury is still out, but what is not in dispute is soy's list of benefits: It is an excellent source of protein, is cholesterol-free and low in saturated fat, and provides calcium, folate, omega-3 fatty acids, and compounds called isoflavones. The following are a few of the more common soy products:

Tofu

Tofu is prepared by boiling soybeans in water, and then grinding the beans into a paste and adding calcium sulfate to coagulate the curd; this makes it a better source of calcium than raw soybeans. In most Japanese and Chinese tofu, however, the curd is coagulated by the addition of an acid, such as lemon juice or vinegar, rather than calcium sulfate.

The coagulated curds are compressed into blocks and stored in water under refrigeration or vacuum-packed. If you do this, the tofu will last for up to one week, and possibly two weeks beyond its sell date if it was very fresh when purchased. If you are going to freeze tofu, do it immediately after purchase, and leave the tofu in its original water and container. It can be frozen for about two months at 0°F. After it is thawed, however, it will be a little bit more fragile and will disintegrate unless added to dishes just before serving.

The proteins in tofu are 90 percent digestible, which is close to the ratio one would get from milk. Reduced-fat tofu is now available in markets.

Tempeh

Made from whole cooked soybeans that have been infused with a starter bacteria and allowed to ferment. This produces very dense and chewy food with a nutty flavor. Tempeh can be fried, grilled, or used to make veggie burgers. It is one of the only vegetable sources of vitamin B12.

Miso

This is a fermented soybean paste. It is high in sodium, but it is also high in protein, isoflavones, and antioxidants. Miso is most commonly used as a flavoring for soups and stews.

Soy Milk

Extracted from soybeans and consumed by people who have an allergy to cow's milk. Soy milk is usually supplemented with vitamins D and B12 and calcium. It is available flavored with carob or vanilla.

Textured Vegetable Protein (TVP)

Made from compressed soy flour, TVP is an excellent source of calcium, and, because of its consistency, it is used as a replacement for hamburger in many recipes. Try replacing 30 to 50 percent of the ground beef with TVP next time you make meatloaf, chili, or sloppy joes.

REPORTED HEALTH BENEFITS
Soy protein has been linked to reducing the symptoms of menopause. Soybeans have been given to athletes because of their high-quality protein.

PINTO BEANS

This is a dried bean that is an excellent source of protein. Pinto beans contain about 22 percent protein, while beef has only 18 percent and eggs 13 percent. They are speckled or have streaks of reddish brown on a pale pink background; fading is a sign of aging or long storage. Try to purchase beans of uniform size; otherwise, the smaller ones might become mushy before the larger ones are cooked. If you think this might be a problem, try adding a small amount of baking soda to the water while the beans are cooking to soften the beans.

STORING DRIED LEGUMES

If legumes are kept in a dry spot below 70°F they will last for up to one year and retain most of their nutrient content. They may be stored in their original bag or container or transferred to a sealed glass jar. Never mix old beans with new beans, as they will not cook evenly. It is not necessary to freeze dried beans, and freezing will not help to retain their nutrient content. Cooked dishes containing beans can be frozen for up to six months, but the beans might become mushy when thawed.

BEAN OVERBOARD

When cooking dried beans, add 1 tablespoon of a pure vegetable oil to the water to help prevent boil overs. Or, cook the beans in a large pot.

COOKING TIPS

◆ To tell whether a bean is fully cooked, squeeze it. There should be no hard core at the center.

- Cooking the beans with an acidic ingredient, such as with tomatoes, will slow down the cooking time, and testing for tenderness is a must.
- The taste of beans is improved by adding a small amount of brown sugar or molasses at the end of cooking.

COOKING TIME VS. NUTRIENT LOSS

Many people worry that beans and legumes will lose their nutrients because they must soak and cook for such a long time. Studies performed by the USDA, however, have proved that legumes, even if they require more than 1 hour of cooking, will still retain 70 to 90 percent of their vitamin content and almost 95 percent of their mineral content. The most affected were the B vitamins, of which about 45 to 50 percent were lost.

THE WELL-COOKED GREEN BEAN

To get the best flavor from green beans, don't overcook them. Boil or steam them for 5 to 10 minutes in salted water; if you boil them, flush them with cold water to stop the cooking.

Bean Cooking Chart

BEAN	PRESOAK	COOKING TIME
Adzuki beans	Yes	30–40 minutes
Black beans	Yes	30–60 minutes
Black-eyed peas	No	30–60 minutes
Chickpeas (garbanzos)	Yes	1½–2 hours
Great Northern beans	Yes	1½–2 hours
Kidney beans	Yes	1½–2 hours
Lentils (green and brown)	No	20–30 minutes
Lentils (red and yellow)	No	5–8 minutes
Lima beans	Yes	50–90 minutes
Mung beans	No	1½–2 hours
Navy beans	Yes	1½–2 hours
Split peas	No	30–60 minutes
Pinto beans	Yes	50–60 minutes
Soybeans	Yes	1¾–3 hours

LINING THEM UP

Soybeans are about the best vegetable source of protein. Lentils come next in the protein stakes, followed by split peas, navy beans, kidney beans, chickpeas, and lima beans.

BEETS

- ◆ Beets have one of the highest sugar contents of any vegetable, but they are low in calories and are an excellent source of vitamins and minerals.
- ◆ Both the roots and the leaves are edible. It is best to buy only small or medium-sized beets, as the larger ones are not very tender and may have a stronger flavor. Never purchase beets that are shriveled or flabby.
- ◆ Beet greens should be used as soon as they are purchased and the roots within seven to 10 days.
- ◆ Cook beets whole and unpeeled to retain their nutrients. Beets contain the chemical pigment betacyanin, which gives them their red color. Some 15 percent of the population can't metabolize this pigment; though it's harmless, it will turn their feces and urine red for a few days.

BEETS ARE COLORFUL

Betacyanin is difficult to remove from your hands, and disposable rubber gloves are recommended when working with beets. When preparing any dish that contains beets, be aware that they will lose some of their color and turn the other foods red.

SWEET BEETS

A two-pound standard beet contains 14 teaspoons sugar. Sugar beets are 20 percent sucrose by weight and have twice the sugar content of standard beets. It takes 100 pounds of sugar beets to produce five pounds of sugar.

REPORTED HEALTH BENEFITS
Beets have been used to relieve coughing, fever, glandular swelling, headaches, and toothaches. Two pounds of raw mashed beets consumed daily have been used to treat tumors and leukemia. Beet greens have a higher iron content than spinach and have been used to treat anemia.

OFF WITH THEIR TOPS

As with any vegetable that has a leafy top, beet greens should be removed after the beets are purchased and before they are stored. The leafy tops will leach moisture from the root or bulb and shorten the vegetable's shelf life. Beet greens can be prepared like chard.

BROCCOLI

◆ A member of the cruciferous family of vegetables that also includes cabbage and Brussels sprouts, broccoli was first grown in United States in the 1920s and is one of the more nutritious vegetables. It will have a higher nutrient content if eaten fresh.

◆ Cooked broccoli still contains 15 percent more vitamin C than an orange.

◆ Broccoli is available year-round, but is best from October through May. The stems should not be too thick and the leaves should not be wilted. The florets of broccoli should be closed and a good, solid green. If the buds are open or yellow, the broccoli is old and will have lost a significant amount of its nutrient content. The florets of broccoli contain eight times more beta-carotene than the stalks.

◆ One cup of broccoli contains 271 percent of the Daily Value of vitamin A, 193 percent of vitamin C, 5 percent of niacin, 9 percent of calcium, 73 percent of thiamine, 57 percent of phosphorus, and 9 percent of iron. It also provides 25 percent of your daily fiber needs and even has five grams of protein.

◆ Broccoli should be washed in a good organic cleanser. The EPA has registered more than 50 pesticides that can be used on broccoli, and 70 percent of these cannot be detected by the FDA after harvesting. In a recent study, it was reported that 13 percent of all broccoli still retained pesticide residues even after the initial processing. Try to buy organic broccoli, or consume broccoli in moderation.

◆ Between 1983 and 1997, consumption of broccoli rose more than 50 percent in the United States, to 23 servings per person per year.

◆ Prepare broccoli stems for cooking by peeling them, and then cutting them into small, even pieces.

◆ Broccoli should be cooked as quickly as possible to retain its green color. Broccoli's color is also very sensitive to acidic foods and will turn a drab olive color if cooked in the same pot with them.

STORING BROCCOLI

Broccoli should be stored in a perforated plastic bag in the refrigerator, where it will keep for three to five days before the florets start opening and it begins to lose nutrients. To freeze broccoli, remove the leaves and peel the stalks, cut the broccoli into small lengthwise strips, and blanch it for 5 minutes. Chill it, drain it well, and place it in a sealed plastic bag. It can them be frozen for 10 to 12 months at 0°F.

A recent study conducted at the University of Kentucky compared the vitamin C content of whole broccoli with plastic-wrapped broccoli. Broccoli that was left out in the air lost 30 percent of its vitamin C content in four days, while the broccoli that was wrapped in plastic only lost 17 percent and retained its color better. The respiration rate of the plastic-wrapped broccoli was slowed, preserving the nutrients.

REPORTED HEALTH BENEFITS
Broccoli has been used to treat constipation, to reduce
high blood pressure, and as a digestive aid.

HEALTHY BUT SMELLY

Broccoli, as well as Brussels sprouts, cabbage, and cauliflower, contains the natural chemical called isothiocyanate that, when heated, breaks down into a foul-smelling compound of hydrogen sulfide and ammonia. And take note: You should never cook these vegetables in an aluminum pot or the reaction will cause an even more intense smell. The longer you cook the vegetables, the more chemicals are released and the smellier the kitchen. Cook florets 2 to 4 minutes, the whole head for 6 to 8 minutes.

If you keep a lid on the pot and place a piece of fresh bread on the top of the vegetable, the bread will absorb some of the odor—but it may disintegrate as well. If you cook broccoli too long, the compounds will react with the chlorophyll that is responsible for its green color, and the vegetable will turn brown. Cooking broccoli in only a small amount of water will slow down this reaction.

TWO OTHER BROCCOLIS

Broccoli raab, from Italy, has succulent leaves and button-sized florets. It has gained in popularity in the U.S., especially in restaurants. Oriental broccoli, called gailon, has leaves and buds with a sweet broccoli flavor.

BROCCOFLOWER

A cross between broccoli and cauliflower, this vegetable looks like a light-green cauliflower. It flavor is milder than that of either of its relatives. To assure maximum nutrition, make sure the florets are tightly closed.

BRUSSELS SPROUTS

This vegetable was named after the Belgian capital, where it originated. A relative of the cabbage family, it even resembles small heads of cabbage. Brussels sprouts were brought to North America from England in the 1800s. They are an excellent source of vitamins A and C.

They are easily overcooked and will become mushy. Store them in the refrigerator to prevent the leaves from turning yellow.

> **REPORTED HEALTH BENEFITS**
> Brussels sprouts are used as a general tonic for blood cleansing, as well as to cure headaches and constipation, and to reduce hardening of the arteries.

X MARKS THE SPOT

If you cut an X on the stalk end of each Brussels sprout with a sharp knife before cooking them, the sprouts will cook quickly and evenly. The small opening will allow the steam to be released through the bottom.

CABBAGE

◆ Cabbage originated in the eastern Mediterranean region and was popular among the ancient Greeks. It is available year-round in three main varieties; red, green, and savoy, which has crinkly leaves. Avoid cabbages with worm holes, and be sure to smell the core for sweetness. Green and red cabbage should have firm tight leaves with good color. Cabbage should be refrigerated in plastic bags, where it will keep for up to two weeks.

◆ Cabbages, like other cruciferous vegetables, are high in a phytochemical called indoles. Because of its indole content, cabbage is being studied for its ability to prevent cancer. Initial studies indicate that if you consume half a green cabbage daily you may prevent a number of cancers.

◆ When making stuffed cabbage, boil the whole head, removing the cabbage from the water and taking off the leaves as they become tender. The individual leaves will come apart without tearing.

◆ Flatulence problems related to the consumption of cabbage can be eliminated by boiling the vegetable for 5 to 6 minutes, draining the water, and continuing to boil it in fresh water. The chemical that causes the problem is released during the first few minutes of cooking.

◆ When preparing a recipe that calls for cabbage wedges, try steaming instead of boiling them; the wedges will retain their shape.

SAUERKRAUT TO THE RESCUE

According to one legend, fermented cabbage was popularized by Genghis Khan, when his marauding hordes brought the recipe from China in the 12th century. The recipe traveled throughout Europe to Germany, where the cabbage was fermented with salt instead of wine and given the name "sauerkraut." In 1772, it took on heroic proportions when Captain James Cook, who had heard of the possible health benefits of sauerkraut, decided to take 25,000 pounds of it on his second journey of exploration to the Pacific Ocean. Because sauerkraut contains vitamin C, Captain Cook lost only one sailor to scurvy in more than 1,000 days at sea. The sauerkraut supply lasted one year without going bad.

CABBAGE VARIETIES

Bok Choy
Looks like a cross between celery and Swiss chard. When cooked, bok choy has a slightly sharp flavor, but the stalks are rarely bitter. Bok choy is an excellent source of calcium and vitamin A.

Green
Has smooth, darker green outer leaves, and paler green inner leaves.

Napa
Has a more delicate flavor than most cabbage and is high in nutrients.

Red
Has solid red-to-purple outer leaves, sometimes with white veins or streaks on the inside leaves.

Savoy
Has crinkled, ruffled, yellow-green leaves and is less compact than most cabbages.

REPORTED HEALTH BENEFITS
Cabbage has been used to control asthma, for blood cleansing, to promote healthier hair and nails, and to cure bladder disorders and skin irritations. It is also reputed to help prevent cancer and lower cholesterol, as well as reduce the symptoms of stomach ulcers and yeast infections such as candidiasis.

DID YOU KNOW?

Don't discard the carrot tops after you cut them off. They are high in vitamins K and E, which are lacking in the carrot itself. You can snip the tops into salads.

CARROTS

◆ With the exception of pumpkin and dandelion greens, carrots contain more beta-carotene than any other vegetable. Studies show that carrots may lower cholesterol levels, but drinking an excessive amount of carrot juice may turn your skin orange.

◆ Carrots are available year-round. They should be well formed, with a smooth skin and a solid orange color. Store them in the refrigerator and don't soak them in water for a length of time, especially if they are peeled. If carrots lose their crispness, refrigerating them in a bowl of ice cubes and water for no more than an hour will refresh them. If they are soaked for too long, the excess water will build up in the spaces between the cells and cause the carrots to become limp.

◆ To slip the skin off carrots, drop them in boiling water, let them stand for 5 minutes, and then place them in cold water for a few seconds. If you're in a hurry or only have a few carrots to peel, a standard vegetable peeler does the job speedily and easily.

◆ Blanch carrots before using them in a stir-fry because they take longer to cook than most other vegetables.

◆ To make carrot curls, peel off slices with a vegetable peeler and drop them into a bowl of ice water.

◆ Retain a portion of the green top to use as a handle while grating carrots. This will keep your fingers from becoming shorter.

◆ The body absorbs the iron in carrots more efficiently than that from most other vegetable sources.

WHY IS THE BETA-CAROTENE INCREASING IN CARROTS?

According to the USDA, scientists have been improving carrots to such a degree that they now have twice as much beta-carotene as they did in 1950. Originally, the increased beta-carotene was designed to help British aviators acquire better night vision during World War II.

STORING CARROTS

Remove the tops from carrots before they are stored. Otherwise, the tops will draw moisture from the carrots, cause them to become bitter, and will reduce their storage life. Carrots should be stored in sealed plastic bags. Carrots are very susceptible to a number of microbes that will cause them to decay. They freeze well with only minimal blanching.

PURPLE CARROTS?

Carrots were red, purple, or black until the early 17th century, when the orange variety was developed in Holland.

COOKED CARROTS ARE BETTER FOR YOU

When carrots are cooked, a percentage of the hemicellulose (fiber) will become softer, making them easier to digest and allowing the digestive juices to reach inside the cells and release the nutrients in the vegetable so that the body can utilize them more easily. Also, cooking carrots causes almost no loss of vitamin A.

CARROTS AND CHOLESTEROL

Studies show that eating 7 ounces of carrots every day for three weeks can lower cholesterol levels by 11 percent, probably because of the calcium pectate, a type of fiber found in carrots. Drinking carrot juice won't help though, because this fiber is usually lost during the juicing process.

FRESH YOUNG ONES ARE BEST

As a general rule, young vegetables are best for freezing. Their nutrient content will be higher, and they will contain less starch. Freeze them as soon as possible. And remember: Freshly harvested produce has stronger cell walls and will handle freezing better.

REPORTED HEALTH BENEFITS
Carrot juice has been used for the treatment of asthma, allergies, anemia, insomnia, bad breath, constipation, diarrhea, fatigue, and colitis, as well as to improve eyesight and to promote healthy hair and nails. It is also an excellent antioxidant.

CAULIFLOWER

◆ A member of the cruciferous family of vegetables, cauliflower has a very compact head and grows on a single stalk. The head is surrounded by green leaves, which protect it from the sun and cause the cauliflower to remain white instead of producing chlorophyll.

◆ Cauliflower is best purchased from September through January but is available year-round. Do not purchase cauliflower whose clusters are open or if it has a speckled surface, which is a sign of insect injury, mold, or rot. A patch of gray on the surface, however, simply means that the sun has reached the surface of the cauliflower. Trim off the gray and the vegetable can be eaten.

◆ Cauliflower should be stored in a perforated plastic bag in the refrigerator.

◆ A small amount of lemon juice added to the water will keep cauliflower white during cooking. Overcooking darkens it and makes it tough.

◆ To reduce the odor of cooking cauliflower, replace the water after it has cooked for 5 to 7 minutes. Cauliflower cooks in 10 to 15 minutes.

◆ Do not cook it in an aluminum or iron pot because contact with these metals will turn cauliflower yellow, brown, or blue-green.

STORING CAULIFLOWER

When handling cauliflower, avoid injuring the florets. This will cause the head to loosen and discolor. Put the unwashed head in a loosely closed plastic bag and store it in the vegetable crisper. It should keep for four to seven days. Wash the head well before eating to eliminate the chemicals that are often used to preserve its freshness. To freeze, cut the cauliflower into small pieces, wash it in cold, lightly salted water, and then blanch it in salt water for 3 minutes. Drain, chill, and freeze it in a plastic bag.

REPORTED HEALTH BENEFITS
Cauliflower is used as a blood cleanser and to alleviate kidney and bladder disorders, as well as anxiety, poor circulation, and headaches. In some cases, it is also used to cure asthma, gout, and high blood pressure.

CELERY

◆ Celery was brought to North America from Europe in the 1800s. It was first grown in the United States in Kalamazoo, Michigan, in 1874 and, to popularize it, was given free to train passengers.

◆ Presently, 2 billion pounds are grown annually in this country.

◆ Celery has a very high water content and is low in calories. It is available year-round.

◆ The ribs should be solid, with no hint of softness, which would indicate the cottony texture that old vegetables acquire. If even one rib is wilted, do not purchase the celery.

◆ Celery will keep in the refrigerator for no more than seven to 10 days and should never be placed in water.

◆ Don't discard the celery leaves. Chop them and use as you would an herb to flavor soups, stews and stock; or add to meat loaf or stuffing.

MEDICAL CONCERNS?

Celery contains the chemical furocoumarin psoralens, an essential oil. The chemical is known to cause contact dermatitis and sensitivity to light in the skin of susceptible individuals. This chemical is also found in other foods such as dill, caraway seeds, and the peelings of lemons and limes. Photosensitivity has also been a problem with workers who handle celery on a daily basis without wearing gloves.

HOW DID CELERY TURN INTO A SWIZZLE STICK?

The idea of using a celery rib as a stirrer in a Bloody Mary was introduced in the 1960s. A celebrity (whose name has been lost to history) enjoying a cocktail at the Ambassador East Hotel in Chicago needed to stir his drink and grabbed a rib of celery from a nearby relish tray.

CELERIAC

This root vegetable resembles a turnip and may be prepared like any other root vegetable. It has an ivory interior and a strong celery flavor with a dash of parsley. Celeriac should be firm and have a minimum of rootlets and knobs. It is excellent in salads and can be shredded like carrots. Celeriac comes into its own in the appetizer found on menus around the world: *céleri rémoulade,* from France.

CELTUCE

A hybrid of celery and lettuce, celtuce does not have a lot of nutritional value. Its interesting flavor is reminiscent of celery and lettuce, and it can be eaten raw or cooked.

A CELERY RELATIVE

The herb lovage is a relative of celery. Its leaves are used in cooking, while its hollow stems (the herb grows 4 to 6 feet tall!) can be cut and used as straws or swizzle sticks in tomato juice or Bloody Marys.

DID YOU KNOW?

Stalk is the term for the bunch of celery; you break individual ribs off the stalk.

255

CELERY STRINGS

Celery is easy to cook; the pectin in the cells breaks down easily in water. However, the strings, which are made of cellulose, are virtually indestructible and will not break down under normal cooking conditions. Even the body has a difficult time breaking the strings down, and many people cannot digest them at all. Be sure to remove the strings with a vegetable peeler before chopping or using the celery. When preparing stuffed celery stalks for a party, it's best to remove the strings first.

REPORTED HEALTH BENEFITS
Celery juice has been used as a tonic to reduce stress.
Other uses include asthma relief, to control diabetes, as a diuretic, and to reduce the incidence of gallstones. It is also purported to reduce the symptoms of insect bites, nervousness, and, not surprisingly to millions of dieters, obesity.

CORN

- Corn was first grown in Mexico or Central America and was a staple of the Native Americans.
- When ground for tortillas, corn releases a high level of niacin. However, as a vegetable, it ranks low on the overall nutritional scale.
- Corn is 5 to 6 percent sugar, making it a taste favorite. Some hybrids of sweet corn are even higher.
- Americans consume about 25 pounds of corn per person annually. There are more than 200 varieties grown worldwide.
- Corn is available from May through September, and the kernels should be evenly colored. Do not purchase husks that are straw colored; they should be green. The straw color indicates that the corn is dried and is fit only for animal fodder.
- Yellow corn kernels are higher in vitamin A than white kernels. Some corn lovers think yellow kernels have a more robust flavor, and that white kernels are sweeter.
- The easiest way to remove the kernels from an ear of corn is to stand the corn on end on a board and cut down the cob with a knife.
- No one from Iowa or New Jersey—or the southwestern United States—will agree, but some people think the best-tasting corn is grown in Florida; it is known as Florida Sweet.

◆ Never add salt to the water when cooking corn; table salt contains traces of calcium, which will toughen the kernels.

◆ Unused fresh corn should be cooked for a few minutes just to inactivate the enzymes. Store it in a sealed plastic bag for up to two days.

◆ To freeze corn, blanch the ears for a minute or two in boiling water, drain it, and immediately flush it with cold water to stop the cooking. Freeze it on a tray, leaving room between the ears so the kernels are not crushed and hold their shape. Once the corn is frozen, place the ears in a sealed plastic bag. Frozen corn will keep for one year.

WHY DOES CORN OCCASIONALLY TURN RUBBERY?

When corn is cooked, the protein goes through a chemical change called denaturization, which simply means that the chains of amino acids (proteins) are broken apart and reformed into a network of protein molecules that squeeze the moisture out of the kernel, turning the corn rubbery. Heat also causes the starch granules to absorb water, thus swelling and rupturing the kernel, thereby releasing the nutrients.

Corn should be cooked for 30 seconds to three minutes, which prevents the protein from becoming tough. When corn is boiled in water, about 50 percent of the vitamin C is destroyed; however, if you cook it in a microwave without water, almost all of the vitamin C is retained.

THE HAZARDS OF STORING CORN

Corn is one vegetable that is always better eaten when it is fresh, preferably on the day it was picked. As soon as corn is picked, its sugars start to convert to starch. The milky liquid in the kernel that makes corn sweet will turn pulpy and bland in as little as two to three days. If you've only eaten corn from a supermarket, stop at a farm stand one day and pick up some ears that have just been picked. You're sure to marvel at the difference in flavor and texture.

WELL, FANCY THAT

When wrapping corn in aluminum foil for grilling, try placing a sprig of a fresh herb within each ear's foil wrap. Marjoram is the most popular choice, but almost any herb will do: try tarragon, Italian parsley, sage, chives, dill, chervil, oregano, and thyme.

DID YOU KNOW?

When boiling corn on the cob, adding a little milk to the cooking water will bring out the sweetness of the corn.

CORN SMARTS

Always store corn in a cool, dry location, and keep the ears separated in order to prevent them from becoming moldy. Remember that as it warms up, the sugar in corn converts to starch very quickly. In fact, when corn is piled high in supermarket bins, the ears on the bottom will be less sweet because of the heat generated by the weight of the ones on top.

COOKING CORN?

Steaming corn for about 5 to 7 minutes is one of the preferred cooking methods. Roasting or grilling corn gives it an appealingly smoky flavor.

ALMOST NO NUTRITIONAL VALUE

The color of a corn chip does not indicate its calories or fat content—white or blue corn chips are no better for you than yellow chips. But if the label reads baked, the chips will probably have less fat.

PICKING CORN

Choosing fresh corn can be difficult unless you have some experience. If the corn still has its husk, peel back a small area and examine the kernels. The kernels should be close together with no gaps between rows. (Gaps between the rows indicate that the ear is over-mature.) If the tip has no kernels, the corn was picked too soon and was not allowed to mature. The kernels should always be plump and juicy and should spurt a milky, starchy liquid. If the center of the kernel is sinking inward, it is drying out and will not be as sweet. Always purchase corn with smaller kernels at the tip of the ear; larger kernels are usually a sign of over-maturity.

WHAT MAKES POPCORN POP?

When a popcorn kernel is heated, the moisture inside turns to steam. As the pressure builds, it has to vent—and the kernel bursts. The explosion forms a fluffy white starch. (Normal corn won't explode because it does not contain as much moisture as the special popcorn corn.) As soon as the popcorn is popped, open the bag or remove the lid so the popcorn does not absorb the steam and become soggy. Popcorn should always be stored in a well-sealed container so it will not absorb moisture from the air.

FLUIDS AND FIBER

Popcorn is composed of a complex carbohydrate (starch), and includes insoluble fiber (cellulose), which may help prevent constipation. It is always best, however, to drink plenty of fluids when consuming a large amount of insoluble fiber, which tends to absorb water from the intestinal tract and add bulk.

SAVING AN OLD MAID

Old maids are kernels that are too pooped to pop. These kernels usually have lost too much moisture and can be revived. Soak them in water for 5 minutes, then dry them off and try again. Or freeze them overnight and pop them when frozen.

WISING UP

Americans consume 17.3 billion quarts of popcorn every year. After a huge brouhaha several years ago, movie houses and other venues stopped making popcorn in high-saturated fat coconut oil and switched to canola oil.

◆ One ounce of air-popped popcorn measures 3.5 cups and provides 107 calories.

◆ One ounce of oil-popped corn measures 2.6 cups and contains 140 calories.

◆ An ounce of potato chips (about 10 chips) contains 114 calories.

PROBABLY NEEDED SALT AND BUTTER

The Aztecs were the first recorded users of popcorn, but they used it for decoration instead of eating.

PASS THE POPCORN TENDERIZER?

It may be healthier to air pop your popcorn; however, air-popping makes larger blossoms that are tougher and not as crisp.

REPORTED HEALTH BENEFITS
Popcorn has been used to cure anemia and constipation.

IS IT WORTH THE PRICE?

Nutritionally, regular popcorn and gourmet popcorn are equals. The only difference is that gourmet popcorn pops into larger blossoms.

CUCUMBERS

◆ Cucumbers belong to the gourd family. They originated in Asia and were brought to the Americas by Columbus.

◆ Cukes are grown in all sizes, from one-inch gherkins to as much as 20 inches long. They have a very high water content and are an excellent source of fiber.

◆ The greenhouse, or English, cucumber is becoming more and more popular; however, the price of this thin-skinned, skinny cuke is considerably higher than that of the standard market cucumber.

◆ Cucumbers should be firm and either light or dark green—but never yellow. Purchase only firm cucumbers and store them in the refrigerator. As with some other vegetables, smaller cucumbers have better texture and flavor.

◆ Cucumbers are capable of holding 30 times their weight in water and, because of this high water content, have only 13 calories per 3.5-ounce serving.

ARE YOUR CUCUMBERS GASPING FOR AIR?

Cucumbers should be stored unwashed in the crisper drawer of your refrigerator in a perforated plastic bag to allow air to circulate. Cucumbers will keep for only four to five days and do best at around 40°F. They do not freeze well because their high water content causes too many cells to burst, making them mushy.

CUCUMBER BITTERNESS REMOVER

This is really surprising, and some think it is just another old wives' tale. But it actually works. Next time you purchase a standard cucumber (not the long, skinny English variety), cut about one inch off the end and rub the two exposed areas together in a circular motion while occasionally pulling them apart. This will cause enough suction to release a substance that causes some cucumbers to have a bitter taste. Then discard the small end you used to release the bitterness.

DID YOU KNOW?

In the 1930s, cucumber was a slang word for a one dollar bill.

WHY ARE CUCUMBERS WAXED?

Cucumbers tend to shrink during shipping and storage, and the wax coating (which is edible) prevents the shrinkage.

DO CUCUMBERS SWEETEN AFTER THEY ARE PICKED?

Cucumbers contain no starch and are therefore unable to produce sugar. They will, however, get softer as they age and absorb more moisture into the pectin. If a cucumber gets too soft, slice it, and soak the slices in lightly salted cold water to crisp them. The unsalted, lower-density water will be drawn from the cells and replaced by the higher-density, salted water.

HOW DOES A PICKLE GET PICKLED?

It all starts with a fresh cucumber arriving at the pickle factory. There are three types of processes to control fermentation. The first begins with a curing stage, during which the cucumbers are stored in large tanks filled with a salt-brine mixture. Next, they are washed and placed in a vat of fresh water, and then they are heated to remove any excess salt residues. After being cleaned and heated, they are packed in a final acid solution that turns them the dark green color we are familiar with.

The second type of processing is for *fresh-pack pickles*. This process eliminates the holding tanks and speeds the cucumbers into a flavored brine or syrup. These fresh-pack pickles are less salty than the cured pickles and are lighter green in color.

The third method of processing is done completely under refrigeration. These special pickles are known as *deli dills*. They are cleaned and graded and proceed directly to the flavored brine. They are never cooked or pasteurized and remain very cucumber-like in flavor and texture. These pickles must be stored under refrigeration.

Sour pickles are completed in a solution of vinegar and special spices. *Sweet pickles* are just sour pickles that have been drained of all brine and bathed in a mixture of vinegar, sugar, and spices. The most popular sweet pickles are small gherkins.

PICKLED CALORIES

Dill pickles have five calories per ounce while sweet pickles have 40 calories per ounce—that is, eight times more.

A LITTLE OFF THE TOP

When making pickles, slice about a quarter inch from the blossom end of the cucumber. The blossom end contains an enzyme that may cause the pickles to soften prematurely.

GRANDMOTHER'S TRICK

If you add a small piece of grape leaf, scuppernong leaf, or cherry leaf to the pickle jar, it will keep the vinegar active while preventing the pickles from becoming soft.

> **REPORTED HEALTH BENEFITS**
> Cucumbers are used as a natural diuretic and to help lower high blood pressure. They have also been used to alleviate symptoms of allergies, diaper rash, insect bites, and eye and skin problems.

EGGPLANT

- Eggplant is a member of the nightshade family of vegetables, which also includes potatoes, tomatoes, and peppers. As vegetables go, it is not very high on the nutrient scale.
- Varieties include Chinese, Japanese, and Italian eggplants, with great variety in sizes and colors.
- Eggplant contains the toxin solanine, which is destroyed when the vegetable is cooked. It is best never to eat raw eggplant.
- Eggplants are available year-round, but they are at their best in August and September. Their purple-black skin should be smooth, glossy, and free of scars, and they should be firm. Soft eggplants are usually bitter. Keep them cool after purchase and use them within three to four days.
- Eggplant should never be cooked in an aluminum pot, as this will cause the vegetable to become discolored.

SAVED BY SALT

Eggplant can be bitter, and the easiest way to eliminate the bitter taste is to slice it, salt the slices, and let them drain on a wire rack for 30 minutes. Then rinse them well and pat them dry. This procedure also reduces the amount of oil they absorb during frying.

WHY IS EGGPLANT SOMETIMES SERVED IN A PUDDLE OF OIL?

The cells of a fresh eggplant contain a lot of air, which will escape when the eggplant is heated. When you fry or sauté eggplant, the air escapes and the cells absorb just about all of the oil that's available. As the cells fill up with oil, and as the eggplant is moved about the pan, the cells will eventually collapse and release the oil. In a recent study, fried eggplant was found to absorb more fat than any other vegetable—even more than an equal portion of french fries.

REPORTED HEALTH BENEFITS
Eggplant has been used to treat abdominal pains, constipation, colitis, alcoholism, gum disease, nosebleeds, ulcers, and various nervous disorders.

FENNEL

Fennel is a member of the parsley family and looks somewhat like a very plump head of celery. It tastes like anise and has a sweet flavor. It is very low in calories, can easily be substituted for celery, and is high in vitamin A, calcium, and potassium.

The bulbs should be firm and clean with fresh-looking leaves. Don't buy fennel that has visible brown spots. It tends to dry out quickly and should be wrapped in plastic wrap and used within three to four days.

COOKING GREENS

◆ Among the most nutritious of all vegetables, leafy greens are packed with vitamins, minerals, and the plant-based substances called phytochemicals.

◆ Because some greens must be cooked to tame their bitterness and mellow their flavors, they are often called cooking greens to differentiate them from salad greens.

◆ Most dark greens are high in calcium, vitamins A and E, beta-carotene, folate, and iron.

◆ Greens can grow in sandy soil and thus should be washed thoroughly. If you sauté them, you don't need to dry them well but can add them to the pan still wet—watch out for splatters!

◆ Choose greens with richly colored leaves—avoid any with yellowing or slimy leaves or tired looking stems.

◆ Store greens in a perforated plastic bag in the crisper drawer for three to five days.

KINDS OF GREENS

Collards

Popular in the South, collards are loaded with the B vitamins; vitamins A, C, E, and K; beta-carotene; and trace minerals like iron, calcium, magnesium, potassium, and phosphorus. They have large, flat leaves.

Kale

Like collards, to which it is very closely related, kale is a nutritional powerhouse. It is high in vitamins A, C, and E, and is a good source of calcium, iron, and the B vitamins. Kale is at its best in the winter—not only does it survive frost handily, but its flavor improves after exposure to cold temperatures. It can be quite pungent, however, and older kale requires long cooking to tame its bitterness.

Swiss Chard

A relative of the beet, chard has been cultivated for thousands of years. Most frequently, it has white or red stems (don't discard them; use them as you would celery).

Turnip Greens

These have the highest calcium content of any green; turnip greens are also high in beta-carotene as well as vitamins C, E, and the B complex.

HORSERADISH

Horseradish can be found year-round and stores very well. Make sure you purchase firm roots with no soft spots or withering. If wrapped in a plastic bag and refrigerated, horseradish should last for a few weeks. After that, it may turn bitter and lose its hot bite.

JERUSALEM ARTICHOKES

These are members of the sunflower family and are also known as sunchokes. They should be firm and look fresh and will keep under refrigeration for about a week. They are easily peeled with a vegetable peeler; however, they contain a fair amount of nutrition in the skin.

The Jerusalem artichoke has a nutty, sweet flavor and should be crunchy when served raw. It can be roasted, boiled, sautéed, or breaded and fried.

DID YOU KNOW?

Hearts of romaine lettuce are sold in plastic bags at some markets. The leaves of the heart have more sweetness and crispness than the outer leaves.

DEGASSING THE SUNCHOKE

The Jerusalem artichoke contains a number of indigestible carbohydrates that cause flatulence in susceptible individuals. About half the carbohydrates can be eliminated through cooking, providing the sunchoke is sliced and boiled for 15 minutes.

KEEP THE COLOR WHITE

Sunchokes are very high in iron, which may cause them to turn gray when cooked. Adding ¼ of a teaspoon of cream of tartar to the boiling water 5 minutes before they are done will prevent the discoloration. Adding 1 tablespoon of lemon juice to the boiling water when you first start cooking will keep the root crisp and also prevent the color change.

JICAMA

Jicama originated in Mexico and is becoming very popular in the United States. It is a root vegetable that can weigh up to six pounds. The skin is brown and the flesh is white, with a crunchy texture similar to that of a water chestnut. It has a slightly sweet flavor and can be substituted for potatoes. It can also be used in salads either diced or cut into small sticks. Choose only unblemished jicama with no soft spots. It's excellent for stir-fries and is a good source of vitamin C.

LEEKS

Leeks are a close relative of the onion family but are milder and sweeter. They are also more nutritious, containing a wide variety of vitamins and minerals. They are best purchased between September and November. They should have green tops and white necks extending two to three inches from the roots. Do not purchase leeks with wilted tops or any signs of aging. Refrigerate and use them within five to seven days.

LETTUCE

◆ Lettuce can be traced back to ancient Rome and was originally named for the Romans—hence, romaine lettuce.

◆ In popularity of vegetables, lettuce is second only to potatoes in the United States. It is mainly used in salads and as a garnish.

◆ Lettuce is available in markets year-round. The darker the leaves of the lettuce you buy, the higher the nutrient content.

◆ Never add salt to lettuce prior to serving, as this may cause it to wilt.

◆ Americans consume about 11 pounds of lettuce per person per year.

LETTUCE SCRUB

There are more than 60 chemical agents that may legally be applied to lettuce. Most of these chemicals can be removed by washing the lettuce with a good organic cleanser or by placing the head stem end up in a sink with six to eight inches of cold, lightly salted water. Shake and swirl the lettuce around for a minute.

OUCH, OUCH!

Before you store iceberg lettuce, you should remove the core by hitting it once against a hard surface and then twisting it out.

SALAD DRESSING SOAKS INTO LETTUCE, SO WHY WON'T WATER?

Lettuce leaves (as well as many other vegetables) have a waxy cuticle, which is a water-repelling mixture of chemicals that prevent the leaves from becoming waterlogged. This cuticle also protects them from losing too much of their internal moisture. The oils in salad dressing are related to the chemicals in the cuticle, and they attract one another—the oil in the dressing clings to the leaves, while water does not. Water molecules, therefore, tend to bead up and fall off the leaves, while the oil spreads out and coats their surface.

TO TEAR IT OR TO CUT IT?

A few years ago, on two different television cooking shows, one chef tore his lettuce while the other cut it with a knife. The chef who tore the lettuce said tearing prevented lettuce from browning quickly. It actually makes no difference. Either way, it will oxidize and turn brown.

STORING LETTUCE

All types of lettuce love the cold, and the closer the temperature gets to 32°F (without going below), the longer the lettuce will last and the crispier it will be. Most refrigerators range between 35°F and 40°F, which is good, but not ideal. The lettuce should be stored unwashed in a sealed plastic bag with a small hole or two for ventilation. Lettuce turns brown if stored near most other fruits or vegetables because of the ethylene gas they give off. Iceberg lettuce remains fresher than any other type because of its higher water content. Iceberg will store for seven to 14 days, whereas romaine lasts for six to 10 days, and butterhead for only three to four days. To crisp lettuce leaves, soak them in ice-cold water for 15 to 20 minutes, then dry them.

LETTUCE CATEGORIES

There are hundreds of varieties of lettuce, and each falls into one of these four categories.

Butterhead

Is a loose head lettuce with a soft, buttery texture. Boston, limestone, and Bibb lettuce are examples. The leaves are dark- to grass-green.

Crisphead

Iceberg, the most popular lettuce in the United States, is the best known of this variety: It is also the least nutritious of all the lettuces and has a water content of 96 percent. Best to choose any other lettuce for nutrition.

Looseleaf

The leaves are loosely packed and joined at the stem. Varieties include red-leaf, oak, leaf, and green-leaf. These are crisp lettuces with mild and delicate flavor.

Romaine

Sometimes called cos, romaine has long, green leaves and is usually very crisp. It is used in Caesar salads. Romaine lettuce has seven times as much vitamin C and vitamin A as iceberg lettuce.

NON-LETTUCE SALAD CHOICES

Celtuce

Has a thick, edible stem approximately six to eight inches long and is widely grown in China. It has a mild flavor.

Arugula

A solid green lettuce with a high beta-carotene and vitamin C content. Arugula has small, flat leaves on long stems and a somewhat peppery flavor. It is a close relative of the radish.

Belgian Endive

A type of chicory, Belgian endives are bullet-shaped, tightly-closed heads of creamy white and yellow leaves. Belgian endive is even lower in vitamins and minerals than iceberg lettuce.

Chicory

Has loosely bunched, very thin, ragged-edged leaves on long stems. The outer leaves are dark green, and their taste is somewhat bitter. The center leaves, however, are yellow and have a mild taste.

Escarole

Has broad, wavy leaves with smooth edges and a bitter flavor.

Mâche

Is very perishable, more expensive than most other lettuces, and is sold only in small bunches. The leaves are delicate green in color and have a fingerlike shape with a mild taste.

Radicchio

A member of the chicory family, radicchio looks like a very small head of red cabbage with variegated, red-and-white leaves.

Watercress

Has dark green leaves and a peppery, mustard-like flavor. It is commonly used in salads.

REPORTED HEALTH BENEFITS
Endive has been used to cure asthma, gout, high blood pressure, arthritis, and liver ailments.

THROW THE LETTUCE IN THE WASHING MACHINE

Greens must be washed thoroughly before they are used, and, if you're in a hurry, drying them can be a problem. Salad spinners are available in housewares stores for as little as $10, or you can put the washed greens in a clean pillowcase, go outside or into the shower, and spin them around. You can also tie the pillowcase closed and put it in the washing machine on the fast spin cycle for no more than two minutes.

MUSHROOMS

- Mushrooms can be traced back to the time of the Egyptian pharaohs.
- Mushrooms are fungi and are an excellent source of nutrients.
- There are approximately 38,000 varieties of mushrooms, and unless you know what you are doing, it can be very difficult to tell the edible from the inedible. It is best never to pick and eat a wild mushroom.
- Mushrooms contain the chemical substance hydrazine, which is found mainly in the stems. Studies from the University of Nebraska have

shown that laboratory mice developed malignant tumors from ingesting large quantities of mushrooms. Cooking tends to neutralize this chemical, so it is best not to eat mushrooms raw—especially the stems.

◆ Mushrooms are available in markets year-round but are best from November through March. Be sure that the caps are closed around the stem and refrigerate them soon after purchase.

◆ Mushrooms can be kept white and firm during sautéing if you add ¼ teaspoon of lemon juice for every 2 tablespoons of butter or olive oil.

MUSHROOMS NEED ROOM TO BREATHE

Fresh mushrooms have a shelf life of only two to three days and must be stored in the refrigerator in an open container. The original container or another paper product will work best. Never use plastic containers, which tend to keep the mushrooms too wet. Never wash mushrooms before storing them; they will retain the water and become soggy. If you must keep them for a few days, place a single layer of cheesecloth on top of the container. If they do become shriveled, they can still be sliced or chopped and used in cooking. To freeze mushrooms, wipe them off with a piece of damp paper towel, slice them, sauté them in a small amount of butter until they are almost done, allow them to cool, then place them in an airtight plastic bag and freeze. They should keep for 10 to 12 months.

THE FLAVOR OF MUSHROOMS, MSG?

The unique flavor of fresh mushrooms is caused by glutamic acid, the natural form of the flavor enhancer monosodium glutamate (MSG). Mushrooms, however, do not have any sodium.

MUSHROOM VARIETIES

Button

This common white mushroom is widely cultivated throughout the world. These are short and stubby with round caps and gills on the underside. They can vary in size from less than one to several inches in diameter. A large majority of the production is dried or goes into cans or jars.

Cèpe

Cèpes, also known as boletes or porcini, are stout, brown mushrooms with pores instead of gills on the underside. Cèpes range in size from one to 10 inches in diameter and are among the best-tasting mushrooms.

Chanterelle

These are shaped like trumpets. They are large with frilly caps and range in color from gold to yellow-orange.

Enoki

These are sproutlike, with very small caps on long, thin stems. Their color is a creamy white and they have a mild flavor. They are best served raw in salads or soups and are sometimes called enokitake mushrooms.

Italian Brown

Also known as cremini, these inexpensive mushrooms are similar in appearance to button mushrooms. They have more flavor but are not as tender as button mushrooms.

Morel

These are among the most highly priced mushrooms. They are dark brown and conical in shape, and their spongy caps have a honey-combed structure.

Oyster

This variety of mushroom can be wild or cultivated. These range in color from off-white to a gray-brown. They grow in clusters and have a very dense, chewy texture. They are more flavorful when cooked.

Portobello

These large mushrooms are overgrown Italian brown mushrooms. They have a hearty flavor, circular caps, and long, thick stems. Cut off the woody part of the stem before using them. They have a meaty texture and can, in fact, be marinated and prepared like steak.

Shiitake

At one time these dark brown mushrooms were grown only in Japan, but they are now cultivated and available in the United States. They are grown on logs and are umbrella shaped. They have a rich flavor and are an excellent addition to many dishes. Shiitakes are also known as golden oak, forest, oriental black, or Chinese black mushrooms. Remove the stems before using them.

Truffles

These fungi grow underground and can be found only by pigs and trained dogs. They have excellent flavor and are a very expensive delicacy. There are two types; the black truffles from France and Italy, and the white truffles from northern Italy. White truffles are even more expensive than black.

Wood Ear

These may have anticoagulant properties, and health claims are presently showing up in the media. There are no conclusive studies at present in relation to their ability to prevent heart attacks. They are mostly sold dried and have ear-shaped caps that tend to vary in size, with a crunchy texture. They have also been known as tree ear and black tree fungus.

REPORTED HEALTH BENEFITS
In Japan, a chemical compound extracted from shiitake mushrooms has been approved as an anticancer drug. Studies show that it represses the growth of cancer cells.

OKRA

◆ Okra originated in north Africa and was brought to the United States via the slave trade in the 1700s. It became a Southern favorite and is used in many Creole dishes, especially gumbos.

◆ Okra tastes like a cross between eggplant and asparagus and, because of its thick juice, is used mainly in soups and stews, or is sliced and fried. It is a good source of vitamins and minerals.

◆ Okra pods should always be green and tender and should never look dry or shriveled. Okra tends to spoil rapidly and should be refrigerated soon after purchase.

◆ It is usually best between May and October. Never wash okra until you are ready to use it; washing removes the protective coating that keeps the pods from becoming slimy.

◆ Try brushing okra with a bit of olive oil and grilling it.

REPORTED HEALTH BENEFITS
Because of its mucilaginous nature, okra has been used as a treatment for stomach ulcers, burns, dermatitis, eczema, poison ivy, and psoriasis.

OKRA IS AN EXCELLENT THICKENER

Okra pods comprise many unripe seed capsules and are very high in carbohydrates, fiber, and starch. Because okra contains a significant amount of pectin and gums, it is an excellent thickener for soups and stews. As okra is heated, the starch granules absorb water and increase in size. They then rupture and release amylose and amylopectin molecules, as well as some of the gums and the pectin. These elements attract additional water molecules, increase in volume, and thicken the food.

ONIONS

- ◆ Onions probably originated in prehistoric times and were popular in ancient Egypt and Rome.
- ◆ The onion family includes more than 500 varieties. They are low in calories, and scallions—also called spring onions or green onions—are an excellent source of vitamin A.
- ◆ Onions should be purchased hard and dry. Avoid those with wet necks; they have begun to decay. Also avoid onions that have sprouted. They are still good to use as onion sprouts, but not as onions.
- ◆ Ideally, onions should be stored in hanging bags that allow the air to circulate around them. Never purchase an onion that has even the slightest hint of decay because the decay will quickly spread to the healthy onions with which it is stored.
- ◆ Onions will keep for two to three weeks in a cool, dry place, but if the weather is hot and humid, their storage time will be cut in half. Refrigerated, they will last for about two months, but they may pass on their aroma to other foods in the refrigerator, even eggs.
- ◆ Remove the smell of onions from your hands or a cutting board with very salty water or some white vinegar.
- ◆ Chives should be wrapped in paper towels, put in a plastic bag, and refrigerated. They will last about a week but should be used within three to four days of purchase to ensure the best flavor. If snipped or finely chopped and frozen, they can be added to food without thawing.

HOW SWEET IT IS

There are several varieties of sweet onions, including the Maui, the Walla Walla, and the Vidalia, which is grown in Georgia. Sweet onions brown better in the microwave than other onions. Combine 2 cups of sliced sweet onions with 4 tablespoons of butter in an uncovered dish and microwave on High for about 30 minutes.

RING MY ONION

When preparing onion rings, make sure you fry only a few at a time. This prevents them from sticking together and ensures even cooking.

PITHY TO THROW IT OUT

If an onion becomes pithy and starts to sprout, place it in a pot on a windowsill and, as it continues to sprout, snip off pieces of the sprouts to use for salad seasoning.

COOKING ONIONS AND GARLIC TOGETHER

When sautéing onions and garlic together, be sure to sauté the onions first for at least half of their cooking time. If you start the garlic at the same time as the onions, it will overcook and possibly burn, releasing a chemical that will make the dish bitter.

TOP OF THE ONION TO YOU

If you need only half an onion, use the top half first, because the root half will store longer in the refrigerator (it won't sprout).

POP GOES THE ONION, INSIDES ONLY

Have you ever cooked a whole onion only to have the insides pop out and ruin the appearance of the dish you were preparing? Piercing the onion with a skewer once or twice will allow the steam to escape and prevent the onion from bursting. Another method, similar to that used to keep chestnuts from exploding, is to cut an X on the root end, which will allow the steam to escape without damaging the onion.

SHEDDING A TEAR FOR ONIONS

A sliced onion releases a substance that reacts with the fluid in your eyes to form sulfuric acid. The eyes protect themselves from the acid by tearing, which rids them of the irritant.

Here are some ways to prevent tearing:

◆ Wear solid plastic goggles.

◆ Cut off the root end of the onion last.

◆ Freeze the onion for 10 minutes, or refrigerate it for 1 hour before slicing.

◆ Ball up a piece of white bread and impale it on the tip of the knife to absorb the fumes.

◆ Chewing gum while you chop onions may also help.

DID YOU KNOW?

Sweet onions actually have less sugar than regular onions. They also have less sulfur, which is what gives onions their pungency.

COOKING AN ONION

Cooking will actually turn the sulfurs in onions into sugars, which is why cooked onions taste sweeter than raw ones. As onions brown, the sugars turn deep-brown and caramelize, which intensifies the flavor. This is called the Maillard reaction. Onions contain a compound called anthocyanin, which should not come into contact with the metal ions in aluminum or iron pots, or it will turn the onion brown. When onions are sliced with a carbon-steel knife, the same reaction takes place, and the onion may change color.

ONION VARIETIES

Bermuda
These are the most common variety of large onions and may be white or yellow. Their flavor is somewhat mild, and they are commonly used in salads.

Boiling
These white onions are about one inch in diameter.

Pearl
These white onions are about the size of marbles.

Purple or Red
These are usually among the sweetest and have the strongest flavor. They are commonly used on hamburgers and in salads.

Spanish
These are light brown and larger than most other onions. They caramelize easily and become very sweet.

White
Smaller than most onions, these are usually used in soups, stews, or dishes that are creamed.

Yellow
The standard onion bought in bags in supermarkets, yellow onions are simply smaller Spanish or yellow Bermuda onions.

REPORTED HEALTH BENEFITS
Onions are used as a diuretic. They also have laxative effects,
and have been used as an antiseptic. Over the ages, onions have been
used to cure countless ailments, including arthritis, asthma, athlete's foot
and other skin conditions including chicken pox, cancer, diabetes,
fever, headache, inflammation, insomnia, mumps, ringworms,
and thyroid problems.

PARSNIPS

Parsnips look like top-heavy, ivory-colored carrots. They have a celery-like, nutty flavor. Parsnips are more easily digested when cooked because they are very fibrous and have strong cell walls. They are often used to flavor soups and can be roasted like other root vegetables.

REPORTED HEALTH BENEFITS
Parsnip is used to alleviate the symptoms of gout, edema, fatigue, gallstone, and hypoglycemia, and as a diuretic.

PEAS

◆ Peas are actually legumes—plants that bear pods with interior seeds. Green peas are one of the best vegetable sources of protein and have been used as a food since ancient times.

◆ Only 5 percent of all green peas arrive at the market fresh; almost all are frozen or canned.

◆ Like fresh corn, fresh peas are best cooked as soon as possible after they are picked, before their sugars have the time to convert to starch.

◆ Always choose pods that are well-filled but not bulging. Never buy yellow, flabby, or spotted pods. Refrigerate and use peas within three days.

◆ When dried peas are placed in water, the good ones will sink to the bottom and the bad ones will float to the top for easy removal.

◆ The peas inside a snow pea pod are so tiny that these pods are never shelled. The pods themselves are quite tender. The easiest way to cook snow peas is to sauté them in a bit of butter, or add them to a stir-fry with scallions, red bell pepper strips, broccoli florets, and baby corn.

◆ Snow peas and snap peas can be served raw in salads or cooked and served in their pods, either whole or sliced in half diagonally. Be careful not to overcook them!

◆ When cooking shelled fresh peas, always add a few washed pods to the water; this will improve the flavor and give the peas a richer green color.

◆ The delicate flavor of peas marries well with many foods but can be overpowered by strong flavors like garlic. Cook them with pearl onions, mushrooms, or top them with minced, fresh mint leaves.

DRIED PEAS ARE BEST IN SOUPS OR STEWS

The difference between fresh green peas and dried split peas is that the dried peas are actually mature seeds and usually have twice as much starch as fresh peas. Dried peas are an excellent source of protein. It is best not to soak split peas before using them, because the discarded soaking water will contain a good percentage of the B vitamins from the peas. When you use split peas in soups or stews, you normally consume the liquid, which will have some of the B vitamins still available.

REPORTED HEALTH BENEFITS
Peas contain nicotinic acid and may help to lower cholesterol levels. Peas have also been used to cure abcesses, blood clots, constipation, and skin problems.

PEPPERS

◆ When purchasing peppers, be sure the sides are firm and the colors are bright. Refrigerate and use them within two to three days.

◆ They are a good source of vitamins A and C. In fact, red bell peppers contain more vitamin C than oranges.

◆ Nutritionally, sweet red peppers are superior to green ones. They are 11 times higher in beta-carotene and have $1\frac{1}{2}$ times more vitamin C.

◆ Hot red peppers contain about 14 times more beta-carotene than hot green peppers; however, their vitamin C content is the same.

◆ Probably one of the earliest spices, chilies may have been used since 7000 B.C., according to archeological digs in Mexico.

WHY WON'T THE COLOR IN YELLOW OR RED PEPPERS FADE?

Green peppers contain chlorophyll as the coloring agent. When the pepper is cooked it releases acids that react with the chlorophyll and cause discoloration. Red and yellow peppers, on the other hand, rely on carotenoid pigments for their color. These pigments are not affected by acids or the heat from cooking.

PEPPER PROTECTION

Peppers contain capsaicin—the compound that gives them heat—and can irritate tissues. The hotter the pepper, the more capsaicin it has. To prevent irritation, wear rubber gloves when working with hot peppers so your hands do not touch the pepper and then, accidentally, your eyes, lips, or other sensitive body parts. If you get hot pepper juice on soft tissues, you will remember the experience for some time to come.

A recent study has shown that New Mexico has one of the lowest incidences of cardiovascular disease and stated that the anticoagulant chemicals in hot chili peppers may actually lower cholesterol levels and increase the amount of time it takes for blood to coagulate.

A MOLE THAT TASTES GOOD

A mole (*moh*-lay) is actually a Mexican sauce made from chili peppers, onion, garlic, ground sesame or pumpkin seeds, and Mexican chocolate. The combination of ingredients, especially the variety of chili pepper used, will determine whether the mole is spicy or mild. The most popular mole is mole poblano, which is a spicy, dark-red sauce that is commonly served over poultry. Green mole is made from green chiles and cilantro.

THE COLOR AND HOTNESS OF CHILI PEPPERS

- ◆ The color of a chili indicates only its ripeness. If the chili is picked before full maturity it will be green and contain more chlorophyll than a red chili, which has matured and lost its chlorophyll.
- ◆ The highest concentration of capsaicin is in the white ribs to which the seeds are attached. If you remove the ribs and seeds and rinse the pepper in cold water, you will reduce the heat by 70 to 80 percent.
- ◆ When a chili is fried or boiled, it will lose even more of its potency. It has also been found that people who consume chilies frequently become less susceptible to their heat.

PUTTING THE FIRE OUT

Capsaicin does not dissolve in water. In fact, if you've eaten a too-hot chili and your mouth is on fire, taking a drink of water or beer only makes it worse—the liquid spreads the capsaicin. Sour cream, yogurt, or even milk are the ideal remedies. A protein in dairy foods called casein breaks the bond between capsaicin and the pain receptors in your mouth.

THE HOTTEST OF THE HOT

The chemical capsaicin acts directly on the pain receptors in the mucosal lining of the mouth and throat. A single drop of this pure chemical diluted in 100,000 drops of water will still cause a blister to form on a person's tongue. Capsaicin is measured in parts per million, which are converted into heat units called Scoville units. This is how the hotness of a chili pepper is measured. One hundred and fifty thousand Scoville units is equivalent to 1 percent capsaicinoids. The hottest known pepper, the habanero, has a Scoville rating of 100,000 to 350,000; next is the Thai chiltepin at 50,000 to 100,000; followed by the Tecpin cayenne at 30,000; the de arbol at 15,000 to 30,000; the serrano at 5,000 to 15,000; the jalapeño at about 2,500 to 5,000; and the cascabel at 1,500 to 2,500.

PEPPER VARIETIES

Bell

A sweet pepper available in many colors, including green, red, orange, white, brown, and yellow. Bells are relatively sweet, but each color has a distinctive flavor. When different colors are mixed in a salad, it is a real taste treat. Bell peppers contain a recessive gene that neutralizes capsaicin, which is why they are not hot.

Bell peppers should be stored in the refrigerator in a plastic bag, where they will stay fresh two to three days. They can be frozen for 10 to 12 months and still retain a good portion of their nutrients.

To seed a bell pepper, hold it tightly and slam the stem end down on the counter. This will loosen the seed core, and it should pull out easily.

Anaheim

A hot chili. One of the most common chilies, with a mild to moderately hot bite, anaheims are consumed in either the green or red stages of maturity. Dried red anaheims are available in long, decorative strings.

Ancho

Dried hot peppers that are flat, wrinkled, and usually heart-shaped. They are mild to moderately hot and are usually ground for use in sauces and salsa.

Banana

A sweet pepper with a mild flavor. They resemble bananas in both color and shape. They are available fresh or pickled.

Cascabel

Moderately hot red chilies with seeds that tend to rattle inside them. When dried, their skins turn a brownish-red.

Cubanelle

A sweet pepper with a tapered shape. About four inches long, the cubanelle ranges in color from yellow to red.

Cayenne

These are among the hottest chilies. They are three to four inches long, with sharply pointed, curled tips, and are usually dried and ground.

Cherry

Shaped like a cherry, this variety ranges from mild to moderately hot. Sold either fresh or in jars.

Habanero

This lantern-shaped pepper ripens to yellow-orange in color and grows to about two inches in diameter. The habanero is the hottest pepper and is known for the lingering effect of its bite. Have milk handy when eating this one.

Hungarian Wax

A moderately hot, yellow-orange pepper. May be purchased fresh or pickled.

Jalapeño

One of the most common hot peppers. Jalapeños are usually moderately to very hot and are sold at their green stage. At the red stage of full maturity, the jalapeño is super-hot. Canned jalapeños are usually milder because they are packed in liquid.

Pimiento

A sweet, heart-shaped pepper generally sold in jars and usually found in gourmet markets.

Serrano

Popular in Mexico, these chilies look like small torpedoes and are very hot.

RADISHES

◆ Radishes are native to the eastern Mediterranean.
◆ They are in the mustard family and contain phytochemicals that are being investigated for their possible use as a cancer preventative. Their green tops are edible and tend to have a peppery flavor.
◆ Radishes are available year-round. The larger ones can be cottony in texture while the smaller ones are usually more solid; squeeze them to be sure they are not mushy or pithy, and don't buy them if the tops are yellow or if there is any sign of decay.

279

◆ Varieties of radish include California Mammoth Whites, Daikons, Red Globe, and White Icicles, among others.

REPORTED HEALTH BENEFITS
Radishes have been used as an appetite stimulant, to relieve body odor, burns, cancer, coughing, fever, indigestion, diarrhea, thyroid problems, nervousness, and constipation, and to dissolve kidney stones and gallstones.

SALSIFY

This oddly shaped vegetable is sometimes called the oyster plant, because its taste is similar to that of an oyster. It grows up to 12 inches long and 2½ inches in diameter.

SPINACH

First grown in the United States in the 1700s, spinach is high in vitamins and minerals and is one of the best vegetable sources of protein. Spinach, however, does contain the chemical oxalate, which binds with certain minerals such as calcium and limits their absorption by the body.

THE EYE IN POPEYE

Spinach contains antioxidants that may be important in preventing an age-related disease of the eye called macular degeneration. This form of blindness is prevalent in people over 65 and is the leading cause of blindness in the elderly. Experts believe that overexposure to sunlight, pollution, and smog over a period of years may contribute to this problem. Regularly consuming foods that are high in these antioxidants, such as kale, collard greens, spinach, red bell peppers, mustard greens, and hot chili peppers, may lower the risk of contracting macular degeneration by as much as 75 percent.

COLOR ME GREEN

One trick chefs use to keep spinach green is to cook it in an uncovered pot. The steam that builds up when a pot is covered causes the plant's volatile acids to condense on the lid and fall back into the water.

SHOULD SPINACH BE EATEN RAW?

While most vegetables can be eaten raw, some—including spinach and carrots—have tough cellular walls that release their maximum nutrients only when cooked. If these vegetables are eaten raw, the digestive system cannot break them down sufficiently to obtain the most nutritional benefits from them. (Of course, uncooked spinach is still a viable source of many nutrients, so you needn't forego spinach salads!) Cook spinach in as little water as possible and as briefly as possible. Spinach boiled in 1 cup of water rather than 2 will retain twice as many of its nutrients.

STORING SPINACH

Spinach will keep in the refrigerator for two to three days, providing it is stored in a sealed plastic bag. Do not wash it or cut it before you are ready to prepare it. If you buy packaged spinach, open the bag when you get home and remove any brown or darkened leaves which, if left in the bag, may cause the rest of the spinach to deteriorate faster.

To freeze spinach, remove the stems, blanch the leaves for 2 minutes, and then drain and freeze. Removing the stems lets the leaves retain more of their moisture. The spinach should keep for 10 to 12 months at 0°F.

REPORTED HEALTH BENEFITS

Spinach has been used to fight blindness, diabetes, eye problems, anemia, tumors, arthritis, high blood pressure, and bronchitis.

SPROUTS

When seeds are moistened, they grow into edible sprouts or shoots. When this occurs, the seed utilizes its carbohydrates and fat and retains a good percentage of its vitamins, making sprouts a healthful food.

◆ When purchasing fresh sprouts, remember that they can be stored for only seven to 10 days.

◆ Sprouts should be left in their original container, lightly moistened, then placed in a plastic bag, sealed, and refrigerated.

◆ Storing sprouts in too much water will cause them to decay.

◆ Sprouts cannot be frozen successfully; they become mushy and bland when thawed.

◆ The shorter the tendril, the younger and more tender the sprout.

SPROUT VARIETIES

Adzuki Bean

Very sweet, with a nutty flavor, this variety looks like grass.

Alfalfa

Threadlike white sprouts with small, green tops and a mild, nutty flavor.

Clover

Looks like the alfalfa sprout, with tiny seeds that look like poppy seeds.

Daikon Radish

Has a silky stem and a leafy top. The taste is somewhat peppery and spicy-hot.

Mung Bean

These are larger than the alfalfa sprouts and have a blander taste. They are thick, white sprouts and are used in many Asian dishes.

Soybean

These sprouts have a rather strong flavor but are a good source of protein. They may contain salmonella and should not be eaten in large quantities. Cooking the sprouts for at least five minutes can kill the bacteria.

Sunflower

Crunchier than alfalfa, with a milder flavor.

SQUASH

◆ Squash is a fleshy vegetable with a solid, protective rind. It has been a staple for thousands of years.

◆ Squash is low in calories and contains excellent levels of vitamins and minerals, which may vary from one variety to another. It is available year-round. The soft-skinned types should be smooth and glossy. The hard-shelled types should have a firm rind. Refrigerate all soft-skinned varieties and use them within four to five days.

◆ Summer squash varieties include chayote, pattypan, yellow crookneck, yellow straightneck, and zucchini.

◆ Winter squash varieties include acorn, banana, buttercup, butternut, calabaza, delicata, golden nugget, Hubbard, spaghetti, sweet dumpling, turban, and pumpkin.

DID YOU KNOW?

One of the best sources of vitamin A and beta-carotene is the pumpkin. An 8-ounce serving provides 40 calories and about 27,000 IU of vitamin A.

◆ Winter squash tend to develop beta-carotene. They contain more of this nutrient after they have been stored than they do immediately after being picked.

◆ The smaller the squash, the more flavorful it is.

◆ Squash blossoms are edible and delicious. They make a great garnish for many dishes and can even be battered and fried. Try stuffing them with cream cheese for a real treat.

◆ If you puree squash in the blender, the strings will be easy to remove because they will become wrapped around the blades.

REPORTED HEALTH BENEFITS
Zucchini has been used to reduce high blood pressure.

JACK-O'-LANTERN MIRACLE

One of the biggest problems every Halloween is that the pumpkin gets soft and mushy soon after it is carved. This occurs because air comes in contact with the inside flesh, allowing bacteria to grow. Spraying the inside of the hollowed-out pumpkin with an antiseptic spray will retard the bacterial growth and increase the time it takes for the pumpkin to deteriorate. Make sure you do not eat a pumpkin that has been sprayed.

TOMATILLOS

Also called Mexican green tomatoes, tomatillos look like small, green tomatoes with a thin, parchment-like skin. They have a somewhat lemon-apple flavor and are popular in salads and salsas. Purchase only firm tomatillos. They are usually available year-round.

TOMATOES

◆ The question of whether the tomato is a fruit or a vegetable was settled by the United States Supreme Court in 1893 when it was officially declared a vegetable—but this was done for tariff purposes.

◆ Botanically, the tomato is a fruit—actually, a berry. It is a member of the nightshade family and is related to potatoes, bell peppers, and eggplant.

◆ Tomatoes are available year-round and should be well-formed and free of blemishes. Green tomatoes will eventually turn red, but will not have good tomato flavor. A vine-ripened tomato is always best.

◆ Never refrigerate tomatoes. Tomatoes can be frozen whole and used as needed for cooking; their texture suffers, though, and they should not be used in salads. When they thaw, the skins slip off easily.

◆ Tomatoes will keep longer if you store them stem end down. Don't let them ripen in direct sunlight, or they will lose most of their vitamin C.

◆ If you expect a frost and have tomatoes on the vine, pull them up by the roots and hang them upside down in a cool basement until the fruit ripens. Green tomatoes will ripen faster if you store them with apples.

◆ Storing tomatoes at temperatures below 50°F will keep them from ripening.

◆ To peel tomatoes, cut an X in the bottom of each tomato and drop them in boiling water, remove the pot from the heat, let them remain in the water for 15 seconds, and then plunge them into cold water. The skins around the X will curl away from the flesh and will become easy to peel away.

◆ Americans consume about 24 pounds of tomatoes per person, per year.

TOMATO AROMA ONLY LASTS FOR THREE MINUTES

If you enjoy the aroma of fresh tomatoes in your salad, don't refrigerate them. Tomatoes should always be stored at room temperature. They should never be sliced or peeled until just before you are going to serve them. The aroma is produced by a chemical that is released when the tomato is sliced open. The chemical lasts at the maximum aroma level for only three minutes before it starts to evaporate.

HOW DO YOU REDUCE ACIDITY IN TOMATOES?

Some people are unable to eat spaghetti sauces and other tomato based foods because of their higher acidic content. Adding chopped carrots to any of these dishes will reduce the acidity without affecting the taste.

WHAT IS A DESIGNER LABEL TOMATO?

A new tomato, called the FlavrSavr, is making an appearance in supermarkets everywhere. This is a genetically engineered tomato that can be shipped vine-ripened without rotting, and it is the first whole food to be born of biotechnology. Most tomatoes are shipped green and treated with ethylene gas to turn them red before they get to the market. The only downside is that the new tomatoes cost about $2 per pound.

PUREE CONCENTRATE

Tomatoes get their pigment from lycopene, a valuable nutritive substance related to beta-carotene, that helps reduce the risk of certain cancers. Cooked tomatoes are higher in lycopene that fresh tomatoes, because the substance is concentrated by cooking.

KA BOOM! KA BOOM!

Never put a whole tomato in the microwave: It will explode.

TOMATO VARIETIES

Beefsteak

Beefsteak refers to a specific variety of tomato, but it is also used in a general sense to describe any large tomato. Beefsteak tomatoes often weigh more than a pound each; those that tip the scales at two or three pounds are not unheard of. As their name suggests, these tomatoes have a meaty texture. Their flavor is sweet and aromatic, with just a hint of acidity.

Cherry

These tomatoes can range in size from smaller than one inch in diameter to almost two inches. Typically, they are perfectly round, with smooth, thin skins that can be red or yellow. They are sweeter than other varieties.

Pear

Like cherry tomatoes, pear tomatoes have red or yellow skins; they are about the same size as the cherries, but pears have a distinct neck. Pear tomatoes are still relatively rare at supermarkets, but you may find them at gourmet markets. Yellow pear tomatoes are a popular heirloom variety.

Plum

Slightly elongated plum tomatoes have a firm flesh with little juice. Because they also contain few seeds and minimal gel, they are ideal for tomato sauce and paste.

SUN-DRIED TOMATO SAVVY

Made from halved and dried plum tomatoes, these succulent little morsels have a concentrated flavor. Those packed in oil can be very high in calories and fat; buy them dry and you can reconstitute them in hot water or low-fat Italian salad dressing.

DID YOU KNOW?

The tomato is native to the Andes, and the peoples of the Americas were growing tomato crops before the arrival of the colonists. Through the centuries, some heirloom varieties have been handed down, literally, by Native Americans.

HEIRLOOM TOMATOES

In the tomato world, growing heirloom varieties has become a popular pursuit with gardeners—and with discerning chefs who buy the green, gold, pink, orange, and yes, even black globes from them. Heirloom tomatoes add scrumptious taste and dazzling colors to summer dishes. If you're lucky, you may find a source at a local food stand or market—or grow your own. Unlike the smooth, round product of modern plant breeders, heirloom varieties often have pin-cushion shapes.

THE WOLF PEACH

The scientific name for the tomato is *Lycopersicon esculentum,* which translates from the Latin as "succulent wolf peach." Botanists assigned the name in the sixteenth century, after it was introduced to Europe. Food historians speculate that the name was chosen because the fruit looks as inviting as the peach but was unfit for human consumption (the tomato is part of the nightshade family, with its many poisonous members).

MARCH OF THE HYBRIDS

The first hybrid tomato available to home gardeners was the Fordhook, introduced by the W. Atlee Burpee Company in 1945. In 1949, Burpee's scored with the hybrid they named Big Boy. Today, the great majority of home garden tomatoes are hybrids, which have higher yields and better disease resistance than open-pollinated, or standard, varieties.

WHAT IS A TREE TOMATO?

If you come across a magazine advertisement touting a "tree tomato" that produces an amazing amount of fruit, don't be fooled. The tree tomato is in fact *Cyphomandra betacea,* the woody, large-leafed plant that yields tart-tasting tamarillos. (Tamarillos are a tomato cousin, but so are potatoes, eggplants, peppers, and tobacco.)

The term "tree tomato" was used until the 1940s to describe self-supporting tomato plants—those with stout central stems that hold a bushy crown off the ground until loaded down with mature fruits. But "tree tomato" gradually took on a different meaning in the minds of gardeners, and came to describe the most vigorous indeterminate types—that is, tomato varieties that keep growing and producing fruits until frost kills the plant. The best known of these are Climbing Trip-L Crop and Giant Tree, which can grow taller than a house if trained on a trellis.

TURNIPS

Turnips are a cruciferous vegetable, and are related to rutabaga and
cabbage (rutabaga, in fact, evolved from a cross between the turnip and
cabbage). They grow easily, even in poor soil conditions, and can weigh
up to 50 pounds. Turnips are a good source of complex carbohydrates,
vitamin C, and fiber, including soluble fiber.

If you find turnips with the tops, or greens, still attached, don't discard
them! Turnip greens are highly nutritious. One cup of boiled greens provides vitamin C, vitamin A, calcium, potassium, and beta-carotene.

WATER CHESTNUTS

Water chestnuts grow in muddy water and are the tip of a tuber. They
must be refrigerated or they will sprout. They are an excellent source of
trace minerals, especially potassium, and also contain vitamin C.

GETTING LOW ON WATER?

If you need to add more water to vegetables as they are cooking, make
sure the added water is as hot as possible. Adding cold water may affect
the cell walls and cause the vegetables to toughen.

Not So Dietetic

Think that salad is low in calories?
Not always—take a look at how the toppings add up.

FOOD	CALORIES	FOOD	CALORIES
1 cup lettuce	8	2 tablespoons salad dressing	120
½ medium tomato	13	¼ cup Cheddar cheese	116
½ cup cottage cheese	120	2 black olives	24
4 cucumber slices	5	1/10 sunflower seeds	75
¼ cup macaroni salad	50	1/10 cup croutons	18

Carbohydrate Content analysis

VERY LOW	Tomatoes	Peppers (green)	Pineapple
Asparagus	Cantaloupe	Pumpkin	Mango
Bean sprouts	Strawberries	String beans	Blueberries
Beet greens	Watermelon	Rutabagas	HIGH
Broccoli	LOW	Turnips	Corn
Cabbage	Beets	Apricots	Dried beans
Cauliflower	Brussels sprouts	Cranberries	Lima beans
Celery	Carrots	Oranges	Pickles (sweet)
Chard, Swiss	Chives	MEDIUM	Avocado
Chicory	Collards	Artichokes	Bananas
Cucumber	Dandelion greens	Kidney beans	Figs
Endive	Eggplant	Parsnips	Prunes
Escarole	Kale	Peas (green)	Raisins
Lettuce	Kohlrabi	Apples	VERY HIGH
Mushrooms	Leeks	Cherries	Potatoes (white)
Mustard greens	Okra	Grapes	Potatoes (sweet)
Radishes	Onions	Olives	Yams
Spinach	Parsley	Pears	

MEATY
MATTERS

MEATS IN GENERAL

As far back as Colonial times, Americans have consumed large quantities of meat. During the 1800s the cattle industry thrived, and methods of transporting and preserving meats were improved, so the entire country could enjoy beef. Meat became the mainstay of the American diet and has remained so until recent years, when it was discovered that eating too much meat—especially the red kind—could increase the levels of fat and cholesterol in blood and cause serious health problems.

Recently, the media has brought attention to other potential risk factors involved in the consumption of meat. The discovery that inspection procedures may not be as thorough or efficient as they should be; the emergence of bovine spongiform encephalopathy, or mad cow disease; E. coli 0157:H7 contamination; and hormone residues in meats are just a few of the problems that have come to light. The number-one food related risk in the United States comes from bacterial contamination, not from pesticides or fertilizers.

Education is key if Americans are to continue their consumption of meat. The public must learn which types of meats are most healthful and safest, how to prepare them, what danger signs to look out for, and even how to clean up after working with raw meat and poultry.

Americans consume one-third of the world's meat, even though they represent less than 1 percent of the world's population. At present, Americans eat about 64 pounds of beef per person per year. Red-meat consumption, however, has declined since the 1970s, while the consumption of poultry has increased significantly.

In recent years, there have been numerous medical studies that leave no doubt that a diet high in saturated fat—of which red meat (as well as butter and other full-fat dairy products) is a primary source—can significantly increase the risk of colon cancer, lung cancer in women, precancerous lesions in men and women, and raise LDL (bad) cholesterol levels. Meat does, however, provide a number of vital nutrients, and eaten in moderation, it should still be considered a healthful food. As a rule, try to keep meat secondary in your meals (as in a taco salad, for example, or in smaller portions than those of vegetables or grains)—not the main focus.

ABOUT E. COLI

In the last few years, E. coli has been in the news a lot. E. coli is a bacterium that normally lives in the human intestine, but the fearsome strain, known as E. coli 0157:H7, can pass from contaminated feces to meat during processing; people can also become infected from improperly handled animal or human waste. This strain is capable of causing severe illness or even death.

The bacteria, however, is normally found on the surface of meat, and is killed by searing or cooking it on both sides. When you cook a steak or a roast, the meat is normally cooked on all sides and the risk is eliminated, even if you are eating it at 145°F, or medium-rare.

There is a more significant risk associated with eating ground or raw meat dishes such as hamburgers or steak tartare. Because hamburger is ground beef, any bacteria present on the surface of the meat is mixed in during the grinding process, and if the ground meat is not cooked to an internal temperature of at least 165°F, the bacteria will still be present on the inside.

USDA MEAT GRADING SYSTEM

The United States Department of Agriculture regulates the terms used to describe meat. Only the first three below are retailed. They are:

Prime
Very tender due to higher fat content, well marbled, most expensive. Almost never available in supermarkets—it goes primarily to high-end restaurants and butcher shops.

Choice
Relatively tender and fairly expensive. Meat of this grade is becoming harder to find in supermarkets.

Select
Relatively inexpensive and, therefore, the grade most commonly found in supermarkets. Has less fat and may need some tenderizing.

Commercial
Tougher beef from older cattle. It is mainly used in low-cost frozen dinners and canned-meat products.

Utility, Cutter, and Canner
Usually leftover bits and pieces, used in processed-meat products. Meat of this grade may be very tough.

BUYER BEWARE

Supermarkets are using their own wording on meat packages to make you think the meat you are buying a better grade than it really is. Most of the major chains are buying more Select-grade beef but may call it by a number of fancy names such as "top premium beef," "prime quality cut," "select choice," "market choice," or "premium cut." Because the public does not want to pay the high price demanded by USDA Choice, purveyors have found a way to market the Select grade more effectively.

THE COW'S INSIDE STORY

There are eight major cuts of beef butchered in the United States. They are shank, flank, brisket, chuck, round, rib, plate, and loin. The eight cuts are given a number of additional names that are more recognizable to most consumers. These include sirloin, porterhouse, top round, eye of round, New York, T-bone, and so on, and they are used to explain the way each of the eight major cuts is actually cut up. The tenderness of beef will depend on the location of the cut and the method of cutting. The tougher cuts are taken from the muscles that do more work—neck, shoulder, brisket, and flank—and are also the least expensive.

Loin Cuts (Tenderloin)

Cut from behind the ribs, these are the most tender cuts. They include filet mignon (steaks), fillet of beef (the entire roasts), porterhouse, and New York strip steaks. The loin includes short loin and sirloin.

Round Cuts (Roasts)

Most round cuts are tender and can be cooked a number of different ways. They include top round, eye of the round, and bottom round. Round cuts can be pot-roasted or spit barbecued.

Rib Cuts (Ribs)

Markets may label these rib steaks, rib roasts, or simply back ribs. For best results, they should be barbecued or cooked slowly in the oven. The taste can be improved by adding a sauce or using a marinade.

Flank and Plate Cuts

Most of the time, if the grade is USDA Select, these cuts need to be tenderized. Choice is a much better grade. These cuts are from the abdomen; they are usually sliced in strips and used for stir-frying or stew.

Brisket Cuts

The brisket is cut from behind a cow's front leg, or it may be cut from the leg itself. Normally a tough cut, brisket should be cooked in liquid for about two to three hours.

Chuck Cuts (Roasts)

These are the toughest cuts; they come from the shoulder. Chuck cuts may need tenderizing and should be braised—that is, cooked over gentle heat in a small amount of liquid.

CONSUME IT OR FREEZE IT

Small cuts of meat will spoil more quickly than larger cuts and should not be kept in the refrigerator for more than a day or two. Liver, sweetbreads, and cubed meats should be cooked within one day, or else frozen.

RUB-A-DUB-DUB

Applying a rub is a common method of seasoning the surface of meats and poultry. A rub is simply a blend of various herbs and spices that do not penetrate the meat. The rub never blends with the flavor of the meat itself, but it does provide a tasty coating, which usually forms a brown crust of concentrated flavor. Rub on the seasoning before you begin to cook the meat, and let it sit awhile for the coating to take hold.

DUNKIN' LAMB?

Adding some black coffee to the liquid when cooking lamb stew gives it a beautiful dark color and adds great flavor.

WHY IS THE FELL LEFT ON LARGER CUTS OF LAMB?

The fell is a thin, parchment-like membrane that covers the fat on a lamb. It is usually removed from certain cuts, such as lamb chops, before they are marketed, but it is usually left on the larger cuts so they will maintain their shape and retain their juices.

FAT FREE-FOR-ALL

Beware of the wording on meat packages. If the steak packaging reads "lean," the beef cannot have more than 10 percent fat; "extra lean" cannot have more than 5 percent fat. (Virtually the only red meat with a fat content this low is bison.) "Lean" ground beef is allowed to have as much as 22.5 percent fat by weight.

DID YOU KNOW?

Lamb is graded Prime, Choice, Utility, or Cull. Prime is sold almost exclusively to restaurants.

COLOR MATTERS

Meat should always be thawed in the refrigerator, and then cooked immediately. The color of fresh beef should be a bright red, which comes from the muscle pigment. The darker the red, the older the cow. The grayish cast of some beef is from oxidation of the pigments; it is still safe to eat. Beef fat, if fresh, is always white, not yellow.

LOW-FAT GLANDS

If you have ever wondered where sweetbreads come from, they are the thymus glands of veal, lamb, and pork. The gland assists young animals in fighting disease, and then atrophies and disappears when they are about six months old. Sweetbreads are a low-fat food, with 3 ounces containing about 2.1 grams, or 19 calories from fat.

CHOLESTEROL-HAPPY FATHER'S DAY

On Father's Day, Americans tend to really outdo themselves, consuming more than 80 million pounds of beef in one day.

LETTUCE EAT

When storing a cooked roast, place it back into its own juices whenever possible. When reheating sliced meat, try placing it in a casserole dish with lettuce leaves between the slices. The lettuce provides just the right amount of moisture to keep the slices from drying out.

PREMATURE AGING

Meats may turn a grayish color if they are cooked in too small a pot. Overcrowding tends to generate excess steam—so, for a nice brown crust, give your meat some room to breathe.

LOW-PROTEIN DOGS

One of the worst sources of animal protein is from hot dogs. A 3-ounce serving (or about two hot dogs from a 10-per-pound package) contains less protein than an equal weight of any other type of meat. Legally, hot dogs may contain no more than 10 percent water, or a combination of 40 percent fat and added water. If they are labeled "with by-products" or "with variety meats," the hot dogs may consist of not less than 15 percent raw meat by-products like heart, kidney, or liver; these must be named

DID YOU KNOW?

The United States consumes more hot dogs than all the rest of the world combined— nearly 50 million hot dogs per day.

individually in the ingredients label. As much as 3.5 percent of the hot dog may be nonmeat binders and extenders, such as powdered milk, cereal, or isolated soy protein; these too must be named on the ingredients label. Sugar is a very common ingredient in hot dogs but may not be named as such; it may be listed on the label as corn syrup.

Fat Content of Nonvegetable Proteins, from Lowest to Highest	
1. FISH	6. VENISON
2. TURKEY	7. LAMB
3. CHICKEN	8. PORK
4. VEAL	9. GOAT
5. BUFFALO	10. BEEF

MEAT MARKET TREASURE HUNT

When purchasing a chuck roast, look for the white cartilage near the top of the roast. If you can spot a roast with cartilage showing, you have found the first cut, which will be the most tender. When purchasing an eye of round roast, look for the one that is the same size on both ends; it will be the most tender. When selecting a round steak, however, you should know that the uneven cuts are the ones closest to the sirloin.

BEST NOT TO EAT READY-TO-EAT HOT DOGS

The bacteria *Listeria monocytogenes* may be lurking in a number of foods, including hot dogs, sausage, raw milk, chicken, and deli-prepared salads and sandwiches. Listeria first came to public attention in 1985, when 48 people died from eating a Mexican-style cheese. The Listeria organism can survive refrigeration or freezing, and more than 1,800 cases of Listeria food poisoning are reported annually; as many as 460 result in death. People with weak immune systems, including children under age 12 and the elderly, are at greatest risk. To avoid this problem:

◆ Be sure to cook all ready-to-eat hot dogs, sausage, and leftovers until very hot. Some lunch kits contain hot dogs; don't send them to school unless your child has access to a microwave.

◆ Cook chicken until the juices run clear.

◆ Drink only pasteurized—never raw—milk.

◆ Keep all foods hot (above 140°F) until they are eaten.

◆ Be aware of "sell by" and "use by" dates on all processed-food products.

CELERY TO THE RESCUE

Roasts will never stick to the bottom of the pan if you just place a few stalks of fresh celery under the meat. This also works well with poultry.

WASTE OF RESOURCES

Chickens require only 2 pounds of feed to produce 1 pound of meat. Pigs require about 4 pounds of grain to produce 1 pound of meat, while cows require 8 pounds of grain to produce 1 pound of beef. The latest statistics indicate that there are 1.6 billion cattle worldwide. These cattle consume one-third of all the world's grain, which is not the most efficient use of this food source.

JUST THE FACTS

In 1997, 16.4 billion pounds of raw beef were sold in the United States, compared with 19 billion pounds in 1976. During this period, raw chicken sales increased from 43 pounds per person to 69 pounds per person.

KEEP MEAT LOAF MOIST

When you are preparing meat loaf, try rubbing the top and sides with a small amount of water instead of tomato sauce. This will stop the meat loaf from cracking and drying out as it cooks. The tomato sauce can be added 15 minutes before the meat is fully cooked.

MOISTER MEATBALLS

If you insert a small piece of cracked ice into the center of your meatballs before browning them, they will be moister. But be careful—you'll need to experiment to make sure the centers don't remain raw and therefore possibly unsafe. Cut open a meatball and check the doneness of the center to determine the proper browning time.

OUCH!

When you burn or scorch a roast, remove it from the pan and cover it with a towel dampened with hot water for about five minutes; this will stop the cooking. Then remove or scrape off any burnt areas with a sharp knife, and put the roast back in the oven to reheat.

MOIST BUNS

When boiling hot dogs, use a double boiler, and put your hot-dog buns in the top to keep them warm.

MUST BE CLEAN LIVING

According to the USDA, only one in 1,000 pigs is found to contain the trichinosis parasite. The trichinosis parasite is killed at 137°F. Because meat can contain other bacteria, the USDA still recommends cooking pork to an internal temperature of 160°F.

BACON BASICS

◆ Bacon, like all cured meats, is very high in nitrites. The highest nitrite content is found in the fat, which means you should choose the leanest bacon you can find.

◆ Bacon can be prepared in the microwave on a piece of paper towel or under the broiler so the fat drips down.

◆ When you are shopping for a bacon substitute, remember that almost all of these products will still contain nitrites. Check the label, and try to find a nitrite-free product.

◆ Once the package is opened, sliced bacon will keep in the refrigerator for only one week.

◆ Never buy bacon that looks slimy; chances are it's not fresh.

A DIFFERENT MINERAL BATH

Cured hams are injected with a solution of brine salts, sugar, and nitrites. The weight of the ham will increase with the injection, and if the total weight goes up by 8 percent, the label is able to claim "ham with natural juices." If the weight of the ham increases by more than 10 percent, the label must read "water added."

HIGH FAT AND FREEZING DON'T MIX WELL

Most sausage products may contain up to 60 percent fat, and don't freeze well. In fact, ground pork products have a freezer life of only two months.

DAMAGE CONTROL

Keep sausages from splitting when cooking them by piercing the skin in one or two places while they are cooking. Rolling them in flour before cooking will reduce shrinkage.

HAM BONE CONNECTED TO THE . . .

To make removing a ham bone easier, slit the ham lengthwise down to the bone before placing it in the pan—but leave the bone in the ham. While the ham is baking, the meat will pull away and the bone will come out easily after the ham is cooked.

DESALTING HAM

Because ham is naturally salty, pour a can of ginger ale over it, and then rub the meaty side with salt at least an hour before baking it. This will cause the salt water in the meat to come to the surface, which in the process will reduce the saltiness of the ham.

EASY-FREEZEY

If you want thin ham slices for a sandwich or cold-cuts platter, place the ham in the freezer for about 20 minutes before you begin slicing.

LAMB FACTS

Lamb from New Zealand is best because it is never treated with hormones. Always buy a small leg of lamb (two, if need be), because larger legs come from older animals and have a stronger flavor.

SITTING AROUND

Stews are usually best prepared a day in advance to allow the flavors to blend—or, as the romantic French say, marry.

KEEP YOUR RIBS COLD

Ribs should always be marinated (in the refrigerator, never on the counter) before cooking. A ready-made barbecue sauce sold at the grocery store works just fine for this. For tender, fall-off-the-bone ribs, be sure to cook them a long time over low heat.

TIMING ROASTS

Don't have a roasting chart nearby? Then follow this rule of thumb: Beef roasts will take about 20 minutes for the first pound and about 15 minutes for every pound thereafter. The USDA recommends cooking beef to an internal temperature of at least 145°F.

IT'S A MATTER OF TASTE

Beef and veal kidneys have more than one lobe; lamb and pork kidneys have only one. Kidneys should be firm, not mushy, and pale in color. Before you cook them, be sure to remove the excess fat and membranes.

JUICING UP LOW-FAT MEAT

If you are preparing hamburger or meat loaf with very low-fat meat, mix in one well-beaten egg white for every pound of meat. Also, adding a package of instant onion-soup mix will really make a difference. Putting a bit of small-curd cottage cheese or instant potatoes in the center of a meat loaf will keep the meat moist and provide an interesting taste treat.

TO FREEZE OR NOT TO FREEZE

When any type of fat-containing meat or lunch meat is refrozen, the fat content may cause the food to become rancid. And this is only one reason why meats should not be refrozen. (In case you need other reasons, the texture of the meat can suffer, and improper thawing can promote bacterial growth.) Leftover cooked meats can be refrigerated safely for four days.

OVEREXPOSURE

Any ground meat has had a large percentage of its surface exposed to air and light, and this means it is potentially dangerous. Oxygen and light cause the meat to break down, change color, and go bad in a very short period. Exposure to oxygen causes the meat to deteriorate. Grinding meats also speeds up the loss of vital nutrients.

BA-A-A-WARE

When purchasing a lamb shank, be sure it weighs at least 3 to 4 pounds. If the shank is any smaller, the percentage of bone will be too high in relation to the amount of meat.

SCIENTIFIC FACTS

A study performed by Dr. Martin Marchello of North Dakota State University's Department of Animal and Range Sciences found that in the meat of 26 species of domestic game, bison meat was lower in fat than beef, pork, or lamb. Three ounces of bison contained only 143 calories, 2.42 grams of fat, and 82 milligrams of cholesterol (the same amount of beef tips the scales at 211 calories, 9.28 grams of fat, and 86 milligrams of cholesterol). It was low in sodium and high in iron. Bison does not have the gamy flavor associated with many game meats.

RABBIT FACTS

The rabbit meat that is from domesticated animals and sold in American markets is all white; this is because the rabbits don't get much time to exercise. European rabbit meat is tougher, because the animals are not farm-raised and get plenty of exercise.

WELL-DONE DANGERS

While undercooked burgers may pose a risk of E. coli poisoning, well-done burgers may pose the risk of a potentially harmful carcinogen called heterocyclic aromatic amine (HAA). This compound is formed when meat is cooked to high temperatures. To avoid HAA, try these tips:

◆ Choose lean cuts of beef. Ask the butcher to remove all the fat from around the edges and put it through the meat grinder twice to break up the remaining fat. Sizzling fat creates smoke, which creates HAA.

◆ Place the ground beef in a microwave oven on high power for 1 to 3 minutes just before you cook it. HAAs form when browning occurs, and meat that is precooked before going onto the grill reduces the amount of time HAAs have to form.

◆ Reduce the amount of meat in your burgers by adding mashed black beans or cooked rice and you will have a safer—not to mention delicious—medium-well burger.

SKELETAL PROBLEM ALERT

Any type of beef consumed in large quantities may inhibit the absorption of the mineral manganese. This increases the chances of the body losing calcium through the urine—and that's bad for the bones.

SETTING A SPEED RECORD

When you are grilling for a large crowd and your grill isn't big enough, you can save time by placing a few layers of hamburgers between sheets of foil on a cookie sheet and baking them at 350°F for 15 minutes. You can then finish them on the grill in only five to 10 minutes. Hot dogs may be done the same way, but bake them only 10 minutes.

SUPER GLUED

If you're going to buy a canned ham, purchase the largest one you can afford. Most smaller canned hams are made from bits and pieces glued together with gelatin.

LIKE A JUICY STEAK

An old wives' tale, handed down from generation to generation, says that searing a steak will keep the juices in. This really didn't seem to ring true, so it was put to the test. The results are in, and it turns out that searing a piece of steak does not help to keep it juicier (many chefs, however, will take issue with this). Searing does cause the browning that creates a good flavor, so it is still recommended. The investigators discovered that steak cooked more slowly and at a lower temperature was not only more tender but also retained more of its juices.

HOW VEAL IS PRODUCED

Veal comes from calves that have been fed a special diet from the day they are weaned until they are slaughtered, which is usually when they are between 16 and 18 weeks old and weigh about 450 pounds. The animals are kept in stalls and are not allowed to exercise, and are fed either a special milk formula (for milk-fed veal) or one consisting of water, milk solids, fats, and special nutrients for growth. When the calves are about three to four months old, the texture of the meat is perfect for tender veal. The most desirable is the milk-fed veal at three months old. However, the second formula has now become more popular because it produces a calf that is larger at four months, thus providing more meat. Veal is tender and contains about the same amount of fat as beef, though it has more cholesterol. By law, veal producers cannot use hormones.

HAM SLICES SALTY? GIVE THEM A DRINK OF MILK

If your ham slices are too salty, place them in a dish of low-fat milk for 20 minutes before cooking, then rinse them off in cold water and dry them with paper towels. The ham will not pick up the taste of the milk. Be sure you only taste a ham labeled "fully cooked."

IS THERE A BLACK MARKET IN DRUGS SOLD TO LIVESTOCK PRODUCERS?

In the 1980s, the FDA cracked down on illegal drug trafficking among livestock producers, but the problem may still exist. Testing of beef by the FDA has shown that a number of drugs are still being used. One commonly used, unapproved drug is the antibiotic chloramphenicol, which in sufficient amounts can cause aplastic anemia and a number of nervous disorders. Among the other illegal livestock drugs that are still showing up are Dimetridazole and Ipronidazole, both known to be carcinogens.

HONOR AMONGST BEEVES

The USDA normally checks only 1 to 2 percent of all beef carcasses for illegal drug residues, or about 1.5 of the total 89 pounds each person consumes in a year. Still, government monitoring and testing indicate that beef remains virtually free from residues.

IS A RARE STEAK REALLY BLOODY?

No! The blood is drained at slaughterhouses and hardly any ever remains in the meat. There is a pigment called myoglobin in the muscles of all meat that contributes to its reddish color, while blood obtains its color from hemoglobin. Those red juices are for the most part colored by myoglobin, not hemoglobin. Beef is redder than pork, for example, because it contains more myoglobin.

TESTING FOR DONENESS

An experienced chef rarely uses a thermometer when cooking a steak. Meat has a certain resiliency, and after testing thousands of steaks, a chef can just press the steak with a finger to tell whether the meat is rare, medium-rare, medium, medium-well, or well-done. As meat cooks it loses water, and the more it cooks, the firmer it becomes.

IS A FATTY, MARBLED STEAK THE BEST?

Those white streaks running through the meat are fat. The fat is a storage depot for energy, and for its meat to be well marbled, an animal must be fed a diet high in rich grains such as corn, which is where we get the old saying that corn-fed beef is best. The fat imparts flavor and provides moisture that helps tenderize the meat. Well-marbled meat indicates that the animal did not exercise a lot, thus the meat will be tender.

BEST WAY TO THAW MEAT

When thawing meat, you want both to minimize any damage from the freezing process and to avoid bacterial contamination. To avoid loss of flavor and reduce the risk of bacterial growth, always thaw meat in the refrigerator. This will require some advance planning. Defrosting in the microwave can partially cook the meat; it will not only cause a loss of flavor but may possibly result in a dried out piece of meat.

SPAM—HAWAII'S FAVORITE CANNED MEAT

In 1937, the Geo. A. Hormel Company introduced Spam, a canned, spiced ham product. Spam was extremely popular as a military ration during World War II. It is actually composed of scraps of shredded pork with added fat, salt, water, sugar, and a dose of sodium nitrite as a preservative and bacterial retardant. The consumption of Spam in the United States is about 114 million cans annually. Hawaii outdoes the rest of the states, with an annual consumption of 12 cans per person. Alaska comes in second with six cans per person. Texas, Alabama, and Arkansas tied for third place with an average of three cans per person.

BUYING THE BEST HAMBURGER MEAT

The news media is constantly telling us to purchase only the leanest meat we can find, and for years doctors gave their patients the same advice. However, after the results of experiments relating to fat content and flavor that were conducted on ground beef were published, some people in the medical field changed their opinions. Now, fattier meats like ground chuck are considered preferable. When meat is broiled or grilled, most of the fat is released and drips below the cooking surface. The flavor of a burger made from chuck is superior to that made from round because the chuck is cut is from a more muscled and fatty part of the animal. Make sure any ground meat you buy is very fresh to avoid bacterial contamination.

HOW MANY HAMBURGERS DO AMERICANS ORDER IN ONE SECOND?

It has been estimated that, in 1997, 252 hamburgers were ordered every second, 24 hours a day, from the more than 150,450 fast-food restaurants throughout the United States.

FRIED RATTLESNAKE

Rattlesnake is actually a tasty meat. To prepare it, just cut off the head— but be careful, because the rattlesnake still has reflexes that allow it to bite even if it's dead. Slit the skin near the head and peel it back an inch or so, then tie a cord around the peeled-back area and hang the snake from a tree limb. This leaves both hands free so you can peel off the skin with a sharp knife. Then slit open the belly, remove the intestines, and then cut the meat away from the bone. Rinse the snake in cold, salted water several times, and then cut into bite-size pieces. (You can also buy rattlesnake from several purveyors in the United States.) Flour and fry it as you would chicken, or add it to soups or stews. Its taste is something like a cross between pork and chicken.

CAREFUL WITH THE LIVER!

An animal's liver acts as a filtration plant for the body, and toxins may concentrate in its cells. These may include pesticides and heavy metals, depending the animal's diet. Liver is also extremely high in cholesterol. A 3.5-ounce serving of beef liver contains 390 milligrams of cholesterol, compared with 95 milligrams in an equal amount of hamburger.

WHEN SHOULD SOUP BONES BE ADDED TO STOCK?

One mistake people frequently make when preparing stock is to place the animal bone in the water after it has come to a boil. This tends to seal the bone and prevent all the flavor and nutrients from being released into the stock. The bone should be added to the cold water when the pot is first placed on the stove. This will allow the maximum release of flavors, nutrients, and especially the gelatinous thickening agents that add body to the stock. Store soup bones in the freezer.

RESTING YOUR ROAST

Let a roast stand for about 15 minutes before you carve it; this gives the juices time to be reabsorbed and evenly distributed. When you cook a roast, the juices tend to be forced to the center as those near the surface evaporate from the heat. Resting the roast also allows the meat to firm up a bit, making it easier to carve thinner slices.

SHOULD YOU EAT MORE WILD GAME?

Restaurants, mail-order food catalogs, and gourmet shops nationwide are now selling more farm-raised game than ever before. The most popular are buffalo, venison, wild boar, and pheasant. Most game has a high price tag (ground venison is $4 per pound, while venison steaks sells for $16 to 18 a pound), but it seems to be selling and gaining in popularity. Most wild animals don't get fat, which means their meat is lower in fat, calories, and cholesterol than domesticated meats. Because it is lower in fat, game may require marinating for tenderness. To remove the gamy flavor, just add some ginger ale to the marinade, or soak the meat in the ginger

DID YOU KNOW?

The acid in tomato juice will tenderize liver. Just soak liver in the juice for 1 to 2 hours in the refrigerator before cooking. Milk will also work as a tenderizer.

ale for an hour before cooking. Also note that overcooking will toughen many cuts of wild game.

ROOM TEMPERATURE HAM

Many times you will see hams on the shelves in the market rather than in the refrigerator case. These hams are actually salt-cured hams, sometimes called country hams. They may have a layer of mold on the skin, which can be scraped off. Salt-cured hams need to soak in water for several hours, then must be simmered for several more, before being baked. They are much saltier than brine-cured hams and are something of an acquired taste, though their devotees think they're heavenly.

PORKERS LIKE TO PLAY WITH PIGSKINS

In England, pigs are given footballs to play with in order to keep them from chewing on one another's ears and tails. Pigs do not like being penned up and pester one another all day. The pigs that have been given footballs seem more contented and are gaining weight at a faster rate.

WHY IS HAM SO POPULAR AT EASTER?

Serving ham on special occasions is a custom that predates Christianity. When fresh meats were not available in the early spring months, pre-Christian peoples buried fresh pork butts in the sand close to the ocean during the early winter months. The pork was cured by the marinating action of the salt water, which killed the harmful microbes. When spring arrived, the salt-preserved meat was dug up and cooked over wood fires.

THE IRIDESCENT HAM

Have you ever purchased a ham that has a greenish, glistening sheen? This occasionally occurs when a ham is sliced and the surface is exposed to the effects of oxidation. It is not a sign of spoilage but is caused by the nitrite modification of the iron content of the meat, which tends to produce a biochemical change in the meat's pigmentation.

THE COLOR OF COOKED HAM

After ham is cured, it contains nitrite salt. This chemical reacts with the myoglobin in the tissue and changes it into nitrosomyoglobin. This biochemical alteration keeps the meat reddish even when it is cooked to a high temperature.

REWRAP ME

If you take advantage of sale prices and stock up on meat with plans to freeze it, take a few precautions if you'll be freezing it for more than two weeks. Always remove meat from the store packaging and rewrap it in special freezer paper. Chops, cutlets, and hamburger should be freezer-wrapped individually to ensure maximum freshness and convenience.

FROZEN FOOD

The Russians claim to have recovered a mammoth, with its meat still edible, from the ice of Siberia. The mammoth is estimated to be 20,000 years old. If the Russians decide to clone it, we may be eating mammoth burgers! In the Yukon, frozen prehistoric horse bones, estimated to be 50,000 years old, were discovered. The marrow was determined safe to eat and was served at an exclusive New York City dinner party.

IS THE BEEF INDUSTRY FORCED TO GIVE COWS GROWTH HORMONES?

If the beef industry did not use growth hormones, the price of beef would increase by about 27 cents per pound. With the use of hormones, cows increase in size at a faster rate and have more body mass to convert to usable meat. More than 90 percent of all cattle raised for beef in the United States are treated by implanting a hormone capsule under the skin on the back of the animal's ear.

COOKING AND MEAT COLOR

While you are cooking beef, you can see the color of the meat change: The red pigment myoglobin changes from bright red in a rare steak to brown in a well-done one. The internal temperature of a rare steak is 135°F, medium-rare is 145°F, medium is 160°F, and well-done is 170°F.

IS THE SURFACE OF MEAT BEING TREATED?

In some instances, the surface of the meat you purchase is a nice red color while the inside is darker, almost brown in color. Butchers have been accused of dying or spraying the meat, but the truth is that when the animal is slaughtered and oxygen-rich blood is no longer being pumped to the muscles, the myoglobin tends to lose some of its reddish color and may turn brown. Then, when the meat is further exposed to the air through the plastic in which it is wrapped, oxidation tends to turn the myoglobin red again. Butchers call this process the "bloom" of the meat. If you would like the inside to be a bright red color, just slice the meat open and leave it in the refrigerator for a short period. The air will turn it a reddish color. Remember, however, that if meat is exposed for too long, the oxygen will eventually turn the meat brown again.

THE SPLATTERING BACON

If bacon were still produced the old-fashioned way, by curing it slowly and using a dry salt, it would not splatter when cooked. Today's bacon is cured in brine, which speeds up the curing process. The additional liquid from the brine gets released when the bacon is cooked, causing the fat to to splatter more. To reduce splattering, use a low heat setting. This will also reduce the number of nitrites that convert into carcinogens, because high heat tends to convert the nitrites faster than does lower heat. You can also soak the bacon in ice-cold water for 2 to 4 minutes, and then dry it well with paper towels before frying it. Also, try sprinkling the bacon with a bit of flour before cooking it, or just put a splatter screen over the pan.

WHY BAD MEAT SMELLS BAD

The surface of meat can become contaminated with bacteria, spores, and mold because of poor sanitary conditions where the animal was slaughtered and processed. These contaminants break down the surface of the meat, liquefying the carbohydrates and proteins and producing a putrid film. This film produces carbon dioxide and ammonia gases, which result in an offensive odor. The meat may also be discolored by this action on the myoglobin (red pigment), converting it to yellow and green bile pigments. The longer this continues, the more the breakdown progresses, eventually converting the protein in the meat into mercaptans (chemicals that contain a substance related to skunk spray) and hydrogen sulfide, which has a rotten-egg-like smell. Meats must be kept refrigerated and should not remain at room temperature for even short periods.

What Is Our Food Composed of?			
MEAT	% WATER	% PROTEIN	% FAT
Beef	60	18	22
Chicken	65	30	5
Fish	70	20	10
Lamb	56	16	28
Pork	42	12	45
Turkey	58	20	20

MARINADE FACTS

◆ If you have ever wondered why meats turn brown so quickly when they are grilled or cooked in a similar method, the answer is: the marinade. Marinades are high in acids that react with the myoglobin (a muscle pigment) in the meat and turn it brown very quickly.

◆ The lower the temperature, the slower the marinade will be to cause this reaction, and, incidentally, to tenderize the meat. If you marinate at room temperature, it will take less time than if you do it in the refrigerator. But it's safer to marinate in the refrigerator.

◆ The acid in most marinades will reduce the meat's capacity for retaining moisture, and the meat may not be as moist as you would expect. This problem is usually offset by the fact that the meat will have a better flavor and may absorb some of the marinade.

◆ Large pieces of meat should be placed in a large plastic bag and tightly sealed to reduce the amount of marinade required. Smaller foods can be marinated in a glass container with excellent results. Never marinate meat in a metal container because the acid in the marinade may react with the metal to give the food an unpleasant flavor.

◆ Never baste food with marinade it soaked in. Bacteria from the food may have contaminated the marinade, and the food may not cook long enough to kill it.

◆ Always cover food that is marinating, and keep it refrigerated. Also, make sure the food is completely covered with the marinade.

Marinating Times Under Refrigeration	
FOOD	TIME
Fish	20 to 40 minutes
Poultry	3 to 4 hours
Meat*	12 to 24 hours

*If the meat is cut in small pieces, the marinade time should be 2 to 3 hours.

THE COOLER THE MEAT, THE TOUGHER IT IS

Meat gets tougher as it cools on your plate, because the collagen, which has turned to a tender gelatin, thickens. The best way to eliminate this problem is to be sure you serve steak on a warmed or metal plate. After carving a roast, keep it in a warmer or put it back in the oven and leave the door ajar.

BACTERIA RISKS—PORK COMPARED WITH CHICKEN

Recent studies have shown that a typical piece of pork found in the supermarket may have only a few hundred bacteria per square centimeter, compared with more than 100,000 bacteria in the same measure of a piece of chicken. This is one of the reasons it is so important to clean up thoroughly after handling raw poultry.

CAN A COW BE TENDERIZED BEFORE SLAUGHTERING?

A number of slaughterhouses in the United States are injecting animals with a papain solution shortly before they are slaughtered. The solution is carried to the muscles by the bloodstream and remains in the meat after the animal is killed. When the meat is cooked, the enzyme is activated at 150°F. This tenderizing method has a disadvantage, however, because the meat occasionally becomes mushy and lacks firmness.

KEEP THE FLAVOR

When you refrigerate cooked beef, the flavor changes noticeably. After only a few hours, the fat, which is the main source of flavor, tends to produce an off taste. This off flavor is caused by the heating process, which encourages oxidation of the fat. If you know you'll be having leftovers, avoid cooking the beef in iron or aluminum pots and pans, and do not salt meats until you are ready to eat them.

SHOULD A STEAK BE SALTED OR PEPPERED BEFORE COOKING?

The jury's still out on this one. One authority says to salt before cooking, another equally respected one says to salt after cooking. The salt tends to draw liquid from the meat. The liquid then boils in the pan, and the surface of the meat may not have the desired texture or brown color you desire. The salt does not work its way into the meat to flavor it unless you puncture the meat, which is not recommended since juices escape. If you want the flavor of salt, or of a seasoning that contains salt, the best method is to season both sides of the meat just before serving. Never use ground pepper on any meat that is to be cooked in a pan with dry heat. Pepper tends to become bitter when scorched by the heat of a dry pan.

THE COMPARATIVE FREEZER LIFE OF CHICKEN AND BEEF

Chicken has a shorter freezer life than does beef because it has a higher ratio of unsaturated to saturated fat. Unsaturated fats are more easily destroyed by oxidation and thus are more likely to turn rancid. This is because there are more hydrogen sites in unsaturated fat to which oxygen can attach. Beef is high in saturated fat and has almost no open sites.

WHY ARE CERTAIN CUTS OF BEEF MORE TENDER THAN OTHERS?

There are a number of factors that account for the tenderness of a piece of meat. These include the actual location the meat is cut from and the activity level and age of the animal. The areas of the animal that are the least exercised are typically the most tender. But even if a steak is labeled sirloin—and therefore ought to be tender—the degree of tenderness will depend on which end of the sirloin it was cut from. If it was cut from the

DID YOU KNOW?

Meat cut across the grain will be more tender and have a better appearance.

short loin end, it will be more tender than if it was cut from the area closer to the round. Kobe beef cattle from Japan are actually massaged to relax them, since stress and tension may cause muscles to flex and this (a form of exercise) increases the development of connective tissue.

How Much Beef To Buy For Each Person?	
TYPE OF BEEF	AMOUNT PER SERVING
Chuck roast/rib roast	½ lb
Filet mignon	5 oz
Hamburger	¼ lb
Pot roast with bone	¼ lb
Ribs	1 lb
Round roast with bone	¼ lb
Round steak	5 oz
Sliced lunch meats	¼ lb
Steaks without bone	5 oz
Steaks with bone	6–8 oz
Stew meat	¼ lb
Fillet of beef	5 oz

TO AGE OR NOT TO AGE?

Aging allows time for the enzymes in meat to soften the connective tissue so the meat becomes more tender. When aging beef, the temperature must be kept between 34°F and 38°F. The meat should not be frozen, because freezing would inactivate the enzymes; too high a temperature, on the other hand, would cause bacterial growth.

SPRUCING IT UP

When preparing a fatty-looking roast, cut off as much fat as possible before roasting. Be sure to cook the roast on a rack or on thickly sliced vegetables to keep it out of any fat that renders from the meat.

WILL FREEZING RAW MEAT MAKE IT SAFE TO EAT RARE?

Unfortunately, freezing will not kill all the bacteria found in meat or chicken, and you will still be at risk if the meat is consumed without having been cooked through. Some microbes survive freezing and will multiply very quickly as meat is thawed.

  If you eat your hamburger rare, purchase a steak, sear it well on both sides, then grind it in a meat grinder and cook it immediately. Searing will kill any microbes on the outside of the meat.

WHY SHOULD MEATS BE WRAPPED TIGHTLY FOR FREEZING?

When you freeze foods, evaporation continues and fluids are lost. The entire surface of the meat must be protected from this process with a moisture-resistant wrap. The best way to wrap meats for freezing is in plastic wrap covered by a protective freezer paper. This will not eliminate evaporation entirely, but it will reduce the risk of oxidation and rancidity.

TENDERIZING MEATS

Generally, the toughness of beef depends on the level of collagen (a protein substance) in the connective tissue. Slow cooking with moist heat breaks down the collagen and softens the connective tissue. If you cook the meat too long, however, it will actually get tough again as a result of another constituent in the connective tissue called elastin, which does not soften and become tender. The best way to cook meat slowly is in a 325°F oven for a few hours, cooking the meat in liquid. Boiling is not effective nor is slow cooking at 140°F for a long period. Meat tenderizers that actually break down the protein are papain and bromelain.

WHAT IS A CHITLIN?

Chitlins, chitlings, or chitterlings are all the same Southern delicacy made from pigs' intestines. One 3-ounce serving of simmered chitlings contains 260 calories, 222 of which are from fat.

313

SHOULD A ROAST BE COOKED IN A COVERED PAN?

The two methods normally used for cooking a roast are dry heat (without liquid) or moist heat (with liquid). When the meat is covered, steam is trapped in the pan. Many cooks use this method to prevent the roast from drying out. Dry heat (with the lid off) will brown the outside of the roast, and, if you wish, you can baste it every 15 minutes to provide the desired moisture. This is the method preferred by most chefs. However, if you do roast with a lid and in liquid, you must lower the temperature by 25°F. Roasts should always be cooked on a rack or with stalks of celery placed underneath. If the meat sits in the liquid on the bottom of the pan, the underside of the roast will be mushy.

WHAT IS AMERICA'S FAVORITE PIZZA TOPPING?

Pepperoni is at the top of the list. Americans consume 300 million pounds of it on pizza every year. If you placed all the pepperoni pizzas eaten in the United States in one year next to one another, they would take up an area the size of 13,000 football fields.

HAM IT UP

Prosciutto is an Italian ham that is never smoked and is prepared by a salt-curing process, seasoned, and then air-dried. *Prosciutto cotto* means that the ham has been cooked and is common delicatessen terminology.

BASTE ME, BASTE ME

When roasting a pork loin, cook it with the fat-side down for the first 20 minutes. This will cause the fat to begin to liquefy. Then turn the roast over for the balance of the cooking time, and the fat will baste the meat.

BURGERS AROUND THE WORLD
Brazil, Argentina, and Chile
Hamburgers in these countries are always broiled instead of fried and are usually served on a piece of pumpernickel (dark brown bread) with a slice of cheese and poached or fried egg on top.

Germany and Austria

Ground beef is mixed with small bits of wet bread or crackers, onions, mustard, and sometimes an egg (to glue it all together).

Switzerland

Hamburgers can be found with the typical toppings of cheese, lettuce, and tomatoes, but they are never held in your hand. Instead, they are eaten with a knife and fork.

Korea, Vietnam, and China

People in these countries eat a unique hamburger, if you can call it that after they get through adding the following: special hot mustards, kimchee, pickled beet sauce, and a brown cream sauce with onions—and even a bit of lingonberry preserves!

Fat and Calories in Meat (per 3.5 Ounces)			
	FAT (g)	% FAT CALORIES	TOTAL CALORIES
BEEF			
Bottom round, roasted	6.0	31	117
Sirloin roast	5.6	28	180
Top round, broiled	4.0	19	190
Chuck arm, braised	6.3	29	198
Flank steak, broiled	10.1	44	207
Club steak, broiled	29.0	36	242
Chuck blade, braised	25.8	67	248
Ground beef (lean), broiled	18.5	61	272
Ground beef (reg.), broiled	20.7	64	289
T-Bone, broiled	23.3	68	309
Porterhouse, broiled	25.6	70	327
Rump roast	27.0	71	344
Sirloin steak, broiled	32.0	75	384

Fat and Calories in Meat (per 3.5 Ounces)

	FAT (g)	% FAT CALORIES	TOTAL CALORIES
PORK			
Tenderloin, roasted	4.8	26	164
Ham leg (butt), roasted	8.1	35	206
Loin, roasted	9.6	41	209
Ham leg (shank), roasted	10.5	44	215
Shoulder, roasted	13.5	53	230
	FAT (g)	**% FAT CALORIES**	**TOTAL CALORIES**
LAMB			
Foreshank, braised	6.0	29	187
Leg (sirloin half), roasted	9.2	41	204
Arm (or shoulder) chop, broiled	10.5	45	210
Loin chop, broiled	11.3	48	211
Rib chop, broiled	12.9	49	235
	FAT (g)	**% FAT CALORIES**	**TOTAL CALORIES**
VEAL			
Sirloin chop, roasted	6.2	33	168
Blade steak, roasted	6.9	36	171
Loin chop, roasted	6.9	35	175
Rib roast	7.4	37	177

12
FOWL
PLAY

FROM FARM TO TABLE

In the United States, all chickens except kosher ones are processed by scalding in 125°F to 129°F water for 30 to 75 seconds to loosen the feathers. These are temperatures at which most bacteria thrive. Hot water also opens the pores of the chickens' skin, possibly allowing undesirable matter that might be floating in the hot, bloody water to enter. The carcasses are then washed to remove debris from the defeathering process.

Recent TV exposés have uncovered the health risks that can result from processing techniques. Inspection procedures cannot detect most of the pathogens associated with poultry. Studies conducted by the National Academy of Science reported that 48 percent of food poisonings in the United States are caused by contaminated poultry. One person in every 50 who eats chicken regularly is at risk of food poisoning.

Commercial chickens must be cooked to an internal temperature of 185°F to kill any bacteria that might be present. If the chicken is fully cooked, traces of pink near the bone do not signify undercooking; the color is probably from bone pigment that has leached out during cooking. This is more common in smaller birds or ones that have frozen and defrosted, and the meat is perfectly safe to eat. Any item that comes in contact with uncooked chicken, whether it is a dishcloth, your hands, a sponge, or the countertop, must be thoroughly cleaned to eliminate the possibility of contaminating other foods and utensils with harmful bacteria.

HOW ARE CHICKS SLAUGHTERED AND INSPECTED?

Chickens are ready for harvesting at about six weeks old. The chickens are packed into cases of 22 birds per case and sent to the slaughterhouse. The chickens are dumped onto a conveyer belt; workers grab them and hang them upside-down with their feet in a locking device. The workers can grab a bird and lock it in about one second. The chickens are then dampened with a spray and sent past a grid, with an electrical charge of 60 volts for five to 10 seconds, just enough to stun them so they won't put up a fight. As the limp chickens move along the conveyer, they pass a mechanical knife that slits the throat, allowing them to bleed freely. After 35 to 50 percent of the blood is drained, the conveyer reaches a bath of scalding water through which the chickens are carried. The 125°F to 129°F water loosens their feathers.

Next, they pass through the defeathering machine, which consists of six-inch, spinning rubber projections that rub off the feathers. The birds are washed, and then arrive at the point where a machine or a worker cuts off the head, cuts open the cavity, and removes the entrails. A USDA inspector inspects the birds at this point for diseases, tumors, or infections. The inspector is given two seconds with each bird to accomplish this task. If the bird has one tumor, the growth is removed, and the bird passes inspection. If it has two or more, it is rejected. Cleaning is accomplished by immersing 5,000 chickens at a time in a bath of chilled water. One billion pounds of chicken are shipped in the United States every week.

THE PROCESSING OF KOSHER POULTRY

Kosher poultry is slaughtered in strict adherence to Jewish dietary laws. First, the bird's throat is slit; it is then put into a special cone to drain blood. The feathers are removed by machine in cold water, after which the bird is rinsed and chilled. It is then inspected by a government inspector and a mashgiah, or Jewish inspector. Afterward, it is soaked in water for 30 minutes, and then covered with coarse kosher salt for one hour. The salt is removed, and the bird is rinsed three times in cold water. Many cooks believe kosher chickens have a fresher, cleaner taste than do standard supermarket chickens. Frequently, kosher chickens that have been approved by government inspectors do not pass the mashgiah's scrutiny and never make it to market.

SAFE STUFFING

Stuffed or cooked poultry should never remain at room temperature for more than 40 minutes. Salmonella, which may be present in the meat, thrives at temperatures of 40°F to 145°F. All stuffing should be removed when the bird is ready for carving. Hot stuffing will keep the interior temperature just right for the growth of bacteria. Stuffing should always be cooked to a temperature of 165°F.

SMART STUFF

Look for stuffing bags, designed to be placed in the cavity of the bird before stuffing it. This is an excellent idea because the stuffing can be removed all at once. If you don't find stuffing bags at your market, lining the cavity with cheesecloth will accomplish the same thing.

DON'T BE TOO SPEEDY

When you make a chicken or turkey salad, be sure the meat has been cooked to 180°F, and then allow it to cool in the refrigerator before adding salad dressing or mayonnaise.

CHICKEN TENDERS

Lemon is a natural tenderizer for chicken and gives it a lovely flavor. Also, try basting chicken with a small amount of white Zinfandel; wine helps crisp the skin, and the sugar in the wine imparts a brown color and glaze to the outside of the meat. A chicken cooked at a constant 375°F will be juicier because more fat and moisture will be retained.

FOWL CUBES

Make do-it-yourself bouillon cubes by freezing leftover chicken broth in ice-cube trays. The cubes can be kept frozen in zip-close plastic bags until needed. They are easily defrosted in the microwave—or just toss them into a soup or sauce, and they'll melt quickly enough.

CLIP, CLIP

To save money, buy chickens whole, cut them up with poultry shears, and freeze in portion-size packages. When you purchase whole birds, remember that larger birds are older, and therefore tougher. Younger chickens and turkeys have less fat.

TRY IT! YOU'LL NOTICE THE DIFFERENCE

Chefs tenderize and improve the taste of chicken by submerging them in buttermilk and refrigerating for two to three hours before cooking.

SMART BIRDS

Chickens in the United States are sold as Grade A, Grade B, or Grade C. Grades B and C are usually blemished and are used only for canning, frozen foods, and TV dinners; they are not available at the retail level. Grade A chickens are sold in supermarket meat departments.

NO CREATURE COMFORTS HERE

Production chickens are raised in large coop farms, each of which house more than 10,000 birds. The chickens are placed in holding boxes and fed around the clock to fatten them up. Poultry in other countries is never subjected to the conditions we allow in the United States, and the flavor of birds from foreign countries is much better.

ASK THE BUTCHER

When you see a chicken labeled "fresh," ask the butcher whether it was previously frozen. Chickens can be stored at 26°F and still be called fresh, even though they will freeze at this temperature. If a chicken has been frozen, it would be best not to refreeze it.

MASS CHICKENDUCTION

One chicken farm may be capable of shipping 26 million chickens per week. More than 43 million chickens are processed in the United States every day, according to the National Broiler Council.

SKIP THE INJECTION

Try cooking your next turkey breast-side down on a V-rack for the first hour. The juices will flow to the breast and make the meat moist and tender. Remove the V-rack after the first hour. After trying this, you will never buy another commercially prepared self-basting bird.

LET'S TALK TURKEY

In 1997, Americans consumed about 28 pounds of turkey per person. In 1991, they consumed 20 pounds; in 1930, they ate only two pounds.

RELAX!

Once a turkey has finished cooking, it should be allowed to rest for about 20 minutes before carving. As with other roasts, this standing time allows the proteins in the meat to reabsorb the juices, so they stay in the meat rather than spilling onto the cutting board.

DID YOU KNOW?

Chicken parts or cut-up chicken should be used within 24 hours. Do not keep uncooked whole poultry in the fridge for more than two days.

BACTERIA HAVEN

Never stuff a turkey or other fowl and leave it overnight, even in the refrigerator. The inside of the bird acts like an incubator, promoting rapid bacterial growth. Cooking the bird may not kill all the bacteria. Hundreds of cases of food poisoning occur every year because birds are stuffed and then left for too long before roasting.

STAYING POWER

To store chicken in the refrigerator, wrap it in clean plastic wrap or waxed paper. The supermarket wrapping often contains bloody residues.

HOME, HOME ON THE RANGE

A free-range chicken has an average of 14 percent fat compared with 18 to 20 percent fat in a standard cooped-up chicken.

RUBDOWN

Brush or apply a thin layer of white vermouth to the skin of a turkey about 15 minutes before you are ready to remove it from the oven. The sugars in the wine will give the skin a rich brown color.

BROWN PARTS

Brushing chicken skin with reduced-sodium soy sauce during the last 30 minutes of roasting will produce a beautiful brown color.

THAWING OUT

Poultry, whether whole or parts, thaws at the rate of approximately 1 pound every five hours in the refrigerator.

SCRUB-A-DUB-DUB

The safest method of thawing frozen poultry is to place it, still wrapped in plastic, in a bowl of cold water; change the water as it warms up.

HERE A DUCK, THERE A DUCK

A farm-raised duck will have more meat than a wild duck. Duck is not a good candidate for stuffing. Its fat content is so high that the fat is absorbed into the stuffing during cooking.

WHERE'S CHICKEN LITTLE?

Miniature chickens are called Rock Cornish game hens. These are a hybrid of Cornish and White Rock chickens that are only four to six weeks old and weigh up to 2 pounds each.

BUYER BEWARE

It is best to compare nutrition labels when purchasing ground turkey or chicken. In most instances, their meats will be as high in fat as lean ground beef. Look for labels that say "ground turkey breast" or "ground chicken breast"—otherwise the poultry has probably been ground with the high-fat skin. If you can't find it at your supermarket, ask the butcher to grind boneless skinless chicken or turkey breast for you, or grind it yourself in a food processor.

OUR TAX DOLLARS AT WORK?

In 1995, the United States Government conducted a study that determined that 80 percent of the public referred to the "stuff" inside a turkey as "stuffing," while 20 percent called it "dressing." Of the 20 percent, most were above the age of 65.

SPUD IT

Do you find that stuffing spills out when you stuff a bird? Next time, seal the opening with a slice of raw potato.

MORE FOWL FACTS

Americans ate an average of 75 pounds of chicken, or about 24 birds, per person in 1998. Approximately 35 percent of all meat sold in the United States is chicken. Chicken farming is a $15 billion industry.

LIKE DARK MEAT? EAT WILD FOWL!

The breast meat on wild fowl is dark because they use their breast muscles, thus providing them with a greater blood supply. The breast muscles of commercially raised birds—even game birds—are rarely used because the birds are cooped up all their lives.

FOWL ANTIBIOTICS

Because of the way chickens are cooped up, and the questionable sanitary conditions they must endure, they are often diseased. Almost all poultry, approximately 93 percent of all pigs, and 60 percent of all cows in the United States are dosed with either penicillin or tetracycline. The fear now is that the animals will develop antibiotic-resistant bacteria. For this reason, many European countries do not allow the indiscriminate use of antibiotics on livestock animals.

REAL SICK BIRDS?

To keep chickens disease-free, chicken farmers purchased $393 million dollars worth of antibiotics in 1997.

CHUBBY CHICKEN

According to the latest USDA reports, chickens are being marketed at higher weights than ever before. Force-feeding and the use of hormones may be the reasons they go to market at top weight in only seven weeks. (Five years ago it took 12 to 14 weeks to bring a chicken to full maturity.) Turkeys reach maturity in 14 to 22 weeks, and their meat is usually lower in fat and more tender than the meat of chickens.

FOWL PLUCKING

To pluck a duck, dip it in water that is at least 155°F; it is easier to pluck the feathers if they are hot and wet. To pluck a goose, pheasant, or quail, the water should be at least 135°F. However, hot-soaking the birds breaks down fatty tissues in the skin, and should only be done if the birds are to be cooked immediately after plucking. If you plan to freeze the game birds or plan to hold them before cooking, pluck them dry.

A CHICKEN BY ANY OTHER NAME

You may find chicken labeled with any number of terms, some of which have only recently been regulated by the government. Here are some:

Free-Range

According to USDA regulations, chickens' cage doors must be kept open, and the exercise they get as a result provides better flavor. The meat is a better quality, and they have a higher proportion of meat to bone. These chickens are usually sold whole.

Organic

Not yet defined by the government, so each producer is free to set its own definition. Reputable chicken farmers will adhere to certain standards, such as raising chickens on land that has not been treated with any chemical fertilizer or pesticide in at least three years, feeding the birds chemical-free grains, and letting them range freely.

Mass-Produced

These are commercially raised in crowded coops and are never allowed to run free. They are marketed in exact sizes and always at the same age.

Kosher

Are slaughtered and cleaned in compliance with Jewish dietary laws.

Broilers and Fryers

These are 2½-month-old birds that weigh up to 3½ pounds.

Roasting Chickens

These are usually hens that weigh 2½ to 5 pounds and contain more fat than broilers.

Stewing Hens

Usually weigh 3 to 6 pounds and are 10 to 18 months old. Basically, these are retired laying hens. They are tough old birds that need to be cooked slowly, but they are very flavorful.

Capons

These are castrated roosters that are less than 10 weeks old and weigh 4 to 10 pounds. They usually have abundant breast meat.

Poussins

The French term that refers to very young, small chickens. Poussins are best when grilled.

Cornish Hens

A special breed of chicken that typically weighs less than 2 pounds. They are best grilled or roasted.

DID YOU KNOW?

A three-pound chicken will yield about 2½ cups of meat, or five servings.

DID YOU KNOW?

Chicken wings, alias Buffalo wings, can supply up to 25 grams of fat per 3-wing serving.

SQUAB

Squab are domesticated pigeons that have never flown; they are no more than a month old and weigh less than 1 pound. They are specially bred to be plump and are usually sold frozen. Look for birds with pale skin; the plumper the better. Squab will keep frozen for about six months at 0°F.

A PUDDLE? YOU'RE IN A MUDDLE

When choosing meat or poultry in the supermarket, make sure that there is no liquid on the bottom of the package. If there is, it means the food has been frozen and thawed; the cells have ruptured, releasing some of their fluids. Never refreeze poultry that has thawed.

WHICH CAME FIRST, THE CHICKEN OR THE TURKEY?

According to history books, Columbus brought chickens to the New World in 1493. The turkey, however, is native to America, and was introduced to Europe by Spanish explorers around the same time.

STICKY CHICKEN SKIN

When grilling chicken, always grease the rack well. Why? Because as the bird cooks, the collagen in the skin turns into a sticky gelatin, which will cause it to stick to the rack. Another way to solve the problem is to sear the chicken on the grill, and then finish it in a preheated oven 15 to 20 minutes, breast-side up.

HOW FAST DO BACTERIA ON CHICKEN MULTIPLY?

If a piece of chicken that has 10,000 bacteria per square centimeter gets to the supermarket, that number will increase 10,000 times if the bird is left in the refrigerator at about 40°F for six days. The Centers for Disease Control and Prevention estimates that 5,200 people die each year from food-borne illnesses, with as many as 76 million others becoming ill from bacterial, chemical, fertilizer, and pesticide residues left on poultry and other foods. According to the USDA, 40 percent of all chickens can be contaminated with salmonella, and even if contaminated, they can still pass USDA inspection.

BEST METHOD OF CLEANING A CHICKEN

Chickens must be thoroughly cleaned inside and out before cooking in order to remove any residues that may be left from the slaughtering process. If you detect a slight off odor when you open the package, rinse the bird under cool water, and then put it in a solution of 1 tablespoon lemon juice or vinegar and 1 teaspoon salt per cup of water (use enough water to cover the bird). Refrigerate one to four hours before cooking.

How Much Chicken to Buy for Each Serving?	
TYPE	AMOUNT PER SERVING
Breast	½ lb
Broiler and Fryer	½ lb
Capon	¾ lb
Cornish game hen	1 bird
Drumstick	2 drumsticks
Thighs	2 thighs
Whole chicken*	10 oz

*One 5-pound chicken will provide about 3 cups of meat;
a 3-pound chicken provides about 2½ cups.

IS BARBECUED CHICKEN A BITTER PROBLEM?

If you use barbecue sauce on chicken, know when to apply it; otherwise, the chicken will have an acidic taste. Barbecue sauces contain sugar, and high heat can burn the sugar as well as some of the spices. Never apply the sauce to the bird until about five minutes before it is fully cooked. Another secret is to use low heat and leave the bird on the grill for a longer period. Never place the bird too close to the coals.

SKIN COLOR VERSUS QUALITY

Because the public prefers to see chicken skin that is nicely yellowish rather than bluish-white and sickly looking, farmers put marigold petals in chicken feed to make the skin yellow. Production chickens are never allowed to run free and soak up the sunlight that would turn their skin

DID YOU KNOW?

The easiest way to skin a chicken is to partially freeze it first. The skin will come right off the bird with almost no effort.

yellow, and because marigold petals are "all natural," they do not have to be listed anywhere on the packaging. Free-range chickens always have yellowish skins in addition to being more flavorful.

WILD QUAIL: A DANGEROUS BIRD?

A number of people have become ill, with symptoms of nausea, vomiting, shivers, and even a type of slow-spreading paralysis, from eating wild quail. The problem may result from the food the quail consumes in certain parts of the country—occasionally hemlock, which is toxic to humans. If you become ill after eating wild quail, contact emergency medical help immediately. Please note that all commercially sold quail in this country is farm-raised and therefore fed a controlled diet—so don't worry.

COOKING WHITE MEAT VERSUS DARK MEAT

When you're cooking chicken parts, remember that dark meat takes longer to cook than white does because of its higher fat content. Start the dark meat a few minutes before the white—assuming the parts are about the same size; smaller pieces of chicken will cook faster than larger ones. The white meat might be too dry if it is cooked as long as the dark.

GIBLET COOKING

When cooking giblets, do not add the liver until the last five minutes. If added too soon, it will impart its flavor to all the rest of the ingredients.

13
SOMETHING'S FISHY

FISH FACTS

◆ More fish than ever are now raised in aquaculture fish farms, and more varieties are now available to consumers.
◆ The fats in fish are high in polyunsaturates and contain the omega-3 fatty acids that may protect us from heart attacks by keeping the blood from coagulating too easily. Studies show that even canned or frozen fish retains most of its omega-3 fatty acids.
◆ Many fish and shellfish harbor certain bacteria and parasites. To avoid food poisoning, always cook fish and shellfish; don't eat them raw. Also, one should never consume the skin or visible fat, which is where most of the contaminants are located.
◆ Fish should never smell of ammonia.

SPOTTING THE FRESHEST FISH

◆ The skin should be shiny; when pressed with a finger, the flesh should spring back to its original shape. Never buy fish whose skin is bruised.
◆ The meat should be firm to the touch, with no visible blemishes.
◆ The eyes should be bulging, not sunken into the head, which is a sign that the fish is dried out. The eyes should also be clear, not cloudy.
◆ The scales should be intact, with a bright and shiny appearance. If you notice loose scales, don't buy the fish.
◆ The gills must look clean, not slimy. Their healthy color is bright red. Gray gills indicate an old fish.
◆ A fresh fish never smells fishy. If the fish does have a strong odor, it is probably because the flesh is decomposing and releasing the chemical compound trimethylamine. Seafood should be as fresh as possible—no more than two or three days out of water.

CHOOSING FROZEN FISH

◆ If frozen fish has an odor, it has probably thawed and been refrozen. Thawed fish should have hardly any odor.
◆ Be sure the skin and flesh are frozen solid, with no discoloration or soft spots. The skin should be totally intact, with no areas missing.
◆ The wrapping should be intact, with no tears or ice crystals.

BIG DIFFERENCE

Saturated fat accounts for only 10 to 25 percent of the total fat in seafood, while it comprises an average of 42 percent of the fat in beef and pork.

SMELLS FISHY

Before handling fish, rub your hands with lemon juice. Chances are, you won't smell fish on them afterward. After frying fish, put a little white vinegar into the frying pan to help get rid of the odor on the surface.

COLD FISH?

When fish is frozen, it tends to lose some of its flavor. If you thaw the frozen fish in low-fat milk, some of the original flavor will return. Frozen fish should be thawed in the refrigerator and cooked as quickly as possible. If your fish is frozen, skin it before you thaw it, because a frozen fish is easier to skin.

TASTE TREAT

If you are going to bake fish, try wrapping it in foil or parchment paper with a sprig of dill and a little chopped onion. This helps to retain moisture and adds flavor.

MILD ACID TO THE RESCUE

To make scaling a fish easier, rub white vinegar on the scales, and then let the fish sit for about 10 minutes. Put the fish in a large plastic bag (hold it by the tail) to keep the scales from flying all over your kitchen.

SAFETY FIRST

Fish, like meat and poultry, should be marinated in the refrigerator because it decomposes rapidly at temperatures above 60°F. But don't overdo it: Because fish has so little connective tissue, it should never be marinated for longer than an hour or two.

THE STEAMY SIDE OF FISH

To steam fish fillets in the microwave, place them in a shallow microwavable dish (a glass pie plate is ideal) with the thinner parts overlapping at the center of the dish. Sprinkle with lemon juice or herbs, if you like, and then cover the dish with plastic wrap (making sure it doesn't touch the fish) and cook for 3 minutes per pound. If your microwave doesn't have a turntable, rotate the dish about halfway through the cooking time.

Fat Content in 3.5 Ounces of Fish			
Cod	0.66	Striped bass	2.3
Haddock	0.71	Oysters	2.4
Pollack	0.8	Salmon, Pacific	3.4
Tuna, yellowfin	0.95	Bass	3.7
Grouper	1.0	Mullet	3.8
Crab	1.1	Swordfish	4.0
Flounder	1.2	Shark	4.5
Sole	1.2	Tuna, bluefin	4.9
Hake	1.3	Butterfish	8.0
Red snapper	1.3	Salmon, Atlantic	8.0
Ocean perch	1.6	Herring	9.0
Shrimp	1.8	Pompano	9.5
Halibut	2.3	Mackerel	13.8

CALL THE FISH HOT LINE

The majority of fish caught in the oceans are safe to eat. If you are fishing in warmer waters, however, call the fish hot line to be sure that the type of fish you are going after is not infected with ciguatera, which has caused a number of cases of food poisoning. The toll-free number for the fish and shellfish hot line, sponsored by the U.S. government, is 800-332-4010.

DUAL-PURPOSE HINT

Fish can be frozen in clean milk cartons filled with water. After the fish is thawed, use the water as a fertilizer for your house plants.

COMMON FORMS OF FISH

Whole Fish
Comes complete with entrails and needs to be prepared soon after it is caught. It is almost never available at supermarkets.

Drawn Fish
A whole fish with only the entrails removed.

Dressed Fish
Scaled and gutted, with head, tail, and fins removed.

Fish Fillets
Sides of dressed fish, cut lengthwise away from the back bones. May be any size; seldom have bones.

Fish Steaks
Slices of larger dressed fish, cut across the body. May have bones.

Cured Fish
Smoked, pickled, or salted fish. If the fish is sold as "cold smoked," it was only partially dried and will have a very short shelf life. If the label reads "hot smoked," the fish is fully cooked and should be consumed within a few days or kept frozen until used.

Dried Fish
Fish that has been processed with dry heat, and then salted to preserve it.

A WORD TO THE WISE

Seafood labels should read "Packed Under Federal Inspection" or PUFI. This signifies that federal inspectors of the Department of Commerce inspected, graded, and certified the fish as having met all the requirements of the inspection regulations, and that the product has been produced in accordance with official standards and specifications.

THE POLLUTION PROBLEM

At present, about 34 percent of all shellfish beds in the United States have been officially closed because of pollution. All coastal waters worldwide are in jeopardy of being closed to fishing. One of the world's best known seaports, Boston Harbor, was at one point so polluted that fishermen were advised not to fish there; currently, it is open to fishermen again. The sewage problem is so bad in the Gulf states of Louisiana and Florida that 67 percent of their oyster beds have been closed to fishing. In Europe, about 90 percent of sewage is still dumped into coastal waters.

I'M JUST A SWEETIE

For the most part, shellfish are sweeter than fish. They have a higher percentage of glycogen, a carbohydrate that converts to glucose. The amino acid glycine also provides some sweetness. Crayfish and lobsters are the sweetest, followed by crab and shrimp. However, if they are stored for more than a day or two, all shellfish will lose some of their sweetness.

DID YOU KNOW?

Fish that feed on the bottom of lakes, such as carp and bass, are the most likely to be contaminated.

ABALONE

Abalone is becoming one of the rarest shellfish to find off the coast of California. The "foot" of the abalone is the tough, edible portion that must literally be pounded into tenderness. To do this, the foot is cut into slices about 3/8-inch thick, which are then pounded even thinner with a special meat-tenderizing hammer. The price is high, and abalone must be cooked within 12 to 24 hours after they are caught; otherwise, they become bitter.

TIME'S UP

Never cook abalone for more than 30 seconds on each side, or it may toughen. Before cooking, cut slashes about an inch apart to avoid curling.

TICKLISH FOOT

When purchasing abalone, make sure the foot muscle moves when touched. Never buy shellfish that is dead.

CLAMS

The most popular clam is the hard-shell clam. The soft-shelled geoduck (pronounced gooey-duck) clam is unable to close its shell because its neck sticks out too far and is too big. It weighs three pounds on average and has juicy meat with a rich flavor.

KNOW WHERE THEY ARE RAISED

All shellfish are called filter feeders. They rely on food entering their systems from the water that flows around them—water which may contain almost any type of toxic material and even sewage. Over time, ingestion of toxic material may increase to a level potentially harmful to humans. Shellfish that fed in areas contaminated by sewage can transmit diseases such as hepatitis. Shellfish are capable of filtering up to 20 gallons of water a day looking for food.

The National Shellfish Sanitation Program controls how shellfish are grown, harvested, processed, and transported, and the FDA oversees state and local officials who inspect fishing areas and shellfish beds. Exercise caution when eating raw shellfish unless they have been farm-raised.

OPEN WIDE, SAY A-A-AH

To open shellfish, wash the shells thoroughly. Hold the clam or oyster in your palm and slip the tip of an oyster knife between the upper and lower shells. Run the knife around the edge of the shell and pry until you hear a pop at the hinge. Loosen the clam or oyster from the shell and remove any shell fragments.

CLEAN 'EM UP

Once clams are dug up, they must be cleansed of sand and debris, or they will not be edible. To accomplish this, the clams should be allowed to soak in the refrigerator in a solution of one part salt to 10 parts water for several hours or overnight. If you're pressed for time, rinse them in several changes of fresh water until no sand remains.

DEAD OR ALIVE?

The shells of healthy clams should be closed when you buy them. The shells will open gradually as the clams cook. If you keep the clams on ice, they will also probably relax and open their shells. To make sure the clam is alive, tap its shell. If the shell doesn't close, the clam is sick or dead and should be discarded. Similarly, if a clam's shell doesn't open by itself when the clam is cooked, it should be discarded.

THIS CLAM WILL REALLY FILL YOU UP

The largest clam on record weighed 750 pounds; it was caught in 1956 off the coast of Manila.

THE CHOWDER TRICK

Chefs always add clams to their chowder during the last 15 to 20 minutes of cooking. If they are added too early in the cooking, clams can become either tough or too soft.

CRAB

Different species of crabs are found in different oceans or seas. Crabs caught in the Gulf of Mexico or the Atlantic Ocean are called blue crabs. Crabs caught in the Pacific Ocean are known as Dungeness crabs. The most prized crabs—and the largest—are king crabs, which are caught off the coast of Alaska and northern Canada. The smaller stone crab is found in the waters off the coast of Florida; only its claws are harvested (it's illegal to take the whole crab).

Crabs should be purchased only if they are active and heavy for their size. Refrigerate all crabs on ice as soon as possible, and cover them with a damp towel. Live crabs should be cooked the day they are purchased.

Soft-shell crabs are blue crabs; they can be found in a variety of sizes. The smallest are "spiders" and measure only about 3½ inches across, which is barely legal. "Hotel primes" measure about 4½ inches across; "primes" are 5½ inches. "Jumbo" crabs measure 6 to 7 inches across.

If canned crabmeat has a metallic taste, soak it in ice water 5 to 8 minutes, and then drain and blot it dry with paper towels.

CLAW RENEWAL

Stone crabs are able to regenerate a new claw when one is broken off. In Florida, commercial crab companies now catch crabs, break off one of its claws, then release the crab to grow another one. The crab is able to protect itself and forage for food as long as it has one claw.

WHAT IS IMITATION CRAB?

Hundreds of years ago, the Japanese invented a way to make imitation shellfish called surimi. In recent years, this has become a booming industry in the United States. At present, we are producing imitation crab meat, lobster, shrimp, and scallops, most of which are made from a deep ocean whitefish called pollack (or pollock).

Surimi is lower in cholesterol than shellfish, contains very little fat, is high in good-quality protein, and is comparable with other forms of shellfish in sodium content. The processing lowers the level of other nutrients that would ordinarily be found in fresh pollack.

COLOR CHECK

Cooking blue crabs? If the shells of blue crab are orange after they are cooked, the crabs may not have the best flavor. The crabs' shells should be a bright red or bright pink after cooking, indicating that the chemical in the shells was still very active.

CRAYFISH

These are related to, and look like, shrimp. The largest supplier in the world is the state of Louisiana, which produces between 75 and 105 million pounds of these little morsels each year.

REMOVING THE MEAT FROM CRAYFISH

Like lobsters and crabs, crayfish are always cooked live. Also known as crawfish or sometimes crawdads, they have a much sweeter flavor than either lobsters or crabs. All the meat is found in the tail of the crayfish. To remove the meat easily, gently twist the tail away from the body, and then unwrap the first three sections of the shell to expose the meat. Next, pinch the end of the meat in one hand while holding the tail in the other, and pull the meat out in one piece. You can also suck out the flavorful juices from the head.

LANGOSTINOS

Langostinos are miniature lobsters; they are usually found frozen in the market and are used mainly for salads, soups, or stews. This small crustacean is also called rock shrimp, Dublin Bay prawn, and *langoustine* (in France; *langostino* is Spanish).

SWADDLE 'EM

If you're eating whole lobster, cover it with a napkin or towel before twisting off the legs and claws. This will keep the juices from squirting about and causing a mess.

COOK WITH CARE

To retain its flavor, lobster meat should not be added to dishes until just before serving. Overcooking will destroy its taste.

WHAT, OR WHO, IS NEWBERG?

In 1876, a businessman named Ben Wenberg brought a recipe for a lobster dish to the chef at New York City's famed Delmonico's restaurant. The chef called the dish Lobster Wenberg. The chef and Wenberg had a falling-out, and the chef took the dish off the menu. His customers, however, raised such a fuss that he returned it to the menu, but reversed the first three letters of Wenberg's name. It has remained a popular way of serving lobster ever since. Most restaurants purchase spiny lobster for this dish; it's less expensive than Maine lobster.

DID YOU KNOW?

Blue crab is the only crab you can buy that isn't already cooked— Dungeness, snow, king, and stone crabs are only available cooked.

THE TWO LOBSTERS

The two most common species of lobster consumed in the United States are Maine and spiny. Maine lobsters are the most prized, and are harvested off the northeastern seaboard. These have excellent flavor, and their meat, when cooked, is snow-white. The spiny lobster is only sold live where it is harvested—the Gulf states and California. It is smaller than Maine lobster and can be identified by its smaller claws. Never purchase a lobster unless you see movement in the claws or its tail turns under when carefully touched.

A LEFT-HANDED LOBSTER?

Believe it or not, Maine lobsters may be either right- or left-handed. They are not symmetrical. Rather, the two claws are very different and are used for different purposes. One is larger, with very coarse teeth for crushing, while the other has fine teeth for ripping or tearing. The flesh in the smaller, fine-toothed claw is sweeter and more tender.

CAN A LOBSTER BE MICROWAVED?

Believe it or note, the taste, texture, and color of microwaved lobster are far superior to boiled or steamed, and microwaving produces an evenly cooked, tender lobster. A problem, however, is that you can only cook one lobster at a time.

To microwave a lobster, place it in a large microwavable plastic bag with ¼ cup water, and knot the bag loosely. A 1½ pound lobster should take 5 or 6 minutes on High, providing you have a 600-700-watt oven. If you have a lower wattage oven, allow about 8 minutes. To be sure the lobster is fully cooked, separate the tail from the body. The tail meat should be creamy white, not translucent.

Even when microwaved, the lobster must still be cooked live because of the enzymatic breakdown that occurs immediately upon its death. If you are bothered by the lobster's movements, which are just reflex actions, put it in the freezer for 10 minutes before cooking to dull its senses; the movement will be reduced to about 20 seconds.

WHY LOBSTERS TURN RED WHEN COOKED

The red coloring is always there, but it is not visible until the lobster is cooked. Lobsters, along with other shellfish and some insects, have an external skeleton that is made up of chitin. Chitin contains a bright red pigment called astaxanthin, which is bonded to several proteins. While the chitin is bonded, it remains a brownish-red color; however, when the protein is heated, the bonds are broken, releasing the astaxanthin and turning the exoskeleton bright red.

LOBSTER LIVER, A DELICACY?

Shellfish lovers seem to think it is a special treat is to consume the green tomalley, or liver, found in lobsters and the mustard found in crabs. These organs are similar to our livers and are involved in detoxifying and filtering toxins out of the shellfish. Many of these organs retain a percentage of those toxins and possibly even some PCBs or heavy metal contaminants. Because you can't be certain of a lobster's exposure to these substances, you should never eat these organs. However, the roe or coral found in female lobsters is safe to eat. Lobster roe is a delicacy in many countries.

STAYING ALIVE, STAYING ALIVE

Lobsters and crabs have very potent digestive enzymes that start to decompose these crustaceans' flesh as soon as they die. The complexity and location of their digestive organs make it too difficult to remove them before cooking. Both lobsters and crabs should, therefore, be kept alive until they are cooked. If you are uncertain as to whether a lobster is alive or dead, pick it up. If the tail curls under, the lobster is alive. Most fish cookbooks and experts recommend plunging lobsters directly into boiling water in order to kill them. If you're squeamish, you can also kill them by severing the spinal cord at the base of the neck with the tip of a knife before boiling them. Some cooks immerse the lobster in beer for a few minutes to get it drunk before placing it in the boiling water.

ROPE ME A MUSSEL

Aquaculture mussel farming has become big business in the United States over the past few years. Mussels are raised on rope ladders that keep them away from any debris on the bottom of the bed. This produces cleaner, healthier mussels and reduces the likelihood of disease. Mussels cultivated in this manner are also much larger.

DID YOU KNOW?

Monkfish is sometimes called "poor man's lobster."

339

When purchasing mussels, be sure they are alive. Tap their shells; if they are open, they should snap closed. Any mussels that don't close their shells are probably goners and should not be eaten. When mussels are shucked, the liquid that comes out should be clear.

NO DOUBLE DECKERS

Live mussels will keep in the refrigerator for two to three days if placed on a tray and covered with a damp towel. Spread them out; never pile the mussels on top of one another.

CUT OFF THEIR BEARD AND THEY DIE

Mussels should be cleaned with a stiff brush under cold running water and their visible "beard" removed just before cooking. Once they have been debearded, mussels will die.

DID YOU KNOW?

Mussels are cooked when their shells open. Discard any mussel whose shell does not open during cooking.

OYSTERS

Oysters are considered a delicacy worldwide. In 1997, 15.4 million pounds were farmed by aquaculture methods; more than 95 million pounds are consumed each year. Different varieties of oysters have distinct flavors and textures depending on where they were harvested.

OYSTERS, A SHELLFISH GAME?

Be cautious of oysters harvested from the Gulf of Mexico between April and October. These summer months are when the oysters may be contaminated with a bacteria called *Vibrio vulnificus*. Cooking the oysters will kill the bacteria, but raw oysters can be deadly to people who suffer from diabetes, liver disease, cancer, and some gastrointestinal disorders. Between 1989 and 1997, the Centers for Disease Control and Prevention received 167 reports of Vibrio contamination; 87 of those cases were fatal.

KEEP 'EM COOL

Store live oysters in the refrigerator in a single layer with the larger shell down, covered with a damp towel. Eat them within two days of purchase.

OYSTERS AND "R" MONTHS

The old saying that you should eat oysters only in months whose names include the letter "r" may have been true in the decades prior to refrigeration—as long as they are cooked. With the exception of oysters harvested from the Gulf of Mexico, there is really no medical evidence to indicate that it is dangerous to eat oysters in any month of the year. However, oysters tend to be less flavorful and less meaty during the summer months, because that is when they spawn.

AGING

Shucked oysters will stay fresh, frozen in their liquid, for up to three months, but they will keep only a day or two in the refrigerator.

TOUGH GUY

Oysters are easy to overcook, which will make them tough. If you are poaching oysters, take them out as soon as their edges start to curl.

SCALLOPS

Scallops have a very short life span once they are out of the water, and they become tough very easily if overcooked. Three types of scallop are available retail: the sea scallop, which is about two inches wide; the bay scallop, which is about ½-inch wide; and the calico, which is slightly larger than the bay scallop. Bay scallops are the most tender of the three. Scallops should be moist and should never have a strong odor.

SHRIMP

Shrimp are sold in a variety of sizes, and to make matters confusing, the quantity of shrimp per pound can vary from store to store—and even from shrimp to shrimp at the same store!

The most common sizes are the jumbo shrimp, which average 21 to 25 per pound; large shrimp, which average 31 to 35 per pound; medium shrimp, which average 43 to 50 per pound; and tiny shrimp, which average more than 70 per pound. If you're lucky, you may find colossal shrimp (10 to 15 per pound) or even extra-colossal (less than 10 per pound). The size is not an indication of their quality.

Shrimp have a high water content and will reduce from 1 pound to about ¾ of a pound or less after cooking. Worldwide there are more than 250 species of shrimp, including prawns. Shrimp can be found in a variety of colors, from white (the most desirable) to brown, depending on where they feed and where they are caught. Brown shrimp feed mainly on algae and have a stronger flavor than white.

OFF WITH THEIR HEADS!

Shrimp with heads are more perishable than those without heads. As a matter of fact, the shrimp's head contains almost all its vital organs and the majority of the digestive system.

IS A PRAWN A SHRIMP?

Biologically, a prawn is different from a shrimp in that it has pincer claws similar to those of a lobster. A relative of the prawn is the scampi, which is the Italian name for the tail portion of several varieties of lobsterettes. When restaurants in the United States have prawns on the menu, they are usually just jumbo shrimp. Jumbo shrimp cost less than the giant prawns and are not as tasty.

GOOD ADVICE

If shrimp develops an ammonia-like odor, it has started to deteriorate and should be discarded. Shrimp cannot be refrozen, and remember, almost all the shrimp you buy has already been frozen. This means that if you don't eat the shrimp the day you buy it, or possibly the next day, it should be thrown out.

NAUGHTY, NAUGHTY

Some of the shrimp that is sold already-breaded may have been overbreaded to increase the total weight of the package. The FDA has taken action against some unscrupulous companies for this practice.

A CANNY SOLUTION

If canned shrimp tastes metallic, soak the shrimp in 2 tablespoons vinegar and 1 teaspoon dry sherry for 15 minutes, or soak them the same length of time in a mixture of lemon juice and cold water.

TENDER LITTLE ONES

Shrimp will always cook up nice and tender if you cool them down before cooking them. Either place them in the freezer for 10 to 15 minutes, or set them in a bowl of ice water for about 5 minutes. If you're boiling them, drop them into hot seasoned broth or court bouillon and boil for a minute, and then turn off the heat and let stand about 10 minutes. Sautéed shrimp are done when they are firm and pink, which takes 3 to 5 minutes. Grilled shrimp are cooked in about 7 minutes.

SQUID

Squid is a member of the shellfish family and may be sold as calamari. It tends to become tough very easily and should be cooked for no more than 3 minutes to obtain the best results. Conversely, it can also become tender if braised or stewed for at least an hour. Squid is the only shellfish that has more cholesterol than shrimp. With the exception of the beak, head, and innards, the entire squid is edible.

"YUK"

The least popular foods among Americans are shark, squid, and snails. Shark, however, is making inroads since people have discovered that it is a healthful, low-fat, good-tasting fish.

DON'T OVERCOOK SHELLFISH

If you overcook shellfish, it will become tough. Clams should steam 5 to 10 minutes, crab for 15 to 20 minutes, and lobster about 20 minutes. Crayfish and mussels need only 4 to 8 minutes. Grilling an 8-ounce lobster tail takes no more than 10 to 12 minutes.

SALTWATER FISH

Anchovies

Surprisingly, anchovies are a popular poultry feed. Most of the more than 200 million pounds caught annually are ground up and used for feed. Anchovies used for canning range in size from 4 to 6 inches, they are commonly used as a pizza topping and in Caesar salad; anchovy paste, sold in tubes, is convenient because it gives the flavor without the mess.

Anglerfish

This is also known as monkfish or by its French name, *lotte*. It has a relatively firm texture and is low in fat. Anglerfish can weigh from as little as three pounds to as much as 25 pounds. They are more popular in France than in the United States, but monkfish is becoming more popular on restaurant menus and is mainly used as a substitute for lobster because its tail is comparable in taste with lobster tail.

Barracuda

The barracuda can weight up to 10 pounds, but it is most commonly found at five pounds. It is a moderately fatty fish, usually caught in the Pacific Ocean. Pacific barracuda is the only edible variety, as most other barracuda have very toxic flesh as a result of ciguatera, a naturally-occurring toxin found in the algaelike organisms barracuda eat.

Bluefish

This fish tends to deteriorate very rapidly and does not freeze well. Bluefish usually weigh three to six pounds and have a thin strip of dark flesh running down the middle that should be removed before cooking, because it may contain higher concentrations of PCBs than other parts of the fish.

Cod

Cod is a low-fat fish and has a very firm texture. The two varieties found in the fish market are Atlantic cod and Pacific cod; scrod is the term for young cod. As a substitute for cod, you might try the similar-tasting cuskfish, which is excellent in soups or chowders.

Croaker

All varieties are low in fat. This is a small fish, usually weighing ½ to two pounds, unless you are lucky enough to catch a redfish, which may weigh more than 30 pounds (redfish fishing is prohibited in some waters). The croaker is a popular chowder fish.

Eel

More popular in Japan and some European countries than in the United States, eel is a firm-textured, tasty fish that can grow to be three to four feet long. The tough skin must be removed before cooking.

Flounder

This is the most popular fish sold in the markets and may appear as "sole." There are more than 100 varieties, all of which have a mild flavor and a light texture. Flounder is one of the lowest-fat fishes and weighs anywhere from one to 10 pounds. Dover sole, which may be found on restaurant menus, is imported from England.

Grouper

A member of the sea bass family, grouper typically weighs four to six pounds but can get up to 15 pounds in the Gulf. Be sure to remove the skin before cooking. It is similar to the skin of the eel and is very tough. Grouper has a firm texture and is an easy fish to prepare either baked, grilled, or fried.

Haddock

Related to the cod, haddock is caught only in the North Atlantic. A common smoked form of this fish, called finnan haddie, is sold in markets. The flesh of haddock is somewhat softer than that of cod.

Hake

A relatively low-fat Atlantic fish with firm texture, hake has a mild flavor and usually weighs between one and eight pounds.

Halibut

Similar to flounder, low in fat and firm of texture, the halibut normally weighs anywhere between 10 and 60 pounds and is marketed as steaks or fillets.

Mackerel

This a high-fat, relatively oily fish similar to tuna. You may find it under a variety of names, such as Atlantic mackerel, wahoo, Pacific jack, kingfish, or Spanish mackerel. There is a red meat variety sold in cans that has an excellent level of omega-3 fatty acids. Mackerel is best cooked in an acid marinade that includes lemon juice or tomato.

Mahimahi

Even though mahimahi is sometimes called dolphin fish, the two are not related. There is a slight resemblance between the two, but mahimahi's bluish-green skin is unique. They may weigh up to 40 pounds and are considered one of the better eating fishes. They are usually sold as steaks or fillets, or whole.

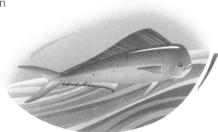

Mullet

Most mullet is caught off the Florida coast. It has a very firm texture and a relatively strong flavor. The flesh is somewhat oily and good for smoking.

Orange Roughy

Almost all orange roughy is imported from New Zealand, usually as frozen fillets. It is a low-fat fish with a slightly sweet taste and a texture similar to that of sole. It may be cooked in many ways.

Pollack

Pollack is mainly used for making fish sticks and surimi. It has a flaky texture and rich flavor. The darker layer of flesh is not as mild as the lighter layer. Pollack is also a very common chowder fish. Atlantic pollack is sometimes called Boston bluefish, though it's not related to the bluefish.

Pompano

Found mainly off the coast of Florida, pompano has recently been affected by overfishing, upping its cost. It is oily and firm-textured.

Sablefish

Commonly called black cod, sablefish has a high fat content but a light texture. Usually found smoked, it can also be baked, poached, or fried.

Salmon

By far one of the tastiest fish you will ever eat. The fattiest salmon is the Chinook, or king, salmon; it is also one of the hardest to find because it accounts for only 10 percent of the total Alaskan catch. The Coho salmon has less fat and is smaller than the Chinook. Other varieties include sockeye, whose flavor rivals king; and pink salmon, which has a dry, sometimes bitter flesh. Coho salmon deposit between 2,000 and 17,000 eggs each year during their five days of spawning.

Sardines

Sardines with bones are an excellent source of calcium. A 3-ounce serving contains more calcium than an 8-ounce glass of milk. Milk has vitamin D added to help metabolize the calcium, but sardines also supply vitamin D and phosphorus. Ounce-for-ounce, sardines can also supply you with more protein than a steak.

A member of the herring family, sardines are normally sold pickled or smoked and served as an appetizer. They are high in fat with a very fine texture. When caught, they weigh only about ¾ pound. The best quality sardine is the Norwegian bristling. Norwegian sardines are an excellent source of omega-3 fatty acids.

Sea Trout

These trout are usually caught along the Atlantic coast from Florida to Massachusetts. They are somewhat fatty but have a solid texture and are good for baking or broiling.

Shad

This is one of the fattiest fishes and is excellent baked, broiled, or fried. It is usually cooked whole, with just the entrails removed, because it is very hard to fillet. Shad roe (the eggs) is one of the more highly prized caviars.

Shark

Shark is becoming more and more popular. It is a tasty, low-fat fish with an excellent level of nutrients. More than 300 species of shark have been identified to date. The most popular, however, is mako shark, which is similar in texture to swordfish. Other common varieties include sand shark, dusky shark, sharpnose, bonnethead, and blacktip.

Skate

A relative of the shark family, the skate has rays or wings that are the most edible part of the fish. The taste is similar to that of the scallop, and the meat looks like crab meat because of its striations.

Sturgeon

Sturgeon roe is one of the finest caviars. These fish can weigh several hundred pounds and are the largest of all freshwater fish. They are high in fat and excellent for grilling. About 52 percent of the calories in sturgeon caviar comes from fat.

Swordfish

Because its flesh was found to contain high levels of mercury in 1971, many people are still reluctant to eat swordfish unless they know it was caught well off-shore. Usually sold as steaks, it is excellent for grilling. Swordfish has good flavor and fairly firm texture.

Tuna

The best kind of tuna is bluefin, but yellowfin is more readily available, costs less, and is nearly as delicious. Bluefin tuna may weigh up to 1,000 pounds. The meat of both bluefin and yellowfin is deep red; albacore is pale pink. Tuna has a very meaty, steaklike texture. The fish swim almost constantly—up to 75,000 miles per year—at speeds up to 55 miles per hour; they are well muscled and have superb flavor. Tuna is quite low in fat and can be grilled, pan-seared, or broiled.

Albacore is the best quality of canned tuna, which may also be labeled light, dark, or blended. These tuna varieties are also very oily and usually higher in calories, even if water-packed. When tuna is packed in olive oil, it is sometimes called tonno, which is the Italian word for tuna.

DID YOU KNOW?

Since swordfish is seriously depleted, chefs all over America are now refusing to prepare it until the overfishing stops.

Turbot

This is a mild, white-fleshed fish. European turbot is superior to American turbot, with a firmer texture and better flavor. It's easy to tell the difference: European turbot is more expensive.

THERE'S A CATCH TO THIS FISH STORY

You probably think that if you purchase canned tuna in water it will have fewer calories than the type that is packed in oil. Well, the truth is that the fat content of an albacore tuna may vary by as much as 500 percent. Tuna manufacturers always try to use fish with about 1 gram of fat per serving. However, when the demand for tuna is extremely high, they resort to packaging higher-fat albacore, which may contain 4 to 5 grams of fat per serving. Always check labels.

PACK IT IN

Solid-pack tuna is made from the loins, with the addition of a few flakes of meat. Chunk tuna may include parts of the tougher muscles, while flake tuna is composed mostly of muscle structure and smaller bits of meat.

NUMERO UNO

In 1997 canned tuna was the most popular fish sold in the United States. Shrimp came in second, with salmon third, then cod, and Alaskan pollack next because of its use in imitation shrimp and crabmeat. Americans consume about four pounds of canned tuna per person annually.

THE SALT OF THE SEA

You can reduce the saltiness of anchovies somewhat by soaking them in ice water for about 15 minutes. Because of their high salt content, anchovies will keep about two months under refrigeration after the can is opened, and up to a year without refrigeration in a sealed can. Once opened, they should be kept covered with olive oil.

SINCE RAW FISH MAY CONTAIN PARASITES, WHAT ABOUT LOX?

Good news for lox and bagel lovers! Smoked salmon, lox, or Nova that are commercially processed should pose no health risk. Lox is heavily salted during processing. According to researchers at the Centers for Disease Control and Prevention and the FDA, no case of contamination

DID YOU KNOW?

If you use anchovies in any dish, taste the dish before adding any further seasoning.

from parasites has ever been reported in lox. Most lox sold in the United States is made from farm-raised salmon. Cold-smoked salmon is always kept frozen, which will kill any parasites.

MMMM, MMMMMM, GOOD

If you go to China, you will find that shark-fin soup is a popular menu item, selling for around $55 per bowl. In Hong Kong, herb shops sell dried shark fins for up to $60 per pound. At the rate sharks are being fished, they may become an endangered species within the next 20 years. In 1997 more than 122 million sharks were caught worldwide.

FRESHWATER FISH

Buffalo Fish

This is a common fish caught in the Mississippi River and the Great Lakes area of the United States. It has a fairly firm texture and enough fat to make it good for grilling. The average weight is eight to 10 pounds.

Carp

Used to make gefilte fish, this scavenger fish may carry some contamination. Carp should be purchased only if it is farm-raised, and only as fillets because it is extremely difficult to skin.

Catfish

One of the more popular and tasty fish. Because catfish are scavengers, 85 percent of those we eat in the United States are currently farm-raised. Catfish are a low-fat fish with a relatively firm texture and are not very good for grilling. Instead, fry, roast, or broil them.

Perch

A true perch is caught only in fresh water; ocean perch is really rockfish. Perch is relatively low in fat, with a fairly firm texture. The majority of perch sold in the United States comes from the Great Lakes. They weigh about one to two pounds and are available fresh or frozen.

Pike

Pike is a member of the perch family; it averages one to three pounds and is delicious pan-fried. If you can find walleyed pike, it is an excellent eating fish, though it has plenty of tiny bones and must be filleted carefully.

Smelt

One of the smallest fish, smelts are usually eaten whole, with just the entrails and head removed. Best prepared pan-fried, they are a high-fat fish with a firm texture.

Trout

Next to catfish, trout is one of the most common fish caught in the United States. The most popular variety is the rainbow trout, which is one of the tastiest. Almost all trout sold has been raised on fish farms.

Whitefish

A relative of the trout, whitefish is also one of the best eating fish. It is high-fat and good barbecued, broiled, or baked. They are found in abundance in the Great Lakes.

CAVIAR

If you see the Russian word *malossol* on the caviar container, it means that only a small amount of salt was used in processing. This caviar will not have a long shelf life. Caviar loses much of its flavor and texture when cooked and is best eaten cold. It should be stored in the refrigerator and will last for two months if the temperature remains at 35°F to 36°F.

Beluga

Comes from the Caspian Sea's beluga sturgeon. The eggs (roe) vary in size but are usually pea-size and silver-gray to black. This is the most prized variety of caviar in the United States.

Osetra

This caviar is somewhat smaller than the beluga. Its color is gray to brownish-gray.

Sevruga

Even smaller than the osetra and gray in color.

Whitefish, Lumpfish, and Salmon

These are the least expensive caviars. Whitefish caviar is yellow-gold, lumpfish is tiny and black; and salmon, sometimes called red caviar, ranges in color from pale orange to deep red.

KNIFE TEST

To test fish for doneness, insert a thin-bladed knife into the flesh at the thickest part. It should be just barely translucent in the center. Even though it might look not quite done, the fish will continue to cook after you remove it from the heat, and it will be fine by the time you serve it.

NEVER OVERCOOK

Many microwave manufacturers suggest that you cook fish at 50 percent power for even results. Just be sure to check the instruction manual for your particular oven.

MODERATION, IF YOU ARE PREGNANT

The latest studies show that pregnant women should avoid eating certain fish that are at high risk for contamination. The white croaker, for instance, has also been found to contain PCBs as well as DDT. Eating fish twice a week is probably safe; if the fish is farm-raised there should be no problem. The safest fish to eat are salmon, halibut, sole, skipjack tuna, and farm-raised catfish, trout, and turbot.

TO SUSHI OR NOT TO SUSHI

There is always the risk that sushi might contain larval nematodes. Violent pains set in about 12 hours after ingestion, but some other symptoms like nausea, vomiting, and diarrhea may not show up for a week. For safety's sake, all fish prepared for sushi should be frozen for three days at -5°F to kill any larvae that might be present. Consuming raw fish too frequently may cause you to become deficient in a number of B vitamins, because raw fish contains an enzyme that affects the absorption of these vitamins.

CONTAMINATION POSSIBLE?

About half of all fish consumed in the United States is imported. As of 1997, the FDA began requiring all seafood companies to follow strict regulations to reduce seafood hazards. As part of this program, seafood importers must verify that their overseas suppliers are providing seafood processed according to these regulations.

HOW DRY I AM

If you are going to broil or grill fish, be sure to purchase steaks that are at least 1-inch thick. Fish dries out very quickly on the grill, and the thicker it is the better. The skin should be left on fillets while grilling and removed after they are cooked. When frying, be sure the surface of the fish is dry before putting it in the oil.

MORE BOUNCE TO THE OUNCE

For the most part, saltwater fish have thicker, denser bones than do fresh-water fish, which have thinner bones. The reason is that saltwater has more buoyancy. If you hate removing the bones, purchase saltwater fish.

FISHERCISE

River fish have more flavor than lake fish because they must swim against currents and thus get more exercise. For this reason, trout is one of the best eating fishes. Fish from cooler waters also have a higher fat content and, therefore, more flavor.

RED SPOTS ARE NOT MEASLES

Red spots on fish fillets indicate that the fish has been handled roughly and is bruised. This may result from throwing it around when it is caught or from poor filleting technique. Too many bruises may affect the flavor of the fillet by causing deterioration of the bruised flesh.

CAN 45,000 MEN BE WRONG?

Researchers at Harvard University tracked the dietary habits of 45,000 men with relation to their consumption of fish. The researchers found that the heart attack rates of the men who ate fish six times per week was the same as for those who ate fish approximately twice a month.

TENDER FISH

Fish and shellfish do not have the extensive connective tissue found in land animals. Because there is so little connective tissue, it gelatinizes quickly when cooked with moist heat. If you overcook fish, the muscle fibers will toughen. Cooking fish with the head and tail on makes it moister because more of the liquid is retained during the cooking process.

AQUACULTURED FISH

Aquaculture, or fish-farming, originated in China in 2000 BC. The first fish to be farmed was the carp. China and Japan currently lead the world in aquaculture fish farms, with the United States coming in fifth. At present, almost 90 percent of all trout sold in supermarkets and fish markets are farm-raised. In 1997, farmed fish totaled more than 792 million pounds, or about 6 percent of the nation's seafood. There are 3,600 fish farms in 25 states raising catfish, salmon, striped bass, sturgeon, tilapia, and trout. More than 569 million pounds of farm-raised catfish and 33 million pounds of salmon are marketed annually.

PUFFER FISH, DELICACY OR POISON?

This fish goes by a number of names, including fugu, blowfish, and balloon fish. It may contain tetradotoxin, a very potent poison, which is concentrated in the liver and ovaries. If the poison is ingested, the person may experience dry mouth, unfocused eyes, and numbness of the lips, tongue, and fingertips, with death following in a few hours. If vomiting can be induced, the person's life may be saved.

Only one person has ever died eating blowfish in a Japanese restaurant, because chefs who prepare the fish must be licensed by the Japanese government and are trained to discard the poisonous organs without contaminating the rest of the fish. In 1975, a Kabuki actor insisted on being served the innards. He died, and the chef was given an eight-year suspended sentence and put on probation for two years.

SHOULD FRESH FISH BE DE-GILLED?

In terms of spoilage, if the fish is caught fresh and prepared shortly afterward, it not necessary to remove the gills. However, if the fish will be out of the water for more than 24 hours before cooking, the gills should be removed because they spoil faster than does the rest of the fish.

In terms of cooking, gills are inedible; they impart a bitter taste and should be removed from any fish that is to be served whole or from any head used in fish stock.

SEAFOOD POISONING

Food poisoning from seafood is becoming more of a problem. Consumers rarely know where seafood comes from or if it has been contaminated. Two types of poisoning are the most prevalent. Mytilotoxin is found in mollusks, clams, and oysters because these filter feeders may have consumed microorganisms that are toxic. Ciguatera may be found in any type of tropical seafood. Both types of poisoning are serious enough to make you very ill or even to kill you. Commercial fishermen know where to find safe fishing beds, but the average person who is just out fishing in a river or lake may be unaware of contaminated areas.

NEVER FISH FROM A BRIDGE

Fishermen in the know will never fish from a highway bridge because auto-exhaust pollution as well as the garbage thrown off the bridge by passers-by affects the water. There's also the chance that you'll hook a car as you're casting your line!

FISH SPOILAGE AND STORAGE

The sooner a fish is gutted the better, because enzymes in the fish's gut tend to break down the flesh very quickly. These enzymes are very aggressive and powerful, which is one reason why fish is easier to digest than beef or chicken. When storing fish, remember that the muscle tissue is high in glycogen, which was the fish's energy source. When the fish is killed, this carbohydrate is converted into lactic acid, which is usually an excellent preservative; however, the fish tends to use up too much of its energy source thrashing around and trying to escape when it is caught. Another reason fish does not keep well is that certain bacteria are located outside digestive tract and remain active even below the freezing point.

FLIP IT CAREFULLY

Fillets are so thin that they cook through in a very short period. The meat of the fillet is also so delicate that it has a tendency to flake apart when overcooked, or if it is even turned. To be sure the fillet does not stick to the pan, use a nonstick cooking spray.

HOT PLATE SPECIAL

Fish tends to cool very quickly. For this reason it should be served on warm plates or a warmed platter.

HARPOON THAT SANDWICH

In 1997, Japan fishermen had 2,000 tons of surplus whale meat. Instead of being discarded, the meat was used for school-lunch sandwiches.

14

ALL
ABOUT
CHEESE

A CHEESE PRIMER

Cheeses come in a wide variety of flavors and colors, few of which are natural. Surprisingly, most cheeses are naturally white—not yellow. Nor are most naturally pink, green, or burgundy.

The cheese industry has perfected methods of changing "milk's leap toward immortality" (in the words of writer and critic Clifton Fadiman) into a chemical smorgasbord. Many of the chemicals used occur naturally as part of the cheese-making process, but some are additives, as are the unbelievable number of dyes and coloring agents.

These chemicals are used to give cheeses their sharp taste, to color them, to make them smell more appealing, or just to change their texture. All of the chemicals have been approved by the FDA and are supposed to be harmless; however, a number of the dyes and coloring agents are now being studied and have been linked to cancer in laboratory animals.

Be more aware of the types of cheese you buy and try to buy cheeses without the added chemicals. If you buy low-fat and nonfat cheeses, you're in a bit of a bind, because these rely heavily on chemical stabilizers and thickeners. Even if the label reads "all-natural," you should still look for the phrase "no preservatives or coloring agents." Consumers need to read labels more than ever these days.

WHY CHEESE MAY REFUSE TO MELT

One frequent error when melting cheese is heating the cheese at too high a temperature for too long a time. When this occurs, the protein is separated from the fat, and the cheese becomes tough and rubbery. Once this happens, the process cannot be reversed, and the cheese is ruined. Remember to keep the heat low, and use a double boiler if the recipe says to do so. Don't try to melt large pieces; cut the cheese into small chunks before you melt it. Grating it will also make it easier to melt, and this method is best for making sauces. Soft cheeses that don't need to be grated are ricotta, Camembert, and Brie, which have a higher water content and lower fat content than hard cheeses. Cheese should be the last item added to most recipes.

Reduced-fat cheeses melt less successfully than their full-fat counterparts; the more fat that is removed, the less likely the cheese is to melt well.

MAYTAG—NOT ONLY A WASHING MACHINE

Maytag blue cheese is one of the finest in the world and is produced from the freshest unpasteurized milk, obtained from Holstein-Friesian herds located in Newton, Iowa. The moisture content is higher than that of most other blue cheeses, making it very spreadable and creamy, and the cheese is aged in a special cellar on the farm that was carved into the side of a hill. The cheese is rather sharp, yet still mellow.

CHEESE CULTURES

One teaspoon of cheese-starter culture can contain 5 trillion living organisms. In the past, cheese producers were never sure of the activity of their culture, which came from milk-souring lactic acid bacteria. Today, there are companies that specialize in producing cultures of bacteria in whey (a protein) that actually separate the curd in the cheese-making process. These companies use lactobacillus and lactococcus bacteria to ferment milk sugar (lactose) into lactic acid. The acid is necessary to prevent unwanted microbes from growing in the cheese.

HOW TO BUY SOFT CHEESES

Two very popular soft cheeses are Brie and Camembert, both of which are sprayed with special mold to form a very thin, white, flexible rind. These cheeses ripen from the outside in and turn creamier, with a more intense flavor, as they age. These cheeses should never smell of ammonia. Ideally, they should be somewhat springy when prodded and should never have a hard core. These cheeses will continue to ripen for a day or two even when refrigerated, and should be eaten within five days of purchase.

Soft cheeses can become too ripe, at which point they may harden in texture until they are cut. Once soft cheese is cut, the ripening process stops. If the cheese appears runny, it has been overaged and may be bitter.

MAY AFFECT THE RECIPE

Many low-fat cheeses are made with low-fat or fat-free milk; examples include part-skim mozzarella and ricotta, and farmer cheese. Many cookbooks advise using a strongly flavored cheese, such as extra-sharp Cheddar or Parmesan; their richer flavors mean you can use less cheese. Use low-fat and fat-free cheeses in dishes that don't require heat, such as salads or sandwiches, because they don't melt well.

A LITTLE SQUIRT OR TWO

When grating cheese, try spraying a liquid vegetable oil or nonstick cooking spray on the grater to make cleanup easier.

DR. ELDRIDGE AND VELVEETA

Elmer E. Eldridge, a chemist at Cornell University, was hired by the Phenix Cheese Company and developed a Velveeta-like product in 1915. The intention was to try to duplicate the consistency of a processed Swiss cheese. Eldridge separated the whey (liquid protein) from the cheese and mixed it with cheese and a small amount of sodium citrate as an antioxidant. The original name of the cheese was Phen-ett, after the Phenix Company. At the same time, Kraft scientists developed a similar product called NuKraft; the two companies agreed to share patent rights.

Velveeta is now called "cheese spread" and contains about 60 percent moisture, not less than 20 percent butterfat, a few gums to hold it all together, and, of course, sweeteners. Velveeta was first marketed in 1928 when Kraft patented a method of packaging the cheese spread in foil-lined wooden boxes. The challenge had been to make the foil stick to the cheese, not the box, creating a hermetic seal that would keep the cheese fresh for long periods.

Velveeta melts beautifully, so it is used in casseroles, on burgers and sandwiches, and in soups. Its mild flavor makes it especially popular with children, as well as with cooks who know that a more assertive cheese would overpower the other flavors in their dish.

CHOOSING A GOOD CHEDDAR

One of the first things to look for when purchasing Cheddar cheese is uniform color. White spots or streaks are a sign that the cheese has been stored too long. The texture should always be relatively smooth, although it is not uncommon to find Cheddars that are grainy and crumbly. If the Cheddar has a rind, be sure the rind is not cracked or bulging, which might mean the cheese will be bitter as the result of poor manufacturing practices. Cheddar will continue to age in the refrigerator for months, and should be stored wrapped in plastic.

Cheddar originated in England, but in the United States it is the most widely produced variety of cheese, with Wisconsin, New York, and Vermont as the major manufacturers.

CHEESE RIPENING CLASSIFICATIONS

Unripened

These are normally consumed shortly after manufacture and include cottage cheese, a high-moisture soft cheese. Examples of other unripened cheeses are ricotta, cream cheese, farmer cheese, and mascarpone.

Soft

These cheeses are cured from the outside, or rind, toward the center. The process involves using particular molds or bacterial cultures that are allowed to grow on the surface of the cheese, creating the specific flavor, body, and texture of that cheese. These cheeses usually contain more moisture than semisoft ripened cheeses. Examples include Brie, Camembert, and triple-cream cheeses like Boursin.

Semisoft

When cheese ripens from the inside as well as the exterior, the curing continues as long as the temperature is warm. These cheeses have a higher moisture content than do firm ripened cheeses. Semisoft cheeses include Gouda, Monterey Jack, and Tilsit.

Firm

These cheeses are ripened by use of a bacterial culture and continue to ripen as long as the temperature is favorable. Firm cheeses have a lower moisture content than the softer cheeses and usually take longer to cure. Parmesan, Parmigiano-Reggiano, and pecorino Romano are the most popular firm cheeses.

Blue-Veined

These cheeses are cured with bacteria and specific mold cultures that grow throughout the inside of the cheese, producing their familiar blue-veined appearance and unique flavor. They are typically quite pungent and include Roquefort, Gorgonzola, Maytag, and Stilton.

COMMON CHEESES OF THE WORLD

American

Pasteurized processed cheese made from shredded Cheddar mixed with dyes and emulsifiers to make a mild, meltable cheese. More than half of all cheese consumed in the United States is, fittingly, American.

Beer

This is a smooth cheese that has been compared with Limburger but is milder. It originated in Germany as Bierkäse.

DID YOU KNOW?

Parmigiano-Reggiano is the authentic Parmesan cheese. Buy a wedge of it and grate it fresh over pasta, or slice it very thinly and sprinkle it in a salad.

Bel Paese

Originating in Italy, this semisoft cheese has a mild flavor. It is usually eaten with fruit for dessert.

Blue (Bleu)

Easily identified by the blue streaks throughout its interior, blue cheese crumbles easily and has a somewhat soft texture. In the United States and Britain, it is often sold in wheels; in France, it is sold in wheels or small medallions. It is also available crumbled.

Brick

A somewhat soft, yellow cheese with a medium-soft texture. It is from the American Midwest.

Brie

Originating in the south of France, this cheese is produced with an edible white coating. It has a mild flavor and a creamy texture. Brie is available in wheels and occasionally in wedges cut from the wheels.

Boursault

A French cheese that is soft, delicate, and mild. It is usually served as part of a cheese board, or in soup, fondue, or sauces.

Camembert

This cheese has a soft, yellowish interior with a thin, dull white, edible coating. It ripens in four to eight weeks and was named by Napoleon, after the Norman village where a farmer's wife first served it to him.

Cheddar

The natural color of Cheddar is white, not yellow. The yellow color is produced by natural dye called annatto, which is derived from achiote seeds. (Manufacturers believe that yellow cheese is more marketable.) Cheddar has a mild to very sharp taste and a fairly firm texture. It is sold in numerous shapes as well as sliced. Cheddar originated in the village of Cheddar, England, and was first imported to the United States in the nineteenth century. Because of its low moisture content, Cheddar will last for years, with its flavor becoming sharper as it ages. Cheddar gets about 70 percent of its calories from fat, of which 40 percent is saturated.

Cheshire

Produced in England, this is a hard cheese with a rich, mellow flavor similar to that of Cheddar.

Colby

Usually sold as a light yellow cheese, Colby originated in Wisconsin and has a somewhat mild flavor with a texture similar to that of cheddar. It is normally sold in wedges cut from a large round.

Coldpack

This cheese is a mixture of natural cheese, typically Cheddar, and other ingredients like spices, artificial flavorings, and port wine. A soft, spreadable cheese, it is available in a variety of colors and flavors.

Cream Cheese

Usually made with whole cow's milk before the cream has been skimmed off, cream cheese gets 90 percent of its calories from fat. It is semisoft and usually white, although flavorings are sometimes added. Some cream cheeses are made with propylene glycol alginate, which is derived from seaweed and is used as a stabilizer.

Edam

This Dutch cheese is commonly available in large spheres with red wax coating. The interior is a creamy yellow-orange color, the consistency is semi soft, and the cheese has a light, nutlike flavor. Edam has a lower milk-fat content than Gouda, which is a similar cheese.

Feta

A soft to semidry Greek cheese usually produced from goat's milk. The taste of feta is somewhat salty and sharp.

Farmer Cheese (Pot Cheese)

A close relative to cottage cheese, farmer cheese is usually pressed into a block shape and is sold mostly in delicatessens.

Fontina

One of the finest semisoft cheeses from Italy, it has a mild, somewhat nutty flavor and a light brown rind. It is often used for fondue.

Gjetost

From Norway, this is a relatively mellow, semisoft cheese that is sold in cubes or rectangles. It is usually a pleasant golden color and is made from a combination of cow's- and goat's-milk whey; the milk is cooked until it is caramelized, and thus the cheese is sweet. Similar to Myost.

Gorgonzola

Mold plays a significant role in the coloring of this Italian cheese. It is always found with blue-green veins and has a soft texture with an off-white exterior. The flavor is tangy and somewhat peppery, and the cheese is quite creamy. It is usually made with whey or cow's milk.

Gouda

Usually sold in a wheel or wedge with a red wax coating, this Dutch cheese has an inside that is semisoft and creamy yellow, with a nut-like flavor. The cheese contains irregular or round holes.

Gruyère

Made in Switzerland and similar to Swiss cheese, Gruyère is usually sold with mold inhibitors added. Check the label.

Limburger

Originally from Belgium, and once among the most popular cheeses in America, Limburger has fallen on hard times and is now produced by only one plant in the United States, the Chalet Cheese Co-op in Monroe, Wisconsin, which manufactures a million pounds per year. It is a smooth, creamy, soft, aged cheese with a pronounced aroma. Limburger will continue to age after it is purchased and will actually develop more flavor. It will last five to six months and should be stored in a well-sealed glass container. (Make that *extra*-well sealed.)

Mozzarella

Produced from either part-skim or whole milk, mozzarella has a firm texture and is sold in rounds, shredded, or sliced. If you live in or near an Italian neighborhood, seek out fresh mozzarella, which is infinitely superior to the stuff in supermarket dairy cases.

Muenster

Usually sold in wedges or blocks, Muenster, from Alsace, is moister than brick cheese. It has a creamy-white interior with a yellowish exterior and possibly small holes throughout. Flavor is mild, and texture is semisoft.

Myost

Sold in pie-shape wedges or in cubes, this Scandinavian cheese is similar to Gjetost. It is light brown in color and has a sweet, caramel flavor.

Neufchâtel

With a soft texture and a mildly acidic flavor, Neufchâtel is lower in fat than cream cheese. It is from France.

Parmesan

Although Parmesan is often sold pregrated, it is best bought in a block and grated as needed. In bulk it is a creamy-white cheese with a hard, granular texture. It is usually produced from partially skimmed milk.

Pasteurized Processed Cheese

This product is a blend of cheeses that varies in consistency from brand to brand. The flavor is relatively mild. This cheese has a low melting point.

Pasteurized Process Cheese Food

Similar to processed cheese, except that milk or whey is added to make the cheese spreadable. These cheeses are softer, with a lower fat content and a milder flavor, than pasteurized processed cheese.

Port du Salut

Creamy yellow with a buttery texture and mild, savory flavor, this French cheese has small holes throughout. It comes in thick cylinders.

Provolone

This Italian cheese has an off-white interior with a somewhat yellowish exterior. It is unsalted, with a mild flavor; the texture is fairly smooth.

Quark

This is a soft, unripened cheese with the texture of sour cream. The flavor is richer than that of yogurt. From Germany.

Ricotta

Produced from either whole or skim milk, ricotta has a somewhat nut-like flavor and looks like small-curd cottage cheese. From Italy.

Romano

A yellow-white cheese with a greenish-black exterior and a sharp flavor, Romano is sold both in wedges and pregrated. It can be made with whole cow's, sheep's, or goat's milk. From Italy.

Roquefort

Mold is introduced to create marbling and blue veins throughout the cheese. It has a white interior and is usually produced from sheep's milk. The flavor is somewhat peppery, and the texture is always crumbly. Sold mostly in wedges or packaged already crumbled. From France.

Stilton

Similar to Roquefort, this English cheese has a pale yellow interior with blue mold streaks. Unlike Roquefort, it is normally produced from cow's milk. Stilton has a crumbly texture and is usually sold in logs or wedges.

Swiss

Usually produced from whole milk, this cheese has a light yellow interior, Swiss cheese has a somewhat sweet, nutty flavor. The texture is firm and the characteristic holes may vary in size. It is usually sold in rectangular blocks or sliced. Do not buy Swiss cheese that has a grayish rind. The flavor will become stronger when the cheese is wrapped in plastic wrap and refrigerated. Cut wedges should last for one or two months.

Tilsit

The inside of this cheese is usually a light yellow color and the texture is semisoft. This German cheese is produced from pasteurized milk and takes about five months to ripen. The fat content runs about 40 percent.

DID YOU KNOW?

There's a hard green cheese that is flavored with mountain herbs from the Swiss Alps. Called Sap Sago, it comes in a small cone, which is grated onto baked potatoes or into green salads.

COTTAGE CHEESE

Cottage cheese is a United States original. It is made from nonfat milk and is either plain-cured or plain-cured with cream. Its texture is always soft, with curds of varying size. If the label says "curd by acidification," it was made with rennet. After processing, cottage cheese retains only 25 to 50 percent of the calcium from the milk it is made from. Because of its high water content, cottage cheese will last only until the expiration date on the container unless it is stored in the container upside down.

HOW DOES SWISS CHEESE GET ITS HOLES?

When Swiss cheese is cured, microorganisms produce a gas that causes pockets of air to form, and these remain after the cheese ripens. The holes should, however, be relatively uniform in size and not too large. The borders of the holes should have a moist, shiny appearance.

CHEESE FACTS

◆ An ounce of cream cheese may contain as many as 110 calories. As advertised, it does have fewer calories than butter by comparable weight, but then again, we tend to use more of it.

◆ Look for cheeses that are low-sodium, low-fat, or reduced-fat. There are new varieties appearing in supermarkets and health-food stores.

◆ Be sure to read the label. If it is not a chemical concoction, the name of the cheese must be preceded by the word "natural."

◆ Most cheese substitutes are produced from soybean or vegetable fats. Many low-fat cheeses substitute water for the fat.

◆ It takes 8 pounds of milk to produce 1 pound of cheese. An average slice of American cheese contains 8 ounces of milk.

◆ The wax coating protects the interior of a cheese. If there is an exposed edge, cover it with plastic wrap or butter to keep it moist and fresh.

◆ To keep cheese longer without mold forming, place a piece of paper towel that has been dampened with white vinegar in the bottom of a plastic container with a tight-fitting lid.

EGG-CELLENT FACTS

EGG CHEMISTRY

Despite all the negative publicity, the fact is that eggs are still about the best and most complete sources of protein. Most of this publicity revolves around the high levels of cholesterol (approximately 213 milligrams) found in the egg yolk.

Some significant studies have recently shown that consuming egg yolks does not, in fact, appreciably elevate blood cholesterol levels. (Consuming saturated fat, not cholesterol, is more likely to raise blood cholesterol levels—though dietary cholesterol still plays a part.) Nevertheless, it is wise to heed the recommendation of the American Heart Association, not to mention most cardiologists and nutritionists, and strive to limit your cholesterol to 300 milligrams per day.

Egg-Quivalents	
CALORIES	**MEASURING EGGS**
1 large egg = 80 calories	1 large egg (2 oz) = ¼ cup
1 egg white = 20 calories	1 medium egg (1¾ oz) = ⅕ cup
1 egg yolk = 60 calories	1 small egg (1½ oz) = ⅙ cup

POURING SALT ON AN OPEN CRACK

If an egg cracks during boiling, remove it from the water and, while it is still wet, pour a generous amount of salt over the crack. Let the egg stand for 20 seconds, then put it back into the boiling water.

IT'S HARD TO GET AN "AA"

There are three grades of eggs: U.S. Grade AA, U.S. Grade A, and U.S. Grade B. Grade B eggs are used by bakeries and commercial food processors. Eggs marked "A" or "AA" on the carton are not officially graded unless they show the USDA shield as well as the letter grade.

A FLATTENED BOTTOM . . .

To keep deviled eggs from wobbling on the platter, cut a thin slice off two sides of the egg before you halve it lengthwise.

. . . AND A ROUNDED BOTTOM

To increase the volume of beaten eggs, use a bowl that's about 10 inches in diameter and five to six inches deep, and that has a rounded bottom. A balloon whisk is the ideal tool for incorporating air into the eggs.

THE UPSIDE-DOWN EGG

Eggs should be stored with the tapered end down to maximize the distance between the yolk and the air pocket, which may contain bacteria. The yolk is more perishable than the white, or albumen, and even though it is more or less centered in the egg, the yolk can shift slightly and will move away from possible contamination.

ANATOMY OF AN EGG

The yolk of an egg is 50 percent water; 34 percent lipids, or fats; and 16 percent protein. The yolk contains most of the cholesterol, three-fourths of the calories, and most of the vitamin A, thiamine, and iron in an egg— the yolk is the source of nutrients for a chick before it hatches. The egg white is mostly water; about 10 percent of it is protein, with traces of minerals, glucose, and lipids. The white's primary purpose is as a barrier against bacteria for the developing chick.

DROWN THEM

If you have used egg whites in a recipe and want to save the yolks for another use, slide them into a bowl of water, cover with plastic wrap, and store in the refrigerator for a day or two.

TOUGHENING 'EM UP

Freezing hard-cooked eggs causes the whites to become tough. When freezing fresh eggs, always break the yolk. The whites and yolks can be frozen separately unless you plan on using them at the same time.

SHAPELY EGGS

To serve the family something different, try frying eggs in metal cookie cutters of various shapes. Just place the cutter in the pan and break the egg into it. Spray the cutter with nonfat cooking spray after placing it in the pan so the egg will be easy to remove.

DID YOU KNOW?

Salt, lemon juice, or vinegar will make the egg white coagulate faster; add it to the water when you're poaching eggs to help them keep their shape.

HARD-BOILED FACTS

◆ You can prevent boiled eggs from cracking by rubbing a cut lemon on the shells before cooking them.

◆ Boiled eggs should be cooled at room temperature before refrigerating them in an open bowl.

◆ To make the eggs easier to peel, add a small amount of salt to the water to toughen the shell. Another trick is to add a teaspoon of white vinegar to the water, which may also prevent cracking. The vinegar tends to soften the shell, allowing the interior more room for expansion. However, eggs cooked in vinegar water may not be as easy to peel.

◆ To remove the shell from a hard-cooked egg, exert gentle pressure while rolling it around on the counter, then insert a teaspoon between the shell and the egg white and rotate it.

◆ Always cool a hard-cooked egg before you try to slice it; it will slice more easily and will not fall apart.

◆ Using unwaxed dental floss makes slicing hard-cooked eggs easy.

◆ Never place peeled hard-boiled eggs in cool water. Eggs have a thin protective membrane that may be removed or damaged when they are peeled. If the eggs are then placed in water or in a sealed container, bacteria may begin to form.

MIXING IT UP

When preparing scrambled eggs, allow 3 per person. Most people eat more eggs when they are scrambled. If other ingredients are added, such as cheese or vegetables, 2 eggs per person will be sufficient.

RISKY HOLLANDAISE?

Eggs have been found to contain the salmonella bacteria even when the shells were not cracked. Because of this, you may be justifiably concerned about using eggs in sauces that are not cooked thoroughly. When preparing a hollandaise or béarnaise sauce, it might be best to microwave the eggs briefly before adding them to the sauce. Use a 600-watt microwave oven and no more than 2 large Grade A egg yolks at a time.

First, separate the egg yolks completely from the whites. Second, place the yolks in a glass bowl and beat them until they are well combined. Third, add 2 teaspoons of lemon juice and mix thoroughly again. Fourth, cover the bowl, place in the microwave on High, and observe the mixture until the surface begins to move.

Cook for 10 seconds past this point, remove the bowl, and beat the mixture with a clean whisk until it appears smooth. Return the bowl to the microwave and cook again until the surface starts to move. Allow it to remain another 10 seconds, remove, and whisk again until smooth. Finally, allow the bowl to stand for about 1 minute. The yolks should be free of salmonella and still will be usable in your sauce.

GENTLY DOES IT

When adding raw eggs or yolks to a hot mixture, be sure to mix part of the hot mixture into the eggs, and then gradually add this new mixture to the hot mixture. This process, called tempering, is extra work, but it makes the eggs less likely to curdle and separate.

PICTURE PERFECT

To guarantee a white film over the yolks of cooked eggs, place a few drops of water in the pan just before they are done and cover the pan.

MISCELLANEOUS FACTS

◆ Egg whites contain more than half of the protein of the egg and only 25 percent of the calories.

◆ When frying an egg, the butter or margarine should be very hot before the eggs are added—a drop of water should sizzle. However, the heat should be reduced just before the eggs are added to the pan. Cook the eggs over low heat until the whites are completely set.

◆ If you are storing hard-cooked eggs with raw eggs, add a small amount of food coloring to the boiling water so that it will be easy to tell which eggs have been cooked.

◆ White or brown eggs are identical in nutritional value and taste.

◆ Egg whites begin to coagulate at 145°F; at 150°F, the yolks begin to set. The entire egg white will be firm yet still tender at 160°F. Be sure to cook eggs over low heat to guarantee a tender white and smooth yolk.

◆ When beating egg whites, remove all traces of yolk with a Q-tip or the edge of a paper towel before trying to beat the whites. The slightest trace of yolk will prevent the whites from beating properly, as will any trace of fat on the beaters or bowl.

◆ When preparing a number of omelets or batches of scrambled eggs, always wipe the pan clean with a piece of paper towel after every two to three batches to prevent the eggs from sticking to the pan.

◆ The fresher the egg, the better it is for poaching. The white will be firmer and will help to keep the yolk from breaking. Bring the water to a boil and then reduce it to a simmer before adding the egg.

◆ For best results, start scrambled eggs in a hot pan, but immediately lower the heat and cook them slowly over low heat.

◆ Did you know? It takes about four hours to digest a whole egg because of its high fat content.

◆ To remove an unbroken egg that has stuck to the carton, just wet the carton. If the egg is broken, throw it out.

EGGNOG FACTS

◆ In many dessert recipes that call for whole milk, eggnog makes a delicious substitute, but it adds lots of cholesterol and calories.

◆ If you freeze eggnog and find upon thawing that it has separated, whir it in a blender before using it.

◆ Eggnog has a short shelf life; use it within five days of purchase.

WILL NEVER SLIP AWAY

If you dampen your fingers a little before handling an egg, it will stick to your fingers and won't slip away.

SAFETY FIRST

USDA regulations state that eggs must be refrigerated during all phases of shipping and in supermarkets. In many instances, however, they are left on pallets in supermarkets without refrigeration. Do not to purchase eggs you suspect have been unrefrigerated, because the temperature of an egg should never rise above 40°F. Unfortunately, there's no way to tell whether eggs have been stored improperly.

EGGS VS. BACTERIA

A soft-boiled egg should be cooked at least four minutes to kill any bacteria that may be present. The whites of fried eggs should be hard, although the yolks may be soft. Eggs are considered safe at 160°F. Some eggshells contain microcracks that allow harmful bacteria to enter. If you find a cracked egg in the carton, throw it out; it is probably contaminated.

ALWAYS IN THE MIDDLE

To keep yolks centered when boiling eggs for deviled eggs, stir the water while they are cooking. When storing deviled eggs, stick toothpicks into the eggs around the edge of the plate, then cover with plastic wrap. The toothpicks keep the plastic off the eggs.

SEPARATION ANXIETY

To separate eggs easily, break the egg into a small funnel placed over a measuring cup. The white will drain through the funnel; just be sure not to break the yolk when cracking the egg. Never separate eggs by passing the yolk back and forth from one half of the shell to the other, because there may be bacteria on the shell that could contaminate the egg.

PLANT ME, PLANT ME

Make an excellent mineral plant fertilizer by drying eggshells and pulverizing them in a blender.

BLACK EGGS?

Aluminum bowls and cookware tend to darken an egg. The reason? The aluminum's chemical reaction with the egg protein.

SUBSTITUTIONS

- ◆ You can substitute 2 egg yolks for 1 whole egg when making custards, cream pie filling, and salad dressings.
- ◆ You can substitute 2 egg yolks plus 1 teaspoon of water for 1 whole egg in yeast dough or cookie batter.
- ◆ If you come up 1 egg short when baking a cake, substitute 2 tablespoons of mayonnaise, but don't substitute for more than 1 egg.

YOLK SUPPORTERS?

The twisted strands of egg white that you find in eggs are called chalazae cords. And what are they for? They hold the yolk in place, and are more prominent in very fresh eggs.

BAD EGG?

Beware of duck eggs, which tend to develop harmful bacteria as they age. They should be eaten within three days of laying. Once the bacteria takes hold, it can be destroyed only by boiling the eggs for 10 to 12 minutes.

SPREAD 'EM!

Determine the quality of your eggs by seeing how much they spread when they are broken. U.S. Grade AA eggs have the smallest spread, a somewhat thick white, and have a firm, high yolk. U.S. Grade A eggs have more spread and a thinner white. U.S. Grade B eggs have the widest spread, a small amount of thick white, and probably a flat, enlarged yolk.

SECRET CODES ON EGG CARTONS

Before eggs are graded they are "candled." This means that the egg is viewed by passing it in front of an intense light that allows the inspector to see through the shell. If a cloud of white obscures the yolk, the egg is very fresh. If the air pocket at the base of the egg is about the size of a dime, this is also an indication the egg is fresh. Grade AA eggs are the highest quality, and grade A are just a bit lower. Grade B eggs are seldom available in stores; they are used in egg products.

Grading is voluntary. All graded eggs have an expiration date on the carton. The date is 30 days or less from the day the eggs were packed. If there is no date, there may be a three-digit code that indicates the day the egg was packaged. The code refers to the day of the year when the egg was packaged. For example, eggs packaged on January 1 would be coded 001; those packaged on February 1 would be coded 032, because there are 31 days in January. Use eggs within five weeks of purchase.

WHAT IS EGG WASH?

Egg wash is a mixture of an egg or egg white beaten with milk, cream, or water. The egg wash is then brushed over baked goods before they are baked to help the tops brown more evenly and give them a shiny, crisp finish. It is also used to hold toppings on rolls and other baked goods.

HOW OLD IS A 1,000 YEAR-OLD EGG?

This Chinese delicacy is really not 1,000 years old. It is often made from chicken eggs (though sometimes from duck or goose eggs) that have been coated with a mixture of ashes, salt, and calcium hydroxide (the lime used in pickling), and are then buried in the ground for 100 days. The insides of the egg turn into a dark, jellylike substance that can actually be eaten without fear of food poisoning. These eggs can even be stored at room temperature for up to two weeks. The combination of the ashes, salt, and lime has a drawing effect on the fluids in the egg, causing the proteins in both the white and the yolk to gel and to be colored by the minerals, which partially decompose and stain the proteins.

THE GREEN EGG

When eggs are overheated or overcooked, they undergo a chemical change that causes the sulfur in the egg to combine with the iron in the yolk and form the harmless chemical ferrous sulfide, which forms a green ring around the yolk. This reaction is more prevalent in older eggs, in which the elements are more easily released. To avoid this reaction, do not cook eggs for more than 12 to 15 minutes, put the cooked eggs immediately into cold water, and peel them as soon as possible.

TELLING THE AGE OF AN EGG

Fill a small, deep bowl about three-quarters full with cold water. Gently drop in an egg. If the egg sinks to the bottom and lies on its side, it's fresh. If the egg stays on the bottom at a 45-degree angle, it is three to five days old. If it stays on the bottom and stands straight up, it is 10 to 12 days old. But if the egg floats to the top, it is bad and should be thrown away. Older eggs are more buoyant because the yolk and white have lost moisture and the air pocket gets larger. Eggshells are porous, and moisture evaporates through them.

THE LIFETIME OF AN EGG

The refrigerator shelf life of eggs is about five weeks from the time you buy them. For longest life, and to avoid the absorption of refrigerator odors, always store eggs in their original carton on an inside shelf of the refrigerator. Never store them on the door.

THE BREATHING EGG

When eggs are laid, they begin to change in a number of ways. For the cook, the most significant is that the pH of both the yolk and the white changes. Eggs "breathe" and release low levels of carbon dioxide after they are laid. The carbon dioxide inside the egg dissolves into the internal liquids and causes the pH of the egg to change. The older the egg, the greater the change. The yolk and the white tend to increase in alkalinity with time, the yolk going from a slightly acidic 6.0 to an almost neutral 6.6, and the white going from 7.7 to about 9.2. Because of the changes in the alkalinity of the white, it tends to go from a deep white color to a very weak, almost clear color. Coating the shell of a fresh egg with a vegetable oil will slow this process. The older the egg, the runnier it tends to be, which may make it more difficult for the chef to work with; the yolk is more easily broken as well.

UP, UP, AND AWAY: SUPER EGG!

A new kind of egg is appearing in supermarkets. The hens that lay these eggs are fed a diet rich in flaxseed so the eggs are higher in vitamin E as well as omega-3 and omega-6 fatty acids. These fatty acids have been shown in studies to cause a marked decrease in triglyceride levels as well as a slight increase in HDL (good cholesterol) levels. The total cholesterol content, however, remains about the same, at about 215 milligrams.

You might also look for eggs with only 190 milligrams of cholesterol, higher levels of vitamin E, and more iodine and unsaturated fat than regular eggs, in your supermarket. Of course, these "super eggs" cost more than do regular eggs, but some feel it's money well spent.

WHAT HAPPENS WHEN EGGS ARE COOKED?

When an egg white protein is cooked, the bonds that hold the proteins together unravel and create a new protein network. The molecules of water in the egg are trapped in this new network, and as the protein continues to cook, the network squeezes the water out. The longer the egg cooks, the more water is released, and the more opaque the white becomes. If you overcook the egg, it will release all its moisture and will develop a rubbery texture. The nutritional value of a dried-out egg is the same as that of an uncooked egg.

THE SECRET TO A FLUFFY OMELET

To make a great omelet, be sure the eggs are at room temperature by taking them out of the fridge 30 minutes before using them. Cold eggs are too stiff to make a fluffy omelet. Also, if you normally add a little milk to your omelet, try substituting a small amount of water. The water increases the volume of the eggs at least three times more than will the milk. The coagulated proteins hold in the liquid, resulting in a moist omelet.

WHERE DID THE FIRST CHICKEN COME FROM?

We are still not sure whether the egg or the chicken came first, but we do know that eggs are millions of years old. The chicken, as we know it today, is only 4,000 to 5,000 years old and not one of the first domesticated animals. The ancestors of the chicken were jungle fowl that were native to Southeast Asia and India. Chickens were probably domesticated to harvest their eggs. Chickens will continue to lay eggs in a nest until a specific number is reached. By removing the eggs at regular intervals, the chicken is made to believe it must lay more eggs, thus providing a steady supply. Some other breeds of fowl will lay only one or two eggs, and no matter what you do to encourage them, they will not lay any more.

HOW THE CHICKEN MAKES AN EGG

The making of a chicken egg is really a remarkable feat. A chicken is born with thousands of egg cells (ova) and only one ovary. As soon as the hen is old enough to lay eggs, the ova will start to mature, usually only one at a time. Each egg cell, riding on a completed yolk, is released from the ovary and enters the oviduct, a tube about two feet long. If the hen has mated in the last few weeks, the sperm may fertilize the egg cell. The egg white is laid down over the yolk and then the shell forms around the white. It takes about 25 hours for the egg to be laid.

COUNTING CHICKENS AND EGGS

In 1997, the chicken population in the United States totaled about 240 million, which means that there are more chickens than people. In 1800, chickens only laid 15 to 20 eggs a year, while they strolled around the barnyard pecking and scratching and generally living a natural chicken lifestyle. Now the fowl are cooped up in temperature-controlled warehouses, fed a special diet, not allowed to move about, and forced to lay egg after egg to produce 300 to 325 eggs per year. Each breeder house

DID YOU KNOW?

Cold water cleans egg off utensils better than hot water. Hot water tends to cause the protein to bind to surfaces and harden.

holds 50,000 to 125,000 chickens and 900 roosters to keep the chickens productive. The record number of eggs laid by a cooped up chicken in a single year is 371, established by the University of Missouri College of Agriculture. The larger chicken farms produce 250,000 eggs per day. Americans consumed about 240 eggs per person in 1997, down from 332 in 1944, as a result of all the negative information about cholesterol disseminated by the medical community.

USE A COPPER BOWL

Always use a copper bowl to beat egg whites. The copper will release ions during the beating process that cause the protein in the whites to become more stable. Using copper means not having to add cream of tartar. The next best material to use is stainless steel; however, you will need to add a pinch of cream of tartar to stabilize the whites. Whatever bowl you choose, make sure it has a rounded bottom to ensure that all the mixture comes into contact with the mixing blades. Also, be sure there is not even a trace of egg yolk in your whites. The slightest hint of fat will prevent the whites from beating properly.

A LITTLE DROP WILL DO YA

Adding vinegar to the water for poached eggs will create a slightly acidic medium that allows the eggs to set and retain their shape, as well as helping the whites to retain their color. The proper amount of vinegar is 1 teaspoon to 1 quart of water. If you use lemon juice the ratio should be ½ teaspoon to 1 quart of water.

WHY EGGS CRACK WHEN BOILED

A newly-laid egg is very warm. As it cools down, the yolk and white cool and shrink, resulting in an air pocket at the large (nontapered) end. This air pocket tends to expand as the egg is heated during boiling, and the gas has no place to go except out of the shell, which can crack. When this occurs, the albumen escapes and solidifies almost immediately in the boiling water. To avoid cracks, bring eggs to a gentle—not vigorous—boil. Or you can prick a hole in the large end of the egg with a pushpin, but this allows water into the egg—which can produce hairline cracks in the shell.

16

DAIRY
DELIGHTS

DID YOU KNOW?

The fat in milk contains carotene, which gives the milk its yellowish color. This is why nonfat milk is whiter than whole milk.

THE MILK OF HUMAN KINDNESS

Milk from dairy animals was first consumed by humans about 4000 BC. Human milk is easier to digest than cow's milk, which tends to be higher in protein. Both cow and human milk protein curdles when it combines with stomach acid, but less of the protein in human milk curdles. The percentage of protein by weight in human milk is about 1 percent compared with 3.5 percent in cow's milk. Heating causes animal milk to form a looser curd, improving its digestibility.

EATING YOUR CURDS AND WHEY

Curds and whey are two proteins found in milk and milk products. The curd is actually casein and tends to be solid in form. The whey may be composed of several proteins (the most predominant being lactoglobulin), all of which are suspended in liquid. The liquid that you see on the top of yogurt or sour cream and other natural dairy products is not water but the protein whey, which should be stirred back into the product.

"A" BIG LOSS

Never buy milk in clear containers. When exposed to light, low-fat or skim milk can lose up to 70 percent of its vitamin A. Markets are now placing this type of container under a light shield. Tinted or opaque containers will protect the vitamin A.

CAN FOODS CAUSE ARTHRITIS?

Recent studies provide some alarming information linking salmonella and other bacteria to arthritis. Recently, people became ill from drinking milk contaminated with salmonella. About 2 percent of them developed arthritis within four weeks of drinking the tainted milk. This newly identified type of arthritis is known as "reactive arthritis." Symptoms include inflammation of the knee and ankle joints and lower back pain.

DO COWS HAVE TO GIVE BIRTH BEFORE GIVING MILK?

Cows, like all mammals, must give birth before they can produce milk; hormones produced when the mammal gives birth activate the mammary glands. If a cow's udders are stimulated regularly, they will produce milk for about 10 months. The gestation period for a cow is 282 days, which means that the farmer has a long wait before the cow will produce milk, and after 10 months, she goes dry.

WE'RE JUST A FEW YEARS BEHIND

Europeans have been drinking milk processed at ultra-high-temperatures for years; it's now available in the United States. The processing preserves milk's nutritional value and makes it possible to store milk for two to three months without refrigeration. It's sold in boxes, often near canned milk, in many supermarkets.

FRESHENING MILK

Adding a teaspoon of baking soda or a pinch of salt to a carton of milk will keep it fresh a few days longer. Leaving milk at room temperature for more than 30 or 40 minutes will reduce its life span.

WHIP IT GOOD

Light cream can be whipped to a firm, mousse-like con-sistency—and will not weep—if you add 1 tablespoon of unflavored gelatin that has been dissolved in 1 tablespoon of hot water for every 2 cups of cream. After whipping, refrigerate it for two hours. Heavy cream will set up faster if you add 7 drops of lemon juice for each pint of cream.

GIVE ME AIR

Have you ever wondered why cream whips and milk doesn't? The reason is that cream has a higher fat content than milk. Heavy cream must contain at least 36 percent fat, while whole milk is only 3.25 percent fat. When the cream is whipped, the fat globules cluster together in the bubble walls, forming a network that holds air.

SAVES A MESS

When you freeze milk, be sure to pour off a small amount from the con-tainer first to allow for some expansion.

OUT OF BUTTERMILK?

If a baking recipe calls for buttermilk and you don't have any, you can make sour milk, which is a reasonably acceptable substitute. To make a cup of sour milk, put 1 tablespoon of white vinegar or lemon juice in a measuring cup, then pour in enough milk to make 1 cup. Stir a few times and let stand 5 minutes before using.

SOUR CREAM 101

It's easy to make sour cream. Combine 1 tablespoon lemon juice with enough evaporated whole milk to make 1 cup, and then let the mixture stand at room temperature for about 40 minutes. You can also mix ¾ cup sour milk or buttermilk with 5 tablespoons melted and cooled butter.

TIMING IS EVERYTHING

Add sour cream to hot dishes just before serving. Dishes containing sour cream must be reheated slowly to prevent the cream from separating.

POWDERED MILK

Dry milk powder comes in three forms: whole, nonfat, and buttermilk. Buttermilk powder is just now becoming available in most markets. Powdered whole milk should be stored in a cool, dry place because of its higher fat content. Other powdered milks will last several months in the pantry or cabinet. Once powdered milk has been reconstituted, it will last about three days under refrigeration.

HOW FRESH I AM

Assuming no one in your house drinks milk straight from the carton, milk will retain its freshness for up to one week after the expiration date.

THEY'RE CAN-VENIENT

Evaporated milk, sold in cans, is available in whole, low-fat, and nonfat varieties. It is sterilized with heat and can be stored unopened at room temperature for five or six months. Partially frozen, evaporated low-fat milk can be whipped to make a low-fat substitute for whipped cream—just remove it from the can before you freeze it. For higher peaks, add a bit of unflavored gelatin softened in water.

GOAT'S MILK: GREAT!

Goat's milk is actually more healthful than cow's milk for humans, especially infants. The protein and mineral ratio is closer to that of human milk, and goat's milk contains higher levels of niacin and thiamine (B vitamins) than cow's milk. Even the protein is of a better quality and is less likely to cause an allergic reaction.

OF ICE CRYSTALS AND ICE CREAM

Ice cream thaws and refreezes slightly each time it is removed from the freezer. When this happens, the fat in the ice cream releases water, and ice crystals form. Home freezers are seldom cold enough to keep ice cream solid; most will not go down to 0°F and hold that temperature for any length of time. Premium ice creams—those with less air whipped into them—will also freeze harder than ice creams of lower quality.

WHO INVENTED THE ICE CREAM CONE?

One account of the waffle cone's invention was that it took place at the World's Fair in St. Louis in 1904. A concession vendor named Ernest A. Hamwi was selling waffle pastries called zalabia. A neighboring vendor was selling ice cream in cups. He ran out of cups and was panicking. The waffle vendor came to his rescue by making a cone-shape waffle that would hold the ice cream. The cone, called the World's Fair Cornucopia, was the food sensation of the fair.

GOOD OLD AMERICAN INGENUITY

In 1943, an article in *The New York Times* titled "Flying Fortress Doubles as Ice-Cream Freezer" stated that airmen were filling special canisters with an ice-cream mixture and attaching them to the tail gunner's compartment of Flying Fortresses—the name for the fighter planes. The vibration of the plane and the cold temperature of the high altitude made ice cream as they were flying over enemy territory.

SECRETS OF MAKING GREAT ICE CREAM

Use these tips to achieve the best results when using an ice cream maker:
◆ Before you start the freezing process, chill the mixture in the refrigerator to 40°F. This will reduce the freezing time.

DID YOU KNOW?

Americans cut their consumption of whole milk by two-thirds from 1970 to 1996. At the same time, they tripled their consumption of low-fat milk.

◆ If you prefer a fluffy ice cream, fill the canister only two-thirds full to allow room for expansion as air is beaten into the ice cream.

ARTIFICIAL GUNK

Avoid any ice cream listing ethyl vanillin on the label. This is a flavoring agent that has caused multiple organ damage in laboratory animals.

FORMERLY KNOWN AS ICE MILK

Reduced-fat ice cream used to be called ice milk. All of a company's ice-cream products containing at least 25 percent less fat than the brand's regular ice cream may use this labeling. By law, any food labeled "low-fat" must have no more than 3 grams of fat per 4-ounce serving.

AERATED ICE CREAM—A MUST

Air is whipped into all commercial ice cream. If the air were not added, the ice cream would be as solid as a brick and you would be unable to scoop it out. The air improves the texture and is not listed among the ingredients. However, a gallon of ice cream must weigh 4½ pounds.

MAKING SENSE OF MILK LABELS

Is low-fat milk really low-fat? Not always. If that sounds confusing, it's because the milk producers mean it to be. Here's a good example: Two-percent milk, which most people think of as low-fat, gets approximately 34 percent of its calories from fat (thus making it not a low-fat product). Whole milk is actually 3.3 percent fat by weight, or about 50 percent, while 1 percent milk gets about 23 percent of its calories from fat.

If fat content is important to you, it's best to use nonfat milk or buttermilk, which is now made from a culture of nonfat milk.

NONSTICK SURFACE

Before heating milk in a saucepan, spread a thin layer of unsalted butter on the bottom of the pan to keep the milk from sticking. Remember to use unsalted, since salted butter may cause the milk to stick.

HOW PERISHABLE IS MILK?

Every half-gallon of Grade A pasteurized milk contains tens of millions of bacteria and if left unrefrigerated, it will sour in a matter of hours. Ideally, milk should be stored at 34°F rather than at the average refrigerator temperature of 40°F. Milk should never be exposed to light, which can diminish flavor and vitamin A content in about four hours. The light actually energizes oxygen atoms that invade the carbon and hydrogen atoms in the fat through a process known as autoxidation.

HOW DRY I AM

Buttermilk can be used to soften cheese that has become too dry. Place the cheese in a shallow dish with a 1-inch layer of buttermilk, cover the dish, and refrigerate overnight.

WHY IS MILK HOMOGENIZED?

Homogenization is the process where milk is forced through a very small nozzle at high pressure onto a hard surface. This is done to break up the fat globules into tiny, uniform particles so the cream, which is high in fat, will not rise and form a layer on top. The fat particles become so small that they are evenly dispersed throughout the milk. After homogenization, milk is pasteurized, and then packaged in cartons or bottles.

LOW-FAT WORKS BEST

If you are low on sour cream and need to make a dip, try creaming cottage cheese in your blender.

CONDENSED VERSUS EVAPORATED MILK

Condensed milk is not sterilized because its high (40 percent) sugar content acts as a preservative, retarding bacterial growth. The milk itself is not very appetizing and is only used as a dessert ingredient. Evaporated milk is sterilized by heating it in the can to 241°F to 244°F. The milk tends to taste burnt and can taste metallic if stored too long.

DID YOU KNOW?

Health-food stores carry a number of nondairy products that can be substituted for milk or milk products.

SKIN SECRETS

When milk is heated, water on the surface evaporates, which causes the proteins there to concentrate and form a skin. When the skin forms, a number of valuable nutrients, protein among them, are lost. To minimize skin formation, cover the pan or stir the mixture rapidly for a few seconds to create a small amount of foam. Both these actions will slow the evaporation and reduce the amount of skin formation.

IS IT TRUE THAT DAIRY PRODUCTS MAY CAUSE MUCUS?

Years ago, people were told not to drink milk when they were sick because it would increase mucus production. In the last several years, the connection between milk and mucus has been studied, with interesting results. In Australia, 125 people were given chocolate-peppermint-flavored cow's milk or an identically flavored nondairy soy milk, so they could not taste the difference. The people who believed that milk produced mucus reported that both beverages produced a coating on their tongue and in their mouth. They also reported that they had trouble swallowing because their saliva had thickened.

In another study, the same researchers infected a group of healthy people with a cold virus, then tracked their dietary habits and cold symptoms. Their finding was that was that those who drank milk produced no more mucus than those who did not drink milk. The researchers concluded that milk did not produce any excess mucus, but that the sensation of excess mucus resulted from the consistency and texture of the milk.

WHAT IS ACIDOPHILUS MILK?

Acidophilus milk is low-fat or nonfat milk to which a bacterial culture has been added. As the milk is digested, the bacteria are released and become active, helping to maintain the balance of beneficial microorganisms in the intestinal tract. It is especially useful when taking antibiotics, as it replenishes the bacteria—especially those that produce B vitamins—which are destroyed by the medication. Other products with a similar bacteria-building effect are yogurt, buttermilk, and kefir. You can also take acidophilus in capsule form; it's available in the vitamin sections of drugstores, health food stores, and natural products stores.

SPINNING OFF THE CREAM

Cream comes from the fat that rises to the surface of nonhomogenized milk. The larger supermarkets generally carry four varieties of cream: the lightest variety is half-and-half, which is at least 10.5 but not more than 18 percent milkfat; next comes light cream, with between 18 and 30 percent milkfat; then light whipping cream, which is between 30 and 36 percent milkfat; and finally, heavy whipping cream, with at least 36 percent milkfat. By contrast, whole milk contains only 3.25 percent milkfat.

STICK VERSUS WHIPPED BUTTER

Unless a recipe specifies whipped butter, it should not be used in cooking. Whipping incorporates air into butter. Whipped butter is 50 percent air by volume and is better to use on toast than in recipes because it will spread more easily.

YOU'D BUTTER BEWARE

Where you store butter will affect how long it lasts. Butter tends to absorb odors and flavors more rapidly than any other food. If you store it near onions, it will have an onion smell. If it's around fish, it will smell fishy, and so on. If butter is refrigerated, it will retain its flavor for about three weeks, after which time it starts losing flavor fairly fast. Date the package to be sure you're getting the most flavor from your butter. To freeze butter, wrap it in two layers of plastic, and then in foil to keep it from absorbing freezer odors. It will last for six months if fresh when frozen; it must be kept at 0°F.

WHAT'S IN IMITATION BUTTER SPRAY?

Butter-flavored sprays are made from water, a small amount of soybean oil, salt, sweet cream buttermilk, gums, and flavorings. A three-second spray has 20 calories, 3 grams of fat, and no sodium.

BEST TO USE UNSALTED BUTTER IN RECIPES

Depending on where you live and what brand you choose, the salt content of salted butter can vary from 1 to 1½ percent. If you use salted butter, taste the dish before you add salt—it may not need any. Unsalted butter tends to taste fresher than salted butter. But salt acts as a preservative, meaning that salted butter can be stored longer.

DID YOU KNOW?

Milk consumption is down in the United States as a result of increased soft-drink advertising. Soda is now the drink of choice.

TO AVOID SCORCHING, USE CLARIFIED BUTTER

When butter is heated, the protein in the milk solids goes through a change that causes the butter to burn and scorch easily. A small amount of canola oil added to the butter will raise the smoke point and slow down this process. However, if you use clarified butter—butter from which the protein and water have been removed—you can cook foods at higher temperatures. You can also store it longer than standard butter.

HOW ABOUT SOME DONKEY BUTTER, YAK, YAK?

While almost all butter sold in the United States is produced from cow's milk, butter may be produced from the milk of many other animals. In other countries, butter is made from the milk of donkeys, horses, goats, sheep, buffalo, camels, and even yaks when cow's milk is not available.

WHY DOES WHIPPED CREAM WHIP?

Cream whips because of the high number of fat globules it contains. As the cream is whipped, the fat globules are encompassed by air bubbles. This action produces the foam and causes the mixture to become stable. The fat globules actually cluster together within the bubble walls. The colder the ingredients and utensils, the more easily the cream will whip. Fat globules are more active and tend to cluster more rapidly at lower temperatures. The cream should actually be placed in the freezer for 10 to 15 minutes before whipping.

Adding a small amount of dissolved gelatin to the mixture will help stabilize the bubble walls so the mixture will hold up better. Sugar should never be added at the start of the whipping process; it will interfere with the clumping of the proteins and will decrease the total volume of the final product. Always stop beating at the point when the cream becomes stiffest. If small lumps appear in your whipping cream, you have over-beaten, and the cream is turning to butter. At that point, there is really nothing you can do to save the situation except to spread the butter on your toast and start with a new batch of cream.

IS LOW-CHOLESTEROL MILK ON THE HORIZON?

Whole milk contains about 530 milligrams of cholesterol per gallon. Certain companies, however, are developing a cholesterol-free milk made with hydrolyzed oat flour.

WHAT'S THE REASON FOR SCALDING MILK?

Scalding—heating milk just to the point where whisps of steam rise off before it starts to boil—destroys certain enzymes and it kills certain bacteria. However, any contemporary recipe that calls for scalded milk has been reproduced in its original form from an earlier source. Scalding is now unnecessary because pasteurization accomplishes the same thing.

IS BUTTERMILK MADE FROM BUTTER?

If you happen to live near a dairy that makes butter, you may be lucky enough to find the old-fashioned kind of buttermilk—that is, the liquid left over from making butter. Virtually all buttermilk is produced from nonfat milk cultures. The milk is incubated for 12 to 14 hours, which is longer than yogurt, and kept at least 40°F cooler than yogurt while it is fermenting. The buttery flavor is the result of citric acid, a by-product of the fermentation process, and is derived from the bacterium *Leuconostoc citrovorum,* which converts citric acid into diacetyl.

WHY IS THERE WATER IN MY YOGURT?

It really isn't water that collects on the top of the yogurt, it's whey—a protein that tends to liquefy easily and should be stirred back in. Use the separation to your advantage to make dips and spreads. Line a strainer with cheesecloth or a coffee filter, set it over a bowl, spoon in plain yogurt, cover with plastic, and refrigerate. The longer it stands, the thicker the yogurt becomes—after six hours it will be like sour cream; if it drains overnight it will be more like cream cheese.

CAN BUTTER GO RANCID?

Oxidation will take its toll on butter just as it does on any other fat. Oxygen reacts with unsaturated fats, causing rancidity. To maintain its freshness as long as possible, butter should always be kept tightly wrapped in the refrigerator or freezer.

MICROWAVING BUTTER

When you try to soften butter in a microwave, it often becomes a runny mess. This is because microwaves cook food from the inside out. It is best to cut the butter into pieces, put it in a glass measuring cup, heat it at 100 percent power for 30 seconds, and then stir it. It should have the consistency of whipped butter.

WHAT IS MARGARINE MADE FROM?

Stick margarine must contain no less than 80 percent fat, along with water, milk solids, salt, preservatives, emulsifiers, artificial colors, and flavorings. The fat may be composed of tropical oils, which are high in saturated fat, or polyunsaturated oils. Better-quality margarines use corn or safflower oil. Tub margarines are the same formulation as stick margarines, but they have had air mechanically incorporated into them. They still contain salt as well as artificial flavorings and preservatives. Liquid margarines are composed entirely of polyunsaturated fat and will not harden in the refrigerator. Light or diet margarines vary from 40 to 60 percent fat content and have more air and water added along with the preservatives, salt, and flavorings.

SAVING THE CREAM FROM SOURING

When cream begins to develop an off odor and you want to use it, try mixing in ⅛ teaspoon of baking soda. The baking soda will neutralize the lactic acid that is causing the souring in the cream. Before you use the cream, however, taste it to be sure the flavor is still acceptable.

DON'T SAVE BABY FORMULA FOR LATER

If there is any formula left in the baby's bottle, it is best to dispose of it, because it is possible for bacteria from the baby's mouth to enter the formula through the nipple. Once the bacteria have been introduced, they will multiply to high levels.

Even if the formula is refrigerated and reheated, there may still be enough bacteria left to cause illness, especially because infants have immature immune and digestive systems. So remember: Formula bottles should be filled with just enough formula for a single feeding.

DID YOU KNOW?

If your milk-based sauce curdles, whirl the sauce in a blender for a few seconds.

BREAST MILK AND EXERCISE DON'T MIX

Studies show that nursing mothers should breastfeed before they exercise. Lactic acid can build up in breast milk during workouts, and its level will remain elevated for about 90 minutes after exercise. Women who know they will need to breastfeed during the recovery period might want to express milk before exercising.

STORING DAIRY PRODUCTS

All dairy products are very perishable. The optimal refrigeration is actually just over 32°F; however, few refrigerators are ever set that low or hold that low a temperature. Most home refrigerators remain around 40°F, and the temperature rises every time the door is opened. Store milk on an inside shelf—never on the door—toward the back of the refrigerator.

BUTTER, GETTING A GOOD GRADE

The butterfat content of any product labeled "butter" must be 80 percent. A natural coloring agent called annatto is added to some butter to give it a deep yellow color. The USDA grades butter by taste, color, aroma, texture, and body. Grading is done on a point system, with 100 being the best. Grade AA must have received at least 93 points, Grade A at least 92, and Grade B a minimum of 90 points. Salt is added to some butter to increase its shelf life; it is sold as salted butter.

HOW TO GUARANTEE A CREAMY CUSTARD

The formula for basic custard calls for 1 egg, 1 cup of milk, and 2 tablespoons of granulated sugar. For a richer custard, add 2 to 3 egg yolks (which will increase the fat and cholesterol significantly). For a custard that is creamy rather than solid, stir the mixture continuously over low heat to keep the protein from setting too quickly.

The milk is not the main protein source in custard, but it contributes fats that separate the egg proteins from one another, allowing the custard to coagulate at a higher temperature, thus reducing the possibility of curdling. Never replace the milk with water, because your custard will not set. The milk and sugar also impede the bonding of the egg proteins, thus promoting tenderness. Never try to speed up the cooking process by increasing the heat. Making the perfect custard takes time and patience.

BUTTER WITHOUT A CHURN

It's easy to make butter at home, especially if you have a food processor. Freeze the bowl and metal blade for 20 minutes. Measure 2 cups of cold heavy whipping cream (try to use pasteurized, not ultrapasteurized) into the bowl and process three to five minutes, scraping down the sides to make sure all the cream is incorporated. Continue processing until all the solids are separated from the liquid. Then pour off the liquid, which is the whey. (Save the whey and use it in place of milk in bread, biscuit, or pancake recipes.) The butter must be refrigerated and used within three to four days. Two cups of cream will make about 6 to 7 ounces of butter.

17

BEVERAGES

IT'S PERFECTLY CLEAR

Water must be filtered if you want clear ice cubes. In addition, boiling the water before filling the trays allows a number of minerals that cause the cloudiness to dissipate into the air.

POOR CENTS

In 1999, people in the United States drank 14 billion gallons of soda and 551 million gallons of wine, spending $58 billion and $18.1 billion respectively. Too bad it wasn't milk or water (especially the soda).

WATER WORKS

The human body is dependent on an adequate and healthful water supply. Every bodily function and organ system relies on water. Water assists in digesting foods, transports nutrients to organs, and then cools the body through perspiration, helping to regulate body temperature. Water washes out contaminants through the kidneys in the form of urine. We require about 10 cups of water daily to replace these losses. On average, we get a little over five cups from fluids, about four cups from solid foods, and just over one cup of water is produced by the metabolism.

By weight, the human body is about two-thirds water; a 150-pound adult is about 90 pounds of water. Here's how it breaks down by percentage of water making up tissues, organs, fluids, and bone.

How Much Water?	
BODY PART OR FLUID	PERCENT WATER
Bone	33
Liver	71
Lungs	71 to 84
Heart	72
Kidneys	76
Brain	77.4
Muscle	79
Blood	82
Saliva	94
Perspiration	95

TYPES OF WATER

Sparkling Water

This comes in two varieties. Naturally carbonated water is found in deep natural springs in many areas of the world. Artificially carbonated water is produced by adding an acid to still water. Because water can undergo treatment, the FDA states that sparkling water must contain the same amount of carbon dioxide that it had when it emerged from the source after treatment and possible replacement of carbon dioxide.

Mineral Water

As the name implies, this is water with minerals. The FDA mandates that mineral water must contain no less than 20 parts per million of total dissolved solids, and that no minerals can be added. Different brands have different levels of minerals. Expensive water from famous spas rarely provides health benefits over other mineral waters.

Club Soda and Seltzer

These are artificially carbonated drinks; soda water contains sodium bicarbonate, but seltzer does not.

Spring Water

This is pure, uncarbonated water. Spring water must come from an underground formation and must flow naturally to the earth's surface.

Artesian Well Water

This comes from a well that taps into a water-bearing layer of rock and sand that lies above the normal water table.

GIVE IT TO THE PLANTS

If you know your house has lead pipes (or if your house is old and you're not sure), play it safe: Always use cold water for cooking, especially making baby formula, and let the water run for two to three minutes first thing in the morning. The longer water sits in the pipes, and the hotter the water is, the higher the chance it may contain lead.

THIRST QUENCHERS?

Have you ever felt thirstier after you drink a soda? Well, they contain sugar, which the body has to break down—and this is a process which requires water. Additionally, the caffeine in soft drinks acts as a diuretic, which makes you lose fluids. Alcoholic drinks also require one cup of water per drink to metabolize the alcohol.

DID YOU KNOW?

If you are really thirsty, the best beverage bet is water.

DON'T CHILL OUT

If you suffer from any form of cardiovascular disease, don't drink ice water. The cold may cause a sudden drop in tissue temperature, resulting in an unnecessary shock to the system. Even if you don't suffer from heart problems, your digestive system functions more efficiently if you drink tepid water (though an occasional glass of ice water won't harm you). Try to avoid drinking water with your meals: It will dilute stomach acids and digestive enzymes.

THE ULTIMATE THIRST QUENCHER

There has been an ongoing debate whether it is better to drink ice water or room-temperature water when you are thirsty. The answer? Drink ice water to quench a raging thirst. Ice water will cause your stomach to constrict, thereby forcing the water into the small intestine, where it will be absorbed into the bloodstream faster.

DRINK UP!

Where you live affects the amount of water you need to drink. At higher elevations, where the atmospheric pressure is lower and the air is drier, water tends to evaporate faster through your skin. Because the air is thinner, you also tend to breathe more rapidly, thus losing additional moisture through exhalation. Denizens of Denver need to consume three or four extra glasses of water per day than do New Yorkers.

A TRICKY QUESTION

Are you more likely to become dehydrated in summer or in winter? While it's true that your body loses more water during the summer months, you're more likely to drink more fluids. You still sweat in winter, but it evaporates more quickly because heated rooms are dry, and perspiration is absorbed by clothing. In the winter, we're less conscious of our need for water, so we drink less.

WASTE NOT . . .

If you leave the water running every time you brush your teeth, you will waste about one gallon of water. The average person in the United States uses 80 gallons of water a day.

DRINK A VEGGIE

Some fruits and vegetables have a high water content. Carrots are 88 percent water and iceberg lettuce is 96 percent water, for example.

WHY ICE FLOATS

When water freezes, the molecules combine loosely, creating air pockets. When water is in its liquid form, these pockets do not exist, making water denser than ice.

THIRSTY FOODSTUFFS

The production of food in the United States uses up 47 percent of our fresh water supply. Feeding one person for one year uses about 1,500,000 gallons of fresh water.

- One large potato requires 18 gallons of water to grow.
- One pat of margarine requires 85 gallons.
- One loaf of bread requires 56 gallons.
- One pint of alcohol requires 110 gallons.
- One pound of flour requires 350 gallons
- One pound of meat requires 4,850 gallons.

The average person drinks more than 15,000 gallons of water by the time he or she is 68 years of age.

A QUICK RINSE

When ice cubes stay in the freezer tray more than a few days, they tend to pick up odors from other foods. Give ice cubes a quick rinse before using them to avoid altering the flavor of your beverage.

NATURE'S CARBONATED WATER

A number of "natural" beverage makers advertise that their drink contains naturally carbonated water. This water is created underground when the water comes into contact with limestone, resulting in the production of the gas carbon dioxide. The water traps the gas under high pressure underground. Artificially, carbonation is helped along with either phosphoric acid or citric acid in most soft drinks.

DID YOU KNOW?

**Most of the
tea sold in
supermarkets
is black tea.**

HAVE A WATER CHASER

It's a good idea to drink a cup of water for every alcoholic drink you consume. It takes eight ounces of water to metabolize every ounce of alcohol.
If you have ever had a hangover, you'll recognize the symptoms of dehydration such as dry mouth, headaches, and an upset stomach.

TEA FACTS

◆ Tea was first grown and served in China. It was originally used to flavor
water that tasted flat after boiling for purification. Tea moved from
China to Japan and throughout the Far East, and now the island of
Sri Lanka leads the world in tea production. Tea is still picked by hand,
and a tea picker can pick about 40 pounds of tea leaves daily.

◆ Iced tea was first sold in the 1870s at New York's Fifth Avenue Hotel on
hot summer days. By 1904, it was a popular beverage at the Louisiana
Purchase Exposition held in St. Louis. The British still think of iced tea
as an American aberration.

◆ The most popular tea in the United States is black tea. In 1996, the
United States imported approximately 140 million pounds of tea, with
annual consumption topping 44 billion cups. The majority of this tea
was imported from India.

◆ Pound for pound, tea has much more caffeine than does coffee.
However, a pound of tea will brew 150 to 200 cups, while a pound of
coffee yields about 48 cups. Brewed tea contains about a third as much
caffeine as instant coffee.

◆ Tea acts as a diuretic and should not be relied upon for providing your
daily intake of water.

CLASSIFICATION OF TEAS

All tea comes from an evergreen related to the camellia family.

Green Tea

This tea is not oxidized—green is the natural color of tea leaves, impart-
ed by chlorophyll. The leaves are steamed, and then rolled and dried.
Gunpowder is a Chinese classification for green tea; basket-fired is a
Japanese classification.

Black Tea

This is made when the insides of the leaves are exposed to oxygen (that
is, they oxidize), which turns them black. The leaves are then dried and
allowed to ferment for two to three hours.

Oolong Tea

This tea is partially fermented and somewhat oxidized. Oolong tea is fermented twice and fired three times. It has a greenish-brown color and is usually sold as Formosa tea; when oolong tea is blended with jasmine tea, it is called Pouchong.

DRINK TO YOUR HEALTH

Studies in Shanghai and Japan showed that drinking green tea was effective in protecting against stomach cancer and lowering cholesterol and triglyceride levels. But be cautious about using tea for any medicinal purpose—drinking large amounts may cause problems because of the caffeine or because of the strong binding properties of the polyphenols in tea. Tea's polyphenic antioxidants are being studied for their potential in preventing cancer; the key one is called epigallocatechin-3-gallate. More research needs to be done to determine the exact activities green and black tea perform, as well as to determine how much tea is both safe to drink and beneficial to your health.

A study from the Netherlands found no relationship exists between drinking black tea and curing cancer. The study was performed on 120,852 men and women between the ages of 55 and 69 who had cancer. Another Dutch study concluded that consumption of black tea was not related to ischemic heart disease and had only marginal benefits in reducing mortality associated with ischemic heart disease.

THE TEMPERATURE MATTERS

Tea experts agree that green teas should be brewed between 180°F and 200°F, oolong teas between 185°F and 205°F, and black teas between 190°F and 210°F. Better quality and more delicate black teas should be brewed at lower temperatures since they tend to release their flavor more readily than do lower quality teas. The higher temperature used to brew lower quality teas seems to stimulate the tea to release its flavor.

THE PERFECT CUBE

Ice cubes used for iced tea or coffee should be made from tea or coffee, not from water. These beverages tend to become diluted rapidly, because they're often enjoyed on sultry summer days, and this ensures the drinks won't become watered down.

CLEARING UP A PROBLEM

Cloudiness is common in brewed iced tea but can be prevented easily. Just let the tea cool to room temperature before refrigerating it. If the tea is still cloudy, try adding a small amount of boiling water to it until it clears up. A number of minerals are released when the tea is brewed, which results in the cloudiness.

GETTING YOUR JOLT FROM TEA

Can't drink coffee but still want caffeine? A cup of English breakfast tea provides you with about 60 milligrams of caffeine—not as much as a cup of coffee, but more than most teas.

UP TO DATE

While the latest studies show that there are no risk factors related to tea drinking, the tannins in tea and red wine can interfere with the assimilation of iron (in an all-vegetable meal), thiamine, and vitamin B2 in the body. These studies did not say that this was a health risk, however, nor did they recommend not consuming wine or tea.

SOME TEAS CAN BE TOXIC

Historically, the blossoms of the germander plant (*Teucrium chamaedrys*) were used for weight loss. However, researchers in France have found that germander blossoms can cause liver damage.

A number of cases of hepatitis were reported in people who took germander for three to 18 weeks. Dosages taken ranged from 600 to 1,620 milligrams a day in capsule form. Teas were also used and may be just as harmful. Most manufacturers have stopped marketing this tea for weight control; however, it is still available.

Several other teas may have risk factors attached and should not be used if you have any medical condition or just want to stay healthy. These include jimsonweed, burdock root, kava-kava, mandrake, oleander, pokeweed, lobelia, senna, and woodruff.

COFFEE IS MADE FROM COFFEE CHERRIES

Coffee trees originated in Ethiopia; Ethiopians were the first to drink the beverage. In time, Turkey became a producer, and the country guarded its monopoly, decreeing at one point that no fertile berries could leave the country without first being steeped in boiling water and partially roasted to prevent them from germinating. Coffee beans were finally smuggled to Holland in 1616 and then to Brazil in 1727.

Coffee trees need 40 to 60 inches of rain annually. Each tree produces about 2,000 "coffee cherries"—enough to make one pound of coffee.

The United States consumes about 50 percent of all coffee worldwide, or approximately 400 million cups per day. Almost half of American adults drink coffee, consuming an average of 1.7 cups daily.

FRESH GROUND COFFEE BEANS, BREW IT FAST

When coffee beans are ground, a large percentage of their surface is exposed to air, which speeds its deterioration. The longer the ground beans sit, the more carbon dioxide, which contributes to the coffee's body and aroma, is lost. For this reason, coffee beans should be stored in the refrigerator and ground fresh as needed. If you choose to buy the vacuum-packed cans, store them in the refrigerator upside down to preserve the taste and flavor. Why upside down? You reduce the amount of oxygen that had contact with the surface of the coffee, slowing down oxidation.

WORLD CLASS COFFEE

The big island of Hawaii is the only location in the United States where coffee is grown. The mineral rich volcanic soil produces Kona coffee, one of the finest and most flavorful coffees in the world.

SURVIVAL AND REVIVAL

When you keep coffee warm in a coffeepot on a hot plate, it will only stay fresh for about 30 minutes after it is brewed. If your coffee needs to be freshened up, add a pinch of salt to your cup before reheating it.

COFFEE FACTS

◆ Ground coffee oxidizes and loses flavor; it should be used within two to three days for best results. Fresh-roasted beans are usually packed in bags that are not airtight, which allows the carbon monoxide formed during the roasting process to escape. If the carbon monoxide doesn't escape, the coffee will have a poor taste.

◆ If you run out of coffee filters, try using a double layer of white paper towels (don't use paper towels with any printing on them—the inks can be released by the hot water).

◆ Clean your coffeepot regularly, and rinse it well. The slightest hint of soap or scum will alter the taste. Baking soda and hot water work well.

◆ The effects of caffeine on your brain that keep you awake may last for about four hours.

◆ If you suffer from stomach ulcers, you should consider giving up coffee, because it can aggravate your condition and may delay the healing time.

◆ Caffeine has a negative effect on zinc absorption. Zinc may play a role in protecting against prostate cancer.

◆ If you're under a lot of stress, you may want to curb your coffee consumption: Caffeine "enhances" the impact of stress, increasing blood pressure and heart rate. Just what you need, right?

A DECAFFEINATION TIME LINE

1906

The first chemical used to decaffeinate coffee was benzol; the beverage was marketed as Dekafa.

1973

The next chemical used to decaffeinate coffee was trichloroethylene. However, two years later it was found that it caused cancer of the liver in mice and use was discontinued.

1975

Processors switched to methylene chloride. In 1981, this was also found to cause cancer in mice when inhaled, but not ingested. The FDA said that the residues that did reach your coffee cup were minimal, and concern that it posed a human health risk was essentially nonexistent.

1981

Coffee companies switched to ethyl acetate, a chemical that is found in pineapples and bananas. Studies showed that a concentrated form of the vapors alone (not the chemical itself) caused liver and heart damage in laboratory animals. This chemical is also used as a cleaning solvent for leathers and production of plastics; it is still used to decaffeinate coffee.

1984

Two companies have developed methods of decaffeinating coffee using water. Swiss and Belgian companies use water to remove the caffeine harmlessly; the coffee suffers a small loss in flavor. A number of U.S. companies are working with the method, but production is still low and more

DID YOU KNOW?

Caffeine can leach calcium from bones. If you're a coffee, tea, or soda drinker, be sure you eat enough calcium-rich foods to offset any ill effects.

expensive than using a solvent. When purchasing coffee, try to choose a coffee that states it has been decaffeinated using a water process.

SO, IS DECAF SAFE TO DRINK?

The Swiss water and the carbon dioxide methods of decaffeination are the two safest methods. In the Swiss water process, green coffee beans are soaked in water for several hours, which removes about 97 percent of the caffeine—as well as a few of the flavor components. The water is then passed through a carbon filter, which removes the caffeine and leaves the flavors. This water is added back to the beans before they are dried.

In the carbon dioxide method, the green beans are dampened with water, then placed into a pot that is then filled with pressurized carbon dioxide. The carbon dioxide has the ability to draw the caffeine out of the beans and can remove almost 100 percent of the caffeine. The coffee beans are then dried to remove the excess moisture. Both methods employ only natural elements to decaffeinate the coffee beans.

THE OTHER DIURETIC

Many people switch from coffee to tea with the hope that they will stop running to the bathroom—but are surprised that the problem is still with them. Caffeine does have a diuretic effect on many people, and tea does contain caffeine (though less per cup than coffee).

DOES A HOT CUP OF ANY BEVERAGE REALLY WARM YOU UP?

From a physiological standpoint, hot drinks will not raise your body temperature. Research conducted by the U.S. Army Research Institute of Environmental Medicine showed that you would have to drink one quart of a liquid at 130°F to generate any increase in body temperature. It also stated that it would be difficult to keep that much liquid down. In fact, hot liquids will cause surface blood vessels to dilate; this may make you feel a slight bit warmer but may actually lead to a loss of heat.

THE DAILY GRIND

The size of the grind does make a difference in the taste and level of caffeine in a cup of coffee. Espresso is typically finely ground, and Turkish coffee even finer. Most American coffee is drip grind. This provides the optimum surface area and will brew a rich cup of coffee that is not bitter.

However, if you grind your own beans, take care they are not too finely ground. The water will take longer to filter through, which can result in an increase in phenolic acids and bitter tasting coffee.

CAFFEINATED WATER?

Yes, it's true—caffeinated water is available and advertised as the latest cure for sleepiness when you are driving. Let's just hope that when you go to a restaurant they won't soon be asking you whether you want your water caffeinated or decaf!

REDUCING ACIDITY IN BEVERAGES

If you're one of those people who is sensitive to acidity in coffee, here's a tip to reduce the acid level. Just add a pinch of baking soda to the drink. (Use this tip to decrease the acid in other high-acid drinks and foods.)

SCALDS THE SKIN, NOT THE TONGUE

There's a simple explanation why you can drink coffee that is hot enough to burn your skin and not your mouth. When you sip a very hot cup of coffee, you suck in cool air. The air lowers the temperature through both convection (air current) and evaporation. Also, saliva partially coats the inside of the mouth, insulating it from very hot liquids.

IT'S ALL WHAT YOU'RE USED TO

If you're not accustomed to drinking coffee after dinner, it will keep you up at night. The more coffee you drink, the higher your tolerance will be, and the more it will take to keep you awake. Some individuals are actually born with a high tolerance and are never kept awake. There's also the psychological effect—studies show that the *belief* that coffee is supposed to keep you awake at night is enough to keep some people awake.

TEMPERATURE MATTERS

When brewing coffee, the proper temperature is important. When coffee is brewed, the water should be between 200°F and 205°F; after brewing, it should be held between 185°F and 190°F. If the temperature is too low, the coffee grounds will not release adequate flavor compounds, and if it gets too high, tannins are released, affecting the flavor of the coffee. Caffeine has very little to do with the taste of coffee.

DON'T BOIL THE BEAN

In 1991, a study reported a connection between coffee and increased blood cholesterol levels. This study was performed in Scandinavia, where boiled coffee is common. Researchers attributed the high correlation to the fact that boiling releases two of the ingredients that are implicated in raising cholesterol, cafestol and kahweol. Filters remove more than 80 percent of these substances.

IS YOUR COFFEE BITTER?

The best coffee flavor can be yours with freshly ground coffee and naturally soft water. Coffee should never be boiled, which can release the tannins that make it bitter.

CARBONATION LASTS LONGER IN COLD SOFT DRINKS

Phosphoric acid and citric acid react with water and form carbon dioxide gas, which produces the bubbles in soft drinks. When sodas are warm, carbon dioxide expands and more of it escapes in the form of bubbles. If you pour a warm soft drink over ice cubes, the gas escapes from the beverage at a faster rate because the ice cubes contain more surface for the gas bubbles to collect on, thus releasing more of the carbon dioxide. This is the reason that warm beverages go flat rapidly, and warm drinks poured over ice go flat even faster. To slow down the process, rinse the ice cubes in cold water for about 10 seconds before adding the soft drink. This will help to eliminate the fizzing, which is when the carbon dioxide escapes.

CAFFEINE

Caffeine is the most widely used behavior-affecting drug in the world. It can be derived from 60 different plant sources, including cocoa beans, cola nuts, tea leaves, and coffee beans.

Caffeine stimulates the central nervous system and is capable of warding off drowsiness and increasing alertness. It also quickens reaction time to both visual and auditory stimuli.

Studies have shown that caffeine does not cause frequent urination in all people, but does cause an acid increase in the stomach after two cups. Chronic heartburn sufferers should avoid coffee completely and limit caffeine from other sources to 300 milligrams per day.

The latest information on pregnancy and caffeine consumption is from studies performed at the University of California, which recommend that pregnant women should try to limit their caffeine consumption to no more than 300 milligrams per day.

Caffeine Content In Common Foods and Drugs

BEVERAGE	PER 8 OUNCES
Drip coffee	137 mg
Instant coffee	57 mg
Jolt Cola	50 mg
Diet Dr Pepper	41 mg
Mountain Dew	37 mg
Black tea	36 mg
Iced tea	36 mg
Instant tea	31 mg
Coca-Cola	31 mg
Diet Coke	31 mg
Sunkist orange soda	27 mg
Dr Pepper	25 mg
Pepsi-Cola	25 mg

Diet Pepsi	24 mg
Cocoa	4 mg

DRUG	PER TABLET
Weight control aids	75-200 mg
Vivarin	200 mg
NoDoz	100 mg
Excedrin	65 mg
Vanquish	32 mg
Anacin	32 mg
Midol	32 mg

CHOCOLATE	PER OUNCE
Milk chocolate	6 mg
Semisweet chocolate	20 mg

CAFFEINE AND CALCIUM

Recent studies released from Washington State University indicate that caffeinated beverages will cause calcium to be excreted in the urine. To replace the calcium losses, try to consume at least 2 tablespoons of milk for each cup of coffee you drink.

BUT IT'S NOT JUST CAFFEINE

Physicians are getting more and more concerned about the number of soft drinks women consume. Most sodas are carbonated with phosphoric acid; excessive amounts of phosphorus can upset the ratio of calcium to phosphorus, which leads to the loss of calcium.

The typical American consumes about 1,500 milligrams of phosphorus daily; the Recommended Daily Allowance is 800 milligrams. One 12-ounce can of cola can provide up to 50 milligrams of phosphorus.

HARD FACTS ABOUT SOFT DRINKS

◆ In a 24-hour period Coca-Cola is consumed 192 million times in 35 countries around the world.
◆ Soft drinks account for 25 percent of all sugar consumption in the United States.
◆ If a child drinks four colas per day, he is taking in the equivalent caffeine in two cups of regular coffee.
◆ The average American drank almost 55 gallons of soda in 1999.

FILE IT UNDER "STRANGE BUT TRUE"

Believe it or not, some lemon furniture polishes contain more actual lemon than commercial lemonade drink mixes.

CONCENTRATE REALLY HARD

Orange juice has a high acid content. If you use frozen concentrate, it will last about a week after it is reconstituted. The nutritional value, especially of the vitamin C, will decrease rapidly, so it's best to consume the juice within three or four days. The oxygen in the water, as well as the aeration when you mix the juice, tends to deplete the vitamin.

HOW DID GATORADE ORIGINATE?

Gatorade originated in 1965 when researchers at the University of Florida in Tampa decided that their football team, the Gators, needed to replace the minerals and fluids lost through strenuous exercise. The drink was developed to provide water (to prevent dehydration), sugar (energy), salt (fluid balance), and potassium (nerve transmission). In 1983, Quaker Oats purchased the brand name and sells the drink in different flavors. More than 423 million gallons of Gatorade are sold every day.

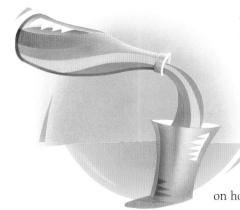

RAINBOW-COLORED BEVERAGES?

Have you noticed that foods marketed to children are becoming more colorful? Kids will purchase blue drinks over any color, and manufacturers are making blue candy, cookies, ice cream, and other foods. Studies performed at the University of Massachusetts showed that younger people "are open to the novelty of unnaturally tinted products" than are a more mature group. It was also discovered that color has an impact on how a food tastes to people.

ALCOHOL

While alcohol is the most familiar of the multitude of available drugs, it has the distinction of being one of the least potent, ounce for ounce. Because it is the least potent, large quantities are often consumed, which can lead to abuse—and a host of societal ills. Alcohol abuse is one of the leading health problems in the United States today, surpassed only by heart disease and cancer.

The following is a brief description of the effects alcohol has on the various body systems after three drinks of an 80-proof beverage:

Mouth

The taste of most alcoholic beverages is not pleasant, which is why mixed drinks are so popular. There is no permanent damage to the mouth, but the risk of oral cancer is increased four times.

Stomach

As the alcohol comes in contact with the stomach lining, the lining may become inflamed and irritated. A number of problems can result, such as small ulcers appearing, tiny blood vessels bursting, and the normally acid-resistant coating losing a high degree of protection. About 20 percent of the alcohol is absorbed directly into the bloodstream from the stomach.

Intestines

As the alcohol finds its way into your small intestine, it is metabolized at the rate of about 7 grams (about ¼ ounce) per hour.

Bloodstream

If alcohol is consumed at a rate faster than the intestines are able to metabolize it, it begins to affect the brain and other organs. The bloodstream transports the alcohol to the liver, which processes it.

Liver

Alcohol reduces the liver's efficiency, and over a prolonged period of use may cause permanent damage. The liver may develop scar tissue and an increase of cellular fats, leading to the disease cirrhosis. In advanced stages, cirrhosis may cause the liver to stop functioning completely and thus become life threatening.

Brain

If you drink more alcohol than the intestines can handle, it returns to the bloodstream and a percentage goes to the brain. When alcohol reaches the brain it affects the frontal lobes first, affecting reasoning powers and judgment. Next the alcohol affects speech and vision centers, then large muscles, causing the staggering and loss of balance. If you drink enough, you will pass out due to alcohol's anesthetic effect on the brain. If you don't pass out, you would eventually kill yourself with a lethal dose if you were to continue drinking. Remember, it is a drug.

VITAMINS, MINERALS, AND ALCOHOL

Alcohol impairs the body's ability to absorb, metabolize, and use vitamins A, E, and D. In addition, alcoholics tend to eat less, which may lead to deficiencies in vitamins C and K, as well as calcium, magnesium, iron, and zinc. If you consume more than two alcoholic beverages a day, consider taking a multivitamin, multimineral supplement.

WILL COFFEE SOBER YOU UP?

After the initial euphoria of alcohol wears off, it will make you drowsy and incoherent. Coffee will make you more alert and awake, but it will have little effect on making you sober. The quickest way to sober up is to consume a glass of water for each alcoholic drink and to take a multivitamin, multimineral supplement while you are drinking. This will assist the liver in metabolizing the alcohol more efficiently, and it may even reduce the effects of hangover.

CAFFEINE NATION

Although caffeine is an addictive drug, cutting back on caffeinated sodas gradually can decrease the likelihood that you'll experience symptoms of withdrawal like severe headaches, nausea, or depression (most of these symptoms are short-lived).

THE PROBLEM WITH ALCOHOL

Alcohol is the major cause of many accidents:

- 83 percent of fatal fires and burn injuries
- 47 to 65 percent of drownings
- 47 percent of industrial injuries
- 38 percent of motor-vehicle fatalities

In addition, separated and divorced men and women were three times as likely as married people to say they had been married to an alcoholic or problem drinker.

SLOW IT DOWN

You can slow down the rate that your body absorbs alcohol if you eat while drinking. Eating fatty foods, which take a long time to digest, will slow down the rate of absorption even more.

SURPRISED?

Alcoholism is most prevalent among those whose incomes are less than $10,000 per year—it affects 17 percent. Only 6 percent of people whose incomes are $25,000 or more are alcoholics.

ALCOHOL CONTENT

Most liquor sold in the United States contain 40 percent alcohol, which means that they are 80 proof. The proof figure is always double the percentage of the alcohol content.

HOW ALCOHOL IS DISTILLED

In its pure state, alcohol is so toxic that even the yeasts that ferment it are unable to survive in a solution of more than 15 percent alcohol. For centuries, beer and wine were the only alcoholic beverages—until the process of distillation was invented. This process makes alcohol production possible because alcohol boils at 173°F, which is 39°F lower than water. When alcohol and water are mixed and brought to a boil, the alcohol will predominate in the vapor. The vapor is then cooled through long curled tubes of cold metal and allowed to drip into a container.

EXTRA, EXTRA! ALCOHOL KILLS VITAMIN!

According to information released by the American Cancer Society, consuming alcohol can promote a deficiency in vitamin A.

MEN BEWARE

Alcohol has the tendency to increase the excretion of the trace mineral zinc, which is very important to prostate health. Magnesium, another important trace mineral, may also be excreted, which may lead to lowering your resistance to stress.

JUST ONE MORE RISK FACTOR

Congeners are chemicals in liquor that are by-products of distillation and fermentation. The more congeners a liquor has, the worse the hangover. The safest beverages—that is, those that produce the lowest levels—are gin and vodka (especially Russian vodka). The beverages with the highest levels are bourbon, rum, and Scotch.

BREAK OUT THE BUBBLY

A seventeenth-century French monk named Dom Perignon perfected the process of making Champagne. He manipulated the presses to make a white wine from black grapes, blended wines from several villages for balance, and enhanced the tendency of white wines to keep their sugars, so the wines would referment, and make more bubbles. He also used cork stoppers to keep the bubbles in the bottle.

By law, anything sold as Champagne must come from the region of France by the same name—anything else must be sold as sparkling wine.

Champagnes are best when served between 44°F and 48°F. But never refrigerate Champagne for more than one or two hours before serving. If left in the refrigerator for long periods, the flavor will be poor.

DID THE ENGLISH OR FRENCH INVENT CHAMPAGNE?

The English invented the cork stopper, which was made from the inner bark of an oak tree that was native to Spain. The English imported still Champagne (wine from Champagne that had not begun to ferment and make bubbles) from France, then would add brandy and sugar, usually in the form of molasses, to the wine and would put it in stronger bottles

DID YOU KNOW?

If you suffer from motion sickness, don't have any alcoholic beverage on the plane. It will make things worse.

with cork stoppers. The wine, helped along by the brandy and sugar, would referment and become bubbly. As a result, some regard Champagne as having originated in England.

A REAL CORKER

Wine should be stored on its side to keep the cork damp. If the cork dries out it will shrink; air will pass through, and the wine will deteriorate. Portugal supplies about 80 percent of the corks sold worldwide.

GIVE IT A SWIRL

Our senses of smell and taste are inextricably linked. When you swirl the wine in the glass, you release its full aroma. Wine may contain 400 different organic molecules, 200 of which have an aroma.

SWEET OR NOT?

Champagnes are available along a continuum of sweet to dry.
◆ Brut is the driest, with less than 1.5 percent sugar.
◆ Extra sec or extra dry is dry; its sugar content is between 1.2 and 2 percent.
◆ Sec is slightly sweet, with 1.7 to 3.5 percent sugar.
◆ Demi-sec is sweeter still, with a sugar content of 3.3 to 5 percent.
◆ Doux is very sweet, with more than 5 percent sugar.
Demi-sec and doux are considered dessert wines.

THROW OUT YOUR SAUCER GLASSES

Champagne and sparkling wine are best served in flutes or tall narrow glasses. These provide less surface for the bubbles to escape. The old-fashioned saucer glasses that are wide and shallow allow the bubbles and bouquet to escape at least twice as fast.

CHEERS!

The quality of Champagne and sparkling wine can be compromised if the beverage is chilled for too long. Never store it in the refrigerator; it should also only be chilled for a matter of hours.

POP! GOES THE CHAMPAGNE

Champagne is produced with a high level of trapped carbon dioxide dissolved in the liquid. The pressure in the bottle is sufficient to keep the carbon dioxide in suspension until the bottle is opened and the pressure immediately drops to room-temperature pressure. The carbon dioxide dissipates and the Champagne goes flat, which will not take very long. The carbon dioxide gas also tends to increase the absorption of alcohol into the bloodstream, allowing you to feel the effects sooner than you would if you were drinking any other type of wine. Wine coolers and spritzers made with carbonated water will give you the same effect.

YOU'RE BLUSHING

Blush wines are produced from red grapes from which the juice has had almost no contact with the grape skins. The color will vary depending on the type of grape and whether a small amount of white grape juice is added. These wines are usually best if served chilled but not icy cold.

FORTIFIED WINES

These wines have alcohol added during wine making. The additional alcohol serves to stop the fermentation by killing the yeast. The most common fortified wines are port, sherry, and Marsala.

VINTAGE WINES

These are wines that are produced from grapes grown in a specific year, frequently from a particular vineyard. The year and vineyard are usually stated on the label. A nonvintage wine is made from grapes that were harvested in different years and never has a date on the label.

WINE CHEMISTRY 101

Wine is composed of water, alcohol, various pigments, esters, some vitamins and minerals, acids, and tannins. It does not remain in a constant state, but is continually changing—even in the bottle. When wines improve in the bottle, they are said to age well; most wines, however, should be drunk within a few years of bottling.

A FIERY SITUATION

If you are making a flambéed dish and have trouble igniting the brandy, it is probably not hot enough. Some chefs warm the brandy gently before adding it to the food to ensure that it will light. If you heat it too much before adding it to the dish, however, it may ignite too soon.

CURDLE UP WITH A GOOD WINE

If you add wine to a soup or sauce that already contains milk or cream, it may curdle; adding the wine and cooking it briefly before you add the dairy product should help prevent this.

A GENTLE TOUCH

When cooking with wine, try not to use too much, or the taste may well overpower the dish. Wine should only be used to improve the flavor. If you wish to make sure that you taste the wine in a recipe, just add it to the recipe about five to seven minutes before completion.

CRYSTALS ON YOUR WINE CORK?

The crystals you sometimes see on corks are tartrates, which are the by-product of tartaric acid used in wine-making. They are not an indication of an inferior or poorly processed wine, they do not affect the flavor of the wine, and they are not harmful if drunk.

TOASTING

The practice of making a toast originated in seventeenth century England where pieces of spiced toast were placed in a carafe of wine or individual glass to improve the taste. It was polite to eat the toast so as not to offend the host. The toast has since been omitted and just the wine consumed.

WINE FACTS

- ◆ The best temperature for storing wine is 55°F. White wine should be served between 50°F and 55°F for the best flavor; serve reds at 65°F.
- ◆ Wine stored at high temperatures will deteriorate rapidly. White wines are more susceptible to deterioration from heat than are red wines.
- ◆ Wine glasses should only be filled between half and two-thirds full—leave room to swirl the wine to release its full flavor and aroma.

◆ Always serve dry wine before sweet and white wine before red.

◆ If bits of cork fall into the wine, strain the wine into a decanter before pouring it.

◆ Red wines more than eight years old tend to develop sediment. This is harmless and the wine can be decanted, leaving the sediment behind.

SOME FOODS NEED CAREFUL PAIRING

A number of foods have flavors that clash with those of some wines. Highly acidic dishes, such as those made with vinegar or citrus, can conflict with wine. Egg yolks contain sulfur, which tends to have a negative effect on wine's flavor. Other potentially problematic foods are asparagus, onions, chocolate, tomatoes, pineapples, and artichokes. Here's a guide to temperamental foods and wine to serve with them.

FOOD	WINE
Eggs	Sparkling wine, not too oaky Chardonnay, medium-bodied Pinot Blanc
Asparagus	Sauvignon, Mosel Kabbinett, young Chardonnay, or red Cabernet Franc
Chocolate	Fortified sweet wines such as Málaga, Muscat, 10-year-old tawny Port; liqueurs; youngish Sauternes
Onion tart	Aromatic fruity dry whites from Alsace, or New World Colombard, Sauvignon, or Chardonnay
Tomatoes	Crisp Sauvignon or Vin de Pays des Côtes de Gascone, or a tangy red such as Barbera
Pineapple desserts	Concentrated sweet white with good acidity such as Côteaux du Layon or New Zealand late-harvest Reisling
Artichokes	Tangy white such as a crisp Chardonnay, Hungarian white, New Zealand Sauvignon, or young white Rioja

BEER BELLY?

It's true: Beer drinking itself is the cause of the beer belly. Across all races and in both genders, beer consumption is consistently and directly linked to higher waist-to-hip-circumference ratios.

DID YOU KNOW?

When you cook with wine, you should use the same beverage you'll pour with the meal. The flavors will mesh. Avoid "cooking wines," because they are almost always inferior.

413

LIGHTEN UP!

In Europe, the term "light beer" refers to the color of the brew. In the United States, it refers to a beer that it is lower in calories.

GETTING A HEAD WITH BEER

The "head retention" on beer is measured by the half-life of the foam—that is, the number of seconds it takes for the volume of the foam to reduce by half. If the head on your beer has a half-life of 110 seconds, it is considered to be very good. The head will last longer if the beer is served in a tall, narrow glass that is scrupulously clean (always be sure to rinse all soap residue off glassware and dry thoroughly). The slightest hint of soap may cause the beer foam to collapse, as well as affect the color.

BRING OUT THE FLAVOR

Beer connoisseurs know: An ice-cold beer might wet your whistle, but it doesn't taste great. In most countries, beer is drunk at what is known as British cellar temperature, or about 55°F. If beer is exposed to light, a chemical change will occur from the intensity of the illumination.

DRAFT BEER VERSUS BOTTLED OR CANNED

Serious beer drinkers will always order a draft beer over a bottle or can. Because all beer is subject to spoilage, beer that is bottled and canned is pasteurized (which is a form of sterilization). This high-temperature processing causes a loss of flavor, which a discerning beer drinker will notice. Draft beer does not go through the pasteurization process because the kegs are kept cold and are never stored for a period that would allow the microorganisms to alter the flavor or spoil the beer.

A DRINK A DAY KEEPS THE DOCTOR AWAY

New studies indicate that having one or two drinks a day may reduce the risk of cardiovascular disease. Beer and wine seem to boost the body's natural levels of a clot-dissolving enzyme. Physicians are using this enzyme to stop heart attacks in progress according to the *Journal of the American Medical Association*. Other studies indicate that moderate alcohol consumption—again, one or two drinks a day—may raise the levels of the good cholesterol (HDL) in the bloodstream.

KEEP YOUR COOL

If you enjoy cold beer, an insulated foam holder will keep the beer close to the original cold temperature for at least 25 to 35 minutes. A glass from the freezer will keep the beer cold for about 10 to 15 minutes longer than a warm glass, but glasses can pick up off odors in the freezer. They can also be uncomfortable to hold, leave water rings from condensation, and can even dilute the beer.

WHAT HAPPENS WHEN YOU COOK WITH BEER?

When beer is heated, the alcohol evaporates, leaving the flavoring agents intact. The acids in beer, however, react with certain metals (especially aluminum and iron) to form a dark compound that can cause those pots to discolor. When cooking with beer always use a pot made of stainless steel, glass, or one with an enameled coating. If you like cooking with beer, try using a bock or ale for the best flavor. Light beers do not contribute much flavor to a dish.

STRAIGHTEN UP AND SETTLE DOWN

Cans and bottles of beer should always be stored upright. When beer is allowed to lie on its side more of the beer is exposed to oxygen. Oxidation will take place and the beer will lose its flavor sooner. Also, beer should not be moved from one location in the refrigerator to another since the slightest temperature change will affect the flavor.

FROTH AWAY

The temperature of the beer controls the amount of foam it produces. A cold beer produces less froth than a room-temperature beer.

The Percentage of Alcohol in Beers			
BRITISH		**AMERICAN**	
Brown ale	4–5.5%	Light	3.5–4.4%
Mild ale	3.2–4%	Lager	3.8–4.5%
Lager	3.5%	Malt liquor	4.8–5.8%
Stout	4.8%	Pilsner	4.1–4.7%

SPEEDY ICED BEER

Chilling beer quickly is always a problem. Freezing the beer usually does not work well, because the can or bottle explodes or the beer turns to slush when you forget it is there. The best way to chill beer rapidly is to fill a cooler chest with water and ice and plunge the beer into the chest. In about 20 minutes, the beer will be ice cold. Ice water is about 32°F and is, of course, warmer than a 0°F freezer. The ice water, however, absorbs the warmth from the bottles or cans more rapidly and more efficiently than the cold air of the freezer does. Just remember that premium lagers should be served between 42°F and 48°F and ales between 44°F and 52°F, so don't let your beer get too cold.

WHICH IS COLDER, A BOTTLE OR A CAN?

Aluminum cans are very thin, and when you hold a can, the heat transfers from your hand to the can, lowering the temperature of the beer. A glass bottle, however, is much thicker. The heat from your hand doesn't penetrate as easily, so the beer stays colder for a somewhat longer period. In addition, aluminum is an excellent conductor of heat; glass is very poor. Whether you buy beer in bottles or cans, connoisseurs recommend that beer always be poured into a glass before serving.

THE YOUNGER, THE BETTER

Unlike wine, beer does not age well and is best consumed as soon as possible. Older beers are inferior in both flavor and overall quality. If beer is not pasteurized, it is best to drink it within a week or two after it is produced. The ideal temperatures for light beers such as lager is 42°F to 48°F, ales and porters should be at 44°F to 52°F.

WORD TO THE WISE

Alcohol may suppress the immune system. It also reacts adversely with more than 100 medications, and reduces the potency of any vitamin supplements you may be taking. If you have a problem with food allergies, drinking alcohol may intensify any adverse effects.

NUTRITION AND BEER

A 12-ounce serving of American beer contains 150 calories, most of which are from carbohydrates. It also provides at least 10 percent of the daily requirement for folate, niacin, vitamin B6, phosphorus, magnesium, chromium, and selenium. Proteins in the grains are usually removed during the brewing process.

Because beer ranges in alcohol content from 3 to 8 percent, and because the calories can add up quickly, it's wise to drink it in limited amounts. Salty snacks like peanuts, pretzels, and chips should be avoided when drinking beer. Snacks that are high in protein, starch, vitamins, and minerals balance beer's high-sugar content better. Try crackers and cheese, eggs, meat, or unsalted peanuts.

TYPES OF BEER

Ale

May range in color from light to very dark amber. It has a slightly bitter flavor and is usually stronger than lager beer. Ales are brewed from hops and barley and are slightly higher in alcohol than beer.

Bock

This is German beer that is usually dark and full-bodied. In Germany, bocks are brewed in the springtime. It is slightly sweet and tends to be heavier than lager beers.

Fruit Beer

This is made from milder lager or ale; it is flavored with a variety of fruit concentrates.

Lager

This is a light-bodied, pale beer that has a somewhat mellow flavor.

Malt Liquor

This is a hearty, dark beer that has a somewhat bitter flavor and a high alcohol content. Avoid American beverages labeled "malt liquor"—they are inexpensive, sweet beers with high alcohol content. German and British malt liquors are of higher quality.

Pilsner

This is a type of lager. It is pale, with a pronounced flavor of hops, and is almost as bubbly as Champagne. Almost all American beer produced by large commercial breweries is an Americanized pilsner that is neither as hoppy nor as aged as are European pilsners.

Porter

This is a relatively strong, full-bodied dark beer that is quite bitter. Porters are made with roasted malt and tend to be higher in alcohol than lagers typically are.

Stout

This is a very hearty, dark beer, with a pronounced aroma of hops and a flavor that can be quite bitter. Stouts are brewed from a dark-roasted barley, malt, or oats.

Wheat Beer

This is produced from malted wheat. It ranges in color from very pale to dark copper. Its flavor is similar to lager.

18

SOUPS, STEWS, & GRAVIES

DOES BLOWING ON HOT SOUP REALLY COOL IT?

Research shows that if you hold a spoonful of very hot soup at room temperature before consuming it, it will take 103 seconds to cool down to a temperature that will not burn your mouth. If you blow on that same spoonful to speed up the cooling process, it will cool down to the same temperature in just 66 seconds. Blowing speeds up the air moving over the soup. This faster air carries away the heat more efficiently than cooler air does, because it forces evaporation from the surface of the soup.

SOUP, BEAUTIFUL SOUP

The varieties of soup are endless, but the most common types are:

Bisque

A relatively thick, smooth, creamy soup, prepared from shellfish or fish, tomatoes, and seasonings. Can be served as a main dish.

Bouillon

A clarified, concentrated broth made from meat, fish, or poultry (and/or the bones from each), and/or vegetables.

Broth

A clear liquid made from simmering meats, fish, or vegetables in water.

Chowder

A relatively thick, creamy soup often made with a fish or clam base, and which contains vegetables, especially potatoes.

Consommé

A very strong, clarified soup made from brown meat or fish stock.

Cream Soup

Usually made with the addition of milk, cream, or butter, or sometimes all three. Make sure you never boil a cream soup; if you do, it will develop a film on the surface.

THE FLOATING FAT

When fat floats to the top of gravies, soups, or stews, it can be easily removed by placing a slice of fresh white bread on top of the fat for a few seconds. After the bread absorbs the fat, it should be disposed of—if you leave the bread on the soup too long, it will fall apart.

ELIMINATING FATS FROM SOUP AND GRAVY

You can de-fat soup and gravy easily even if you don't have time to refrigerate it. Remove it from the heat for five to 10 minutes. Put four or five ice cubes in a piece of cheesecloth and swirl it around in the soup or gravy. Alternatively, stir a few lettuce leaves into the soup for a few minutes, and then discard them. Fat is attracted to the cold and to the lettuce leaves. A third method is to make a mop from a few paper towels (crumple, then hold the corners together), and swish it over the soup.

STOP GRAVY FROM SEPARATING

Does your gravy separate? When it does, simply add a pinch or two of baking soda to emulsify the fat globules in a matter of seconds.

READ THOSE LABELS

Spaghetti sauce is really best if it is homemade. Commercial sauces are almost always much higher in fat and calories. One brand's extra chunky with sausage and green peppers is 47 percent calories from fat, and another brand's marinara is 40 percent calories from fat. Read labels and choose those that are low in fat and additives, and high in vegetables.

WHAT CAN YOU DO TO STOP CURDLING?

Whenever you prepare a cream soup or sauce, there's always the risk it will curdle. One easy way to avoid the problem is to thicken the mixture with flour or cornstarch before adding any acidic ingredients, such as wine, citrus, or tomatoes. Remember, too, that the heavier the cream the less likely it is to curdle.

A CHEMICAL BUFFET

Whenever possible, make your own sauces and gravies. Packaged items, whether from bottles or mixes, typically contain numerous additives, preservatives, and coloring agents.

A LITTLE MEAT, A LITTLE MYSTERY

Commercial spaghetti sauces that contain meat may have very little. By law, companies need to include only 6 percent actual meat. Add your own meat to a marinara sauce, and you will know what you are eating.

SAVING CURDLED HOLLANDAISE

The secret to saving hollandaise sauce is to catch the problem as it starts. As soon as the sauce begins to curdle, vigorously beat in 1 to 2 tablespoons of cold water for every ¾ cup sauce until the sauce is smooth. Repeat this for the balance of the sauce, never adding more than 1 or 2 tablespoons at at time. If the sauce has already curdled, beat 1 tablespoon of cold water into the sauce to help bring back the smooth texture.

GRAVY SAVERS

Use your blender to smooth lumpy gravy, or add a pinch of salt to the flour before adding any liquid. If your gravy burns, just stir in a teaspoon of peanut butter to cover up the burnt flavor without altering the taste.

A SAUTÉING SECRET

If you sauté with butter, be sure you use the unsalted kind. When salted butter melts, the salt can separate from the butter and may consequently impart a bitter taste to the dish.

DARK, RICH GRAVY

Here's a trick to give your gravy to have a rich, dark-brown color. Spread the flour in a dry skillet and cook over low heat, stirring frequently, until it browns. Add a bit of coffee (no milk, no sugar, please!) to the gravy during the last few minutes of cooking.

IN OLDEN TIMES

Nineteenth century cooks added onion skins to the gravy while it cooked to give it a brown color. If you try the trick at home, just make sure you remove the skins after a few minutes and discard.

SHAKE IT!

To help a semisolid or condensed soup slide right out of the can, shake the can first, and then open it from the bottom.

GENTLY, GENTLY

For the best results and to keep the flavors intact, soups and stews should simmer, never boil.

DO IT YOURSELF

Easiest-ever pot pies: Put leftover stew into individual baking dishes or small casseroles, cover with prepared pie crust or biscuits, or dumplings made from a mix, and bake until the topping is golden brown.

FLAVOR: UP, UP, AND AWAY

Herbs are often used in soups and stews, but tend to lose much of their flavor after about 15 minutes of cooking. For maximum flavor, always add herbs, whether fresh or dried, during the last 10 minutes of cooking.

KEEP 'EM HANDY

To make dips and sauces, look for dry soup mixes made with dried vegetables and seasonings and few, if any, additives. Keep in mind that these mixes are usually high in salt.

REMOVING LUMPS

Wire whisks work better than any other kitchen tool for removing lumps in soups and sauces.

STIR GENTLY TILL THE LUMPS ARE GONE

To thicken a stew or to make a sauce of medium consistency, dissolve either 1½ tablespoons of cornstarch, 2½ teaspoons of potato starch, or 2 teaspoons of arrowroot in 3 tablespoons of water for every cup of liquid, then add this mixture to the food. Let it simmer for three to five minutes.

SOUTH-OF-THE-BORDER FLAIR

To enhance your stew a little, stack a few corn tortillas and cut into thin strips. Add them to the stew during the last 15 minutes of cooking.

TEA AS A TENDERIZER?

The tannic acid in strong black tea can tenderize meat in a stew, as well as reduce the cooking time. Just add ½ cup of strong tea to the stew when you add the other liquid.

DID YOU KNOW?

To make soup go further, just add cooked pasta, rice, or barley to it.

COOL TRICK

Freeze homemade beef, chicken, or fish stock in an ice-cube tray, and then use the cubes in soups and stews at another time. If you have left-over soup, put it in zip-close freezer bags. Squeeze out as much air as you can, and then stack the bags in your freezer.

QUICK THICKENERS

An easy method of thickening stews is to add a small amount of quick-cooking oats, a grated potato, or some instant-potato flakes.

SALT REDUCTION

If your soup or stew is too salty, pick one of these methods based on the flavors you prefer: Add a can of peeled tomatoes; add a small amount of brown sugar; or stir in a slice or two of apple or raw potato, let simmer a few minutes, then discard the apple or potato.

CARROTS PROVIDE SWEETNESS

To give your soup or stew a sweeter taste, stir in a small amount of pureed carrots. Use one of the sweeter carrot varieties.

BAD BONES

Dark-colored bones should never be used for cooking. They are probably too old and have deteriorated.

A MILK-CURDLING EXPERIENCE

Cream-of-tomato soup can be tricky to make from scratch. To keep it from curdling, try adding the tomato base to the milk instead of the milk to the tomato. Stirring a small amount of flour into the milk first also helps.

A REAL WINNER

Next time you make stock, put all the ingredients in a metal pasta insert or basket. Set the insert into your pot and cook. When the stock is done, remove the insert—and all the veggies, meat, or bones—easily.

THE PARSLEY MAGNET

When you overdo the garlic in a soup or sauce, place a few parsley flakes in a tea ball to soak up the excess garlic. Garlic is attracted to parsley.

ON A CLEAR SOUP

To make a clear noodle soup, cook the noodles, then drain and rinse before adding them to the soup. When noodles are cooked in the soup, the excess starch will turn the soup cloudy. Use this trick for any soup with pasta or dumplings, from wonton soup to tortellini in brodo to chicken noodle soup.

SMOOTH OPERATOR

To make a lower-fat cream soup, try adding a little flour to milk instead of using cream. The flour adds a little body and results in a thicker soup without additional fat. It even works with 1 percent milk.

SOUP SECRETS

Always make soup at least a day ahead of time, so the flavors have time to blend. Wait to season with salt or pepper until the soup is almost done; both of these seasonings will intensify and may give the soup too strong a flavor. Always cook soup with the lid on to help the flavors become better absorbed. When you make a cold soup, remember that it needs more seasoning than a hot soup; cool temperatures mute flavors.

TAPIOCA

A thickener, tapioca is usually sold as a pudding mix, and is actually a starch that is extracted from the cassava root. It is found in three forms:

Pearl Tapioca

This usually has to be soaked for a number of hours before it is soft enough to use.

Quick-Cooking Tapioca

This is the type used for puddings. It is normally sold in granular form, needs no presoaking, and is popular for use as a thickening agent.

Tapioca should be mixed with water until it forms a thin paste before adding it to the food that needs thickening. Adding undiluted tapioca directly to the food will cause it to become lumpy. Try not to over-stir tapioca when it is cooking, or it may turn into a thick, unpalatable paste.

Tapioca Flour

Normally found only in health food stores, this is also very popular as a thickening agent for soups and stews.

WHAT IS ARROWROOT?

Arrowroot is derived from the rootstalks of a South American tuber; it is finely powdered and used as a thickener. Its thickening power is about one to two times that of all-purpose flour, and like cornstarch, it should be mixed into a paste with adequate cold water before it's added to a hot mixture. Unlike some thickeners, arrowroot will not impart a chalky taste if it is overcooked, and it does not become cloudy—your sauce will remain clear. It's best not to over-stir a mixture that contains arrowroot or it will become thin again. If your recipe calls for arrowroot and you don't have any, you can substitute 1 tablespoon of cornstarch or 2 tablespoons of all-purpose flour for every tablespoon of arrowroot.

HOW FOODS BECOME EMULSIFIED

Emulsification is the process of combining two liquids that do not normally blend: Oil and water is one example. Oil and vinegar is another, and if you've ever made a salad dressing, you know that it takes a bit of doing to combine them. When the oil and vinegar solution is whisked vigorously or shaken, the oil breaks into small droplets for a short period of time, resulting in a temporary emulsion. There are a number of emulsifiers that will help keep the oil suspended in the vinegar. Prepared mustard is one, which is one reason why Dijon mustard is often added to a vinaigrette (flavor, of course, is another reason).

GELATIN, THE GREAT THICKENER

Gelatin is pure protein, derived from animal hooves, muscle, bones, and connective tissue. (Agar, made from seaweed, and carrageenan, made from Irish moss, are vegetable-based thickeners.)

Gelatin granules have the capability of trapping water molecules and then expanding to 10 times their original size. The firmness of a food will depend on the ratio of gelatin to water. Fresh figs, kiwi, papaya, and pineapple contain enzymes that break down protein, which keeps gelatin from setting. Bromelain, the enzyme in pineapple, can be neutralized by simmering the fruit for a few minutes.

When using gelatin for a dish, be sure to moisten the gelatin first with a small amount of cold water, and then use hot water to dissolve the gelatin completely. If you combine the gelatin with hot water, some of the granules will clump together so they won't all dissolve, and the finished dish may be somewhat grainy. If your recipe calls for an equal amount of sugar and gelatin, the cold-water step is not required, since the sugar will stop the clumping. However, never pour hot water into the gelatin; instead, sprinkle the gelatin into the water.

THE JELLY THICKENER

Pectin, a carbohydrate, is the only thickener for jellies. If your jelly doesn't set, it's probably because you used too little pectin or the wrong proportions of other ingredients. Jelly requires a number of ingredients to set properly, and pectin is only one of the most important. The acid and sugar content will both affect the setting properties of the jelly, and cooking the jelly for too long will destroy the pectin.

Certain types of fruit jellies need only a small amount of pectin, because most fruits are relatively high in pectin. Higher-pectin fruits include apples, cranberries, and all citrus. Those with less pectin include peaches, cherries, raspberries, apricots, and strawberries. To make the most of the fruit's natural pectin, the fruit should be very fresh.

WHO REALLY INVENTED KETCHUP?

The original name for what we know as ketchup was *ke'-tsiap*. The sauce was invented in China in the 17th century and was the brine of pickled fish or shellfish. It was made from fish entrails, vinegar, and hot spices. The Chinese exported the sauce to the Malay Peninsula, where it was called kechap. The Malayans sold the kechap to English sailors during the 17th century, who brought it back to England; the English substituted mushrooms for the fish entrails. In *The New Art Of Cookery, According to the Present Practice; Being a Complete Guide to All Housekeepers, on a Plan Entirely New*, a 1792 cookbook by Richard Briggs, the sauce is referred to as *catsup* and includes tomatoes as a main ingredient.

HANDY CONTAINERS

Empty plastic ketchup and mustard containers are great for holding icings and oils. Allow a mixture of warm water and baking soda to sit overnight in the containers, and then rinse thoroughly with hot water.

ALL ABOUT VINEGAR

Vinegar can be made from a number of liquids; common vinegars include apple cider, white distilled, red wine, white wine, barley, malt, rice, and balsamic. Vinegar is a mild acid called acetic acid. The actual amount of acid varies from 4 to 7 percent, with the average being 5 percent. Grains refer to the acetic acid content of vinegar. A 5 percent acetic acid content is known as 50-grain vinegar. Vinegar has a shelf life of six months.

HOW WAS WORCESTERSHIRE SAUCE INVENTED?

Actually, what we know as Worcestershire sauce was not invented—it was produced by accident by John Lea and William Perrins. In 1835, Lea and Perrins were running a small drugstore in Worcester, England when Lord Marcus Sandys came in and asked whether they could duplicate an Indian sauce he had enjoyed while in Bengal. They mixed up a batch but didn't like the smell or flavor, and stored the mixture in their cellar. Two years later, they came across the sauce, tried it, and were surprised at the taste. Lea & Perrins Worcestershire sauce is now one of the most popular steak sauces in the world. It's unlikely the sauce they ended up with bears much relation to the sauce they were trying to duplicate.

   The recipe has hardly changed from the original, which uses anchovies, tamarinds, molasses, garlic, vinegar, chiles, cloves, and shallots. The mixture is still aged for two years, at which point the solids are filtered out and preservatives and citric acid are added.

19

LOOKING GOOD

SLIPPERY WHEN WET

For an inexpensive bath oil, mix some sunflower oil with either crushed lavender or rose petals. Let stand a few days before using.

A REVIVAL

Revive hair brushes and combs by soaking them in a pot of warm water and 1 tablespoon of baking soda or ammonia.

UPON REFLECTION

If you lose a contact lens, turn off the lights and turn on a flashlight. The lens will reflect the light.

HIGHLIGHTING HAIR

For maximum hair shine, mix a cup of water with a teaspoon of white vinegar (for blond) or 2 tablespoons of apple-cider vinegar (for red and brunette). Pour it over your hair after rinsing out the shampoo, and then rinse out the vinegar. Redheads and brunettes can also rinse their hair with either black coffee or orange pekoe tea to add luster, then rinse with clear water.

RING AROUND THE FINGER

If you are unable to remove a ring from your finger, run your hand under very cold water for a few seconds.

GLOVES WORK, TOO

To keep dirt from getting under your nails when you garden, rub your nails over a bar of soap before starting work.

A CLEANER-UPPER

Laundry detergent makes an excellent hand cleaner for very dirty hands. To freshen your feet, rub a few fresh lemon slices over them.

WHY DIDN'T I THINK OF THAT?

Dab a small amount of vegetable oil on the threads of nail polish bottles and the caps won't stick.

THIS WILL SNAP YOU AWAKE INSTANTLY

Believe it or not, freezing panty hose can keep them from running. Before you wear them the first time, stick them in the freezer overnight; this will strengthen the fibers. Just make sure you thaw them before wearing them—unless you are having trouble waking up in the morning.

TASTES GOOD, TOO

Here's an inexpensive facial treatment for normal to somewhat oily skin. Blend 1 cup plain yogurt, 1 teaspoon fresh lemon juice, 1 teaspoon fresh orange juice, and 1 teaspoon carrot juice. Apply to your face for 10 to 15 minutes, and then rinse with warm water.

NEW USE FOR BREAKFAST FOOD

For a gentle yet effective facial scrub, make a paste of oatmeal and water. Apply the paste, then let it dry until your skin feels tight. Remove it and dead skin by rubbing back and forth with your fingers.

EAU DE REFRIGERATOR

Perfume is very volatile—the fragrance breaks down rapidly when exposed to heat and air. If you're not going to use the entire bottle within thirty days, store it in the refrigerator to extend its life.

MONSTER OR MOM?

Alleviate dry skin by mashing ½ avocado and spreading it thickly on your face. Wait 20 minutes, and then wash off with warm water. A piece of advice: Don't let your kids see you!

A LITTLE DAB WON'T DO YA

The American Dental Association counsels against brushing your teeth with only baking soda. It has not been shown to have any preventative effect on periodontal disease. If you like the taste or feel of baking soda, use a baking soda toothpaste.

BURN RELIEF

For a bad sunburn, apply a paste of baking soda and water. Or, sponge the sunburned skin with apple-cider vinegar.

431

SWEET SOLUTION

To remove garden stains from your hands, add about ½ teaspoon of sugar to the soap lather before you wash your hands. You will be amazed how easily the stains will come off.

THE MAD SCIENTIST

It's silly to buy expensive liquid soap when it's so easy to make it. Grate one 4-ounce bar of soap (preferably one with moisturizing cream) into a bowl, and then add 3 cups water. Microwave on high till dissolved, stirring every few minutes. Let cool completely before using.

A LITTLE SQUIRT

To keep your makeup fresh longer, first mist your face with mineral water and let it dry. Then apply your makeup.

HOT AND COLD

If your lipstick breaks, heat the broken ends over a match until they are soft, then press them together. Then put the lipstick in the freezer until the pieces harden and fuse together.

BABY YOURSELF

Don't waste your money: Baby oil will do the same job as a fancy cleansing cream at a fraction of the price.

BREAK OUT THE BUBBLE MACHINE

To make your own bubble bath, try placing soap slivers in a mesh drawstring bag. Attach the bag to the tap while the water is running. Place herbs in the bag for a pleasant fragrance.

STRETCH THE BAR

If you want to make a bar of soap last longer, unwrap it before you use it and let it dry out.

SKIN-ADE

Skin blemishes can be cleared up quickly by dabbing them with lemon juice four to six times per day.

A LITTLE ACID GOES A LONG WAY

Before polishing your nails, wipe them with a small amount of white vinegar. This simple treatment will clean your nails, and they'll stay shiny longer. To bleach any stains, soak your fingernails in lemon or lime juice. The mild citric acid will do the job.

NO HANGING AROUND

Many women have found that rubbing a little vitamin E oil around the cuticles is a good way to prevent hangnails.

THE EYES HAVE IT

To combat puffy eyes, place slices of cucumber on them. Cucumbers have a mild anti-inflammatory action. Parsley seeds also work. To make a compress, mix 1 tablespoon parsley seeds with 1 cup boiling water, then let it cool. Soak a washcloth in the liquid, wring it out and fold it in thirds lengthwise to make a compress. Lie down and place it over your eyes.

PERFUME HOLDER

Do you find your perfume fading after a few hours? To make it last longer, rub a small amount of petroleum jelly onto your skin before you start dabbing on the perfume.

BALANCING ACT

If you want to restore the natural acid balance to your skin, pour ½ cup of apple-cider vinegar into a basin of warm water. Splash it on your face, then allow it to dry before removing with a towel.

TEA BAG TREATMENTS

Don't throw out that used herbal tea bag. Empty the leaves into a pot of boiling water, lean over it with a towel tented over your head (test first to see if the steam is too hot), and enjoy a scented herbal facial sauna. Bags or sachets of black tea have their uses, too: If your eyes are tired or swollen, place moist tea bags over your eyes for at least 15 minutes.

DID YOU KNOW?

If you don't happen to have any vitamin E oil on hand, massage olive oil—or any vegetable oil—into your cuticles to prevent hangnails.

HOMEMADE HAIR CONDITIONER

This oil and honey mixture softens dry hair and helps prevent split ends. Place ⅓ cup olive oil, ⅓ cup vegetable oil, and ⅓ cup honey in a small saucepan and set over low heat until just boiling. Remove from heat and let cool for 5 minutes. Transfer to a 1-pint plastic spray bottle. Spray on hair and rub in thoroughly. Wet a towel with warm water and wrap around the head for 1 hour. Shampoo well to remove, then wash and style hair as usual. Store the conditioner in a cool, dry place.

WASHCLOTH FOR THE THRIFTY

When bars of soap are almost used up, save any slivers too small to use and stuff them in a nylon sock. Knot it well, then use this self-soaping washcloth in the bathtub or shower.

ALOE AND HONEY FACE MASK

To soothe and moisturize dry skin, cut two aloe vera leaves in half lengthwise and scoop 1 teaspoon of their gel into a cup. With a spoon, beat in 1 egg yolk and 1 teaspoon warmed honey. Add enough powdered milk (usually about 1 tablespoon) to make a thin, spreadable paste. Apply the mixture with cotton balls, being careful to avoid the area around the eyes. Leave the mask on for about 15 minutes.

20

FEELING GOOD

THE MECHANICS OF METABOLISM

Metabolism is the process by which the body releases energy derived from nutrients. It is the sum of all chemical reactions of the body's cells. The cells produce the energy in the form of heat, or in muscle cells in the form of mechanical work. The basic fuels are proteins, carbohydrates, and fats, which the liver converts into glucose. Glucose travels to the cells for chemical processing by way of the Krebs cycle, a complex biochemical pathway, and is turned into usable energy.

Metabolic rates vary depending on age, sex, body size, activity level, and thyroid activity. Basal metabolism is first in line when the body distributes the energy it produces; the body must have energy to run the heart and vital organs before anything else. Physical activity energy is available only after these more important needs are met. Physicians are often asked how to increase the metabolic rate as we age, but no pill will raise it. Many supplement companies claim to have invented different herbal combinations and special nutrients to raise metabolism, but no claims have been proven true, nor have any products been proven to work in double-blind studies performed by a reputable lab. In fact, the only way to lose weight is to burn more calories than you ingest.

Men tend to have higher metabolic rates throughout their lives than do women. This may be due to men's greater percentage of lean body mass; muscle requires more energy to keep it going than does fat, so higher levels of muscle tissue increase metabolic rate. The thyroid gland's activity also has a direct influence on the basal metabolic rate. The thyroid secretes a hormone called thyroxine; the less it secretes, the lower the energy requirement for the running of the body.

Women's Energy Output	
The following is an example of the total energy output by a moderately active woman.	
Energy for basal metabolism	1,400 calories
Energy for moderate physical activity	500 calories
Energy to burn 2,000 calories	200 calories
TOTAL	2,100 calories

THE ENERGY BALANCE

Approximately 60 to 75 percent of all food we consume is utilized in keeping the essential life processes going, such as the heart pumping and the liver functioning. The other 30 percent is turned into "external energy," which is used for activities such as walking or playing sports.

The actual energy value of foods is determined by their caloric content. A kilocalorie (abbreviated Kcal) is a measure of energy needed to raise the temperature of one kilogram of water one degree centigrade (one calorie is a thousandth of a Kcal).

When we discuss energy balance, the input-output aspect of weight control usually is mentioned. This means if you burn more calories than you take in, you will lose weight. While this is true, of course, it is still the type of calories you consume—that is, the nutrients those calories provide—that will ultimately determine your actual level of health.

EXERCISE

Exercise is a must for everyone, regardless of age. The type of exercise you do should be one you enjoy and can be continued over an extended period of time. Many people are motivated initially, but end up doing exercises they really don't enjoy and ultimately don't stick with.

It is not the intention of the information on the next few pages to suggest one form of exercise over another. You need to choose the one that fits your lifestyle; the easiest for most people is walking.

Before starting any exercise program, have a complete physical from your physician, not just a series of tests by a local athletic club. If you will be walking, swimming, jogging, or doing any very intense exercise, a treadmill stress test is a must. A resting cardiogram is a poor test in detecting early heart disease or how your heart will respond to exertion.

A FAMILY AFFAIR

Parents can do their children a favor by interesting them in exercising from an early age. And it's not that hard to make exercising fun. Cycling on a bicycle-built-for-two is a good way to get older children involved, and you get to spend time together to boot. Another good idea is to give a child a stopwatch so she can time herself and try to break her records, whether for riding a bicycle around the park, jogging or sprinting a certain distance, or climbing up the monkey bars.

BENEFITS OF EXERCISE

Here are some of the good things exercise will do for you.

Cardiovascular System

- ◆ The heart grows stronger and pumps more blood with each beat, reducing the number of beats necessary.
- ◆ Increases the number and size of your blood vessels, as well as your total blood volume. Enhances oxygenation of cells.
- ◆ Increases your body's maximal oxygen consumption by increasing the efficiency of the red blood cells. By doing this, it improves the overall condition of the body, especially the heart, lungs, and blood vessels.
- ◆ Improves the muscle tone of your blood vessels, changing them to strong and firm tissue, possibly reducing blood pressure.

Lungs

- ◆ Improves the efficiency of your lungs, making them capable of processing more air with less effort.

Aging

- ◆ Slows the aging process and physical deterioration that accompanies it.

Stress

- ◆ Helps you relax more easily and develop a better self-image.
- ◆ Relieves the tension and stress of daily living.

Job

- ◆ Allows you to get more work done with less fatigue.
- ◆ Enhances your ability to concentrate.

RESTING HEART RATE

Heart rates will vary widely among individuals and also within an individual from one moment to another, so the term "normal heart rate" is meaningless. We may say that the average heart rate is 72 beats per minute for men, 80 beats per minute for women, but we cannot suggest that a variation from these figures is borderline or abnormal.

To determine your own resting heart rate; first take your pulse three times, either radial (on the side of the wrist) or carotid (on the side of the neck), and count for 60 seconds each time. Average the three figures to obtain your resting pulse rate. It is important that you take your resting pulse rate when you are calm and have not exerted yourself.

After 10 days of exercising, repeat the procedure to determine your new resting heart rate. Your new rate should be lower than the first one, demonstrating the positive effects of exercise.

FACTORS AFFECTING HEART RATE

Age
The resting heart rate at birth averages 120 beats per minute; it can vary between 100 and 150 beats per minute. It gradually decreases until the teens, when it averages out to about 72 beats per minute.

Sex
The resting heart rate in adult females is five to 10 beats faster than in the average male.

Size
In the same way that infants have higher pulse rates than adults, resting heart rates vary among adults as well. All other things being equal, a larger adult will have a slower resting heart rate than a smaller adult.

Posture
A change from a sitting to a standing position may increase the heart rate 10 to 12 beats per minute.

Food
Ingesting food affects the resting heart rate, as well as the exercising heart rate. Both rates are higher during digestion than before eating.

Emotion
Heightened emotions increase the resting heart rate as well as the exercising heart rate. They also tend to slow the recovery rate.

Environment
An increase in ambient temperature causes an increase in the exercising heart rate.

Smoking
Even one cigarette will increase the resting heart rate.

INCREASING LUNG POWER

Your lungs have a porous lining to absorb the oxygen you need for energy, and they are strengthened by regular exercise. The more your lungs can inflate, the more oxygen they can absorb. When you are inactive for a long time you begin to breathe more shallowly, with the lungs being inflated only as much as necessary keep your body working. This can leave you feeling listless and tired and make you susceptible to chest infections. Regular physical activity improves the elasticity of the lungs, which lets them inflate more easily. During exercise, your lung capacity increases five to seven times. Some of this capacity stays with you when you are not exercising, so you breathe more deeply to produce more power for the muscles and more fuel for the brain.

DID YOU KNOW?

Larger animals have slower heart rates than smaller ones. The heart of the hummingbird beats 1,000 times a minute, while an elephant's heart beats 25 times.

EXERCISING IN WATER

Because water offers resistance to your movements, water-based exercise builds muscle strength and endurance while improving your stamina and suppleness. Water's buoyancy also reduces impact on the joints. Water aerobics is a newly popular form of group exercise, and then there are such water sports as water polo—and, of course, swimming.

AEROBICS AND FITNESS

The term "aerobics" refers to the type of metabolism that utilizes oxygen in the production of energy. It relates to modes of training that are designed to improve the efficiency of the body's oxygen exchange system, thus delivering more oxygen to the cells while improving the efficiency of the cardiovascular system (heart, lungs, and blood vessels).

The degree to which the cardiovascular system becomes more efficient (and healthier) is dependent upon the total work performed by a particular exercise and its effect on the system.

By gradually increasing the amount and intensity of an exercise program, your fitness level will also increase.

The following is a listing of activities in their order of aerobic value. These are goals to work toward. If you are unaccustomed to physical activity, consult your physician before beginning any exercise program.

Aerobics in Order of Value		
EXERCISE	MINUTES	TIMES PER WEEK
Jogging 6 mph	20	4
Bicycling 12 mph	30	5
Swimming 25–50 yards per minute	20	4
Walking 4 mph (0 elevation)	30	5
Rowing machine	20	5
Tennis (singles)	45	4
Handball (singles)	30	4
Ice-skating or roller-skating	45	5
Racquetball (singles)	25	4

DIFFERENT MUSCLE FIBERS

Slow-Twitch Muscle Fibers

These muscle fibers are usually utilized first during a sport or exercise until the body determines the need for the fast-twitch muscles. Following are some facts about slow-twitch muscle fibers:

◆ Slow-twitch fibers are used for low-intensity aerobic activity, where glucose burns in the presence of oxygen to produce needed energy.

◆ Used for long-distance or endurance exercises or sports.

◆ The number of slow-twitch muscles and the intensity of their movement are usually determined by heredity.

◆ The size and strength of the fibers can be improved with exercise.

◆ The fibers are also capable of burning fatty acids, which reduces the body's fat stores.

◆ The leg muscles of a long distance runner may contain up to 90 percent slow-twitch fibers.

Fast-Twitch Muscle Fibers

Activated when a higher level of force is demanded of the muscle, such as when sudden bursts of energy are needed in a dash or when lifting weights. The following are facts related to fast-twitch muscle fibers:

◆ These muscle fibers are for the most part anaerobic, which means they burn fuel without the presence of oxygen.

◆ The leg muscles in world-class tennis players may contain up to 70 percent fast-twitch muscle fibers.

◆ As with slow-twitch muscle fibers, the number of fast-twitch muscle fibers is controlled by heredity.

◆ With training, the size of the fibers can be increased and provide faster response.

MUSCLES: ALWAYS ACTIVE

Muscle is metabolically active, even if you're not doing anything. This means that putting on extra muscle through exercise will burn more calories even when you're sitting still. So if you exercise regularly, your increased muscle mass will act as a metabolic booster, meaning you'll gradually become more efficient at converting fuel to energy and therefore less likely to store it as fat.

DID YOU KNOW?

Many people find that walking is the easiest exercise. It requires no special equipment (other than a good pair of shoes) or skills, and has real benefits when your walk lasts for 30 minutes or more.

HAZARDS OF NOT EXERCISING

People who are sedentary run a far greater risk of developing high blood pressure and high cholesterol, which lead to heart attack and stroke. A lack of exercise also weakens the skeleton and increases the risk of developing osteoporosis, a condition that results in fragile bones that fracture easily. What's more, people who don't exercise are more subject to lung ailments like bronchitis and disorders like diabetes, and generally have a weaker immune system than those who regularly exercise.

HOME FITNESS EQUIPMENT

Rowing Machines

An all-around exerciser involving numerous muscle groups. These machines are excellent for the legs, upper body, and arms. However, they are not recommended for persons who are not in good condition, nor do they provide the best aerobic workout.

Treadmills

These machines vary widely in price and quality, with the more expensive models offering more features. They employ a moving belt, which may be motorized. Most motorized models will allow you to adjust both the speed and elevation. The most frequent complaint is that treadmills become boring after a short period. Earphones with music or a TV to watch seems to solve the problem. Computerized models are best.

Mini-Trampolines

These are best avoided. In 1996, more than 83,000 trampoline-related injuries were reported.

Stationary Bike

Provides good aerobic training without the problems that may be caused by the continual pounding on the leg and feet muscles by jogging, especially for the unfit. Combining workouts on the rowing machine and the bicycle provides a well-rounded exercise program. The cost of the bicycle often determines the overall quality, ease of making adjustments, and the degree of comfort. Many of the less expensive models do not have adjustable handlebars, which is a comfort feature. Computerized models tend to hold your interest better and provide feedback.

Multi-Gyms

Usually expensive, but competition has brought the prices down in recent years. Incorporates a multitude of different exercises into one unit, which makes it handy for home use. Be sure to try out a unit before buying one, either in a store or a gym. Many of the more unusual units will not hold your interest too long. Be wary of some of the new ones advertised on TV unless you can send the product back if you don't like it. Watching a person use a machine on TV is different from using it yourself.

INJURIES AND PREVENTION

Blisters

Blisters are common, particularly if you've worn an ill-fitting pair of shoes (properly fitted shoes don't need to be broken in). Prevention begins with properly fitting shoes, and socks that stay in place and do not creep down or bunch up. When blisters occur, avoid breaking the blister. Apply a topical antiseptic solution, and then cover with an adhesive bandage.

Arch Problems

Painful arches are usually the result of improperly fitting shoes, being overweight, excessive activity on a hard surface, faulty posture, or fatigue (or a combination of these). The symptoms are divided into three stages:

◆ Slight soreness in the arch.
◆ Chronic inflammation that includes soreness, redness, swelling, and a slightly visible drop in the arch. See your physician.
◆ Completely fallen arch, accompanied by extreme pain, immobility, and deformity. See your physician.

Caring for arch disorders might include the following suggestions:

◆ Shoes should be properly fitted.
◆ Anti-inflammatory medication.
◆ Arch orthotics (supports).

Sprained Ankle

Generally caused by a lateral or medial twist that results in external- and internal-joint derangement. Sprains may be classified as first, second, or third degree. The majority of ankle sprains are the inversion type, resulting in the stretching or tearing of the lateral ligaments. In handling a sprained ankle, these first-aid measures should be followed:

◆ The ankle should be compressed with an ice pack and then elevated for 24 hours. Think RICE: Rest, Ice, Compression, and Elevation.
◆ Protect the affected area by keeping it immobile. This encourages healing and helps to prevent further injury.
◆ If swelling is more than minor or if a fracture is suspected, contact your physician; X-rays may be necessary.
◆ With severe ankle sprains, continue cold applications through the second or even the third day.
◆ Apply heat therapy if swelling has subsided by the third day.

Knee Problems

Although the knee is the largest joint in the body, it is extremely vulnerable to traumatic injuries because of poor bone arrangement, particularly in women. Knee injuries fall mainly into four categories: compression injuries, lateral and medial sprains, torsion injuries, and hyperextension injuries. See your physician if you have any knee problems.

Lower-Back Pain

Lower-back pain is usually the result of poor flexibility, weak abdominal and back muscles, and poor posture. Stretching and strengthening exercises, combined with a concerted effort to improve posture, can improve the problem in the majority of cases. However, if any back pain persists, see your physician.

Muscle Soreness

Engaging in activities that call on seldom-used muscles or overexerting conditioned muscles can produce muscular soreness. In some cases, pain can occur during the latter stages of high-intensity exercise. More often, it occurs as many as 24 to 48 hours after you stop the activity. This type of pain is not understood as well as immediate pain is, but it most commonly occurs after an endurance workout rather than a short burst of activity. Reports show the delayed pain to be caused by alterations in the muscle connective tissue (stretching of the elastic components). Warm compresses or warm baths, accompanied by light exercise to help prevent adhesions during the healing process, can enhance recovery from this type of soreness.

Side Stitch

A side stitch usually develops in untrained individuals during aerobic activities or exercise. It is manifested by mild to agonizing pain in the area of the lower rib cage and may be felt on either side of the body. There are several explanations for this occurrence, none of which is completely satisfactory. It is probable that all the following factors contribute to the discomfort of a side stitch:

◆ Accumulation of metabolic wastes (lactic acid) in the diaphragm.

◆ Severe shaking of the abdominal contents, which causes pain in the supporting structures.

◆ Formation of gas in the ascending colon.

◆ Reduced blood flow to the affected area due to the rerouting of blood to other areas.

Relief is usually accelerated by the application of pressure on the affected side; stop or slow down when you have a stitch. If the pain becomes too severe, the alternative is to terminate the workout and rest.

Achilles Tendon Rupture

This usually follows a history of chronic inflammation and gradual degeneration caused by tiny tears in the tendon. When the rupture occurs, it feels like a snap or as though something has hit you in the lower leg. Severe pain, tenderness, swelling, and discoloration are usually associated with the trauma. Signs of a rupture are obvious indentations at the tendon site; they also show up on a CT scan.

Achilles-Tendon Bursitis and Tendinitis

Bursitis and tendinitis usually occur from the over-stretching of the Achilles tendon, resulting in a constant inflammatory condition of the Achilles bursar. The condition is the result of small tears in the tissue caused by strenuous exercise. Rest, ice, and switching to a different, less strenuous exercise routine are often all it takes for the tendon to heal. Heel lifts should be placed in the shoe to relieve the Achilles tendon of as much tension as possible. After a workout, the tendon should be cooled with ice packs or ice massage. Gradual heel cord stretching is recommended.

Shin Splints

These are characterized by pain and irritation in the shin region of the leg, and are usually attributed to an inflammation localized mostly in the muscles and tendons of the lower leg. Inflammation in this area is often a mystery. Speculation of cause includes repeated pounding on a hard surface, jogging, basketball, tennis, marching (in military recruits), muscle fatigue, or overuse stress. All these factors, singly or in combination, may contribute to shin splints.

While rest is the only sure cure, limited exercise is possible with an ice massage and a leg wrap. You can prevent shin splints by wearing proper shoes, running on soft surfaces, stretching, and strengthening the surrounding musculature.

A FOLK CURE FOR SPRAINS

Turmeric is used as a spice, but it also has a long history of medicinal use in India and Asia. You can use it to make an anti-inflammatory paste that will ease the pain of a sprain. Mix 2 parts powdered turmeric root and 1 part salt with just enough water to get consistency. Apply to the sprain once a day for 20 minutes to an hour, covering snugly with cotton or muslin. A warning: Turmeric can irritate sensitive skin and the mucous membranes; it can also temporarily stain clothing and skin.

LEG CRAMPS

To quickly relieve a muscle cramp in the leg, slowly stretch the cramped muscle and massage it. For a thigh cramp, straighten your leg. For a cramped calf, pull your toes gently toward your knee.

WALK THIS WAY

Ever wonder how long you'd need to work out to burn off a snack or meal? The charts on these two pages show how far a 150-pound adult would have to walk at three miles an hour to burn off popular foods.

SANDWICHES	SERVING	CALORIES	MILES
Ham	½ oz. w/butter	267	2.9
Cheese	½ oz. w/mayo	286	3.2
Peanut butter and jelly	2 tbsp. peanut butter, 1 tbsp. jelly	375	4.2
Hamburger on bun	3.5 oz. patty	429	4.8
Tortilla w/cheese	1 oz. cheese	167	1.9
BEVERAGES	**SERVING**	**CALORIES**	**MILES**
Soda	12 oz.	146	1.6
Chocolate malted	12 oz.	344	3.8
Ice cream soda	12 oz.	324	3.6
Whole milk	8 oz.	150	1.6
Tea or coffee	8 oz. (w/2T cream & 2t sugar)	70	0.8
Beer	12 oz.	147	1.6
Martini	2.5 oz.	156	1.7
Sherry	4 oz.	180	2.0
Scotch or bourbon	1½ oz.	105	1.2
FRUITS	**SERVING**	**CALORIES**	**MILES**
Apple	1 medium	81	0.9
Orange	1 medium	60	0.7
Pear	1 medium	98	1.1
Grapes	1 cup	58	0.6
Banana	1 medium	105	1.2

SALTED NUTS	SERVING	CALORIES	MILES
Almonds	1 oz. dry-roasted	166	1.8
Pecans	1 oz.	189	2.1
Cashews	1 oz. dry-roasted	163	1.8
Walnuts	1 oz.	182	2.0
Peanuts	1 oz. dry-roasted	166	1.8
CANDY	**SERVING**	**CALORIES**	**MILES**
Chocolate bar	1¼ oz.	233	2.6
Caramel	l inch pc.	34	0.4
Jelly bean	1 avg.	6	0.1
DESSERTS	**SERVING**	**CALORIES**	**MILES**
Doughnut	1 medium	140	1.6
Ice cream cone	1 scoop	218	2.4
Ice cream sundae	2 scoops w/chocolate topping, whipped cream, and peanuts	589	6.5
Cake w/frosting	⅛ of 8-inch cake	243	2.7
Pie (fruit)	⅙ of 8-inch pie	260	2.9
Cream puff	4 inch	335	3.7
Brownie	2¾ x ⅞-inch	227	2.5
Graham cracker	1	30	0.3
MISCELLANEOUS	**SERVING**	**CALORIES**	**MILES**
Potato chips	1 oz.	152	1.7
Popcorn (air-popped)	1 cup	54	0.6
Butter	1 tablespoon (modest amount for popcorn)	108	1.2
Saltine crackers	4	52	0.6
ICE BOX RAID	**SERVING**	**CALORIES**	**MILES**
Light-meat chicken, no skin	1 oz.	44	0.5
Chicken leg	1 roasted, no skin	76	0.8
Hard-cooked egg	1 medium	78	0.9
Gelatin salad	½ cup	80	0.9

EXERCISE AND CALORIES

The purpose of the following information is to create an awareness of which foods are higher in calories and the number of minutes needed to work off calories. The information is based on a 150-pound adult.

	Calories	Walking 3 mph 270 Kcal per hr	Bicycling 15 mph 711 Kcal per hr	Jogging 5 mph 620 Kcal per hr
BREAD & CEREALS				
Raisin Bran (½ cup)	133	30	11	13
Special K (½ cup)	55	12	5	5
Cornbread (2-inch square)	176	39	15	17
White bread (1 slice)	67	15	6	6
Whole-grain bread (1 slice)	71	16	6	7
Doughnut, iced (1 medium)	192	43	16	19
Blueberry muffin (2¼-inch)	158	35	13	15
Pancake (med.)	86	19	7	8
Waffle (7-inch)	218	48	18	21
White rice (¾ cup)	154	34	13	15
Egg noodles (¼ cup)	53	12	4	5
Popcorn, air-popped (1 cup)	31	7	3	3
Macaroni & cheese (1 cup)	430	96	36	42
Spaghetti & meatballs (1 cup)	332	74	28	32
Beef taco (3 oz.)	185	41	16	18
Saltine cracker (1)	13	3	1	1
FRUITS				
Apple (medium)	81	18	7	8
Banana (1 medium)	105	23	9	10
Cantaloupe (1 cup pieces)	56	12	5	5
Grapefruit (½ small)	40	9	3	4
Orange (1 medium)	60	13	5	6

	Calories	Walking 3 mph 270 Kcal per hr	Bicycling 15 mph 711 Kcal per hr	Jogging 5 mph 620 Kcal per hr
MEATS				
Bacon (2 slices)	140	31	12	14
Beef hash (½ cup)	220	49	19	21
Reg. hamburger (3.5 oz.)	306	68	26	30
Lean hamburger (3.5 oz.)	225	57	22	25
Beef pot pie (⅓ of 9-inch pie)	517	115	48	50
Chili (with beans & meat) (1 cup)	420	93	35	41
Hot dog with bun	242	54	20	23
Lean ham (2 oz.)	90	20	8	9
Lamb (3 oz. lean roast sirloin)	223	52	20	23
Meat loaf (3 oz.)	155	34	13	15
Fried chicken TV dinner (9 oz.)	470	104	40	45
Bologna (1 slice)	89	20	8	9
Sausage (1 regular link)	48	11	4	5
T-bone steak (3.5 oz, fat trimmed)	309	69	26	30
FISH & SHELLFISH				
Baked flounder (3 oz.)	100	22	2	10
Broiled lobster (2 lb.)	233	62	28	39
Fried oysters (3 oz.)	168	37	14	16
Broiled salmon (4 oz.)	233	52	20	23
Fried shrimp (3 oz.)	205	46	17	20
Tuna in water (4 oz.)	132	29	11	13
Tuna in oil (4 oz.)	211	47	18	20
POULTRY				
Fried chicken (½)	603	134	51	58
Fried chicken leg	120	27	10	12
Roast turkey (3 oz. skinless breast)	157	35	13	15

	Calories	Walking 3 mph 270 Kcal per hr	Bicycling 15 mph 711 Kcal per hr	Jogging 5 mph 620 Kcal per hr
NUTS				
Almonds (1 oz. dry-roasted)	166	37	14	16
Cashews (1 oz. dry-roasted)	163	36	14	16
Peanuts (1 oz. dry-roasted)	166	37	14	16
Pecans (1 oz.)	189	42	8	18
PREPARED SALADS				
Coleslaw (1 cup)	82	18	7	8
Carrot-raisin (3 oz.)	150	33	13	15
Macaroni salad (1 cup)	400	67	30	41
Potato salad (1 cup)	358	80	30	35
DAIRY PRODUCTS				
Milk (whole) (1 cup)	150	33	13	15
Milk (nonfat) (1 cup)	86	19	7	8
Buttermilk (1 cup)	99	22	8	1
Amer. cheese (1 oz.)	106	24	9	10
Cottage cheese, 2% (½ cup)	102	23	9	10
Ice cream, premium (½ cup)	220	49	19	21
Yogurt (plain non-fat) (1 cup)	130	29	11	13
SOUPS				
Cream of mushroom (1 cup)	129	29	11	12
Chicken noodle (1 cup)	75	17	6	7
Split pea (1 cup)	190	42	16	18
Tomato (1 cup)	85	19	7	8
RESTAURANT SANDWICHES				
Club (3 slices of bread)	654	145	55	63
Egg salad	462	103	39	45
Tuna salad	285	63	24	28

	Calories	Walking 3 mph 270 Kcal per hr	Bicycling 15 mph 711 Kcal per hr	Jogging 5 mph 620 Kcal per hr
SWEET TREATS				
Hershey's bar (1.5 oz)	233	52	20	23
Milky Way (2.15 oz)	258	57	22	25
Banana split (2 scoop)	694	154	59	67
Apple Pie (⅛ of 9-inch pie)	296	66	25	29
Brownie (2¾ x ⅞-inch)	227	50	19	22
BEVERAGES				
Beer (12 oz.)	147	33	12	14
Light beer (12 oz.)	110	24	9	11
Brandy (1 oz.)	97	21	8	9
Martini (2.5 oz.)	156	35	13	15
Wine (4 oz.)	80	18	7	8
Champagne (4 oz.)	80	18	7	8
Chocolate shake (10 oz.)	359	80	30	35
Eggnog (8 oz.)	342	76	29	33
Soda (12 oz.)	146	32	12	14
VEGETABLES				
Asparagus (½ cup)	22	5	2	2
Broccoli (½ cup)	22	5	2	2
Cabbage (½ cup)	17	4	1	2
Sweet corn (1 ear)	120	27	10	12
Sweet pickle (1 lg.)	41	9	3	4
Baked potato (1 med.)	220	49	19	2
French fries (3 oz.)	156	35	13	15
Mashed potatoes (½ cup)	111	25	9	11
Potato chips (1 oz.)	152	34	13	15

Just For the Fun of It

SPECIAL EXERCISE CALORIE CHART

Beating around the bush	75	Turning the other cheek	75
Jogging your memory	125	Wading through paperwork	300
Jumping to conclusions	100	Bending over backward	75
Climbing the walls	150	Jumping on the bandwagon	200
Swallowing your pride	50	Balancing the books	23
Passing the buck	25	Beating your head against the wall	150
Grasping at straws	75	Running around in circles	350
Beating your own drum	100	Chewing nails	200
Throwing your weight around	50–300	Eating crow	225
Dragging your heels	100	Fishing for compliments	50
Pushing your luck	250	Tooting your own horn	25
Making mountains out of molehills	500	Climbing the ladder of success	750
Spinning your wheels	175	Pulling out the stops	75
Flying off the handle	225	Adding fuel to the fire	150
Hitting the nail on the head	50	Pouring salt on the wound	50

21

EAT
WELL
EATING
OUT

FAST FOODS: THE GOOD AND THE BAD

Fast-food restaurants have made a number of changes to their menus. Most now offer a number of low-fat alternatives to their usual fare of high-calorie, high-fat foods. In many cases, these changes have been in response to consumer demand.

IT'S THE REAL THING

If you are going to roast-beef fast-food restaurants, you might be surprised. One nationwide chain reports that its "roast beef" is just processed ground beef, water, salt, and sodium phosphate. But it is lower in cholesterol and fat than real roast beef or the average hamburger, so it's a healthful choice when it comes to fast-food fare.

SALT SHAKE?

Most thick shakes contain so many additives that are derived from sodium that one shake can contain more sodium than an order of French fries.

CHOCOLATE, OR FAT?

Steer clear of soft-serve ice cream dipped in chocolate coating. There's very little chocolate—it's actually a high-fat product made from fats that have a very low melting point.

THE ROASTED-CHICKEN INVASION

Roasted chicken chains provide some healthful choices, but they can also have artery-busting food. A roasted half chicken with skin can contain between 650 and 750 calories and about 3 tablespoons of fat. Choose skinless chicken, and stick with lower-fat side dishes.

IT'S STILL NOT HEALTH FOOD

Many fast-food chains advertise that they do not use any animal fats for frying. What many neglect to mention is that they have switched to tropical oils like coconut and palm—both of which are high in saturated fat. Another thing you should know: Some chains precook their fries at a central location to reduce cooking time on-site. This prefrying may be done in high-saturated fat vegetable oils.

WELL, SHIVER MY TIMBERS

Fish is healthful, right? Not if you order a fried-fish sandwich. Otherwise low in fat, fish gets 50 percent of its calories from fat when it's fried.

HAR, HAR, HAR

Some seafood chains offer baked fish, which provides about 200 calories less than fried fish; it also clocks in with about one-half as much sodium.

ONE FATTY CHICKEN

If you think you are getting a low-fat meal by ordering a burger chain's chicken sandwich, think again. Most chicken sandwiches contain 20 to 29 grams of fat, but some contain more than 40 grams—which is like eating a pint of regular ice cream in one sitting.

WHY BOTHER?

Just because it's chicken doesn't mean it's healthful. If it's fried, if the skin is still on, and if there are special coatings, a chicken sandwich has in most cases got more calories and fat than a regular burger.

GREAT BUNS

Some fast-food restaurants offer multigrain buns, which are an excellent source of fiber—and, to many people, have more flavor.

ALL OF ME, WHY NOT TAKE ALL OF ME . . .

Beware of claims of "100 percent pure beef." Legally, this label can be given to any processed meat that contains ground bone, gristle, fat, and almost any other part of the animal.

GOOD GOING

Many chains identify healthier menu offerings. At some restaurants, you may see a small red heart next to an item. One chain even has a few sandwiches that are approved by the American Heart Association.

Common Fast-Food Meal	Calories	Cholesterol	Sodium	Fat
Hamburger on a bun	550	80 mg.	800 mg.	57 percent
Regular fries	250	0 mg.	115 mg.	52 percent
Thick shake	350	31 mg.	210 mg.	8 percent
Apple pie	260	6 mg.	427 mg.	21 percent
TOTAL	1,410	117 mg.	1,552 mg.	no percent was given

HOLD THE BAD STUFF

Always order fast food as a special order so that you can specify that you do not want the special sauce (loaded with fat), ketchup (sugar), mayonnaise (fat), and pickles (salt).

EASILY BEATS THE BURGERS

Pizza is the most popular fast food in the United States, and pepperoni is the number one topping. In Japan, the favorite pizza toppings are tuna and scallops—maybe one reason the Japanese have fewer heart problems.

STUFF IT?

As tasty as they are, stuffed pizza crusts add about 4 grams of fat to the pizza and at least 150 to 160 more calories.

FAT CITY

If you really want a high-fat meal, try a Double Western Bacon Cheeseburger from Carl's Jr. This one is on top of all charts with 1,030 calories and 63 grams of fat, half of which is saturated. Double the fat by adding a thick shake and a large order of fries.

SALAD FAT?

Think that a salad is a better choice? Add one packet of ranch dressing to a McDonald's Chef's Salad, and it will have more fat than a Big Mac.

THE BETTER CHOICE

Nutritionally, pizza is a reasonably good choice. The tomato sauce provides vitamins A and C, the cheese provides calcium, and if you have veggie toppings instead of sausage or pepperoni, you'll get additional nutrients without much fat.

IT'S A HOLY CATASTROPHE

In 1997, Americans ate more than 11 billion doughnuts. What's more, 90 percent of us eat doughnuts on a weekly basis.

KEEPING CARDIOLOGISTS BUSY

The three biggest national burger chains sell almost 4 million pounds of French fries daily—that's a total of 1 million pounds of saturated fat.

BLAME IT ON THE DEEP-FRIED BOWL

One of the worst meals for calories and fat is a taco salad from a taco chain. It can tip the scales with as many as 905 calories and 61 grams of fat, 16 grams of which are saturated.

ADDING THEIR OWN TOUCH

If you are curious about additives in fast foods, send away for the list of ingredients in the fast foods, or log on to the company's Web site. You may be surprised at the number of additives such as MSG in chicken and roast-beef seasonings; dyes in shakes, soft ice cream, chicken nuggets, hot cakes, and sundae toppings; and so on.

GET A GOOD PIZZA

Your best bet for flavorful, nutritious pizza is a local pizzeria, not a national (or even regional) chain. A mom-and-pop place is more likely to make the crust and sauce every day and use top-quality ingredients.

DID YOU KNOW?

Most fast-food restaurants have Web sites, where they post the nutrient analysis of their food.

Reasonable Fast Food Choices

FOOD	CALORIES	FAT GRAMS	FOOD	CALORIES	FAT GRAMS
BURGER KING			Clam Chowder (w/cod)	140	6
Chef's salad	178	9	Cod, baked (1 piece)	90	2.5
Garden salad	95	5	Hushpuppies (1 piece)	60	2.5
CARL'S JR.			Rice pilaf	140	3
Chicken salad	200	8	Seafood salad	380	31
Hamburger, plain	320	14	**McDONALD'S**		
DOMINO'S PIZZA			Apple bran muffin	180	0
Cheese pizza (2 large slices)	375	10	Chunky chicken salad	150	4
Ham pizza (2 large slices)	417	11	Garden salad	50	2
			Hamburger, plain	255	9
HARDEE'S			Hash Browns	130	8
Fried chicken leg (no skin)	170	7	**SUBWAY**		
Grilled chicken sandwich	290	9	Ham sandwich	317	3
Roast beef sandwich	270	11	Roast beef sandwich	326	2
JACK-IN-THE-BOX			Turkey sandwich	312	8
Chicken fajita pita	290	8	**TACO BELL**		
Hamburger, plain	270	11	Pintos and cheese	190	9
Taco	190	11	Chicken taco, soft	213	10
KFC			Steak taco, soft	217	9
Baked beans	132	2	Taco	183	11
Chicken Little sandwich	169	10	Tostada	243	11
Cole slaw	114	6	**WENDY'S**		
LONG JOHN SILVER'S			Garden salad	110	6
Chicken Plank	120	6	Grilled chicken sandwich	290	7
Chicken, baked (1 piece)	110	3	Jr. cheeseburger	320	13
			Jr. hamburger	270	9

RESTAURANT CHOICES

When it comes to healthful eating, fast food restaurants are one thing, and restaurants with table service are another. At the latter, you have more control over the amounts of fat, sodium, and sugar that end up on your plate. There are more items to choose from, of course, and you can ask that rich sauces or dressings be served on the side or not at all.

APPETIZERS TO AVOID

In restaurants, avoid fried appetizers such as breaded jalapeños stuffed with cheese, breaded zucchini sticks, and any appetizers that mention cream or butter in the menu description. On salads, avoid creamy and cheese-based dressings—especially blue cheese and thousand island—and choose a simple oil-and-vinegar dressing instead. Good alternatives to fatty appetizers are a clear soup or a shrimp cocktail.

REMOVE POULTRY SKINS

If you order chicken or turkey, remove the skin before you eat it and you'll end up with less fat. (As for duck, it's fat through and through.)

IS IT REALLY A DIET PLATE?

A lot of so-called diet plates feature a ground beef patty, cottage cheese, and some kind of salad. But a 3-ounce patty can have as much as 19 grams of fat, and even cottage cheese has 5 grams of fat per half-cup.

SMART BREAD CHOICES

From the bread basket, choose breadsticks, hard rolls, French and Italian bread, pita bread, wafers, and melba toast. These don't have as much butter or sugar as soft rolls, biscuits, croissants, and muffins.

WATCH THAT SODIUM!

If you are on a low-sodium diet, be aware that relish trays and antipastos are extremely salty. Avoid pickled vegetables, relishes, and cured meats. Also watch out for mustard, Worcestershire sauce, steak sauce, salsa, barbecue sauce, and ketchup—all very high in sodium.

Healthy Restaurant Eating

CHINESE

Soup Choices: Wonton or hot-and-sour soup

Main Courses: Stir-fried vegetable dishes, white or brown rice, chow mien dishes, and most vegetable-based dishes

Stay Clear Of: Anything bread or fried, especially egg rolls, sweet-and-sour dishes (very high calorie), and any dish sautéed in large amounts of oil

ITALIAN

Soup Choices: Minestrone

Main Courses: Any grilled lean meat or seafood, vegetable dishes without cream, pasta with marinara sauce

Stay Clear Of: Antipasto, garlic bread, cream sauces, dishes topped with cheeses, breaded and fried foods

FRENCH

Soup Choices: Broth or vegetable soups

Main Courses: Any grilled lean meat or seafood, stews with a tomato base, vegetable dishes without cream sauces

Stay Clear Of: French onion soup topped with cheese, pâté, anything in butter or cream sauce, croissants, au fromage or au gratin dishes

MEXICAN

Soup Choices: Corn-tortilla soup

Main Courses: Bean-and-rice dishes without cheese, chicken fajitas without cheese, corn tortilla or taco

Stay Clear Of: Flour tortillas and chips, cheese sauces, guacamole, beef dishes, fried tortilla dishes, enchiladas, and burritos

FAST-FOOD CHAINS

Breakfast: Scrambled eggs, English muffin with no butter, orange juice

Lunch: Small burger with no cheese or sauce, grilled chicken sandwiches without sauce, salads with low-cal dressing, small single layer cheese pizza with vegetable toppings, Wendy's chili, Jack-In-The-Box Club Pita

Stay Clear Of: Everything else

22

SUPERMARKET SMARTS

CLEAN IS IN

The cleanliness of a supermarket is critical. This includes the floors, counters, and even the employees. Check the bathrooms, too.

THE TEMPERATURE MAKES A DIFFERENCE

The meat freezer cases should have a thermometer in plain sight, which should read between 0°F or below. Dairy should be stored at 40°F or below. Frozen foods should be between 0°F and 10°F. If you see ice crystals, don't buy the item; it means moisture has crept in.

RING AROUND THE BOTTOM

Want to see whether lettuce is fresh? Look at the bottom. Check to be sure that the stem ring is white, not brown.

WHAT'S IN A NAME?

Many supermarkets sell beef under a house brand to make you think that the item is a higher grade than it really is (most stores sell USDA grade Select). These names are usually similar to ones used by the USDA, and include Premium, Quality, Select Cut, Market Choice, and Prime Cut.

SUPERMARKET SAVVY

◆ Shop when the store is not crowded so you can see the specials.
◆ Never buy food in a sticky jar or a dented can.
◆ Most weekend specials start midweek.
◆ Foods on the lowest shelves are usually the least expensive. The most commonly purchased items are always found at eye level on the shelves.
◆ Processed hams should be kept refrigerated.
◆ If the market has a sale, buy by the case whenever possible.
◆ Don't be afraid to return poor-quality goods.

KOSHER FOODS: BETTER OR WORSE?

Although kosher foods do not contain any edible offal or animal-based additives such as lard, they still may contain tropical oils (palm and coconut), which are high in saturated fats. Kosher meats usually have a higher sodium content than other meats due to the heavy salting during processing. For the most part, kosher products are no more healthful than others are, and the additional cost is not worth it—unless, of course, you adhere to the dietary restrictions.

NUTRIENTS IN FOODS

Nutrients in fresh supermarket foods—produce, meat, and fish, for instance—vary so widely that any nutritional breakdowns are ballpark figures at best. Nutritional contents vary because of different storage and transportation times; original quality of the food; washings in the markets; effects of direct light, packaging, and freezing techniques; preservatives used; processing; and variations in the nutrient content of the soil or feed. The following are results from one study.

Vitamin A Content in 3½ oz. Servings Ranged Between:	
Calf's liver	470–41,200 IU
Carrots (with skin)	70–18,500 IU
Tomatoes	640–3,020 IU
White cheddar cheese	735–1,590 IU
Eggs	905–1,220 IU
Vitamin C Content in 3½ oz. Servings Ranged Between:	
Oranges (no skin)	Trace–116 mg
Tomatoes (with skin)	9–38 mg
Calf's liver	15–36 mg
Carrots (with skin)	.1–8 mg

SHOPPING CARTS

Shopping carts are a necessity, albeit an expensive one. Supermarkets lose about 1.8 million carts every year, at a cost of $175,000. The number of carts a store has is also an indication of its total dollar business. Most markets average $1,000 per week for every cart they have in service. If the market has 200 carts, then it probably does $200,000 per week in business, which equals $10.4 million dollars a year.

DID YOU KNOW?

Give bags of frozen foods a quick squeeze before putting them in your cart. If the food is solid, it has thawed and refrozen. Choose another package.

THE LAW OF AVERAGES

In 1997, the average American consumed:

- ◆ 132 pounds of refined sugar
- ◆ 61 pounds of fats and oils
- ◆ 339 cans of soft drinks
- ◆ 195 sticks of chewing gum
- ◆ 21 pounds of candy
- ◆ 15 pounds of potato chips, corn chips, popcorn, and pretzels
- ◆ 792 doughnuts
- ◆ 52 pounds of cakes and cookies
- ◆ 22 gallons of ice cream
- ◆ 105 tablespoons of peanut butter
- ◆ 7 pounds of carrots
- ◆ 5 pounds of bell peppers
- ◆ 4 pounds of broccoli

SALES PRODUCED FROM PRODUCE

The produce department in a supermarket is one of the more lucrative. In 1997, produce sales totaled about $35 billion. Apples are the most popular item, followed in order by oranges, lettuce, potatoes, and tomatoes. Some of the least popular are broccoli, squash, asparagus, and cauliflower. Fruits account for 44 percent of sales, and vegetables account for 56 percent. According to law, tomatoes (which are classified botanically as a fruit) are counted as vegetables, and watermelons (which are actually a vegetable) are counted as fruits.

BRIMMING OVER WITH POSSIBLE CONTAMINATION

Be careful around the holidays. Many stores place foods in chest freezers, piling the food higher than the freezer line. Chickens and turkeys over the line have probably thawed and refrozen a number of times. When you are ready to use them, they may have gone bad.

WHAT ARE THE MOST COMMON ITEMS STOLEN FROM SUPERMARKETS?

Shoplifting is a real problem in supermarkets, with losses estimated to be $5 billion per year. The most common stolen items are cigarettes, health-

and-beauty aids, meats, fish, and batteries. Two of the most common problems are internal: stock staff who steal and cashiers who don't ring up items for friends or family.

When Were America's Most Popular Foods Introduced?

DATE	FOOD	DATE	FOOD	DATE	FOOD
1790	First patent for a food additive	1917	Moon Pie marshmallow sandwiches	1941	M&M's
				1946	frozen French fries
1853	potato chips	1919	All Bran cereal	1947	Almond Joy candy bar
1867	hot dogs	1920	Baby Ruth candy bar	1950	Hawaiian Punch
1876	Heinz ketchup	1922	Mounds candy bar	1950	Minute Rice
1896	Tootsie Roll	1923	Milky Way candy bar	1950	Sugar Pops cereal
1897	Grape Nuts cereal	1923	Reese's Peanut Butter Cup	1952	Sugar Frosted Flakes cereal
1897	Jell-O	1927	Kool-Aid	1953	Sugar Smacks cereal
1900	chocolate bars	1928	Rice Krispies	1958	Jif peanut butter
1906	Planter's peanuts	1928	Velveeta cheese	1965	Cool Whip
1907	Hershey's Kisses	1930	Snickers candy bar	1965	Shake 'n Bake
1909	Instant coffee	1930	Twinkies	1965	Tang orange drink
1911	Crisco shortening	1932	3 Musketeers candy bar	1969	Pringles chips
1912	Goo Goo Clusters	1933	Ritz crackers	1976	Country Time lemonade
1912	Oreos	1937	Spam	1978	Weight Watchers foods
1913	Life Savers	1941	Cheerios		
1914	Clark Bar				
1917	Mary Janes				

SUPERMARKET STATISTICS

For every $100 spent on food, almost $18 goes for meat, seafood, or poultry. Produce takes almost $10, snack foods take just more than $5, and beans, rice, and dried vegetables take $1. More than 80 percent of households buy potato chips every two weeks. In 1997, $55 million worth of Twinkies were sold.

SNIFF, SNIFF...THAT'S AN ORANGE

Checkout counter scanners may soon have aroma detectors that will identify every kind of produce to save the cashier time.

SUPERMARKET PROFITS ARE ON THE EDGE?

Almost 50 percent of a supermarket's profits come from the perimeter of the store: produce, meats, dairy, and the salad bar. The produce department is the showcase of most stores, and they want to stimulate your appetite by making you walk past the great-looking fruits and vegetables first. Meats are often at the back of the store so you notice them at the end of every aisle. Since many people run in for milk mid-week, dairy is usually as far from the entrance as possible to get you to walk past other food. Anchor displays are placed at the end of each aisle. These are products the market needs to rid its inventory or are higher profit-items. Breakfast cereals make more money than any interior store product and are given a large amount of space.

PERFECT PRODUCE

The produce area usually has the most influence on where you choose to shop. Produce is the second highest profit for the market (meat is always first). In supermarket terms, the aisles (as opposed to the perimeter) are called the prison, because once you enter you cannot get out until you reach the other end. The prison, however, in most instances is where the least profitable foods are found.

GETTING CANNED

The United States cans more than 1,500 different kinds of foods, with billions of cans being sold annually. There are more than 40 varieties of beans alone, 75 varieties of juices, and more than 100 different types of soups. A can of food will last for about two years and still retain a reasonable level of nutrients if stored in a cool, dry location.

PETS AND FOOD

North Americans spend an unbelievable amount of money on pet foods. In 1997, people in the United States spent almost $2.29 billion a year on cat food and more than $3.14 billion on dog food.

◆ The higher-quality pet foods contain more protein and less sugar, as well as fewer artificial dyes and additives.

◆ Veterinarians estimate that about 30 percent of cats and dogs are over-weight. One study linked overweight pets to overweight owners.

◆ Feeding cats a saucer of milk may not be a healthful treat. Some cats are lactose intolerant and a treat with less lactose, like cottage cheese or yogurt, would be better for them.

◆ Chocolate is toxic to dogs, but cats won't even touch it because they can't taste sweets.

LABEL TERMINOLOGY

Low-Calorie
Meats and main dishes are allowed to contain 120 calories per serving; all other foods can contain 40 calories per serving.

Reduced-Calorie
Must have at least 25 percent fewer calories than the original product.

Diet or Dietetic
The product may be lower in calories, sodium or sugar than a comparable product. The FDA has not defined this term.

Lite or Light
This is one of the more confusing terms. If 50 percent or more of the calories are from fat, the fat must be reduced by at least 50 percent from the original food. If less than 50 percent of the calories are from fat, the fat must be reduced at least by 50 percent, or the calories must be at least one-third of the original food. For main dishes or meals, the item must also meet the definition for low-calorie or low-fat.

No Cholesterol
This means that the item has less than 2 milligrams per serving amount. But it still may be high in saturated fat.

Low-Cholesterol
Cannot contain more than 20 milligrams of cholesterol per serving.

Low-Fat
The food must contain no more than 3 grams of fat per serving and no more than 30 percent of calories from fat per serving size.

DID YOU KNOW?

If you prefer fruits and veggies with the peels, try to buy organic produce. You'll still need to wash it, but there will be less need to worry about pesticide residues.

Lean
Meat and poultry must have no more than 10 grams of total fat, 4.5 grams or less saturated fat, and less than 95 milligrams of cholesterol per serving amount.

Extra-Lean
Meat and poultry must have no more than 5 grams of total fat, less than 2 grams of saturated fat, and less than 95 milligrams of cholesterol per serving amount.

Sugar-Free
Must contain less than 0.5 gram of sugars per serving.

Sodium-Free
Must contain less than 5 milligrams of sodium per serving.

Very Low-Sodium
Must contain 35 milligrams or less of sodium per serving.

Low-Sodium
Must contain 140 milligrams or less per serving.

Reduced-Sodium
The sodium content in the food has been reduced by at least 25 percent.

No Salt Added
Salt cannot be added during processing, though the food may have other ingredients that contain sodium. If so, the label must state "This is not a sodium-free food."

Imitation
A food substitute, usually nutritionally inferior, and may contain the same calories and fat as nonimitation. Any new food with less protein or lesser amount of any essential vitamin or mineral must be labeled imitation.

The following terms are not yet regulated by the FDA.

Organic
Usually means a food that is grown without the use of artificial fertilizers. There are no consistent guidelines nationwide for food growers. If organic foods are important to you, shop at a reputable store.

Natural
May mean anything. No regulations apply, and the word may be seen on foods that have no additives and preservatives.

Enriched
A processed product that is sometimes fortified with a percentage of the nutrients that were originally there.

IT'S GETTING EASIER

A survey was done in 1988 to see whether the public read nutrition labels on food items before purchasing them. The study reported that 97 percent of people who purchased processed foods never read the label. In 1994, the survey was repeated and showed that 84 percent still did not read the labels. In 1998, however, 56 percent of consumers checked labels for ingredients to avoid. Since the labels were standardized in the mid-1990's, consumers have found it easier to make smart choices.

SCRATCHING YOUR HEAD YET?

If a label says that a food is 80 percent fat-free, it's necessary to understand what that really means. For example, let's look at two hot dogs.

Hot Dog		Light Hot Dog (80 Percent Fat Free)	
NUTRITIONAL INFORMATION PER SERVING 8 LINKS PER PACKAGE		NUTRITIONAL INFORMATION PER SERVING 8 LINKS PER PACKAGE	
Portion Size	1 link (56 g)	Portion size	1 link (56 g)
Calories	180	Calories	130
Protein	6 g	Protein	7 g
Carbohydrate	2 g	Carbohydrate	1 g
Fat	17 g	Fat	11 g
Cholesterol	35 mg	Cholesterol	25 mg
Sodium	600 mg	Sodium	600 mg
17 grams of fat multiplied by 9 calories per gram equals 153 calories from fat. 153 divided by 180 calories X 100 = 85 percent of calories from fat.		11 grams of fat multiplied by 9 calories per gram equals 99 calories from fat. 99 divided by 130 calories X 100 = 76 percent of calories from fat	

If this seems confusing, it is! This is just another way to trick consumers into thinking they are getting a better product than the full-fat version, when, in fact, there is only a minor difference. Manufacturers can list the percent of nutrients by weight (which includes water weight), not percent of fat by calories. The "light" hot dogs are 80 percent fat-free by weight, which is determined by the total weight including water content, not by the actual food value.

NEEDS SUNGLASSES

If you can, avoid milk in clear plastic containers. When they are exposed to light for four hours, low-fat and nonfat milk lose 44 percent of vitamin A. Supermarkets in some areas of the country now package milk in yellow containers to shield it from light, and some markets have even installed "light shields" or store the milk under counters to protect them.

Light can also affect the nutrients in juices, especially vitamin C. Avoid juice in clear containers.

CRACKING LABEL CODES

Food labels contain a large amount of important information. To make the information useful, you must first understand the labels. The following facts may make it somewhat easier.

Food Label Decoding and Terminology
Proteins contain 4 calories per gram
Carbohydrates contain 4 calories per gram
Fats contain 9 calories per gram
Alcohol contains 7 calories per gram

23

SAFETY FIRST

KNOWLEDGE IS POWER

In recent years, food safety has become a paramount concern. Reports of illness and death as a result of contaminated foods and water have been national news. Meats, poultry, and fish can harbor dangerous bacteria or chemicals; soil is lacking vital nutrients so produce is less nutritious; we allow a degree of contaminants in our foods; and hundreds of chemicals are used in the growing and processing of our foods.

Although it's impossible to avoid food-borne pathogens completely, there are things you can do to lessen your risk of falling prey to a debilitating—or potentially fatal—bug. You'll find them in the next 15 pages.

CUTTING BOARD CONTROVERSY

Studies keep going on and on regarding the safety of cutting boards. Plastic cutting boards were thought to be the better than wood because they are less porous. Then, a 1996 study commissioned by the Food Research Institute reported that bacterial levels on wooden cutting boards were low after only a few minutes. A subsequent study, however, indicated that bacteria burrowed deeper into the wood, not that the wood was inhospitable to them.

While the jury is still out on which is safer—plastic or wood—here are some critically important rules to follow:

- Reserve one cutting board only for raw meats, poultry, and fish; use other cutting boards for prepping vegetables, cheeses, and cooked meat, poultry, and fish.
- Wash all cutting boards immediately after use in very hot soapy water. Run them through the dishwasher to sterilize them (hint: plastic withstands the higher temperatures better than wood does), or wash them with a weak bleach solution.
- Remember that it's harder to scrub bacteria out of nooks and crannies; discard cutting boards whose surfaces have deep knife marks.
- Avoid setting hot pans on wood cutting boards or butcher-block countertops. Bacteria love heat, and the hot pan may serve to activate them or draw them to the surface of the wood.

GERM SPREADERS

Dishcloths and sponges should be washed or run through the dishwasher every day. Paper towels are safer to use in most instances. Can openers also have the potential to spread germs; wipe them clean after each use.

IS YOUR FAVORITE RESTAURANT CLEAN?

There are 1,800 strains of salmonella, most of which cause food poisoning. The Centers for Disease Control and Prevention estimates there are 2 to 4 million cases of salmonella poisonings every year, with 200,000 serious enough to warrant medical care and 1,000 to 2,000 resulting in death. Most cases are caused by human error and many have been associated with restaurant and employee uncleanliness.

SHOULD BE CALLED "POT RISK"

Many food poisonings are linked to potluck parties. When protein-based dishes—meat, poultry, egg, or dairy—are left at room temperature for more than two hours, bacteria multiply rapidly.

BEST TO USE THEM FOR A VASE

Imported lead crystal decanters, as well as some imported ceramics and pottery, are best used as decoration rather than for storage. A number of liquids—especially vinegar and wine—can leach the lead out of crystal over time.

BACTERIAL SAUNA

A number of cooks insist on roasting their turkeys on low heat overnight. Although this results in a juicy bird, it also gives the bacteria plenty of time to multiply, because it takes longer to get to a temperature that's high enough to kill all the bacteria. If the bird is not heated to 180°F, food poisoning is a possibility.

UPSIDE DOWNER

When you go out for a drink, avoid drinking from a glass that has been stored upside down over the bar. Smoke and other contaminants get into the glass and remain there.

SNIFF, SNIFF

Never purchase a can or jar if there is a bulge or any sign of damage. When you open a can or jar always smell the contents and check for mold. Never put a utensil that's been in your mouth into a container. This includes fingers, for those who love peanut butter or to nibble olives.

DID YOU KNOW?

You should always wash your hands before preparing food. Bacteria that cause food-borne illness can't be smelled or tasted, but are probably on your hands, nevertheless.

MED FACT

If you're given antibiotics, ask your doctor or pharmacist whether you should take them on an empty stomach. Food tends to slow down the absorption of the medication, and this may reduce its potency.

WHAT ARE THE INSPECTORS INSPECTING?

Food-borne illnesses sicken more than 81 million Americans every year. The majority of these cases are relatively mild, and most people get over the illness in two to three days. However, about 9,000 of these cases are fatal, with 75 percent of the fatalities caused by salmonella and campylobacter, primarily found in meat and poultry.

RUN, DON'T WALK, TO NEAREST EXIT

If you ever spy a restaurant cook with a cigarette, do yourself a favor and leave as soon as possible. Saliva cross-contamination when smokers touch a cigarette then food is relatively common.

HEAT THEM FOR SAFETY

If you refrigerate leftovers for more than 36 hours, they should be reheated to 165°F. Refrigerator temperatures are usually not cold enough to slow bacterial growth for much longer than a day and a half.

EITHER HOT OR COLD

When you're setting out a buffet, keep foods either warm or cold—not lukewarm. Cold foods should be kept at 40°F at the most, while hot foods should stay at 140°F in a Crock-Pot or chafing dish.

A DEFINITE NO-NO

When grilling, never put cooked meat or poultry back onto the same plate that held the raw food. This form of cross-contamination has been the cause of many cases of food poisoning.

DON'T EAT CHILLY CHILI

If you make chili with beef or poultry, be sure and heat it to a temperature of 165°F before serving it. Follow this rule whether the chili is being served for the first time or you're reheating leftovers.

WASH AND REWASH

When preparing a buffet, pay special attention to the cleanliness of your kitchen equipment. Always rewash any plates, cutting boards, and knives that have come into contact with raw meat or poultry.

SMALL PORTIONS, PLEASE

Instead of setting out the food for a buffet all at once, keep most of it in the fridge. Then, before replacing a food, either wash the platter or get a new one before adding fresh food. Put out larger servings of foods that are going quickly and smaller servings of foods that are less in demand.

A SULFITE BY ANY OTHER NAME

Sulfites are used less and less frequently in foods and beverages. Occasionally, however, they appear in processed foods. Labels must clearly state that the item contains sulfites, but if you suffer from asthma, read the ingredients lists and watch out for:

- Sodium metabisulfite
- Sodium sulfite
- Sodium bisulfite
- Potassium metabisulfite
- Potassium bisulfite
- Sulfur dioxide

STERILIZATION A MUST

When canning anything by any method, sterilizing is an important part of the process. Be sure to sterilize the jars and lids, as well as utensils like spoons or ladles, by boiling them for 10 minutes before you fill the jars.

PLAY IT SAFE

Preservatives, additives, or artificial colorings should never be added to home-canned foods. Clean all food residue off the jar exteriors by wiping them with white vinegar before storing.

SEAL SAFETY

As long as the seal is intact, freezer-preserved foods are still safe to eat. However, as with all frozen foods, the taste and texture may be different.

BE AFRAID OF THE DARK

If you see a black deposit on the lid after you open a canned food, it is not a good sign. Throw the food out.

HELP! I'M EXPANDING

Foods high in starch such as corn, lima beans, and peas need to be packed loosely because they tend to expand during and after processing; leave 1 inch of head space in their jars. Fruits and berries should be packed with about ½ inch of head space because of shrinkage and the fact that their texture does not stop the heat penetration.

KEEP IT IN THE CLEAR

If the liquid in a food jar is cloudy, the food inside is probably spoiled. Dispose of the jar without even opening it, or harmful spores may be released into the air.

BEST VINEGAR FOR CANNING

Any vinegar with 4 to 6 percent acetic acid is acceptable for canning. But pick your vinegar wisely: Some have distinctive flavors that might not be suitable for all pickling recipes.

SOLVING A SOFT-PICKLE PROBLEM

Keep the crunch in your pickles when you make them. Be sure that your vinegar is adequately acidic and that you use enough. Other causes of soft pickles include not covering the cucumbers completely with brine during fermentation; not sealing the jars so they're airtight; using moldy garlic or spices; or processing the jars for too long—or too short—a time. Storing the pickles in the refrigerator will help keep them firm.

INDEFINITELY IS NOT FOREVER

As long as the seal is intact, canned foods can last for years. The nutrient content will diminish, however, the longer the food stays on your shelf.

RING IT UP

After canning food, tap the lid of the jar. You should hear a clear, ringing note. If the food is touching the top, this will not occur. Be sure to leave the proper amount of head space.

SWEETNESS

Always thaw frozen fruits in the refrigerator. The fruit will have time to reabsorb the sugar as it thaws.

NO DUNGEON? A CELLAR WILL SUFFICE

Canned foods need to be stored in a cool, dark place. Heat causes dormant bacteria to become active and multiply.

SCRATCH THE WAX

Avoid using paraffin or wax of any kind to seal jars of preserves. Wax seals fail more frequently than do the two-piece caps of rings and seals. The result: Mold can grow.

COOL CUSTARD

If you order a dish made from custard or whipped cream, or one that has a cream filling, be sure it is served cool to the touch. These are all supposed to be refrigerated desserts.

WATER SAFETY

If the server touches the rim of your glass, you might want to ask for a new glass or for a straw.

A TEST FOR FRESH CREAM

If, when you're drinking coffee, you are unsure whether your cream is fresh, don't waste the whole cup of joe. Pour a little coffee into your mug, then add the cream. If you see small white flecks floating around, the cream is starting to go sour. Don't use it.

DID YOU KNOW?

When you're concerned about food safety, you can call the USDA Meat and Poultry Hotline at 1-(800) 455-4555.

RADIATION: YES OR NO?

Many scientists and doctors believe that foods exposed to radiation are as safe to eat as foods that have not been irradiated. According to the Centers for Disease Control and Prevention, researchers have noted that levels of thiamine in food are slightly reduced, but not enough to result in a deficiency. In addition, there are no significant changes in levels of amino acids, fatty acids, or the vitamin contents of foods.

In well-controlled studies, irradiated foods have been fed to animals and people. Some of these animal studies have lasted for several generations in several species, including mice, rats, and dogs. Researchers have found no evidence of adverse health effects in these studies. Nevertheless, many people prefer to avoid irradiated foods. If you have any questions, call the Consumer Nutrition Safety Hotline: 1-(800) 366-1655.

CAUTION

Symptoms of food poisoning will vary depending on the amount and type of the bacteria or virus ingested. Symptoms usually include chills, stomachache, nausea, muscle aches, and diarrhea. If diarrhea occurs shortly after a meal, it is usually a sign of food poisoning. If you experience any symptom or even suspect that you have eaten a contaminated food, contact your doctor immediately.

NUTRIENT PROTECTION

Have you wanted to try salads, broccoli florets, spinach, and other vegetables packed in plastic bags but suspected they might be inferior to bulk produce? Be reassured: Studies have demonstrated nutrient content is excellent, even to the point of surpassing those sold loose. Two caveats: Wash packaged produce before eating it, and heed the "use by" dates.

SCARY STATISTIC

Every day in the United States, more than 220,000 people get sick from eating foods that are contaminated. This explains why there are so many telephone hotlines devoted to food safety, including the Consumer Nutrition Safety Hotline: 1-(800) 366-1655.

Common Food Poisoning Bacteria/Viruses

ORGANISM	SOURCE	ONSET	DURATION
Bacillus Cereus	Cooked grains & vegetables left at room temperature	1–6 hours	Less than 24 hours
Campylobacter Jejuni	Raw poultry & milk; contact with infected animals; contaminated water	12–36+ hours	2–4 weeks
Clostridium Botulinum	Improperly canned foods; chopped garlic in oil; foil-wrapped baked potatoes; raw honey	8–36 hours, but can be up to 8 days	Nerve regeneration can take months
Clostridium Perfringens	Improperly handled foods	6–24 hours	24 hours
Escherichia Coli 0157:H7	Undercooked meat, especially ground; raw milk; any food or water contaminated with manure	5–48 hours	3 days–2 weeks
Listeria	Processed meat; deli-type salads; unaged cheese; dairy products; raw vegetables	24+ hours	2–7 days
Norwalk Virus	Fecal contamination on food or hands	1–3 days	1–2 days
Salmonella	Undercooked or raw meat or poultry; eggs; raw milk	12–48 hours	1–4 days. Can be contracted from contact with pet reptiles
Shigella	Food contaminated with feces	12–36+ hours	10 days. Most common in overpopulated areas with poor sanitation; most prevalent in children 1 to 4 years old
Staphylococcus Aureus	Improperly handled cooked food, especially custards; cream-filled pastries; milk; processed meats; fish	2–8 hours	Less than 12 hours
Vibrio Vulnificus	Raw or undercooked shellfish	15–24 hours	2–4 days

LEAVE THEM WHOLE

Cutting fruits and vegetables, especially those like citrus fruits and melons that are high in vitamin C, can speed nutrient loss. It's best to buy them whole and cut them yourself, rather than purchase tubs of cubed fruits at supermarkets or salad bars.

JUST THE OIL FACTS, MA'AM

Oils break down and become rancid over time, especially if exposed to light. If you buy large containers of oil, look for dark containers and store them in the refrigerator if the oil will not be used within 30 days.

CONCERNING WATER

Almost every day it seems as if we hear about another incident involving contaminated water supplies. These contaminants may include heavy metal salts, inorganic compounds, and suspended solid particles.

Disease outbreaks are easily traced to chemical or bacterial contamination of local water supplies. Remember that almost all of our drinking water originates in streams, rivers, and lakes. Even if the water source is a mountain steam, it may have contact with impurities in suspension as it flows down the mountain. Surface water frequently contains fertilizers and insecticide residues as well as pollutants from manufacturing plants and motor vehicles. At water filtration plants, chemicals like chlorine, fluorine, phosphates, and sodium aluminate are added for purification.

We should be able to rely on a safe water supply and not worry about its safety every time we take a drink. Water may contain a number of inorganic minerals that cannot be utilized by the body and are instead deposited in bones, joints, and organs.

GET THE LEAD OUT

Over 5 million private wells in the United States may be exposing as many as 23 million people to high levels of lead. A warning has been issued by the Environmental Protection Agency that certain types of submersible pumps may leach lead into the water. The problem pumps have fittings made from brass that contains copper and zinc and 2 to 7 percent lead. It is possible to drink water with 51 times the allowable limits of lead in water prescribed by the EPA. Pumps should be made from stainless steel or plastic to eliminate the risk. For more information call the EPA's Safe Drinking Water Hotline at (800) 426-4791.

WATER-TREATMENT METHODS

Since it cannot be taken for granted that the water we drink is healthful, a home-filtration device is a must (unless your budget allows for regularly purchasing bottled water). Some options are:

Charcoal Filtration

Most units filter the water through activated charcoal. This method is good for removing odors, pesticides, chlorine, and other organic matter. However, not all are effective in removing bacteria and heavy metals like lead. When the filter reaches a saturation level, it needs to be replaced. You can purchase an inexpensive carafe with a replaceable filter, or install a filtration system on a faucet or under the sink. Charcoal filtration systems range in price from $5 to $200.

Reverse Osmosis

This treatment method has a dual-filtration system utilizing a sediment filter and an activated filter system. It is effective in removing up to 90 percent of the majority of minerals and inorganic materials. The drawbacks are that it does not allow the production of large quantities of water and its cost: around $750.

Distillation

This is a very effective method of filtration. Boiling the water produces steam then the vapor is trapped and cooled to produce water. Gasses, however, do not seem to be eliminated completely through this method. Prices for distillation systems start at $100.

Aeration

If you live in the Midwest and have a radon gas problem with your water, the best method to remove it is aeration filtration. Recent EPA estimates are that more than 80 million people may be at risk.

Ultraviolet Radiation Purifiers

Effective for the removal of bacteria. Usually installed on wells with other types of filters. You may need to double up with a sediment filter, because ultraviolet purifiers are less effective when it's overcast.

Water Softeners

Use a method of ion exchange to remove hard minerals like calcium and magnesium and replace them with sodium or potassium. Sodium has a softening effect on the water and creates more suds, making it more effective for washing clothes, bathing, and doing dishes. It is best to avoid drinking soft water because of its high sodium content. These range in cost from $500 to $1,500.

Note:

Water filters are going to keep your water safe only if they remove the particular problem in your area and are serviced properly; this includes changing the filter at regular intervals.

WATER PURITY STATS

◆ According to the National Cancer Institute, nine recent studies correlated water quality and cancer with drinking waters in Pittsburgh, New Orleans, a number of cities in Ohio, New York, and New Jersey. In 1998 in the United States, 40,000 water systems violated testing requirements and purity standards, putting 58 million people at risk.

◆ In 1993, 110 people died and 403,000 became ill from drinking tap water in Milwaukee, Wisconsin. The water contained the parasite cryptosporidium. The problem is usually caused by agricultural runoff and sewage leaks.

◆ In 1996, a report was released that listed 28 cities' water supplies that may be at high risk for the same parasite; some of the high-risk cities were Baltimore, Boston, Chicago, Houston, Los Angeles, Denver, New York, San Diego, West Palm Beach, and San Francisco. Numerous other cities were listed at a lower risk.

◆ In 1994 to 1995, the Environmental Working Group released a report stating that 2,726 water supplies affecting 11.9 million Americans had a high level of fecal coliform from animal wastes.

◆ The same report stated that radioactive contamination of water is a problem for 2.3 million Americans. It is caused by natural radioactive elements such as radon and uranium seeping into groundwater. If you feel that this may is a problem in your area, call (708) 505-0160 for information regarding special filter units.

◆ Chlorine is a double-edged sword. On one hand, it protects us from a number of waterborne diseases. On the other hand, the latest findings are that it reacts with organic matter to produce a class of carcinogens called trihalomethanes. This problem may affect about 640,000 Americans. Long-term exposure has been associated with increased cancer risks and other adverse health effects

Call the EPA Safe Drinking Water Hotline at (800) 426-4791 for a free booklet. Additional water information and literature may be obtained by calling the Environmental Working Group at (202) 667-6982 and the Natural Defense Council at (212) 727-2700.

SO WHAT'S NEW?

A new bacterial water contaminant, *Helicobacter pylori*, is now being studied as a possible link to diseases of the stomach. Studies to find ways to control this bacterium are ongoing.

RELEASE ME

There is a higher level of contaminants in hot tap water than in cold tap water; the heat tends to hold the contaminants better. Boiling-hot tap water, however, tends to release contaminants.

WELL WATER? THINK AGAIN!

Something important to remember in the country: Well water should be tested every year, without fail. Many farmers never have their water tested and assume that well water is always clean and healthful.

ADD A GOOD ORGANIC CLEANER

Rinsing vegetables in a sink filled with water (instead of under running water) will save about 200 gallons of water per month for the average family. You will waste another 200 gallons waiting for tap water to warm up. Best to save the cold water for the plants.

DOESN'T SAY MUCH FOR THE GOVERNMENT

The bottled-water industry is a $3.2 billion industry. More than $450 million were spent in 1996 on home filtration systems. Home-filter systems are only capable of removing larger particulate matter still leaving a good percentage of the small ones, such as some bacteria and viruses. One out of 12 households in the United States uses bottled water as its main source of drinking water.

RAINDROPS...

Rainwater is considered to be mineral water and may have a number of impurities. (We have all heard of acid rain, after all.) The purest water is distilled water.

Health Hazards in Everyday Items

ALUMINUM CONTAMINATION

ENVIRONMENTAL CONTAMINANTS

Air wastes	Coal burning	Nasal sprays
Alum	Cooking vessels	Packaging material
Aluminum cans	Dental amalgams	Pesticides
Aluminum foil	Deodorants	Refining
Antacids	Emulsifiers	Smoke
Baking powder	Foods	Soil
Beer	Industrial utensils	Table salt
Bronze paint	Lab equipment	Toothpaste
Cables/wiring	Medicines	Vanilla powder
Cigarette filters	Milk equipment	Water supplies

OVEREXPOSURE SYMPTOMS

Back pain	Heart problems	Osteoporosis
Emphysema	Hyperactivity	Psychosis
Fatigue	Kidney problems	Rickets
Flatulence	Memory Loss	Senility
Gastric upset	Muscle aches	Skin reactions

LEAD CONTAMINATION

ENVIRONMENTAL CONTAMINANTS

Ammunitions	Hair coloring	Plaster
Batteries	Insecticides	Plating
Ceramic glazes	Lead pipes	Printing
Cigarette smoke	Machine shops	Putty
Enamels	Mascara	Solder
Foundries	Newsprint	Toothpaste
Gasoline additives	Old paints	Urban atmosphere
Glass	Paints	Wines (lead caps)

OVEREXPOSURE SYMPTOMS

Abdominal pain	Dizziness	Loss of appetite
Anxiety	Drowsiness	Memory loss
Ataxia	Gout	Muscle aches
Confusion and fatigue	Headaches	Nervousness
Constipation	Hyperactivity	Seizures
Crying	Hypertension	Weak muscles
Depression	Insomnia	Weight loss
Disorientation	Irritability	Withdrawal

CADMIUM CONTAMINATION

ENVIRONMENTAL CONTAMINANTS

Air particles	Galvanized pipes	Processed meats
Auto exhaust	Incineration	Rubber carpet backing
Auto tires	Instant coffee	Rustproofing
Batteries	Iron roofs	Sewage sludge
Candles	Jewelry making	Shellfish
Cigarette smoke	Motor oils	Silver polish
Cisterns	Paint manufacturing	Soil
Cola drinks	Pigments	Soldering
Drinking water	Plastic tapes	Solders
Electroplating	Plastics	Welding metal
Fungicide manufacturing	Process engraving	Zinc smelting

OVEREXPOSURE SYMPTOMS

Arthritis	Fatigue	Liver damage
Bone softening	Glucosuria	Loss of smell
Cancer	Hypertension	Pain in back and leg
Dyspnea	Increased mortality	Renal colic
Emphysema	Iron deficiency and anemia	Teeth discoloration

MERCURY CONTAMINATION

ENVIRONMENTAL CONTAMINANTS

Adhesives	Chemical fertilizers	Ointments
Antiseptics	Cosmetics	Pesticides
Batteries	Dental amalgams	Pharmaceuticals
Body powders	Fabric softener	Plastics
Burning coal	Fish and shellfish	Talc
Camera film	Floor waxes	Thermometers
Canvas	Florescent lamps	Water-based paints

OVEREXPOSURE SYMPTOMS

Anxiety	Irritability	Paralysis
Ataxia	Loss of appetite	Psychosis
Depression	Loss of self-confidence	Renal damage
Dermatitis	Lack of self-control	Speech problems
Drowsiness	Memory loss	Tremors
Hearing loss	Muscle weakness	Vision problems
Insomnia	Nervousness	Weight loss

24

HOUSE AND GARDEN HINTS

MODERATION IS A MUST

Painting doors? It's easier to get paint off hinges if you coat them lightly with petroleum jelly before you start.

PAINT DROPS KEEP FALLING ON MY HEAD...

Cut a tennis ball in half, then cut a thin slot in the bottom. Slide it, open side toward the bristles, over the brush handle to catch the drips.

THE DISAPPEARING ACT

If you are sure you will use up the paint in a can or if you are nearing the bottom of it, notch a few holes along the rim. The paint that you wipe off the brush will go back into the can instead of running down the outside.

NOT A SHOCKING EXPERIENCE

To remove a broken lightbulb from the socket, turn off the electricity or unplug the lamp, and then push half of a raw potato or small apple into the broken bulb base. Turn it to unscrew the base.

CALL SMOKY

To give the charcoal filter in your range hood a new lease on life, set it in a 450°F oven for 30 minutes—but clean the frame completely first. Any grease on the frame may catch on fire or smoke up the house.

DUNK IT, DIP IT

When painting anything, dip a three-by-five-inch index card into the paint to make it easier to match at a later date.

A SECOND USE FOR SOAP

If a pin or needle will not penetrate an article, stick the pin into a bar of soap to make it nice and slippery.

I CAN SEE A RAINBOW

To add color to a campfire, soak pinecones in a solution of 1 quart of water and 1 cup of baking soda. Let them dry for a few days before tossing them into the flames.

REAL SHARPIE

An easy way to sharpen scissors is to fold a piece of aluminum foil three or four times, then cut through it several times.

RETURNING TO LIFE

Dented table-tennis, or ping pong, balls can be revived by submerging them in very hot water for about 20 minutes. The air inside the ball will expand enough to pop out the dents.

DON'T GET ZAPPED

Microwave doors may become misaligned, especially if you pull down on them when opening them. They can leak radiation and should be checked periodically with a small, inexpensive detector, which can be purchased in any hardware store.

FILLER UP

If you need to repair a hole in a piece of wood, add a small amount of instant coffee to the spackle or to a thick paste made from a laundry starch and warm water. The coffee tints the spackle.

DON'T BUY A NEW LID

Did you lose the knob of a pot lid? Place a screw with the thread side up in the hole, and then attach a cork to it.

SNOW SLIDE

To keep snow from sticking to your shovel, save your empty butter wrappers and wipe the shovel off before using it. The snow will slide right off. You can also spray the shovel with nonstick cooking spray.

SEEING THE LIGHT

Cleaning agents can leave a thin film on mirrors. Brighten mirrors by rubbing them with a cloth dampened with alcohol.

GETTING A NEW LEASE ON LIFE

If your flashlight batteries become weak, set them in the sunlight for six to eight hours. This should give them some life back.

DOING THE TWIST

Blow-dryer cords can be kept neat using ponytail holders. This will work for any small electrical appliance, of course.

A SWEETER YULE

To extend the life of your Christmas tree for a few days, add a small amount of sugar or Pinesol to the water.

NATURAL FERTILIZERS

A number of food scraps make excellent fertilizers. Banana skins and egg shells are on top of the list. The minerals they provide are not found in many fertilizers. Flat club soda also makes an excellent fertilizer. To perk up colors, give your plants sip or two occasionally.

SMOOTH OPERATING

Hanging wallpaper? Use a paint roller instead of a sponge to smooth out wallpaper when hanging it.

HOPSCOTCH

When you paint steps, paint every other one. When those are dry, go back and paint the rest. This way, you'll still be able to use the stairs—but only if you're careful.

COLA WORKS WELL, TOO

If you're having a problem removing a rusty nut or bolt, put a few drops of ammonia or hydrogen peroxide on it, and let it stand for 30 minutes.

MAY HAVE A NEGATIVE EFFECT

If you run out of salt or sand to keep ice at bay on your walkway, try kitty litter. Keep the cat in the house!

BE FIRM WITH YOUR GUTTERS

The ideal tool to clean gutters? An old fan belt. It has excellent flexibility, yet is firm enough to do the job without scraping off paint.

DON'T TREAD ON THEM

Linoleum or vinyl floor tiles are excellent for covering picnic tabletops. Linoleum can also be used instead of contact paper on kitchen shelves. It will last longer and is easier to keep clean.

ELECTRICIAN'S TRICK

To avoid tangled electrical cords, fold them up and store in paper towel tubes. Label which appliance each tube goes to.

GETTING ON THE RIGHT TRACK

The windows in your house will open and close more easily if you rub a bar of soap across the track occasionally.

RUST PREVENTION

If you place a few mothballs, a piece of chalk, or a piece of charcoal in your toolbox, you will never have any rust on your tools.

OUCH!

Use a split piece of old garden hose to cover saw blades when storing them in the tool shed or workshop.

DID YOU KNOW?

Drop a few charcoal briquettes into the baby's diaper pail (under the liner). You'll be amazed at what you *don't* smell.

GOING DOWN?

If you need to use a ladder on soft earth, set the legs inside empty coffee cans so that they won't sink in from your weight.

BIG BAGGIE

No space to bring outdoor furniture inside in bad weather? Protect lawn chairs and tables by covering them with large plastic bags.

GLUB, GLUB

When cutting flowers from your garden, be sure to cut them only in the late evening or early morning. Have a bucket of water with you and use very sharp shears. After you cut the flowers, immediately submerge the stems in the water, and cut them again on the diagonal. The stems will then take in water and not air, and the blooms will last longer.

WEED-A-WAY

Keep paved areas looking spiffy with this trick. To remove unwanted grass or weeds from sidewalk and driveway cracks, squirt them with a solution of 1 gallon vinegar, 1 cup salt, and 8 drops liquid detergent.

HOW DRY I AM

When transplanting, always use premoistened soil and peat moss to help retain the moisture.

A CLEAN LEAF IS A HAPPY LEAF

If you want your plant's leaves to shine, wipe them with glycerin, or clean the leaves with a cotton ball dipped in milk or mineral oil.

CLAY IS POROUS

Never place a clay pot on wooden furniture. Water will seep through and can damage the wood finish.

PLANT SAVER

If you are going a long vacation and are unable to find someone to care for your plants, try placing a large container of water near your plants. Then place long pieces of yarn in the water, laying the the ends of the strands across the stalks of the plants. Capillary attraction will keep the plants in good shape until you return.

GETTING POTTED

If you are going to repot a plant, put a small coffee filter on the bottom of the new pot to keep the soil from leaking out.

ROCKY TOP

To keep mud from spattering when you water plants in window boxes (or when it rains hard), top the soil with a one-half-inch layer of gravel.

RECYCLED TAPES AND TRAYS

Broken cassette tapes make excellent ties for plants; and old ice cube trays make excellent herb starters.

GETTING A LEG UP

Nylon stockings or panty hose make excellent storage holders for plant bulbs during the winter. Air is able to circulate, avoiding a problem with mold. Store in a cool, dry location.

THE LIVING CUP

Plastic-foam cups make excellent plant starters and are easy to break apart when it's time to plant the garden.

IT WON'T MAKE THE ICE GROW

You'll distribute sand or salt in a thin, even layer on ice if you use a lawn seeder or fertilizer spreader.

THE HOLE TRUTH

To repair a small hole in a window screen, cover it with a number of layers of clear nail polish.

MR. CLEAN

If you place masking tape on the rim of a paint can before pouring the paint out, you can remove the tape later and the rim will be clean.

LUMPLESS PAINT

If you have lumps in your paint can, cut a piece of screen just under the size of the can and let it settle to the bottom. It'll carry the lumps with it.

TO THE RESCUE

Squeaky door and cabinet hinges, as well as sticky locks, benefit from a light spritz with a nonstick cooking spray.

SAFETY FIRST

To get a closer look at your roof or second story, use a pair of binoculars before deciding whether you need to climb a ladder.

FINDING A REAL STUD

No stud finder? Try this. Hold a compass level with the floor and at a right angle to the wall, then slowly move the compass along the surface of the wall. When the needle moves, that's where you will find a stud.

HOW TO GET A RUN IN YOUR PANTY HOSE

If you're sanding wood and want to know when it's smooth enough, use the panty-hose test: Slip an old nylon stocking over your hand and run it over the wood. You'll have no trouble finding the slightest rough spot.

LESS MESS

Do you hide a key outdoors? Keep it clean by stashing it in a plastic bag before you stick it under a rock or bury it under a shrub.

CULTIVATE THAT DRIP

You can keep your water lines from freezing during a cold snap by leaving one of the taps running very slightly. If you have a two-story house, open a tap on the first floor.

DON'T PAINT YOUR PORES

Slather on a heavy layer of hand moisturizer before painting or doing other dirty chores. It will prevent dirt and paint from seeping into your skin and make personal cleanup easier.

HANDY RULER

If you just need a ballpark measurement, a dollar bill is just more than six inches long. Its actual dimensions: 6⅛ by 2⅝ inches.

BUBBLE, BUBBLE, TOIL AND TROUBLE

Stir varnish thoroughly from the bottom of the can, but don't stir vigorously. Stirring creates air bubbles, which may ruin a smooth finish.

SCRATCH AND SNIFF

To restore the aroma—and moth-repelling properties—to cedar blocks or a cedar chest, rub the wood lightly with fine sandpaper.

ALL-PURPOSE, OF COURSE

If you are painting old woodwork that has small holes that need patching, try filling the holes with flour and some of the paint. It will harden and will not be noticeable.

STICKY DRAWERS?

Wooden drawers with wooden runners will glide smoothly if you rub a candle along the tops of the runners.

DID YOU KNOW?

Air bubbles in varnish can be brushed out while the varnish is still wet. If you notice them when it's dry, gently buff them out with very fine steel wool.

A CHILLING SOLUTION

If you don't feel up to the job of cleaning a paint roller, wrap it in foil or in a plastic bag and place in the freezer. This will keep the roller moist and usable for a few days.

AND A LO-O-NG EXTENSION CORD

If your pipes freeze but do not burst, use a blow-dryer to thaw them. As always, though, take care that the appliance doesn't get wet.

TRY TO KEEP IT TOGETHER

Lightweight materials that need to be glued together are easily held in place with spring clothespins.

SOFTENING THEM UP

If a paint brush hardens, soften it by soaking in full-strength white vinegar, and then clean it with a comb.

KEEPING GREASE IN ITS PLACE

If you have grease spots on the wall after removing wallpaper, apply a coat of clear varnish to the spots. The grease won't soak through to the new wallpaper.

BALLOONING

To keep a partially used can of paint fresh longer, blow up a balloon until it is about the size of the space in the can; then put it in the can before covering. It will reduce the amount of air in the can and keep paint from drying.

SUN-DRIED CHAIR BOTTOM

Caning can loosen on chairs, but it can be tightened. Apply very hot water to the underside, then dry the chair direct sunlight.

A WASTE OF A COOL ONE

To temporarily "frost" a bathroom window, mix a solution of 1 cup light beer and 4 tablespoons Epsom salts. Then paint the mixture on the window. The paint will wash off easily.

PEEL PREVENTOR

Bathroom light fixtures should be painted with a special epoxy paint because of their frequent exposure to moisture.

A SHINING EXAMPLE

Enamel or oil paint can be removed from your hands easily. Rub with floor paste wax, then wash with soap and water.

SKIN TIP

To prevent a skin forming on top of the paint, try placing a piece of waxed paper the size of the opening on top of the paint.

OIL YOUR BRISTLES

After you clean out a paint brush, rub a few drops of vegetable oil into the bristles to keep them soft.

FOR A WHITER WHITE

If you add seven to 10 drops of black paint to each quart of white paint, it will keep the white from yellowing over time.

TILL YOU'RE OLD AND GRAY

If you allow wood to "weather" before you apply a stain, the stain will last years longer. This is a case where patience pays off.

DON'T CRACK UP

To prevent plaster walls from cracking when driving in a nail, place a small piece of tape over the spot before hammering in the nail.

DON'T FENCE ME IN

Never hang lights on a metal fence, even if the lights are approved for outdoor use. There is the hazard of electric shock.

SWIMMING POOL SAFETY

They're wonderful on hot summer days, but swimming pools require vigilance—particularly in terms of safety.

In 1994, 900 people drowned in their homes; 350 were under age four. If you have a swimming pool, it should be surrounded by a fence, ideally isolation pool fencing. This is a fence that separates the pool from the house, has gates that close and latch by themselves, and cannot be scaled. Your state may require that you have additional security precautions, such as alarms on doors that lead to the pool. Whether such safety features are mandated by law in your area, if you have small children or play host to small children on a regular basis, you may wish to install such devices.

◆ Keep all toys out of the pool area. Remove pool toys and store them out of sight, so small children are not tempted to go in unsupervised.

◆ Empty small wading pools of water after each use. Children can drown in them, and they are breeding ground for mosquitoes.

◆ Whenever children are near water, they require constant adult supervision. Don't take your eyes off them, not even for one second. If there's a large group of children, the number of adults in the immediate area should always be proportionate to provide adequate attention.

25
CLEAN UP YOUR ACT

TWO CRUCIAL RULES FOR STAIN REMOVAL

◆ Never wash any fabric before attempting to remove the stain. Washing in a detergent and the heat of the dryer may actually set the stain and make it impossible to remove later.

◆ Stains on washable fabrics should be treated as soon as possible. Remember, fresh stains will come out more easily than old ones. Items that normally go to the dry cleaner should be taken there as soon as possible. Point out the stain to the dry cleaner, and identify what caused it. Different stains can require very different treatments.

DRY VS. LIQUID BLEACH

Bleach doesn't remove stains, but simply masks them. Dry bleach is made of sodium perborate, which is converted to hydrogen peroxide, which continues to break down, liberating oxygen. This action ultimately oxidizes the clothing. Liquid bleach contains the chemical sodium hypochlorite, which causes the release of chlorine gas that oxidizes the clothing, thus bleaching the stain out. Of the two, liquid bleach is more powerful and effective, but not necessarily safest.

MAGICAL SPOT REMOVERS?

Don't be taken in by TV commercials and newspaper ads touting cleaners that take any spot or stain out of any fabric. They're often just a combination of a detergent and bleach. Most do work well, but you can make them effectively at home.

DON'T WASTE YOUR MONEY

If you wash clothes in cold water, you don't need to purchase a special cold-water detergent. The difference between detergents formulated for hot and cold water washing is insignificant. The only compound that is capable of changing the effectiveness of a detergent is a surfactant, and most detergents have similar amounts. Surfactants actually make the water "wetter" by changing the surface tension, so the water and detergent enter the fibers of the garment more freely.

LIGHTS ON

When trying to remove stains at home, make sure you do it on a clean, well-lit work surface. Always use clean rags or a towel.

RUST REMOVAL

Remove rust stains by wetting the spots with lemon juice, then sprinkling with salt. Let the fabric stand in direct sunlight for 30 to 45 minutes.

THAT BURNING SENSATION

Scorch marks will come out if you rub the area with a raw onion and let the onion juice soak in thoroughly—for at least two to three hours—before washing. Try this on ink stains, too.

MAKE SURE IT'S CHILLED

Blood stains may be cleaned with cold club soda. Just pour it on and rub with a soft cloth.

A SHINING EXAMPLE

To shine chrome fixtures, dampen them, and then rub them with newspaper. Baby oil and a soft cloth work well, too.

A WORD TO THE WISE

If you are going to use a commercial stain remover, be sure to follow directions to the letter.

TESTING, ONE, TWO

Always test a stain remover on an area of the fabric that will not show to be sure how colorfast the fabric is. Allow the product to stand on the area for at least three to five minutes before rinsing it off. If there are any changes in the fabric's color, do not use the remover.

OUT, DAMNED SPOT

When treating a spot, place the cloth with the stain facedown on paper towels, then apply stain remover to the back of the cloth, allowing the stain to be forced to the surface and not back through the fabric. If the stain is stubborn, replace the paper towels frequently.

Did You Know?

Most solvents are highly volatile. Heed all warnings on bottles as to use, storage, and proper disposal of empty containers to prevent disasters.

STAIN BEGONE

As soon as the stain is removed, launder immediately with your favorite laundry detergent. This will also remove the residues from the stain remover.

STAIN REMOVAL PRODUCTS

Prompt treatment is the key to stain removal, and it's wise to have the supplies on hand at all times. In the following lists are some of the more common items needed for most stain removal. In case you run out of an item, look in this chapter for natural stain removers, as well as tips for using common cleaning products.

Cleaner Uppers	
BLEACHES	Chlorine bleach Fabric color remover Nonchlorine, all-fabric bleach
MISCELLANEOUS REMOVERS	Ammonia Rust-stain remover White vinegar
DETERGENTS	Enzyme detergent Enzyme presoak Liquid detergent
SOLVENTS	Dry-cleaner spot remover Nail-polish remover Rubbing alcohol Turpentine
SOAPS	Laundry detergent White bar soap
SUPPLIES	Clean white cloths Paper towels

CAUTION

Some stain removal materials are flammable, while others are poisonous or toxic. Store them safely and use them with care. Never allow chemicals near your face and eyes; wear rubber gloves and safety goggles in case they splash. Wash any spilled chemicals off your hands as soon as possible.

CHEMICAL ALERT

Keep stain removal supplies out of the reach of children. They should be stored in closed containers, ideally their original ones, with childproof lids and in a cool, dry location away from any food products.

SMELLS NICE, TOO

Lemon extract will remove black scuff marks from shoes and luggage. So will rubbing alcohol.

DON'T WRITE IT OFF

Ball-point-pen ink stains can be removed with hair spray. Rubbing alcohol may remove a number of ink-pen stains, too.

CONTAINER SMARTS

Empty and wash all stain-removal containers immediately after using them. It is best to store stain removal supplies in their original containers. If you need to transfer them to smaller containers to use, opt for glass or unchipped porcelain containers. Solvents will ruin plastic. Rusty containers should never be used.

WEAR A GAS MASK

Use chemicals that give off vapors only in a well-ventilated location, preferably outside. A mask specifically designed to protect from fumes is necessary so you don't inhale harmful vapors.

PO-O-OF

Caution! Never use a solvent near an open fire or even something that seems as benign as a lit cigarette or an electrical outlet. Nearly all solvents are extremely flammable.

MACHINE MANAGEMENT

Never add solvents directly to the washing machine. Always let a solvent-treated fabric dry before washing or putting it into the dryer.

A WITCHES' BREW

Never mix stain removal materials, especially ammonia and chlorine bleach. If it necessary to use both, make sure one is thoroughly rinsed out before adding the other.

SAFE CLEANING PRODUCTS

Any recipes below are safe when mixed exactly as directed. Varying from these quantities or from these products may be dangerous.

All-Purpose Household Cleaner

Add 1 teaspoon of any liquid soap and 1 teaspoon of trisodium phosphate (TSP) to 1 quart of warm water. This is a very effective cleaner for many cleaning jobs, including countertops and walls. However, try an area of the wall that will not show before using it, in case your walls are painted with a poor-quality water-based flat paint.

Chlorine Bleach

Best to use a hydrogen peroxide–based bleach.

Degreaser (engines, etc.)

Use a water-based cleaner that is well diluted (instead of kerosene or turpentine) or a commercial engine degreaser, available in auto-parts stores. Look for labels that say "nonflammable," "nontoxic," or "store at temperatures above freezing." These are water-based products and will do the job.

Degreaser (kitchen, grill)

Add 2 tablespoons of TSP to 1 gallon of hot water, or use a scouring pad or steel-wool pad sprinkled with a nonchlorinated scouring cleanser.

Fabric Softener

Fabrics made of from natural fibers do not need fabric softeners; only synthetics do. Add ¼ to ½ cup of baking soda to the wash cycle to soften synthetic fabrics.

Floor Cleaner

For mopping vinyl floors, use ½ cup of white vinegar added to 1 gallon of warm water. For wood floors, damp-mop with a mild liquid soap.

Furniture Polish

Mineral oil may be used, however, most wood surfaces may be cleaned with a damp cloth.

Oven Cleaner

Mix 2 tablespoons of baking soda or TSP in 1 gallon of warm water and scrub with a very fine steel wool pad (0000 grade). Rubber gloves should be worn and the area rinsed well. For difficult baked-on areas, try scrubbing with a pumice stone. If this fails, use an oven cleaner that states "no caustic fumes" on the label.

Glass Cleaner

Fill a 3-cup spray bottle with ½ teaspoon of liquid soap, 3 tablespoons of white vinegar and 2 cups of warm water. If the windows are very dirty, use more liquid soap.

Laundry Detergent

Use laundry soap instead of detergent. Washing soda may be used in place of a fabric softener. An alternate would be to use a detergent with no added bleaches or softeners. Bleach should be used in moderation, and only when needed.

Mildew Remover

Scrub the area with baking soda; if very stubborn, scrub with TSP.

Scouring Powder

Baking soda will work well in most instances.

Toilet Bowl Cleaner

Use a nonchlorinated scouring powder and a stiff brush. To remove hard-water deposits, pour white vinegar, a mixture of white vinegar and baking soda, or a commercial citric acid-based toilet bowl cleaner into the toilet and allow to sit for several hours or overnight before scrubbing.

AN IMPORTANT NOTE

Washing soda and TSP are caustic and should always be kept out of the reach of children. TSP is a skin irritant—so always wear rubber gloves to protect your hands.

FABRIC ADVICE

To clean garments, tablecloths, and other items properly, refer to the attached care label. If you remove sewn-in labels, save them and note which item they came from to avoid problems.

Any durable press or polyester fabric will hold soil and stains very well. A dry cleaning solvent may be necessary. If the stain remains after the first treatment, try once more. If the fabric has been washed or has been put in a dryer, the stain may never come out.

DID YOU KNOW?

If candle wax drips onto candle holders, put them in the freezer until the wax hardens. It will pop right off.

◆ Never use chlorine bleach on silk, wool, or Lycra spandex.

◆ Never try to remove a stain from leather. Take it to a dry cleaner that specializes in cleaning leather.

SUEDE STRATEGIES

Water spots can be removed from suede by rubbing lightly with an emery board. If there are grease spots on suede, blot with white vinegar, then brush lightly with a suede brush.

CAN'T PERFORM MAGIC

Remember, even the best enzyme detergent or enzyme presoak product is not capable of removing all types of stains. Grease and highly colored stains may require special pretreatment before laundering. Because many stains require a variety of different treatments and techniques, it is important to identify a stain before trying to remove it. A number of stains may actually be set if the wrong method is used.

The following stains can usually be removed with the recommended methods that are specified. Use these treatments on washable fabrics only. Treat the stain, then make sure it is gone before drying the fabric. Once it dries, the stain may never come out.

Stain	Method of Removal
Alcoholic beverage	Sponge the area with cold water or soak, then sponge again. Launder with oxygen bleach and the hottest water that is safe for the fabric.
Blood	Soak the fabric in cold water as soon as possible. If the stain persists, soak in warm water with a presoak product before laundering. Try club soda.
Candle wax	Scrape off surface wax with a dull knife. Place the item stained side down on paper towels and sponge the remaining stain with dry cleaning solvent. Let dry, and then launder. If traces of color from the wax remains, try soaking it in an enzyme presoak or an oxygen bleach before laundering again. If the stain is still present, launder again using chlorine bleach, if the fabric is chlorine-bleach safe.

Stain	Method of Removal
Ketchup and tomato products	Remove excess with a dull knife, then soak in cold water 30 minutes before laundering in the hottest water the fabric will stand.
Chewing gum, adhesive tape, rubber cement	First apply ice to the adhesive to harden it. Scrape off as much as you can with a dull knife. Place the item face down on paper towels and sponge with a dry-cleaning solvent.
Chocolate and cocoa	Soak the article in cold water 30 minutes, then launder with oxygen bleach using the hottest water the fabric will stand.
Coffee and tea	Soak in an enzyme presoak or oxygen bleach using the hottest water that is safe for the fabric for 30 minutes, then launder. If the stain is still present, launder again using chlorine bleach if it is safe to do so.
Cosmetics	Dampen stain with water and rub gently with white bar soap, then rinse well and launder.
Crayon	If there are only a few spots they can be treated the same as candle wax. If there are many items that are stained, first wash the items with hot water and laundry soap (e.g., Ivory Snow)—not laundry detergent—and 1 cup baking soda. If the spots remain, have the clothes dry-cleaned.
Deodorants and antiperspirants	Apply white vinegar, then rub and rinse. If the stain remains, saturate the area with rubbing alcohol, rinse, then soak in Biz or an oxygen bleach, and launder. If the stain remains, wash in chlorine bleach if it is safe for the fabric.
Dye transfer	If you have white fabrics that have picked up dye from a colored garment that bled, restore the white by using a fabric color remover. If any of the dye remains, launder using chlorine bleach if it is safe for the fabric.
Egg and meat juice	Remove excess with a dull knife, then soak in cold water 30 minutes. Then launder in oxygen bleach in very hot water.
Fabric softeners	Fabric softener stains usually result from accidental spills and can be removed by rubbing the area with a piece of cloth moistened with bar soap before laundering. You can also try a paste of water and detergent, or a prewash stain remover.

507

Stain	Method of Removal
Infant Formula	Soak in warm water, then launder with oxygen bleach in the hottest water that is safe for the fabric.
Fruit and fruit juices	Soak in cold water before laundering.
Grass	The green area should be sponged with denatured alcohol before washing in very hot water and oxygen bleach.
Grease stains	The stained area should be placed facedown on paper towels. Blot with dry cleaning solvent on the back side of the stain, then brush from the center of the stain to the outer edges using a clean white cloth. Moisten the stain with warm water and rub with bar soap or mild liquid detergent, then rinse and launder.
Gum	Rub with ice and carefully remove the gum with a dull knife before laundering.
Ink stains	To remove ink ball-point pen ink, place the stain face down on paper towels and sponge the back of the stain with dry cleaning solvent. If there is some ink left, try rubbing the area with moistened bar soap, rinse, and then launder.

For ink except ball-point or felt-tip pen ink, try to remove the stain with a dampened cloth and bar soap, rinse, and soak in an enzyme presoak or oxygen bleach using very hot water. If the stain won't come out, try chlorine bleach, if the fabric is safe. Some permanent inks may never be removed.

For felt-tip pen ink, rub the area with Fantastick or Mr. Clean, rinse, and repeat if necessary. These stains may be impossible to remove. |
Iodine	Rinse the fabric from the underside with cool water, then soak in a solution of fabric color remover, rinse, and launder.
Lipstick	Place so the stain is face down on paper towels, then sponge with dry-cleaning solvent, replacing the paper towels frequently. Moisten the stain with cool water and rub with bar soap, then rinse and launder.
Mildew	The fabric should be laundered using chlorine bleach if it is safe for the fabric. If not, soak it in oxygen bleach before laundering.

Stain	Method of Removal
Milk	The fabric should be rinsed in cold water as soon as possible, then washed in cold water using a liquid detergent.
Mustard	Moisten the stain with cool water, then rub with bar soap, rinse and launder using a chlorine bleach, if it is safe for the fabric. If not, soak in an enzyme presoak or oxygen detergent using very hot water, then launder. It may take several treatments to remove all of the stain.
Nail polish	Blot up the excess from both sides of the fabric with paper towels. If the fabric can withstand acetone or nail-polish remover, work it in from the inside of the fabric by pressing it in gently with a paper towel.
Paint	Treat the stain while it is still wet; latex, acrylic, and water-based paints cannot be removed once dried. While the paint is wet, rinse in warm water to flush the paint out, then launder.
	Oil-based paints can be removed with a solvent; your best bet will be to use one recommended on the paint can. If none is mentioned, blot with turpentine, rinse, and rub with bar soap, then launder.
Perspiration	Moisten the stain and rub with bar soap. Be gentle, as perspiration may weaken some fibers, especially silk. Most fabrics should be presoaked in an enzyme presoak or detergent and then laundered in hot water and chlorine bleach, if it is safe to use on the fabric.
Perfume	Same as alcoholic beverages.
Rust	Apply a rust stain remover, rinse, then launder. You can also use a fabric color remover and then launder, or if the stain is really stubborn, dissolve 1 ounce of oxalic-acid crystals (or straight warm rhubarb juice) in 1 gallon of water in a clean plastic container. Soak the garment in this solution until the stain is gone, then rinse and launder. Never use chlorine bleach on rust.
Scorch marks	For washable fabrics, use all-fabric bleach. For non washables, use hydrogen peroxide.
Shoe polish	Try applying a mixture of 1 part rubbing alcohol and 2 parts of water for colored fabrics and only the straight alcohol for whites. Sponge this on, then launder.

509

Stain	Method of Removal
Tar	Rub gently with kerosene until all the tar is dissolved, then wash as usual. Test a small area first to be sure the fabric is color fast.
Tobacco	Moisten the stain and rub with bar soap, then rinse and launder. If the stain persists, try soaking it in an enzyme presoak or oxygen detergent before laundering. As a last resort use chlorine bleach, if it is safe for the fabric.
Urine, vomit, and mucus	Soak the fabric in an enzyme presoak or detergent, then launder using chlorine bleach, if safe for the fabric. If not, use an oxygen bleach with a detergent.
Wine and soft drinks	Soak the fabric with an enzyme presoak or oxygen bleach using very hot water, then launder. Use chlorine bleach if needed and if it is safe for the fabric.

TOTALLY THRIFTY

If you wish to use less detergent and save money, put slivers of old soap in a sock with the neck tied. Put the sock into the washer and you can get away with using less detergent.

SETTING IT PERMANENTLY

To make a possibly problematic garment more colorfast, soak it in cold, salty water for 30 minutes before laundering for the first time.

STAIN REMOVAL FROM WASHABLE FABRICS

A number of stains can be removed right in your washing machine. Laundry detergents that state that they contain enzymes will provide the best cleaning and stain removal. Enzyme presoak products provide extra cleaning and stain removal for fabrics that may have more difficult stains.

An enzyme detergent or enzyme presoak product should be able to remove the following common stains: blood, gravy, body soils, egg, fruits, milk, chocolate, grass, cream soups, infant formula, baby foods, pudding, vegetables, ice cream, and most other food stains.

GET THE YELLOW OUT

Yellowed fabrics can be restored to white and even old, unknown stains may be removed by soaking in an enzyme presoak before laundering.

ZIPPER TRICK

After washing a piece of clothing with a zipper that has been sticking, rub beeswax on the zipper to solve the problem.

THE OLD BUBBLE MACHINE

Adding too much soap to the washing machine can cause bubbles to overflow, and it won't get the clothes any cleaner than if you used the correct amount. If you add too much, pour in 2 tablespoons of white vinegar or a capful of fabric softener to neutralize some of the soap.

BEGONE, OLD SOAP

If you suspect the rinse cycle isn't getting all the soap out of your clothes, add 1 cup of white vinegar while they are rinsing. The vinegar will dissolve the alkalinity in detergents as well as give the clothes a pleasant fragrance.

NATURAL SOLUTIONS

Get this—you can get rid of grass stains with toothpaste. Scrub it into the fabric with a toothbrush before washing. Or rub the stain with molasses and let stand overnight, then wash with regular dish soap by itself. If all else fails, try methyl alcohol, but be sure the garment is colorfast.

RETIRE YOUR IRON

Banish wrinkles easily by removing clothes from the dryer the second it stops. Fold or hang them up immediately.

THE RIGHT WAY TO WASH

Your clothes will get cleaner if you turn the washer on while it's empty, add the detergent, and let the detergent dissolve and mix with the water before you add the laundry. Putting detergent onto clothes that are still dry can cause dyes to fade.

DID YOU KNOW?

Your clothes will get cleaner if you don't overload the washer. They need to be able to move freely during the different cycles.

CATCH THAT COLOR

Washing colored material for the first time may be risky unless you wash it in salt first. Add ¼ to ½ cup salt to the wash water (about 1 teaspoon per gallon of water). The colors will not run.

THE DISAPPEARING ACT

If you have nongreasy stains on washable fabrics, an excellent spot remover can be made using 2 parts of water to 1 part of rubbing alcohol. Test for colorfastness by applying to an inconspicuous area first.

A DIRTY JOB

To remove dirt from difficult areas like shirt or blouse collars, mix ⅓ cup water, ⅓ cup of liquid detergent, and ⅓ cup ammonia in a spray bottle. Rubbing shampoo into the area may also do the job. Just be sure you never mix ammonia with bleach.

INSIDE OUT

To keep corduroy garments from retaining lint, wash them inside out. This also will keep acrylic sweaters from pilling.

DARK AS NIGHT

Two tricks for keeping dark clothes dark: Wash them inside out, and air dry them; if you dry them outside, keep them inside out or dry them out of direct sunlight. Rubbing darks against other clothes as well as the insides of the washer and dryer will fade them fast.

ONE OF THE TOUGHEST

Iodine stains can be removed using a mixture of baking soda and water. Allow to remain on for about 30 minutes, then rub gently.

IT'S PRETTY MESSY

Petroleum jelly will remove tar from clothing; just rub it in until the tar is gone. Remove the jelly with any type of spray-and-wash product.

BEWARE OF A TIGHT FIT

If you wash slipcovers, put them back on your furniture while the covers are still damp. Not only will the slipcovers be easier to get on, but they will also not need to be ironed.

BLOW-DRYING

If cuffs or necklines of woolen sweaters are stretched out of shape, dip them in hot water and dry with a blow-dryer.

A SPOT OF TEA

Remove tea stains from tablecloths with glycerin. Let it sit overnight before washing. Glycerin, which is available at pharmacies, is a wonder for softening old stains before laundering.

INTO THE FREEZER

Candle wax on tablecloths? Remove it by rubbing with an ice cube and then scraping with a dull knife.

HOLD THE SHAVING CREAM

A pilling problem with your sweater? A disposable razor does a wonderful job of removing small pills from sweaters.

EASY DOES IT

Wash woolen garments with great care, since wool fibers are very weak when wet. Don't pull, stretch, or wring out the garment. Instead, roll it in a towel and squeeze the excess water out, and then dry flat.

NEUTRALIZER

For difficult blood stains on fabric, try making a paste of meat tenderizer and cold water. Sponge it on the area; let stand for 20 to 30 minutes. Rinse in cold water, and then wash. Hydrogen peroxide may also work.

BATHING STUFFED ANIMALS

To clean stuffed animals that cannot be placed in the washer, just place them in a cloth bag or pillowcase, add baking soda, and shake.

A SLIPPERY SUBJECT

Vaseline will help loosen lipstick stains, grease, and tar. Use a solvent afterward, and then launder.

HONEY, I SHRUNK THE SWEATER

If you shrink a woolen garment, soak it for 15 minutes in a mixture of ½ cup hair conditioner and 1 gallon lukewarm water, then squeeze out the excess solution. This will help to soften the fibers so you can gently stretch the article back to the original size. Another method is to dissolve 1 ounce Borax in 1 teaspoon hot water, and then add it to 1 gallon warm water. Place the garment in the solution, stretch back to shape, and then rinse it in 1 gallon warm water with 2 tablespoons white vinegar added.

BE STINGY, BE SMART

When you are doing a small wash load, tear the fabric-softening sheet in half and get the same results.

A SOLID FACT

To make your own spray starch, purchase a bottle of liquid starch concentrate and mix equal parts of liquid starch and water in a spray bottle.

SECURING A BUTTON

When buttons pop off, sew them back on with unwaxed dental floss, which is much stronger than thread.

THEY WERE CLEAN WHEN THEY WENT IN THE WASHING MACHINE . . .

Does it seem as though your clothes get greasy stains on them in the laundry? It may not be your imagination. One cause: adding undiluted fabric softener. Always dilute it, because it can cause stains that look greasy. Remove these stains by pretreating the fabric with a paste made of water and detergent, or with a prewash stain remover.

BRING IN THE SUB

If you prefer not to use bleach when doing laundry, substitute 3 tablespoons hydrogen peroxide in the wash load.

SAVE THE BUTTONS

A tip for the thrifty (and clever): Always remove buttons before discarding a garment. They may come in handy later.

ATTRACTIVE SALT

Clean silk flowers easily by placing them, bloom end down, in a plastic bag with 2 tablespoons of salt. Hold onto the stems and close the bag, then shake vigorously. Salt tends to attract the dust.

BE COOL, BE SMART

Always start your ironing with silk, rayon, and other delicate fabrics that require a cool temperature, before the iron heats up.

DEW TELL

Remove mildew from plastic shower curtains. Wash the curtain with two large white bath towels in ½ cup bleach and ½ cup powdered detergent in a washing machine filled with water. To prolong the life of the shower curtain, add 1 cup white vinegar to the rinse cycle.

MAKING COLORS FAST

To prevent jeans from fading, soak them in ½ cup white vinegar and 2 quarts of water for one hour before you wash them for the first time.

JEAN SMARTS

To minimize shrinking, wash blue jeans in cold water, dry them on medium heat for only 10 minutes, and then air dry them the rest of the way.

JUST A SHADE CLEANER

Smudges and stains on your window shades? Lay the shades on a table or countertop and rub the spots with an art-gum eraser.

DID YOU KNOW?

Always used distilled water in your iron. Tap water contains impurities and minerals that will ruin the iron over time.

DOLLAR SAVER

Dry-cleaning wool blankets can break the bank. Save money by washing them with mild dishwashing liquid in cold water on the gentle cycle, then air fluff to dry.

NO ONE WILL EVER KNOW

If you scorch a garment when ironing, cover the scorch mark with a vinegar-dampened cloth, then iron with a warm iron (not too hot). Scorch marks on cotton, however, tend to remove better with hydrogen peroxide.

BUTTON, BUTTON....

Dab a small amount of clear nail polish in the center of every button on a new garment. This seals the threads and makes them last longer.

A SHOCKING SITUATION

Dip a pipe cleaner in white vinegar and use it to clean the holes in an iron after it is completely cool. Just make sure the iron is unplugged!

IF YOU'RE IN A SPOT

Glass cleaner sometimes makes an excellent spot remover if you need something clean in a hurry. Make sure the fabric is colorfast.

BRIGHTEN UP

To get the whitest whites, add a cup of dishwasher detergent with the laundry detergent. This even whitens sweat socks.

ANY PENCIL WILL DO

A sticky zipper will respond to rubbing with a lead pencil. The graphite in the pencil does an excellent job of lubricating it.

A TEMPORARY SOLUTION

If a button comes off, try reattaching it with the wire from a twist tie. Just tear the paper off each side of the tie.

DON'T SUCK YOUR THUMB

Do you use a thimble to sew or sort papers? If you wet your finger before you put the thimble on, you'll create suction so the thimble stays put.

A SEALER

After you wash cotton sneakers, spray them with spray starch to help them resist stains in the future.

DIRTY BOTTOM

If the bottom of your iron gets dirty, clean it with a steel-wool soap pad (don't use steel wool if your iron has a nonstick finish). To make it shiny again, just run a piece of waxed paper over it.

A LITTLE BUBBLY

Don't fret over spilled red wine. Just wet the tablecloth with club soda, and let it stand for 20 minutes before washing.

AND AWAY WE GO

To dry the insides of shoes or sneakers quickly, try placing the blower end of the vacuum cleaner hose inside.

NO MORE DAY TRIPS

Shoelaces are more likely to stay tied if you dampen them before tying.

A BLOODY MESS

Blood stains can be incredibly difficult to remove. If the blood is fresh, make a paste of water and talcum, cornstarch, or cornmeal and apply it to the stain. Let it dry, then brush it off. If you have a powdered meat tenderizer, cover the stains with that and cool water. Sponge it off with more cool water after about a half-hour.

SAVES MONEY, TOO

No matter which temperature you choose to wash your clothes, always use a cold-water rinse. It will help the clothes retain their shape and color, and you'll save money and energy by not taxing your water heater.

DID YOU
KNOW?

**Don't use a terry
cloth towel to
cover silk before
ironing—the slubs
in the towel will
"pock" the silk.
Use a pillowcase
or cotton knit
shirt instead.**

A WORD OF CAUTION

If a clothing label of a silk garmet doesn't specify dry-cleaning only, you
can wash it by hand. Silk should be hand-washed using cool water with
mild liquid soap. Always air dry—never place silk in the dryer—and then
iron on the wrong side of the fabric, placing a soft, smooth piece of cloth
over the garment as protection.

COFFEE TALK

Spilled coffee can be very problematic, particularly if it has milk in it
(milk proteins require solutions different from coffee compounds). Here
are three methods that may remove coffee from fabric or carpet:

◆ Dip a white cloth in a beaten egg yolk. Rub the yolk into the stain, then
   rinse with clean water.
◆ Blot denatured alcohol into the stain, then rinse with water.
◆ Mix a solution of ½ teaspoon of mild detergent and 2 cups of warm
   water. Blot this solution into the stain. If the stain remains, blot with a
   50-50 solution of white vinegar and water.

If the inside of your cup is stained, one of these methods should have it
looking like new. Be sure to wash the mug thoroughly afterward.

◆ Mix a paste of coarse salt or baking soda and water; or use a 50-50 mixture of salt and white vinegar. Scrub the mug with this, then rinse well.
◆ Dissolve a denture cleaning tablet in the mug and let stand overnight.
◆ For a lot of stained mugs, put them a solution of ½ cup of household
   bleach and 2 quarts of water. Let the cups stand overnight.

IN VINO VERITAS

If you spill wine on a tablecloth, blot up as much as you can as soon as
you can with a cloth, then sponge with cool water. If the fabric is not
machine washable, cover the stain with a small cloth dampened with a
solution of detergent, water, and vinegar, then rinse. Get the cloth to the
drycleaner as soon as you can.

TOY STORY

Stuffed animals and plush toys can be vacuumed; use the upholstery
brush attachment. If they're still dirty and cannot be machine-washed, put a
few cups of cornmeal into a large bag, add the toy, and shake the bag vigorously. Then brush the cornmeal off the toys.

26
GRAB BAG

SOMETHING TO CUDDLE UP WITH

A one-liter plastic soda bottle can make an excellent hot-water bottle in an emergency. Just make sure that you wrap it in a hand towel before you place it against your skin.

A FOREIGN PROBLEM

Imported dinnerware, especially pottery and some types of crystal, may still contain traces of lead and other heavy metals. Acidic foods, like vinegar in salad dressings, lemon juice, or even tomatoes, may be strong enough to release these metals.

SHAKE, RATTLE, AND ROLL

To remove an unsightly residue buildup inside a vase or bottle, try a solution of 2 tablespoons salt, enough raw rice to create friction, and 1 cup white vinegar. Cover and shake vigorously.

DECAL BEGONE

Transparent decals may be easily removed using a solution of lukewarm water and white vinegar. Place the solution on a sponge and dampen the area thoroughly for a few minutes. If this doesn't work, saturate the decal with straight vinegar and let stand for 15 minutes.

COVER UP

To cover a scratch on your refrigerator or freezer, try using the same color enamel paint. This really works great and will last a long time.

GREASE REMOVER

To clean your electric can opener, run a piece of paper towel through it. This will pick up the grease and some of the gunk.

STREAKER

If the sun is shining on your windows, wait until they are in the shade to wash them. When they dry too fast, they tend to streak.

PUT A LID ON IT

If there's a grease fire in a pan, cover the pan with a lid. You'll cut off the oxygen supply and the fire will go out.

ALCOHOL TO THE RESCUE

Remove unsightly black soot marks from candles of any kind by sponging them with rubbing alcohol.

BE GENTLE

Buff away a nick on the rim of a glass with an emery board. Don't use a nail file or sandpaper; both are too coarse and will scratch the glass.

PASS THE PEANUT BUTTER, HOLD THE HAIR

One of the best methods of removing chewing gum from a child's hair is to use a small amount of smooth peanut butter.

LEATHER REVIVAL

To revive the beauty of leather, lightly beat two egg whites, then apply to the leather with a soft sponge. Allow the egg whites to remain on the leather for three to five minutes, and then wipe it off with a soft cloth dampened with clear warm water. Dry immediately, and buff off any residue.

ODOR EATERS

Besides baking soda, a number of other foods are capable of removing odors. Pour a little vanilla extract into a bottle cap and set in the refrigerator to absorb odors. Dry mustard is commonly used to eliminate fish odors from hands and cutting boards. Just don't get it in your eyes!

ON A CLEAR DAY

To prevent windows from steaming up, rub the insides with equal amounts of glycerin, followed by methyl alcohol (also called methanol). This combination will neutralize the buildup of minor condensation.

DID YOU KNOW?

To make your house smell great, simmer apple cider with a cinnamon stick and a few whole cloves. Also add a bit of orange peel, if you like.

DON'T POUR IT DOWN THE DRAIN

Stale milk will do a great job of cleaning plant leaves. The protein in milk called casein has a mild cleansing effect on the plant cell walls.

SOLUTION FROM THE PANTRY

If you run out of furniture polish, try vegetable oil on wood furniture. A very light coat will help protect the finish, but be sure to rub it in well so that it doesn't leave a residue. Leftover tea and mayonnaise can also be used on wood furniture.

POURING SALT ON AN OPEN SPILL

If you spill red wine on your carpet, pour salt on the area as soon as possible and watch it absorb the wine almost instantly. Wait until it dries, then vacuum it up. Salt tends to provide a special capillary attraction that will work for most liquids. Baking soda, with its high sodium content, works with wine, too. Salt also works on mud stains.

MONEY SAVER

Don't bother buying fancy dust cloths that are treated to attract dust! Instead, simply sprinkle a piece of cheesecloth with a few drops of lemon oil. Let the cheesecloth air dry, and it will do just as good a job as an expensive cloth.

SHAKE, BABY, SHAKE

If you wish to make a quick and unique salad dressing, just place a small amount of olive oil and wine vinegar inside an almost-empty ketchup bottle and shake.

LEMON TREE, VERY USEFUL

For a brighter shoeshine, place a few drops of lemon juice on your shoes when you are polishing them. Also, a small amount of lemon juice mixed with salt will remove mold and mildew from most surfaces. The juice is just acidic enough to do the job.

TRY IT—YOU'LL BECOME A BELIEVER

To remove glue residue on almost any surface, try vegetable oil on a rag. Residue from sticky labels is also a breeze to remove this way. The vegetable oil tends to neutralize the glue's bonds.

A GIRL'S BEST FRIEND

A 50-50 solution of white vinegar and warm water can easily clean gold jewelry and all gemstones except opals, pearls, and emeralds. (Opals, emeralds, and pearls are too delicate for this type of treatment and should be professionally cleaned.) Dip a soft toothbrush into the solution and brush gently. Hot sudsy water and a bit of ammonia also work. Costume jewelry should be cleaned only with a weak solution of baking soda and water to avoid damaging the glue bonds.

EXTINGUISHING THE OLD FLAME

Baking soda is one of the best fire extinguishers. It cuts off the oxygen supply and the flame goes right out. Always keep an open box next to the stove to dump onto grease fires—and *never* use water!

A POPPER OUTER

Tough nut and bolts are easy to remove after you pour cola or another carbonated beverage on them and allow it to sit for about 20 minutes. The citric or phosphoric acid is just strong enough to loosen any corrosion or gunk that's making the metals stick.

NEUTRALIZE ME

The corrosion around your car battery posts can easily be cleaned with a thick solution of baking soda and water. Let it stand for 10 to 15 minutes before washing it off. Baking soda is a mild alkali and will neutralize the weak acid on the battery.

SMILE!

Here's a method of cleaning dentures that works as well as the expensive spreads: Soak them overnight in white vinegar.

RING AROUND THE TABLE

Does your wood furniture sport white rings left from wet glasses? Remove them with a mixture of 2 tablespoons corn oil and enough salt to make a paste. Apply the paste to the rings and let stand for at least one hour before rubbing the area gently. If the finish on your furniture is very delicate, you can substitute baking soda for the salt (it's less abrasive).

A NUTTY SOLUTION

To mask scratches in wood furniture, rub gently with the broken edges of nut meats (not the shells!); the results will surprise you. Just find a nut that matches the color of the wood. The most common ones for this purpose are pecans, walnuts, and hazelnuts.

IT REALLY HITS THE SPOT

Have a load of greasy clothes? Pour a can of cola into the load along with the detergent. It will really improve the cleaning action of most detergents. Colas contain a weak acid that will help to dissolve the grease. Cola can also be used to clean the rings off toilets. Pour into the bowl, let sit for one hour, and then brush and flush.

FILL 'ER UP

A trick used by antique dealers to hide hairline cracks on china plates or cups is to simmer the piece in milk for 45 minutes. Depending on the size of the crack, casein (which is the protein in the milk) may fill in the crack. If your china is old or fragile, though, this could backfire—heat can cause pieces to expand and crack.

BUG SLIDE

Spray vegetable oil on a clean car bumper before a trip to make it easy to remove the bugs when you return.

A GREAT GRATER TIP

Cleaning a cheese grater will never be a problem if you grate a small piece of raw potato before trying to wash it out. Sometimes an old toothbrush also comes in handy for cleaning graters.

GREASE CUTTER

If you are expecting to have a problem cleaning a real greasy pan, add a few drops of ammonia to the pan with your soapsuds.

SLOWING DOWN TARNISH

If you place a small piece of chalk in a silver chest, it will absorb moisture and slow tarnishing. Calcium carbonate (chalk) absorbs moisture from the air very slowly. If you break the chalk up and expose the rough surface, it will be more efficient.

BAG 'EM

Professional cooks worldwide keep a small plastic bag handy in case both hands are covered with dough or food and they need to answer the telephone. Or, you could put your hands in plastic bags before mixing meatloaf or kneading dough.

LUCKY FOR YOU

If you have ever wondered why you can reach into a 350°F oven and not be burned, the answer is simple: Air does not conduct heat well. Water conducts heat more efficiently and will easily burn you at lower temperatures. At 140°F, liquids can burn in five seconds; at 160°F, in one second.

MESSY!

The glue on any type of contact paper will melt if you run a warm iron over it or use a blow-dryer on high heat.

SPRINKLE, SPRINKLE

If you want to sharpen up your carpet colors, try sprinkling a small amount of salt over the carpet before you vacuum. The salt provides a mild abrasive cleaning action that won't hurt the fibers.

VERY UPLIFTING

An easy method of raising the nap of a carpet after a piece of furniture has matted it down is to let an ice cube melt into the matted area; wait until the next day to vacuum.

DID YOU KNOW?

Storing sterling silver and silver-plate in an airtight container—or wrapping each piece in plastic wrap—prevents tarnishing.

REMOVING ODORS

To eliminate refrigerator odors, leave a small cup of fresh coffee grounds on two shelves. Deep-frying a small amount of cinnamon will chase all odors from the home. Another excellent method of removing kitchen odors is to keep a few washed charcoal briquettes in a shallow dish on top of the refrigerator.

ROUND AND ROUND WE GO

Have you ever wondered how to get the last drop of ketchup out of the bottle? All you have to is to hold the neck of the bottle and swing the bottle in a circular motion from your side. Hold on tight!

MEASURING UP

To use the fewest cooking utensils possible, first measure out all the dry ingredients, then the wet ingredients. This way, you can reuse the measuring spoons or cups with having to rewash and dry them.

SMART MOVE

Used microwave food containers should be saved and used for leftovers. (Many plastic containers are not microwave safe.) Either store them in the cupboard or fill with food, freeze, and reheat.

MICROWAVE SMARTS

It is always wise to check and see whether a dish is microwave safe and will not melt. Just place the container next to a cup half filled with water and turn the microwave on high for about $1\frac{1}{2}$ minutes, or until the water is boiling. If the dish is hot when you touch it, you should not cook with it.

SLIPPERY SUBJECT

Save the wrappers from unsalted butter. When you need to grease a pan, simply wipe the pan with them. Don't use wrappers from salted butter, since they may cause foods to stick.

DON'T BURST YOUR BUBBLE

Here's an inexpensive solution for children to use when blowing bubbles: Mix 1 tablespoon glycerin with 2 tablespoons a powdered laundry detergent in 1 cup warm water. Any unpainted piece of metal wire can be shaped with a circle on one end to use with the solution. Blowing into the mixture with a straw will make smaller bubbles float into the air. For colored bubbles, add food coloring.

ONE FOR THE GRIPPER

If your drinking glasses are slippery, put a wide rubber band around them so that children can get a better grip.

SAVES ON THE WASHING

To keep melted ice cream from leaking out of ice cream cones, just drop a marshmallow into the bottom of the cone to act as a plug.

A STICKY PROBLEM

Plastic wrap loves to hug itself. If you hate this problem, just keep the box in the refrigerator. The cold keeps the wrap from sticking to itself.

SALVAGE JOB

If you accidentally burn or scorch a food, set the pot or dish into cold water immediately. This will stop the cooking action and minimize the damage. Carefully remove the unburned food—don't scrape—then discard the damaged food. When you reheat the salvaged food, set a fresh piece of white bread on top to remove the burnt odor.

CRUMMY SOLUTION

Too much mayonnaise or salad dressing can ruin a dish. To fix the problem, try adding breadcrumbs to absorb the excess.

REVIVAL

Almost all soft rubber balls, including tennis balls, can be brought back to life and the bounce returned by leaving the balls in an oven with only the pilot light left on overnight. The heat causes the air inside the ball to expand. Just be sure to remove the balls before you turn the oven on!

SUMMERTIME

To keep salt flowing freely in high humidity, add some raw rice to the shaker to absorb the moisture. Rice absorbs moisture very slowly under these conditions and lasts for a long time.

EDIBLE CANDLE HOLDER

Make natural birthday-cake candle holders from small marshmallows. If they are kept refrigerated they will work better.

CLEAN LIVING

If you have a problem with mildew forming in your refrigerator, just spray the inside walls with vegetable oil. Spray the freezer after it has been defrosted and next time it will be easier to defrost.

PUT ON A THIN COAT, PART I

To keep your blender and mixer in top working order, be sure to lubricate all moving parts with a very light coating of mineral oil (not vegetable oil). This should be done every three months.

PUT ON A THIN COAT, PART II

Before using a measuring cup to measure a sticky liquid, coat the inside with vegetable oil or nonstick cooking spray—the liquid will flow freely.

SLICK IDEA

If you have a problem with ice-cube trays sticking to the bottom of the shelf, try placing a piece of waxed paper under the tray. Freezing temperatures do not affect waxed paper.

FREEZER MELT

A common problem with icemakers is that they freeze up. Next time this happens, just use the blow-dryer to defrost the problem. (For safety's sake, keep the dryer away from any pooling water.) This problem won't occur if you release a few ice cubes every few days.

WORKS LIKE MAGIC

The next time you have two drinking glasses stuck together and can't get them apart, try this: Fill the top glass with ice water and then place the bottom one in a few inches of hot tap water in the sink. It should only take a few seconds for them to come unstuck.

GETTING IN SHAPE

Butcher-block and wooden cutting boards can harbor bacteria deep down in the cracks and can be difficult to clean. The boards need to be washed with a mild detergent and then dried thoroughly and covered with a light layer of salt to draw any moisture that may have gotten into the crevices. Leave the salt on overnight before scraping it off. The wood can then be treated with a very light coating of mineral oil. Make sure it is only a light coat, because mineral oil may affect the potency of a number of vitamins in fruits and vegetables.

TIME SAVER

Here's a chef's secret for keeping a grater clean so you can use it repeatedly without washing: Simply grate the softest items first, then grate the firmer ones.

COMING UNGLUED

If your postage stamps are stuck together, place them in the freezer for about 10 minutes. This does not work with self-adhesive stamps.

THRIFTY IDEA

Dishwasher soap can be expensive. If you want to save money, just purchase the least expensive one and add 2 teaspoons of white vinegar to the dishwasher. You dishes will come out spot-free.

CAN PROTECTION

If you've only used part of a can of motor oil, cover the can with a coffee-can lid to keep dust and debris from contaminating the oil.

DID YOU KNOW?

Never put a wooden cutting board into the dishwasher. The high temperatures can damage it.

GETTING BACK ON SOLID GROUND

If you get stuck in snow or mud, try using your car floor mat for traction. Or you could keep a blanket in the trunk for the purpose.

NO NIPPING, IT'S POISON

If your windshield wipers are smearing the windows, wipe the blades with some rubbing alcohol.

LET THERE BE LIGHT

Used plastic or coated-paper milk containers can be filled with old candle wax and kept in the car for emergencies. Place a long candle in the center for the wick. It will burn for hours.

RUB-A-DUB-DUB

To prevent the rubber around your car doors from freezing, rub the rubber moldings with vegetable oil.

BE GENTLE

Steel-wool pads make an excellent white-wall tire cleaner. It's best to use as fine a steel-wool pad as you can find.

THE HALF-GALLON SIZE

Come winter, fill a few old milk cartons with sand or kitty litter and keep them in your car's trunk. If you get stuck, sprinkle the sand on the ice to improve the tires' traction.

TO THE SEAT OF THE PROBLEM

If you place a sheet of fabric softener under your car seat, it will keep your car smelling fresh.

CHURCH KEY TO THE RESCUE

When you can't open a jar, set it in a bowl with a little hot tap water for a few minutes, and then try again. If it's still stuck, carefully work the pointed tip of a puncture-type can opener under the lid and gently loosen the cap. This should release enough pressure to allow you to open the jar.

A SALTY SOLUTION

If you live in a snowy area, keep a container of salt in your glove compartment or trunk. It will help to melt the ice on your windshield.

STUCK ON YOU

A nail polish remover is what you need if you ever glue your fingers together by accident when you're working with a quick-bonding glue or epoxy. If you get stuck working with rubber cement, try lacquer thinner; you may need to let the thinner soak in for a few minutes before gently pulling your fingers apart.

KEEP IT CLEAN

Always clean dust mops after using them. To avoid making a dust cloud, cover a dry dust mop with a damp paper bag before you shake it out. If your mop has a removable head, put it in a large mesh lingerie bag and toss it into the washer.

HOW DRY I AM

Water can collect in umbrella stands. Prevent this by cutting a large sponge to fit in the bottom. Remove it and wring it out as necessary.

WHO'S GOT THE BUTTON?

An easy way to keep your earrings together: Thread the posts through buttons, then attach the backs.

KEEPING IT SHINY

- Polishing silver is never a neat chore, but an old sock can make it easier. Slip the sock over your hand; use one side to apply the polish and the other to buff it out.
- If you have large silver items that are not used with food, consider having them lacquered by a jeweler to prevent tarnishing. Candelabras, vases, and trophies are good candidates for this treatment.
- Sulfur compounds in the air cause tarnish; keeping your silver in airtight containers, or wrapping it in tarnishproof cloths or paper, will help to keep tarnish at bay.
- Never wrap silver in plastic food wrap, though. It will keep air away, but it can also cause stains and corrosion.

531

◆ To remove tarnish from the tines of a fork, coat a piece of cotton string with silver polish and rub between the tines.

◆ Silver can spot easily if you air dry it. It's better to dry it right away with a lint-free cloth and store it properly.

STRAIGHT UP

If you're moving a large piece of marble like a tabletop, always transport it upright. If you carry it flat, it can crack under its own weight.

A COULD-BEE CATASTROPHE

If a bee or other stinging insect gets trapped in the car with you, don't swat at it! Instead, pull your car off to the side of the road, open all the windows or doors, and let the critter fly out.

SAVE THOSE BABY FOOD JARS

Do you have a "junk drawer" in your kitchen? Baby food jars are perfect storage containers to keep it tidy. Use them for screws, brads, rubber bands, push pins and thumb tacks, sugar and artificial sweetener packets, loose change, and anything else small that clutters your life.

27

PETS AND PESTS

VITAMIN C FOR PREGNANT DOGS

If you find your pregnant dog searching the garbage for citrus peels, don't get upset; she knows what she's doing. Give your pet a vitamin C supplement three to four weeks before she whelps; the vitamin makes the process easier for her. Even though dogs (unlike humans) produce vitamin C, they tend to use more than they can make during pregnancy.

HERBS AS REPELLENTS

A number of herbs will ward off crawling insects. The most potent are fresh or dried bay leaves, sage leaves, and cloves. Placing any of these herbs in locations where a problem exists will cause the critters to do an about-face and leave the premises. Ants, roaches, and spiders may be more difficult to get rid of. If the above herbs don't work, try mixing 2 cups borax with an equal amount of sugar in a large container, and sprinkle the mixture in areas that you know the pests frequent. When crawling insects cross a fine powder, it removes the waterproof layer of their bodies, causing water loss and, ultimately, death.

NATURAL INSECTICIDE

If you have a problem with any type of flying insect, keep a basil plant or two around the house. Keep the plant well watered from the bottom; this will cause it to release additional aroma. Drying the basil leaves and hanging them in small muslin bags will also repel flying insects.

YOU WON'T NEED THE ROD AND REEL

To get rid of silverfish, mix 1 part molasses with 2 parts white vinegar. Apply the mixture to cracks and holes where the pests reside. Treat the baseboards and table legs as well.

OOPS!

If your pet has an accident on the rug, blot it with a paper towel to soak up as much liquid as possible, then spritz it with white vinegar or a mild solution of hot soapy water to remove the odor. However, first test a small, hidden area to make sure the carpet is colorfast.

ROTTEN EGGS TO THE RESCUE

Keeping deer, antelope, reindeer, and other pesky animals away from your garden and trees is a breeze with eggs that have gone bad. Just break them open (outside of the house) around the area that you want to keep the critters away from. The smell of hydrogen sulfide from rotten eggs is not one of their favorite aromas and is sure to repel them from the areas that you want to keep pest-free.

MULTIPLYING FLIES

If you don't keep trash cans and compactors sealed tight, you can end up with 1,000 or more flies in a week. But flies are repelled by lavender oil. Soak a sponge with the oil and leave it in a saucer, or saturate a few cotton balls with the oil and toss them into your garbage at the beginning of each week. Other natural repellents that will send flies in the other direction are oil of cloves and wintergreen mint sprigs.

LOOKS NICE, TOO

If you are going to plant in window boxes, try whitewashing them first. This will deter insects and reduce the risk of dry rot.

BUG KILLER

If you place a few drops of liquid detergent in the water you use to clean a plant's leaves, it will keep the bugs off, and if they go into the soil at night, they will die.

FLEA SUCTION

Fleas can be eliminated from upholstery and carpets by vacuuming with a high-powered vacuum cleaner (ideally with a canister) with a bag that seals well. Remove the bag and dispose of it outside as soon as you finish.

THE CABBAGE-PATCH SLUG

If you're having problems with slugs eating your flowers, here is a simple solution: Just plant a few cabbage plants in your garden. Slugs go crazy for cabbage, and will make a bee-line for it.

NO MORE MOSQUITOES

Citronella oil candles will rid your home of mosquitoes. The smell is pleasant and not at all offensive to humans. Adding a few drops of citronella oil to tall gaslights and placing them around the yard will keep the area clear of not only mosquitoes but also of moths.

MOTH TRAPPER

Trap moths by mixing 1 part molasses with 2 parts white vinegar and placing the mixture in a bright yellow container. Or make a 10 percent solution of molasses in water and hang it from a tree in a quart jar. Use an old-fashioned clamp jar and keep the lid off.

NUTRAPET

Vitamins and minerals are very important to your pet's health. Save the water from steamed or boiled vegetables or liquid from a slow cooker and mix it with your animal's food for additional nutrients.

TRAPPER TOAD

Finding a toad in your garden is really good luck. One lonely toad will feast on more than 100 slugs, cutworms, grubs, caterpillars, and assorted beetle larvae every night. If the toad is in top form, it can consume more than 10,000 invaders in three months.

SNAIL-ZAPPER

Whenever you need to get rid of snails in the yard or garden, pour stale cheap beer in a shallow container just below ground level. Snails are attracted to beer. The beer has a diuretic effect, causing snails to lose vital liquids in a short period, and then die.

RODENT REPELLER

Moles, squirrels, gophers, rats, and mice hate the aroma of peppermint. If you plant mint around your home chances are you will never see one of these pests for any length of time. Soak a cotton ball with peppermint oil and drop it down a gopher hole. You will never see the varmint again.

HERE, KITTY, KITTY

To remove a grease stain from your concrete driveway, rub kitty litter into the stain and let stand for one to two hours before sweeping it up. (Just don't let the cat out.)

NO FLEAS, PLEASE

To ward off fleas from a pet's sleeping area, try sprinkling a few drops of lavender oil in the area. Fleas hate lavender oil.

WRIGLEY'S FOR WRIGGLERS

Mealworms will avoid pasta and grains if you keep a wrapped slice of spearmint gum in or near the products. Be sure to use spearmint—using a flavor like Juicy Fruit will actually attract them.

BANISHING BAMBI

Hanging small pieces of a deodorant bar soap on trees (especially fruit trees) will keep the deer away. Or, try a piece of your clothing—deer don't like the smell of humans.

TAKE TWO AND SEE ME IN THE MORNING

Chigger bites respond to a thick paste of a few aspirin tablets dissolved in water. The paste should ease the pain and itching.

CAT FOOD FOR CARPENTER ANTS

It's not necessary to drive the family out of the house for a week or risk poisoning your pets to get rid of carpenter ants. Just mix up a batch of 4 ounces of cherry or grape jelly in 3 tablespoons of canned cat food and 1 tablespoon of boric acid. Place small amounts in locations that the ants frequent (but keep it away from your cat). They will take the food to the queen and the colony will be eliminated.

SLIPPING AND SLIDING

Smearing petroleum jelly around the base of plant stems will make ants and other crawling insects slide right off, protecting your plants.

DID YOU KNOW?

Meat tenderizer can be used to treat an insect bite. Commercial meat tenderizers contain papain, an enzyme from papaya. Moisten a teaspoon of tenderizer with a little water and rub it immediately into the skin. Papain's protein-digestive properties will help to decompose the insect venom.

WORRIED ABOUT MOTH EGGS IN YOUR WOOLENS?

All you have to do is place your woolens in a plastic bag and leave it in the freezer for at least 24 hours to kill the eggs. When you do store the garments, place them in a bag that is as airtight as possible.

A SPOT OF TEA, WITH A DASH OF AMMONIA

If you want to keep bugs off your indoor plants, try spraying the plants with a solution of 10 parts weak tea and 1 part ammonia. Try it first on a few leaves to test for damage. An important note of caution: Keep the solution out of reach of children!

SHINE ON, SHINE ON…

Most animals are afraid of anything bright and shiny. Try hanging strips of foil on trees or shrubs to repel unwelcome visitors.

TRAPPING MICE WITH PEANUT BUTTER

Mice love the flavor of peanut butter even more than cheese. If you're having problems trapping them with cheese, give peanut butter a try.

MOSQUITOES SMARTER THAN ZAPPERS

Studies have proven that electric bug zappers have no effect on mosquitoes. They seem to have a special sense that keeps then away from magnetic fields. Citronella lamps will do the trick.

COMMON HOUSEHOLD PRODUCTS

28

AN EFFECTIVE GROUT CLEANER

Make an inexpensive yet very effective grout cleaner by mixing ¼ cup chlorine bleach with 2 tablespoons phosphate-based liquid floor cleaner, ¾ cup rubbing alcohol, and 1 cup plus 2 tablespoons water in a plastic spray bottle.

ABOUT PHOSPHATE DETERGENT

◆ Phosphates make water more alkaline. They bind with certain metal salts found in hard water and change it into soft water, which helps detergent get into the item in need of cleaning.
◆ Sometimes phosphates are called sodium tripolyphosphate (STP), which is harmless to humans.
◆ Phosphates can cause algae bloom and foam in lakes and streams.
◆ Products made from phosphates have higher levels of heavy metals—arsenic in particular.

A LAUNDRY LIST OF INGREDIENTS

Most laundry detergents are made not only of soap but also of antiredeposition agents, bleach, perfumes, enzymes, surfactants, and even a few chemicals to prevent your washer from being damaged. Antiredeposition agents coat the clothes with a cottonlike substance called carboxymetacellulose that prevents the dirt and grime that has been washed from the garments being redeposited back on the clothes during the wash cycle. This substance washes away during the rinse cycle.

HOW FABRIC SOFTENERS WORK

Fabric softeners are made from chemicals that possess a positive charge and have an affinity for wet, negatively charged garments. They form an even layer on the surface of the garment, removing the negative charge that gives your clothes a scratchy or rough feel—and static electricity.

RINGS AROUND THE TOILET

The ring around a toilet bowl is caused when dirt accumulates and becomes embedded in minerals in the hard water. A mild acid will easily remove the stains. Oxalic acid is one of the most common and least expensive; it is available in a powder or flake form. In some instances, a cola that contains phosphoric acid and has gone flat will also do the job.

THE SOAP THAT FLOATS

Way back when, Ivory soap sank. In 1930, an employee fell asleep on the job instead of watching the machinery and stopping the mixer at the appropriate time. Air was incorporated into the soap, which provided the buoyancy necessary for floating. Rather than discard the batch, the company marketed the flotation as a bonus, and consumers bought it.

OF CREAMS, COLD AND CLEANSING

Cleansing creams and cold creams are basically the same. They are often made of camphor, clove oil, eucalyptus oil, menthol, phenol, linseed oil, water, stearic acid, soybean oil, calcium hydroxide, and aluminum hydroxide. The camphor, clove oil, and eucalyptus oil provide fragrance; the menthol has some antibacterial and astringent properties; soybean oil adds a smooth texture; stearic acid prepares the skin so the cream will penetrate; linseed oil is a softening agent; and phenol is a relatively strong antibacterial agent. These ingredients are all acidic; the hydroxides increase the pH, neutralizing the acidity.

DON'T USE SOAP

Shampoos are formulated differently from soaps and are much gentler for your hair. Hydrolyzed animal protein helps to repair split ends; lauramide DEA produces lather, lecithin imparts shine; glycol stearate helps to detangle and add luster; methylparaben is a preservative; methylisothiozoline is an antibacterial agent; and citric acid lowers the pH.

THE TRUTH ABOUT HELMET HAIR

Hair spray is basically a resin dissolved in a volatile solvent or alcohol. When you spray it on your hair, the solvent evaporates rapidly, leaving a thin layer of plastic.

Don't believe it? Try this experiment: Coat a mirror with a thick layer of hair spray and let it dry for a minute or two. You should be able to peel off the layer in one thin sheet.

TAKING IT ALL OFF

Depilatories remove body hair with a concentrated chemical solution that breaks the sulfide bonds in hair. When these bonds break down, hair disintegrates and can then be rinsed off.

YES, YOU WANT THEM IN YOUR MOUTH

Toothpastes contain a number of chemicals and substances that work in concert to polish off stains, help prevent cavities, wash away food debris, and impart a pleasant taste. (Even if you're tempted to avoid these chemicals, don't use plain baking soda—the American Dental Association does not recommend it because it is much too abrasive.) Some natural toothpastes not only list their ingredients but also what function they serve.

ANTIPERSPIRANTS VERSUS DEODORANTS

Skin is covered with bacteria (don't worry; it's supposed to be). Because bacteria need a certain amount of moisture to reproduce, sweat provides a perfect medium for them to thrive. *Antiperspirants* actually prevent normal perspiration by causing sweat glands to constrict. Sticks are more effective than creams or sprays, which lose their effectiveness too soon.

Deodorants have no effect on perspiration. They contain antibacterial agents, even the most effective of which lasts for about two to three hours. Most deodorants contain perfume to mask odors.

THE BENEFITS OF AFTERSHAVE LOTIONS

Aftershave lotions are astringent—that is, they tighten pores and promote healing from the irritation of shaving. *Preshave lotions* are only used with electric shavers and are skin lubricants that help the shaver glide more easily across skin. Some have ingredients that make facial hair stand up, enabling you to get a closer shave.

KEEP A TUBE ON HAND AT ALL TIMES

Petroleum jelly, the most popular of which is Vaseline, is a must for every medicine chest. It seals off the skin and protects it from surface damage, especially from irritations and mild abrasions.

OVER-THE-COUNTER PAIN RELIEVERS

The most common analgesics (pain relievers) found in drugstores are aspirin, acetaminophen, ibuprofen, and naproxen.

◆ Aspirin reduces fever and inflammation in joints, but some people find it irritating to the stomach.
◆ Ibuprofen is also an anti-inflammatory and is supposed to be more effective for deep muscle pain.

- Acetaminophen does not seem to relieve swelling and is not as good a pain reliever as aspirin, but it generally does not irritate the stomach.
- Naproxen is similar to ibuprofen—it relieves muscle pain, backache, discomfort of arthritis, and menstrual cramps—and tends to remain in the bloodstream longer. However, it may irritate the stomach just as much as aspirin, and those who have conditions that sodium worsens—fluid retention, heart problems, high blood pressure, peripheral edema—should not take naproxen without consulting their physicians.

GLUG GLUG GLUG

If you suffer from stomach irritation when you take aspirin or other analgesics, be sure to take them with a full glass of water. Stomach irritation is usually the result of too little water when taking the product.

HOW LINIMENTS WORK

Liniments have been used for hundreds of years on animals and humans to relieve pain, especially from sore muscles. They actually irritate the skin to such a degree that they cause mild pain, which causes the pain receptors deeper in the area to be switched off. Liniments for use on animals should not be used on people; some can dilate blood vessels in the skin, allowing foreign substances into the bloodstream.

THAT NEW CARPET SMELL

The smell of new carpets can be overpowering, but take heart: The smell will dissipate over time. The fumes are caused by oils added to plastic during manufacturing. Most of the oils are absorbed by the plastic; you smell those that are left on the surface. Over time, oils come to the surface of the plastic, but they are not strong enough to produce fumes.

THEY'RE NOT INTERCHANGEABLE

Most aerosol oven cleaners contain lye, also found in drain cleaners. When you spray lye on burned fats and carbohydrates, it converts them to soap that can be wiped off with a damp cloth. If possible, choose one of the newer oven cleaners that use organic salts—they're less noxious. Whichever type you use, make sure that your kitchen is well ventilated or the cleaner fumes may burn the lining of your mouth and throat.

DID YOU KNOW?

Topical muscle rub ointments can contain substances called salicylates, which work by irritating the skin. This increases blood flow to the area and reduces deep muscle or joint pain.

CAN COLA REALLY CLEAN MY CAR BATTERY?

Carbonated beverages, especially those that contain phosphoric acid, dissolve the powdery gunk on battery terminals. However, a better way to clean terminals is to sprinkle on some baking soda to neutralize the acid, and then brush with a metal brush. Never clean battery terminals with water, or the battery may short out and explode.

LEAVE THE JUMPER CABLES IN THE GARAGE

Car engine won't start? It may not be the battery. Cold temperatures can turn motor oil into a thick sludge, so the battery has to work harder to turn the engine over. If you live in colder climes, look for a higher amp battery, or use an electric blanket (one made for cars, not a household blanket), which will keep the motor oil from becoming a semisolid.

ANTISEPTICS AND DISINFECTANTS

Antiseptics are chemicals that kill some (not all) bacteria. They inhibit the growth of most bacteria quite effectively, and are commonly used on cuts or abrasions to prevent infection. Disinfectants kill all bacteria and viruses but are too harsh to be applied to skin. They are used in kitchens, bathrooms, and other places where bacteria and viruses thrive.

KEEP YOUR FIZZLE IN

The refrigerator is a good place to store many chemicals such as hydrogen peroxide. It will stay active for a longer period. Nail polish is another chemical that likes the cold. It will last longer if you keep it in the refrigerator, but bring it to room temperature before your manicure.

HOW DO THE INSTANT HOT SHAVING CREAMS WORK?

A number of shaving creams purport to provide a more comfortable shave. They contain mild skin irritants that increase blood circulation.

YOU STILL HAVE TO CLEAN THE BOWL

Those tablets you place in the toilet tank are not a substitute for a thorough scrubbing. They're designed to help keep the bowl clean, but they won't clean a bowl that's already dirty.

YOU DON'T ALWAYS GET WHAT YOU PAY FOR

Most bathtub cleaners advertise that they contain powerful disinfectants that will kill bacteria as well as clean off the soap scum and dirt residue. While they do contain disinfectants, the chemicals are only effective for a matter of hours, and then the bacteria come right back. The grout cleaner on page 540 is just as effective as most commercial bathtub cleaners.

SAME THING, DIFFERENT COLORS

Think you're getting extra benefits from your striped toothpaste? Think again—most are simply the same product dyed different colors. That said, there is a toothpaste that's fairly new to the market. It has two compartments that contain two different cleaners. Check with your dentist before using this, because it contains hydrogen peroxide.

BEWARE OF BREATH MINTS

Breath mints contain sweeteners, moisturizers, and may contain a germ killer. Most brands are sweetened with sorbitol, which may cause diarrhea or stomach problems if susceptible individuals consume too much. Chronic bad breath can indicate a medical condition; see your doctor if you rely heavily on breath fresheners.

MAKING SENSE OF THE PERFUME COUNTER

So you're confused by the difference between perfume, cologne, and eau de toilette? The main variant is the concentration of the compounds that are responsible for the aroma of each of these products. *Perfumes* are produced with the highest concentrations, and that is why they last longer. (Hint: Before you apply perfume, dab a bit of petroleum jelly on those areas; the perfume will last twice as long.) *Colognes* contain less of the same compound and more fillers, and *eau de toilette,* or toilet water, is just diluted cologne. Here's another thing worth knowing when you're browsing the perfume counter: The cost of a perfume has more to do with its advertising and marketing expenses than the cost of its ingredients.

YOU GET WHAT YOU PAY FOR

When it comes to toilet tissue, most people have no trouble telling a better (often more expensive) brand. All toilet tissues are made from purified wood pulp, but the better brands also include skin softeners; lesser quality products do not go through any softening process. Colored toilet paper contains traces of metals that produce the different colors. People with very sensitive skin may experience a reaction from the colored papers.

GENTLY IS THE OPERATIVE WORD

Acne medications do not cure acne; they only provide a measure of control. Gently cleaning the face with soap and water seems to work almost as well as some of the medications.

CAN COLA STOP NAUSEA?

Antiemetics control the gag reflex, which comes into play when you're nauseated. But in most instances, cola syrups that contain sugar and phosphates are every bit as effective. Most pharmacies sell cola syrup; ask your pharmacist. Regular or diet colas will not work—just cola syrup.

ODOR EATERS

Baking soda is inorganic, which simply means that it is not produced from living matter. Household odors are composed of organic oils, and they get stuck in the inorganic powder, which neutralizes them.

GET THE ICE OFF

Most windshield deicers work fairly well, but the thicker the ice, the longer it will take to melt. Deicers are similar to antifreeze, though they tend to be much more expensive. An inexpensive yet effective solution: Fill the windshield washer fluid reservoir with a mixture of 1 part antifreeze, 4½ parts alcohol, and 4½ parts water. Never pour hot water on your windshield. The glass may expand from the heat and then contract as it cools, causing the windshield to crack.

A PRIMER PRIMER

Paint primers are usually colorless or white, so you might wonder if you need them. They serve many functions: Primers seal the surface to be painted, so paint does not soak in. Colored primers hide colors already on the wall that may bleed through; they can also lessen the appearance of an uneven paint job. If you're painting metal, primers can help prevent corrosion; they also help paint adhere better.

MAKING NONSTICK PANS NONSTICK AGAIN

For the most part, these plastic-coated pots are easy to keep clean, but they do stain, and over time grease and oil may build up. If this occurs it will adversely affect the efficiency of the nonstick surface. To clean, mix 2 tablespoons baking soda, ½ cup white vinegar, and 1 cup water in the pot, set on the stove, and boil for about 10 minutes. Wash the pot, then rub vegetable oil on the surface of the plastic coating to re-season it.

UNCLOGGING DRAINS ON THE CHEAP

If a plumber's helper doesn't work, try this: Remove all standing water so you can access the drain. First pour 1 cup of baking soda, then 1 cup of table salt, and then ½ cup of white vinegar into the clogged drain; these will start dissolving any organic matter and grease immediately. Let stand for 5 minutes, then flush 1 to 2 quarts of boiling water down the drain.

ELIMINATE THERMOS ODORS

The easiest way to eliminate the odors and stains from a vacuum bottle? Fill the container with hot water and drop in a denture-cleaning tablet, and then let stand overnight. Baking soda will also work, but not as well.

MAKING CANDLES DRIPLESS

Prepare a solution of 2 tablespoons of salt per candle in just enough water to cover the candles. Let the candles soak in the salt water for 2 to 3 hours, and then rinse them, let dry, and wait at least 24 hours before you use them. The salt water hardens the wax, which makes it burn slower and more cleanly, reducing the chance of drips onto linens or furniture.

AN EASY METHOD OF OVEN CLEANING

If your oven is not self-cleaning, here's a way to get the gunk off without a lot of scrubbing: Set a small bowl with ½ cup of ammonia on the center rack, close the oven, and let stand overnight. The next day, open the oven and let it air for 30 minutes in a well-ventilated kitchen. Wipe up the mess with warm, damp paper towels.

DID YOU KNOW?

Commercial drain cleaners can be made from very dangerous, volatile chemicals. Be sure to follow the manufacturer's instructions to the letter when using these products.

547

HOT STUFF

When you wash dishes, be sure to use hot water. It activates the detergent better than cold water, and it's more effective at rinsing off the soap.

CAULK ONE UP FOR ALCOHOL

Isopropyl alcohol belongs in the bathroom for more than first-aid purposes. It cleans the caulking around the bathtub, and it shines chrome and glass.

KILL THEM WHERE THEY THRIVE

Humidifiers often are hotbeds of bacteria—which means that you may be filling the air with germs as well as moisture. Add a drop or two of chlorine bleach for every gallon of water when you refill the humidifier to help keep bacteria at bay.

29

VITAMINS, MINERALS, & SUPPLEMENTS

WHY WE NEED SUPPLEMENTS

How often have you heard that if you eat a balanced diet with all the food groups in the right proportions, you will be able to obtain all the nutrients your body needs? This may have been true many years ago, but with so many chemicals in our foods and environment, free radicals will get you no matter how good your diet is. Free radicals are highly reactive molecules that cause tissue damage. We've been bombarded with more environmental insults than our bodies can cope with. This chapter explains why dietary supplements are mandatory for optimum health.

Every week there seems to be another news report telling of yet another problem with our food supply. There are not enough inspectors to check our foods properly, produce and other fresh foods are stored too long before they are sold, and many nutrients are processed out of foods. For example, tests have shown that a potato that has been in storage for four to six months will have lost at least 50 percent of its vitamin C content.

Then we take a supplement that has probably lost a percentage of its potency. If you bought inexpensive supplements to save a few dollars, they may well have a low level of "biologic activity." Many supplements cannot provide you with the level of nutrients you expect.

The following information will give you some insight into nutrition and the many factors that relate to obtaining nutrients from the foods you purchase. It will also provide some additional information regarding the need for supplementation in relation to a variety of lifestyle factors.

TEMPERATURE AND NUTRIENT LOSS

Fried Foods

The higher the temperature and the longer the food is fried, the higher the nutrient loss. Most frying temperatures reach 375°F, making canola oil best for frying because of its high smoke point.

Canned Foods

Vitamins, but not minerals, are lost during cooking and sterilization processes in canning. But canned foods are convenient, and without canning, many foods would spoil before they could be used.

Frozen Foods

The level of nutrient loss depends on how long the foods were harvested before freezing and whether they were cooked prior to freezing. Frozen foods also provide us with convenience and year-round availability.

Dehydrated Foods

If these are processed using a high-quality dehydrator, the nutritional content for the most part will be retained.

Dairy Products

The pasteurization process takes its toll on nutrients. Many vitamins either lose their potency or are destroyed, although vitamins A and D are added after pasteurization.

REFINING OUT AND REPLACING NUTRIENTS

Many refined foods have nutrients removed during processing; only rarely are these nutrients returned to the food. In bread, for example, many nutrients are processed out of flour, and only a few are replaced. Whole-wheat breads go stale faster than breads made from processed flours that have the oil-containing (and very healthful) germ removed. Almost all breakfast cereals are fortified with vitamins and minerals, whether or not they contain the whole grain. Vitamin C and calcium are added to numerous products.

White and wheat flours (not the 100 percent whole-grain flours) may lose up to 90 percent of their vitamin E potency during processing. Cereals and grains, especially rice, may lose up to 70 percent of their vitamin E when processed.

STORAGE AND NUTRIENT LOSS

Canned and Packaged Products

The length of time a food is on a shelf at the supermarket, as well as the time it spends at the warehouse and in transit, may result in reduced potency of many vitamins and minerals. Look for products that are stamped with a freshness date and use by the suggested date.

Fruits and Vegetables

Frequently fruits and vegetables are picked before they are fully ripe, and then allowed to ripen while being transported to the supermarket. Produce departments often cut fruits into smaller, more salable pieces, and this causes more of their surfaces to be exposed to the effects of air and light. Oxidation takes place more rapidly, thus reducing their nutrient content. Buy fruits and vegetables whole and cut them up just before consuming them to minimize nutrient loss.

AND DON'T FORGET . . .

Rotation of Foods

When you bring home food from the supermarket, always put newer foods behind older foods so older ones get used first. Not doing this is one of the more frequent mistakes people make.

Warehousing

Most foods are warehoused before they are shipped to supermarkets. The time they are delayed has a lot to do with the ultimate level of nutrients.

Restaurants

To save money, restaurants purchase in large quantities, possibly resulting in long storage before the food is served. Most fast-food restaurants avoid this problem because they serve a great number of people. Restaurant management should make it a priority to train personnel in prudent food storage methods, stock rotation, and proper sanitation.

ENVIRONMENT AND NUTRIENT LOSS

Organic farming is one of the fastest growing segments of agriculture. Between 1992 and 1997, certified organic cropland more than doubled in the United States. In 1997, farmers in 49 states dedicated 1.3 million acres of land to organic farming. A more natural approach to farming and consumer demand for organic produce is driving the growth. Farmers are adopting minimum tillage and crop-rotation methods that result in less soil erosion and herbicide use. Small and large farms are experimenting with using biologically-based pest-control products to reduce the use of insecticides, and soil quality is being improved by composting, growing cover crops, and adding animal manure.

MINERALS IN SOIL

Some minerals in soil that are crucial to crop growth can be replaced; these include phosphorus, potassium, and nitrates. Selenium, a trace mineral, can vary considerably across the United States, and even foods that should be adequate sources can be low in this vital nutrient. Wheat, for example, may contain from 50 micrograms to 800 micrograms of selenium depending on where it is grown. Two other important minerals, chromium and zinc, are also critically deficient in the soil. This problem is significant and is presently under study by the USDA.

DID YOU KNOW?

Too few people plan their meals in advance. This results in poor combinations of foods, leading to inadequate vitamin and mineral intake.

SMOKING AND HEALTH

The smoke from cigarettes, cigars, and pipes all impact the oxygen-carrying efficiency of your red blood cells. Smoke contains carbon monoxide, and this is one reason why smokers get short-winded; a percentage of their red blood cells carry carbon monoxide instead of the needed oxygen. Also, recent studies have shown that smokers require approximately 40 percent more vitamin C than nonsmokers to achieve adequate blood levels. Every cigarette may reduce bodily stores by about 30 milligrams, so if you smoke a pack of cigarettes a day, you need to increase your vitamin C intake by at least 600 milligrams. Smoking rates are dropping in the U.S., but 1997 estimates indicate that 48 million adults still smoke.

SMOG FIGHTERS

All major cities in the United States have some form of chemical air pollution. This pollution will effect your lungs' capacity to deliver oxygen efficiently to the cells of the body. The antioxidant vitamins A, C, and E, the minerals selenium and zinc, and proanthocyanidin have proven to be effective in combating some of the effects of chemical pollution.

DAIRY PRODUCT INTOLERANCE

The mechanism to produce the enzyme to break down lactose loses it efficiency over time in many people. Between 30 and 50 million Americans are lactose intolerant. This may lead to calcium deficiencies. Dark-green leafy vegetables (such as kale and broccoli) and canned fish with soft, edible bones (such as salmon and sardines) are excellent non-dairy sources of calcium.

The McNeil Consumer Healthcare Company offers products under the brand name Lactaid that make milk products easily digestible. Lactaid tablets are taken before eating foods containing lactose, and Lactaid drops are added to milk before drinking to break down the lactose. The company also sells Lactaid milk, available in most grocery stores, that contains no lactose and can be used for cooking and baking as well as drinking.

HORMONES AND NUTRIENT LOSS

Aging and hormonal changes may lead to an increase in the loss of calcium, and supplementation should be considered. If you're a woman taking birth-control pills, you need more vitamin B6.

WATCH THOSE COOKING METHODS

Don't plan to get your B vitamins from fish, shellfish, Brussels sprouts, and red cabbage. All of these foods contain thiaminase, a chemical that may destroy the B vitamins. And though cooking inactivates the thiaminase, cooking itself will reduce the B vitamins. As for vegetables in general, you will retain more of their nutrients by stir-frying, steaming, or microwaving whenever possible.

COFFEE, TEA, OR WINE

The tannins in teas and red wines may interfere with the utilization of iron, thiamine, and B12. Iron absorption can be also be affected by coffee consumption. Vitamin C is required to assist in the metabolism of iron. If vitamin C is not present in adequate amounts, less than 30 percent of the ingested iron will be utilized by the body.

Recent interest in the health benefits of the antioxidants contained in green tea has spurred a profusion of research. Among the findings are that the polyphenols in green tea may protect against arthritis, heart disease, and cell damage that leads to cancer. The "French paradox" is a theory that the French are able to eat a high-fat diet without experiencing a high rate of heart disease because of their red-wine consumption. Recent research has found that the heart-protecting substances contained in red wine are flavonoids—specifically resveratrol and quercetin, both of which act as powerful antioxidants.

C-RATIONING

The Recommended Daily Allowance for vitamin C is 60 milligrams. Two hundred milligrams per day is the upper limit recommended. An excess of pectin or zinc in the diet may decrease vitamin C absorption, but on average, 80 to 95 percent of vitamin C is absorbed.

FABULOUS FAT

Vitamins A, D, E, and K are best absorbed in the intestines when a small amount of fat is present. If you are taking a vitamin E supplement as a single supplement, it is best to take it with food containing a small amount of fat, such as 2 percent milk, low-fat cheese, or low-fat yogurt.

SUPPLEMENTAL SECURITY

Americans spent $27 billion on nutritional supplements in 1997. The Dietary Supplement Health and Education Act of 1994 (DSHEA) brought a boon to the supplement industry. It allows companies to introduce supplements without FDA approval with the caveat that there be a history of use or other evidence establishing that when used under the conditions recommended in the labeling it can reasonably be expected to be safe. The burden of proof is on the FDA, though the responsibility for safety is on the manufacturer. According to DSHEA, dietary supplement labels can make structure or function claims without FDA review (such as "helps you relax"), but not disease claims (such as "prevents osteoporosis"). In other words, the supplement label cannot assert a claim to cure disease.

The American Medical Association has called for dietary supplements to meet standards of identity, strength, quality, purity, packaging, and labeling before being sold to the public. This standardization, however, would not be an endorsement of safety or efficacy of the supplement.

In April 2000, the FDA announced its intention to expand monitoring of serious adverse reactions to herbs, vitamins, and other dietary supplements and to expand its role in establishing manufacturing standards for the dietary supplement industry.

MOVE IT

Keep your digestive system in good working order by consuming at least five to six servings of fresh fruits and vegetables as well as several servings of whole grains every day.

A RACE TO LOSE

Caucasian women begin losing calcium stores around age 18. Caucasian men and African-American women start to lose calcium around age 30, but studies show that they lose it at a faster pace than the rest of the population. (African-American men don't seem to have the problem.) Adults require between 1,000 and 1,500 milligrams of calcium every day; an 8-ounce glass of milk provides about 300 milligrams. Recognizing that Americans need to increase their calcium intake, food manufacturers are introducing calcium-fortified foods every day, including orange juice, cereal, pasta, and tofu.

DID YOU KNOW?

Studies reveal that eating excessive amounts of foods that are high in vitamin A, such as liver, carrots, and cantaloupe, may result in headaches and nausea.

GETTING THE MOST

Calcium supplements are best absorbed when taken with meals, because calcium likes an acid medium. Calcium absorption increases in the presence of vitamin D and when taken with foods that contain lactose—so it's a good idea to have a glass of milk with your calcium supplement.

Calcium is also best utilized by the bones when boron is present. Good sources of boron include prunes, raisins, almonds, peanuts, dates, and honey. Studies have also shown that if you consume a small amount of sugar the absorption rate will improve.

THE IMPORTANCE OF A

Vitamin A is important for a healthy immune system. It also helps the body retain vitamin C and metabolize zinc.

BEWARE THE HIGH-PROTEIN DIET

A high-protein diet does not build muscle and burn fat. Too much protein can shorten life expectancy, increase the risk of cancer, deplete calcium from bones, cause fluid imbalances, stress and damage the liver and kidneys, cause obesity, and increase the need for vitamin B6. A diet high in protein can mean that nutrients from fruits, vegetables, and grains are missing and that the intake of fat and calories is too high. People who do lose weight on these diets are losing mainly water, not body fat. A high-protein diet is not a healthful lifelong eating plan.

JUST WEAR SUNSCREEN

Studies are being done relating low vitamin D levels to breast cancer. Areas of the country with low sunlight levels seem to have a higher incidence of breast cancer. New FDA regulations restrict companies from labeling products with a sun protection factor (SPF) higher than 30. In addition, sunscreen labels will no longer have terms like "waterproof" or "all-day protection." Swimming reduces the effective time of sunscreen to as little as 80 minutes, and the "all-day protection" is misleading. We do need sunlight to synthesize vitamin D, and protective measures such as wearing protective clothing, limiting sun exposure between 10 a.m. and 4 p.m., and liberal use of sunscreen can help to make the sun safe.

VITAMIN ROBBERS

The chart below provides information regarding some of the environmental factors, drugs, and everyday products that can significantly affect the potency and availability of many nutrients.

Vitamin and Mineral Robbers	
VITAMIN/MINERAL	ROBBER
Vitamin A	Mineral oil, air pollution, fertilizer nitrates, antacids, corticosteroids.
Vitamin D	Anti-convulsive drugs (dilantin), stressful situations, oral contraceptives, mineral oil, antacids, alcohol.
Thiamine	Antibiotics, excess heat/cooking, sugar, alcohol, antacids, heavy coffee or tea consumption.
Riboflavin	Antibiotics, exposure to light, diuretics, alcohol.
Niacin	Excessive heat, alcohol, penicillin.
Pantothenic Acid	Alcohol, diabetes, inflammatory bowel disease.
Folate	Oral contraceptives, stress, vitamin C deficiency, alcohol, smoking.
Vitamin B12	Prolonged iron deficiency, stress, oral contraceptives.
Biotin	Excess heat, antibiotics, sulfa drugs, oral contraceptives.
Calcium	Antacids, aspirin, corticosteroids, diuretics, lidocaine, aging, alcohol.
Magnesium	Thiazides, alcohol, diuretics, diabetes, pregnancy.
Vitamin C	Overexertion, fatigue, stress, aspirin, smoking, alcohol, corticosteroids, antihistamines, fluoride, oral contraceptives, barbiturates, infection.
Vitamin E	Oral contraceptives, food processing, rancid fats, mineral oil.
Vitamin K	Antibiotics, mineral oil, radiation, anticoagulants, phenobarbital, alcohol.

NEWS ABOUT PHYTOCHEMICALS

These chemical extracts from fruits and vegetables are substances that give them their color, flavor, and aroma, and provide us with their natural defense system against diseases. Phytochemicals are not vitamins or minerals. Researchers have known about them for years, but these substances have started receiving press of late because of studies linking them to cancer prevention in laboratory animals.

Numerous agencies and universities, including the National Cancer Society and the National Academy of Science, are conducting studies on phytochemicals. Phytochemicals are presently showing results in animals, arresting cancer in all stages of cellular development. Exactly which phytochemicals will be beneficial to humans and in preventing which types of cancer are questions that will take years to answer.

We have always known that whole grains, fruits, and vegetables should be consumed in adequate amounts on a daily basis for optimum health, and that cancer was not as prevalent in the early part of the century as it is today. A possible explanation is that our grandparents ate a healthier diet with fewer processed foods and more fruits and vegetables. The compounds in these foods provided a degree of "natural" protection.

Cancer has only become more prevalent since the 1940s, when processed and chemically altered foods came into vogue. Phytochemicals may, however, be one answer to reducing the incidence of cancer.

One very important factor is that phytochemicals are not destroyed by cooking or processing; the problem is that we just don't eat enough of them. Cooking methods such as microwaving and steaming increases their availability.

Researchers have identified more than 100,000 phytochemicals, and as research equipment becomes more sophisticated as time goes on, scientists will undoubtedly identify even more. A number of plants provide more than one phytochemical—in fact, many more. Broccoli, for example, contains at least 40; orange juice has 59; and garlic and onions have 50 phytochemicals. In addition, many phytochemicals can be found in several foods, so if you hate one vegetable, there might be another vegetable or a fruit that you do like to eat that provides the same phytochemical.

The charts on the next six pages are current as of 1998 on the more potent and important of these extractions. All information has been taken from laboratory-animal-testing only.

Phytochemicals in Fruits, Vegetables, and Herbs

FOOD	PHYTOCHEMICALS
Broccoli, cauliflower, Brussels sprouts, kale, turnips	SULFORAPHANE Activates enzyme that aids in removing carcinogens from the body. DITHIOLTHIONE Triggers production of enzymes that may block carcinogens from damaging DNA.
Sweet potatoes, yams, artichokes, berries, red grapes, red wine, strawberries, citrus fruits	FLAVONOIDS AND POLYPHENOLS May reduce the risk of cancer and cardiovascular diseases by attaching to free radicals and flushing them out of the body. Flavonoids block estrogen-producing enzymes, thereby reducing the risk of estrogen-induced cancers. Phenols block enzymes that cause inflammation and prevent blood platelets from clumping. This group of phytochemicals may help to explain why, despite their high fat diet, the French have lower heart-attack rates than do Americans. However, it would be wise to avoid red wine and consume the foods until additional studies are more conclusive. Recommendations are ⅓ cup per day.
Cabbage, turnips, dark green leafy vegetables	INDOLES Bind chemical carcinogens and work in the gastrointestinal tract to detoxify enzymes. Studies show that these may improve immune system function by allowing the body to eliminate toxins more easily. Stimulate the production of an enzyme that may make estrogen less effective, which may give a degree of protection against breast and ovarian cancers. Three to five ½ cup servings per day are recommended.
Kidney beans, chickpeas, soybeans, lentils	SAPONINS Slow the growth and replication of cancer cells and may lower LDL cholesterol.

Phytochemicals in Fruits, Vegetables, and Herbs

FOOD	PHYTOCHEMICALS
Soybeans, dried beans, mung bean sprouts	**GENISTEIN** A type of phytochemical called a phytoestrogen which blocks enzymes that promote tumor growth. It regulates estrogen levels and may protect against heart disease and lower LDL cholesterol. Genistein may also offer protection against breast, skin, and colon cancers, and osteoporosis. Additional phytochemicals found in soybeans may help reduce cholesterol levels and slow replication of cancer cells. Three 4-ounce servings of tofu or 3 cups of soy milk daily is recommended.
Chili peppers	**CAPSAICIN** This anti-inflammatory substance prevents carcinogens from attaching to DNA and discourages the growth and replication of cancer cells. Other potential uses are killing bacteria that may cause stomach ulcers and as a treatment for bronchitis and colds. Capsaicin also blocks pain sensation and is helpful in relieving arthritis pain. Eat in moderation, as red chili peppers tend to stimulate gastric acid, causing indigestion and general stomach irritation. Recommendations are no more than two to four small peppers per day if tolerated well.
Citrus fruit	**LIMONENE** The active substance d-limonene has been shown to offer protection against breast cancer in laboratory animals. It also increases the production of additional enzymes that may help the immune system dispose of carcinogens. Future studies may also show that this phytochemical reduces plaque in arteries. Extracts of limonene have been found to clear the congestive mucus from the lungs of patients with pulmonary disease. The more pulp in the fruit or juice, the more benefits you'll reap. Recommendations are 16 to 24 ounces of pulpy orange juice daily or three to four pieces of fruit.

Phytochemicals in Fruits, Vegetables, and Herbs

FOOD	PHYTOCHEMICALS
Garlic, onions, leeks, chives	ALLIUM COMPOUNDS Recent studies show that these vegetables may lower HDL (bad cholesterol) and detoxify the body by increasing the production of glutathione S-transferase, which may cause carcinogens to be excreted more easily. They may also slow reproduction of carcinogens, allowing more time for them to be destroyed. They may reduce the incidence of heart disease by having a mild blood thinning effect, which protects against atherosclerosis and stroke. Allium compounds may decrease the risk of stomach cancers and when combined with the mineral selenium, may have an effect on breast cancer. Compounds in garlic may prevent cancers from forming by acting as a stimulant to the immune system and by inhibiting growth of malignant cells. Allicin, a compound that develops when garlic cloves are cut up, is a strong antibacterial agent. Too much garlic powder may interfere with anticoagulants and cause stomach upsets. Recommendations are two to four fresh garlic cloves or ½ cup raw onion daily. Keep mints handy!
Grains, especially rye, wheat, rice; sesame seeds; peanuts	PHYTIC ACID Binds to iron, thus reducing a free radical production mechanism. Studies are being conducted relating to preventing colon cancer and reducing the severity of intestinal cancers.
Tomatoes, green peppers	COUMARIC AND CHLOROGENIC ACIDS Kills cancer-forming substances in their formation stages. This group of antioxidants contains more than 10,000 phytochemicals.
Red, yellow, dark-green vegetables and fruits, including carrots, seaweed, winter squashes, tomatoes, zucchini, asparagus, peaches	CAROTENOIDS (including beta-carotene) Fight free radicals which may invade the DNA causing an abnormal cell to be produced. Tend to improve vitamin A effectiveness and improve immune-system responses, as well as decreasing the risk of lung cancer in laboratory mice. Carrots should be cleaned thoroughly and left unpeeled to preserve the phytochemicals. Recommendation is one to two servings of red, yellow, or dark green vegetables or 1 cup seaweed daily.

DID YOU KNOW?

Vitamin supplements will maintain their freshness longer if stored in the refrigerator. Most will maintain a good level of potency for about two years.

Phytochemicals in Fruits, Vegetables, and Herbs

FOOD	PHYTOCHEMICALS
Licorice root	**GLYCYRRHIZIN** Has disease-fighting properties. Still under investigation. Increases the effectiveness of the immune system and tends to slow the rate at which cancer cells replicate. Also useful in treating gastrointestinal problems, ulcers, and shingles. Contains antibacterial properties and helps fight tooth decay and gingivitis. Prevents breast cancer in laboratory animals by activating the production of liver enzymes, reducing the level of tumor-promoting estrogens. Persons with high blood pressure should not eat licorice root. Anise, a licorice flavoring, does not contain the phytochemical; most licorice-flavored candy does not contain licorice.
Green tea/black tea (Not herbal teas)	**CATECHINS** These substances in tea act as antioxidants and free-radical scavengers. They stimulate the body's detoxification systems through enzyme action. Laboratory studies have found that compounds in green tea may inhibit tumor initiation and the rate of cell replication, thus inhibiting the growth and development of tumors. May have a tendency to increase fat metabolism as well as increasing the effectiveness of the immune system and lowering cholesterol. Recent studies have found that phenols protect tissues from oxidation. Tea must be brewed for at least five to 10 minutes to get maximum catechin content. Excessive consumption may cause stomach upsets and provide a large dose of caffeine. Moderation is the key.
Rosemary	**CARNOSOL** An antioxidant that tends to reduce the development of certain types of tumors and may protect fats in the body from oxidizing. Used for headaches, indigestion, nausea, fever, and inflammation of joints. May be used freely on salads or other foods.

Phytochemicals in Fruits, Vegetables, and Herbs

FOOD	PHYTOCHEMICALS
Flaxseed	LIGNANS Antioxidants. Flaxseed contains elements that are capable of producing lignans, which act as estrogens and contain omega-3 fatty acids that may have anticancer properties. Lignans help balance estrogen, and laboratory studies have found that they reduce the risk of heart disease and some cancers. Recommendations are to use ground fortified flaxseed with B6 and zinc added. Daily dose is 1 tablespoon of grain or 1 teaspoon of oil.
Red grapefruit, tomatoes, watermelon, apricots	LYCOPENE An antioxidant that protects DNA and cells against damage from free radicals. May decrease the risk of colon and bladder cancer in laboratory mice as well as reduce the risk of heart disease. Data are also suggestive that lycopene may prevent cancers of the pancreas, mouth, breast, and cervix. Fruits should be uncooked and as fresh as possible, though results have been found with processed as well as fresh tomatoes. One cup daily is recommended.
Yellow squash, spinach, collard, mustard and turnip greens, eggs, citrus, corn	LUTEIN AND ZEAXANTHIN Contribute to maintaining healthy vision. Slows growth of cancer cells. Reduces the risk of lung cancer, strengthens the immune system and may have a role in the prevention of colon, prostate, and esophageal cancers. Steam the greens using a small amount of water for a short period. Two-thirds cup daily is recommended.
Cranberry juice	ANTHOCYANINS Long known to prevent and cure urinary tract infections, cranberry juice may have other healthful benefits. The anthocyanins in the juice have shown anticarcinogenic activity in laboratory experiments and gallic acid in cranberries can lower LDL cholesterol. Best to use unsweetened cranberry juice. Two 8-ounce glasses per day is the recommendation.

DID YOU KNOW?

Boiling any food for more than five to 10 minutes will destroy 100 percent of the vitamin B and C content.

Phytochemicals in Fruits, Vegetables, and Herbs	
FOOD	**PHYTOCHEMICALS**
Ginger root	GINGEROL Relieves motion sickness. Has anti-inflammatory properties and may relieve symptoms of headaches. Ginger has been used as an appetite stimulator, to relieve gas, and as a treatment for colds, asthma, and burns. Recommendations are 1 teaspoon fresh ginger, or or 2 to 3 cups ginger tea (simmer several slices in 2 to 3 cups water for eight to 10 minutes, then strain).
Horseradish, cabbage, turnips	PHENETHYL ISOTHIOCYANATES Tends to reduce tumor growth by activating enzymes that block carcinogens from damaging the DNA. Studies show these substances may inhibit cancer of the lungs, pancreas, and esophagus.
Basil, carrots, parsley, mint, caraway seeds, citrus fruits, cabbage	MONOTERPENES Interfere with the replication of cancer cells. In laboratory studies, monoterpenes have been shown to effectively prevent and treat mammary cancer.

CLAIM CHECK

Nutraceuticals, at present, are regulated by the FDA as dietary supplements only and are not classified as drugs. They are extractions from foods, and to date no definitive, extensive studies on humans have been completed.

Claims made for products that offer cancer protection and cure should be viewed with caution. Products that contain herbal or botanical ingredients should indicate the part of the plant the product was derived from. Labels should list all ingredients that are present in significant amounts.

In the future, nutraceuticals may include a label that might read, "This food product is not intended to treat, cure or prevent any disease." In the future, phytochemicals will be transferred to different foods and added to foods that will be called "functional foods." One that is now available is the margarine product Benecol, which incorporates sitostanol, a derivative of pine oil, that has cholesterol-lowering properties.

Major Carotenoids		
CAROTENOID	**FOOD SOURCE**	**POSSIBLE BENEFIT**
Alpha-carotene	Carrots	Neutralize free radicals, increase immune system response.
Beta-carotene	Broccoli, cantaloupe, carrots	Same response as alpha-carotene, with the additional decrease of colon, bladder, and skin cancers in mice.
Beta-cryptoxanthin	Mangos, oranges, papayas, tangerines	Provides vitamin A.
Canthaxanthin	Natural food coloring added to jellies, jams, soft drinks, and tomato sauce	Found to slow skin cancer as well as slow the growth of cancer cells and improve immune response in mice.
Lutein	Broccoli, dark-green leafy vegetables	Contributes to maintaining healthy vision.
Lycopene	Tomatoes, tomato products	Decreases the risk of colon and bladder cancer and slows the replication of cancer cells in mice.
Zeaxanthin	Cress, Swiss chard, okra, beet greens	May prevent macular degeneration, blocks peroxide free radicals.

CAROTENOIDS

Fruits and vegetables contain more than 600 carotenoids. These are pigments that give these foods their colors.

Ongoing studies may show that carotenoids are more effective when taken together. In the mid-1990s, researchers believed that beta-carotene had the power to prevent lung cancers. After a few years, however, researchers noticed that cancer rates in those who took beta-carotene supplements had actually increased. It is now believed that carotenoids work together to slow down or stop cancer cells from replicating.

One of the more interesting findings is that carotenoids improve communications between premalignant cells and normal cells. Tumor growth is slowed when they receive regulating signals from the normal cells.

There is consistent evidence that a diet sufficient in fruits and vegetables can reduce risk for a number of diseases. There is no evidence at present that consuming small amounts of beta-carotene, such as the amounts in foods or in a multivitamin tablet, is unwise for any population.

Animal studies have shown that when a combination of carotenoids were given there was a decrease in the number of cancer cells.

SHARK CARTILAGE

Studies are continuing in many countries regarding the use of shark cartilage in the prevention or treatment of cancer. Some of the research has found that there is a component of shark cartilage that seems to reduce the growth of tumors. The following results have been taken from a small study of only 21 patients and should be viewed in that context: 61 percent had a reduction in tumor size; 87 percent stated that they had improved their quality of life; and 100 percent of prostate cancer patients had a lower PSA level.

ANTIOXIDANT ENZYMES

Proanthocyanidin

Proanthocyanidin (PAC) is a relatively new antioxidant to the market (you may have seen it sold as Pycnogenol). It is a natural plant product extracted from grape seeds and pine bark; it is also found in many other plants, but it is relatively expensive to extract from most of them.

Proanthocyanidin is said to be 20 times more powerful than vitamin C and 50 times more powerful than vitamin E. It also may be able to protect other antioxidants from being destroyed before they are able to perform their functions or be utilized by cells. Studies are underway to explore the possibility of using PAC to treat vascular problems and eye disorders.

PAC is one of the most efficient free-radical scavengers known. It has the unique ability to actually adhere to collagen (connective tissue) fibers and ward off the potential damage that might be done by circulating free radicals. This function may be the emphasis of future studies that relate to aging of the skin and joint diseases, such as arthritis.

PAC is water-soluble and has the ability to be absorbed and used by cells very shortly after ingestion. PAC remains in the body for three days, circulating in body fluids, and is gradually eliminated. If PAC is taken regularly, cells will acquire a saturation level, which provides a continuum of beneficial antioxidant activity.

Coenzyme Q10 (Ubiquinone)

Coenzyme Q10 is an enzyme that the body can produce. It is necessary for cells to produce energy and has proved to be an active antioxidant in reducing free radical production. Dietary sources of the nutrients needed to produce coenzyme Q10 are lean meats, nuts, vegetables, and grains.

Many factors may reduce the available coenzyme Q10 in the body, causing lower energy levels. Studies have shown that if levels of coenzyme Q10 are low (below 25 percent of normal levels), cells cannot produce enough energy to live and will start to die until the level increases. The elderly, malnourished, and chronically ill have lower levels of coenzyme Q10 and may need supplements. However, if a sufficient supply is always available energy levels are maintained.

Coenzyme Q10 may be active in keeping the immune system healthy and has been shown to enhance the heart's pumping capacity. It may also accelerate weight loss for those on a low-calorie diet.

Superoxide dismutase (SOD)

One of the first lines of defense the body has from free radicals is from a substance called superoxide dismutase, or SOD. SOD is a natural antioxidant that keeps free radicals under control and eliminates them. SOD always has a partner called "catalase," which helps carry away some of the debris when SOD reacts with a free radical. The most dangerous element of the debris is hydrogen peroxide, which if left alone will create additional, even more destructive free radicals.

This partnership is one of the most effective free radical eliminators in our bodies. A deficiency of SOD can reduce the body's effectiveness in fighting free radicals and increases the risk and severity of a number of diseases such as arthritis, bursitis, and gout.

Glutathione Peroxidase (GP)

The main components of this antioxidant enzyme are the amino acid glutathione and the mineral selenium. One of selenium's main functions in the body is to become a component of the GP enzyme.

The key role of GP in the body is to protect lipids in cell walls from being destroyed by a group of free radicals known as lipid peroxides. In relation to heart disease, premature aging, cancer, liver and pancreas damage, and skin disorders, studies are being done to determine the significance of the cell damage by peroxides when adequate GP is not present.

Methionine Reductase (MR)

This antioxidant enzyme has been effective in neutralizing another free radical called a hydroxyl radical. These are formed by the reactions involving heavy metals and other free radicals. Hydroxyl radicals are also formed by the exposure of the body to Xrays and radiation. MR plays a significant role in the destruction and neutralization of these free radicals, especially those formed by athletes or during strenuous exercise periods.

Hydroxyl radicals are a by-product of fat metabolism that occurs after the depletion of the body's carbohydrate stores. Athletes who can keep a high level of MR during a strenuous exercise period or sport may be able to improve their performance.

CHLORELLA

Chlorella is derived from freshwater algae and is one of the newest green algae products. It has 50 times the chlorophyll content of alfalfa, and scientists estimate it has survived for approximately 2.5 billion years. Studies have concluded that the longevity of chlorella is due to the strength of its hard cell wall and unique DNA repair mechanism.

Only recently has science discovered a method of breaking down the hard cell wall and been able to produce it as a health food. At present, chlorella is the fastest-selling health-food product in Japan and is used as both a dietary supplement and for medicinal purposes. Chlorella has a protein content of approximately 60 percent (compared with soybean's 30 percent), making it an excellent nonmeat protein source.

Chlorella contains over 20 vitamins and minerals and is an excellent source of vitamin B12, especially for vegetarians. Chlorella is far superior to spirulina (another algae) in all categories. Studies are surfacing showing that chlorophyll has been related to improved metabolism, tissue growth (wound healing), and lowering cholesterol levels. Additional studies are ongoing relating to cancer prevention because chlorella may stimulate the immune system to produce macrophages, which kill abnormal cells.

30

WHAT'S IN YOUR FOOD?

BHT

Sulfit

MSG

Did You Know?

Not all additives are harmful or undesirable. For instance, when cut apples are sprinkled with lemon juice to prevent browning, the juice is an antioxidant additive.

ABOUT ADDITIVES

Most of us are unaware of the vast quantities of additives we consume. In 1997, more than 820 million pounds of additives were used in the manufacturing of foods. Almost all these additives require vitamins and minerals to assist with their breakdown so that they can be properly disposed of, usually by the liver. The problem is that when vitamins and minerals are used to metabolize these additives, they are no longer available to the body as nutrients.

The additives and chemicals discussed in this chapter are the more common, recognizable ones. This information pertains only to the more pertinent facts regarding these substances and will not be overly technical.

THE CLASSIFICATIONS OF FOOD ADDITIVES

Moisture-Control Agents

These include anti-caking and free-flowing agents that are added to foods that are finely powdered or in crystalline form to prevent them from caking or becoming lumpy.

Humectants

Substances added to foods to assist in retaining moisture. Other additives in this category include water-binding agents, protective coatings, and anti-dusting agents.

Antimicrobial Agents

Substances used in food preservation to prevent the growth of bacteria that might cause spoilage.

Antioxidants

Substances used to preserve foods by limiting deterioration, rancidity, or discoloring caused by oxidation (exposure to oxygen). Oxygen is one of the worst enemies of food.

Coloring Agents

Substances used to enhance the color of foods. This category is broken down into color stabilizers, color fixatives, and color-retention agents.

Malting and Fermenting Aids

These are used to provide flavor and retard bacterial growth, as well as increase shelf life.

Emulsifiers

These are substances that keep oil and water in suspension so they do not separate after being mixed.

Firming Agents

Substances that are added to assist in increasing the firmness of plant tissues to keep the food from collapsing during processing and storage.

Flavors and Flavor Modifiers

Substances that impart, supplement, intensify, or modify the taste and/or the aroma of a food. This category excludes sweeteners.

Leavening Agents

Substances used to produce or stimulate the production of carbon dioxide gas in baked goods. This helps give the food a light texture. A number of yeasts or salts are used.

Sweeteners

Sweeteners are classified as nutritive and nonnutritive. The nonnutritive type of sweeteners contain less than 2 percent of the caloric value of sucrose (table sugar) per equivalent of sweetening capacity. The nutritive sweeteners must have more than 2 percent of the caloric value of sucrose per equivalent unit of sweetening capacity.

Nutrient Supplements

Substances added to a food to restore or increase its nutrient content.

Propellants, Aerating Agents, and Gases

Substances used to add force in expelling a product or to limit the amount of oxygen that comes into contact with food during packaging.

Sequestrants

Substances that combine with metal ions to change them into a metal complex that will blend into water or other liquid. The purpose is to improve the stability of that product.

Stabilizers and Thickeners

Substances used to produce a blended solution or disperse substances to give foods more body, improve the consistency, stabilize an emulsion, and assist in the setting of jellies.

Surface-Tension-Control Agents

Substances that enhance the compatibility of the liquid, solid, and gas phases of foods. Dispersants, wetting agents, rehydration enhancers, and whipping agents are included in this category.

Surface-Finishing Agents

Substances that increase the palatability of foods, preserve their natural gleam, and inhibit discoloring. These substances include glazes, polishes, waxes, and other protective coatings.

Texturizers

Substances that affect the appearance or "mouth feel" of the food.

PROCESSING ADDITIVES

Processing aids are used to enhance the appeal or the utility of a food or ingredient of a food. Some of the most common types are listed below.

Material-Handling Aids

Used to bring about a desired physical characteristic or texture in the food. These include carriers, binders, fillers, plasticizers, film-formers, and tableting aids.

Sanitizing and Fumigating Agents

Used for pest and insect control.

Lubricants and Release Agents

Added to surfaces of food manufacturing equipment that come into contact with foods to stop foods from sticking to them.

Oxidizing and Reducing Agents

Enhance or reduce oxidation in foods. They prevent of darkening of foods, are used to bleach flour, or to modify the protein content of flour.

pH-Control Agents

Added to assist in the maintenance of acid-alkaline balance in foods. These include buffers, acids, alkalis, and neutralizing agents.

Solvents

Used to extract or dissolve substances before placing them into a solution.

Catalysts

Enzymes or metals used to initiate reactions that improve the characteristics of the food or facilitate processing.

YOUR OVERWORKED LIVER

The foods we consume today contain more than $500 million of additives. This amounts to more than 820 million pounds of additives every year, which means that the typical American eats approximately six to nine pounds of these substances annually.

HIDE-AND-SEEK

Many preservatives may be hidden in the wrappers of foods. Even white bread has preservatives in the plastic bag to keep it fresh. Whether this means that any of the preservatives will be leached from the wrapper and affect the food is open to question. That said, federal safety regulations regarding packaging means that any tainting is highly unlikely.

IT'S THE OTHER 2 PERCENT . . .

By weight, almost 98 percent of food additives are sugar, corn syrup, pepper, mustard, baking soda, baking powder, citric acid, salt, or a vegetable-coloring agent. It is the other 2 percent of additives that are of possible concern to the consumer.

ACETIC ACID

Acetic acid is the acid found in common household vinegar—the substance that gives vinegar its tang. It occurs naturally in apples, cheeses, cocoa, coffee, oranges, pineapples, skim milk, and a number of other fruits and plants. A solution of about 9 percent acetic acid is used to pickle condiments and relishes, and an 0.8 percent solution is used as a flavor enhancer in cheese.

ACID-MODIFIED STARCHES

Used in soups, gravies, baby foods, and salad dressings, acid-modified starches are made by mixing starch with acid and water at such low temperatures that the starch does not gelatinize. The mixture is then neutralized and the starch is dried for use in foods.

ALUM

Alum is also known as aluminum sulfate, which is used in making pickles and acid-modified food starches. In a non-food application, alum is the main ingredient in styptic pencils (now rarely seen in these days of electric and cartridge razors), which are used to stop the bleeding caused by shaving nicks and cuts.

AMMONIUM BICARBONATE

This common leavening agent is made from carbon dioxide and ammonia. It is used in all types of baked goods, chocolate, and antacids.

AMMONIUM CHLORIDE

Baked goods and other foods that are made with yeast are the principal application for aluminum chloride. The substance has a slightly salty taste and is sometimes prescribed as a diuretic.

AMYLASE

Used in flour processing, this harmless enzyme is derived from the pancreas of swine. It breaks starch down into sugar.

BETA-CAROTENE

Beta-carotene is a compound that occurs naturally in vegetables such as carrots, yellow squash, and pumpkin. The body converts beta-carotene to vitamin A. Beta-carotene is being studied as a cancer-preventing antioxidant. In food processing, it is used for coloring.

BHA AND BHT: FRIENDS OR FOES?

Both substances are used to preserve foods by acting as antioxidants to retard rancidity. They are used in beverages, ice creams, shortenings, chewing gum, potato flakes, baked goods, dry breakfast cereals, gelatin desserts, and soup bases. The total, or combined, amount of BHA and BHT that is allowed in foods is 200 parts per million in shortenings and 50 parts per million in breakfast cereals and potato flakes, with the amount allowed dependent on the fat content of the food. One study found that with a diet of 0.5 to 1 percent BHA or BHT, mice developed abnormal behavior patterns and their offspring were born with brain abnormalities.

BROMELAIN

This enzyme, extracted from pineapple, is used to tenderize meat, condition dough, and clarify beer.

CAFFEINE

Caffeine is a psychoactive drug found naturally in coffee, tea, and chocolate. It is also used to flavor root beer and other sodas. Taken in excess, caffeine can cause nervousness, insomnia, and irregular heart rhythm.

CALCIUM CARBONATE

Also known as common chalk. Calcium carbonate is highly alkaline and is used in the food industry to lower the acidity of wine and ice cream. It is also used in antacids and in antidiarrheal medications.

DID YOU KNOW?

Bromelain prevents gelatin from setting. If you want to use pineapple in a gelatin salad or dessert, use canned—the heat from processing inactivates the bromelain.

CALCIUM HYPOCHLORITE

Found in common household bleach, calcium hypochlorite has applications in the food industry as well. In dilute solutions, it is used to sterilize produce, to wash cottage cheese curd, and to kill germs and bacteria on food-manufacturing equipment.

CALCIUM LACTATE

This chalky, odorless powder is used as a bread dough conditioner and oxidizing agent. It is also an ingredient in some calcium supplements.

CALCIUM PROPIONATE

This is a preservative. Its primary purpose is to inhibit mold in cheese and baked goods.

CALCIUM SULFATE

A fine white powder used as a firming agent and dough conditioner. It is found in baked goods, jellies, cereals, and canned tomato products. It is the abrasive in most toothpastes and is also known as plaster of paris.

CARRAGEENAN

Derived from Irish moss, this natural additive is used as an emulsifier in dairy products such as cheese spreads and ice cream. It is also used in processed-meat and poultry products, and in gelatin desserts and reduced-calorie jellies.

CHLORINE GAS

This greenish-yellow gas is dangerous to inhale. It is used as a food bleaching agent, most commonly on flour.

CHLOROPHYLL

The same substance responsible for light absorption in photosynthesis is also used to give a green color to olive and soybean oils. It is also used in mouthwash and as a natural deodorant.

COLORINGS

Each batch of synthetic color additives produced in the United States goes through a certification process in which it is tested by the manufacturer and by the FDA to assure safety, quality, consistency, and strength prior to use in foods. Colors from natural sources do not have to go through the strict certification process but are subjected to rigorous standards of safety prior to approval for use in foods.

DIACETYL

Found naturally in cheeses, pears, and berries, diacetyl is a flavoring agent added to butter, ice cream, baked goods, and confections.

DISODIUM PYROPHOSPHATE

Used in meats and poultry to help retain juices and as a leavening agent in biscuits and doughnuts. Also found in hot dogs and poultry products.

ETHYL ACETATE

Ethyl acetate occurs naturally in berries, pineapple, and pears. A synthetic form of ethyl acetate—a colorless liquid with a fruity aroma—is used as a flavoring in fruit drinks, candy, chewing gum, ice cream, and pudding.

ETHYL VANILLIN

This synthetically produced vanilla flavoring is used in baked goods, ice creams, beverages, and dessert sauces.

EUCALYPTUS OIL

Eucalpytus oil has a camphor-like odor and is used in flavorings for beverages, ice creams, and baked goods.

GLUTEN

Gluten, a combination of the two proteins gliadin and glutelin, occurs naturally in wheat flour. Gluten is sometimes added to breads to give them a smooth yet firm texture.

GUAR GUM

Extracted from the endosperm of the seeds of a plant grown in India, guar gum is used as a thickener in salad dressings, cream cheese, baked goods, and ice creams. In the pharmaceutical industry, it is used as a tableting agent in the manufacturing of pills.

GUM ARABIC

This odorless, colorless, and flavorless substance is derived from the stems and branches of the acacia tree, which grows in Africa and areas of the southern United States. Gum arabic, also known as acacia, is considered a natural gum and has the ability to dissolve very quickly in water. It is used to stop sugar crystallization, as a thickening agent in candymaking, and in chewing gum. Gum arabic is used in the soft drink and beer industry to retard foam.

INVERT SUGAR

Equal parts glucose and fructose, invert sugar is used to sweeten icings, candy, and soft drinks. In baked goods, it not only sweetens but also holds moisture, preventing cakes and cookies from drying out.

LECITHIN

A natural antioxidant and emulsifier derived from soybeans and egg yolk, it is used in cereals, candies, chocolate, baked goods, and margarine.

MALIC ACID

Malic acid occurs naturally in apples and cherries. It is used to flavor frozen dairy products, candies, preserves, and baked goods.

MANNITOL

Mannitol is a sugar alcohol used in sugar-free candies and gum. It is not calorie-free, though it is lower in calories than table sugar. Unlike sugar, mannitol does not promote dental cavities or cause a sudden increase in blood glucose. Consuming excess mannitol can have a laxative effect.

DID YOU KNOW?

If you're sensitive to the effects of MSG, avoid foods with "hydrolyzed vegetable protein," "hydrolyzed plant protein," or "natural flavoring" listed on the label.

METHYLENE CHLORIDE

A gas used in one method of decaffeinating coffee. Residues may remain, and the kicker is that coffee companies do not have to disclose on the label which method they used to decaffeinate. It's best to drink decaf whose label states that it was decaffeinated with water—it's a more expensive process and results in a better tasting, possibly more healthful, brew.

MODIFIED STARCH

This chemically altered starch is used as a thickener for jellies. It is also gives baby foods a smooth, homogeneous texture.

MONOSODIUM GLUTAMATE (MSG)

Monosodium glutamate is the sodium salt of glutamic acid, a common amino acid. MSG is used to flavor soups, condiments, processed meats, and baked goods. Glutamic acid is responsible for the transmission of nerve impulses, and too much MSG temporarily disrupts the glutamic acid balance in the nerve endings. This is one possible explanation for the headaches and tingling feelings reported by some after consumption of MSG. A study released by the Federation of American Societies for Experimental Biology in 1995 stated that MSG was safe for most people. However, other reports indicate that people with asthma may be affected by as little as half a gram of MSG.

NITRATES AND NITRITES

Nitrates and nitrites are used in meat processing as preservatives to guard against botulism. These compounds also give hot dogs, ham, and luncheon meats their rosy color. In the body, they form nitrosamines, which have been found to cause cancer in laboratory animals.

When humans ingest nitrites, two potentially harmful reactions can occur. In babies whose intestinal tracts have not developed enough acid-producing bacteria to block nitrite formation, the nitrites may react with hemoglobin to produce a pigment called meth-hemoglobin, which may seriously lower the oxygen-carrying capacity of red blood cells. Because babies are not often fed nitrite-cured meats, this rarely poses a problem.

Second, there is a possible cancer connection when the nitrites are biochemically altered into a nitrosamine, which occurs in the stomach if certain proteins are present when the nitrites arrive. Nitrosamines are formed naturally in the human digestive tract, and only about 20 percent of the nitrite available for this reaction is from cured meats. The other 80 percent is formed in the body from nitrates that are found in produce, especially that grown on land where high-nitrate fertilizers are used.

If you drink some orange juice or chew a 500-milligram vitamin C tablet just before consuming foods that contain nitrites, you may reverse the adverse reaction. Vitamin C can neutralize the reaction that takes place in the stomach by interfering with the protein combining with the nitrite. As a result of recent studies about this neutralizing effect, some hot dogs are now made with ascorbic acid as an additive.

PAPAIN

Papain is naturally derived from the milky juice of papaya skin, and is used as a meat tenderizer. It is rendered inactive at temperatures above the boiling point and so must be used before the meat is cooked, usually as a marinade. An interesting footnote: Papaya has a long history as a digestive aid, and is eaten after meals in countries where papaya grows. The enzyme responsible for aiding digestion is papain.

PECTIN

Pectin occurs naturally in citrus fruits, apples, and beets, and in lower amounts in the roots and stems of many other plants. Pectin thickens fruit syrups, jellies, salad dressings, puddings, and ice creams. It stabilizes and adds body to foods, functioning as a binding agent.

PEROXIDE

Peroxide is used as a bleaching agent for cheeses, shortening, and flour. It is also used as a dough conditioner, as an oxidizing agent, a preservative, and as a starch modifier. Its uses extend to the dairy industry, where it is employed to reduce bacteria in milk products.

POTASSIUM CHLORIDE

This crystalline, odorless powder has a salty taste and is used by people on sodium-restricted diets as a replacement for sodium chloride. It is also employed by the brewing industry to control pH during fermentation and is used to improve the gelling of jams and jellies. Taken in excess, potassium chloride can cause gastrointestinal irritation.

SODIUM BENZOATE

Sodium benzoate is used to retard bacterial growth and as a preservative in carbonated beverages, jams and jellies, margarine, and salad dressings.

SODIUM BISULFITE

A type of sulfite used to prevent browning and as a preservative in beverages, dehydrated potatoes, dried fruits, sauces, soups, and some wines. Sodium bisulfite destroys vitamin B1 (thiamine) when added to foods.

SODIUM CARBONATE

Derived from seaweed, this odorless powder is used to control the pH of dairy products and olives. It is also used in antacids.

SODIUM CASEINATE

Used as a thickener and texturizer, this protein is obtained from milk. It is used in coffee creamers, frozen custards, and ice cream products.

SODIUM CHLORIDE

This is the chemical name for common table salt. It is used in numerous food products both as a preservative and flavor enhancer. It readily absorbs water. Your daily intake should not exceed 2,400 milligrams.

  Table salt is sold as mined salt or sea salt (see page 161). Mined salt is actually sea salt, albeit very old. The great undergound salt domes near Chicago, for example, were originally formed hundreds of millions of years ago when seawater, trapped behind ocean reefs, evaporated.

SODIUM CITRATE

An emulsifier in ice cream, processed cheese, and evaporated milk, sodium citrate also controls acidity and retains carbonation in soft drinks.

SORBITOL

Sorbitol, like mannitol, is an alcohol sugar. It has fewer calories than table sugar and it does not promote tooth cavities. The substance is used to sweeten sugar-free candies and soft drinks and as a stabilizer in frozen desserts. Eating an excess of sorbitol can have a laxative effect.

SULFITES

There are three types of sulfites that may be used as anti-browning agents: sodium, potassium, and ammonium. All may be used on most foods except meats or other foods that have a high thiamine content, as sulfites destroy this vitamin.

The FDA estimates that one in one hundred people is sensitive to sulfites, and that 5 percent of people with asthma are at risk of having an adverse reaction to sulfites. Sulfites are banned for use on fresh-cut vegetables, such as those served at salad bars, but are used on dried fruits and dehydrated potatoes. Sulfites are also used to prevent "black spot" on shrimp and lobster, to discourage bacterial growth when fermenting wine, to bleach food starches, and to condition dough. If you are sulfite sensitive, read food labels carefully.

TANNIC ACID

Tannic acid is found in many commonly-eaten foods and is the substance that gives red wine, tea, and coffee their astringency. In the food industry, tannic acid is used to clarify beer and wine and is used as a flavoring for beverages, baked goods, and candy.

ACCIDENTAL ADDITIVES

Sometimes you're ingesting additives that weren't puposely added to the food, but got there nonetheless. In fact, as many as 10,000 substances overall can make their way into food during the growing, processing, and packaging phases. And some of these accidental additives are more of a threat to health than preservatives and other direct additives. For example, some foods contain traces of pesticides that were sprayed on crops or applied in the soil. Then there are environmental pollutants such as PCBs, mercury, and lead, all of which are harmful when ingested in large quantities.

ADDITIVE OVERKILL

Some cereals that are highly fortified with vitamins and minerals claim to provide 100 percent of the Recommended Dietary Allowance (RDA). But it is unrealistic to expect a bowl of cereal to deliver on that promise. A high-fiber, whole-grain cereal is just as healthful, and costs less to boot.

INDEX

························◆◆◆·············

A

abalone, 334
acacia. *See* gum arabic
accidents. *See* safety
acerola, 187
acetaminophen, 543
acetic acid, 573
Achilles tendon, 445
acid-modified starches, 573
acidophilus milk, 384
ackee, 193
acne medications, 546
acorns, 140
Adams, Thomas, 108
additives, 570-81
  accidental, 581
  candy, 102
  classifications of, 570-72
  consumption of, 572
  in fast food, 457
  overkill, 581
  processing, 572
  by weight, 106, 573
  See also specific additives
adhesive tape, 507
aerating agents, 571
aeration filtration, 481
aerobics, 440
aflatoxin, 137-38
aftershave lotion, 542
aging, 438

air pollution, 553
alcohol
  absorption, 408
  in breads, 76
  as cause of accidents, 408
  coffee and, 407
  content, 408
  cooking with, 24
  distillation, 408
  effects on body systems,
    406-7, 416
  freezing dishes with, 39
  and motion sickness, 409
  stain removal, 506
  and vitamin A, 409
  water to metabolize, 393,
    396
  and zinc, 409
alcoholism, 408
ale, 417
allergy, 134
allium compounds, 561
all-purpose flour, 52, 54, 55
allspice, 147
  roasting, 165
  substitution, 166
almond paste, 135
almonds, 135, 137
aloe, 434
alpha-carotene, 561, 565
altitude, and boiling point,
  25
alum (aluminum sulfate),
  573

aluminum contamination,
  484
aluminum cookware, 16, 22,
  371
aluminum foil, 44, 190
amaranth, 128
American cheese, 359
ammonia, 48, 491
ammonium bicarbonate, 573
ammonium chloride, 573
amygdalin, 192
amylase, 139, 574
amylopectin, 139
anaheim peppers, 279
analgesics, 542-43
ancho peppers, 279
anchovies, 343, 348
Anderson, Alexander P., 132
angel food cake, 65, 83, 87,
  91
anglerfish, 344
animals
  accidents on rugs, 534
  deterrents outdoors, 535,
    538
  vitamins and minerals for
    pets, 536
anise, 147
ankle sprain, 443
antacids, 219
anthocyanins, 562
antibiotics, 302, 324, 474
antimicrobial agents, 570

antioxidants, 566-68, 570
  See also phytochemicals;
    specific antioxidants
antipastos, 459
antiperspirants, 507, 542
antiseptics, 544
ants, 537
Appert, Nicolas-François, 40
appetizers
  amount needed for party,
    46
  in restaurants, 459
apple butter, 199
apple cider, 196
apple-cider vinegar, 164, 433
apple juice, 196, 198
apples, 464
  baked, 197, 236
  facts, 193-94, 198-99
  health benefits, 199
  preferred by teachers, 199
  tips, 197-98
  varieties, 194-96
applesauce, 198
apricots, 199-200
aquaculture, 352-53
arch, 443
argol, 70
aromas, 12, 285, 521
  See also odors
arrowroot, 426
artesian well water, 393
arthritis, 233, 378
artichoke, 236-37
artificial sweeteners, 100-101
arugula, 230, 268
asparagus, 238-39
aspartame, 100
aspirin, 542
astringency, 186
atemoya, 200
automobile. *See* car
avocado, 184, 200-201, 431

B

babáco, 187
baby food jar, 532
baby formula, 388, 508
baby oil, 433
Baby Ruth candy bar, 107
back pain, 444
bacon, 297, 308
bacteria, 38, 188
  in food poisoning, 479
  and hand-washing, 474
  in poultry, 310, 322, 326
  in seafood, 340
  See also specific types, e.g.,
    E. coli
bagel, 56, 75
baked goods
  cooling of, 58
  expansion of, 82
  fat content, 72, 77
  mold on, 79
  sticking to bottom of pan,
    81
  sugar in, 111
  See also specific baked goods
baked potato, 13, 175, 176,
    178, 179
baking
  blending ingredients, 89
  with buttermilk, 59, 64,
    119, 380
  greased and floured pans,
    76-77, 84, 88, 119
  at high altitude, 93
  moisture lost in, 55
  oils in, 125
  pans, 53-54
  potatoes, 13
  preheating oven, 56
  sinking of dried fruits, 92
  sources for equipment, 75

spacing pans in oven, 56
  at temperatures in recipes,
    74
  vegetables, 10
  warm ingredients for, 55
  See also baked goods
baking powder
  in biscuits, 68
  and chocolate, 70
  home formula, 64-65
  workings of, 63
baking sheet, 86
baking soda
  and B vitamins, 15
  facts, 70-71
  and tooth brushing, 431
  uses for, 432, 523, 524,
    546
  and vegetable cooking,
    182, 234
ball, 527
balloon fish, 353
balsamic vinegar, 164
banana, 184, 201-3
banana pepper, 279
barbecue sauce, 327
barbecuing
  chicken, 326
  cross-contamination
    during, 474
  and gender, 19
  for large crowd, 48, 301
  tips, 17
bar cookie, 85
barley, 128, 139-40
barracuda, 344
basil, 147, 534
Bath bun, 73
bath oil, 430
bathroom
  bathtub cleaner, 545
  caulking cleaner, 548
  light fixture, 497

toilet bowl cleaner, 505, 540, 545
batter
 cake, 81
 cookie, 90
 deep-frying, 118
 mixing, 84
 raw eggs in, 91
 stirring, 57
battery, car, 523, 544
bay leaf, 148
beans, 239-43
 cooking tips, 245-46
 facts, 239-40
 and flatulence, 241
 phytochemicals, 559
 storing, 242
 varieties, 241-43
 See also specific types
peanut butter, 136
béarnaise sauce, 368-69
beef. See hamburger; meat; roast beef; steak
Beef Wellington, 47
beer
 age of, 416
 alcohol in, 415
 coldness of bottle versus can, 416
 cooking with, 415
 draft versus bottled or canned, 414
 foam/head, 413, 415
 to get rid of snails, 536
 and health, 414
 light, 413
 and nutrition, 417
 speedy iced, 416
 storage, 415
 temperature of, 413, 415
 types of, 417
beer belly, 413
beer cheese, 359
beets, 230, 247-48

beet sugar, 109
Belgian endive. See endive
bell pepper, 236, 279
Bell's Seasoning, 166
bel paese cheese, 360
beluga caviar, 350
Benecol, 564
berries, 204-6, 208
 See also specific types
beta-carotene, 561, 565, 574
 in carrots, 252, 253
 in pumpkin, 283
beta-cryptoxanthin, 565
beverages
 acidity in, 402
 calories burned off in exercise, 446, 451
 colorful, 406
 hot drinks, 401
 ice cubes in, 47
 See also specific beverages
BHA/BHT, 574
bicarbonate of soda. See baking soda
Birdseye food company, 40
biscuits
 color of, 79
 cutter, 59
 fluffy, 70
 heavy, 69
 mixing dough, 86
 reheating, 77
bison, 300
black beans, 138
black tea, 396, 397
black walnuts, 139
bladder, 206
blanching, 42
blankets, 516
bleach, 500, 502, 504
bleached flour, 52
blender
 hand-held, 31
 lubrication, 528

bleu cheese. See blue cheese
blisters, 443
blood stains, 501, 506, 513, 517
bloodstream, and alcohol, 406
blow-dryer
 cord, 490
 for defrosting, 528
blowfish, 353
blown sugar, 109
blueberry, 204, 205
blue cheese, 357, 360
bluefish, 344
blush wines, 411
bock beer, 417
boiling point, 14
 and altitude, 25
 temperature of, 19
Bok Choy, 251
bolts. See nuts and bolts
bones, dark-colored, 424
bottles, 44, 520
 See also jars
bouquet garni, 172
boursault cheese, 360
Braeburn apple, 194
brain, and alcohol, 407
bran, 128, 130, 134
brandy, 412
Brazil nuts, 140
breadcrumbs, 527
breadfruit, 206
breading, 13, 25bread machine, 59
breads
 browning too fast, 92
 burned, 79
 calories burned off in exercise, 448
 checking while baking, 77
 cooling, 58
 crispy crust, 60

dough, 55, 57, 79
flour, 52, 55, 56, 57, 78, 134
freezing, 78
French, 61
garlic, 79
keeping top from cracking, 62
kneading, 56, 68
labeling, 56, 59, 134
liquids in, 76
nutritional value, 54
plant output, 62
potato water in, 57, 76
pumpernickel, 78
removing from pan, 69
replacing moisture in, 79
in restaurants, 459
rising of, 67-68, 71, 78, 79
salt in, 60, 78
sourdough, 58, 63
stale, 62
storing, 60, 93
structure of, 73
sweeteners in, 61
tips, 78
types of, 77
See also yeast
bread sticks, 59
breast cancer, 556
breastfeeding, 389
breath mints, 545
brick cheese, 360
Brie cheese, 357, 360
brisket, 293
broccoflower, 250
broccoli, 248-50
broccoli raab, 249
broccoli, oriental, 249
bromelain, 313, 574
brown rice, 130
brown rice flour, 52
brown sugar, 104, 105, 109

Brussels sprouts, 250, 554
bubble bath, 432
bubble blowing, 527
buckwheat, 129
buffalo, 305
buffalo fish, 349
Buffalo wings, 326
buffets, 49, 474, 475
bulgur, 133
buns
    Bath, 73
    multigrain, 455
burns, 105
burritos, 120
bursitis, 445
butter
    balls, 49
    in cake recipes, 84
    clarified, 386
    in cookies, 89
    creaming with sugar, 82, 83
        fancy pats, 49
    grades, 389
    highest quality, 116
    making at home, 390
    microwaving, 388
    not from cow, 386
    in preserves and jellies, 193
    rancidity, 387
    sautéing with, 422
    smoke point, 14
    stick versus whipped, 385
    storage, 385
    terra-cotta dish for, 116
    unsalted in recipes, 385
    whipped, 119, 120, 385
    wrappers, 526
butter-flavored sprays, 385
buttermilk
    in baking recipes, 64, 380
    contents, 387
    in mashed potatoes, 178
    in pastry, 119

in quick breads, 59
to soften cheese, 383
button mushrooms, 270
buttons, 514, 515, 516
B vitamins, 15
    in barley, 140
    and honey, 112
    and thiaminase, 554

C

cabbage, 189, 250-51, 535, 554
cadmium, 485
Caesar salad, 235
cafestol, 403
caffeine, 398, 400, 574
    and calcium, 404
    content in common foods and drugs, 404
    physical properties, 403-4
    in sodas, 407
    in water, 402
caimito, 226
cake(s)
    angel food, 65, 83, 87, 91
    bubbles in batter, 81
    checking while baking, 77, 82
    cheesecake, 81, 106
    chiffon, 65
    chocolate and baking powder in, 70
    cutting, 91, 92
    "dome", 69
    eggs in, 82
    fats in, 83
    flour, 52, 82, 90
    heart-shaped, 87
    keeping insides from drying out, 80
    keeping layers together, 80
    lower-fat, 64

one-bowl, 75
problems, 65
removing from pan, 69
shortened, 65
sponge, 65
stale, 81
storing, 92
texture, 84
toppings, 57
warm ingredients for, 55
See also icing
calamari, 343
calcium
in almonds, 137
and caffeine, 400
and lactose intolerance,
553
loss of, 555
and manganese, 301
and oxalic acid, 234
supplements, 556
calcium carbonate, 525, 574
calcium hypochlorite, 575
calcium lactate, 575
calcium proprionate, 575
calcium sulfate, 575
calories
burned off in exercise,
448-51
burned off in walking,
446-47
and energy balance, 437
in fast foods, 456-58
fat, 119, 126
humorous chart, 452
in meats, 315-16
Camembert cheese, 357, 360
campfire, 489
campylobacter, 474, 479
cancer
carcinogens in burgers,
300
carcinogens in vegetables,
230

and fat intake, 120
and flaxseed, 141
and nitrites, 578
and peanut butter, 137-38
and phytochemicals,
558-64
and shark cartilage, 566
and shiitake mushrooms,
272
and vitamin D, 556
candleholders, 528
candles, 506, 513, 521, 547
candy
additives, 102
Baby Ruth, 107
calories burned off in
exercise, 447, 451
carob, 120
consumption, 111
cooking tips, 22, 103
freezing, 103
fudge, 103
Hershey's Kisses, 108
history of, 112
recipes, 102, 103
storing, 105
thermometers, 11
and tooth decay, 102
See also chocolate
cane sugar, 109
caning, 496
canned food
black spot on lid, 476
damaged can, 473
facts, 466
history of, 40
home-canned, 233, 475,
477
seal, 476
vitamin loss in, 550
canola oil, 14, 22, 122
can opener, 520
cantaloupe, 188, 207

canthaxanthin, 565
capers, 148
capon, 325
capsaicin, 278, 560
car
battery, 523, 544
bumper, 524
jumper cable, 544
stinging insect in, 532
tips, 540
carambola, 207
caraway, 148
carbohydrates, 288
carbonated water, 393, 395
carbon monoxide, 19
carbon steel cookware, 22-23
carbon steel knife, 29
carcinogens. *See* cancer
cardamom, 148
Cardini, Caesar, 235
cardiovascular disease, 394
cardiovascular system, 438,
440
carnosol, 563
carob, 110, 120
carotene, 378
carotenoids, 123-24, 561,
565-66
carp, 349
carpenter ants, 537
carpets and carpeting
colors, 525
fleas in, 535
odors, 543
pet accidents, 534
raising nap, 525
red wine on, 522
carrageenan, 575
carrot family, 229
carrots, 236, 252-54
in soups or stews, 424
water in, 395
cascabel peppers, 279
casein, 524

cashew nuts, 141
castor oil, 125
catalysts, 572
catechins, 563
catfish, 349
cattle, 296, 310, 378-79
cauliflower, 253-54
caulking cleaner, 548
caviar, 350
cayenne pepper, 149, 280
cedar, 495
celeriac, 255
celery, 236, 254-55
celery flakes, 149
celery juice, 256
celery seed, 149
celiac disease, 134
cellulose, 232
celtuce, 255, 268
Cèpe mushrooms, 270
cereals
    calories burned off in
        exercise, 448
    fortified, 551
    hot, 133
    protein from, 137
    puffed, 132
ceviche, 217
chairs, 496
chalazae cords, 371
chalk, 525, 574
Champagne, 409-11
chanterelle mushrooms, 270
charcoal filtration, 481, 488
chayote, 226
Cheddar cheese, 358, 360
cheese, 356-64
    buttermilk to soften, 383
    chemicals in, 356
    common types, 359-63
    cultures, 357
    facts, 364
    grating, 358, 524

low-fat in recipes, 357
melting, 356
in pizza, 46
ripening classifications,
    359
soft, 357
See also specific types
cheeseburger, 456
cheesecake, 81, 106
cheesecloth, 522
cherries, 47, 207-9
cherry peppers, 280
chervil, 149
Cheshire cheese, 360
Chess pie, 62
chewing gum, 108, 110,
    506, 508, 521
chicken
    amount per serving, 327
    cleaning, 327
    consumption of, 323
    eggs from, 375
    facts, 320-21, 322, 326
    fast food sandwich, 455
    feed to produce, 206
    freezing of, 311
    fried, 454
    grilling, 326, 327
    and health risks, 318, 322,
        324, 326
    history of, 375
    population, 375
    roasted, 455
    skin color versus quality,
        327-28
    skinning, 328
    slaughtering and
        inspection, 318-19
    types of, 325
    weight, 324
    white meat versus dark,
        328
    wings, 326
    yields, 325

chicory, 268
chiffon cake, 65
chile pepper, 149, 278, 560
chili, 240, 474
chili powder, 149
Chinese dates, 189
Chinese five-spice powder,
    167
Chinese gooseberry. See kiwi
Chinese lantern fruit, 186
chitlins, 314
chives, 150
chlorella, 568
chlorine, 482
chlorine gas, 575
chlorogenic acid, 561
chlorophyll, 575
chocolate
    and baking powder, 70
    bunnies, 49, 103
    curls, 91
    facts, 101-2
    Hershey's Kisses, 108
    icing, 80
    making in cool weather,
        103
    and migraines, 112
    phenols in, 106
    plastic, 107
    shaved frozen, 49
    stain removal, 507
    stiffening, 107
cholesterol
    and cocoa powder, 106
    and coffee, 403
    in eggs, 374
    and exercise, 442
    in fast foods, 456
    and garlic, 152
    in milk, 387
    and stearic acid, 121
    and trans-fatty acids, 116
chow-chow, 228

chowder, 335
Christmas trees, 490
chrome fixtures, 501
chuck cuts, 292, 295, 304
ciguatera, 332, 353
cilantro, 150
cinnamon, 150, 165
cis-form fatty acids, 115
citron, 186
citronella candles/lamps,
    536, 538
citrus fruits, 224, 560
    See also specific types
citrus peel, 188, 191
clams, 334, 335, 343
cleaning products, 502
    bathtub, 545
    grout/caulking, 540, 548
    oven, 505, 543, 548
    safe, 504
    toilet bowl, 505, 540, 545
    See also detergent; soap
cleansing cream, 433, 541
clementines, 188
clover, 283
cloves, 150, 167
club soda, 393
cobblers, 74
Coca-Cola, 110, 405
cocoa butter, 120
cocoa powder, 106
cocoa stain removal, 507
coconut, 135, 210
cod, 344
co-enzyme Q10, 567
coffee
    acidity in, 402
    and alcohol, 407
    bitter, 403
    boiled, 403
    brewing fresh ground
        beans, 399
    decaffeinated, 400-401

diuretic effect, 401
facts, 399-400
fresh cream, 477
iced, 397
and insomnia, 402
origins of, 398-99
size of grind, 401-2
stains, 507, 518
storage, 399
temperature, 402
cola, 523, 524, 544
    See also Coca-Cola
cola syrup, 546
Colby cheese, 360
cold cream, 541
coldpack cheese, 361
collagen, 310
collard greens, 264
cologne, 545
colorings, 570, 576
compound fats, 114
condensed milk, 383
conduction cooking, 26
confectioners' sugar, 92
congeners, 409
constipation, 185
contact lens, 430
contact paper, 525
containers
    baby food jars, 532
    icing, 428
    milk, 378, 470
    oil, 119, 122, 428
    stain removal, 503
    used microwave, 526
convection cooking, 26
convection oven, 17, 24-25
Cook, James, 251
cookbooks, 32
cookies
    baking sheet for, 86
    browning, 90
    burned, 85, 86
    chewy, 87

crisp, 90
crunchy, 89
dough, 73, 86, 91
facts, 73-74
fats used in, 83
heavy, 83
hermits, 72
jumbles, 72
margarine in, 74
Mexican wedding cakes,
    62
oatmeal, 87
sharp edge on, 91
snickerdoodles, 69
soft, 90
storing, 55
sugar, 88
types of, 85-86
warm ingredients for, 55
cooking
    with alcohol, 24
    aromas, 12
    burned foods, 527
    chemistry of, 18
    gadgets, 31
    heat used for, 26
    with salted water, 24
    temperature, 12
    utensils, 526
    vegetables, 10-11, 15, 24
    See also specific foods and
        cooking methods
cookware
    aluminum, 16, 22, 371
    baking pans, 53-54, 76-77,
        88, 119
    buying, 31
    carbon steel, 22-23
    copper, 17, 22, 376
    for cruciferous vegetables,
        24
    enamel-coated, 23
    glass, 17, 23

greasing pans, 76-77, 84, 88, 119, 526
and heat distribution, 20
iron, 14, 16, 22-23
microwave safe, 526
multi-ply, 23
nonstick, 16, 23, 547
for roasts, 15
slow-cookers, 10, 28-29
sources for baking equipment, 75
Teflon, 23
types, 16-17, 22-23
warped, 25, 93
copper cookware, 17, 22, 376
coriander, 150
corks, 48, 410, 412
corn, 129, 256-58
corn flour, 53, 136
Cornish hens, 323, 325
corn syrup, 96, 97, 106
corn tortillas, 423
Cortland apples, 194
cottage cheese, 364, 383
cough medicine, 106
coumaric, 561
cows. See cattle
crabs, 335-36, 339
cracked wheat, 133
crackers
high-fat, 118
and tooth decay, 102
cranberry, 205-6
cranberry bean, 243
cranberry juice, 206, 562
crayfish (crawfish; crawdad), 336-37, 343
crayon stain, 507
cream
fresh, 477
light, 92
souring, 388

varieties, 385
whipped, 80, 379, 386, 477
cream cheese
colored, 47
defined, 361
at room temperature, 81
cream of tartar, 70
cream-of-tomato soup, 424
cream soups, 421, 425
Criterion apples, 194
croaker, 344
Crock-Pot, 28-29
cruciferous vegetables, 24
Crum, George, 175
crumbs, 137
cubanelle peppers, 279
cucumbers, 260-62, 433
cumin, 150
curdling
of cream soup or sauce, 412, 421, 424
of dairy products, 15, 388
of hollandaise, 422
curds, 378
curry powder, 151
Curtis, John Bacon, 108
custard, 389, 477
custard apple, 226
cutting board, 472, 529
cyanide, 192, 198
cyanogen, 198
cyclamates, 100

D

dairy, 378-90
calories burned off in exercise, 450
intolerance, 553
low heat for, 15
and mucus, 384
pasteurization, 551

storing, 389
substitute products, 383
in supermarket cases, 462
See also specific products
dandelion, 230
dates, 188, 209
decaffeination, 400-401
decals, 520
decanters, 473
deep-frying
sticking food, 15
temperature of oil, 20, 125
thermometer, 118
deer, 537
degreasers, 504
dehydrated foods, 551
dehydration, 394
denture cleaning, 523
deodorants, 507, 542
depilatories, 541
derived fat, 114
desserts
calories burned off in walking, 447
flambéed, 47
most popular, 106
See also specific types, e.g., pastry
detergent, 500, 502, 510, 524, 540
deviled eggs, 366, 371
Dewar, James, 61
diacetyl, 576
diaper pail, 491
Diat, Louis, 180
Dietary Supplement Health and Education Act of 1994 (DSHEA), 555
diet plate, 459
diet terminology, 467-68
digestive system, 555
dill, 151
dill pickle, 262
dinnerware. See tableware

dip(s)
  dry soup mixes for, 423
  high-fiber, 48
  holders, 46
dishwasher soap, 529
dishwashing, 548
disinfectants, 544
disodium pyrophosphate,
  576
distillation filtration, 481
distilled water, 515
dithiolthione, 559
dogs, 534
Dom Perignon, 409
doors, squeaky, 494
dough
  bread, 55, 57, 71, 79
  cookie, 73, 86
  cutting down on rising
    time, 58
  hook, 55
  and humidity, 55
  kneading, 80, 525
  pastry, 85
  pie, 85, 88
doughnuts, 90, 457
drains, 547
drawers, 495
dressing. See salad dressing
dried fruit, 192
drinking glasses. See glasses
drinks. See beverages
drop cookies, 85
drugs
  on empty stomach, 474
  and grapefruit, 212
  in livestock and poultry,
    302, 324
dryer, 511
dry skin, 431
DSHEA. See Dietary
  Supplement Health and
  Education Act of 1994

duck, 323, 324, 372
durum wheat, 132
dust mop, 531
dye stain removal, 507

E

earrings, 531
Easter eggs, 48
eau de toilette, 545
E. coli, 188, 217, 290, 291,
  300, 479
Edam cheese, 361
eel, 344
eggnog, 370
eggplant, 262-63
eggs, 366-76
  age of, 373, 375
  and bacteria, 368, 370
  in baking, 64, 82, 83
  beating, 93, 376
  "breathing", 373-74
  chemistry, 366
  of chicken, 375
  Chinese delicacy, 372-73
  consumption, 375
  cooking of, 366-68, 374
  cracking when boiling, 376
  Easter-egg dyes, 48
  exploding, 14
  facts, 369-71
  grading, 366, 372
  green, 373
  healthy, 374
  raw, 91, 376
  rotten to deter animals,
    535
  separating, 371
  stain removal, 507
  storing, 373
  telling quality by spread,
    372
egg substitute, 119, 371

egg wash, 372
Eldridge, Elmer E., 358
electric can opener, 520
elephant garlic, 151
emulsification, 426, 570
enameled cookware, 17, 23
endive, 230, 268
endosperm, 128
energy balance, 437
enoki mushroom, 270
entertainment, 50
escarole, 269
Escherichia coli. See E. coli
ethyl acetate, 576
ethylene gas, 184, 196-97
ethyl vanillin, 382, 576
etrog, 186
eucalyptus oil, 576
eugenol, 167
evaporated milk, 380, 383
Evert-Fresh bags, 42-43
exercise, 437
  aerobic, 440
  benefits of, 438
  and breastfeeding, 389
  and calories, 448-51
  hazards of ignoring, 442
  home fitness equipment,
    442-43
  injuries and prevention,
    443-45
  lung power during, 439
  and muscles, 441
  in water, 440
eyes, puffy, 433

F

fabric, 505-6, 510, 512
fabric softener, 504, 507,
  514, 540
facial treatments, 431,
  433-34

Fadiman, Clifton, 356
farmer cheese, 361
fast food, 454-60
  See also specific foods
fast-twitch muscle fibers, 441
fat(s)
  bad side of good, 115
  in baked goods, 72, 77, 83
  calories in common foods,
    126
  and cancer, 120
  chemistry of, 114
  color of, 122
  consumption of, 121
  cost of reduced-fat foods,
    60
  in crackers, 118
  in dairy products, 378
  dietary guidelines, 123
  digestion of, 121
  drippings, 117
  in fast food, 456
  in fish, 332
  in folk medicine, 125-26
  and freezing, 298, 299
  and frying meat in oil, 14
  frying temperature, 118
  and insomnia, 122
  in meats, 315-16
  and obesity, 121, 122
  smoke point, 21
  in soups, stews, or gravies,
    420
  in spaghetti sauce, 421
  substitutes, 123-24
  thermometers, 11
  and vitamins, 554
fatty acids, 114-16
fava beans, 243, 246
feet, 430
feijoa, 187
fell, 293
fennel, 151, 263
fenugreek, 151

fermenting aids, 570
fertilizers, 371, 490
feta cheese, 361
feverfew, 529
fiddlehead fern, 231
figs, 210-11
fire, 521
fire extinguisher, 523
fireplace, 490, 491
firming agents, 571
fish, 330-54
  aquacultured, 352-53
  baked, 331
  calories burned off in
    exercise, 449
  common forms, 332-33
  contamination, 332
  cooking, 351, 354
  cooling, 354
  de-gilling fresh, 353
  facts, 330
  fast food, 455
  fat content, 332
  freshest, 330
  freshwater, 349-50, 352
  frozen, 330, 331, 332
  and heart attack, 352
  imported, 351
  labeling, 333
  microwaving, 331, 351
  and pregnancy, 351
  raw, 351
  red spots on fillets, 352
  saltwater, 343-48, 352
  scaling, 331
  smell, 331
  spoilage and storage, 354
  test for doneness, 350
  thiaminase in, 554
  See also shellfish; *specific
    types*
fishing, 354
fishing sinker, 488
fitness. *See* exercise

flambéed dishes, 47, 412
flank cuts, 292
flashlight batteries, 490
flatulence, 240-41
flavonoids, 559
flavors/flavor modifiers, 571
flaxseed, 141
fleas, 535, 537
Fleer, Frank, 108
flies, 535
floor cleaner, 504
flounder, 344
flour
  bleached versus
    unbleached, 66, 72
  in breads, 52, 55, 56, 57,
    78, 134
  bug infestation, 54
  in cakes, 52, 82, 90
  facts, 52
  in gravy, 26
  in pies, 85
  tasting to determine type,
    54
  types of, 52-53
  vitamin C in, 57
  weighing, 88
  whole-grain, 134
  See also specific types
flowers
  cutting, 492
  slugs eating, 535
fondant icing, 68
fontina cheese, 361
food
  additives, 106, 457,
    570-81
  average American
    consumption, 464
  fast food, 454-60
  introduction of America's
    most popular, 465
  paired with wines, 413,
    414

pectin in, 183
preservation, 38-44
rotation, 552
salt content in, 160
water used to grow, 395
See also nutrients; food
    poisoning; food safety;
    specific foods
food poisoning
    common bacteria, 479
    E. coli, 188, 217, 290,
        291, 300, 479
    from fish, 332, 353
    from fresh produce, 188
    Listeria, 295-96, 479
    and pot luck parties, 473
    symptoms, 478
food safety, 472-79
    facts, 474-77
    germ spreaders, 472
    irradiation, 478
    meat, 474, 478
    unsafe herbs, 168-71
    See also food poisoning;
        restaurant(s)
fool (dessert), 67
formula, 388
fowl, 324
frankfurters. *See* hot dogs
free radicals, 550, 566-67
free-range chicken, 322, 325
freezing
    bread, 78
    candy, 103
    dishes with alcohol, 39
    fats, 298, 299
    grapes, 49
    meat, 43, 307, 311, 313
    milk, 379
    negative effects of, 41
    pancakes, 56
    panty hose, 431
    pipes, 496
    potatoes, 156, 175

storage times, 43
tips, 38-44
vegetables, 41, 42, 231
See also frozen food
French bread, 61
French fries
    fast food, 454, 457
    and trans-fatty acids, 116
    twice fried, 177, 179
French toast, 56
fried food. *See* French fries;
frying; *specific foods*
frosting. *See* icing
frozen food
    Birdseye, 40
    and nutrient loss, 550
    seal safety, 475
    supermarket, 462, 464
    temperature of, 11, 462
    See also freezing; *specific
        foods*
frozen water lines, 495
fructose, 101
fruit beer, 417
fruit pie, 88
fruits, 182-227
    browning, 185
    bruised, 197
    calories burned off in
        walking, 446
    carbohydrates in, 288
    carotenoids, 565-66
    coatings on, 184
    consumption, 200
    cooking, 189, 233
    and digestive system, 555
    dressing for, 192
    dried, 192
    frozen, 43, 477
    fructose in, 101
    grades of, 233
    nutrients in, 182, 192, 480
    peeling, 191
        with peel on, 468

phytochemicals, 558-64
pits, 192
preparation of, 16
presentation of, 46
refrigeration, 184
ripening, 184
sale of, 464
selecting, 182
sinking in baking, 92
stain removal, 508
storing, 43
sugar in, 188, 189
See also specific fruits
frying
    heat of fat, 118, 125
    oil, 20, 125
        and paper toweling, 14
    and salt, 19
    See also deep-frying
fudge, 103
Fuji apple, 194
fugu, 353
fumigating agents, 572
furniture polish, 504, 522
furniture rings, 524
furocoumarin psoralens, 256

G

gailon, 249
Gala apple, 194
game, 305-6
garden stains, 432
garlic, 151-52
    cloves, 147
    cooking, 231
    and onions, 274
    in soup or sauce, 425
    storing, 39
garlic bread, 79
gases, additive, 571
gas range, 21, 27
Gatorade, 405

gelatin
  and bromelain, 574
  salad, 92
  as thickener, 426-27
genistein, 559
germ, 128
germander plant, 398
giblets, 328
ginger, 153
gingerol, 562
Gjetost cheese, 361
glass cleaner, 505
glass cookware, 17, 23
glasses
  clean, 473, 477
  nick on rim, 521
  rings on furniture, 524
  slippery, 527
  stuck together, 529
  wine, 410
glucose, 436
glue and gluing, 496, 523,
    531
glutamic acid, 578
glutathione peroxidase, 567
gluten, 134, 576
gluten flour, 53
glycyrrhizin, 562
goat's milk, 381
Golden Delicious apple,
    194-95, 199
goose, 324
Gorgonzola cheese, 361
Gouda cheese, 361
graham crackers
  crusts, 91
  and tooth decay, 102
grains
  mealworm repellent, 537
  nutritional guidelines, 128
  protein from, 137
  testing for freshness, 139
  varieties, 128-30
  See also specific types

Granny Smith apple, 195,
    199
grapefruit, 211-2
grapes, 49, 187, 212-14
grass removal, 492
grass stains, 508, 511
graters, 524, 529
gravy
  fat in, 420-21
  flour in, 26
  making own, 421
  separation, 421
  tips, 422
grease removers, 496, 504,
    508, 520, 524, 525, 537
green beans, 246
green peppers, 277
green plums, 193
greens, 229-30, 236, 263-64
  See also lettuce
green tea, 396, 397, 554
grilling
  oils on grill, 17
  See also barbecuing
grouper, 345
grout cleaner, 540
grunt, 74
Gruyère cheese, 362
guar gum, 577
gum. See chewing gum
gum arabic, 577
gutters, 491

H

haddock, 345
hair brush, 430
hair conditioner, 430, 434
hair remover, 541
hair spray, 541
hake, 345
halibut, 345

ham
  canned, 301
  facts, 306-7
  labeling, 297
  prosciutto, 314
  removing bone, 298
  salty, 302
hamburgers, 299-301
  around world, 315
  buying best, 304
  consumption, 304
  and E. coli, 291
Hamwi, Ernest A., 381
hand cleaner, 430, 432, 497
hand-held blender, 31
hand-washing, 474
hard-boiled eggs, 367-68, 372
headaches, 112, 529
heart attack, 352
heartburn, 404
heart rate, 438-39
Helicobacter pylori, 483
hens, 323, 325
hepatitis, 398
herbes de Provence, 172
herbs, 146-47
  adding to dish, 165
  drying, 172
  on hot coals, 17
  medicinal, 168
  as repellents, 534
  rub, 293
  in soup and stew, 423
  starters, 493
  substitutions, 166
  unsafe, 168-70
  See also specific herbs
hermits, 72
Hershey's Kisses, 108
high blood pressure, 157,
    442
hinges, 488, 494
hollandaise sauce, 368-69,
    422

home fitness equipment, 442-43
homogenization, 383
honey
    and B vitamins, 112
    for facial mask, 434
    facts, 97-98
    for hair, 434
honeydew melon, 215
hormones
    in beef, 307
    and nutrient loss, 553
hors d'oeuvres, 48
horseradish, 264, 563
hot dogs, 294-95, 297
hot-water bottle, 520
humectants, 570
hydrogenation, 115
hydrogen peroxide, 491, 544
hydrolyzed oat flour, 124

I

ibuprofen, 542
ice
    flotation, 395
    kitty litter for, 491, 530
    sand/salt distribution on, 493
    on windshield, 531, 546
    See also ice cubes
iceberg lettuce, 268
ice cream, 106
    aerated, 382
    cone, 381
    consumption, 104
    ice crystals, 381
    leaking from cones, 527
    making, 381-82
    reduced-fat, 382
ice cubes
    filtered water for, 392
    for iced coffee or tea, 397

keeping from melting, 46
rinsing, 395
soda fizzing over top, 48
sticking trays, 528
stock for soups or stews, 424
uses, 47
icemakers, 528
ice milk, 382
ice water, 394
icing
    chocolate, 80
    dried out, 88
    fondant, 68
    tips, 80, 82, 93
Idared apple, 195
indoles, 559
ink stains, 508
insects
    meat tenderizer for bites, 538
    repellents, 534
    trapped in cars, 532
insomnia, 122, 402
instant flour, 53
intestines, and alcohol, 406
invert sugar, 577
iodine, 508, 512
iron, 554
iron cookware, 14, 16, 22-23
ironing, 515-18
irradiated food, 478
isoflavones, 136
isopropyl alcohol, 548
Italian brown mushrooms, 270
Ivory soap, 541

J

jackfruit, 187
jalapeño peppers, 280
jams, 103
jars, 473, 475-77, 530

jasmine rice, 132
jeans, 515
jellies
    in cookie batter, 90
    labeling, 103
    pectin as thickener, 427
    preservation, 193
    vitamin C in, 104
"jelly-bean rule", 108-9
jelly beans, 108
Jerusalem artichoke, 264
jewelry cleaning, 523
jicama, 265
johnnycake, 228
Jonagold apple, 195
Jonathan apple, 195
juices, 185, 232
    See also specific types
jujube, 189
jumble/jumbal cookies, 72
jumper cable, 544

K

kahweol, 403
kale, 230, 264
kamut, 133
ketchup, 427, 506, 526
keys, 495
kidneys, 299
kilocalories, 437
kitty litter, 491, 530, 537
kiwano, 190
kiwi, 215-16
knee, 444
knives
    buying of, 30
    sharpening, 30
    storage of, 30
    types of, 29-30
    types to own, 31
Kona coffee, 399
kongoroko, 193

kosher foods, 319, 462-63, 325
kosher salt, 161

L

labeling
 beef, 292, 293, 455, 462
 bread, 56, 59, 134
 confusing, 469
 jam and jelly, 103
 milk, 382
 nutritional, 469
 seafood, 333
 sulfite, 475
 terminology, 467-68
lactose, 553
ladder, 492
lager beer, 417
lamb, 293, 298, 300, 316
langostinos, 337
lard, 14, 118
latkes, 57
laundry, 510-18
 See also ironing; stain removal
lavender oil, 535, 537
lawn chair, 492
Lea, John, 428
lead, 393, 473, 480, 520, 484-85
leather, 521
leavening agents, 571
lecithin, 577
lectin, 240
leeks, 265
lees, 70
leftovers, 474
leg cramps, 446
legumes, 240, 245
lemon, 189, 320, 405
lemon juice
 for shoeshine, 522

 as skin treatment, 433
lemon tart/pie, 83
lentils, 139
lettuce, 265-68
 categories, 268
 freshness, 462
 storing, 267
 washing, 269
 water in, 395
licorice, 147, 165, 562
lid
 canned food, 476
 jar, 475
 pot, 14, 26-27, 489
lightbulb, 488
lighting, 497
lignans, 141, 564
lima beans, 243
Limburger cheese, 362
lime, 188
lime juice, 217
limetta, 190
limonene, 560
liniment, 543
linoleum, 491
lipstick stains, 508, 514
liquid soap, 432
liquor, 408, 409
 See also alcohol
Listeria, 295-96, 479
litchi, 191
liver (body part), 407, 572
liver (food), 305, 339
livestock, drugs in, 302
lobster, 333, 337-39, 343
lobster Newberg, 337
locks, sticky, 494
loin cuts, 292
lollipops, 102
lovage, 255
lox, 348-49
lubricants, 572
lumpfish, 350

lungs, 438, 439
lutein, 562, 565
lycopene, 564, 565
lye, 543
lysine, 128

M

mace, 153
mâche, 269
mackerel, 345
mahi mahi, 345
Maillard reaction, 54
Maine lobster, 338
makeup, 432, 507
malic acid, 577
malting aids, 570
malt liquor, 417
malt vinegar, 164
mamey, 217
Mammoth, 307
M&Ms, 111
manganese, 301
mango, 217-18
mannitol, 577
maple syrup, 89, 98-99
maraschino cherries, 47
marble, 532
Marchello, Martin, 300
margarine
 contents, 388
 in cookies, 74
 facts, 120, 121
 smoke point, 14
 storing, 43
marinades, 309-10
marjoram, 153
marshmallow, 89, 103, 104, 528
marzipan, 135
masa harina, 136
mashed potato, 177-78, 179
material handling aids, 572

mayonnaise
 facts, 118
 overuse, 527
 and weather, 120
McIntosh apple, 195, 199
mealworms, 537
measuring cup, 528
meatballs, 296
meatloaf, 296, 299
meats, 290-316
 aging, 313
 beef color, 294, 307
 beef cuts, 292
 beef fat and calories,
  315-16
 beef labeling, 292, 455,
  462
 beef refrigeration, 311
 beef tenderness, 311-12
 browning in microwave, 13
 calories burned off in
  exercise, 449
 composition of, 309
 consumption of, 290, 294,
  296
 cooling, 310
 cut across grain, 311
 freezing, 43, 307, 311, 313
 frying in oil, 14
 grading, 291
 ground, 300
 herbs and aromatics for,
  146
 hormones in beef, 307
 marinades, 309-10
 moist heat for, 18
 odors, 308
 purchasing, 314
 safety, 474, 478
 sautéing, 18
 seasoning, 293
 in spaghetti sauce, 421
 stain removal, 507

storing, 43, 294
 in supermarket freezer, 462
 tenderizing, 187, 211, 216,
  313, 538
 thawing, 303
 thermometers, 11
 treating of surface, 308
 See also specific types
Melrose apple, 195
mercury, 486
meringue, 87, 88
metabolism, 436
methionine reductase, 568
methylene chloride, 578
Mexican green tomatoes, 284
Mexican wedding cakes, 62
mice, 538
microorganisms, 38
microwaving
 butter, 388
 facts, 27
 fish, 331, 351
 invention of, 28
 leaking radiation, 489
 lobster, 339
 meat browning, 13
 and plastic wrap, 26
 positioning of foods, 16
 and rising time of bread,
  67-68
 safety, 13, 526
 sandwiches, 59
 tomatoes, 286
 vegetables, 10
migraine headaches, 112
mildew, 505, 508, 515, 528
milk
 acidophilus, 384
 calcium from, 137
 to clean plant leaves, 522
 condensed, 383
 consumption, 381, 385
 containers, 378, 470
 for cracks in china, 524

custard, 389
 evaporated, 380, 383
 facts, 378-79
 fat in, 378
 freezing, 379
 freshness, 379, 380
 heating in saucepan, 382
 homogenization, 383
 labels, 382
 low-cholesterol, 387
 perishability, 383
 powdered, 380
 scalding, 387
 skin when heated, 384
 stain removal, 509
 in supermarket, 466
millet, 129
mineral oil, 528
minerals, 407
mineral water, 393, 432
mirrors, 490
miso, 245
Mitchell, Earl, 75
mixers, 55, 528
modified starch, 578
MOG (material other than
  grapes), 187
moisture control agents, 570
molasses, 99, 109
mold, 38, 79, 236
mole, 278
monkfish, 339
monosodium glutamate
  (MSG), 578
monounsaturated fats, 114,
  115
Moon Pie, 75-76
morel mushrooms, 270
mosquitoes, 536, 538
moths, 536, 538
motion sickness, 409
motor oil, 529
mouth, and alcohol, 406

mozzarella cheese, 362
MSG. *See* monosodium glutamate
mucus, 384, 510
Muenster cheese, 362
muffins, 79, 92
mullet, 345
multigrain buns, 455
multi-gyms, 442-43
mung beans, 283
muscles, 441, 444
mushroom(s), 268-71
    facts, 268-69
    flavor, 270
    quiche, 28
    storage, 270
    varieties, 270-71
mussels, 339-40, 343
mustard, 153-54, 509
Mutsu apple, 195
myoglobin, 303, 309
myost cheese, 362
mytilotoxin, 353

N

nail polish, 431, 433, 544
nail polish remover, 509, 531
nails, 430
naproxen, 543
nausea, 546
nectarines, 218
Neufchâtel cheese, 362
Newton Pippin apple, 195
nitrates, 578-79
nitrites, 230, 297, 578-79
nitrosamines, 230, 578-79
nondairy products, 383
nonstick cookware, 16, 23, 547
noodle soup, 425
Northern Spy apple, 195

nutmeg, 154
nutraceuticals, 564
nutrients
    in beer, 417
    in bread and toast, 54
    and freezing, 39
    in fresh supermarket foods, 463
    in fruits and vegetables, 15, 182, 192, 227, 229-30, 480
    labeling, 469
    loss of and environment, 552
    loss of and storage, 551
    in pizza, 457
    in refined foods, 551
    in steak, 138
    supplements, 550, 555, 571
    and temperature, 550-51
    in white rice and black beans, 138
nuts, 135
    calories burned off in exercise, 447, 450
    chopped, 138
    shelling, 139
    types of, 136-37
    See also specific types
nuts and bolts, 491, 523

O

oat flour, 124, 131
oatmeal
    cookies, 87
    as facial, 431
    toasted, 88, 131
oats, 129, 131
obesity, 121, 122
odors
    baking soda for, 546

car, 530
carpet, 543
cooked vegetable, 235
meat, 308
removing, 521, 526
thermos, 547
ohelo, 191
oil(s)
    in baking, 125
    coating with, 12
    containers for, 119, 122
    disposing of used, 116
    flash point, 21
    flavored, 167
    frying meat in, 14
    frying temperatures, 20, 125
    on grill, 17
    heated, 125
        rancid, 480
    refrigerating, 123
    reuse of, 20, 117
    smoke point, 20, 117
    use and obesity, 121
    versus shortening, 124
    See also specific oils
okra, 271-72
Olestra, 123-24
olive oil, 117, 167
omelet, 374
onion(s)
    cooking, 275
    and crying, 274
    facts, 272
    and garlic, 273
    in quiche, 28
    skins in gravy, 422
    storing, 39, 178
    tips, 272-74
    varieties, 275
oolong tea, 397
orange juice, 219
orange juice fizz, 220

orange marmalade, 104
orange roughy, 345
oranges, 218-20
oregano, 154
Oreos, 60, 61
organic chicken, 325
organic farming, 552
organic food, 468
oriental broccoli, 249
osetra caviar, 350
osmosis, 41
osteoporosis, 442
ostrich fern, 231
oven(s)
    cleaners, 505, 543, 547
    convection, 17, 24-25
    electric, 27
    opening door of, 19
    reaching in, 525
    self-cleaning, 27
        temperature, 12, 31
    thermometer, 12
oxalic acid, 234
oxidizing agents, 572
oyster mushrooms, 271
oyster plant, 281
oysters, 335, 340-41

P

pain relievers, 542-43
paint and painting
    primer, 547
    stain, 509
    tips, 488, 490, 494-97
pancakes
    cooking tips, 66
    freezing extras, 56
    griddle, 89
    stirring batter, 57
    syrup in batter, 89
    turning, 57
panty hose, 431, 493

papain, 187, 310, 313, 538, 579
papaya, 193, 221
paper towels, 14
paprika, 155
parcooking, 18
Parmesan cheese, 362
parsley, 150, 155, 425, 433
parsnips, 275
parties
    pot luck, 473
    shopping for, 50
pasta
    and atmospheric pressure, 31
    converting measure to cooked, 141
    from durum wheat, 132
    facts, 142
    mealworm repellent, 537
    meaning of names, 143-44
    and protein, 141
    rinsing, 133
    shapes, 143-44
pasteurization, 551
pastry
    buttermilk in, 119
    cold ingredients for, 55
    dough, 85
    flour, 53
    puffy ends, 76
pawpaw, 221
peaches, 221-22
peanut butter
    as carcinogen, 137-38
    history of, 140
    reduced-fat, 122
    to remove chewing gum, 521
    spoilage, 138
    to trap mice, 538
peanuts
    facts, 137
    for peanut butter, 140

for protein, 135
roasted, 240
pears, 222-23
peas, 158, 275-76
pecans, 235
pectin, 182-83, 189, 197, 427, 579
peppercorns, 155-56, 167
peppermint, 156, 536
pepperoni, 314
pepper(s), 155
    facts, 276-77
    hot, 277-78
    shaker, 14
    varieties, 278-79
    See also specific types
perch, 349
perfume, 431, 433, 509, 545
peroxide, 579
Perrins, William, 428
persimmon, 223-24
perspiration stains, 509
pesticides, 234, 468
pesto, 166
pet food, 467
petroleum jelly, 542
pets. See animals
pH control agents, 572
pheasant, 305, 324
phenethyl isothiocyanates, 563
phenols, 106
phenylethylamine, 112
phosphate detergent, 540
phosphoric acid, 405
Physalis peruviana, 186
phytic acid, 561
phytochemicals, 558-64
pickles, 261-62, 476
picnic tabletops, 491
pie(s), 106
    chess, 62
    crusts, 83, 84-85, 91

cutting, 90
dough, 85, 88
fruit, 88
lemon, 83
shoofly, 67
shrinkage, 88
thickeners, 64, 89
pigs, 296, 297, 306
pigs in blankets, 119
pike, 349
pilsner beer, 417
pimiento, 279
pineapple, 224
pinecone, 489
ping pong ball, 489
pinto bean, 245
pitanga, 187
pith, 191
pizza
  cutting, 78-79
  as fast food, 456, 457
  fat in, 72
  favorite topping, 314
  homemade, 46
  nutrients in, 457
plantains, 203, 204
plants
  cleaning leaves, 492, 522
  repelling bugs, 535, 537, 538
  tips on, 492-93
plaster, 497
plastic bags, 42-43, 235, 478, 525
plastic chocolate, 107
plastic wrap
  and microwaving, 26
  sticking to itself, 527
plate cuts, 292
plums, 225
poached eggs, 367, 376
pollack, 346
pollution, 333, 480, 553

polyphenols, 554, 559
polyunsaturated fats, 114, 115
pomegranates, 225-26
pompano, 346
popcorn, 259-60
popovers, 79
poppy seeds, 54, 135, 156
pork, 310, 314, 316
Port du Salut cheese, 363
porter beer, 418
portobello mushrooms, 271
postage stamps, 529
potassium chloride, 579
potato chips, 119, 175, 180
potatoes
  baked, 13, 175, 176, 178, 179
  cold soup, 180
  cooking of, 178, 179
  facts, 174, 176-77
  firming up, 179
  freezing, 175
  green, 177, 180
  mashed, 177-78, 179
  new, 177
  newleaf, 178
  peeling boiled, 180
  purchasing from bulk bins, 176
  skin, 179
  soaking in water, 177
  solanine in, 233
  storing, 176, 177, 178, 179
  varieties, 176
  See also French fries
potato salad, 176, 450
pot cheese, 361
pot luck parties, 473
pot pie, 423
pots and pans. See cookware
poultry
  calories burned off in exercise, 448

ground, 323
kosher, 319
safety of, 474
seasoning, 156, 166
skin, 459
stuffing, 319
thawing, 322, 326
See also chicken; turkey
poussins, 325
powdered milk, 380
prawns, 342
pregnancy
  and caffeine, 404
  and fish consumption, 351
  vitamin C for dogs, 534
preservatives, 475, 572
See also additives
preserves, 189, 193
pressure cooking, 24
  vegetables, 10
pretzels, 60, 73
prickly pears, 226
primer, 547
proanthocyanidin, 566-67
produce, 182-285, 464, 466
  and bacteria, 188
  bagging, 192
  organic, 552
  See also fruits; vegetables
propellants, 571
prosciutto, 314
prostate, 409
protein
  fat content of non-vegetable, 295
  from grains and cereals, 137
  high-protein diet, 556
  and pasta, 141
provitamin A. See beta-carotene
provolone cheese, 363
prunes, 185

pudding, 15
puffball mushroom, 228
puffer fish, 353
pulses, 139
pumpernickel bread, 78
pumpkin, 283, 284
pumpkin pie, 89
punch bowl, 47

Q

quail, 324, 328
quark cheese, 363
quercetin, 230
quiche, 28
quick breads, 59, 77
quinoa, 129

R

rabbit, 300
radiant heat, 26
radiation. *See* irradiated food
radicchio, 269
radish, 279-80
rainwater, 483
raisins, 214-15
rambutan, 186
range(s)
  charcoal filter in hood, 488
  convection cooking, 26
  gas, 21
  See also oven(s)
rapeseed oil. *See* canola oil
raspberry, 206
raspberry vinegar, 164
rattlesnake, 304-5
reactive arthritis, 378
recipes
  bread, 57, 61
  butter in, 385
  buttermilk in, 59, 64, 380

cake, 84
candy, 102, 103
common substitutions,
  33-36
low-fat cheese in, 357
seasoning substitutions,
  146
Red Delicious apple, 196,
  199
red pepper, 277
reducing agents, 572
red wine, 106, 522
refined foods, 551
refrigerator
  for chemical storage, 544
  mildew, 528
  odors, 526
  scratches, 520
release agents, 572
relish trays, 459
restaurant(s)
  cleanliness of, 473
  fast food, 459
  healthy eating in, 460
  and nutrient preservation,
    552
  smoking by cook, 474
reverse osmosis, 481
rib cuts, 292, 299
rice, 129-30
  brown, 130
  burned, 130
  cooking, 131
  to help salt flow, 528
  jasmine, 132
  nutritional data, 138
  parboiled, 132
  rinsing, 131
rice flour, 53
ricotta cheese, 363
ring removal, 430
roast beef
  cooking time, 299
  cuts, 292

fast food, 454
purchasing, 295
roasting
  cookware for, 15
  in covered pan, 314
  resting before carving, 305
  tips, 296, 297
  vegetables, 10
Rock Cornish game hen, 323
rock salt, 161
rodents, 536
rolls
  Bath buns, 73
  color of, 79
  glaze for, 80
  keeping warm, 58
  reheating, 77
romaine lettuce, 230, 267,
  268
Romano cheese, 363
Rome Beauty apple, 196
Roquefort cheese, 363
rosemary, 156, 563
round cuts, 292, 295
rowing machine, 442
rub, 293
rubber cement, 507
rubbing alcohol, 521
rug. *See* carpets and
  carpeting
ruler, 495
rust, 491, 501, 509
rye, 130
rye bread, 56, 130

S

sablefish, 346
saccharine, 100
safety
  alcohol as cause of
    accidents, 408
  in cleaning products, 504-5

hazards in everyday items, 484-86
microwave, 13, 526
swimming pool, 498
See also food safety
saffron, 156
sage, 156
salad dressing
creamy without cream, 122
with dairy product, 184
fast food, 456
on lettuce, 267
overuse, 527
quick, 522
salads
Caesar, 235
calories burned off in exercise, 450
calories in, 287
most popular items in, 236
non-lettuce choices, 268-69
soggy, 233
salsify, 281
salmon, 346, 348, 350
salmonella, 188, 368, 378, 473, 474, 479
salt
in bread making, 60, 78
for carpet colors, 525
consumption, 158
content in common foods, 160
in cooking water, 24, 233, 235
on cutting board, 529
facts, 157
in fast foods, 456
foods high in, 159, 459
and frying, 19
in humidity, 528
as microbe inhibitor, 158
savers, 172

shaker, 14
in shakes, 454
sodium-free seasonings, 158
in soups or stews, 424
for stains, 522
table salt, 580
types of, 161
sandwiches
animal-shaped, 48
calories burned off in exercise, 446, 450
colorful, 47
easy-finger, 46
fast food, 455
freezing, 39
microwaving, 59
sanitizing agents, 572
sap, 98
saponins, 563
sapote, 226
Sap Sago cheese, 363
sardines, 346
saturated fatty acids, 115
sauce(s)
barbecue, 327
curdling, 388, 421, 422
dry soup mixes for, 423
garlic in, 425
hollandaise, 368-69, 422
lumps in, 423
making own, 421
of medium consistency, 423
Worcestershire, 428
sauerkraut, 251
sausage, 298
sautéing
with butter, 422
heat of oil, 125
tips, 18
savory, 161
saw blades, 491
scallops, 341

scissors, 489
scorch marks, 501, 509, 516
scratches, 520
screens, 494
scuff marks, 503
seafood, 330-54
poisoning, 332, 353
See also fish; shellfish
sea salt, 161
seasonings, 146-72
for meat and poultry, 293
sodium-free, 158
See also specific seasonings
sea trout, 346
seeds, 135
selenium, 552
self-cleaning oven, 27
self-rising flour, 53
seltzer, 393
semolina, 53
sequestrants, 571
serrano peppers, 280
sesame, 162
sevruga caviar, 350
shad, 347
shakes, 454
shallots, 39
shampoo, 541
shark, 343, 347, 349
shark cartilage, 566
shark fin soup, 349
shaving cream, 544
shell beans, 243
shellfish
overcooking, 343
pollution, 333
raising of, 334
sweetness, 333
thiaminase in, 554
See also specific types
sherry vinegar, 164
shiitake mushrooms, 270, 271

shin splints, 445
shoelaces, 517
shoe polish, 509
shoes, 517
shoeshine, 522
shoofly pie, 67
shoplifting, 464-65
shopping cart, 463
shortening
    creaming with sugar, 82
    versus oil, 124
shrimp, 341-43
side stitch, 444
silk flowers, 515
silk garments, 518
silverfish, 534
silverplate, 525
silver polishing, 531-32
simple fats, 114
skate, 347
skin treatments, 431, 433
slipcovers, 513
slow-cookers, 10, 28-29
slow-twitch muscle fibers,
    441
slugs, 535
slump (dessert), 67
smelt, 349
smog, 553
smoke-curing, 42
smoking
    and nutrition, 553
    by restaurant cook, 474
    and sugar, 103
snails, 536
sneakers, 517
snickerdoodles, 69
snow shovels, 489
soap
    to deter deer, 537
    dishwasher, 529
    Ivory, 540
    liquid, 432

making bar last longer,
    433, 434
    uses for, 488, 491, 502
soda
    caffeine in, 407
    for car battery, 544
    carbonation in, 403
    consumption, 110, 385,
        392, 405
    to remove nuts and bolts,
        523
    and thirst, 393
sodium benzoate, 580
sodium bisulfite, 580
sodium carbonate, 580
sodium caseinate, 580
sodium chloride. See salt
sodium citrate, 580
soft drinks. See soda
soil, 552
solanine, 177, 233
Solomon, Isaac, 40
soluble fiber. See pectin
solvents, 502, 503, 572
soot, 490
sorbitol, 545, 580
sorghum, 109
soufflés, 61, 89, 93, 94
soup(s)
    barley as thickener, 139
    blowing on hot, 420
    bones added to stock, 305
    calories burned off in
        exercise, 450
    carrots in, 424
    cream, 421, 425
    cream-of-tomato, 424
    curdling, 421, 424
    dried peas in, 276
    fat in, 420-21
    frozen stock cubes in, 424
    garlic in, 425
    herbs in, 423
    lumps in, 423

noodle, 425
    removal from can, 422
    salty, 424
    shark fin, 349
    simmering, 422
    tips, 425
    turnips in, 286
    types of, 420
    vichyssoise, 180
sour cream, 92, 380, 383
sourdough bread, 58, 63
soybeans
    beanut butter, 136
    facts, 243-44, 247
    roasted, 240
    sprouts, 283
soy flour, 53
soy foods, 244-45
soy milk, 245
soy sauce, 322
spaghetti sauce, 421
Spam, 304
sparkling water, 393
Spartan apple, 196
spearmint, 537
spelt, 133
Spencer, Percy, 28
spices, 146-47, 165, 166,
    167, 293
    See also specific spices
spinach, 230, 234, 280-81
spiny lobster, 338
sponge cake, 65
spot removal, 500, 501, 516
sprain, 443, 445
spray starch, 514, 517
spring water, 393
sprouts, 281-82
squab, 326
squash, 189, 282-83
squid, 343
stabilizers, 571
stainless steel cookware, 16
stainless steel knife, 30

stain removal, 500-514
  blood, 501, 506, 513, 517
  grease, 496, 504, 508, 520,
    524, 525, 537
  lipstick, 508, 514
  tobacco, 510
  wine, 510, 517, 518, 522
star apple, 226
starch, 57, 132, 476, 573,
  578
starter, 58
stationary bike, 442
Stayman Winesap apple, 196
steak
  fatty, marbled, 303
  labeling, 293
  nutritional value, 138
  rare, 303
  salting/peppering before
    cooking, 311
searing, 301
steaming
  fish, 331
  vegetables, 11
stearic acid, 121
steps, painting of, 490
sterilization, 475
sterling silver, 525
Stevia, 101
stew(s)
  black tea in, 423
  blending, 298
  carrots in, 424
  corn tortillas in, 423
  dried peas in, 276
  fat on top of, 420
  frozen stock cubes in, 424
  herbs in, 423
  salty, 424
  simmering, 422
  thickening, 139, 423, 424
  turnips in, 286
Stilton cheese, 363

stir-frying
  tips, 27-28
  vegetables, 10
stock, 305, 424
stomach, and alcohol, 406
storage. See food,
    preservation; specific foods
stout, 418
strawberry, 193, 204, 205
strawberry jelly, 104
stress, 198, 438
Strite, Charles, 29
stroke, 229
stud finder, 494
stuffed animals, 514, 518
stuffing, 21, 319, 322, 323
sturgeon, 347
sucralose, 101
sucrose, 109
suede, 506
sugar
  in baked goods, 111
  in bananas, 202-3
  beet, 109
  blown, 109
  brown, 104, 105, 109
  butter creamed with, 82,
    83
  on cake plate, 91
  cane, 109
  in common foods, 105
  consumption, 96, 106, 111
  in cough medicine, 106
  craving, 106
  dusting confectioners', 92
  in fruit, 188, 189
  in lemon tart or pie, 83
  lumpy, 105
  in pastry dough, 85
  raw, 99
  and smoking, 103
  on strawberry, 204
  and yeast, 61, 78
sugar cookies, 88

sugarless gum, 110
sulfites, 475, 581
sulforaphane, 559
sunburn, 432
sunchoke. See Jerusalem
    artichoke
sunflower seeds, 135, 139
sunflower sprouts, 283
sunscreen, 556
supermarket, 462-66
superoxide dismutase,
  567
supplements, nutritional,
    550, 555, 571
  See also vitamins
surface-finishing agents, 571
surface tension control
  agents, 571
surimi, 336
Surinam cherry, 187
sushi, 351
sweaters, 513, 514
sweetbreads, 294
sweeteners
  artificial, 100-101
  in bread making, 61
  in cakes, 84
  classification of, 571
  consumption of, 102
sweet potatoes
  facts, 174
  freezing, 175
  peeling, 174
  storing, 175
sweets
  babies' ability to taste, 107
  calories burned off in
    exercise, 447, 451
  craving for, 107
swimming pools, 498
Swiss chard, 265
Swiss cheese, 363, 364
swordfish, 347

syrup
  boiling, 105, 109
  crystallization, 109
  maple, 89, 98-99
  running down side of
    botttle, 104

T

tabbouleh, 134
tableware
  hairline cracks in, 524
  lead in, 520
  See also glasses
taco salad, 457
tangelo, 226
tannic acid, 423, 581
tannin, 140, 186, 398, 403,
    554
tapioca, 64, 89, 425-26
tarnish, 525, 532
tarragon, 162
tar removal, 510
tartrates, 412
tarts, 83
tea
  brewing temperature, 397
  caffeine in, 398
  classifications, 396-97
  diuretic effect, 401
  facial sauna, 434
  facts, 396
  green, 396, 397, 554
  and health, 397
  iced, 397-98
  stain removal, 507
  in stew, 423
  tannin in, 398, 554
Teflon cookware, 23
tempeh, 244
temperature
  in baked goods recipes, 74

beer, 413, 415
of boiling, 19
coffee, 402
cooking, 12
of fats, 118
of foods at buffet, 49
freezer, 39
of milk, 379
and nutrient loss, 550-51
oven, 31
for stuffed turkey, 21
in supermarket cold cases,
    462
tea, 397
tendinitis, 445
tetradotoxin, 353
textured vegetable protein,
    245
texturizers, 571
theobromine, 102
thermal bottle, 44
thermometers
  deep-frying, 118
  oven, 12, 74
  types of, 11-12
thermos bottle. See vacuum
    bottle
thiaminase, 554
thiamine, 554
thickeners
  arrowroot, 426
  definition of, 571
  gelatin, 426-27
  for jellies, 427
  okra, 272
  for pies, 64, 89
  for soups, 139
  for stews, 139, 423, 424
thimble, 517
thioglucoside, 234
thirst quenchers, 393, 394
thyme, 162
thymus gland, 294
thyroid gland, 234, 436

Tilsit cheese, 363
tin can, 40
tires, 530
toads, 536
toast and toasting, 54, 55
  history of toast-making,
    412
  invention of toaster, 29
  radiant heat for, 26
tobacco stains, 510
tofu, 244
toilet bowl cleaner, 505, 540,
    545
toilet tissue, 546
tomatillo, 283
tomatoes
  baking, 236
  chopped, 15
  facts, 283-87
  largest, 189
  in microwave, 285
  storing, 39
tomato juice, 305
tools, rust on, 491
tooth brushing, 431
tooth decay, 102
toothpaste, 542, 545
topping(s)
  cake, 57
  crisp, 13
  nut, 138
tortilla chips, 74
tortillas, 74, 423
trampoline, 442
trans-fatty acids, 116, 120
treadmill, 442
trichinosis, 297
triglycerides, 123, 374
triticale, 130
trona, 70
trout, 346, 350, 352
truffles, 270
tuna, 347, 348

turbinado, 99
turbot, 347
turkey
  in brown bag, 24
  facts, 321-22, 326
  roasting overnight, 473
  stuffing, 21, 323
Turkish delight, 71
turmeric, 162, 445
turnip greens, 265
turnips, 287
Twinkies, 61

U

ubiquinone10, 567
ugli fruit, 226
ultraviolet radiation purifier,
  481
umbrella stand, 531
urine stain removal, 510
utensils, 526
    See also cookware

V

vacuum bottle, 44, 547
vanilla, 163
varnish, 495
vase, 520
Vaseline, 542
veal, 302, 316
vegetables, 227-88
  browning, 163
  calories burned off in
    exercise, 451
  carbohydrates in, 288
  carcinogens in, 230
  carotenoids, 565-66
  coatings on, 184
consumption, 228
  cooking, 10-11, 15, 24,
    182, 233, 235, 236, 287

and digestive system, 555
freezing, 41, 42, 231
in garden catalogs, 184
grades of, 233
losing color in, 232
new, 232
nutrients in, 15, 182, 227,
  229-30, 480
with peel on, 468
phytochemicals, 558-64
in plastic bags, 478
preparation, 16
refrigeration, 184
sale of, 464
snack chips, 232
storing cooked, 231
tenderizing, 232
tips on, 234-36
See also specific vegetables
Velveeta, 358
venison, 305
vichyssoise, 180
vinegar
  as facial treatment, 433
  facts, 163-64, 428
  as nail cleaner, 433
  in poached eggs, 376
  uses for, 523, 529
vitamin A
  and alcohol, 409
  excessive amounts, 556
  in fresh foods, 463
  importance of, 556
  in pumpkin, 283
  sources, 557
vitamin B, 564
vitamin B12, 554
vitamin C
  and boiling of food, 564
  in flour, 57
  in fresh foods, 190, 463
in fruits and vegetables, 16,
  190
  and iron, 554

in jellies, 104
for pregnant dogs, 534
in prepared juices, 185
recommended allowance,
  554
vitamin D, 556
vitamins
  and alcohol, 407
  and fat, 554
  freshness, 561
  robbers of, 557
  See also specific vitamins
vomit stain removal, 510

W

waffles, 56, 57, 92
walking, 446-47
wallpaper, 490, 496
walnuts, 136, 139
warehousing, food, 552
washing machine, 511, 514
water
  bottled, 483
  caffeinated, 402
  conservation, 483
  consumption, 395
  contamination, 480, 483
  frozen, 395
  at higher elevations, 394
  in human body, 392
  lead in, 393
  purity statistics, 482
  as thirst quencher, 393
  treatment methods,
    481-82, 483
  types of, 393
  usage, 394
  See also ice; ice cubes
water chestnuts, 287
watercress, 269
Waterhouse, Andrew, 106
watermelon, 189, 226-27

water softeners, 481
waxy cuticle, 267
weed removal, 492
well water, 393, 483
Wenberg, Ben, 337
whale, 354
wheat, 130
  allergy, 134
  bran, 134
  bread, 134
  cracked, 133
  flour, 56
  pasta, 132
wheat beer, 418
wheat germ, 133
whetstone, 30
whey, 378, 387
whipped cream, 80, 379,
    386, 477
White, William J., 108
white bread, 56
white chocolate, 105
whitefish, 350
whole-wheat bread, 57, 134
whole-wheat flour, 53, 55,
    57, 89, 134
wild boar, 305
wild einkorn, 133
wild fowl, 324
wild game, 305-6
wild rice, 132
window
  opening more easily, 491
  steamed up, 521
  washing, 520
window box, 535
window shade, 515
windshield deicer, 531, 546
windshield wiper, 530
wine
  aroma, 410
  blush, 411
  chemistry, 411

consumption, 392
  cooking with, 320, 412,
    413
  cork, 48, 410, 412
  in cream soup or sauce,
    412
  facts, 412-13
  fortified, 411
  glasses, 410
  and health, 414
  paired with foods, 413,
    414
  phenols in, 106
  in soup or sauce, 412
  stains, 510, 517, 518, 522
  storage, 410
  tannin in, 398, 554
  vintage, 411
  in waffle batter, 92
wine cooler, 47
wine vinegar, 164
wok, 27-28
wood
  cutting board, 472, 529
  drawers, 495
  repairing hole in, 489
  sanding, 494
  stain, 497
wood ear mushroom, 271
wooden board, 56
woodwork, 495
woolens, 513, 516, 538
Worcestershire sauce, 428
work, 438
Wrigley, William, 108

Y

yams, 174
yeast, 38
  in bread machines, 59
  in breads, 71, 77, 78
  dough, 55, 71

dry and compressed, 69
  and hard water, 66
  proofing, 72
  rising, 58, 71
  and sugar, 61, 78
  uses, 67
yellow pepper, 277
yogurt, 387

Z

zeaxanthin, 562, 565
zest, 191, 192
zinc, 400, 409
zipper, 511, 516
zucchini, 189

Notes